HISTORY OF FRANCE,

FROM THE EARLIEST TIMES

TO

MDCCCXLVIII.

BY

THE REV. JAMES WHITE,

AUTHOR OF "THE EIGHTEEN CHRISTIAN CENTURIES."

NEW YORK:

D. APPLETON AND COMPANY,

443 & 445 BROADWAY.

1868.

PREFACE.

This book makes an attempt to furnish a readable account of the country with which we are in closest neighbourhood, and yet of whose history the generality of us know less than of that of almost any other kingdom. It aims at something higher than a mere epitome, for it founds itself on a great deal of various reading, and gives results more than abstracts. At the same time, it devotes sufficient space to any occurrences which seem to have a general bearing on the progress or character of the nation. But it does not profess to be very minute in its record of trifling or uninfluential occurrences, nor philosophic in searching out the causes of obscure events.

If it gives new information to any youthful student, or induces him to search in other quarters for more, or if it recalls to maturer readers scenes and incidents they have nearly forgotten, one of the objects of the writer will be gained. He believes, however, there is a large class of persons, at the present day, neither ambitious schoolboys nor forgetful middle-aged men, but members of Mechanics' Institutes and other societies for voluntary education, who are anxious for historical as well as other kinds of knowledge, but who are repelled from the attempt to acquire it by the dryness of the narrative and the uninteresting style of the smaller volumes devoted to this subject, and by the time and labour required for the perusal of the larger and more valuable works. If this short and easily-mastered History of France is found to supply the want hitherto experienced among those associations, as well as by the classes named above, the Author's highest ambition will be gratified.

CONTENTS.

CHRONOLOGICAL TABLE OF THE FRENCH KINGS.

KINGS OF THE FRANKS.

Merovingian Line.

A. D.
496. Clovis.
511. Thierry, Clodomir, Childebert, Clothaire.
559. Clothaire.
561. Charibert, Gontran, Chilperic, Sighebert.
584. Childebert.
596. Theodebert, Thierry II., Clothaire II.
628. Dagobert.
638. Clovis II., Sighebert II.
656. Clothaire III., Chilperic II.
673. Thierry III., Dagobert II.
690. Clovis III.
695. Childebert III.
711. Dagobert III.
716. Chilperic III.
720. Thierry IV.
741. Chilperic IV.

Carlovingian Line.

752. Pepin.
768. Charlemagne.
814. Louis (the Debonnaire).

KINGS OF FRANCE.

843. Charles (the Bald.)
877. Louis (the Stammerer).
879. Louis III., and Carloman.
884. Charles (the Fat).
887. Hugh (or Eudes).
898. Charles (the Simple).
923. Raoul.
936. Louis IV.
954. Lothaire.
986. Louis V.

Capetian Line.

A. D.
987. Hugh Capet.
996. Robert.
1031. Henry I.
1060. Philip I.
1108. Louis VI. (the Fat).
1137. Louis VII. (the Young).
1180. Philip II. (Philip Augustus).
1223. Louis VIII.
1226. Louis IX. (Saint Louis).
1270. Philip III. (the Hardy).
1285. Philip IV. (the Handsome).
1314. Louis X. (the Hutin, or Quarrelsome).
1316. Philip V. (the Long).
1322. Charles IV. (the Handsome)

Valois Branch.

1328. Philip VI. (de Valois).
1350. John (the Good).
1364. Charles V.
1380. Charles VI.
1422. Charles VII.
1461. Louis XI.
1483. Charles VIII.

Valois-Orleans.

1498. Louis XII.

Valois-Angouleme.

1515. Francis I.
1547. Henry II.
1559. Francis II.
1560. Charles IX.
1574. Henry III.

Bourbon Branch.

1589. Henry IV.
1610. Louis XIII.
1643. Louis XIV.
1715. Louis XV.
1774. Louis XVI.
1793. The Republic.
1804. The Empire—Napoleon.
1814. Louis XVIII.
1824. Charles X.

KING OF THE FRENCH.

Bourbon-Orleans.

1830. Louis Philippe.
1848. Republic.

HISTORY OF FRANCE.

CHAPTER I.

THE GAULS.—THE ROMANS.—CLOVIS AND THE FRANKS, A. D. 482.—PEPIN, A. D. 752.—HUGH CAPET, A. D. 987.

This little book is not presumptuously intended for the perusal of the wise and learned, but for those who wish to recall the historic knowledge which time has nearly obliterated, and also for that larger and increasing class who desire to be informed shortly and intelligibly of what is most important to be known in the annals of various states. We have, therefore, undertaken to be their conductor through the devious windings and varied scenery of the History of France. But, like a cautious guide who is not very sure of his ground, especially at the beginning of his journey, we will avoid, as much as possible, all obscure and dangerous places, and merely ask them to take their station every now and then on some commanding eminence, and contemplate at their ease the prospect at their feet. They will see unrolled before them, like a series of dissolving views, the strongly-marked periods of a great nation's career; wild populations reclaimed by contact with their Roman conquerors, and sinking into barbarism again under the trampling heels of another race of invaders from the forests of Germany. A little time longer, and they will see the civilising element, which was never entirely obliterated, asserting its power over the mixed mass of the Franks and Gaels; and, gradually combining, gradually re-forming, gradually softening, and giving way to the bent of their inborn genius, they will see the descendants of those ferocious tribes claiming to be the most polished, the most warlike, the most accomplished nation in Europe. If we do not go quite so far as to grant them the position they arrogate, and agree with their own historians, that they are at the head of modern civilisation in all its branches, we shall not be blind or disingenuous enough to deny that, in all the departments of intellectual exertion, they hold a foremost place; that if they have no Newton, no Locke, nor Shakespeare, they have many philosophers and many poets; that the fleur-de-lis and the tricolor have waved in many a glorious field; and that the elegancies of life and the charms of manner were never carried to such a pitch before.

Some years ago it would have been an unexampled stretch of liberality to have confessed that France had any good qualities at all. We were in the habit of wrapping ourselves up very comfortably in the folds of our own conceit, and looking down on the rest of mankind as a very inferior race of mortals. We took the additional precaution of maintaining our own superiority by calling our neighbours by the most insulting names. We pictured them as the most ludicrous imitations of humanity, as if one of Nature's journeymen had made the Frenchman, and not made him well. He was a lean, half-starved, lanky-legged creature, looking in hopeless despair, with watery mouth and bleared eyes, at a round of English beef. His attitudes were grotesque, his language even became immensely amusing, because he did not speak our tongue with the slang of a hackney-coachman and the pronunciation of a Cockney. We called him Jack Frog, because we believed he fed on those unsubstantial animals, which we also fancied the exact image of himself in hoppiness of motion and yellowness of skin. His cowardice was unvarying. One Englishman was always equal to half-a-dozen of the "mounseers;" and, in short, we were a most unjust, narrow-minded, pudding-headed set of self-glorifiers, adding to the isolation that belongs to the whole nation in right of its four seas the still more separating insularity of our own individual opinions. We were islands altogether, nowhere connected with the rest of mankind. Our country was an island, we despised the rest of Europe ; our county was an island, we despised the other shires ; our parish was an island, with peculiar habits, modes and institutions ; our households were islands ; and, to complete the whole, each stubborn, broad-shouldered, strong-backed Englishman was an island himself, surrounded by a misty and tumultuous sea of prejudices and hatreds, generally unapproachable, and at all times utterly repudiative of a permanent bridge. We are better now. The sea, where it is not drained off, is very calm and very shallow. We look with clearer eyes upon distant and unaccustomed objects. We can believe that the marshals of the Emperor and generals of the Restoration can be chivalrous soldiers and kind-hearted men ; that a Dutchman does not wear seven pairs of trousers ; that an Italian sometimes succeeds in *not* murdering his mother ; and that, granted the same conditions, the conduct of a Swede, of an Austrian, of a Prussian, and even of a Muscovite, would be very much the same. It is lucky that this change of opinion and widening of our sympathies has taken place ; for if all our inquiries in these historic sketches were to end in the production of the cringing, grinning, trembling mountebank and impostor it was anciently the fashion to consider the Frenchman, the labour would be greatly misapplied. But our investigation will not be so poorly rewarded as this. It will end with the presentment of a nation filled with many grand recollections, and, in spite of present appearances, buoyant with grander future hopes—a people so ingenious, so intellectual, and so active, that its influence thrills through the thoughts of Europe with the rapidity and clearness of the electric wires ; and so powerful, by the size and situation of its domain, and the bravery of its armies, that the authority of its sword in the political government of the world is as great as of its genius and philosophy in the regions of literature and science.

Both as friend and foe that great country has proved itself worthy of our respect. None ever fought more bravely against us, as many a bright and some melancholy names in our annals can witness, and none ever stood shoulder to shoulder, or advanced foot to foot more gallantly or more truly, as Alma, the trenches of Sebastopol, and the great day of Inkermann have written in the heart of England. Therefore, with the feelings of brotherhood and kindness cemented by such ties, or at all events with the manly respect due to a brave and chivalrous race with whom our relations may no longer be those of political union or mutual aid, let us see what steps were necessary before the present France attained her proud position.

The first element in the greatness of a nation is its possession of strong and well-defined boundaries. We will say nothing of our own, for no barrier has yet been found equal to the sea. France wants but little to put her within limits which would make her almost as impregnable as if she were ringed all round by

> "The beached verge of the salt flood,
> Which twice a-day with its embossed froth
> The turbulent surge doth cover."

If you look at any map of Europe you will see how comfortably France would repose with her south guarded by the Mediterranean and the Pyrenees ; her west by the Atlantic ; her north by the British Channel ; and her east by the Alps, the Swiss mountains, and the strong current of the Rhine. If this were her position, her people would possess their land in peace ; for no enemy could reach them behind those unassailable ramparts. This was the circumference of Gallia or Gaul, and if Nature had her way, would be also the circumference of France. But geography books tell us that in this instance Nature has not been allowed to have her way. A line is arbitrarily drawn across from a certain part of the

Rhine, and confines France within boundaries on the east and north, which it is evident to every Frenchman are not the proper limits of his country. He looks on the Rhenish Prussians, the Belgians, and the Dutch, as Irish landowners used to look on the squatters on their estates ; and has the same kindly feelings towards the public law of Europe, which guarantees those portions of territory to their present occupiers, as the same Irish landowner entertained towards the common law of England which gave the said squatters a right to their lands by the length of their possession. But even with this drawback to the perfect defencibility of the French territory, and this slice off the original domain, its situation is the best in continental Europe. It is a rich, compact, thickly-peopled land, nearly square, with every variety of soil and climate, from the cold of the northern channel at Calais, where the winters are as severe as ours, to the sunny south at Avignon and Marseilles, where tropical plants are reared. It has great alluvial plains where agriculture may yet be carried to its fullest development. It has hills where the grape flourishes in rich luxuriance, and fills the vats of Burgundy and Champagne. It has mountains where a hardy population rears innumerable herds of oxen and sheep. Its harbours are numerous and commodious. It has easy access to the three chief seas of Europe. It contains upwards of two hundred thousand square miles, being more than twice the size of Great Britain, and is occupied by a strong, healthy, and energetic population, amounting to thirty-four millions of souls. It has many more elements of strength. Its populations have all got amalgamated in the course of time in one mixed and congenial people—not divided into races hating each other like the Czetches and Magyars of Hungary, or the Wallachians and Turks. Then they speak one language—not a number of distinct and unconnected dialects, where the tongue of the conquered still survives and stands up hostilely against the conqueror's, as the Polish against the Russian, and, till lately, the Welsh and Gaelic against the English. Language is the greatest element of combination in the formation of states. It seems as if the necessity of articulating the same words produced the same class of ideas, and the same turn of thought. Patriotism goes from end to end of England, because the man of Cornwall and the man of Cumberland equally, with mere varieties of accent, speak the English tongue. They read the same books; they pray in the same words; and when they meet together in the business of the world, the bond of Englishman is equally upon them both. The French, in spite of a greater diversity of provincial speech, have the same advantage. Their authors, statesmen, warriors, belong to them all; and on the Seine and on the Rhone the feelings and expressions, the hopes and recollections, bear the same national impress. It is possible that, in this sense, the possession of Belgium and Holland, and the rich dependencies of Aix-la-Chapelle and Cologne, might not be an increase to the power of France. The law would have difficulty in joining together what language, tradition, and, as regards the Dutch, religion had put asunder. And where law is not effectual, the application of force is a source of weakness to all parties concerned.

But though we have thus begun with a geographical view of what France is or might be, we are not to forget that a nation does not consist of the Land, but of the People. The square piece of territory which we now call France, was at one time not France at all. Its earliest recognition by History is as Gallia, the land of the Celts or Gael. These were a tribe or race originally springing from the farthest East. Wild, brave, and impetuous, loving war for the sake of glory and conquest, almost irresistible in attack, but greatly dispirited if their first dash was unsuccessful; boastful in speech and variable in disposition, they bear an unmistakable resemblance to their lively and gallant successors on the soil of France. What became of them in the long series of years after their first settlement was effected, nobody can say. We can only discover in the darkness of savage life, that the original possessors of the land, whoever they may have been, were driven before the new-comers, and found refuge in the extreme West; that, after intervals more or less prolonged, the colonisers were joined in their first acquisition by tribes of cognate descent from the North; and that, on one or two occasions, they burst across the boundaries of their still unconsolidated dominion, and carried terror and devastation to the walls of Rome and the fertile lands of Greece. Rome, fighting with her neighbours, and crushed by the barbarian numbers, was not able to expel them entirely from the lands of Italy. At the foot of the Alps, therefore, in the rich level plains beyond the Po, the retreating squadrons took up their abode. Wives and children, and all the cattle they had seized on their southern march, constituted the contented warriors into a nation, and their territory was recognised by the Roman authors as Cisalpine Gaul, or Gaul on this side the Alps. The dwellers, in the mean time, on the other side, pursued their course. The growth of the population required some exertion in clearing the ground. The rivers were traversed in coracles in search of fish. They hunted for wild game on the hills, and led their cattle where the pastures were greenest. There were vast assemblages for the decision of public questions, and for the ceremonies of religion. Long-bearded Druids guided the simple peasantry by the hopes and terrors of a dreadful faith—denounced curses on any one who might be disobedient to their commands, and sacrificed human victims to appease the angry gods. Meanwhile Rome was waxing great, and stretched her boundaries on every side. Gallia Cisalpina, or Cisalpine Gaul, became a subject state. All the level tract along the Mediterranean Sea and up to the Garonne was reduced to a Roman province; and finally, when the fulness of time was come, Julius Cæsar—greatest of soldiers and wisest of politicians—crossed the boundary, and carried his conquering eagles throughout the land. We need not follow minutely the course of his battles and campaigns, much less shall we waste any virtuous indignation on the destruction of Gallic freedom and the ambition of the Roman chief. The freedom of a barbarian is only an independence of general law, and an ignorant impatience of the restraints of subordination. When a wandering population, combined only for the purposes of plunder and destruction, forces its way into the peaceful domains of a people in a more advanced stage of civilisation, the historian is justified in being as eloquent as he can, in denunciation of the invasion. But when, as in the case of Cæsar, the conquest achieved by the sword was accompanied by the arts of life and all the advantages of settled government and intelligible laws, we have too much sense to lament the fate of a crowd of miserable tribes, whose defeats bring them such benefits, and whose submission to the mightier power removes their contests from the slaughter of their battle-fields and the treacherous murders of their feasts, to the impartial decision of a Roman Emperor—bad and cruel, it is possible, in his individual capacity, but following certain laws in his formal judgments, and guided by the precedents and principles of four hundred years of liberty and power. Æduans, Nervians, Allobroges, and Veromandians, were compelled to accept the securities of citizenship—not the loss of liberty—at the point of the sword; and before many years elapsed, the inhabitants of the whole of Gaul looked back without regret to the stormy period of their savage independence, and almost forgot the sound of their original Gaelic in their devotion to the language of Cicero and Virgil. Many Gallican towns had colleges of their own, which rivalled the schools of Athens and Alexandria. Patricians sent their sons to finish their education in Marseilles; and gradually the tide of eloquence and learning went on, till the grandsons of harsh-named warriors, who had worn the plaid and trunk-hose, the long hair and wooden shoes of their country, were dressed in the Roman toga, and wore the robes of senator or prætor. It became a point of honour to follow Roman customs, and even to take Roman names. One gentleman, of the uneuphonious name of Vercundaridub, whose fathers had evidently been drummers to the tribe, changed it into the easier sounded Caius Julius, and became a priest in the

Temple of Augustus. It was, indeed, impossible for a people who had mastered the Roman tongue, and tasted the pleasures of literature and science, to continue their belief in the religious tenets which had satisfied them in their original state. That religion had been adapted for the deep woods and shady hill-sides of its native seats, and had not become softened by its migration to the West. It still breathed its ancient harshness in its mysterious rites and bloody practices. But when Roman agriculture irrigated the fields, and cut down the forests, and deepened the rivers, it was found that the time of Thoth and Tanaris had long gone by. A faith that derived its sanctity from the darkness of the primeval woods, died out when the woods were thinned, and the sunshine admitted to their depths. It did not require an order from the Emperor, or missionaries from the heathen temples, or any attempts at proselytism by the governing power, to overthrow the old belief. The Romans, for the first hundred years of their dominion, made no effort to silence the teaching of the Druids, but merely interdicted the cruelties which those sacred fanatics—those earlier Brahmins—consecrated with the name of devotion. Human sacrifices, and pretensions to supernatural prescience, were prohibited by the law; but the conquering people achieved their object without offending the feelings of the conquered. They neither blindly oppressed the religion of the natives, nor meanly concealed their own. On every altar burned a flame to Jupiter or Minerva; their daily duties commenced with prayer and sacrifice for the safety of the Emperor and the State; their language was used as the means of communication of all their benefits, and the decisions of their courts. The trembling native saw something sacred in a tongue which could extend its orders over half the world; which uttered the praises of the immortal gods and the sentences upon Asiatic kings; and all the varying clans and kindreds were converted to the Roman faith, by respect for the Roman name, and gratitude for the blessings of Roman rule.

Those blessings, however, were soon mingled with many

disadvantages. The towns increased in size and number beyond the requirements of the land. Whole tracts of territory were deserted, while thousands crowded into the seats of wealth and luxury. Autun, under the courtly name of Augustodunum, contained a hundred thousand inhabitants. Science and the arts attracted immense numbers to Arles, and Lyons, and Vienne. Within the walls, rich Romanised nobles occupied their palaces, and left their rents to be collected from the diminished and overburdened peasantry. The arena at Nismes disputed the palm for size and grandeur with the Coliseum itself. The nation had, in fact, fallen into the greatest misfortune which can befall a state; the ranks were separate and hostile. The old patriarchal system had lost its charm. The man who had been chief of the family, became master of the land; and the man who had been tenant or clansman, became a slave. There was no class between. The graceful gods of Parnassus had expelled the grim divinities of the original mythology, and for a time had satisfied the longings of the Gael, for they were the embodiments of irresistible power in heaven, as the Emperors were upon earth. While the supreme State was prosperous, and the inhabitant of Gaul was safe from foreign aggression under the shelter of the Roman name, and from intestine trouble by the presence of fifty thousand soldiers, all went well. Jupiter and the rest were worshipped in their stately fanes, and the citizens of Amiens and Troyes were proud of the magnificence of the building, and the number of victims slain. But when sorrow and commotion were in the land, when the oppressions of their native lords were multiplied a hundredfold by the tyrannous exactions of the central government; when the treasury at Rome was empty and had to be filled from the half-stored granaries of the serfs of Gaul, something more was needed than games in honour of Apollo, and hymns in the purest Latinity to Venus and the Graces. The ground was now prepared; the noblest of languages was universal in the land; the human heart was bowed down with distress; the groans of the prisoners arose from the dungeon;

and there was no hand to save. It was at this time that the people that sat in darkness saw a great light. The tidings of the gospel reached them in the midst of their despair, and from henceforth they had a refuge against the woes of life. Delightful stories are told of the earliest preachers of the Word; and we forgive the fond credulity which invests them with miraculous power, and traces them at two removes to the very foot of the Cross. It was in the year 160, we are told, that a certain Pothinus and St. Irenæus landed from Asia Minor at Marseilles, and established the first congregation, and built the first church, in Lyons, the capital of Gaul. Irenæus had been the disciple of Polycarp, who himself had imbibed wisdom from the lips of St. John. Seed so planted was sure to flourish in the end; and, passing over some centuries of the alternate persecution and triumph of the new faith, we come at the same moment to the universal Christianity, and the total ruin and personal misery of the people. More helpless than the Romans themselves, more overwhelmed with luxury among the nobles, and starvation among the mass, the two extremes of life were brought face to face in the light of day. Bursting from the plains and forests of Germany in the year 481, the Franks, repulsed in former trials by the legions of Rome, dashed across the Rhine without opposition, and took possession of the land. There was no fighting or parleying, or flights or treaties. The used-up population, the effeminate noble, the enfeebled serf, the trembling townsman and scattered labourer, could neither fight nor fly. Hope had died out among them; for Rome, to which they used to turn in all their distresses, was now the author of all their woes. Tyrannical Emperors had squeezed the last farthing of their coin, the last bushel of their meal, in the name of tax. What worse could the wild soldier of Chlodoveg, with his sharp sword and hungry followers, be than the Curial, or tax-gatherer, who sold them into slavery if they were deficient in the payment, and the noble who flogged them if they failed in their servile work? So, welcome a fresh invader! A change of sorrows will be almost a relief. But Chlodoveg had other claims to their submission. In the year 453, at the great battle of Chalons, where the devastating Huns under Attila were defeated, and scattered by a combination of all the tribes and languages which were still in the service of Rome, the Franks under their leader Meroveg, and the Goths under their own chief, had been of essential service. Often repulsed by the authorities of Gaul when they had tried to seize the country, and driven over the Rhine, they were now received as deliverers ; and Franks and Goths contended for the gratitude and favour of the rescued population. But the Goths, who had learned some lessons of government by their intercourse with the polished rulers of Constantinople, had imbibed also some of the false doctrine at that time prevalent in the Eastern Church. They were Arians in faith, and the clergy of Gaul were uneasy at their obligation to such heretical intruders. To Chlodoveg, therefore, the grandson of the warrior Meroveg, they turned, because, as he was still an unconverted heathen, he would be less hostile than their rival sect. Welcomed accordingly by all—by bishop, and lord, and citizen, and slave—the savage king came on. The Goths fled before this new defender of the faith, and set up their power in Spain and Italy ; the Burgundians paid him tribute—nobody could offer any resistance to his exactions, and he found himself at the head of a successful band, located in far better quarters than their late settlements had supplied, and supported by all the influence of the now rich and powerful church.

It is a strange mixing up of almost opposite conditions which now meets our view. The old Roman intelligence, its elegance of manner and purity of taste, had never died out. The educated gentleman of Gaul wrote as good Latin verses almost as the authors of the age of Augustus. Noblemen of old descent, who traced up to the Consuls of the ancient time, and were near relations of the reigning Emperors of the East, accepted bishoprics and other church dignities, without altogether ceasing to look with benignant eyes on the inhabitants of the mythological Olympus; the Romanised cities were still entire, and even to us it gives a strange feeling of the uninterrupted flow of history when we come, in the incidents of the sixth century, upon names which are still in everyday times—Toulouse, Bordeaux, Paris, or Cologne. Their walls, and theatres, and temples, were yet erect; but, better than those inanimate records of their former greatness, their municipal privileges remained; their self-government and elective magistracy were not interfered with; their ecclesiastical rulers were also appointed by the votes of priests and people; and along their streets passed busy crowds hurrying to hear their favourite preacher, or, perhaps—for Paganism lived in the amusements of the people long after their religion was changed—to some flower-crowned celebration which had descended from the worship of Venus or Pomona. Luxury in dress and festival kept up its ancient reign; and a Roman of the last days of the Republic, if suddenly transplanted into the drawing-room of Avitus, the prelate of Vienne, or Sidonius Appollinaris of Clermont, would have heard as learned conversation, in as grammatical phrases, as in his own villa five hundred years before.

Outside of this cultivated society—ruling it, guarding it, and scarcely comprehending either its feelings or its language—was the conquering, wondering, and admiring Frank. The cognate tribes who had settled in the south and east were impressed with a still profounder awe of the wonders of that antiquated civilisation they had been commissioned to destroy. They were subdued by the old Roman majesty which shone before them in the architectural grandeur of their captured towns, and gazed with reverence on aqueducts and bridges, which combined so much gracefulness with so much strength. But the Frank in the north of the land, proud of his personal prowess—devoted to the wild faiths of the northern pantheon, where Odin sounded the note of battle and called his followers to the joys of a sensual paradise—closed his ears and heart to the teaching of Christianity. Even when Chlodoveg—or let us henceforth call him Clovis—conformed to the faith and underwent the ceremony of baptism, the pagan reigned supreme in all his thoughts. His feasts were attended by nobles who would have looked on him with disdain if they had believed in his attachment to a faith which forced him to forgive, to pity, to repent. His court at the same time, at Soissons—if court you can call a grand old Roman palace converted to the uses of a barbaric chieftain, who retained the manners and habits of the tent in his native wilderness—was attended by priests and poets who explained the doctrines of the gospel, and led a purer life than the savage warriors at their side. The perplexed and politic king did not know what to do to reconcile the jarring interests by which he was surrounded ; and at last (perhaps by way of a compromise) gratified his bishops by incursions on the lands of their heretical opponents, the Arians, on the Loire and the Saone ; and satisfied his warriors at the same time by placing no restraint on their cruelties and oppression. No follower of Thor or Odin was ever more false and pitiless than the newly christened king. No missionary was ever more zealous in the extermination of unbelievers than the pagan warriors of the Frank. Gradually this dreadful race, uniting the ferocity of savage courage with the fanaticism of religious enmity, extended its power. Clovis was never without a reason for a fresh assault on his neighbour. "It is a shame," he said, as he looked on the rich fields across the Garonne, "that such territories should belong to villains who have a different creed from ours. Onward ! let us take possession of their land." The same eloquence was exerted on the east as well as the south of his dominions, and the result was, that in a few years he was acknowledged king and conqueror from the Channel to the Mediterranean. He is the founder of the first royal race of France, which, however, does not take his name, but is known from his grandsire Meroveg as the "Merovingian Line."

Here is a state of society which never existed before. In the destruction of the other great monarchies of the world, the conquering people were of an equal organisation with the subdued. In the case of the Persian monarchy, indeed, the circumstances were reversed. The arts and sciences were in the tents of Alexander; and on the fall of that wondrous Macedonian empire, where the eloquence and learning of Greece had penetrated farther than its arms, and exercised an influence on the thoughts and feelings of the myriads of Central India, the invaders were not barbarians from the hills, or tribes from hitherto undreamed-of lands, but Roman legions cognisant of law, and proud of their obedience to constituted authority. But when the Roman Empire was in turn to be subdued, the new intruders were summoned from the woods of Germany and the long steppes of Scythia,—ignorant of the language, the arts or manners of the millions among whom they came—devastating the fields, overthrowing the temples,—murdering the helpless. Nothing was left but the prospect of a complete renewal of savagery, and the desolation of all the lands, when gradually it was found that the divine light of Christian faith was penetrating those darkened minds. Goths, Alans, Burgundians, and other immigrants, lent patient ears to the new revelation; and by the time Clovis completed his subjugation of all the Gauls, the Franks themselves, however barbaric in reality, were professedly a nation of Christians. And this is a vast step in advance, whether the profession be false or true, for it gives a starting point for future improvement; it contains an acknowledgment of certain laws, and furnishes a standard by which all actions may be measured. Clovis, barbarian, warrior, conqueror, Christian, and king, died in 511, at the age of forty-five. To show how powerful the old name of the vanished empire still was, it will amuse you to hear that this irresistible potentate was thought to have reached the pinnacle of his greatness when the powerless Anastasius of Constantinople bestowed on him the fasces and mantle of a Roman consul. A tyrant speaking Greek on the Bosphorus sent the insignia of Cicero and Scipio to a despot speaking Teutonic upon the Seine.

We need not occupy your time or fatigue your memory

with the acts and names of the successors of this great adventurer. His four sons spread ruin and misery over the land by their crimes and quarrels. Brought under one man's power again by the superior skill or wickedness of Clothaire, it was only to go through the same process of dissolution by partition between his children. Again there was a King of Paris, and a King of Orleans and Burgundy, a King of Austrasia, and a King of Soissons. All the passions of barbarism, and all the vices of a more polished state of society, were allowed full play among those fratricidal chiefs. But, crueller than all the barbarians, more false than all the statesmen, the crown of bloodthirstiness and deceit fell upon two women. The names of Fredegonde and Brunehild are still whispered with awe as incarnations of the evil principle. Both ambitious, relentless, mercenary, and beautiful, their rivalry plunged the whole land in blood. Fredegonde, relying on her treasures and powers of fascination, bribed or smiled her attendant warriors into the wildest crimes. She paved her way to the throne of Soissons by the murder of her predecessor the sister of Brunehild, and vowed implacable hatred to the family of the hostile queen. One day at this time, Gregory of Tours, the historian of that wretched period, was walking near the palace of Soissons with Sylvius the Bishop of Albi. "Do you see anything on that roof?" said Sylvius. "I see the standard which Hilperic the King has set up," replied the monk. "And you see nothing else?" inquired the Bishop. "No; do you see anything?" "I see the sword of divine vengeance hung over that wicked house." And so must many others, with eyes as clear as the Bishop of Albi's. When human endurance is at an end, the sentence of offended Heaven is close at hand. The curse of outraged humanity fell upon the royal line. Brother against brother, uncle against nephew, and when age came on, the white locks of the still vengeful Brunehild against the faded charms of the relentless Fredegonde. These were the spectacles presented to the eyes of the offended nations. Powerless kings dominated by the loftier spirit of their wives; their sons so subdued by the energy of those detested mothers, that they never obtained independence when they were placed upon the throne ; even the grandchildren held in a timid subjection which unfitted them for the struggles of war or policy ; it is no wonder the Franks held more resolutely than ever to the Salic law, by which females were excluded from the succession. At the same time they provided themselves with a compensation for the unworthiness of their lineal rulers by the election of an officer, who at this time made his first appearance in history, but who played a wonderful part in the succeeding events. This was a Mayor of the Palace ; a noble chosen by the nobles to be the guide and controller of the sovereign,—the leader of the armies in war, and President of the Council in peace. The humility of the name for a long time hid the real nature of the appointment ; and long after Fredegonde had died amid the execrations of the country, and Brunehild had excited a momentary feeling of compassion by the sight of her dying struggles at the age of eighty, lashed hand and foot to an untamed horse, the kingly title indeed remained to their descendants, but the power had passed into other hands. The tendency of a warrior tribe which owes its settlement to the sword, is towards monarchy— the concentration of authority into one hand secures the unity of action which is essential to success in war. But when the strong bond of mutual danger is removed, the pride of enriched nobles and powerful possessors of land revolts against the supremacy of one of their own order. Aristocracy is the next step in the progress of a nation, and Gaul (as it was still called), or the nation of the Franks, reached this period when the frightful tragedy of the sons and grandsons of Clovis came to a close. Lords of vast domains, and hereditary leaders of numerous vassals, the counts and marquises looked on the puppet who professed to wear the crown as their inferior in everything but name. His commands were disobeyed, his domains infringed upon to such a degree as sometimes to be insufficient for his support. On great occasions, when a royal procession took plaee, the lowly appearance of the legitimate king must have formed a humiliating contrast with the pomp and dignity of the nobles who rode by his side. Sitting alone, sad and silent, the descendant of Clovis was paraded from the palace to the church in a waggon drawn by bullocks, the mark of the remote and primitive simplicity of his ancestral line, but unappreciated unless in its ludicrous or degrading aspect, by the rough and ambitious warriors who reverenced nothing which they did not fear. One great opportunity was offered for the restoration of the kingly office, by the incursion of the Saracen armies in 730. On this occasion all Europe was on the gaze. Crowding all the plains of France, holding already the rich realms of Spain, the African shores of the Mediterranean, the illimitable levels of Asia, and the gorgeous cities on the Tigris, the Mohammedans were in the very act of establishing their power over the distracted populations of the west. But the gallantry of the Franks came to the rescue. If there had sat upon the throne a man like Clovis, the greatness of the peril would have restored to him all the advantages of his position. The king, however, was an idle and dissolute youth, trembling at a word from priest or necromancer, and retaining of all the royal attributes of his ancestors only the long hair and loose raiment which marked the kingly line. But at his side was found a man as brave as Clovis, and wiser than that barbarian chief. Karl Martel, or Charles the Hammer,—an unmistakable Frank in name and epithet—General of the army, and wielding all the powers of the state as Mayor of the Palace, dashed down to Orleans at the head of the collected hosts of Germany and Gaul, and with one fatal shock scattered the light battalions of the Moslem, so that they never combined again. Europe was Christianised by the victory, and the crown transferred to the proper wearer. Loudest in expressing the thanks of Christendom for this great deliverance, was the chief bishop of the Christian Church. No eminence was too high for the champion of the faith, and though Charles Martel was satisfied with the title of Duke, and the reality of sovereign power, the pontiff insisted upon showing his appreciation of the services of the father by his benevolence to the son. This son was Pepin, successor to Karl's name and authority, wielding the sword with as much power, and ruling the land with as much wisdom ; and when, in the year 751, the old dynasty actually died out from the public mind, and the poor representatives of the heroic founders of the monarchy exchanged the premature debaucheries of their youth for the living sepulture of a convent, the grateful and politic Pope Zacharias found that the time was come. He said, "It is right that the kingly title should rest where the kingly power now is." He crowned Pepin King of the Franks, and thus consecrated the second or Carlovingian race. But King Pepin was not to be outdone in generosity by a priest, and proclaimed the successors of St. Peter sovereign pontiffs and lords of the city and territories of Rome. By this arrangement, two shadowy impostures were abolished, and two strong realities substituted in their stead. The Western Church was freed from its nominal vassalage and subserviency to the Eastern Cæsar ; and the true King of the Franks, the man who "could rule and dared not lie," delivered from the apparent superiority of a phantom chief, from whom all life had long passed away. Visits and benefits after this were interchanged between the Frankish monarch and the Roman Pope. Twice Pepin hurried into Italy to the support of the tottering chair. Stephen in return crossed the mountains, and anointed with holy oil not only the king himself, but his two sons Charles and Carlaman.

To be a crowned king in those days, was to have the sanctity of Religion added to the reality of earthly power. After that ennobling ceremony the office of king became invested with loftier attributes than merely the reverence of men. It was considered something divine and sacred ; resistance to its authority grew to be not only rebellion, but sacrilege ; and henceforth, however nearly a great noble might approach the monarch in power, he was immeasurably inferior to him in dignity and rank. Pepin died in 768, and the greatest monarch the world had seen since the Roman Empire began to decay, inaugurated a new state of society, and different modes of thought. Charles the Great, contracted by French pronunciation into Charlemagne, is the last of barbaric kings, and the first of feudal monarchs. Ancient history disappears at the death of Pepin, and what is called Mediæval life begins. There was, however, one institution, which formed a stronger connecting link between the two states of society than the personal predominance of the king. This was the Church, which, in all those earlier years, had acted as mediator between the oppressor and the oppressed, and endeavoured to calm the ferocity of the Frank, and revive the confidence of the Gallo-Roman, by declaring the great and elevating doctrines of the faith. It had also supported its claim to authority by many signs and wonders above the powers of men. It will not be necessary to inquire too curiously into the miracles by which the simple spectators were impressed. If a saintly visitor astonished a king by throwing down a vase of matchless beauty, the spoil of some assault on one of the great cities of the Roman period, breaking it into pieces, and then by two or three words of prayer, restoring it in all its pristine integrity, we are to bear in mind, at the same time, the humanising advice by which this incident was accompanied. If fire burst regularly forth, kindled by invisible hands on spires and church roofs, wherever the march of the barbaric chief was directed, we are to remember that the priests of those illuminated fanes preached mercy and compassion in ears which were yet strangers to the sound. All through the stormy years of the first or Merovingian life (from 481 to 751), the monasteries, which had been richly endowed by the later Emperors of the West, maintained a kind of sacred neutrality in the struggle of the contending nations. Strongly fortified, and generally of immense size, presided over by an abbot chosen for his talents or influence, they acted as garrisons, to which all the learning of the time fled for refuge. The monks, at a very early date, began to copy the books of the great authors of the Augustan and succeeding ages. All the inventions and sciences of past periods were here preserved, and strong-armed kings stood rebuked and awestruck in presence of those powerless but omniscient ecclesiastics.

The parts played by the respective nations, the Frank and Gallo-Roman, were at last by these means almost reversed.

The conqueror obeyed, the vanquished issued his commands. For it has been observed, by a modern inquirer who went carefully over the names of priests and soldiers, recorded in the annals of two or three hundred years after Clovis, that the preponderating majority of Romans were in the service of church and abbey, and of the Franks in the army. The warrior was either too modest or too proud to pore over books, and acquire the almost miraculous power of writing with a pen. Gallo-Romans were chiefs of abbeys, lords of church lands, preachers in crowded cities, confessors of repentant lords, guides of devout princesses. It needs little observation to perceive that the unhappy Frank, buckled up in his armour of proof, was getting ten times more subdued than his Gallo-Roman subject ; and we accordingly perceive, that before the accession of Pepin, the kings, the counts, the dukes, had all nearly stript themselves of their houses and lands. Death-bed terrors, love, expiation, contempt for earth, and zeal for heaven, all the passions and energies of the human mind, were enlisted in favour of the church. Cupidity won over new supporters whom the mere truths of Christianity had failed to move, and, long before the time of Charlemagne, we observe a strong mixture of Frankish names among the dignitaries of so secure and wealthy an establishment.

Here, then, we see the universal course of human affairs exemplified in the history of Gaul. First the sword ; then the intellect. No nation is secure and happy without the combination of the two. Without the first, the second becomes degraded into cunning and cruelty, as among the Greeks of the Lower Empire, or the Hindoos of our own time ; without the last, the sword becomes an instrument of tyranny and oppression, as in the ferocious onslaught of the Huns, or the desolating fanaticism of the Mohammedans. Happiest state of all, where a people, strong in courage and clear in intellect, possesses the wisdom to devise a constitution in which all are subject, yet all are free ; and a sword never drawn in an unjust quarrel, nor idle in a just one ; which protects and guards the blessings which the intellect has won.

> " A land of settled government,
> A land of just and old renown,
> Where freedom broadens slowly down
> From precedent to precedent;
> Where faction seldom gathers head,
> But by degrees to fulness wrought,
> The strength of some diffusive thought,
> Hath time and space to work and spread."

Charlemagne is the greatest name in European history, with the exception, perhaps, of Alexander the Great and Cæsar. A more modern name has been added as recalling in a closer manner the wonders of his career, and commanding the same populations. Napoleon has the farther resemblance that he governed the same soil as a portion of his dominion, and is claimed by the vanity of the French as their countryman, though an Italian by blood and name, in the same way as the grandson of Karl, who spoke no word of their language and never resided in any part of their country, is claimed as one of their compatriots. The Britons, by this rule, might have claimed kin with the Roman Antonines, because they were subject to their power. From his great castle at Aix-la-Chapelle, the Frankish ruler looked over all the lands, and watched the motions of the most distant tribes. Perpetually listening for the slightest sound of opposition, he started off without a moment's delay, and carried surprise and destruction among the Saxon heathen, or the rebellious Lombards, or the Mussulmans of Spain. A new system of government was instituted, by which the various peoples were constituted separate and almost independent states, with the one bond between them of the great Sovereign who stretched his authority over all alike. Each territory was governed by its native chiefs, appointed to certain duties, and invested with a portion of the kingly power. There were dukes, and counts, and commissioners of the crown, who ruled, and raised troops, and collected taxes in the two Burgundys, and Navarre, and Germany, and Italy,—but their authority was limited to the districts to which they were sent. A duke in Milan had no power in Vienna ; the chief governor in Paris had no influence in Bavaria, any more than a lord-lieutenant of Ireland has any authority in Bengal. The councils also of this great statesman were composed of national advisers. He went with very few attendants from one of his subject provinces to the other, and consulted on their local interests with the wisest of their respective populations. Wherever he extended his sceptre, he sent the crozier and the cross along with it. All the recesses of heathenism were penetrated by his missionaries first, and then by his armies. The vanquished were condemned to submit to just laws and to be baptised—a severe punishment, as it appeared at first to the ferocious Saxon, who sometimes refused to accept his life on these conditions, but in the end working great things for Europe and mankind. From all quarters the eyes equally of friend and foe were directed to the seat of such wisdom combined with such power. It seemed to those who could read, or who knew only the traditions of the old Imperial time, that the days of Augustus and Trajan, and the Antonines, were returned. Brimful with gratitude for past protection, the Pope of Rome was ready to give outward form to this universal thought. On the eve of Christmas, in the year 800, he placed on the head of Charlemagne the crown of Italy, and hailed him Emperor of the West. Immediately fresh dignity was believed to rest on the person of the Frank. Something of the old reverence which had made the worship of the Emperor the great bond of unity among the different religions and territories of the Roman world, would still linger about the very name. To be Emperor of the West was to be the greatest, and almost the holiest, of mortal men. The Pope himself could only bless the wearer of that mysterious crown, and was the creature of his breath, the hearer of his commands, and owing dignity and office to his grace and favour. Charlemagne, Emperor of the West, could nominate kings and pontiffs at his pleasure. All the little potentates of the time thought it an honour to be admitted to his presence, or even to wait in his antechamber. Laws and ordinances were issued for the regulation equally of Church and State. Great public works were undertaken to improve the internal communication of his dominions. Learning was encouraged, not merely by largesses to scholars, but by the example of the sovereign himself. He was surrounded in his hours of retirement by a select band of poets, historians, and philosophers from all countries: Alcuin, from England, was the chief; and here, in easy conversation, in essays on Virgil or Horace, and the lighter amusements of wit and repartee, let us hope that the great man forgot that he was great. After three-and-thirty years of battle with the Saxons, after fifty-four military expeditions, all crowned with success; after overthrowing the Lombards in Italy and the Saracens in Barcelona, he saw one day, when he was residing in Southern Gaul, a small fleet of vessels manœuvring off a harbour on the Mediterranean. A common enough sight, you will say, for the Mediterranean at that time was the highway for all the traffic in the world; but Charlemagne burst into tears. "These are not merchants," he said, "from Africa, or adventurers from Britain: these are the Norsemen—not that I fear such enemies can do any harm to me, but I weep for the calamities I perceive they will bring upon my realms." And shortly after this, in 814, he died.

Forty-six years of so vigorous and beneficent a reign had accustomed all Europe to the supremacy of a master mind. When the master mind was withdrawn, the feeling of obedience still remained. But it could not long stand the shock to which it was now exposed by the weakness and wickedness of the royal line. Louis, his son, had the imperial name, and all the kingdoms, states, and principalities, except the kingdom of Italy, which was left to his nephew for his share. Never was a man in such a false position as Louis, the meek and lowly. Excellently qualified for a monk, or even for a ruler in happier times, he did all that gentleness and superstition could do to render the name either of king or emperor contemptible in the eyes of his men-at-arms. He made conscience, forsooth, of restoring to the church the lands and houses torn from it by those grasping barons. He would not benefit by the rapine of his friends, or even by what he thought the unjust conquests of his father. What was a rough soldier, whose wealth arose from plundered enemies, to think of such a leader as this? He complained also of the bishops and other dignitaries of the church, that they had departed from the simplicity of apostolic life, and contended more for superiority in rank and riches, than for the conversion of souls. What could an ambitious and energetic hierarchy think of a crowned friar who taught them their Christian duties, and showed them an example in his own person of all the Christian virtues? Too scrupulous for the soldiers, too religious for the priest, Louis the Debonnaire (a word that means the weakly pliant) was deserted by both parties. He was dethroned by his more warlike sons, and degraded by his offended clergy. Twice immured in a cloister, he was twice brought out to stop the mortal enmities of his children. To each of his three sons he had allotted a portion of his vast domains during his lifetime; and when he died, after a sad and troubled reign, in 840, the separation of the component portions of the empire became complete. The great name of emperor fell to Lothaire, his eldest son, who instantly asserted its rights over the kingdoms of his brother Charles the Bald, and Louis the German. But they resolved to defend their independence, and took arms against his claims. In this quarrel all the nationalities took part; and in 841 there gathered to the banks of a little streamlet at Fontenay, near Auxerre, in Burgundy, the forces of all the empire of Charlemagne, only now they were in separate camps. On one side of the river stood Lothaire with the men of Italy, and Helvetia, and Provence, who, though conquered by Charlemagne, and ruled over by his son, were recalled by the sound of their language, in which no German words were intermixed, to the memory of a time when they were the masters of the world, and gave laws both to Germany and Gaul. On the other there stood with Charles of Neustria (the north-west of France, including Paris) the men of the conquest—Franks in descent and name—but by this time so intermingled with the subject population that they had all the feelings of Gallo-Romans, and resisted the sway of the Frankish emperor as a memorial of their defeat. With Louis the German, side by side with Charles and the Franks, were the men of the ancient line—the Teutons from the original seat of the Frank confederacy, the warriors of Almagne and Saxe and Thuringia, throwing off their community with a distant and, practically, a foreign people, with whom they had no ties in common, either of origin, or law, or language.

This battle it is necessary to dwell upon, because, though apparently fought on behalf of rival chiefs, it was in reality the bursting forth of national life. There were to be henceforth introduced into European history feelings which had not yet been perceived—feelings of patriotic love for the natal soil, of pride in the national greatness, and of equity and moderation in the intercourse between state and state. Up to this time the individual was all in all. The chief was a warrior encamped on a certain piece of ground. He took possession of it yesterday, he might leave it to-morrow; but from henceforth the tenure of his estate is changed. He sees in long perspective his sons' sons and his remotest successors living in the same tower and governing the same dependants. Property, in short, gets established under the protection of general law, and woe to the man beyond the Rhine, beyond the Alps, beyond the sea, that from this time should do the Frenchman wrong! His cause would be taken up—not by a solitary baron, or even a combination of petty chiefs, but by the collected state.

The three brothers, after the battle of Fontenay, in which Lothaire was vanquished, made a peaceable partition of their lands. The empire remained to the eldest along with Italy. He obtained also a long strip of ground extending from the mouths of the Rhone to the mouth of the Scheldt in the North Sea ; and on the eastward from Istria and the Alps to the mouth of the Weser. All to the west of this arbitrary line was France ; all to the east of it was Germany. Placed like an embankment between the two families of Franks, this narrow band has been a debatable land between them ever since. Bit by bit the Frenchman has pressed his way, absorbing portions of this territory as he went. Burgundy is his, and Lorraine and Alsace ; but his natural boundary he has never permanently regained. The Teutonic tongue has kept a firm hold of the noble river ; and all the hearts of Germany, from Cologne to the Black Forest, have made the Rhine ! the Rhine ! the rallying-cry against aggression. For language in this instance, as in many others, has been found a more powerful demarcation than geographical limits. The treaty by which the partition was made, was written in the tongues of the great cognate, but now widely separated peoples. The Franco-Roman, parent of the present French, was addressed to the subjects of Charles,—and veritable German, which is intelligible at the present day, to the followers of Louis. Henceforth each was to be recognised as sovereign of a distinct and independent state ; and though for some time longer the title of Emperor was given to the eldest lineal descendants of Charlemagne, their principal occupation was the government of the kingdom of France. This, however, was no easy task, and the men to whose lot it fell were not qualified for the great duty. Their kingship, indeed, over a great portion of the land, was merely nominal. There were rival princes claiming independence as dukes of Aquitaine, marquises of Septimania, and counts of Brittany, and twenty potentates besides. But more weakening to the unhappy monarchs than the presumption of too powerful vassals were the unintermitted invasions of the Norsemen, which the sagacity of Charlemagne had foretold. They pushed their light boats up the rivers as far as they could go—

burning, slaying, and spoiling throughout their whole career; and when water failed, or a force was collected to oppose them, they carried their vessels across the level plains and launched them on some pastoral brook, where their very names were still unknown, and carried on their depredations as before. When it was found that the crown was inadequate to the defence of the people, the possessors of the great estates, who had hitherto held them by the policy or favour of the king, retained them on their own behalf; promising a shadowy sort of fealty to the monarch, but exercising in their own names and on their own authority all the rights and privileges which they had held by appointment from the crown. The church was far from being left behind in the race of aggression upon the properties of the crown. Vast domains accrued to it by the generosity or feebleness of the successive kings. Bishops and lordly abbots disputed the precedence with the highest of the nobility, and did suit and service in person, armed in complete steel, for the lands they held as fiefs. The smaller proprietors followed these great examples, and soon all the country was filled with square towers and fortified castles; with which, and his handful of followers, the stalwart baron guarded his crops and cattle, or made head against the assault of northern freebooter, or unscrupulous neighbour.

But against Norman activity every defence was vain. Pirates, warriors, and fanatics for their hideous faith, they swarmed on every coast—forced their way up the Seine, and for two years besieged the city of Paris. A strong man rose among them of the name of Rollo. Too weak to resist, and too impoverished to buy off the assailants, Charles the Simple (properly so called) brought one of his feudal attributes into play, and by the ceremony of homage, converted the savage conqueror from an enemy whom he could not meet in the field, into a vassal who swore to be submissive to all his commands. On this condition the powerless king conveyed Normandy, with all its rights and privileges, to the triumphant chieftain, and Brittany, in so far as it depended on the crown. But as if to show that the submission was merely nominal, and the liegeman superior to his lord, the act of investiture was accompanied by an insult to the monarch, which must have interrupted the solemnity of the scene. When the recipient of the fief was required to conclude the ceremony by kissing the sovereign's foot, the haughty Norman signed to one of his attendants to go through the form in his stead. The burly soldier grasped the uplifted leg with all his force, and raising it to his lips, upset the unprepared monarch upon his back. In this unseemly manner the pirate of the Baltic, and worshipper of the almost forgotten Odin, took his place among the Christian chivalry of Europe as Duke of Normandy, and one of the twelve Peers of France. The old anarchy of the days of the last of the Merovingians seemed to be returned. But let us not be afraid. A new principle, if not of legal obedience, at least of personal independence, was spread among the owners of the soil. And faint as the light of royalty was, and in abeyance as all its active powers were held, there still hung over it the sacred feeling of supremacy and law. The forms of feudalism might be destitute of effect at the time, but they had an internal significance which only awaited a favourable moment to develop itself in act. And this moment came in the year 987, when the chief of all the feudal magnates was called upon to reunite the reality of power to the name of king. Hugh Capet, duke of France and Burgundy, connected by marriage and treaty with Normandy and other dukedoms, celebrated for valour and skill, and looked up to as the sole hope of an exhausted people and dishonoured crown, was summoned to the throne, not so much by the voice of his country as by the necessity of the time. From Rome again came forth the words which overthrew an ancient dynasty, and inaugurated a new. Hugh Capet was declared by the Pope to be "king of France in virtue of his great deeds," and the third race began.

CHAPTER II.

FROM HUGH CAPET, A. D. 987, TO PHILIP AUGUSTUS, A. D. 1180.

THE Merovingian dynasty lasted two hundred and seventy years, from Clovis to Pepin; the Carlovingian lasted two hundred and thirty-six years, from Pepin to Hugh Capet.

The Franks, during those lengthened periods, had gradually yielded to the humanising influences of association with the conquered peoples. Their language softened; they obtained some knowledge of old Roman institutions and laws; they professed submission to the church, but the wildness of their native forests was never altogether quelled. Wherever they had power, they exercised it harshly; they quarrelled among themselves; and when Hugh Capet came to the throne, he succeeded to the chieftainship of a race more than the government of a nation. The king had no influence, and scarcely any acknowledged rights, beyond the limits of his own domain. In Burgundy and France he was a real substantial king, because in both he was a long-established duke; but in Normandy, Brittany, and Aquitaine, and Toulouse, and Flanders, as he held none of the ducal authority (originally communicated as a trust by Charlemagne), he was not in possession of any kingly powers. Each of these territorial potentates claimed now to hold his lands with as high a sanction as the king held his crown. When Capet reminded a disobedient vassal of his duties, by asking "Who made you Count?" the warrior answered, "Who made you King?" —not, as may be supposed, with the vulgar insolence of a rebellious subject, but with the pride of an equal, maintaining that the throne of France and the countship of Perigneux were equally by the grace of God.

The struggle henceforth was to be between the principles of Royalty and Aristocracy. At first the forces were equally balanced, and very slight circumstances might have affected the result. Both parties for a long time seem to have been profoundly ignorant that, in addition to crowned Prince and armed Chevalier, there was another body whose fortunes were interested in the debate, and that the masses of the people would be a tower of strength whichever side they espoused. Humbled, trodden down, and almost without life or hope, the multitude still bore within it the means of future power. It had arms and a heart—it could be won and trained ; and while envious chief and ambitious monarch were watching each other's motions, calling round them their immediate retainers, and relying solely on sword and spear, there was a third order in the State which seized the ground left unoccupied by the contending factions, offered refuge, peace, and consolation to the wretched who had no other friend, and bound the affections and interests of the poor and destitute to the holy and compassionate Church. The Church undertook the championship of the weak and helpless, and by their aid very nearly succeeded, not only in France, but through the length and breadth of Christendom, in establishing an ecclesiastical domination, to which both king and noble would have been forced to submit. This, then, is the combat which we are called on to witness : the aggressions of a proud nobility on the theoretical supremacy of the sovereign —the gradual elevation of the kingly office above the competition of all or any of its subordinates, with the great part played by priests and bishops in the strife, till finally, by the junction of these last with the crown, and their desertion of the people, they converted a government, in which power was divided, though unequally, between the three Estates, into a despotic monarchy, for which the subject of the Turkish Sultan would have been loth to exchange the freedom and independence left him by the traditions of his race.

Now, the period of the class-antagonism of king and peerage, extending from the accession of Hugh Capet, in 987, to the reign of Louis the Eleventh, in 1461, is called the Middle Ages ; and of all this time of trouble and action, of universal personal activity and deep mental torpor, the great characteristic is the Feudal System. We will therefore take a short view of the condition of France at the date we have now reached, divided as it is between the rivals for supreme influence ; and then we can proceed with more assurance in estimating the nature of the dispute, and the prospects of success. Some people say the feudal system existed in full force among the original tribes from which the Franks proceeded, and that even in the time of Clovis it was established among all the Gauls. And very likely it was ; for the feudal system was not the result of any legislator's institution, with all the covenants arranged and settled beforehand, like the clauses of an act of Parliament, but was the natural growth of the circumstances in which people were placed, developed itself more and more as the good effects of it were seen, and only assumed the force and stability of written law when the principles from which it came were reduced into systematic order. These principles are very plain, and may be stated to consist in the reciprocal obligation of protection and obedience. As long as the superior afforded security against oppression, and guaranteed the inferior in the possession of his lands, he was bound to assist his lord by every means in his power. But, on the other hand, as long as the inferior was ready to perform the services required, his lord was equally bound to guard him from all wrong. The whole country was distributed on these conditions. The king was nominally the lord of all the soil. Portions of this were held by great proprietors, who vowed submission and service ; aid in war, and counsel in peace, in return for their vast domains, and the serfs and townsmen who occupied the ground. They swore this in a formal and binding oath, placing their closed hands between the king's palms, and kneeling at his feet, and on rising were presented with the emblems of investiture, and were the liegemen or homagers of the chief. These great proprietors. however, had others dependent upon them, to whom they allotted, in a similar way and on similar conditions, portions of their domain. These again subdivided their portion among still smaller holders, till there was nc more land to assign in fief, that is, on feudal terms; and thus the great hierarchy went on and on, from the occupant of a few hundred acres and a rugged tower, to the possessors of miles of mountain and plain, and the great princes who held whole countries in their hands,—till finally it reached the sovereign himself, unapproachable in the theory of his grandeur and power, but dependent in practice, for his influence and authority, on the number of his own personal retainers and the wealth of his hereditary domains. Two immense advantages, however, were on the side of the king. He was crowned as the visible and heaven-appointed chieftain of all the rest, and the estates of his liegemen lapsed into his hands on breach of covenant, such as rebellion and treason, and on failure of heirs. Here was always a chance for the suzerain lord; for, in those disturbed and lawless times, the deaths of whole families were by no means uncommon. Battles, assassinations, and the unwholesomeness of houses and lands, swept off entire lines of stalwart youths and blooming maidens; and tower and hall, and all the territories, and all the serfs, and scarcely less valuable cattle, reverted to the original bestower. This paralysed the efforts of the mightiest nobles against the Crown; for their subtenants—the men, for instance, who held their grounds from the Dukes of Toulouse or Aquitaine, and were fighting under their banner against the king—were never sure that a desolating fever or dangerous war might not exterminate the family of their chiefs, and then the sovereign whom they were now opposing would be, not only their national and paramount lord, but their own immediate superior, Duke of Toulouse or Aquitaine, as well as King of France. But the establishment of well-defined feudalism at the accession of the Capets was contemporaneous with what appeared a total dissolution of all the bonds of society, and an almost universal belief in the approaching end of the world. The world might well indeed be supposed to be near its end, when misery was so universal, and the prospect of improvement so hopeless. It was supposed to have been prophesied in the Book of Revelation, that at the end of a thousand years from the birth of Christ the great dragon was to be let loose, and the earth and all its inhabitants destroyed. As the dreaded hour drew near, the symptoms of advancing doom grew clearer and clearer. The husbandman left off his labour—the baron divested himself of sword and buckler, and took refuge in the church. Famine was universal over Europe. Pestilence followed, and want of confidence between man and man. Battles were fought between nearest relations for scraps of food, and, worst calamity of all, the instincts of nature were set aside under the great agony of hunger and despair, and human flesh was eaten almost without concealment. Marshes covered the plains. Bridges were few, and, being only of wood, had fallen into decay. Travelling was very difficult, and trade almost impossible; for the enterprising merchant had to seek out the fords on the swollen rivers, and avoid the castle of the rapacious freebooter on the hill; and even the peaceful ecclesiastic, who was generally safer than his countrymen, was condemned to remain in his abbey, from the mere impossibility of traversing the land. An abbot of Cluny, invited by Bouchard, Count of Paris, to bring his religious to St. Maur des Fosses, excused himself from making so long a journey in "a strange and unknown country." It was about the distance of Portsmouth from London.

Such was the state of France when Robert, the son of Hugh Capet, mounted the throne in 996. If gentleness and meekness had at that time been thought qualities befitting a king, the French would have gathered round the new monarch, and protected him from the enemies whom his very virtues raised against him. But they submitted to see him rebuked and humbled, and rewarded him for his humiliation with the vain appellation of Saint. This was the reason of his punishment: he had taken to wife Bertha, widow of the

Count of Blois, and was devotedly attached to her. But Bertha was his cousin in the fourth degree, and Robert had acted as godfather to one of her children by her previous husband. Whereupon the Pope, who had by this time stretched his authority into all the relations of life, ordered him to dismiss his unhappy queen, as he had married her without a dispensation from the Holy See. The relationship of blood, and the closer bond established at the baptism of her child, made the union illegal, and now it must be dissolved. Robert refused, protested, pleaded and prayed, but all in vain. The haughty bishop was Gregory the Fifth, and the dreadful sentence of excommunication was passed. From that moment the king was treated as the Jews of old treated the lepers in their towns. His servants deserted him ; the offices of the Church—prayer, communion, penance and absolution —were forbidden ; nobody was allowed to speak to him, or comfort him, or aid him in any way. The few victuals which the compassion of his friends allowed him, were swallowed in silence ; the plate on which they had lain was passed through the fire, and the fragments thrown to the dogs. The pious and guiltless Robert yielded at last. Bertha left him, and the haughty and imperious Constance, a daughter of the Count of Toulouse, was forced on him in her stead. Robert obeyed the orders of the Church, and looked back with unavailing regret on the vanished happiness of his home. In the succeeding reigns we shall meet with this terrible instrument of power wielded by the Popes in furtherance of their own designs ; and we will only, therefore, now add, that when an interdict and excommunication were pronounced on a whole kingdom, in order to bring a refractory king to reason, the privations, which were limited to Robert personally, were extended to every house and family in the land. The churches were shut up ; marriages, christenings, burials, all ceased ; trade was suspended ; and the whole machinery of social life brought to a dead stand. We are, therefore, not to wonder at the effects produced by the mere threat of this tremendous infliction ; we can only wonder that the folly and superstition of mankind ever allowed it to be carried into effect. The policy of Hugh Capet, which consisted in allowing the feudal chiefs to weaken themselves by mutual quarrels, was so far pursued by Robert, that he left them almost entirely to themselves. He attended all the services of the Church, dressed himself in a surplice, and joined the choristers in hymns of his own composition. No warlike triumphs fill this reign ; and even when the furious ambition of his wife, the successor of the gentle Bertha, raised enmities between her husband and her son, the benevolent Robert defeated her machinations by throwing himself into the arms of the malcontent Prince, and bringing him back to his duty by tears and prayers. When he died at sixty years of age, in 1031, the attendants at the grave wept bitterly, and said, "We have lost our Father. He governed us in peace, and under him our goods were secure." A noble epitaph, which could be repeated at that period over the grave of no other ruler in France. Wars and spoliation never ceased in all the land, and the Chronicles contain little but a confused medley of battles and negotiations, treaties broken as soon as made, and quarrels patched up again between the Counts of Blois and Champagne, the Dukes of Burgundy, and Counts of Anjou.

The year after Robert's death the effect of these commotions was shown in the total exhaustion of all the combatants. A bad harvest added to the distress, and half the population lay dead or dying. Men's hearts were touched at last, even through their coats of mail. The harshest and bloodiest laid by the sword, and built monasteries and chapels to appease the wrath of Heaven. The clergy stepped nobly forward and proclaimed the "Truce of God," by which it was rendered sinful to wage war on any private account between Wednesday night and Monday morning of each week during the whole of Advent, and from the Monday before Lent to Pentecost. When they added that this respite for humanity was to be extended to all the holidays and festivals of the Church, we are to look with reverence on the admirable motive from which those numerous observances originally sprang, and even listen kindly to the absurd legends of the Roman Catholic calendar; for to the canonisation, perhaps of some altogether incredible saint, a day's immunity from suffering was given to the peasantry of France. Never let us mind whether St. Denis walked some miles with his head off, or not. His festival saved many a head from being broken, and that, in those days, was almost as great a miracle.

But church-building, and abstaining from slaughter a few days in the year, did not satisfy the conscience of some of the wilder chiefs. In all great calamities it was already an established practice to make a pilgrimage to Rome. There, in the city of the martyrs and apostles, the repentant warrior kissed the sacred relics of the saints, and bent in prayer over the graves of Peter and Paul. A holier grave and more sacred soil at this time rose strongly to the general mind. One by one, or joined in small companies, excited penitents turned their steps to the distant and unknown Jerusalem, and by one touch of the Sepulchre and one night watch on Calvary compensated for all the errors of their lives. Few came back, for the journey was far, and the conquerors of Syria, the Fatimite Caliphs, hostile. But the great custom spread. In the first year of this century, Sylvester the Second, one of the best and most learned of the Popes, had cried almost prophetically, "Arm, soldiers of Christ!" and pointed to the birthplace of the Faith. Many obscure men had listened to the command; but at this time, when the good King Robert died, and was succeeded by his son Henry the First, pilgrims of higher rank set out on the perilous journey. Among these, the most distinguished was Robert of Normandy, the father of William the Conqueror. He died at Nicæa, in 1035, on his return, and his duchy passed peaceably to his son, in spite of the illegitimacy of his birth. This sagacious ruler was too young at first for personal exertion, and then too busy with his domestic troubles to look beyond his own territory; and the realm of France enjoyed comparative repose. The Truce of God had produced excellent effects, and the energy of lord and abbot, being diverted from war and spoil, expended itself in raising the most gorgeous architectural buildings, cathedrals, and churches and abbeys, of which the remains, and in some instances the perfect fabric, are everywhere visible in France. Greatest of all the builders was William of Normandy, and to his dukedom the student of art still turns for matchless specimens of the early style, which has combined in marvellous proportions the lightness and grace of individual details with the grandeur and solemnity of the general effect. Thus we see that church-building, pilgrimages, and their inevitable accompaniments, employment of the poor, and improvement of the roads, succeeded to the chaotic state of society before the rules of feudalism were established. Every village was enriched with a house of worship, every warrior's hall became a centre of intelligence and life. The mason who worked the tracery of the abbey walls could not be destitute of other kinds of skill; the colourist who stained the windows, the carver who fretted the screen, brought their local information to the general stock. The man who had traversed the Alps and rested in the streets of Rome, or, grander still, the man who had taken ship at Venice and passed the Grecian Isles, and sprung ashore at the harbour of Aleppo, and climbed the Mount of Olives, could not fail, however deficient in art or education, to bring back with him vast stores of new and elevating thoughts. Nor were their pilgrimages altogether without reward even in a pecuniary sense. From the early seats of the Faith they brought back relics and memorials which were worth their weight in gold. Already the new-built churches were glorified with the possession of cartloads of real bones and chips of holy wood. Even a fragment of stone from the floor of Pilate's judgment-hall, or a pebble from the garden of Gethsemane, was set in costly frame, and placed with prayers and processions on the altar. Elevated, ennobled, almost sanctified by the mysteries of art and the treasures of superstition, the priest exercised a sway over the simple crowd which it is impossible to understand, and which it would be wrong to undervalue ; for the priest was the patron, friend, and protector to whom, in all their woes, they were certain to have recourse. Though in later times ambition and the natural corruption of prosperity combined to raise the priestly office above the other orders in the State, in the early days of priestcraft its influence was beneficial. It established a barrier between brute strength and individual weakness. It was an idea ; and great progress is always made when the mind is able to realise something which is not tangible by the hand or visible to the eye. It is in fact the first triumph of mind over matter. Sword and spear were blunted against the great thought represented by the church, for it embodied all we have ever fought for since—the equality of man in the sight of God, and the necessity of justice, mercy, and peace.

Henry the First died in 1060, and was succeeded by his son Philip at the age of seven. The Empire fell at the same time into the hands of an infant, and France and Germany would have been the prey of a thousand petty barons and rebellious princes, if it had not been for the insane perseverance of young and old in pushing onward to the Holy Land. Castles and hamlets were left deserted when those long files of peaceful wanderers took their way ; and gradually as the few survivors returned and related their adventures, and dwelt on the insolence and cruelty of the unbelieving Moslem who defiled the sacred place with their presence, a feeling arose, strengthening with every fresh report, that the sepulchre of Christ should be freed from its pagan masters, and the banner of the Cross be waved on the walls of Jerusalem. At the same time the designs of William upon England acted as a safeguard to France during the minority of its king. Instead of breaking through the feeble barriers which a regency presents to the powerful and discontented, all the ambitious or impoverished cavaliers and strong-handed adventurers, who were " lords of their presence and no land beside," betook themselves to the levies of the Norman duke. Some pretence he made to a rightful title to the

English throne when his kinsman Edward died ; but all men felt that his true title was the phalanx of sixty thousand gallant desperadoes who had sworn fealty to his cause. Such a builder of churches and payer of tithes was not without the support of the ecclesiastical power, and blessed accordingly by pope and bishop, and attended by innumerable priests and friars, the vast expedition set sail. The sagacious governors of France were not displeased to see the dukedom weakened by the absence of all its warriors. If the adventure succeeds, they thought, the settlement of England will occupy all their forces ; if it fails, the fief of Normandy will easily be annexed. William had great reason for speed in all his proceedings ; and while with pitiless hand he was riveting the feudal chain upon the Saxon people, parcelling out the land and substituting everywhere a foreign priesthood for the native clergy, who still preferred their diocesan liberty to the tyranny of Rome, Philip saw with dismay, in 1071, when he attained his eighteenth year, that the vassal who had yielded him so scanty a reverence as Duke of Normandy, was elevated far above him in power, and equal to him in rank, as wearer of the English crown. It was, indeed, fortunate for the French king that the attention of William was required in other quarters ; fortunate also that the knighthood of the land was either engaged in penitential pilgrimage to the East, or fiery onsets on the Saracens of Spain, against whom the Cid was raising all the forces of Christendom ; for if the barons of the realm had been retained at home, and had witnessed the meanness, dishonesty, and cowardice of their feudal chief, they would have burst out in uncontrollable excesses, and probably have swept him from his dishonoured throne. But though the nobles were too busy to take advantage of the state of affairs, there was that other power we spoke of, perfectly awake to the opportunity offered to its ambition. The Church availed itself of the weakness of the king, and the disunion or preoccupation of the lords. At the very time when William was trampling on England, and Philip dishonouring the name of France, a sallow-faced, contemptible-looking monk of Cluny was elected to the Papal Chair. He had been for some time archdeacon of Rome, and had ruled with the superiority of an indomitable will the successive pontiffs, whom he appeared to serve. But when the monk Hildebrand formally took possession of the supreme power, in name as well as reality, under the title of Gregory the Seventh, there was poured out upon Europe a torrent of ecclesiastical arrogance and assumption, which would appear mere madness and self-inflation if we did not see how admirably calculated it was to attain its end. He insulted the kings of France, and Hungary, and Poland, and Spain, and yet none of all these princes could eventually stand up against his extravagant claims. And the secret of his success is this: There was not a miserable hut in any hamlet in Europe, or a wretched workshop in any town, where the voice of the man who trampled on the pride of the oppressor was not hailed as a sign of deliverance. The Pope, it was known to the humblest in the land, was of no higher origin than themselves, and they rejoiced in perceiving that there was a power upon their side different from the baron's sword, and even the monarch's sceptre, and superior to them both. The monasteries and churches, of course, prided themselves on the pre-eminence of their representative, the strong-willed monk in Rome; and as there were greater numbers among the poor, and greater intelligence among the clergy, the two great instruments by which causes are won, were in the hands of the Church. The nobility, however, might have interfered with its schemes, and some method must be found of thinning their numbers and diminishing their power. The kings were equally anxious for the weakening of their rivals; and monarchs and popes watched the course of events, and beheld with satisfaction the commencement of the First Crusade in 1095. In this apparently mad but really beneficial expedition, France was stripped of warriors and money to an incredible extent. Poor barons sold or mortgaged their estates, and died in the Holy Land. The rising towns purchased fresh franchises from their needy owners. Shipping increased.

at all the seaports on the Mediterranean, and trade started at once into activity; so that the two potentates, the French king and the Roman bishop, had merely exchanged the antagonist whose opposition they feared. A worse foe took the place of the rebellious lords, for after the First Crusade wealth and intelligence—which are the most fatal enemies to absolute power, whether civil or ecclesiastic—began to be diffused; and from this time we find a new element in French society—capitalists who could lend money to the extravagant freeholder, and merchants whose warerooms were filled with all the commodities of the East.

Philip—as trifling but not so harmless as one of the idle kings of the Merovingian line—was succeeded by his son Louis. He was already the sixth of that well-known name, but was indebted to his personal appearance for the epithet by which he is distinguished from the others. He shines in history as Louis the Fat. But his obesity was equalled by his goodness. He perceived the changes which altered circumstances were making on the great body of the inhabitants. They were no longer the unreasoning, uninquiring multitude they had been before. Their minds were now opening, and their purses getting filled. He had the political wisdom to assist them in their upward progress, and brought over to the royal cause the masses of the towns by the establishment of "Communes," with franchises and privileges, and the humblest of his subjects by the emancipation of many of the serfs. He kept the Church in good humour, by obedience to its commands, and generosity to the clergy; and would in all things have been wise and beneficent if he had not had the misfortune to be opposed and thwarted in all his plans by Henry the First of England. This potentate, after recovering the duchy of his father by force of arms, to the exclusion of his elder brother, was a perpetual thorn in the side of the French king. Powerful as Normandy had been before, its importance was now greatly enlarged by the increased rank of its ruler, and by the knowledge that, in addition to its own forces, the wealth and warriors of Britain were ready to rise in its defence. The vassal looked with contempt on the resources of his lord, and cherished, even then, high notions of what his united Normans and Saxons would do for the English crown. The troubled years of Stephen's reign gave some respite to the overmatched suzerain ; but an incident of the Second Crusade rendered the affairs of his successor, Louis the Seventh, or the Young, more desperate than ever. Roused by the preaching of St. Bernard, the great Abbot of Clervaux, almost all the gentlemen of France, their gentle and pious king, and Henry of Normandy—afterwards Henry the Second of England—and the flower of European nobility, had hurried to the East. Along with the splendid host went princesses and queens ; high-born ladies, emulous of the hardihood and enterprise of the warriors, and ready like them to unite the utmost fervour of religious zeal with the luxuries and immorality of a court. Highest in rank, and most eminent in vice, was Eleanor, the unworthy wife of the French monarch. Contemning all the restraints of relationship and faith, she outraged all the feelings of the time by the profligacy of her behaviour. Louis the Young drove the degraded woman from his home, and repudiated her on his return to Europe. But Henry of England, who was fully aware of her improprieties, and knew the scorn and shame she had brought on the Christian and queenly character, would see nothing in Eleanor but the lands, and towers, and castles of which she was possessor. She was lady of Poitou and Aquitaine, and of all the territories from the Pyrenees to the Loire—and when Henry, by marrying her six weeks after her divorce, added these to the duchy of Normandy, to which he succeeded through his mother the Empress Maud—and to the county of Anjou, which he inherited from his father, his domains were equal to a fifth of the whole of France, while the monarch's direct authority did not extend over more than a tenth. When England was finally thrown into the opposite scale by Henry's accession to the throne in 1154, the chances seemed very much against the guileless Louis, who perhaps regretted when it was too late the fastidious delicacy which had made him sacrifice the principal part of his power, and throw it into his rival's hands. He did not affect the glory of a warrior—and his influence was limited to his own domains. Henry, in opposition to this, had the vigour and unscrupulousness of his race—was a bold chevalier and politic king—rich in the support of a great kingdom, and in possession of a fifth of the hostile realm. Yet Louis was the successful combatant in this duel of honesty with violence. The length of his reign enabled him to lay the foundation for future increase. His reputation for justice attracted references to his decisions, from nobles who might have been too proud or too politic to submit their differences to a more ambitious chief. The oppressed, even among the subjects of Henry and the other princes, appealed for protection to the good king, and seldom appealed in vain. His was a moral greatness, which it is delightful to see recognised among all those fiery and illiterate freebooters, who combined the pride of knighthood with the cruelty and rapacity of barbarians. Henry, on the other hand, in a reign of equal length, established nothing, because he tried to force everything to his will. The wife he had married from ambition was the evil spirit of his home. She stirred up rebellion in his family, and sent forth her sons to fight their father in the field. Even his contest with the ecclesiastical power, which we are apt to look upon with favourable eye, sprang in him from a mere desire of personal aggrandisement; and when in addition to his family and his wife, the great body of the clergy turned against him, and he was held up as a tyrannical oppressor of his sons, an unfaithful spouse to Eleanor, and a murderous opponent of the Church, all the props upon which his greatness rested were removed. A'Beckett, his friend and favourite, now Archbishop of Canterbury and champion of his order, fled to his rival Louis for defence. The Pope joined in the outcry against him, and we see the greatest of European sovereigns, the unhappiest of husbands, fathers, and rulers, doing penance before the tomb of a revengeful and ambitious priest, gaining a verbal absolution indeed, for the sin he had committed in wishing the death of his opponent, but burdened with the disgrace of a useless humiliation, and thwarted in all his projects both at home and abroad.

Louis died in 1180. The new French king, Philip Augustus, was four-and-twenty years of age when his rival, Richard the First of England, succeeded to his father's throne in 1189. The contest seemed now to be on more equal terms, for Richard was not more warlike than his liege lord, nor Philip Augustus more unscrupulous than his liegeman: we shall see how their enmity proceeded. But now that we have brought France and England as it were face to face, it will be necessary to take a very short view of the state of society at this time, and see what progress has been made since our last survey.

The increase of trade and the impoverishment of the nobility, both the results of the Crusades, had made great changes in the relative positions of the lord and the citizen. Large estates, with all their rights and privileges, were mortgaged to wealthy individuals or corporations, to enable the owner to make a dignified appearance in the Holy Land. In addition, however, to the title-deeds and conveyances, the needy baron was obliged to sign away his extravagant powers of oppression, his portage and tax on entrance within the walls, his claim of military service or pecuniary support; and as it had become the policy of the king to find both money and adhesion from the burgher class by an increase of their liberties, and a guarantee of the franchises they had already acquired, there were soon seen in all parts of France flourishing little commercial towns, with regard to which the manorial tower beside it had entirely changed its relations. It was no longer a castle raised to awe and dominate the peaceful workman, but a fortification held in his defence by a burly cavalier, who was glad to receive wages from the citizens, and even to share in the profits of their trade.

King and noble, at all events, were not now united to oppress the lower order, and by this means a great part of the Church's peculiar duty was taken away from it. A walled town, with charters of independence from the Crown or great nobility, was as sure a refuge from injustice as the monastery had been, and offered greater chances for the acquisition of wealth and information ; for the gradual increase of riches, and the opening of men's minds by the expeditions to the East, had given leisure and inclination for far higher studies than former years had known. People in the enjoyment of competence, without the fear of starvation or the necessity of work, began to inquire. Inquiry led to doubt, and in the reign of the gentle Louis was presented the strange sight of a lecturer on theology who was not in holy orders, and who ventured to assign to reason some weight in the balance of religious truth. This was Abelard, more famous among us now by his love of Eloïse and the beautiful lines of Pope, but in his own day the most eloquent, the most learned, and the most accomplished man in Europe. His speculations were condemned by the Council of Soissons, and he retracted his statements, and died in the monastery of Cluny. But Abelard had been the most popular professor ever known. His pupils were so numerous that they could not find room in the towns where he lectured, but encamped in the open fields. Among all these the germ of inquiry was spread, and merchant, and baron, and educated scholar, all began to open their eyes to the state of the Church, and to examine into its claims. The state of the Church was deplorable, and its claims higher than ever. There was a schism in the Chair of St. Peter itself. Two Popes professed each to be the lineal successor of the Apostle, and that his rival was Antichrist. Alexander the Third and Victor the Fourth were supported by different factions, and offered for eighteen years, from 1159 to 1177, the edifying spectacle of the two contending fathers of Christendom interchanging their threats and curses. The lives of the clergy were in worse keeping with their profession than even their ambition and wealth. They were almost universally sunk in sensuality and vice. The literature, such as it was, of which they had been the sole custodiers, had passed into other hands. Abelard and his disciples knew more than any of the monks or clergy. The Gay Science, or ballad poetry of Provence, had taken its first beautiful rise, and kings and nobles sang sweet sonnets to their harps, and followed them with bitter satires on the manners of their priests. The Church saw its danger, and had recourse to the secular arm. Heretics were burned, and laws passed against recusants. Excellent guide up to a certain time of a barbarous and believing people, defender and guardian of the weak against the masters who were superstitious as well as tyrannical, the Church, about this time, found that its pupil had outgrown its lessons, and that its ward, whom it had succoured and enslaved in his nonage, was now strong enough to do battle for himself. A fourth element is henceforth added to the composition of French society: in addition to king, and church, and nobles, there is now the people.

CHAPTER III.

FROM PHILIP AUGUSTUS, A. D. 1180, TO THE DEATH OF SAINT LOUIS, A. D. 1271.

PHILIP AUGUSTUS, ready of hand, false of tongue, was an adversary to the English kings very different from peaceful Louis the Sixth and honest Louis the Young. Henry the Second found the change before the Frenchman had been many years on the throne. His eldest son was supported in rebellion to his authority. Cabals and parties were made among the lesser vassals against the pretensions of the now foreign Duke of Normandy, and every enemy he made, whether in England, or Poitou, or Aquitaine, was sure of a warm ally in the person of the suzerain lord. Nor had the nobility of France itself much cause for rejoicing. He pursued the same plan of weakening and division in his own domains. Baron was roused against baron. He chastised with fire and sword the great feudatories of the Crown, if they raised forces that might be dangerous, under pretence of making private war upon each other; and thus, by courage and cunning, by establishing boroughs as a counterpoise to lords, and encouraging colleges and universities as a counterpoise to the Church, he in a short time taught the whole nation to look to the throne as supreme in all matters ecclesiastical and civil. When Henry the Second died in 1189, his successor Richard the First was actually in the French king's camp, and only pausing for a while from active war against his father, because the old man was too broken-hearted to continue his resistance. John, whom his father's kindness had spoiled, had also been won over by the promises of Richard, or more probably of Philip Augustus, and suddenly the unfeeling son and disobedient vassal found himself in possession of all the kingdoms and estates which it had been his selfish and short-sighted policy to sever from the English crown. His friendship with the French monarch was of course not long maintained. Both young, both utterly unprincipled and selfish, their only struggle henceforward was to do as much mutual damage as they could. Richard hurried over to England, and inaugurated his reign by an indiscriminate and almost entire slaughter of the Jews. The unhappy members of that race who had settled in France under the gentle governance of Louis the Seventh, had been spoiled and murdered by Philip Augustus as soon as he mounted the throne. With matchless generosity he paid off the debts of his Christian subjects by making it death for the Hebrew creditor to accept a shilling; and to reward himself for this great benefit, he forced all the debtors to pay one-fifth of their obligations to himself. Fired with noble emulation, Richard plundered the sons of Abraham with a fiendish sort of glee. He took their riches and confiscated their bonds, and set them up to ransom. The homeless nation found no rest in England. The oriental seclusion of their families was rudely broken in upon by armed assailants. The Rabbi of York called on the husbands and fathers of his flock to deliver their wives and maidens from the pollution with which they were threatened. The community was gathered into one house. The elders stabbed the young girls, who smiled as they died, and then themselves. The solitary survivor set fire to the building and perished in the flames. But king, and noble, and priest, and peasant, felt no remorse: they looked on the Jews as the personal enemies of the Saviour, and thought their presence among them was sufficient to bring down the wrath of God.

Delivered from their debts, the knights and citizens were now perhaps in a position to purchase whatever the King wished to sell. That needy and greedy warrior sold everything he could lay his hands upon. He sold the domains of the Crown, and the domains also of other people. He sold the prerogatives of the king, and the rights of the nobles.

All the treasures of his father were seized and catalogued ; and on the great plains of Vezelay, in the summer of 1190, the two greatest sovereigns of Europe, and perhaps the two most unprincipled men, placed themselves at the head of the greatest army which had yet been assembled to chastise the Saracen ; and after professions of friendship and fidelity to their words, which were very soon forgotten, they started for Jerusalem. One curious thing is worth observing here, that Richard the English king embarked from Marseilles ; and Philip Augustus, who as yet had no port on the Mediterranean, embarked from Genoa. Marseilles was a free port, but was a fief of the kings of Aragon. The main body of the English forces sailed down channel, like our transports of the present day ; and the armies were joined together once more in Sicily. Philip Augustus kept a suspicious eye upon his rival, and saw in him a deadlier enemy than the Paynim Saladin. Richard, who seems to have had an irrepressible inclination for blows and violence, got into a variety of scrapes, some so undignified that it is wonderful they are recorded in the chronicles of the campaign. One day he heard the cry of a hawk in a working man's cottage. Not a very treasonable cry, you would think, but all the blood of the Norman kings was boiling up in a moment. A peasant to have a knightly bird—the bird which sat with embroidered hood and silver bells on wrist of high-born cavalier and noble lady ! He rushed into the house, seized the bird, and was making off with it, when the Sicilian peasant, who perhaps himself had some Norman blood in his veins, rose up in anger, drew a knife against the king, and called his neighbours to the rescue. The chivalrous Richard, unable to draw his sword in so low a dwelling, and unsupported by his train, was hustled into the street with a shower of blows from stick and stone, and, greatest indignity of all, an amount of kicks which would have been a more appropriate punishment for a humble-born robber. Shortly after this, Philip Augustus had another gratification at his enemy's expense. Richard had offended the inhabitants of Messina, by seizing on a convent, which he converted into barracks for his troops. They refused admittance to his army one day, and stood to their arms. Nothing could be more agreeable to the English king. He forced his way in, slew the resisting citizens, and, in sign of victory, hoisted his Norman standard on the walls of the town. This was too much for the pride of the feudal chief. Normandy was but a fief of the Crown of France, and Philip Augustus ordered his vassal's flag to be pulled down, and his own raised in its stead. From this time forth there was scarcely a concealment of the enmity of the two crusaders. They accused each other in good broad language of the basest crimes, and finally went through the form of a reconciliation, and continued their voyage. History and romance have rendered the main incidents of this the Third Crusade well known to us all; but not even the enchanting colouring of poetry and imagination can hide from us the coarser features of reality. After two years of gallant achievements against the Saracens, and undignified quarrels among themselves, the chiefs of the expedition broke out into open separation. Philip Augustus, to quiet Richard's apprehensions, made oath on the Gospels and the relics of saints that "he would be true to his cause, and maintain his interests in England and Normandy with all his power;" and, full of these professions of amity and justice, left the crusaders' camp, and returned to Europe. On his way through Rome he took the opportunity of being relieved from all his vows of friendship and protection to his absent brother, by the easy connivance and absolution of the Pope; and the moment, accordingly, he reached his capital, he set every engine in motion to disturb the peace of England, and destroy the independence of the English fiefs in France. Richard, in the mean time, was perfectly contented with battles all day and festivals all night, and did not hesitate to offend beyond forgiveness the greatest of the European princes who had still remained with the array. This was Leopold, Duke of Austria. In reply to an insolent observation of his Highness's, Richard, remembering perhaps the incident of the hawk in the cottage of Sicily, bestowed kicks on the recusant, which were perhaps more effective than any eloquence could have been. One by one he converted all his friends into enemies, made terms with Saladin, which, however favourable to the Christian cause, appeared a concession to the claims of the unbelievers ; and finally, on hearing of the proceedings of his rival in France, determined to return home. But the reputation he had acquired in Palestine was of the worst. Right or wrong, he was accused of great crimes : of suborning assassins to murder the Marquis of Montserrat, the nominal King of Jerusalem ; of attempting to poison his liege lord, the King of France ; of disregard of his own followers, and ferocious cruelty to his captive enemies. On one occasion, indeed, he drew up two thousand five hundred Saracens in a field near Acre, and slew every man of them in cold blood. His announcement of this massacre is conveyed in a tone of triumph to the Holy St. Bernard ; and it is added, by the historian of the time, that it was done "with the assent of all." Two years of warfare, and sufferings from climate and disasters, had seen the expedition dwindle away. Out of three hundred thousand men who took the Cross, but six thousand remained alive ; and, with a few faithful attendants, Richard embarked for England. Philip Augustus took measures for a struggle for life or death, when he heard that he was on the voyage home. Other princes, also, refractory vassals, rebellious brother, insulted dukes, were all at gaze when it was ascertained the Lionheart was close at hand. Philip Augustus surrounded himself with a body-guard in the heart of Paris. John trembled at the sound of his name among his sycophants in London. Leopold of Austria nursed bitter recollections of his controversy with the heavy-booted King ; and even the Emperor of Germany thought so fierce and so valiant a champion better employed in the slaughter of unbelieving Moslem, than in spreading terror and confusion among Christian states.

Richard's voyage was not prosperous. Shipwreck forced him on the shore of the Adriatic, from which he determined, disguised in palmer weeds, to find his way to the West. He was recognised and arrested, for he was in the territories of the Duke of Austria, and had little to expect from the mercy of the man he had so offended. Moved about from castle to castle, he was at last surrendered, for the sake of safe custody, into the hands of Henry the Sixth, Emperor of Germany. Philip Augustus wrote to his new jailor to hold his prisoner fast. The relations of the leaders he had insulted in the crusade made the same request. But, strange to say, the instinct of generosity aroused the people. The moment the arrest was known, rebellion against his authority ceased in England and on the Continent. The multitude recognised him now only as the man with the great heart and conquering sword, who had fought for the deliverance of the Holy Tomb and the wood of the true Cross. The men of Rouen, under the guidance of Robert of Leicester, repulsed the French king, who made an assault upon the town. The other powers waited in silence to see what the event of those strange incidents would be; and, flying about like a vengeful fury, threatening, praying, promising, by turns, was the old and still undaunted Eleanor, the mother of the captive knight—writing eloquent petitions to the Pope, and shrieking imprecations against the disloyalty of Austria and the injustice of the Emperor. Henry the Sixth was overwhelmed with the obloquy he had excited. He summoned a diet of the States, and Richard appeared before them. A more eloquent defence has never been made. He was accused of the high crimes and misdemeanours we have named; and this was his answer, as regarded his dissensions with Philip Augustus, his negotiation with Saladin, and the poisoning of the Marquis of Montserrat:—"As to my quarrels with Philip, let the Crusaders reply. Which has best served the cause of religion—the perjured King who fled before the victory, or the faithful King who fought in the Holy Land while there was a horse left to carry one of his men-at-arms? I have treated with Saladin—well—but the treaty was glorious, since Jerusalem is henceforth open to every pilgrim; since the princes of Edessa, Antioch, and Tripoli, are confirmed in their power;

since we have a king in Judea, and a king in Cyprus to defend our brothers. And, lastly, it is said I poisoned the Marquis of Montserrat. To this I make no reply, save that I carry the cross of my Saviour on my breast, and the crown of England on my head. Let the accuser show himself, with arms in his hand. I appeal to the judgment of God, who is protector of the honour of kings."

He was acquitted by acclamation, and the Emperor promised to set him at liberty on payment of an enormous ransom for the expenses of his keep. A tax was raised in all his realms. Eleanor contributed from her own stores. Richard took his way towards England, and Philip Augustus wrote to John, "Be on your guard, the devil is broke loose." Two years of petty warfare, of sudden attacks upon Normandy, or unexpected marches into France, were the very inadequate termination of a death-feud between the two most famous fighting men in Europe. The crusade and the ransom had exhausted the wealth and population of Richard's states. Philip Augustus used other arms against his vassal, and was loth to meet him in the field. At last necessity imposed a peace, and there was even an interview between the kings. Richard sat in a barge upon the Seine, and Philip Augustus on horseback on the shore. If they had met foot to foot one of them would have died. They agreed on this occasion to a truce for five years, and parted never to meet again. Richard heard that one of his feudatories in Limoges had found a hidden treasure. He set out at once and made a demand of all. A part was offered and refused. When the siege began, a certain archer upon the wall took aim at the king, and sent his arrow deep into the shoulder. The assault, however, was given, and the garrison taken prisoners. The archer, Bertrand de Gourdon, was brought to the side of the dying king. "Why did you point your weapon against the Lord's anointed?" he asked. "Because with your own hand you slew my father and my two brothers, and I glory in avenging their fate." The king, conscience-struck, and moved with the bravery of the youth, forgave him and died. A noble forgiveness, and worthy of a repentant soldier; but in vain, for the infuriated attendants slew the archer with unheard of cruelty, and stained the memory of their lord with their useless zeal.

France breathed more freely when the terrible Crusader was no more. England felt the want of his strength of will, though delivered from his tyrannous grasp, when it fell upon the evil days of a dastard like John. Better be trampled on by a man, than sold and degraded by a coward. Philip Augustus saw his advantage, and in a short space obtained the object which had excited the ambition and cupidity of the French monarchs for three hundred years. He made himself master, by conquest and confiscation, of the dukedom of Normandy, and the other possessions of the Norman kings, with the exception of Rochelle. This was achieved in the year 1204; and the last news which reached Eleanor, who had retired into the convent of Fontevrault, was, that all the principalities and towns which she had brought to the French and English crowns, were torn from her unworthy son, and attached forever to the sovereignty of France.

From this time forward, the development of the internal policy of the two kingdoms took a different direction. Released from their obligations as Norman landholders, the great nobles of England limited their views to their island possessions. There was no longer a rival interest between their estates near Warwick and their estates near Rouen. Their position in England was higher and more independent. In this country they held directly of the crown, and in Normandy were the vassals of a chief who was himself a vassal to the king of France. They were under two masters, and liable to the wrath of each for deeds performed in the other's service. The Duke of Normandy revenged himself for their delay in bringing him aid upon the borders of the Loire, by confiscation and fine upon their lands upon the Trent. The king of France punished them for furnishing Lancashire levies to his enemy the English king, by carrying fire and sword among their territories upon the Seine. Gradually they felt that they were considered strangers, and began to hate the land from which they had been expelled. Anglo-Saxons, the great-grandsons of the Franklins of Hardicanute and Edward, were enrolled among the tenants and men-at-arms of the descendants of the warriors of Hastings. An approach was made between the races, and the sign of the union between conqueror and conquered was made by a curtailment, by the barons, of the prerogatives and tyranny of the king, who was the enemy of both. This junction of high and low, and rapid growth of nationality among the nobles, produced the famous Magna Charta, or Great Charter, by which the liberties of all generations of Englishmen were secured. In France, on the other hand, the march of affairs was in a totally opposite path. Kingship grew in the one country as rapidly as citizenship in the other. In France, the nobility became altogether subordinate to the crown ; in England, it became amalgamated with the people. The result is, that the throne in France became despotic, and in England the people continued free. Without a hereditary class to stand between the chief and the multitude, the government grows either a despotism or a republic, or fluctuates with bloody alternation between the two. By the reabsorption, therefore, of Normandy into France, it is not too much to say, that England gained infinitely more than her rulers lost. It gained concentration of interests, and perfect identity of blood and feeling between all classes of the inhabitants. They lost a barren coronet which kept them feudatories of a rival king, and mixed them up in all the fights and squabbles of a savage and discontented peerage.

Philip Augustus had now extended his personal power over a large portion of the land called France, and had realised in a great extent the idea of Hugh Capet, the founder of his house. Internal division had so weakened the great nobles who at first had maintained an equality with the Crown, that they could no longer resist his claims as feudal chief. They attended his councils, summoned his refractory vassal John to appear before their court as his jury of peers, and on his recusancy assigned his domains by irrevocable sentence to the suzerain as lapsed to the Crown. This was the death-sentence of the peerage, properly so called. The wiser nobility of a former age would have guarded against such a preponderance being given to the royal power, and might have pronounced John unworthy to rule without depriving his family of its succession. Nothing was spared by Philip Augustus to win over his new subjects to his cause. They were confirmed in all their rights and privileges, and the old customs of Normandy guarded by oath. Satisfied with these, the wretched tyrant, who wallowed in sensuality at London, was rapidly forgotten. No friendship, of course, existed between the disinherited barons of England and the successors to their Continental estates. Another conquest of England was talked of by the Norman knights; and a conquest of France was not obscurely hinted at by the English nobles. Meanwhile great things took place in the southern provinces of Philip Augustus's realm, in which he showed the masterly policy of inaction, and reaped all the fruits of victory without the dangers of the fight. In fact, no fighting was required from anybody else when there was such a pugnacious pontiff sounding the trumpet of battle as Pope Innocent the Third. Never since the departure of Gregory the Seventh had so tremendous an apparition alarmed the potentates of Europe. Thick and fast flew his anathemas and excommunications. Philip Augustus himself lay under the curse of the Church for resisting the spiritual aggressions of St. Peter on the liberties of his national clergy. Otho the Emperor was his tool; and as to John of England, he trembled at the sound of his name. Now it chanced that a certain Raymond of Toulouse was too much addicted to the Gay Science, and listened with too eager ears to the songs of the troubadours and their "sirventes" against the Pope. His subjects were no less inclined for poetry and independence than himself; and clothing their hatred of their sensual and overbearing priests in a doubt of some of the tenets of Rome, they ceased to be considered merely disobedient sons of the Church, and became enemies of the Faith. From insolent metre-ballad-mongers they became heretics of the blackest dye. They denied transubstantiation, the supremacy of the Pope, the necessity of celibacy in the clergy, invocation of the saints, and the fires of purgatory. Innocent maintained, on the other hand, that they hated the Cross, vilified the Gospel, and worshipped the devil. Philip Augustus merely perceived that the territories of Raymond of Toulouse had several ports on the Mediterranean, and that France would be immensely benefited by an outlet to the sea. A crusade, not against distant Paynims or the swarthy chivalry of Spain, but against the most refined, the most musical, and the most effeminised population in Europe, was proclaimed with great solemnity by the Father of the Christian world. All the villains in all lands joined the banner of the truculent John de Montfort, and rushed forward at the call. Dominic, a Spanish friar, more furious than his master, hounded on the slaughterers. Alas for the beautiful towns and valleys of Provence! Blood, and fire, and spoliation, and outrage everywhere. But when all the towns were desolate, and all the fields ravaged, and all the villages depopulated, the Church had effected its triumph. The voice of heresy was heard no more; no, nor the voice of song, nor the verses of passion, nor the harp of the minstrel. The gay science died utterly out, and the very language, with all its delicate inflections and musical pronunciation, disappeared from human ken. Raymond, the heretic troubadour, was despoiled of his estates; and, noticeable fact, in the midst of that confused story of suffering and wrong, France acquired, in direct sovereignty, the harbours of the Narbonnaise, and set her firm foot on the Mediterranean Sea. This crowning gain, however, was reserved for the successor of Philip Augustus. That politic ruler laid the foundation, and left the building to other hands. His policy, indeed, had been too successful, and awakened the fears of the other princes. The Emperor Otho, and John of England, and the Count of Flanders, entered into a league against him in the year 1214, the object of which was not only his displacement from the throne, but the division of France among themselves. John had qualified for this effort by surrendering his kingdom of England into the hands of Innocent the year before, and receiving it as a liegeman of the Pope. Otho also had made his submission to the Papal chair ; and a vast body of Germans and Flemings, and strangers from all quarters, blest by the apostolic chief, took the field against the successor of Clovis, and Pepin, and Hugh Capet, who had all been declared the true champions and eldest sons of the Church. John landed at Rochelle, and on coming into presence of the knights and citizens who defended his ancient patrimony of Anjou, took to flight and returned home. In Flanders the enemy were more dangerous. An emperor of Germany and a king of France were face to face. The Emperor had summoned to his aid all his supporters, the feudatories and princes of the Empire, and dependants on his various crowns. Philip Augustus, who had enlisted the affection of the townsmen to his side in his struggle with his nobility, continued his confidence in them during the war. The contingents of fifteen of the Communes or municipalities appeared in his array. The battle was fought at Bovines, on the bank of the river Mark, and was decisively in favour of the French. Otho, after a narrow escape from the hands of William des Barres, a natural brother of Simon de Montfort, who twice got hold of him by the neck, made his escape, and hid his disgrace in Saxony. Submission was made by the few survivors of the fight ; and, illustrative of the manners of the time, the gallant citizens who had contributed to the victory were presented with hundreds of the captive knights, and enriched their towns with the amount of the ransoms they exacted. This appearance of burghers on the same field with mounted retainers and armed cavaliers, is not without its significance as a sign of approaching change. A townsman who could wield a sword, and march under the banner of his craft, was not quite so helpless as the knights, in their supercilious ignorance, supposed. Take notice, therefore, of this, and we shall see that the nation which trusted most largely to its yeomen, achieved a mighty superiority in liberty, and wealth, and arms, to those which relied too long on "helm and hauberk's twisted mail." This victory, besides strengthening the personal authority of Philip Augustus, is memorable as being the first in the long series of national triumphs which have given France the pre-eminence in military power. The battles before this, in which French blood had been shed, were decided on French soil and between French combatants. Here France ranged itself in one compact and irresistible battalion. Her enemies were foreigners, and her glory spread over the whole realm. Enough of Norman feeling survived on the other side of the Channel, to make the knights and gentlemen of England take pride in the prowess of their former countrymen at Bovines; and when the disheartened noble and discontented spearman compared the courage and energy of the French monarch with the falsehood and effeminacy of their own, they felt shame as well as anger at their subjection to such a man. Accordingly, when in the following year, 1215, it was spread over England that Pope Innocent, out of his plenary authority and love for kings, had absolved John from the oaths he had sworn at Runnymede, and recommended him to annul the charter it had cost them so much trouble to obtain, the barons threw off their blind submission equally to John and Rome, and conveyed an offer of the crown of England (guarded by the covenants they had imposed upon its unworthy wearer) to Louis, the son of the French king. The ground on which they placed the offer, was the tyrant's originally defective title to the throne, his nephew Arthur being alive; his murder of that unhappy prince, and many other crimes. They then maintained that failing him by death or deposition, Louis, in right of his wife, Blanche of Castile, was the legitimate successor to Henry and Richard. It did not much matter whether these pretexts were correct or not. The law, indeed, was so clearly against Louis, that Philip Augustus declined to give him any open assistance in his recovery of England,—by this skilful abstinence from action disarming the national jealousy

—and Louis crossed over with some armed attendants in the spring of 1216, and threw himself on the outraged barons, not as invader or conqueror, but as the rightful heir. His best ally in this enterprise was the unpopularity of his rival. He might have succeeded if he had been opposed by the craven and assassin who dishonoured the name of man and the dignity of king ; but the sword which might have cut its way through living enemies, fell blunted upon a coffin. John died in the same year, and the hopes of the foreign candidate expired. The English heart softened to the English king, a boy of ten years old, and Henry the Third became the rally-ing-cry of all parties in the State. Louis's army was defeated near Lincoln, and his fleet near Dover. No fresh adherents came to his standard, and he resolved to retire. Not like a defeated enemy, nor like a lawless freebooter, did the noble Louis conduct his retreat. He made terms for his supporters ; they were to be maintained in their houses and estates. He bound his adversaries to respect the privileges of London and the other burghs, and stipulated for the mutual interchange of prisoners without ransom. He made no complaint of disappointment, or of the expenses to which he had been put, but behaved in all things like a true and loyal cavalier ; and gained more fame by his defeat than many would have gathered from success.

But the reign of Philip Augustus was drawing to a close. He had made great changes in France, and converted the separate interests of the feudal nobles into a confederation of powers strictly subordinate to the Crown. A tumultuous republic of knights and barons had become a well-balanced kingdom, with local privileges and a centralised authority. The Church, satisfied with its progress, and now relying on law for its support in crushing its adversaries, had imbibed a monarchical spirit not known in the days of its early struggles in defence of the helpless people. The Communes were rich and flourishing, and had made their voice already potential in the State, by holding the purse, and even by keeping men-at-arms in their pay. The great mass of the population were in easier circumstances than before, and not so entirely exposed to the oppressions of their local tyrants. Learned men, even from the lower class of the laity, were admitted into the national councils, and administered justice in the king's name. The nearest approach to the polity of a modern State was made by this wise and unscrupulous ruler. But when he died in 1223, and left the throne to Louis the Eighth, who was absorbed, during the three years of his reign, in fatal enmities with those who might have become his affectionate subjects, if he had not warred with them as heretics—there was a pause in the onward progress of the land. Besieging towns in Provence, torturing the affrighted inhabitants in the name of God and the Church, was an unworthy employment for the husband of Blanche of Castile, and the father of Louis the Ninth. He died in 1226, of a fever caught at the siege of Avignon, and Christendom attained its highest moral elevation when it saw the proudest of its thrones adorned and glorified by the best and purest of its sons. Louis the Ninth would have been impossible at any other period of history. His tenderness in the earlier ages would have been weakness ; his zeal in later ages would have been fanaticism. He appeared at the exact period when justice, mercy, and truth, were recognised as kingly no less than Christian virtues, and when hatred of dissent and unreasoning submission to authority were proofs, not of a dull and uninquiring spirit, but of a humble and contrite heart. It is, therefore, only as a monarch of the thirteenth century that this illustrious character deserves our unmixed approbation. Judged by our ideas, some of his actions would have fitted him for Bedlam, and some for Tyburn ; but, compared to the rough and brutal natures by which he was surrounded —the quarrelling, feeble, godless, superstitious barons of France and monarchs of Europe—he is an apparition of meekness, and faith, and purity, to which the heart turns with honest delight. Between the death of his father and the attainment of his majority, his admirable mother was virtually regent of the kingdom in his name. Strange that the French, with the strictest law of exclusion of females from the throne, have been oftener than any other people under the governance of women. The Salic law might have been safely abrogated in honour of such a ruler as Blanche of Castile. Already the strong hand of Philip Augustus began to be forgotten by fiery baron and ambitious great vassal, who prepared for a resumption of independence. But new powers had arisen in the State, which bore a very keen memory of the blessings of Philip Augustus's reign. The towns gathered round the Regent in her struggle with the Dukes of Boulogne and Brittany, the Counts of La Marche and Poitou, and far in the south, the open enemy of Christ and the king, the heretical Raymond of Toulouse. The malcontent nobles assembled their power. They tried to intercept the queen and her son in their progress to Paris, and forced them to take shelter in Montlhéry. The alarm-bell was rung in the city. Burgher, and knight, and gallant volunteer, armed in all haste, and set off for the rescue. They dispersed the followers of the discontented barons, and escorted the royal party into the town. Not till they saw them safe in the palace did the triumphant citizens lay by their swords. This junction of crown and people was of evil augury to the feudal lord, if he could have foreseen how fatal it would be to his class. Of evil augury to the people, if it could have been foreseen how fatal the destruction of a nobility is at all times to the liberties of a nation. A woman of thirty-eight, and a boy of eleven, were tempting adversaries, even when supported by the trainbands of a town. Some of the lords refused their homage, others disobeyed the orders of the Regent, and it was necessary to show rigour as well as wisdom. The queen besieged the fortresses of Brittany; detached the Duke of Champagne from the rebel cause; won over De Burgh, the minister of the English king, Henry the Third; and finally scattered their whole forces in the year 1229, when they were engaged in the siege of Troyes. A woman was not henceforth to be utterly despised. Many of them made their peace, and among them no less a person than Raymond, the Seventh of Toulouse, heretic, warrior, poet, and now curtailed of all his powers, and ousted of all his lands. He came to petition the King of France at Meaux. He did penance, scourge in hand, and barefooted, at the porch of Nôtre Dame, for the support he had given to the enemies of the Faith. And now came the fruit of the policy of Philip Augustus. The whole shore of the Mediterranean, from Maguelonne to the county of Barcelona, was attached to the Crown, at the expense of the luckless Troubadour. France became a maritime power on three seas, and could send fleets from the Seine, and the Loire, and the Narbonnaise.

It was now time to provide the youthful monarch with a wife, and his mother cast her eye on one of the four daughters of Raymond Berenger, Count of Provence. The eldest was but twelve years old ; but her states, if she should be appointed heiress, were of inestimable value to France, and the marriage took place in 1234. Henry the Third of England had the same idea of the value of the succession of the dying Raymond, and in 1236 married the second daughter Eleanor, and, by way of keeping so good a chance in the family, obtained the third daughter for his brother Richard of Cornwall. Two kings and a royal duke for sons-in-law seemed sufficient honour for a vassal, however powerful ; but Raymond, considering that his elder children were now provided for, constituted his youngest and sole unmarried one heiress of all his estates. All the marriageable princes and potentates were immediately on the alert. She was still, however, too young to be married, and Louis awaited his opportunity, and employed himself in the mean time in extinguishing the last spark of opposition to his royal supremacy. By courage in the field he subdued the refractory Count of La Marche, and the again recalcitrant Raymond of Toulouse ; and gained over to himself peasantry, and knight, and churchman, and, finally, the rebellious nobles themselves, by a tenderness and generosity very unusual at any age of the world, and at that period totally unexampled and unknown. When the time came, and Beatrice the heiress of Provence was of a marriageable age, there were suitors as numerous as those of Penelope besieging her in her house. Raymond of Toulouse, pouring out the burdens of love and compliment, and Pedro, the Prince of Aragon, relying on his rank, were the chief. But if Raymond got possession of Provence, he would be powerful enough to recover his former territories in Languedoc; if Pedro obtained her, they would make the Spanish possessions in France too dangerous for its peace. So Louis, who fortunately possessed a brother of five-and-twenty years of age, and still unmarried, proposed him to the states of Provence as a fitting husband for their lady; but scarcely waiting for her answer, which, however, was in the affirmative, he despatched the youthful wooer with an escort of five hundred sharp-sworded cavaliers, who made very short work with the rival candidates. Raymond and Pedro escaped from this formidable bridegroom with the utmost speed, and Charles of Anjou carried off the prize. He married the heiress in 1246, and secured her noble heritage from going into hostile hands.

Louis, it will be seen, did not consider earthly policy inconsistent with the highest duties of his religion. Above all things he was a Christian, next he was a King, and next he was a Frenchman. Never for a moment were these three characters absent from his thoughts. God, the crown, and the people, might have been embroidered on his banners, as they certainly were united in his prayers. He thought it was the highest offering he could make to all the three, when, in 1248, he prepared himself for a crusade. It was the seventh which had exhausted the nobility of Europe, and given an impulse to knowledge and trade. Already it was believed that success must attend the efforts of so intrepid a warrior and holy a pilgrim, and a great multitude of all classes of the people gathered to his command. His wife could not be persuaded to remain behind. His three brothers and the Count of Flanders, and many who might have been dangerous if left to cabal during his absence, were companions of the expedition, which this time was directed to Egypt, where the Saracen power had achieved new triumphs. A sad and painful story, but not without a parallel in former times, is the pilgrimage of 1248. There was a great deal of courage displayed, and little generalship. At the siege of Damietta, and battle of Massoura, the king was the most prominent of the combatants. But combats are of no use without a good commissariat. The bravest of men could do nothing when provisions were not to be had; when the diseases of the country came upon them, and the Nile began to rise. Louis and his surviving brothers, and half the nobles of his train, weakened by want and illness, were surprised and taken near the Thanis on their retreat to Damietta. On payment of a reasonable ransom the massacre was stopped; and by a farther treaty, the king bound himself not to bear arms against the Moslem for ten years. But nothing quelled the devoted spirit of the crusader. As he could no longer fight the enemy, he spent four years in the East, strengthening the positions held by the Christians, and alleviating with money and personal care the misfortunes of his countrymen. At the end of that time Blanche of Castile, whom he had left Regent in his absence, died; and the presence of the king was imperatively demanded by his States. Failure and disappointment could not blind the nations of Europe to the virtues and merits of the French king. He was received as a Christian hero, if not a conquering monarch, in the good city of Paris. Henry the Third of England came over to congratulate him on his return; and in the old palace on the Island in the Seine, that day, there met the basest and the best of kings—for baseness was the atmosphere in which Henry lived. Unable to understand the solemnity of an oath or the obligation of a promise, he must have looked on the brave knight and truthful gentleman beside him as a creature of another species; very likely with contempt, for he knew that the man had scruples of conscience; that he had actually resigned some possessions of his predecessors which he did not think honestly acquired; and even now offered to submit his title to the ancient French territories of the English Crown to an impartial court. A treaty was soon after concluded between the kings. Louis restored the Limousin, Perigord, Guienne, and other places, to Henry; and Henry resigned all claim to the States of Normandy, Anjou, Maine, Poitou, and Touraine.

A wise regulation of the French king, founded avowedly on the text that no man can serve two masters, had disqualified the feudal landlords from holding property under different crowns. They were delivered from the dangerous claims of a double allegiance by the choice which was given them of which suzerain they would serve. This was the severest blow that could be inflicted on the English interests in France. Henceforth the French king was a foreigner to the English nobles, and the acquisition of French estates an impossibility, unless at the expense of their English lands. A closer connection at once began between the nobility and commons in this country, when they were thus for ever condemned to inhabit the same soil and submit to the same laws. It was in 1262 that Simon de Montfort, who had acquired the earldom of Leicester, and by the above-named regulation of Louis had lost his great holdings in the south of France, summoned for the first time the representatives of towns and boroughs to aid the deliberations of parliament. He was in rebellion against the imbecile and faithless Henry, and required the support of public favour. The barons who defended the crown, he felt, were nearly a match for his adherents, but the accession of the citizens turned the scale. From that time a community of interests has been established between the different classes in this country; and a balance never for a moment lost sight of between the liberality of the people in voting supplies, and the wisdom of the rulers in the granting of privileges. The English representatives seldom voted a subsidy without bargaining for a right. We seem, indeed, to have been a nation of shopkeepers from the beginning, and never to have given anything without an equivalent. If this foundation of our freedom is not very dignified, it is at all events very secure. It lasts, in fact, unimpaired to the present time, and shows how broad and deep it was settled in the soil, compared to the more showy, but unsubstantial, fabric furnished by the Establishments of Saint Louis. This is the first time we have given him the appellation of saint, and we dwell upon it here to say that the papal canonisation was never bestowed upon a worthier name.

While England was convulsed with civil conflict, and Germany was distracted by quarrels between the Empire and the Pope, and Spain was engaged in interminable hostilities with her Moorish populations, the land of France lay in profound peace. The brother of the king, Charles of Anjou, had passed onward to secure the throne of Naples, to which he had been invited by the rebellious nobility and the Pope ; the other great holdings were in the hands of the princes of the blood or the attached friends of the Crown ; and Louis sat under a tree, like the patriarchs of old, and distributed justice to the poorest man in his realm. He established public Assemblies, which also bore the name of Parliaments, and summoned wise counsellors, and men learned in the Roman Institutes, to devise laws for the common good. At first they assembled only at stated intervals, but he soon constituted them his permanent courts, and published the result of their consultations as ordonnances of the Crown. No power of the purse was given to these assemblies ; but he made them respected from one end of France to the other by making them courts of appeal from the judgment of the feudal tribunals, and investing them with the dignity of a Royal Council. The high-spirited baron, residing in thick-walled castle, and surrounded by armed retainers, was surprised to see his influence gradually gliding away from him like the water of a retiring inundation ; he heard the judgments and argumentations of an order of men he had never seen before ; he heard these new dispensers of the law declare the trial by combat a barbarous injustice, and private war a crime to be punished with death. He heard them talk of words and things he could scarcely understand—custom.

right, precedent, principle, pandects, rescripts, and other phrases, and felt that a new power had come into the world And truly it was a new power before which he and his steel-clad brethren were forced to bow ; for whether Louis meant it as a blow to feudalism or not, its effect was fatal to that institution. The baron was unseated from his chair of state in the great hall where he gave a rude justice to his followers, and Legalism took his place. Whether the change was for the best or not it is difficult to say, for Europe is only now endeavouring to cast off the technicalities with which those ancient masters thought they were protecting the weak against the strong, but which turned out to be an intolerable burden by which justice itself was oppressed.

Reconciling all classes to his rule—the baron by his courage, the priest by his religion, the peasant by his justice—Louis found himself in a position to stretch the royal authority beyond its previous bounds. He restrained the rights and privileges of the highest nobility, and made his coin and his laws current in all the states. Many cases of crime and misdemeanour were reserved exclusively for the royal court ; and, as if to show that he was governor of all conditions of men within the realm, he interdicted various assumptions of the Pope, and protected the Church from the arbitrary impositions of its spiritual chief. His one dominant idea was the supremacy of the Crown. What the ambition and cunning of Philip Augustus had commenced, the gentleness and wisdom of his grandson enabled him to achieve. Piety was more successful than force. France became consolidated into a powerful undivided monarchy, under a ruler who avowedly held all worldly distinctions vain. Nobody could resist the claims which, coming from Louis, were certain to be thought founded on higher motives than his own advantage. All men relied on the well-proved character of the heavenly-minded King: the baron on his justice, the Church on his faith, the people on his kindness. Even what we consider blots upon his fame were elements of his influence at the time. No fanatic in the darkest ages had ever attributed such sanctity to relics and outward forms. Barefooted and bareheaded, he walked in solemn procession from Vincennes to Paris, carrying a portion of the Crown of Thorns, which had been sent him by the Emperor Baldwin, and deposited it in the gorgeous Sainte Chapelle, which he built for its reception. Jew and heretic were never exposed to such enmity or merciless persecution as by this model of a Christian king. No monk was ever more ignobly under the dominion of a morbid delicacy, or forswore with more unnatural abnegation the "sweet domestic charities of life." Yet this extreme zeal, and self-denying abstinence from the pleasures and duties of his condition as husband and father, were only additional claims to the admiration of his contemporaries. If we can look upon those portions of his behaviour with the same eyes, we shall see before us the most perfect of rulers and most innocent of men. We shall see that the feudal period has achieved its consummation, when a saint, girt with a sword and looking to the cross, is seated on a throne. Knighthood has nothing farther to hope for. It has given a king to the greatest of Christian nations, and a saint to the Christian Church. It was now going to give a victim to chivalry and Christianity at once; for Louis, in 1270, prepared for his last pilgrimage. Hatred to the Moslem had now extended, from the custodiers of Jerusalem and the warriors of Syria, to the whole Mohammedan race. Wherever they were to be found was the proper end of a crusade. As on a former occasion he had been diverted from the Holy Land to Egypt, he was now attracted to the shores of Africa by a report of the wealth and insolence of the Soldan of Tunis. Charles of Anjou, the brother of the King, whom we saw the successful wooer of the heiress of Provence, had by this time forced his way into Italy, and mounted the throne of Sicily. The expedition to Africa is said to have been at his suggestion; but whether with a view to his personal interest, in the weakening of a power so near to his new dominions, or for some other reason, cannot now be discovered; whatever was the cause, the voyage was speedily accomplished, a landing effected near the ruins of Carthage, and the half-crumbling walls taken by assault. It was in the month of July, and the desert was glaring all round the soldiers with inextinguishable heat. The sands were driven against them by the simoon, like little balls of fire; the water was dried up, and fever began its course. It struck down the heads of the expedition. Philip of France was ill; the Counts of La Marche and Vendôme, and Montmorency, had died. Funerals every hour frightened the camp from its calmness. The vast array of the Tunisians came in sight, and no reinforcements from Naples. Active, truthful, vigilant, the King performed the duties of warrior and priest. He roused his soldiers with spirited exhortations, and prayed with the dying. At last the blow fell upon himself. He struggled for a few days, continuing to the last the same noble cavalier and Christian believer he had ever been. With his last breath he dictated advice to his successor on the throne, and gave directions to restrain the excesses of his brother of Anjou. When that dilatory brother made his appearance in the port it was too late. The good King had died; and when the Sicilian ruler entered his tent, he found the noblest of kings and of Frenchmen lying upon ashes, with a crucifix on his breast.

> "Who is the happy warrior? This is he
> Whom every man in arms would wish to be."

There is a great resemblance between the characters of this justly venerated king and his despised predecessor Louis the Debonnaire. But what a cheering view it gives us of the progress of right feeling, when we perceive the strange difference between the contemporary appreciation of the two! The very names by which they are known are more a contrast than a similarity; for Debonnaire, which, besides being weakly pliant, contains the idea of a pious disposition at the same time, is used as a term of reproach, and was chiefly earned for the first Louis by the exercise of the same qualities which obtained for Louis the Ninth the epithet of Saint. In the earlier time, we saw how priest and noble were equally unable to understand the workings of a conscience which scrupled to be benefited by the injustice or violence of others. The Debonnaire was cast down from the throne he had degraded for proposing to restore wealth and properties, which had been wrongfully obtained, to their proper owners. The Saint was raised above the throne he had glorified for actions and sentiments precisely of the same kind. The difference consisted entirely in the better and purer intelligence of the time. Too far removed from Roman civilization to have retained any portion of the light radiated from that long-extinguished centre, the period we have now reached begins to be illuminated by the dawn of the coming day. Already we trace the risings of many modern thoughts and usages; and from this time we may look hopefully forward, for, however interrupted by wars and policies our onward course may be, certain it is that the light will daily increase; and when next we pause to survey the country we have passed over, we shall find that our progress has been as great as between the reigns of Louis the Debonnaire and Louis the Saint, for we shall have a fresh region added to our observation—the rise of a new and brilliant literature, and the first glorious appearance of science and art.

CHAPTER IV.

FROM PHILIP THE HARDY, A. D. 1271, TO CHARLES THE FIFTH, A. D. 1364.

WITH the death of St. Louis the crusading spirit came to an end. Calculations have been made by which it appears that the eight expeditions against the Saracens, extending from 1095 to 1270, cost to Europe the lives of two millions of men. It was now found that denuding Christendom of its soldiers was not the surest means of weakening the Mohammedan power; and from this time the energies of kings and peoples were directed to the settlement of their national affairs. Sufficient had been done during the eight crusades, by giving a common direction to the enterprise of many states, to spread the same principles of action among them all. The gentlemen of the most distantly situated kingdoms became acquainted during their common triumphs or dangers, under the walls of Jerusalem or Acre. A sort of freemasonry of knighthood ran through all lands. The Scottish cavalier interchanged ideas and feelings of brotherhood and amity with a knight of Sicily or Spain. But now this fraternity of nations, founded on a community of hopes and fears, was to be exchanged for quarrels among themselves. Yet the remembrance of the league which once had bound them, acted as a civiliser between the warriors of all lands in their intercourse with each other. The names of the early crusaders had now become historic. Heraldry had established itself as the highest of sciences, and the bearings on shields, and mottoes on pennons, revealed to the hostile squadrons, when drawn up in battle-array, who their antagonists were. In the same way as mutual respect was thus established among the knights and nobles of different kingdoms, there was a feeling of kindliness produced between the knights and other classes of the same realm. The destruction of so many followers had thinned out the original vassals to such an extent that new possessors arose in all quarters, men of the same blood with the peasantry around them—so that by this time the distinction between a conquering and a conquered race was becoming very slight. The Norsemen in Normandy were now completely French, and their countrymen in England almost completely English. The Saracen sword had nearly undone the work of Rollo and William; and the dullest spectator of the termination of those periodic paroxysms of heroic insanity must have read in the accompaniments of this last attempt, that the favour of Heaven was visibly withdrawn. Philip the Third, the son of the sainted king, left the shores of Carthage with five coffins in his train. A great storm near Sicily scattered and sunk the largest part of his fleet, and when the melancholy cortege at last reached the mainland, the population of France was awestruck at the greatness of their loss. They received in the same mournful silence the living king and the corpses of his father, his queen and infant son, his brother, and his brother-in-law, the king of Navarre.

Charles of Anjou had a more wretched struggle before him, and atoned, by his misery and disappointment, for his cruelty and want of faith. Five years before this, in 1265, he had established his power in Naples under the protection of the Pope, who desired a counterpoise in Italy to the preponderance of the German Emperors of the Hohenstaufen family. The last Emperor, Frederick the Second, had left a natural son of the name of Manfred, and a grandson, Conradin. Manfred resisted the French intruder, and was conquered and killed in a great battle at Grandella. Charles made his triumphant entry into Naples, where he soon inaugurated his reign with the bloody execution of the youthful and innocent Conradin. The guiltlessness and beauty of the highest born of the chivalry of Europe clung long to the affectionate and revengeful hearts of the Neapolitan people; and the animosity which the heedlessness and harshness of the French dominion had sown among the Italians, broke forth in the ferocious massacre of Palermo in 1282. It was on the 30th of March, at the first sound of the vesper-bell, that the infuriated natives rose against their invaders. Nobody was spared ; man, woman, and child, soldier and priest, all were stilettoed by surprise or slaughtered by superior numbers. As the news spread, the same tragedy was repeated in every town. And when the morning of the first of April came, there was scarcely a Frenchman alive in Sicily. This is known in history as the Sicilian Vespers.

Charles hurried across and laid siege to Messina. The terrified townsmen were reduced to great straits, and had little to expect from the forgiveness of the most unmerciful man of his time, when, in the last extremity, they were astonished with the sight of a great fleet sailing into their bay, bringing help and safety, under the command of Peter the King of Aragon, who had married the daughter of Manfred. Pope, and kings, and princes, ranged themselves on different sides. Martin the Fourth, continuing true to the French, declared Peter's throne of Aragon vacant, for rebellion against the Holy See, and offered it to the King of France. Peter and Charles were equally enraged, and agreed to solve their difference in a combat of a hundred on each side, to meet at Bordeaux, in the territory of Edward of England. When the appointed day came, the combatants, in fulfilment of the letter of their agreement, presented themselves in the town named ; one, however, at early dawn, and the other in the afternoon. Neither of them wished to fight, and both were obliged to keep their knightly words, taking shelter from the laughter of the disappointed spectators in the plea that Edward gave no safeguard for the meeting, and made no preparation for the lists. Charles of Anjou died of wrath and disappointment. The battle of Spanish and French interests which he had provoked, went on in the kingdom of Naples for two hundred years ; and it might give rise to some moralizing on the strange turn of human affairs, when we find the descendants of St.

Louis seated on the thrones of both the subsidiary kingdoms, while not one of his name or kindred is permitted to touch the soil of France.

The exploits of Philip, called the Hardy—the origin of which complimentary title it is difficult to trace—left no mark in history. His foreign politics were obscure and various ; and it can only be said for him that he had the good taste to leave almost entirely unchanged the internal principles of government of his illustrious father. The glory of St. Louis shed a light upon the fifteen years of his son's reign, and the impetus he had given kept France in forward movement without the interference of the King. This impetus, you will remember, was towards the centralisation of the royal authority, and the elevation of the lower class. Philip continued his patronage of the legalists, and took refuge against the occasional outbursts of his barons behind the decisions of his lawyers. But now there appeared upon the throne of France a man who united the rather incongruous characters of a sharp practising attorney and a crowned king. When Philip, the eldest son of Philip the Hardy, made his first public appearance in the Church of Notre Dame du Puy, in the Velay, he was only seventeen years of age. Tall and manly, with fair complexion and fascinating manners, he was hailed with universal acclaim as Philip le Bel, or the Handsome, and it was not for some time that the nation began to perceive that the sword of France had been converted into a quill, and the oriflamme itself changed into a vast roll of sheepskin written over with unintelligible words. Prepared to fight, and always ready to quibble, the new leader of the chivalry of Europe was a mixture of Brian de Bois-Guilbert and Gilbert Glossin. Where he could not force, he swindled, and hid all his tricks and manœuvres, and false claims and arrogant pretensions, under the terrifying name of law. Foreign kings and domestic princes, and even popes themselves, did not know what to do against a man who produced documents whenever they were required, and who brought worm-eaten deeds out of old repositories where they had quietly been gathering the dust of two or three hundred years. The law phraseology, which is at all times liable to several interpretations, and the fulsome adulation derived from the practice of the Roman Empire, by which the most unbounded powers are attributed to the Crown, were made excellent use of by the successor of Clovis and Pepin. If by any deed a privilege was conveyed, and there was added the usual clause, "saving nevertheless the rights of our lord the king," it was very soon found that the rights of our lord the king were totally inconsistent with the privilege, and it was accordingly withdrawn. There were covenants, we saw, in the mutual obligation of suzerain and vassal, a breach of which was fatal to the tenure of the liegeman. It was easy, by some musty old record or chronicle in an abbey, to prove that every covenant on both sides had been broken a hundred times; that the lord had not defended the tenant, that the tenant had opposed the lord. Out came the dignitaries of the law with a sentence of deprivation, and a royal garrison was speedily established in the baron's tower. It was the King's policy above all things to abolish the municipalities, for those establishments were centres of strength and freedom, and might be rallying places for resistance to his despotic attempts. Now these municipalities are called in French "communes," because they were formed for the purpose of common defence, and were combined by the use of a common seal and government of their own. In the south of France, we observed, the grand old cities of the Roman time retained more or less the municipal privileges granted them by the policy of the Emperors. In proud memorial of the past, they had bestowed on their civic rulers the majestic title of consul. In the north, when some community of feeling with these ancient "boroughs" had been established by intercourse and trade, the citizen, the shopkeeper and labourer, who had settled themselves in the neighbourhood of some chieftain's tower, and who now were oppressed and trampled on by the successor of their original lord, sighed for some refuge against his lawless authority, and applied sometimes to the king, sometimes to a neighbouring baron, for a place of shelter on his domain. The king gratified a town, especially if it happened to be on one of his vassal's lands, with a charter of incorporation, granting it the feudal indispensable signs of independence, "bailliage," "common seal," "town clock," "bell and belfry," and did not scruple, on receiving a bribe in money, to give the same privileges to a third-rate town or inconsiderable village on his own territory. Where there was no means on the part of the citizens to assert their liberties by force of arms, the kings granted them whatever nominal franchise they desired at its proper price. An ambitious or compassionate baron in the same way received the prayer of the persecuted dependants of a neighbouring chief, and set apart a small portion of his land, enclosing it with a wall, and giving it the guarantee of his sword and influence against all who should infringe his charter. Nay, we sometimes read of a count or earl, in answer to an appeal from a municipality to defend it against the assaults of the king himself, inviting the inhabitants to remove into his peculiar territory, and once off the soil of the royal domain, he will defend them, their charter, their bells and belfry, against the army of the Crown. And this was the feeling which alarmed the legal mind of Philip le Bel. Many of these institutions had secured to themselves the protection of powerful chiefs, by the grant of handsome salaries. The castle which had been built to overawe the unruly townsmen, was now their fortress against all comers. The lord of it was in their pay, and they themselves could buckle on their armour on occasion, and play no inconsiderable part in the defence of their goods and families. If the municipalities kept alive a spirit of liberty and equality, and were protected in these pretensions by any number of the nobility, the king perceived that the scheme of a true and unlimited monarchy could never be brought to bear. But there was another body in the State who stood equally in the gap against the overweening attempts of the Crown. This was the Church, which, starting so humbly, as we saw it under the blessing of Irenæus, and forming a bond between conqueror and conquered, which improved the condition of both, had by this time lost all remembrance of its original institution. Though many of the historians of this period are priests, and inclined to take a partial view of the interests of their order, it is easy to see that the Christian, or even the ecclesiastical character, had almost entirely departed from the higher dignitaries, while ignorance and evil living were the characteristics of the inferior clergy. A bishop in early times availed himself of the sacredness of his profession to calm the troubles of a town, which was exposed to the violence of a Gothic or Frankish assault. The civil governor had deserted his post, and by the force of circumstances, the man who possessed the greatest personal authority succeeded to the direction of the community. In quieter periods the bishop succeeded in retaining, as inherent in his office, the power which he had so auspiciously usurped. The great prelates of the realm, therefore, exercised as plenary powers in the formation of communes, and the protection of their tenants, as the proudest of the lay nobility. Many towns owed their charters of incorporation to their clerical lord. Many communities fled from the persecution of their feudal superiors, to the milder sway of the magnates of the Church ; so that when Philip the Handsome looked around, he saw those citadels of freedom dotted over all parts of his kingdom, some under the protection of his barons, and some under the safeguard of his bishops. The Church, moreover, could wield a two-edged sword in her combat with the King. At the same time that the highest of the clergy strengthened themselves by the adhesion of populous towns, the serf or injured labourer found a sure refuge for his weakness or wrongs by enrolling himself a priest. Once in holy orders, the stain of his lowly origin clung to him no more. Church and State seemed in this manner equally prepared against the aggressions of the King. The high nobility had not forgotten their old claims of equality ; and now were encouraged to exercise a more independent authority, by the fact that the inhabitants of their lands, who were rapidly increasing in wealth, had in many instances already commuted their personal service for a pecuniary payment. They were now masters of fixed revenues, and could raise mercenaries for their permanent service, who were exempt from the obligation of feudal obedience. The hierarchy limited the sovereign's power by their ecclesiastical privileges, and their allegiance to a foreign and permanent authority—the Pope; the lower priesthood took the peasantry from his direct rule, by admission into their ranks. The rising middle class of the towns took care of their interests, by the establishment of communes. Nor were these called citadels of freedom by a mere figure of speech. They were guarded by actual square towers, and vast castles, which, before the invention of gunpowder, resisted all assaults. It is difficult to give an idea of the number of those edifices, unless by asking you to ornament with turret and bartisan all the gentlemen's houses you see in a railway excursion,—where gentle lawns sloping downward from the door must be converted into a foreyard, crossed by a drawbridge, and enclosed within high walls. The plate-glass windows also, and nice conservatories at the side of the drawing-room, must be exchanged for narrow arrow holes in the thickness of the masonry, and a dark stable leaning against the donjon keep. A survey was made a few months ago of the ancient Chateaux of France. There remained twenty thousand three hundred and twelve, and of these there were no less than three hundred and eleven which had seen the reign of Philip le Bel. How many seats are there in England which claim such antiquity as this? Not Windsor itself, nor Chatsworth, nor Warwick. And if, after the wear and tear of five hundred and fifty years, three hundred and eleven are still standing, we must make allowance for the crowds of them which have disappeared, and wonder at the audacity of the man of legality and special pleading, who threw down the gauntlet to so many burgesses stout and strong, so many wielders of the sword, and so many leaders of the Church.

Edward the First was at this time King of England, and was deeply engaged in his schemes for the subjugation of Scotland and Wales. A quarrel very soon arose between the kings, and it gives us a proof of the complete separation between the Norman duchy and the English crown, that the war was caused by a riotous scuffle between some English and Norman sailors. Philip demanded justice on the culprits, and Edward declined to take any steps. Philip then summoned Edward to appear before his court as feudatory of Guienne, and answer for his conduct in person. Edward was too busy setting up John Baliol, and oppressing the Scotch nobility, to prepare for the next step of his rival. Guienne was seized with little remonstrance on the part of the native barons, and annexed to the French crown. At the same time, Philip arrested Guy, Count of Flanders, as aiding and abetting his rebellious vassal, and terrified or cajoled the King of Aragon into a surrender of the island of Sicily, in which he did not possess an acre of ground, to the Duke of Anjou. This surrender, though not supported by force of arms, was a weapon in the armoury of the politic king, which he was ready at any time to bring forth, if the princes of Italy gave him any umbrage. His possession of Guienne was more practically useful, as it enabled him, in 1296, to detach the powerful Edward from the party of his enemies, by making restitution of the duchy as dowry of his daughter Isabella, whom he betrothed to Prince Edward, afterwards Edward the Second. But even this restitution was under more stringent conditions of fealty and submission than pleased the English king. That potentate, who had dated his charters and coins, in the county of Guienne, from the year of his own reign in England, was now obliged to date them from the accession of Philip.

On taking note of his forces in the year 1299, the French monarch had no reason to be discontented with the state of his affairs. He had silenced England, reunited Champagne to the throne by his marriage with the heiress of that duchy, and gained possession of Flanders by a mere breach of his word. A legal quibble was more agreeable to him than a campaign. His brother, Charles of Valois, had agreed on terms with the Count of Flanders, and advised him to wait upon the king. The king was delighted to see him in his power, declined altogether to ratify the conditions of his surrender, and threw him and his two sons into prison. Charles of Valois, not being of so legal a mind as his brother, was insulted by the discovery of a flaw in his contract with the noble captives, and retired from court. The Pope, who began to hate and fear the French king, rewarded his brother's enmity with the crown of Constantinople; and, as a farther proof of affection, made him Apostolic Vicar of the whole of Italy.

Philip had already a bitter feeling towards the imperious Boniface the Eighth. A papal aggression on his royal authority, by the erection of the bishopric of Pamiers without his consent, had roused his wrath some years before this date. He had retorted by receiving at his court the Colonnas whom the Pope had banished from Rome. The Pope retorted again, by sending a certain Bernard Saissetti, who was no other than the intrusive Bishop of Pamiers, to rebuke the king for his manifold offences against the Holy See, particularly for continuing to raise a tax from the clergy, on pretence of fitting out a new crusade to the Holy Land; whereas it was well known that neither he nor Edward of England had the remotest idea of going to the East. The king's retort upon this was an order to let no money leave the realm of France, whether for Rome or elsewhere, upon pain of death for treason. The bishop, as a parting blow, had accused the king of being a forger, or at least a passer of base money, which, though perfectly true, was not complimentary, and ordered him to release the Princes of Flanders, whom he had imprisoned without any cause; and the king, not knowing how else to retort, sent down a body of bailiffs to the town of Pamiers, who arrested the bishop in his bed, and brought him in safe custody to Paris. Boniface was not to be excelled in violence, and gave his final retort on this part of the question, by summoning the whole clergy of France to meet at Rome, and to consult on the defence of their ecclesiastical privileges, and the best method of curbing the excesses of the king. Philip took higher ground. He told the audacious pontiff that there were kings in France before there were bishops, and he would rule within his realm in total disregard of what such a blinded, fraudulent, simoniacal pretender could say. He appealed to the College of Cardinals to proceed to a new election, and guarded himself in the mean time by summoning a great Council in Paris, to which came, for the first time, the third order in the State, equivalent almost to our members for the boroughs. The order for all the French clergy to appear at Rome roused the wrath of the assembly. They resolved unanimously to support the king in maintaining the privileges of the Crown; and as the first proof of national independence, the quick eyes of Philip having detected the departure of forty-five bishops who preferred the Pope's commands to the King's, all their goods and chattels were confiscated, without a moment's delay, to the public exchequer.

War was now openly declared between the King and the Church. In this he was supported by the representatives of the towns and the great mass of the nobility. But he was now resolved, whenever the opportunity arose, to try conclusions with the towns themselves; and, as a preparatory measure, determined to curb the liberal tendencies, and diminish the overgrown riches of the burghers of Flanders. During his first royal progress, the wealth of the Flemish merchants had struck him with surprise, if with no more dangerous feeling; the pride of the queen also was offended beyond forgiveness by the magnificence of the attire in which she was received by the citizens' wives. "There are five hundred queens here, I think," she said, and looked with covetous eyes on the masterpieces of the looms of Ghent and Bruges. French governors and soldiers, left as garrisons in the great manufacturing towns, had vied with each other in oppressing the inhabitants. Royal taxes, local rates, forced contributions, and, above all, the tampering with the coinage, had irritated the citizens past endurance. At last they burst forth in open rebellion, overpowered the foreign troops, and at Bruges gave way to the utmost excesses of popular vengeance. Never was such an opening for revenge and plunder presented to a Christian king. Philip raised an army, and sent all his knights and nobles to chastise the insolent workmen, and pillage the magnificent shops. At Courtrai they were met by a phalanx of armed burghers, who blocked up their further course. With shouts of contempt and hatred, the nobles put spurs to their steeds. But there was a ditch in the way; confusion fell upon their ranks; the stout weavers plied their staves, which were tipped with iron, and bore the very inappropriate name of "good day;" and in a bruised mass of flesh and armour, the bodies of horse and gentlemen covered all the plain. This is called the battle of the Spurs, on account of the four thousand pairs of those knightly ornaments which were gathered after the fight; and it is not impossible that Philip, who meditated a diminution in the privileges of his nobility, derived some little compensation for his national defeat, in considering the advantage so many deaths would give him in his contest with the survivors. Without loss of time he raised another force, consisting of the Ban and Arrière Ban of the kingdom; and it is a circumstance worthy of notice, that while the horsemen of this array amounted to twelve thousand, the infantry reached the number of forty thousand men. The usual proportion between horse and foot was entirely changed, and the result justified the measure, for the Flemings were now entirely defeated, and left thirty thousand dead upon the field. But what were the foot-soldiers of all France to the countless artisans of the Low Countries? Undismayed by their misfortune, the gallant townsfolk gathered fresh levies, and presented themselves wherever the army moved. Philip was amazed. "Does it rain Flemings?" he said; and when they had collected an overwhelming force, they sent over a messenger with the two words, "Battle or Peace?" The king chose the latter. He sent back his prisoner, Robert, the son of their legitimate ruler; and reserving to himself a few border towns, and a subsidy of a hundred thousand francs, he returned to resume his contest with his greatest enemy, the Pope. It would have been wiser to have shown a little more moderation in his transactions with that misguided and untamable old man. When an interdict was launched against the king and kingdom—which, however, had entirely lost its effect—and accusations were denounced by the barons of France against the Sovereign Pontiff, Philip despatched a trusty officer apparently to lodge an appeal in his name, but with orders to arrest his enemy wherever he might be found, and to bring him prisoner to Paris. This man was William de Nogaret, one of the legal functionaries on whom the king relied for the execution of his plans—a man who, in the dark robe of his profession, and with the bonnet of the law upon his head, exercised more real authority than any one in the kingdom. But the long-winded sentences of William de Nogaret, who rose, by dint of prolixity and shrewdness, to be Chancellor of France, would not be sufficient to impress the hostile ear of Boniface the Eighth. A man of the sword also was required, and the person chosen was Schiarra Colonna, whose brothers the Pope had banished, and heaped their estates on his nephews—whose family he had vowed to exterminate, and declared incapable of any office, civil or ecclesiastical, in all time to come. Colonna was an ancient Roman in the vigour of his hatred, and kept all these things rankling in his heart. He found his victim in the small town of Anagui, and seized him with unnecessary violence in the church. Boniface, who saw his fate in the countenance of his enemy, resolved to die with dignity, and, like the English à-Beckett, awaited the final blow in the raiment of his rank. The brutal soldier struck the old man with his iron gauntlet on the face, and was proceeding to further extremities when the townsmen rose; the assailants were speedily outnumbered and dispersed, and Philip the Handsome had only the satisfaction of having embittered an octogenarian's last days with personal humiliation, and sufferings beyond his strength to bear. He died in a few weeks after the outrage, and the new pontiff inaugurated his reign by fulminating his sentence against the persecutors of his predecessor. A contest with the Church was not now what it had been in previous times. The clergy had lost their influence with the increase of general knowledge, and consoled themselves with sensual indulgences for the diminution of their spiritual power. Their gluttony and drunkenness were the subjects of every ballad, and their less excusable vices were spoken of in harsher terms. They were not in a position to give much moral assistance to their head at Rome, and, in fact, were not inclined to do so, for the exactions of the Pope were more intolerable than those of the King. They preferred to pay subsidies, which were spent in France, to sending half the revenues of their parishes and free lands across the Alps. Philip was also encouraged by the support of the third estate, the representatives of the communes, and prepared for the coming storm. In answer to the criminations and threats of Benedict the Eleventh, he sent large sums for distribution among the Cardinals. There was a French party established in the conclave itself, and the King could look forward to the next vacancy of St. Peter's chair as the crowning-point of his quarrel with the Holy See. This vacancy occurred sooner than was expected. At supper, one night, the Pope was presented with a basket of figs by a female closely wrapped in a veil, and was dead before the morning Philip saw his time. He discovered the most sensual, dissolute, and mean-spirited of the prelates of France, in the person of Bernard de Got, the Archbishop of Bordeaux, and receiving a promise of complete obedience to all his orders, if he were elected Pope, sent off a command to the servile conclave, and the obsequious pontiff kissed his hand, and professed his eternal gratitude under the name of Clement the Fifth. The seat of the Christian government was transferred to France. The pontiff was but the paid servant of the Crown, and was used in the further schemes of the now triumphant monarch, exactly as the other retainers of his government were used. Clement was a mere instrument in his hand, like his chancellor, Peter Flotte, or his counsellor, William de Nogaret. To appoint a Pope was not enough, it was necessary to degrade the office ; for this purpose he insisted on a process being raised in the Papal Court, to blacken the memory of Boniface the Eighth. Witnesses were found who deposed to the most frightful crimes on the part of the victim of Anagui, and even the soul of Clement the Fifth began to recoil from the hateful work he had undertaken. He begged the king to desist from the prosecution; and the king agreed, yet not without conditions. The Papacy was at his feet; the Church, through its leader, was entirely in his hands; but there was another body in the State whom it was necessary to destroy. Would the Pope consent to his instituting a process against the Templars—the guardians of the Holy Sepulchre—the defenders of Jerusalem—the Christian warriors; uniting the nobility of the loftiest knighthood to the personal humility of monks and friars? The bargain was struck, and the king began. In one day all the brotherhood was arrested. They were accused of the most revolting and impossible crimes; they were kept in dark dungeons, and starved, till the bodily weakness affected the mental power, and then were tortured till they confessed whatever William de Nogaret put into their mouths. When their strength returned, they recanted their confessions, and were instantly burnt as relapsed heretics. The process dragged its slow length along; for the confiscation of their goods, and the occupation of their castles and preceptories was a work of time. At last, when nothing more was left to be seized, the final sentence was passed in a grand consistory presided over by the Pope, where, in presence of the King and the Princes, the men of law and the men of birth, the Order of the Templars was declared abolished, and their possessions conveyed to the Knights Hospitallers, on payment of such sums as might be claimed by the King. It is only fair to say, that the example of Philip was followed in many other kingdoms, and the Order dissolved; a convincing proof of the decay of the glory of knighthood, as the treatment of the Pope had evidenced a decay of the influence of the Church. In passive endurance all Europe saw the Father of Christendom transformed into a French judge, and the abolition, on evidently false pretences, of the highest order of chivalry. That the spectacle of degradation might be more complete, Clement reserved to himself the trial of the Grand Master, Jaques de Molay, and three commanders of the Order. They were condemned to perpetual imprisonment; but the courage of the old man revived. When brought out to the front of Nôtre Dame to hear the sentence read, he protested his innocence, and retracted the confession forced from him and his two friends by the rack. Philip was close at hand in the palace, on the island where the Hall of Justice now stands. He heard of the retractation, and ordered the faggots to be laid. He commanded them to be executed without delay, as given over to the secular arm; and on another little islet, where the statue of Henry the Fourth still stands, to remind his countrymen of the most clement and patriotic of their kings, Jaques de Molay and his noble companions went through the dreadful ordeal, and died with the firmness of martyrs. It is said that from the midst of the flames the old man summoned his persecutors to appear at the bar of God within a year; but this report probably arose when the deaths of both the wicked workers in this great tragedy so soon followed their success; for Clement died in April, and Philip in November of the year 1314. The supremacy of legalism was now fairly established over both the sword and crozier. The third estate was admitted to a seat and equal vote with the other orders in the realm. Parliamentary deliberations were regulated by the judges, and the judges were appointed during pleasure by the king. If to this we add, that in this reign an ordonnance was passed by which a commoner, on purchasing a noble fief, became himself noble, and a title, with all its privileges, could also be conveyed by the mere nomination of the king, we shall see what powerful assaults were made on the sacredness of the feudal nobility, and what an impulse was given to the personal ambition and political power of the free burgesses of France.

Philip the Fourth left three sons, who all successively attained the throne: Louis the Tenth, called the "Hutin," or Quarrelsome; Philip the Fifth, or the Long; and Charles the Fourth, who succeeded also to his father's epithet of the Handsome. He left also a daughter, Isabella, whom we saw married to Edward the Second of England, and who was the cause, perhaps, of more misery in both countries than any woman who ever lived. The fourteen years of the three reigns of Philip the Handsome's sons were distinguished by nothing but the discontent of the people at the amount of taxation, and by the destruction of the royal family itself. Louis held the throne for less than two years, and had only time to take vengeance on his wife, Margaret of Burgundy, grand-daughter of St. Louis, for her life of infamy. She was strangled in the Chateau Gaillard. His successor, Philip, was no less unfortunate in the partner of his throne, Jane, a daughter of the Count of Burgundy, but, for political reasons, was more merciful in his anger. He mounted a doubtful throne on the death of his brother, for a party arose who defended the superior claims of the daughter of the late King; the question of the exclusion of females from the throne of France never having practically been tried. In all other holdings the female was as eligible as the male. Half the provinces now attached to the Crown had come to it by marriage. At the coronation itself of the new king, his crown was supported on his head by the hands of a Countess of Artois, as one of the peers of France. But the men of legality came in, and decided that the customs of local tenures had no relevancy in a discussion about the crown. The King of France was lord paramount over all the realm; and "the kingdom could never fall to the distaff, though females were capable of all other fiefs."

Already the collateral branches of the royal family, from which France has suffered so much at various times, began their baneful influence, and overshadowed the throne. Charles of Valois, the son of Philip the Hardy, and uncle of the King, exercised the chief influence in the State. He oppressed the people with fresh burdens, and brought back the Jews, on pretence of toleration, for the purpose of pillaging them again. He carried forward, however, the plans of the late king for the strengthening of the Crown, and excluded the bishops from their seats in the parliament, on the plea that "the King made conscience of detaining their lordships from the duties of their sees." But, in spite of some advances made in the formal elevation of the royal authority, nothing could counterbalance the discontent created by the exactions of the Court and the divisions among the nobility. Rebellious and mad processions of the irritated peasantry took place in all parts of the country under the name of Pastorals. Armed with staves and stones, those infuriated sufferers professed to reform the State. They were subdued and exterminated with the hatred of fear. Leprosy, also, the worst of woes with which humanity can be afflicted, had been imported from the East. It spread among the starved and houseless masses with such rapidity that it was looked on as a judgment on the land. No one was allowed to associate with the sufferers, unless at the price of sharing their seclusion for ever. Wrapped in a thick veil, and ringing a bell to warn passengers of their approach, they were only admitted to the wider streets and open places of a town; they must touch nothing, breathe on nothing, go near to nothing which might be required for the use of man. A prayer was read over them, and sentence of banishment for ever from human society passed upon them. And all men were liable to the visitation. Noble lords and gentle ladies were not beyond reach of the fatal pest, and where all were equally exposed, alarm was equally diffused. In the reign of Philip the Long this terror reached its height. Compassion, if it ever existed, gave way to hate. The lepers were accused, along with the Jews, of poisoning wells and bewitching cattle. They were slain with pitiless sword, or starved to death in their miserable dens, not by popular fury alone, but by order of the King, and with the blessing of the Church. Pope John the Twenty-second headed the good work, and the clergy superintended the massacres. Meanwhile money was required for the purposes of the State, and to satisfy the cupidity of the supporters of a still doubtful title. Counties were conveyed away from the Crown to raise the needful funds ; and, as a last resource, Philip made freedom itself an article of merchandise, and forced his serfs to buy their liberty with all the wealth they had saved. Vast numbers were thus forcibly emancipated, and as a consequence, not expected by their lord, were compelled to assume the loftier aspirations befitting their new condition.

Charles the Fourth succeeded, on the death of Philip, in 1322. He tried to put some restraint on the fanaticism of the public against the Jews and lepers, and took both under his protection. The Jews were restricted to certain portions of the towns they inhabited, and hospitals were erected outside the city walls for the reception of the diseased. Those leproseries, as they were called, amounted to several thousands before many years had elapsed ; for we are entering on a period of public misery and distress which was very unfavourable for the cure of a distemper depending in a great measure on filthiness of living and poorness of blood. It is therefore scarcely too much to say, that the great support of leprosy in France was Edward the Third of England, whose inroads began at this time. We are not to pay our English kings so poor a compliment as to suppose they were ignorant of the advantage of legality which they saw so flourishingly established by Philip the Handsome in their contests with their nobility and people. They were almost as much alive to the power of "whereas" and "notwithstanding" as the humbler practitioners of the noble science of the present day ; and though occasionally disconcerted by the unlegal minds of certain barons, who pointed to their swords as the title-deeds by which they held their lands, they pursued, when they could, the same course of chicanery and pettifogging which gave such new dignity to the fleur-de-lis. Edward the Second, you remember, married Isabella, the daughter of Philip the Handsome. In 1328 Charles the Fourth, the last of her family, died without sons, and Philip the Sixth, the son of that Charles of Valois who had been the despotic minister of the three unfortunate brothers, mounted the vacant throne, as nearest male descendant of St. Louis. But the right of female succession, though rejected by the decision of the lawyers, was not by any means banished from the hearts of ambitious pretenders. And when kings were the clients in such a cause, it was easy to find learned gentlemen on one side of the Channel who replied to learned gentlemen on the other. The English advisers took a distinction between the direct accession of females and their power of transmitting their claim to a son. Isabella, it was confessed, in her own person was incapable of reigning, but Edward was next in blood to the late monarch, and took precedence of so distant a collateral as the heir of the Valois, who was removed by one degree more. Unluckily for Edward, if this doctrine held good, there were descendants of the daughter of a former king still alive, and the three brothers through whom he claimed were usurpers. But, however legal sophistry might display itself, everybody knew that the final umpire was the sword. Edward the Second had been deposed by his Parliament on account of his cowardice, tyranny, and falsehood, and when the wretched drama was brought to a conclusion by his frightful murder in the dungeon of Berkeley Castle, and the hated queen received her punishment, far less than she deserved, by confinement to one of the royal houses, the king, radiant in strength and courage, held the sceptre, though only in his eighteenth year, with so firm a hand, that all England felt there was again a man at the head of affairs who would compensate for the disgraces of his predecessor's administration. All France also was very soon of the same opinion, and in a short time the Hundred Years' War began. Quarrels and misunderstandings were on a gigantic scale in those days. With us the Thirty Years' War of the German Reformation is quoted as a very long one; the war of the Revolution from 1793 to 1815 seems an enormous tract of time devoted to the arts of destruction. But from 1337 to the loss of the English possessions in 1450 —for the historians give good measure in their valuation of a hundred years—there was no pause in the mutual wrath and slaughter of the greatest of European states. The spirit in which the war began was sufficient to insure its permanence while there was a power of fighting on either side. The declaration is worth quoting as manifesting the animosity already established between the nations. A combination of pirates off the Spanish main never inaugurated a voyage with such ferocious sentiments. The knights and gentlemen of England, assembled in a cour plenière, that is, in a full assembly under the presidency of the Crown, bound themselves upon the Heron—a touch of conscience, let us hope, prevented them from swearing it upon the Gospels—"to ravage and massacre without pity, to spare neither mill nor altar, nor pregnant women, nor relation, nor friend." Amenities of the same kind were professed on the other side, and Edward for a while left off his overbearing cruelties and lawyer-like quibbles in Scotland, and threw himself heart and spirit into the French quarrel. A wise man, though careless of blood, and sagacious enough to forego his personal feelings when his interests were concerned, haughtier than his predecessors, despising the commonalty with more vigorous contempt than even the Valois to whom he was opposed, Edward saw that the power by which victories were gained had changed its seat. It rested no longer in square stone tower or battle-axes, but was found in busy looms and swarming factories, in broad-bottomed ships, and bales of Indian silks. So he made the rough mechanics of Flanders his friends, gave them privileges of trade, invited their extra numbers to come under his guardian solicitude into England, and wrote delightfully familiar letters to his "good friend and cousin" James Van Artarveld, a brewer in the great city of Ghent. He turned to his own people also, and spoke to them of the advantages of commerce, and the duty of rich citizens to furnish men-at-arms, not steel-clad horsemen as in the olden time following their chiefs in fulfilment of their feudal obligations, but stout wielders of the sword and drawers of the bow, men in buff jerkins and leather helmet, with whose assistance he could rout the chivalry of France. The truth of this apparent boast was proved by the annihilation of the hostile fleet in the harbour of Sluys in 1340, and by a series of successful advances during the following years. Intestine troubles broke out in France in addition to foreign war. There were revolts in Brittany and other dukedoms ; and everywhere support was furnished to the malcontents by England. Many of the nobles were in England's pay, the sea was open to his ships, for Philip had lost every vessel at Sluys, and all the oppressed Frenchman could do was to stir up troubles in Scotland to attract his enemy's attention nearer home. Truces were occasionally patched up,—by the connivance, apparently, of the rival kings,—during which one went and punished his refractory vassal in Brittany, and the other carried fire and sword from the Tweed to the Forth. By the great victory of Crecy in 1346, the balance turned greatly in favour of the English claimant. Philip could no longer ride out to a campaign in the midst of an escort of kings and great vassals. The flower of French chivalry was swept away, and little reliance could henceforth be placed on the old resources of mounted tenants and personal adherents. At the siege of Quesnay in 1341, there had appeared a ridiculous-looking hollow mass composed of plates of iron tied together with strong hoops and loaded with a black powder, which projected round stones, about once in the four hours, against the walls with tremendous force. This was the first cannon employed in European war, and far-sighted chevaliers might have seen in the first flash that their occupation was gone. A few shots were also fired at Crecy. But more palpable to the common observation was the now established fact that the strength of battle was in a line of "yeomen good." It took a long time to infix this very unwelcome circumstance on the hearts of stout knights and hopeful squires. The fallacy of chivalry lingered on, and waving plumes and burnished armour were in use long after muskets, and even pistols, had rendered them of no avail.

The terrible day of the 26th of August, 1346, had cost to

Philip the lives of eleven princes, twelve hundred knights, and thirty thousand men. A popular king might have risen up under so great a misfortune, but Philip of Valois was hated by his subjects. His oppressive taxation had reached its height when it forced a groan from every cottage, and a witticism from Edward the Third. To talk of those grim historical personages being jocular and addicted to laughter like other men, seems a contradiction in terms, and a derogation from the cheerless dignity in which they ensconce themselves. But it will reconcile us, perhaps, to the hard-hearted Plantagenet that he gave utterance to a pun, which may farther endear itself to our memory by the fact of being a horribly bad one. When all other means of raising the revenue were exhausted, Philip, in an evil hour, laid on the Gabelle, which was a tax upon salt. "This is the real author of the *Salic* law," exclaimed the son of Isabella, and perhaps resolved to overturn it in favour of the people, as well as of himself. Fortunately for the independence of France, the English invaders roused everywhere the hatred of high and low. Whether in fulfilment of their vow of the Heron, or merely to gratify their love of blood, these leaders of the expedition were unpitying in their treatment of the vanquished. Fear of the foreigner supplied the place of attachment to the national crown, and every fresh success of Edward against the soldiery called forth fresh animosity from the millions of the land. Calais was taken after the field of Crecy, and only, as we are told, on the intercession of his wife Philippa could Edward be prevailed on to pardon the burgesses of the town, who were given up to his vengeance by the exhausted inhabitants. Whether this be true or not, it paints the manners of the time ; and this, at all events, admits of no dispute, that the conqueror drove every resident of the devoted place to find subsistence or starve, as the case might be, outside of the walls, and repeopled the whole city with a great colony of English. Philip, on the other hand, came to the rescue of the exiles in a way which probably produced no benefit to the sufferers for it was by an ordonnance appropriating "all the fines and forfeitures which might fall to the Crown, along with the salary of all offices which might become vacant, till their losses were entirely made up." There were too many courtiers and applicants for grants around the person of the sovereign to allow any forfeitures or salaries to find their way to the good folk of Calais; and Eustace St. Pierre and his gallant companions are likely to have died in poverty. If they lived, it was in obscurity, for their names are heard no more.

The French nobles began now to look with divided interests on the fortune of the war. Edward, by the advice of his gossip the Brewer of Ghent, had boldly taken the royal name, and borne the lilies on his shield and banner; for, as the sagacious Fleming observed, "if you continue a mere invader, the knights and feudatories, and especially the great Earl of Flanders himself, will have scruples in assisting you against their sovereign lord. Be their sovereign lord yourself, and it will be their feudal duty to aid your enterprise." So two kings ravaged the country, and the men of lands and hereditaments saw nothing but the chance of forfeiture from disobedience to one or other of their majesties. But a truce came unexpectedly in the midst of those civil agitations; for the most dreadful plague ever known in Europe made the boldest and most thoughtless tremble at what was evidently the wrath of Heaven. Pope Clement the Sixth proclaimed the double unholiness of war when so great a calamity darkened all lands. This is known in history as the plague of Florence. Originally coming from the East, it gradually extended its ravages in the West and North, and in France found a fitting place for the display of its horrors; for the late wars had wasted the farms, and ruined the towns, and withered the hopes of the people. Prelates, and nobles, and princes, felt the fatal stroke. The Queen of Navarre and the Queen of France were the first royal victims; and while the whole country lay in this wretched state, and every man expected his last hour, property seemed to lose all its value. Many great land-owners retired into convents; and the legalists availed themselves of the general insecurity to advance the interests of the King. Dauphiny was bought for his grandson Charles, who thence took the name of the Dauphin, for two hundred thousand florins ; and James of Majorca sold Montpellier for a hundred thousand crowns. When the terror had in some degree subsided, and popular fury had vented itself in cruel persecution of the Jews, and even of notorious swearers and blasphemers, and the plague had gone on to exercise its strength on yet unexhausted realms, the King applied for the hand of Blanche of Navarre for his eldest son. But when the old man saw the beauty of the princess, who was said to be the loveliest woman of her time, he determined to keep her to himself, and consoled his disappointed heir with the widow of the Duke of Burgundy. While the festivals and rejoicings for these double espousals were going on, the King, who was in his sixtieth year, perhaps repented of his precipitancy, and after a short illness died in 1350—a man of personal courage and resolute mind, but with none of the nobler virtues which make kings respectable even when they are unfortunate.

John, King of France, was thirty-one years of age at the time of his father's death, and was in all respects, except in the wisdom and lofty sentiment of the Spanish Hidalgo, a royal prefiguration of Don Quixote. His whole education consisted in books of chivalry, and his models were impossible beings like Amadis de Gaul. The fate of a fantastical and imaginative person like this, when opposed to the crushing common sense and unscrupulous pertinacity of Edward the Third, might easily have been foreseen. There were Crecys and Poictiers written in every line of their characters. At his coronation at Rheims he armed chevaliers, his brother Philip, his son the Dauphin, the young Duke of Burgundy, and the two Princes of Artois, with all the ceremonies of knightly initiation. He then made a royal progress through the portions of the realm which were yet in his power, and thought he was consolidating his interests by tournaments and Feasts of the Peacock. Wherever he went there was emulation in expenditure and show. Feudalism had reached the period of its existence when it hid the harshness of its real features under the gloss of romance and sentiment. Songs and poems were everywhere sung and recited, recording the great deeds and hapless loves of long-forgotten heroes. Charlemagne and all his peers, and a mixed literature of Oriental grandeur and Western superstition—palaces of gold and jewels on the banks of the Tigris, and enchanters and transformed damsels on the banks of the Garonne—recollections evidently of the wild fables which had overshadowed the true history of the Crusaders, and of the wilder beliefs of Gael and Frank softened by time and distance ;—these were the intellectual food on which the upper classes were fed. And foremost in the ring, and most believing of the listeners, was the man whose crown was tottering on his head, and whose competitor was the strongest-armed and most inflexible-hearted warrior, statesman, and legislator the world could show. As if in mockery of the terrible realities by which he was encompassed, the King gave himself up to the enjoyment of an imaginary world in which his word was supreme. He amused himself with what he thought a resuscitation of the noble times of the championship of forlorn damsels and the siege of enchanted castles ; and surrounded with high-born dames, and barons who looked back to Arthur and the Paladins of the Round Table as their ancestors in chivalry, held high feast and tournay ; and created, in imitation of the Garter instituted in 1350, the second Order of Knighthood recognised in Europe, the Order of the Star or of the Noble House. Now at this time there was a man in France who presented in his own person the double spectacle of actual and fictitious chivalry. This was Charles of Navarre, Chevalier and King—one-and-twenty years of age, handsome and eloquent—from spur to plume a star of tournament—and married to the French King's daughter. Nobody could dwell more gracefully on the duties of armed chevalier—on courtesy, justice, generosity, and aid to the weak and feeble. And yet it is painful to say this ingenious, brave, liberal, and royal gentleman, was known by the name of the Bad. Charles the Mauvais was the truest knight in theory, and the greatest rascal in practice ever known. He claimed the appanage of Angoulême in right of his mother, but John had unfortunately given it to the Constable Charles of Spain. The Constable was refreshing in a hostel near L'Aigle, in Normandy, suspecting no evil, and never thinking that the acceptance of a gift from the King of France would be a sentence of death against him by the King of Navarre. But the latter potentate was judge by his office, and executioner by his own desire. He rushed with many men into the room, and slew the unhappy Constable, his brother in chivalry, unarmed and surprised. The county of Angoulême was now vacant, he thought, and he claimed it more earnestly than before. There was no rising of horror in the King's heart at this treacherous act. There was only an enemy to be gained over, and a friend to be forgotten. So he forgot the Constable, and gave Charles his demand. In less than a year the young King of Navarre had established his power so firmly in his new acquisitions, that he began to look higher, and thought, with the help of Edward, he might expel his cousin from the throne of France ; and accordingly he exerted himself as a popular orator, and declaimed, in town-hall and market place, against taxes and oppressions, and professed himself a reformer of all the abuses in Church and State. Charles, the Dauphin, became alarmed, and made overtures of friendship to the murderer. A treaty was concluded, and in 1356 a great festival was given at Rouen, by the heir to the crown, to the now reconciled monarch of Navarre. When the dinner was going on, John broke furiously into the apartment. He had ridden across from Orleans, and came in the nick of time. "Down, traitor!" he cried, and seized the Navarrese by the throat, striking him, and sparing no act of brutality. "By my father's soul," he cried, "I will neither eat nor drink, methinks, as long as you live!" On a sign, the captive was grasped by the men-at-arms, and hurried off to the dungeon of the Louvre, in Paris. Another sign was the death-warrant of every attendant the unsuspecting king had brought with him ; they were decapitated in the hall where they were at a friendly meal ; and John rejoiced as King in the dignity of his behaviour, and as Knight of the Star, in its courage. This, however, was not the only field in which he showed his prowess in this fatal year 1356. The brothers and friends of the imprisoned King of Navarre applied to Edward of England for revenge. The English monarch called it justice, and sent his son, the Black Prince, to administer it with a great army. The fame of Crecy had not yet died out, and the approaching struggle was looked on as a return game to be played by the same players ; John, therefore, at the head of all his knights, hurried down to Poictiers, where the wickets were set up, and guarded by the bowmen and billmen of the former match.

There is a wonderful amount of sameness in our three great battles against the French. Our army is caught in an unsafe position, and is threatened by overwhelming numbers. The leaders try to temporise, and offer great sacrifices to avoid the fight. The French, presumptuous and self-willed, refuse all accommodation, assault with impetuous courage, and are exterminated horse and man. This is not complimentary to the generalship of our chiefs, but speaks trumpet-tongued of the courage and endurance of our men. On this occasion, Ban and Arrière Ban of France, amounting to eighty thousand men, drew up in battle array against exactly one-tenth of their numbers. Eight thousand men stood upon that memorable ground, prepared to fight or die ; and doubtless their joy must have been mingled with surprise when the result of their engagement met their eyes. The French king, many princes, many counts, and rich feudatories, were their prisoners ; their enemies utterly destroyed, and spoil enough lying in the deserted tents to enrich a Nottingham archer or Suffolk burgess for life. We may doubt whether John was not consoled for his misfortune by the strictly chivalrous manner in which the conqueror received him. No captive monarch of Abyssinia was ever received at the gate of a castle built entirely of jasper and diamonds by El Tenebroso, the knight of Troy, with more rigorous adhesion to the rules laid down in chivalry, than was the prisoner of Poictiers by the Prince of Wales. From the field of battle to Bordeaux he was led in a sort of triumph, where the places of the victor and the vanquished in the old Roman pageant seemed absolutely reversed ; for John held the first seat, rode the best horse, fed at a table too sacred for any one to sit at but himself, and was waited on, cap in hand, knee on ground, by the heir of England, the best-known warrior in Christendom. The same conduct—farce would perhaps be too harsh a word—was continued in the following year, when the Prince and his captive made their famous entry into London. Royally treated at the Tower, and surrounded by lords who still spoke his language, though with the difference between the pronunciation of Paris and that taught at Stratford-le-Bow—invited to jousts and tournaments, and with all the dignity of a king without his cares, we shall scarcely think it so great a stretch of magnanimity in John as it was in Regulus, to return to the scene of his captivity, when he had been permitted on his word of honour to go home to negotiate for his release. John came back to the courtesies of a generous hospitality, and, if report speaks true, to the presence of a noble lady, to whom he had devoted his heart ; and Regulus went back to Carthage to be tortured with inhuman malignity till he died. Nor was the condition of France at that time such as to tempt his stay. The Dauphin stepped forward in the absence of the King, and found the whole country in disunion and distress. A meeting of the States-General was held, and, in emulation of their English contemporaries, the assembled representatives of the nation made hard terms with the Crown. They demanded the dismissal of many of the legal functionaries whom they distrusted, and the nomination of the receivers of taxes ; and on these conditions they granted a supply. But the supply granted by the assembly was to be raised among the people, and where was the money to come from ? Despair took possession of the hearts of the wretched peasantry. Jacques

Bonhomme—the pitying or contemptuous name by which the unfranchised classes were known—grew wild with hunger and rage. He broke through all bounds, and destroyed what he could not enjoy. Castles, houses, farms, and even monasteries, were sacked and burned ; and down upon him, in remorseless hatred and irresistible strength, poured the mounted and armed soldiery. The Jacquerie was crushed out by main force, and the royal and noble party rejoiced in the removal of their enemies, forgetting that from the masses only of those enemies could they hope to gather friends. For the English were perpetually at their gates. Paris was in insurrection ; and our old acquaintance, Charles the Bad, was collecting all the wild and discontented spirits of the land to aid him, not only in escaping from the Louvre, but ascending the throne of France.

It seems like meeting with a page descriptive of the Revolution in 1793 in its wrong place, when we come to certain transactions of the year 1358. Charles the Bad had been allowed to slip out of confinement, and was now in Paris. Streets were barricaded, and harangues made in all quarters. Charles himself brought his power of popular oratory into play, and addressed the wondering citizens from a tribune near the Abbey of St. Germain. Roused by his inflammatory language, crowds forced their way into the Dauphin's presence, and compelled him to restore all his chateaux and other property to the king of Navarre, and to proclaim the innocence of his comrades, who were treacherously slaughtered at Rouen by the King. But early next year the effects of this extorted clemency were known. One of the treasurers being assassinated by a citizen, the Dauphin ordered the murderer to be seized in the Church, to which he had fled for safety, and executed without delay. Robert of Clermont, Marshal of Normandy, and John of Conflans, Marshal of Champagne, carried the sentence into effect. But two feelings were roused to madness by this righteous violence. The priests, encouraged by the Bishop of Leon, cried out against the infraction of their asylum ; and the Parisian populace exclaimed against such severity to one of themselves, who had merely put a royal tax-gatherer to death. Led by the turbulent Stephen Marcel, provost of the town, dressed in red bonnets trimmed with blue, the tumultuous citizens presented themselves to the prince. In the midst of clamour and confusion the provost pointed to the marshals, who stood at the Dauphin's side. In a moment they were stabbed in a hundred places, their blood spurting out upon their master's clothes. "Do you wish to spill the blood of France?" inquired the prince. "No," answered the provost, and to protect him from popular fury, exchanged caps with him, putting the red bonnet on the head of the Regent, and leading him with the shoutings of a countless multitude to the Hôtel de Ville. Arrived there a window was opened, and the prince, in a long speech, pronounced his friends the Marshals of Champagne and Normandy enemies and traitors, and that they were justly punished for their misdeeds. This man was a lineal ancestor of Louis the Sixteenth. It is pleasant to know that justice overtook the provost ere many months expired. The Regent had again established his authority in Paris, and Charles the Bad was laying siege to the walls. Marcel had agreed to open the gate to the enemy, but he was overtaken by a worthy bailiff of the name of John Mallard, and knocked on the head with an axe when he was in the very act of applying the key.

Who could tell, in that distracted period, whether he was fighting for the good cause or not? Government was not more disorganised in the great shipwreck of the Roman Empire, for at this time there was no Clovis with the strong hand and military discipline to come to the rescue of the weltering mass. The want of money had released all the mercenaries from their obedience, and want of employment had reduced the peasantry to starvation. The Jacquerie, therefore, broke out from time to time; and while the barons and freeholders gathered in large numbers for the protection of their houses and lands, countless hosts of discharged soldiers joined the opposite side. Free lances or "companies," following a leader of their choice, and living by plunder, appeared everywhere.

Adventurers from England and Navarre were companions in those frightful scenes, and all France, you may almost say, was given up to pillage and conflagration. Knightly John, in the mean time, entered into a bargain with Edward in England, by which, in exchange for his liberty, he was to strip the French crown of all its late acquisitions, and give over to his vassal, in full sovereignty, the whole of the territory which now, or at any time, had belonged to the English crown. Charles the Dauphin took courage from despair. He summoned a national parliament, and refused to ratify the selfish arrangement. Better, he said, have open war for ever, than sacrifice the dignity of France. John was once more led back to his apartments in the Tower, and Edward took over an army to Calais. He found no enemy to oppose his march. Crecy and Poictiers had taught the Frenchmen wisdom : they retired step by step, and saw the invader gradually weakened by the want of provisions and other comforts, in the ruined and depopulated country. He invested Rheims, with the intention of being crowned in that sacred city, but was repulsed by the archbishop, after a six weeks' siege. He showed himself before the walls of Paris,—but what was the use of camping, or marching, or even of capturing the capital of the kingdom, when everything was a prey to disorder and desolation? The wearied-out King agreed to terms at Bretigny, by which peace was concluded in 1360. Edward was now contented with Aquitaine, and some of its dependencies released from obligation, and a ransom of three million golden crowns for his royal prisoner. He reserved, at the same time, his claim to the French throne, and left some minor questions for future settlement,—a convenient arrangement for enemies who are only out of breath for the time, and wish to renew the engagement when they have recovered their wind. Three million golden crowns! All France could scarcely have found the sum necessary to release the King, even if his presence had been thought worth the money. But a foreigner came to the rescue. John Galeaz had obtained supreme power in Milan, and was anxious to connect himself with the established dignities of Europe, by a royal marriage. He offered to pay a large portion of the ransom, provided he might have the hand of John's youngest daughter, and, thanks to the gold wrung from the oppressed inhabitants of an Italian dukedom, the King of England opened the prison doors to the King of France. The emancipated monarch resumed his old train of thought. He drew plans for a confederation of knights and gentlemen, against the free companions and the serfs. The Pope aided him in this, by publishing a crusade against them, and after he had issued the sentence, trembled within the walls of Avignon ; for he heard that a countless host of those desperadoes were coming down the valley of the Rhone. Short shrift would his holiness have had if he had fallen into the hands of a free lance of Navarre. But a safeguard was found in the Marquis of Montserrat, who met the multitudes as they hurried to their prey, took them into his pay, and led them across the Alps, with a promise of the plunder of Milan. The Pope blessed the happy movement that carried his enemies so far away, and even John was not displeased that the storm should fall upon his plebeian son-in-law rather than himself. The conduct of the Marquis of Montserrat seemed an excellent model for his own. As Avignon and the south were freed from those frightful freebooters by a transplantation to Italy, why should not Europe itself be freed from its dissolute and impoverished population by a revival of the crusades ? Already he saw himself at the head of a glittering host, emulating the deeds of Richard Cœur-de-Lion and Philip Augustus. Waldemar, king of Denmark, was at the court of the Pope ; so was Peter of Lusignan, King of Cyprus, who asked the aid of all good Christians against the Sultan of Cairo. Urban the pope was zealous in his favour, and preached the holy cause with the fervour of Saint Bernard. But the days of Saint Bernard had long passed away ; men's thoughts had now a more practical direction ; the voice of the papal chief had lost much of its thunder since the degradation of Boniface the Eighth and the meanness of his successors. The provincialism also of a residence at Avignon had tarnished the dignity of a chair whose proper place was the eternal Rome ; and kings, princes, and a few archbishops, had it all to themselves. Nobody would mortgage house and home to fit out for the Holy Land. And yet the enthusiastic king would not surrender his hope of success. If he could get Edward of England to join in the expedition—Edward the conqueror of Crecy and Poictiers—the lord of England and Ireland, and Aquitaine, what might not be expected from their united forces ? Louis of Anjou, his favourite son, who had been left as hostage in the Tower, broke his parole and came over to see him while engaged in these meditations. The feeling of the knight overcame the affection of the father, and as the young man would not go back to prison, he resolved to resume his confinement in his stead. The kings who so deeply cherished the idea of a new assault on Islam, had already exerted their influence on that subject in London. David Bruce, of Scotland, had added a fourth crown to the conclave in favour of a crusade. But Edward was deaf to all their arguments. Years had brought to him the philosophic mind, and also the debilitated body ; and John, in fulfilment of the noble words, which he perhaps quoted from some romance of chivalry, "Good faith, if banished from the earth, ought to find itself in the heart of kings," remained a contented prisoner ; not in the fortalice of the Tower, but in the spacious rooms of the palace of the Savoy. There, surrounded by the noble hostages, his brother of Orleans, the Duke of Berry, the Duke of Bourbon, and many more, he led the life he had pictured to himself in all his dreams. There were feasts and balls—dinners of the most amazing size, and suppers till daylight did appear—little excursions on the Thames from Westminster to the Savoy, or from the Savoy to Westminster—junketings with noble dames, and jokes and songs and corantos from the accomplished Enguerrand de Coucy, whose graces as a dancer, and beauty of person, won him the hand of the Princess Royal of England. And pity would be wasted on a captive who enjoyed his captivity so much. It is more probable he died of too frequent a repetition of those gorgeous festivals, than of grief for the loss of freedom; but whatever it was, he brought his strange life to a close—a life of thoughtless happiness in the midst of personal and national calamities which would have broken any other spirit—of little true ambition—and much individual injustice—in the April of 1364.

CHAPTER V.

FROM CHARLES THE FIFTH, A. D. 1364, TO THE RECOGNITION OF HENRY THE FIFTH OF ENGLAND, A. D. 1420.

CHARLES THE FIFTH was seven-and-twenty when he began to reign, and if he had followed the example of his father, he would have played the part of feudal king and fighting cavalier, as that for which he was ordained. But the young monarch saw that France had need of other defenders than feudal kings and fighting cavaliers. It needed a clear eye and a steady hand, a man at the helm, not a gilt figure at the prow, for never was there a time when the vessel of the State seemed in such danger. There was a whole people to feed and satisfy—rebellious vassals to reclaim—an open foe to guard against—riotous bands in the very heart of the kingdom to be discomfited; and for all this he had an empty treasury, a discontented parliament, ambitious communes, and a disunited nobility. But the French heart of courage, and chivalrous spirit of loyalty, was still entire. Bertrand du Guesclin was the sword of France, and Charles was her shield. "You shall risk nothing in a pitched battle against the English," he said. "You shall divide into small bodies and harass the enemy. You shall seize his towers by surprise and make up by rapidity of march for fewness of number. Meanwhile I will win over the municipalities whose protecting castles are turned against me. I will defend the farmer in his work, and guard the harvest when the corn is ripe. I will prevent extortion of the tax-gatherers, and assault from the freebooters. Law shall resume its power, and the great feudatories of the Crown shall unite for the common defence." Wise plans, and successfully executed, while the governing hand remained. But Charles was weak in body, and over him always hung the sentence of death, passed on him by the physicians in his youth. Charles the Bad, in return for his arrest at Rouen, had mixed poison in the Dauphin's food. The prince escaped destruction by the opening of a perpetual wound in his left arm. "Whenever the sore heals over," the doctors said, "the Dauphin must die." This issue was probably only a sign of a feeble constitution, but it silenced the sneers of his enemies, who were not accustomed to see a king except in armour; it doubled the respect of the few discerning potentates of the time, who began to perceive that a cabinet might be quite as great a scene of glory as a field of battle. Edward the Third said he was never so resisted in open fight, as by the calm sagacious counsellor who had never drawn a sword. Before the first year was over all men perceived that kings were greatly changed. There were no tournaments at the Louvre—no feasts at the palace. The King lived like an anchoret, except on state occasions, when he outshone the magnificence of oriental princes; and paid his men-at-arms their wages, and granted privileges to the trading towns, and did not increase a single tax! People must have grown ashamed of sustaining the cause of Charles the Bad, against so true a Frenchman and gracious a king as Charles the Wise; yet the war continued. It had been Du Guesclin's policy to recover as much of the valley of the Seine as he could from the hands of the King of Navarre. He had already secured Nantes and Meulan, and now the valorous Captal de Buch came to the rescue with a great number of discharged soldiers and desperate adventurers in his train; Englishmen and Brabanters, and Dutchmen and Bohemians, and Navarrese and Gascons. Du Guesclin's troops were a little alarmed at the appearance of the foe; but he only said, "Stay quietly where you are, and I'll take the Captal prisoner and destroy the rest." He waited long and patiently on the rising ground. The enemy were also on a hill. But English impetuosity could stand inaction no longer, and the mercenaries from all lands were thirsting for spoil. The French pretended to retreat, and the Captal moved from his formidable position into the plain. Du Guesclin exclaimed, "He is mine!" and charged down with great force. Thirty knights dashed through all impediments, and laid hands on the astonished Captal. Enclosed on all sides, he was led off through his own men, and taken without pulling bridle to the strong post of Vernon. The King and his young Queen were kneeling at the altar at Rheims with the crown upon their heads on their coronation day, when this news was brought to them by a messenger from the camp. "'Tis a bridal gift for the king," Du Guesclin had said before the battle, "and the Captal is his captive to ransom or keep." But the course of true war, any more than of true love, never did run smooth. Two pretenders were in arms for the dukedom of Brittany; the Count of Montfort, supported by the English, and Charles of Blois by the king. The English this time were not led by a foreign adventurer, but fought under their own standard, and were commanded by the famous John Chandos, the only rival in Europe to the fame of Du Guesclin, as general and knight. Another celebrated warrior, Oliver Clisson, was on the English side, and the star of Du Guesclin for a moment was obscured. He was taken prisoner at the combat of Auray in the September of the same year which saw him conqueror of the Captal de Buch, and the French interests seemed at the lowest ebb. But the politician in his cabinet at Paris knew how to make up for losses in a battle. One of the pretenders, Charles of Blois, was killed in the engagement, and the King of France, accepting this as a providential decision of the quarrel, recognised the title of the survivor on condition of his doing homage for the dukedom. He also arranged a marriage at the same time between the rival families, which might reconcile the contending factions. Peace was concluded on these terms at Guerande in 1365, and Du Guesclin was restored to liberty. Peace also was concluded with Charles of Navarre, who was glad to accept the city of Montpellier in exchange for the places he had lost upon the Seine, and a period of rest was promised to the distracted land. But rest was impossible with so many conflicting interests to arrange, and such a spirit of unrule diffused by the recent struggles. Thousands of armed men were in all parts of the country, discharged from the service of the dukes and princes who had now made up their quarrels, but not by any means inclined either to return to their own lands or to submit to the laws of the kingdom. Forming themselves into large bodies, they besieged and ransomed towns of the greatest size ; or uniting by fifty or a hundred at a time, they lived at free quarters in the villages and farms of remote districts, and were always ready to come to each other's assistance whenever the central authority threatened to stop their proceedings. France, differing in no respect from the position of a conquered country in the hands of its invaders, sighed for the time of more regular warfare, where the English companies were held in some restraint by the presence of their chiefs, and the rules of chivalry were not altogether disregarded in the intercourse between the armies. Charles the Wise looked back with fond regret to the time of the Crusades, and meditated another exportation of the restless adventurers of all surrounding countries to the East. But the Brabanters, English, and Saxons were very well satisfied with their present position, and had no desire to distinguish themselves against the enemies of the Faith, when they could live so comfortably on the fat of abbey-lands, and occasionally put a bishop to ransom at home. The example of Montserrat, who had saved the Pope at Avignon by leading the Free Lances of the south against the wealth of Milan, occurred also to the anxious thoughts of the King ; and just at the moment when he was in greatest distress, a circumstance occurred in Spain which gave him the wished-for opportunity. Pedro, known in general history as the Cruel, but recognised in Spanish annals as the Great Justiciar, had offended a great proportion of his subjects by his relentless executions and harsh behaviour. He had poisoned his wife, a princess of Bourbon, at the instigation of his favourite Maria de Padilla, and threatened death to the surviving natural children of his father. Of these, Don Henry de Trastamar was the most popular and the best ; he fled to France, and implored the aid of Charles against the murderous husband and unpitying brother. Du Guesclin saw the opening. "Sir," he said, "the Free Lances are anxious for work, and will gather from all parts if I hoist my banner. Better neighbours will they be on the other side of the Pyrenees than on this." Charles adopted the party of the banished brother, and preparations were instantly made. Du Guesclin himself had begun as a leader of Free Lances, and knew their ways. Thirty thousand of them joined him in an incredibly short space of time, and he marched southward down the Rhone. The Pope was as much alarmed as his predecessor had been, and sent out to know the object of their approach to Avignon. Bertrand answered with a grim smile, "We are thirty thousand poor Christian pilgrims bound on a crusade against the Saracens of Granada, and we want the Holy Father's absolution, and also two hundred thousand livres." "Touching the absolution, my son," replied the nuncio, "you shall have it without fail ; but with regard to the money, that is a different thing." "Sir," replied the knight, "there may be many here who reck not of absolution, but many who desire the money, for we make them prudent men in spite of themselves." Their prudence was rewarded with both the absolution and the coin. They made a detour, and Avignon was saved. When they reached Toulouse, the object of the expedition was for the first time declared to them. Plunder and battle was all they required, and a deluge of cruelty, carnage, and destructiveness poured down on devoted Spain. Pedro was expelled from the throne, and fled to Portugal. Henry was crowned at Burgos with Du Guesclin at his side, and was joyously received in the other cities of Castile.

Both nations now seemed ready for repose, and the triumph of having restored an exile and created a king was added to the other glories of the French monarch. But the Black Prince held his court at Bordeaux. Feasts and tournaments were celebrated according to the strictest rules of chivalry, and noble ladies listened to the songs of troubadours, and the picturesque narratives of Froissart, and the adventures of fabulous warriors, as their predecessors were said to have done in the days of Charlemagne and Arthur. Suddenly a dethroned and powerless king threw himself at the feet of the master of the lists; and half the stories of kingdoms lost and won by the irresistible sword of a single champion immediately rushed to their minds. All the blood of knighthood was on fire at the insolence of a people who had rebelled against their anointed lord, and Edward of Wales, as became a knight and man of honour, vowed to restore his suppliant to the throne. Crecy was renewed over again in the great field of Navarette in 1367. Du Guesclin himself fell into the enemy's hands, and all the work of the Free Lances was utterly undone. Pedro was king and justiciary in one, and let loose his royal vengeance on all the land. Murders, executions, confiscations, threw the whole kingdom into despair, and the English bitterly repented of their interference in behalf of so unchivalrous, unpitying a tyrant. The dreadful heats of the south came to the support of Henry. The English died of fever and excess, and discipline became relaxed. The reinstated king declined to pay the stipulated rewards; mutiny broke out among the discontented conquerors; and in the scorching summer, and amid these disturbances, the health of the Black Prince began to fail. Meantime, Charles the Wise endeared himself to his subjects by diminishing their burdens, by encouraging agriculture, and giving greater influence to the parliaments he convoked. The contrast was great and striking. Conquest in the field was of no avail against the steady advance of a popularity so justly founded and nobly sustained, as now grew on the vanquished side. The Free Lances, who had joined the prince, if not paid by the treasuries of Pedro, must be satisfied by the wealth of their employer. Edward returned to Bordeaux with barren laurels, and an empty exchequer. He laid fresh burdens on his unhappy subjects in Aquitaine, to pay for the expenses incurred in Castile, and when the population of that trampled province compared their position with that of their neighbours under the Crown, dissatisfaction took a wider range, and they complained of their rulers, not only as oppressors, but as foreigners. The English, indeed, even when the languages were the same, never became acclimated in France, and now there was added the great distinction of a different tongue; for the Norman portion of the English people had now become so small, that English at this time was declared to be the language of law, as it had long been of religion and commerce. Anglo-Saxon bowmen, who never spoke a word of French, served in the ranks of the Black Prince, and, of course, offended the nations by their brutal contempt for everything they did not understand. The Prince, therefore, in the midst of failing health and military disappointment, perceived that his countrymen were not the masters of the land he claimed, but were only forcibly encamped on it. From England no help was to be had. The king was old, and had fallen into the hands of a designing favourite, Alice Perrers, and her accomplices, who ruled him at their will. And nothing was wanting to the French monarch in these favourable circumstances, but warriors who could carry his plans into effect. Du Guesclin was a prisoner at Bordeaux, and all the wiser spirits in the court advised the Prince on no account to let so dangerous an enemy go. But Edward was made of penetrable stuff; and on one occasion when they were in familiar conversation, he said, if the captive could collect a hundred thousand francs, he should be set at large—a vast sum in those days; but the sight of Du Guesclin, sword in hand, and released from bondage, was worth forty times the amount to the French king. The money was sent at once, and Du Guesclin lost no time in showing his arm was as strong and his heart as brave as ever. A rapid incursion into Spain established Henry de Trastamar once more upon the throne, and freed him from the rivalry of Pedro, by the death of that ferocious tyrant. He was stabbed to the heart by his infuriated brother, after a personal struggle which lasted a long time. Henry was now undisturbed, and attributed his prosperity to the favour of the French king.

Charles was not slow in seeing the advantage of his position. Strengthened by the gratitude of his new ally, and the general favour of all his subjects, he spoke in a tone of defiance and majesty to the English Prince, which sounded strange in his ears within twelve years of the battle of Poictiers. He summoned the Prince of Wales to appear before his court of peers, as one of the feudatories of the realm, to answer for high crimes and misdemeanours. Edward answered, with much submission, that he would not fail to obey the summons, but would bring sixty thousand men along with him—helmet on head and spear in rest. Charles knew too well that this was but a vain boast, for the warrior was now too feeble to ride, and advanced in the exorbitance of his claims. He repudiated the article of the last treaty by which he surrendered Aquitaine in free sovereignty, and reclaimed it as a fief of the Crown. Edward of England took up the game of brag on behalf of his son, and retorted from Windsor by reasserting his claim to the French throne, and calling himself, in formal documents, King of England and France once more. War was openly declared, and Charles summoned his states in Paris. Never was meeting so unanimous and so sedately firm. Taxes were voted, forces were raised, and defiance hurled against the English both in their island fastness and the lands they usurped in France. Every village, in imitation of the enemy they had learned to fear, had butts for practice of the bow; games of manly exertion were encouraged; freedom was extended to the serfs, and the municipal towns enriched with further privileges. Du Guesclin returned from the Spanish triumph, and visited the king. The feeling in favour of illustrious birth was then so strong, that though Charles had bestowed the highest commands on the Breton soldier, they were offices which gave him only a temporary superiority over the forces employed, and implied no permanent pre-eminence when peace should be restored. But on this occasion a stately assemblage was called. All the princes of the blood, nobles of highest rank, chancellors, judges, warriors, were assembled in the great palace of St. Paul, and Charles gave his sword to Du Guesclin, and said, "Du Guesclin, take my sword, and use it against my enemies. Henceforth you are Constable of France." This was the highest dignity a subject could hold, and Bertrand excused himself on account of his humble extraction; but Charles persisted, and the Montmorencies, and De Coucis, and Courtenais, and Bourbons, thought the sword could not be in better wielding, and did obeisance to Sir Bertrand Du Guesclin, who was now the foremost man in all the land. The whole of Poitou fell in a short time. Rochelle itself was taken. The example of submission was contagious; and by the end of the year 1371, there remained nothing to the English interest in all the dukedom of Brittany but the town of Brest. Aquitaine continued in uneasy subjection to its foreign lords; and when the parties came to a truce in 1375, the glory of the English achievements was utterly obliterated by the disasters of their later years, and Charles could look forward to happier times than his predecessors had ever seen. The Black Prince lingered painfully for four years, and died at last at Eltham in 1377. Edward the Third, broken down with labour and disappointment, followed his heroic son to the tomb in a few months; and the accession of Richard the Second was marked by quarrels in the royal family, and a dissolution of military discipline, which encouraged the invigorated French to the hardiest undertakings. A landing was even made on the coast of Sussex; Calais was threatened; Normandy overrun as a supporter of the English; and if Charles and the Constable had lived, there was a chance of a complete expulsion of the enemy fifty years before it actually occurred. But many things conduced to weaken the health of the too thoughtful king. Dissensions among his brothers renewed in Paris the scenes of falsehood and partisanship which were going on in London. The influence he possessed over Europe as long as the Pope resided in Avignon, was taken from him, first, by the removal of Gregory the

Eleventh to Rome; and in a short time after that, the usefulness of the papal chair in his schemes of advancement was altogether destroyed by the schism which broke out at the election of the next Pope. For many years no one but natives of France had been chosen to preside over the spiritual affairs of Christendom, for the arts introduced by Philip the Handsome in securing a French majority among the cardinals had never been discontinued. But on this occasion the conclave assembled at Rome was surrounded by a furious mob. The patriotic Italians insisted on an Italian Pope; and as a compromise, and under compulsion, the electors fixed on a temporary pontiff, who promised not to avail himself of their nomination, and took, merely for form's sake, the name of Urban the Sixth. He immediately, however, used his apostolic authority to free himself from the oaths he had taken, and insulted the astonished cardinals to such a degree that they convoked a meeting in a place of safety, and called Robert of Geneva to the tiara. He assumed the name of Clement the Seventh, and fulminated curses on the impostor who disgraced the chair at Rome. France accepted the Frenchman, who resided at Avignon as his predecessor had done; and half the rest of Christendom, including England, adhered to his Italian rival. This is the commencement of the great schism which afforded such vantage-ground not only to the enemies of priestcraft, but of Christianity itself. Charles felt the blow equally as Christian and king, and perceived that the Germans, Venetians, Genoese, or any other authority, who were nearer to Rome and could pull the strings more conveniently by which the puppet was moved, would have a great gain in any future discussion with the kings of France. While mourning this unhappy event, his grief was increased by the fall of the Constable. Bertrand was besieging one of the strong castles in Auvergne which was rebellious against the royal authority and strengthened with an English garrison. The commander—it is a pity his name is not mentioned, for he is an honour to our land—had agreed to surrender if not relieved within a certain time. Fever, pain, and anxiety, laid Du Guesclin low ; and when the appointed day came he was lying on his bier, and preparations making to carry him to the grave. The governor, true to his word, hauled down the flag of independence, and marched out with all his men, head bare and sword drawn, and laid the keys of the fortress on the hero's coffin. So died the best soldier and truest gentleman of France. His last words to his comrades who bent over his couch were these, "Remember that whenever you are at war, the churchmen, the women, the children, and the poor, are not your enemies." Blow followed blow upon the tender heart of Charles. Brittany threw off its obedience, and Flanders joined his enemies. The sword of his country was broken, and his own arm was too weak to bear the shield. He lingered a few days, and died in September 1380, in the forty-fourth year of his age ; and the immediate change in the fortunes of his country shows how much, in those ages of unsettled law, depended upon the personal character of a king.

The entire secret of this wise ruler's success was reliance on his people ; and perhaps the most valuable portion of this reliance was in the fact that in the word people he included the whole population of France. This great word was not limited, in his interpretation of it, to the tax-paying inhabitants of the towns or free labourers on the farms. The very serfs on the soil were fellow-countrymen of the great successor of St. Louis. His laws had reference as often to the interests of the lowest of his subjects as to the rights of the richest cities. He was the first and the last to put arms into the hands of the whole nation. Each man had his bow and quiver of arrows, his short sword or iron-pointed staff. He was openly practised in the use of them, and was taught that it was dishonourable for a Frenchman to be unable to defend his wife and children with his own hands. The experiment was so successful against even such generals as Chandos and the Black Prince, that it might be expected to continue one of the standing institutions of the kingdom. But these feelings of self-respect were only useful against a foreign enemy, and might be dangerous against a domestic master. So, ere many years elapsed, the system was abolished ; the butts were destroyed, the bows and swords withdrawn, for fear the "small people" should find themselves too powerful; and the result was—as we shall speedily see—Henry the Fifth of England and the battle of Agincourt. It was not more in the formation of new establishments that Charles showed his wisdom, than in the purification and improvement of the old. The legalism so strongly encouraged by Philip the Handsome, as a preservative against the power of the nobles, had now become an oppression to the people. The civil servants of the Crown absorbed a vast portion of the taxes they were employed to raise, and the paid offices about the provincial courts and local parliaments were innumerable. He diminished them both in number and amount of salary, and tried to save his subjects from the intricacies of technical pleadings, as almost an equal evil with the violence of lawless force. The only people, indeed, he could not bring within the rules of mercy and justice, were the lords and gentlemen, who were the ornaments of chivalry and the strength of his armies. Bertrand Du Guesclin was a trained leader of "Free Companies," and, solely by the excellence of nature, was enabled to soar out of those bloody confederacies, and set an example of honourable war. But the rest of the great men of the time presented specimens of the most savage atrocity, which seemed to derive new lustre from the extent of suffering it caused. Next to Du Guesclin in fame, and next wielder of the Constable's sword, was Oliver Clisson, a knight of Brittany ; and this is the manner in which he considered an enemy was to be treated—not a blameless enemy, let us say, for ferocious passions were excited on both sides, and mutual excesses had deprived either party of a right to complain. But the knightly code still remained in force. The chevalier was to keep his sword for open fight, and his spear for the breast of opposing horsemen. Blood, however, with some men, is pleasant, whose soever veins it flows from, and Oliver Clisson was of that sanguinary number. An English governor of the small fortress of Benon, the

French call him David Oligrane—which is probably not in the slightest degree like the real name—had killed and wounded some unfortunate inhabitants of Rochelle, when that city, which was near at hand, had treacherously gone over to the enemy. The people of Rochelle retorted by hanging all the English they could catch. When the English of Benon were devising how to reply to the last move, a great body of French besieged them in their tower. Resistance was obstinate, though the defenders were few, and the walls not strong. At length the fatal time arrived; nothing could be had to eat or drink; no help was near, and the garrison came forth, surrendering at discretion. Clisson, the commander-in-chief, armed himself with a sharp two-edged battle-axe, and waited at the doorway. As the emaciated soldiers tottered out, he swung the axe and crushed in their skulls. When the blood of fifteen fainting wretches had dimmed its shine, he laid the instrument aside, and left the slaughter to inferior hands. It is not known whether it was in horror, or with an agreeable facetiousness which gives a comic name to a popular act, that the witnesses of this achievement called him the "Butcher;" but it will not be uninteresting for us to remember his feats at the gateway of Benon, when we meet with this heroic character again. Feudalism, in fact, was dissolving, and chivalry, which was its poetic ideal, could not stand the trial of actual war. Knights were still mere gladiators—sometimes more for show than action; and gentlemen, in our sense of the word, were not yet in existence.

Charles the Sixth, a child of twelve years of age, seated on the throne of a kingdom torn by so many dangers as France, presented a spectacle of helplessness and weakness which was not long of being darkened into the deepest tragedy, by the aberration of his reason and the loss of half his realm. His three uncles, the Dukes of Anjou, and Berri, and Burgundy, fought round the undefended crown like vultures round a corpse; and for forty years the feuds of the royal family brought royalty itself into danger. We need not dwell minutely on that unhappy time, for there are few trustworthy guides to any of the great events, all were so distorted by party spirit; and men's feelings at length became so blunted by the perpetual recurrence of crimes and misfortunes, that the distinctions between right and wrong were nearly obliterated, public orators were permitted to plead in extenuation of notorious murders, and massacre was resorted to as a legitimate political movement. The example of evil actions came from the highest quarters. The Duke of Anjou was a pitiful villain, and scarcely soared above the dignity of thief. He consented to shorten the period of his regency, which he held as senior of the blood, on condition of no inquiry being made as to his appropriation of a vast amount of jewels and gold plate which he had seized the moment his brother died. But all the jewels and plate in the kingdom would not have satisfied this estimable prince, and he made the best use of the period of authority which remained. He knew that the wisdom and economy of Charles had amassed a large treasure, which was carefully deposited in the castle of Melun—so carefully, indeed, that nobody but the late king and his confidential treasurer, Philip de Savoisi, knew the exact spot of its concealment. The Duke of Anjou paid a visit to the mysterious castle, taking Philip de Savoisi in his train, and on their arrival he led the treasurer into a certain hall, and commanded him to show where the money lay. Savoisi hesitated—a thing which Anjou did not; for in a moment he ordered some hangmen into the room, who presented themselves with cords and instruments of torture. Savoisi yielded, and pointed out a stone in the wall, which, on being removed, revealed bags and boxes of silver and gold, to an incalculable amount. Seventeen millions of livres, equal to more than a million of our present pounds, rewarded the ingenuity of the duke, and he put the spoil under watch and ward in one of his private towers. Uproars occurred in many of the great towns, and the honourable regent was always at hand to profit by the event. Rouen declined to admit the youthful king, unless on some assurances of safety. Force was applied; the wall was thrown down, and the child of thirteen, dressed in armour, rode his horse through the breach, as a signal that the town was taken by asault. Submission was made, after great suffering among the citizens. Some were executed ; but when murmurs arose on account of the frequency of these displays, the regent endeavoured to satisfy the public by putting a stop to the headsman's axe, but made up for this concession to popular clamour by causing great numbers to be sewn up in sacks, and thrown at midnight quietly into the Seine. Paris, at the same time, rose in insurrection, and demanded the presence of the king. The Court returned to the capital, on condition that the inhabitants should be disarmed. Great acclamations hailed the young king's arrival, and, with fitting generosity, he granted the demands of the oppressed people, and presented them with a donation of a hundred thousand francs. Happy people ! liberal young king ! The Duke of Anjou was at his side, and put every farthing of the money into his own stores. Fortunately for his family, thus loaded with the wealth and curses of France, he soon departed for Italy, where he had been adopted as son and heir by the infamous Joanna of Naples. This personage was now too old to marry, and resorted to the system of adoption, to revenge herself on her natural successor, Charles de Darus. Louis of Anjou, it is pleasant to think, arrived too late ; he waited to be crowned by the French Pope, Clement, at Avignon, as his rival candidate was crowned by the Italian Pope, Urban, at Rome. The expectant mother had perished, before his coming, by the halter—the mode of death she had administered to her first husband and many of her friends ; and nothing was left to him but a claim to the vacant throne. His ill-got treasure was spent in support of what he called his rights, which consisted entirely in the nomination of the late queen ; and in 1384 he found an obscure ending to a mean and dishonourable life.

But things got worse and worse in Paris. Anjou had represented the interests of petty larceny and the smaller vices, but Philip of Burgundy shone in the nobler characters of murder and ambition. This was the favourite son of John, who gained the name of the Hardy by some insolence to his elder brother, and who now, by his marriage with the daughter of Louis le Mlâe, Count of Flanders, had added the richest provinces of Europe to his hereditary state. Under his influence the whole power of France was directed against the insurgent burghers of Ghent, led by Philip Van Arteveldt, a son of the famous brewer who had been so intimately connected with our Edward the Third. At Rosbec the crowded ranks of the artisans were crushed by the charge of mounted and heavy-armed soldiers. Forty thousand of them were slain in the field, and confiscation and cruelty reduced the flourishing city to the lowest ebb. Paris was daunted by the fate of the unfortunate Flemings, and for a while submitted to the tyranny and exactions of its masters—surrendering its arms, and giving up the right to the chains with which they could defend their narrow streets by extending them from strong stone pillars at either side. This was the commencement of the system of barricades for which that loveliest and most tumultuous of cities has been since so famous. And now that the public opinion of those days (which seems to have consisted in organised bands of burly shopmen and an easy recurrence to staves and paving-stones) was withdrawn, the guilty crew at the head of affairs did what was right in their own eyes. Within five years of the death of Charles the Wise, every vestige of his government had disappeared from the land. His successor had been married at sixteen to the handsomest and wickedest princess in Europe, Isabelle of Bavaria, and social morals fell into as deplorable a state as political honesty. If we can imagine all the bad passions that torment and degrade humanity, not only let loose without the restraints of shame, but embodied in the highest personages of the State, we shall form but a feeble idea of the situation of France at this time. The first conditions of civilised life were utterly ignored. The Duke of Brittany, in full peace, seized Oliver Clisson, the highest officer of the Crown, the hero of the memorable massacre of

English prisoners at Benon, and ordered him to be put intc a sack and thrown into the sea. The nobleman appointed to this honourable office hesitated to run the risk of drowning the Constable of France, and kept his prisoner concealed. Racked with fears, after his wrath was appeased by the reported death of his enemy, the duke was greatly relieved in mind when the executioner confessed his disobedience. He took a highly lucrative method of showing his satisfaction, and exacted an enormous ransom from the man he had so unjustly imprisoned; and the gentle Oliver returned to court breathing vengeance against his captor. Our old friend, Charles the Bad, continuing his career of infamy to the end, instructed one of his adherents to go into the apothecaries' shops as he walked to Paris, and buy arsenic enough to poison the king, the princes, and any of the nobility who might be of the royal party. While gloating over the pleasing prospect of such a noble banquet, he comforted himself, as he was now chilly with age, by having a cloth wrapped round him, after it was steeped in spirits of wine. The domestic neatly sewed up the envelope to his throat, and finding no scissors close at hand, took a lighted candle to burn off the ends of the thread. Spirits of wine are very inflammable, and perhaps his hand was not very steady, or his heart very affectionate. The cloth burst into a flame, and the wickedest and most unrelenting of mankind found a death which would be melancholy in the case of any other man, but was only a feeble and condign punishment for the perpetration of so many crimes.

The Archbishop of Saon, compassionating the sufferings of the people, proposed that the king should assume the reins of government without the superintendence of his uncles, Burgundy and Berri, whom he described in no flattering terms. The truths were so undeniable, and the measure itself so reasonable, that no objection could be made. The king was emancipated from the control of his guardians—but the archbishop, good, easy man, was poisoned in a week. Burgundy returned to his dukedom, and Berri went off to his castle ; but it was observed that all the ornaments of the king's apartments, his golden candlesticks and ebony cabinets, had disappeared. The houses of the discontented dukes were known, at the same time, to be brilliantly supplied with articles of the same kind, and of exactly the same pattern as those which had been missed from the royal halls. Paris looked with blank surprise on these extraordinary proceedings of the highest men in the State. Law and order seemed at an end, and the thoughtless king, and his extravagant and beautiful wife, led the revels in the wildest excesses of luxury and show. Oliver Clisson was at a brilliant ball at the queen's palace in the Hôtel de St. Paul. At one in the morning he was returning home, with only eight or nine attendants, when all of a sudden he was waylaid by forty horsemen, who assaulted him from behind. At first he thought it a practical joke of the Duke of Orleans, and made no defence ; but when he heard the voice of Peter de Craon, the envoy and confederate of the Duke of Brittany, and the most inveterate of his enemies, he knew his hour was come. He resisted as long as his unarmed state allowed, but a blow with an axe from the hand of Craon felled him from his horse, and he lay across the narrow pavement with his bleeding head against a door. The assassins had done their work, and Craon and his party galloped away. The Constable lay in the silent street, and became insensible. But the owner of the shop against which he pressed was a baker, and came to open his door at a very early hour. The gory head fell down in the passage, and the man was greatly alarmed. He pulled the body in, and saw some signs of life. In a few minutes the courtiers who had heard the news, the men-at-arms, and, at last, the king himself, came in all haste to see what had occurred. The baker then knew he had saved the life of the Constable, and great joy was expressed by the spectators. The perpetrator was well known. Peter, Baron de Craon, was a nobleman of the usual stamp—brave and dishonest ; and having been intrusted with some funds by the Duchess of Anjou to carry to Italy, in support of her husband's attempt on the Neapolitan throne, had kept the money, and astonished everybody with the splendour of his equipage ever after. But the king at once perceived that a greater than Peter de Craon was engaged in this assault on the Constable of France. He declared vengeance on the faithless vassal, and summoned his followers to a campaign against the harbourer of the assassin, for Peter had fled to Brittany, and was received with favour by the Duke. Oliver rapidly recovered his strength in the expectation of wreaking his vengeance on foes. The Dukes of Burgundy, and Berri, and Orleans, were all ready for war, in hopes of confiscations and plunder, and Charles found himself, in the August of 1393, at the head of a large army, marching through the deep forest of Mons. The weather was oppressively hot; there was not a breath of air in the depths of the wood. The king's life had been full of excitement, and his health had never been very strong. All of a sudden a dreadful figure rushed out of a shadowy dell, and seized the bridle of the astonished youth, uttering some incoherent gibberish, and telling him he was betrayed. The attendants came up, for they had been riding a few paces behind, but the madman or emissary of some secret friend had disappeared. Charles moped and was silent, but in a minute or two a frenzy seized him; he imagined that he was surrounded by enemies—no false imagination if he had seen into their hearts—and clapping spurs to his horse, drew his sword, and before rescue came, put two of his pages to death. After a while the access of fury departed; he was easily mastered and disarmed; and France, in addition to the ruin of her cities, the oppression of her people, and the quarrels of her nobility, had now to mourn the madness of her king. Glimpses of returning reason, from time to time, enabled the custodiers of his person to advance their own interests under his revived authority, but the royal name was no tower of permanent strength. His nobles despised him, his wife deserted him, and often the hapless Charles was left to the charity of his servants for a mess of food, while the shameless Isabelle was filling the palace with the sound of wassailing, or presiding at the "Courts of Love," where the tender passion was treated of as a regulated science; and princes and princesses, bishops and doctors of divinity, were not ashamed to appear as pleaders before the judgment-seat of the most abandoned woman alive. All these things require to be dwelt on, for it is to this universal corruption of manners that the national humiliation is due. One by one the rallying-points of a people's greatness were taken away. The administration of justice was suspended; the dignity of noble rank was degraded; the honour of man's word was at an end; the feminine virtues, on which alone the future of a nation can be securely built, were unknown. The people looked up from the midst of their abasement, and saw no help even in the Church. Fiercest among the brawlers for power, falsest among the breakers of oaths, were the clergy, high and low. Men's minds were thrown loose from the steady anchorage of an unreasoning faith, when they saw the instability of the rock itself, to which they had moored their bark. There was a claimant of their belief (and money) at Avignon, and another, quite as loud-toned, and quite as anxious for their contributions, at Rome. Dominicans and Franciscans were fighting with unholy rancour, on the doctrine of the Immaculate Conception. Livings were kept vacant that the patrons might enjoy the stipends. Churches fell into disrepair; and the adherents of the great nobles, and even the forces of the king, being irregularly paid, levied black-mail on the wretched cultivators, or helped themselves to what they required, as if in an enemy's land. The ties, in short, between the different classes—protection from above, reverence and obedience from below—were utterly broken, and never were re-knit. This, indeed, is henceforth the peculiarity of French history as compared with ours. You will see gallant warriors, glittering princes, and obedient subjects; but the endearing relations which exist between a resident and popular gentry and their dependants—between a landed aristocracy, exercising both its rights and duties amid an observant and trustful population, never found a place among our neighbours. Their nobility was never anything but a military array, till it sank into a titled courtierdom—men without pity in the first character, and without dignity in the second—ornaments, or sometimes opponents, of the Crown, but never the natural-born leaders of the people. The bitterness of feeling against their oppressors, which rose in the hearts of the poor in the reign of this fatuous Charles, and was strengthened by the degradation to which they submitted on the conquest of their throne and country by the victorious English, never wore out. Jacques Bonhomme had a longer memory than his representative on this side of the water; and while the descendants of Wat Tyler's followers were comfortable church-and-king men, when the great trial came, in 1793, the men of the Jacquerie were boiling with revenge for centuries of wrong, and poured forth the concentrated wrath of nine generations, on clergy, noble, and Crown.

But for a long time there was a similarity in the position of the two countries which must have led to the same results, if the dispositions of the two populations had been the same. Even in the minutest things the resemblance was carried out. When the gallant Black Prince and the wise Charles the Fifth left their sons to maintain the struggle carried on between themselves, both their representatives were boys of very tender years; both were surrounded by father's brothers, who weakened the kingdom by their quarrels and ambition. Old John of Gaunt, the uncle of Richard the Second, preferred his interests in the crown of Castille (which he claimed in right of his wife) to the interests either of his nephew or his country, in the same way as the Duke of Anjou frittered away the wealth of France in establishing his claim to Naples. The harshness and cruelties of the Duke of Burgundy were equalled by those of the Duke of Gloster. Even the fatuity of the unhappy Charles was not less hurtful to his country, or degrading to himself, than the thoughtless selfishness and blind favouritism of the equally unhappy Richard. In England, the safeguard against a total dissolution of society was formed by the bold front assumed by Parliament. Legislation, by the reign of Edward the Third, had assumed the place of force, and laid down principles by which all actions were guided. It is painful to us at this present day, after so many fruitless efforts to simplify the rules under which we live, to read the glowing description of its former state by the great historian of the law, Sir Matthew Hale: "The judges and pleaders at this time are very learned. The pleadings are more polished than those in the time of Edward the Second, yet they have *neither uncertainty, prolixity, nor obscurity.* So that, at the latter part of this King's reign, the law seemed to be near its meridian." The foundations of this noble science were so deep, and its usefulness so universally acknowledged, that the law stood like a fortress to which all looked for support in the threatened anarchy. Instead of hiring an assassin to get quit of an overpowerful enemy, the discontented party appealed to Parliament, and impeached the greatest persons in the land. The responsibility of members was established in this reign by the banishment of the Earl of Suffolk and the Archbishop of York, for "certain counsels they had given to the King;" and the position was not obscurely stated, that a king who was dangerous to public liberty might lawfully be displaced.

The weakness, however, of both France and England, had the fortunate result at this period of preventing a regular and continuous war. Battles were, of course, occasionally fought; for the English garrisons of French towns were under the necessity of displaying their nationality by raids upon the surrounding lands. French cavaliers, in the same way, made dashes into the English pale, just to show that their horses were as fresh as ever, and their swords as sharp. But there were truces succeeding each other, and festivals on the borders of the respective territories; and at last a marriage between the silly English monarch and the daughter of the silly French one, gave an opportunity for a more formal declaration of peace. Isabelle of France was intrusted by her father, in one of his lucid intervals, to the ambassadors of his rival, and conducted to England in solemn state. She was not of much use in sustaining or comforting her royal husband, for she was at this time only six years old; but her portion of a million livres would have been of extraordinary value to her new relations—if it had ever been paid; for nothing interfered in either country with the madness of display and luxury. In France affairs were worst. In the midst of national distress and divided councils, and unsettled governments, splendour held its way. When an insurrection of starving peasantry was expected, a tournament was held with wilder dissoluteness of behaviour than before. The kings, indeed, had a meeting where there was a rivalry of magnificence and fatuity. Both nations were exhausted; men's minds in both countries were uneasy with the feeling of some great approaching change; and the chivalry of France, as if judicially blinded to the results of their actions, took this opportunity of advocating an expedition to the East, to resist the approach of Bajazet the Turk. But this great enemy of the Christian faith, reviving the fanaticism and ferocity of the early Saracenic invasions, could only be successfully opposed by a united Christendom, led by the great chieftain of the Christian Church in whom all parties believed. The Pope of Avignon was acknowledged by the French, and gave his blessing on the crusade. The Pope of Rome was acknowledged by the English, and would have nothing to do with a proceeding countenanced by a heretical impostor. The only glimpse of wisdom shown amidst the assembled kingship and chivalry of the two nations, was a proposition submitted to them by the University of Paris, to disown both the pontiffs, and let Benedict and Gregory fight it out as they would. But the Pope was still too useful a political instrument to be altogether thrown away, and the knights of France, proud of having the honour of so holy an expedition, unshared by other nations, contented themselves with the blessing of the pretender of Avignon, and wasted their lives and fortunes in fruitless marches and a disastrous battle in Bulgaria.

The defeat of Nicopolis was as complete as Poictiers. Royal prisoners illustrated both, and immense ransoms impoverished the country. When the news of the calamity was first whispered in Paris, the unfortunate messengers were thrown into the Seine. It seemed impossible that John de Nevers, the heir of Burgundy and Flanders, Philip of Artois, the Earls of Bar and La Marche, John de Vienne, and the Sires de la Tremouille and de Coucy, with ten thousand of the bravest warriors of the West, could be slain or captured by turbaned unbelievers. But the truth came out ere long. Not more than eighty out of all that array of knights and princes, returned to tell the tale. The survivors, indeed, said that Bajazet only spared John de Nevers—afterwards fatally known in French history as John the Fearless—because he saw something so sinister and cruel in his countenance that he was persuaded his life would be more injurious to the Christian cause than his death could be. The same feeling was perhaps the cause of the barbarian's moderation to them all. He sent them back to spread additional misery among their retainers by exacting the stipulated sums, and lower still farther the public estimate of the upper orders by the spectacle of their meanness and unsuccess. It might seem that France, the first of European kingdoms, the richest and most populous, the country of Philip Augustus and Saint Louis, had fallen to its lowest point ; but beyond its present depths there was a lower depth still. The pageant tyrant who disgraced and weakened the throne of England was about to suffer the punishment of his crimes. By a long persistence in cunning and intrigue he obtained for awhile the mastery of the land. Parliament itself was silent before his exactions and extravagance. He imbrued his hands in the blood of his nearest relations, and spared no lower heads in his assertion of supreme power. The necessities of self-preservation produced a leader in resistance who was worthy of the office. This was Henry of Bolingbroke, a son of old John of Gaunt. He had been arbitrarily banished, and now went back to England to claim a restitution of his estates. The Parliament felt its power when it had a cause to rally round. It formally met and deposed the unworthy king. If the deposition was soon followed by his death, we have only to look to the whole course of his idle and wicked existence to dry our tears for his fate. A strong man's hand now guarded the house, and all his efforts were devoted to strengthen his position. Fortunately for the land, he felt the want of a lineal claim to the succession (for his father was a younger son of Edward the Third), and compensated for the weakness which might be supposed to reside in a merely parliamentary title, by increased attention to the interests of the realm. He extended good laws to all his subjects, and put an end to the violence of the nobles. Looking across the narrow sea, he saw what must have appeared like the shipwreck of a mighty kingdom. France lay like a great hulk upon the waters, with maddened crew and incompetent commanders.

But it is only by embarking in the vessel, and seeing what was going on within, that we can judge of the insubordination and danger. Philip the Hardy—Duke of Burgundy by the appointment of his father, and Earl of Flanders by his marriage—died in 1404, and it might have been hoped that one of the enemies of France was removed from the scene. But scarcely was he cold in his grave when John de Nevers, the prisoner of Bajazet, and ten times more ambitious than his father, rushed among the contending factions, seized the regency as a matter of right, to the exclusion of the Duke of Orleans (the brother of the king), and the shameless Isabelle, who had pretended to be guardian of her husband's person. Orleans and the queen retired from Paris, and the reign of John the Fearless began. Who, indeed, was capable of resisting so strong-willed and powerful a combatant? In addition to his predecessor's possessions of Burgundy, Flanders, and Artois, he had secured as dower of his wife, Margaret of Bavaria, the counties of Hainault, Holland, and Zealand, and all the plains and cities up to the North Sea. His uncle, the dissolute and grasping Duke of Berri, was governor of Languedoc, and his nephew Louis, of Provence. The family held in firm hands the greater part of the country, and the fatuous king was also in their power. England was never more dangerous to the independence of her neighbour when Edward the Third was master of all her western lands, with the whole force of his island kingdom sustaining him from abroad, than John of Burgundy now was with so many strong places in his custody, and the wealthy Low Countries backing him up in all his claims. But he was not above the arts of the lowest deceiver, though apparently strong enough to attain his object by open violence. He doffed his cap and spoke kindly to the starving populace of Paris, and commiserated them for the oppressions they suffered from the extortions of Orleans and the queen. He gave them back their pikes and staves, and even restored to them the iron chains with which they could barricade their streets against a charge of horse, and was in all respects the model of a demagogue of the vulgarest kind. Meantime Orleans was outside the gate with a great body of his retainers, and everything threatened the extremities of civil war. But John the Fearless was a man of policy as well as action. He easily gave in to a reconciliation with his cousin of Orleans, and admitted him into the city. There they exchanged visits and feasts, but fortified their respective houses as if in an enemy's country, and collected their friends about them. Isabelle, the queen, lived in sumptuous splendour in the Hôtel de Montagne ; the king lived in dreary seclusion in the Hôtel St. Paul ; the Duke of Berri lived at the Hôtel de Nesle ; the other princes in the Louvre and their family houses. Nothing could be more magnificent or friendly than their mutual entertainments. On Sunday, the 20th of November, 1407, a religious ceremony consecrated the novel friendship of the contending parties. Orleans and Burgundy partook of the holy communion together, and on the following Tuesday they dined at the Duke of Berri's in the Hôtel de Nesle. They were in high spirits and very amicable all the time of the festival, and at parting embraced each other with marks of mutual affection, and promised to meet on the following Sunday at a dance in the Hôtel d'Orleans. John the

Fearless had now gained his object. On the following night Orleans was supping with the queen. He was summoned to go at once on important business to the Hôtel St. Paul, where the unhappy Charles wished to see him. He went, little thinking what was to happen, for before he had gone many yards, just when he was passing under a high-walled house, which kept him from the moonlight, a dozen ruffians rushed upon him with swords and axes, and the gayest and not the wickedest of the French princes lay a disfigured corpse on the deserted street. A figure, as soon as all was still, emerged from a dark recess. He was dressed in a cloak of rich colour, and had armour under his gala clothes. He stopped and touched the head to satisfy himself that all was over, and quickly disappeared. The Duke of Burgundy next morning went to see the body as it lay in state, and was loud in his denunciation of the crime. He attended the funeral, and wept long and bitterly as the body was lowered into the grave. But when the forms of law had to be gone through, and some inquiries made as to the perpetrators of the murder, he pulled the Duke of Berri to one side and said, "It was I that slew the man. The devil tempted me." "Rash nephew," said the Duke of Berri, "you will have to answer for this with your life."

But there was no risk of speedy vengeance overtaking the Lord of Flanders and Brabant. He retired to his own possessions for a time, and then came up at the head of a great force of Flemings and other foreigners, and proceeded to justify his crime. A great assemblage was summoned in the Hôtel St. Paul, where the king presided at what was called the "justification of my Lord of Burgundy." A talking, pedantic, eloquent and avaricious Cordelier of the name of John Petit, who practised as a counsellor before the courts, commenced an oration in defence of murder. He ransacked all history, sacred and profane, and brought the dagger of Phineas, and the spear of Joab, and the smiles of Judith into play. Limiting his reasons to twelve, in honour of the twelve apostles, he accused the deceased of ambition, treachery, magic and sorcery; and finally demanded an honourable acquittal of the patriotic citizen who had delivered his country from a tyrant. Tyrannicide was never so openly advocated in the tent of Brutus and Cassius. It was not to be a subject of apology, but of praise, and the reverend doctor worked himself into such virtuous indignation that he claimed a reward for his illustrious client, in "humble imitation of the benefits bestowed on my Lord St. Michael for his putting the devil to death." The king, who had been forced into the throne, though not even in momentary possession of his reason, sat unmoved during the whole discourse. Sad and statue-like, he gave no sign of apprehension, and when the business was concluded, was conducted out without having said a word. Many sympathised, both with the king, who was warmly attached to his brother, and with the beautiful Valentine of Milan, the wife of the murdered man; but no one dared to show anything but a face of rejoicing. Valentine lived long enough only to exact an oath from her children, of vengeance for the slaughter of their father, and died. Among those children she included Dunois, who was afterwards so famous in the wars as the Bastard of Orleans, and whom she loved as if he had been her own son. She used often indeed to say, "I have been robbed of him, and now," she added, "no child of mine is so well able to avenge the family loss." But policy was of more force than justice. An accommodation was patched up between the king and his rebellious vassal, and even between the orphans of Orleans and the butcher of their father. All that Burgundy condescended to do was to express a wish in full court to be taken again into the king's favour; and Charles, starting out of his dreamy abstraction sufficiently to repeat the lesson he had been taught, said, "Fair cousin, we accord you your request, and pardon you all." The children of Valentine were less easily moved, and it was only at the express command of the king that they accepted the murderer's hand, and did so at last with tears.

And now the Burgundian influence knew no check. In

his own country, he had trampled down an insurrection at Liege, with such ferocious cruelty that the hearts of his subjects were subdued. In Paris, he played the part of a leader of the poor; promised to take off their burdens; and gratified the populace with a sight of the execution of the rich and powerful. Montagne, the chief minister of finance, glutted the bloodthirsty propensities of the people, and the avarice of the prince, at the same time. He was hated as collector of the taxes, and envied as immensely rich. So he was tortured and executed, and his money and estates divided among the successful faction. Isabelle, the queen, began to perceive that she was no longer on the winning side. Gradually she allowed herself to be gained over, and considered her victory secure when the duke acceded to her request, and pronounced her son, the Dauphin, now in his fourteenth year, capable of reigning during the madness of his father. She flattered herself she was once more mistress of the kingdom; but Burgundy had already married the Dauphin to his daughter, and was now appointed superintendent of his education. It was soon evident that the authority of the father-in-law and tutor was superior to that of the mother. Isabelle sank into the second rank, and became more infamous, if possible, than before, by her attachment to the murderer of her former lover. Meantime the young princes of Orleans were approaching man's estate, and the eldest at this time married the daughter of the most powerful of the great vassals of the south, Bertrand, Earl of Armagnac, a lineal descendant of Clovis, and already a sworn foe to the Burgundian. When the alliance was known in Paris, John the Fearless prepared himself for a struggle. He gave up the rule and management of the city to the vilest of the mob. The corporation of the butchers, armed with knife and hammer, kept order in the streets by indiscriminate massacre day and night. They dressed themselves in a blue bonnet, with the St. Andrew's cross upon their cloaks; and, in a short time, were replied to from the outside of the ramparts by the party of the Armagnacs, distinguished by a white scarf across their shoulders. From this time there was nothing but mutual slaughter throughout the whole of France. Men's passions were let loose in the wildest license. Again the dens of villany in all other countries were emptied out upon the fated soil. Every city was the scene of internecine contest ; and it is painful to confess that, in the midst of those dreadful excesses, the English name is heard. The leader of the Burgundians, we are to remember, was Prince of Flanders ; and Henry the Fourth could refuse nothing to a man who might impoverish the woolstaplers of England by closing the Flemish ports. Favourable terms for English trade were exacted from the Lord of Ghent and Bruges, on condition of assistance in his death-struggle at Paris. It was for this reason the men of Surrey and Hampshire were found in the battles of the French parties. With their aid, the Burgundians so quelled the opposing princes that they sued for peace, and the English forces were withdrawn. Yet it is not impossible that the reports carried home by those bands awakened the hopes of Henry the Fourth, and his more adventurous son, of triumphs over the faction-weakened land. All the contending parties were willing to sell their country for revenge upon their foes. The spirit of patriotism and loyalty had entirely died out in the higher ranks, and it was not known, either to the foreign enemy or the domestic oppressor, what a warmth of courage and love of country still glowed in the hearts of the common people.

Henry was perhaps induced to turn his attention to the affairs of France, in the hopes that military success would give a new guarantee to the crown he had assumed. But while in the midst of his preparations for a descent on the distracted country, he was carried off by an illness from which he had suffered a long time. His gallant son was more anxious than his father had been to win over the hearts of his subjects by a restoration of the old glories of the Edwards ; but civil dissensions raged in his own kingdom. The adherents of the legitimate line were still powerful, and it was not till after two years of vigorous government at home that he was enabled to look abroad. The state of France had grown worse than ever. No parallel can be found in history so close to the condition of that wretched land, during the reign of its insane king, as that of Oude before its annexation to the English possessions. Great hereditary landholders, released, in both, from the obligations of law, had forgotten all the principles of justice and honour. The noblest families were engaged in secret assassination ; rich persons were seized in open day, and ransomed by their captors. Peaceful towns and castles were stormed and pillaged without warning by neighbouring lords. Even the bloodthirstiness of the Indian character, when revenge for fancied wrongs converts the mild Hindoo into a ravening savage, was more than matched by the frightful excesses of the knights and nobles who called themselves the Christian chivalry of Europe. First, the Duke of Burgundy got possession of Paris, and starved his enemies in secret dungeons, or drove them by thousands into the Seine. Next, the Count of Armagnac, descendant of Clovis, and worthy of that gory genealogy, retorted upon the supporters of his rival, and hung and decapitated his enemies till the executioners were exhausted with fatigue. Feelings of truth and confidence were as entirely discarded as those of pity and honesty. There were frightful mutilations, and nameless violences, and hideous tortures, inflicted in the wantonness of success by the alternate parties. It is almost a relief when we read of the vengeance of Heaven let loose on those depraved and dishonoured bearers of ancient names, when the battle of Agincourt thinned for the last time the bead-roll of the feudal nobility. Henry the Fifth (himself far from the model of heroic manliness we read of in the magical pages of Shakespeare) sailed from Southampton in 1415, and, after besieging and taking Harfleur, proceeded across the country towards Calais. Midway, at the village of Agincourt, he was intercepted by such an array of mounted cavaliers and princely enemies as had not been seen since Poictiers. The same steady imperturbability as in that famous combat gave the victory to the yeomanry of England.

Massed up in inextricable battalions, the great array of the French nobles was incapable of moving from the narrow gorge in which they were confined. The earth was wet and marshy from a fortnight's rain. Horse and man sank beyond the power of retrieval, and the yard-shaft of the English archer plied its terrible trade, and knight and charger were thrown into helpless confusion. They could not retreat, the land was so deep ; they could not fight, their ranks were so close ; they could only die or yield themselves prisoners. The list of the killed and taken is the most remarkable which ever was the result of a single fight. Princes of the blood, feudatories of the Crown, warlike bishops, and innumerable knights, perished on this fatal day ; and yet the conqueror, regardless or unconscious of his position, pursued his march to Calais, embarked in his transports, and left the prey, which was apparently lying at his feet, to recover from its wounds and renew its efforts of offence. It seems to show that the war, so glorious to the English arms, was not yet a favourite with the English people, that the victor was forced to pawn his jewels and private property to raise money enough for each of his campaigns. It was not till the year 1419 that he felt sufficiently strong to lay siege to the town of Rouen. Burgundy, a traitor to his country, had aided the English cause, and was reaping the fruit of his treason by obtaining forcible possession of Paris. The cruelties of the Armagnacs were repaid. The mob rose with cries of "Burgundy ! Burgundy !" broke open the prisons, burnt and slew and drowned many thousands of the inhabitants, and tearing the Constable in pieces, carried portions of his body through the streets ; and, as a dreadful rehearsal of what was to come, they stuck fresh bleeding heads upon their pikes, and made an assault on the Bastile. When peace in this manner was secured, the Duke and the detested Isabelle made their solemn entry into the city, where the miserable king was brought out by his keeper to give them a friendly welcome. While festivities were going on within the blood-stained walls, Henry the Fifth took possession of Rouen, and added publicly to his titles that of King of France. He held—and in this was supported by all the lawyers who had any regard for the safety of their heads—that the right to the French crown was inherent in the English king, and that the claims of the late royal house passed over to their successor along with the other attributes of the throne. Henry kept high state at Rouen, and was visited there by the Duke of Burgundy and the shameless queen. They brought with them the Princess Catherine, whom Henry had taken this rough method of wooing. And though he professed his love and admiration on this occasion, he rose extortionately in his demands before he would offer her his hand. He required a dowry of a million crowns, the surrender of Normandy in addition to the English conquests, and sixteen hundred thousand crowns still due for the ransom of King John. It was very evident that the English bridegroom would absorb all the wealth of the country, and for a moment the Dauphin Charles made a stand,—the Dauphin, or his advisers,—for that young prince was not yet sixteen years of age. Burgundy threw the blame of the interrupted negotiation on the party of his opponents, and prepared to make terms for himself in the final spoliation of the kingdom.

Charles invited him to an interview ; and after much hesitation, and many warnings of the peril he incurred, John the Fearless repaired to the place appointed, which was a pavilion, built in the middle of the bridge over the Seine at Montereau. Each was to be accompanied by a few friends ; and there were barriers at the ends which neither party could pass. John went with a few attendants into the enclosure, and knelt before the heir of France. He bent his unhelmeted head in deepest courtesy ; and Tanneguy du Chatel, one of the Dauphin's attendants, at that moment crashed through the skull of the unsuspecting Duke with his battle-axe ; and the Dauphin, with his followers, retired. John lay weltering in his blood on the spot where he had fallen, and his train, when they had recovered from their surprise, drew the body away. Thus was the murder of the

Duke of Orleans avenged, and another blood-feud begun between the houses of France and Burgundy. Who now could be safe? It was better to have a strong government which could restrain all the contending factions, even though it consisted of foreigners and enemies like the English. Philip of Burgundy, the son of the slaughtered John, acknowledged the Englishman for his lord. Others gave in their adhesion, and the treaty of Troyes was signed in 1420. By this, Henry was to marry Catherine, to exchange the name of King of France for that of Regent during the life of Charles, and then to take full possession of the throne, to the exclusion of the Dauphin. The Parliament, the University, and Municipality of Paris, agreed to these shameful conditions. France was a conquered country, a mere dependency of her island mistress, and looked for indemnification for the loss of her glory and independence in peaceful submission to the will of her imperious lord. Only one voice was heard in reclamation, and that was of Charles the Dauphin. He wakened to a momentary feeling of the duties of his place, and appealed against the treaty to God and his sword.

CHAPTER VI.

FROM CHARLES THE SEVENTH, A. D. 1423, TO LOUIS THE ELEVENTH, A. D. 1461.

WE have now reached the lowest point of depression to which a great nation was ever reduced and recovered from it again. A foreign invader has overcome all opposition, and is acknowledged lord and master of the land. Everybody saw through the thin disguise with which Henry endeavoured to hide his triumph from the eyes of his new subjects, by calling himself Regent, and carrying on the administration in the name of the king. The name of the king was, indeed, a subject of deep reverence in places where the courtiers and sycophants of authority never turned their eyes. In the midst of all his distresses, in his abandonment by wife and friends, and now in his subjection to enemies and strangers, the pale face of the patient and almost unconscious Charles rose before the fancy of the peasants and townsfolk at a distance from the centre of affairs ; and at this time, when the nation seemed on the verge of dissolution through the inadequacy and weakness of its sovereign, he was talked of as "the gentle," "the well-beloved." The "Well-beloved," indeed, is his name among French historians, and contrasts in a delightful manner with the epithets of his foes and kinsmen, Philip the Hardy or John the Fearless. These village talks and patriotic tendencies had their effect in due time, and were found surer guarantees for the liberties of the country than the debauched and useless chivalry which made its last appearance on the field of Agincourt. If Henry, in his selfish ambition, did nothing for the permanent benefit of his conquest by kindness or legislation, he was still the greatest benefactor the French people ever saw, by scattering for ever the horde of highborn robbers and oppressors who could neither defend the honour of their country nor obey its laws. When great political changes are about to take place, it has been remarked that they are heralded by the perpetration of enormous crimes. These are the ground-swell, as it were, which show the approach of the great tempest before the wind is heard. Princes had put princes to death by cowardly surprise or open violence. The two eldest sons of the king had been poisoned, within a year of each other, by contending factions. Great officers had been seized and imprisoned till ransom was paid. Estates were forcibly taken possession of, and held at the point of the sword, without even a pretence of law or right. In every county there were barons who kept their retainers by the plunder of the surrounding country; and prisoners—peaceful pilgrims or enterprising merchants, who risked the danger of passing from place to place—were inhumanly tortured till they yielded their stores, or put to death with every circumstance of mutilation and dishonour. Any observant spectator must have seen that these things portended a change—that the forms of society itself required a complete alteration, and that the time for insolent bullies in steel helmets and emblazoned shields was fairly past. Romance and sentiment have unfortunately obliterated the real features of that condition, so that we look back through the magical glass of *Ivanhoe* and the other records of a fanciful state of manners, and see nothing of the actual scene. Sir Walter and his followers perform feats like those of the Mesmerists, who tell their adepts to see flowery meadows or waving woods on the blank wall of a dungeon; or to hear enchanted flutes and delicious harmonies in the sharpening of a saw. But let us go to the fountain-head of all these imaginings, to the contemporary chroniclers of knightly deeds; or better still, to the authenticated statements of the sufferings of the weak and unprotected. You find no instance of generosity or justice. Moral feeling and

Christian charities are choked up by the coat of mail. Of all the gallant array who fought and fell at Agincourt, not one in twenty could write his own name. Du Guesclin himself, after much labour, had acquired penmanship enough to write Bertrand, and no more. Reading, as a general rule, was equally beyond their power, though there were instances, at a former date, of cavaliers who could compose agreeable verses, and sing them with expression to the lute. But anarchy and violence had deteriorated the race of nobles. Life was too active and too insecure to devote any time even in youth to education in any arts but those of horsemanship and the management of arms. We need, therefore, only form an idea of what such a state of things would produce—relaxed government, ineffectual laws, brutal ignorance, and remorseless cruelty—and we find its fulfilment in the state of French chivalry during the reign of Charles the Sixth. It would be easy, from Froissart and Monstrelet, to justify all that has been said, but the results speak for themselves. A nation saw eighty thousand knights and noblemen as its champions trampled under foot, and no man regretted their fall. We shall come, in a future chapter, to another total extirpation of a powerful and haughty class, and shall find that both deserved their fate, for neither performed their duties.

The Church, which by its theory was the appointed guardian of the helpless, had no less fallen away from the principle of its institution than the feudal lords. A palsy had fallen upon its arm since it first lifted the sword and torch against heretics in the crusade against the Albigenses. Force, before that date, had been applied only to the Mussulman and idolator. From that time it was used against Christians who differed in opinion on points of doctrine or church discipline; and no trusting peasant or inquiring parishioner could fly to it for refuge or satisfaction, for a hostile neighbour might insinuate doubts of his perfect orthodoxy, and he became exposed to the Inquisition. While the Church extended its claim to obedience by fire and sword, it lost some of the arms which would have been of more avail in its behalf. The unity of faith, which the inquirers of England and Bohemia, such as Wickliff and Jerome, disturbed in many countries of Europe, received a heavier blow by the schism in the government of the Church, which raged for forty years. Two popes, one at Rome and one at Avignon, seemed a sufficient blot on the oneness of the Great Shepherd's authority. But a greater blot was still to follow, for a third pontiff appeared, and farther divided the obedience of Christendom. Each arrogant pretender to supremacy surrounded himself with a court of cardinals who were prepared to nominate a successor to their own adopted chief; and the sight might have been presented of an infinite number of popes, for every minority of the electors seemed disposed to indemnify itself by electing a pontiff of its own. France, torn by political faction, was saved by the wisdom of the University of Paris from the complication which the claims of such a divided infallibility would produce, and rejected the authority of all the three, regulating its own ecclesiastical affairs by the hands of its native priests and bishops. At last, tired out by the contumacy of the popes, the decision of Christendom was taken at the Council of Constance, in 1418. The three successors of St. Peter were deposed, and Martin the Fifth nominated to the vacant chair. All the nations gave in their adhesion; and as a thank-offering for this restoration of Christian peace, the unhappy John Huss and Jerome of Prague—who had appeared before the Council under a guarantee of safe-conduct, to answer for their heretical opinions—were burnt as deniers of the doctrine of transubstantiation, and maintainers of the sufficiency of Scripture as a rule of faith.

The Dauphin seemed about as inadequate to the duties of his perilous condition as his unfortunate father had been. Thoughtless and self-indulgent, he appeared to have no appreciation either of his rights or of his hopes. Knightly festivals, when he happened to have money enough to defray the expense, and the society of joyous though disreputable companions, made his retreat beyond the Loire take the semblance of a party of pleasure ; and rumours were not altogether unheard that his resignation under the insults and injuries of the victorious Henry arose from a cowardly regard for his own personal safety. In spite, however, of his manifold faults and deficiencies, he was still the hope of France, and rallying-point for all the patriotic spirits of the land who feared or hated the English domination. Bands of his adherents still maintained themselves in several districts of the north, and occasionally dashed into the counties which owned the sway of the Regent. Greater efforts were made, and French spirit appeared to revive. Henry was at Windsor in the early part of 1422, rejoicing over the birth of his son, the unfortunate Henry the Sixth, when news was brought him that a great battle had been fought at Beaugé, in Anjou, in which his brother Clarence had been defeated and killed ; and that the strength of the Dauphin's army consisted of seven thousand Scottish spearmen, under command of John Stewart, Earl of Buchan. Buchan with his own hand had slain the unhappy Clarence, and a great body of Scottish auxiliaries were to follow immediately, commanded by Earl Douglas. The King was instantly on board, and hurried to Paris. His two dependent kings were still in his power : Charles of France, feeble and unable to resist ; and James of Scotland, close guarded in the tower of London, into which he had been thrown seventeen years before by Henry the Fourth, having been seized in a time of profound peace between the nations, when quietly making a voyage to France in 1405. His leaders were also all ready at his word, and more gallant leaders never led the English array to victory. There were Talbot and Salisbury, and Bedford and Arundel ; and in addition, the richest prince in Europe, Philip of Burgundy and Flanders. He had little cause to fear the result of all the efforts of his enemies, aided by the courage and animosity of the Scotch ; but while in the midst of his designs, in his palace of the Louvre, the hand of death fell upon him. He had only time to appoint Gloster Regent of England, and Bedford Regent of France ; to warn them both against releasing the prisoners of Agincourt till his son attained his majority, and to commit that infant of eight months old tc the tenderness of his relations. A pompous funeral took its way through the draperied streets of Paris, and deposited the body of the politician and conqueror in the royal vaults at Windsor. The grief in both kingdoms was equally deep in appearance ; we cannot believe that France was sunk so low as that the grief in both was equally sincere. In two months more a simpler cavalcade accompanied the body of the helpless Charles to the tomb of his ancestors, and the stage was left for the struggle of the new generation.

Charles the Seventh was twenty years old, and seldom has fortune poured her gifts in the lap of one who appeared at first so unworthy of her favours. Some men have honours thrust upon them, and he was of the number. Nothing seemed to rouse his courage or sink his spirits. Whatever news of loss or disgrace reached him, found him perfectly unmoved. He was the centre of a set of gay young cavaliers, who considered life a continued tournament, where he was the happiest knight who gained the most prizes from the Queen of Beauty, and fought in the most graceful manner with a blunted spear. An old leader of the Free Companies, who was afterwards a subject of patriotic enthusiasm under the name of La Hire, could not understand the feelings of the youthful king, and limited his praise to the statement, "that nobody ever lost a kingdom so joyously." The kingdom, indeed, seemed gone beyond hope of recovery. With no dissentient voice, the great assemblage of peers and counsellors, lawyers, judges, doctors of divinity, and fathers of the Church, crowds of citizens, and all the municipal authorities of Paris, had seen the herald Montjoie break his staff of office over the coffin of Charles the Sixth, and cry, "The king is dead, God save King Henry of England, our Sovereign Lord of France !" Bedford had revenged the defeat of Beaugé by a decisive victory over the Scotch, and the French adherents of the Dauphin, at Verneuil, where Buchan, who had been created Constable, and Douglas, who had been named Duke of

Touraine, were both killed. Town after town gave in its adhesion to the English Regent. Brittany had joined the stranger, and Charles was reduced to a few territories on the south of the Loire, and the hidden good wishes of every true Frenchman in all the land. He was called in derision, "King of Bourges," as that little city was the chief part of his restricted dominions ; but his name all this time ascended in the prayers of all the people. The brave young king—the handsome cavalier—the descendant of St. Louis—the joy of France—these were the ideas called up by his position throughout the whole extent of his ancient kingdom. The despair and misery of his suffering subjects invested him with qualities to which he had no claim ; and love as usual worked its own miracles, and saw generosity and nobleness in the most selfish and indifferent of mankind. When the sky was darkest, a little star began to appear. A quarrel arose between Burgundy and Gloster ; and a dispute no less bitter broke out between Bedford and the Earl of Richemont, brother of the Duke of Brittany.

Jacqueline of Holland was the richest heiress in the world, and all the hungry princes went off in full pursuit. Married in her childhood to John the Dauphin, she had lost him by poison in 1416. Forced then into a betrothal with the Duke of Brabant, nephew of the Duke of Burgundy, she refused his hand, and fled for protection to England. Gloster, who had as full an appreciation as his rivals of the charms of Holland and Hainault, thought the safest way of defending her from her Flemish husband was to marry her himself. But the offence against morals and propriety was too open, and the sanction of the Church was refused. Jacqueline left her English claimant, and lost her Flemish one by death at the same time. But instead of going back to Gloster, now that she was free, she gave her heart and hand to a simple gentleman of her States called Borselen, and the magnificent Philip of Burgundy knew now how to proceed. He cast Borselen into prison, and hinted unutterable woes, till Jacqueline, anxious to save the only one of her numerous husbands she ever cared for, surrendered her princedom, lands, and tenements to the overjoyed Burgundian, and retired to love and a cottage. There she might have lived as long as she pleased, but Gloster could by no means rest satisfied without a portion of his late spouse's property, and put in a claim for her dower. Philip kept fast hold of all he had got, and turned benevolent eyes towards Charles, the enemy of England. Richemont, at this inopportune period, demanded a high command in the English service; and Bedford, who should have conciliated the brother of his ally the Duke of Brittany, refused the application. He showed little knowledge of character if he did not expect an immediate defection from the English cause. The King of Bourges was more considerate, and gave the Constable's sword to the haughty Richemont, who instantly went over to his side. He submitted to his guidance in all things, even to the dismissal of some of his old favourites, on which the new champion insisted. He even made no scruple of sacrificing to the same imperious mandate the lives of some of his more useful followers. Louvel, his chancellor, was disgraced without a trial. The Seigneur de Giac was seized by force, sewn up in a sack, and cast into the Loire, by sentence of a pretended council; Camus de Beaulieu was assassinated by order of the Earl of Richemont, without any council at all. The court of Bourges was purified by these vigorous murders of the old set of misleaders, but was amply supplied by the same hand with a fresh assortment of sycophants and buffoons. The Earl tried to immerse the king deeper than ever in sensual enjoyments and degrading amusements; and the Duke of Brittany, satisfied with the power his brothers had attained, withdrew from the English alliance. Charles, however, was uneasy under his tutelage, and rejoiced greatly when a defeat, sustained by his unprincipled dictator in the year 1426, at St. James de Beuvron, lessened his authority; and at last when old John Talbot, in the following year, retook all the towns and places he had seized within the English pale, no farther terms were kept with the discomfited tyrant, and Richemont was unceremoniously dismissed. Brittany, however, did not rise in consequence of this proceeding, and the Duke of Burgundy was quiescent, if not favourable. All that threatened an increase of danger to the national interests, was a report that the famous Salisbury was coming over the sea with a great reinforcement of Englishmen, and that the war was to be prosecuted with the utmost vigour.

Charles, who was the Mark Tapley of kings, bore himself with his usual jollity under this afflicting news, and was probably excited to fresh ebullitions of satisfaction, when he heard that on the 12th of October, 1428, the city of Orleans, the best of all his possessions, and the only security of his adherents, was besieged by a great body of his English enemies, led by Salisbury and Talbot, and all the rough Saxons and Anglo-Normans whom these perpetual wars had raised to fame. Gradually it became known that all the great names also on the French side had crowded to the same point. Xaintrailles, La Hire, La Fayette, Gaucour de Giresme, and the Bastard of Orleans, had thrown themselves within the walls. Trumpets and banners answered each other in deadly defiance, and on both sides was seen the royal standard of France ; the golden lilies waved over the tent of Salisbury and the citadel of the besieged. Volunteers from all parts of the land, of humbler rank and deeper interest in the decision, poured into the devoted town. The strength of the two kingdoms was fairly matched, as in the case of Sebastopol, and victory depended upon the result of the siege. We can form no idea of the tremendous arbitrament dependent on apparently so small an issue as the fate of a wretched little city of twelve or thirteen thousand souls. But in all France, and in all England too, the operations were followed with the intensest eagerness, and hopes and fears alternately predominated as the tide of fortune seemed to flow towards one side or the other. Salisbury was killed at the commencement of the struggle, and the French heart beat high. A convoy of provisions for the besieged, guarded by several thousand Scotch, was defeated and dispersed, the barrels of salted herrings which constituted their stores being scattered on the road, and giving their name to the engagement,—and England blew a note of triumph. Charles himself was at last so far roused from his epicurean carelessness, that he advanced within a convenient distance of the seat of action;—and fresh summonses on the other side were issued for support to the English force. The townsmen fought well ; the gallant cavaliers made brilliant sorties, but slowly and surely the invading lines were drawn round the city. The siege was changed into a blockade. Walls were run from point to point, and strengthened at proper intervals by bastions and towers. Pickaxe and spade supplied the place of spears and arrows. And though the English, as usual, despised their opponents, and undertook more work than their numbers justified, and accordingly lost more men by over fatigue than the weapons of the enemy, it was evident that their indomitable perseverance and brutal ignorance of the fact of their being beat, would reap its common reward, and that Orleans would fall into their hands. Now let us enter into the feelings of the French peasantry, when it flew from village to village, at this time, that a country maiden of eighteen years of age had been summoned by celestial voices to the rescue of the country ; that she had seen and conversed with angels and glorified saints, who bade her fight for France ; and that captains, and knights, and nobles had given credence to her communications. Then they were told that the Lord of Baudrecourt at Vaucouleurs had been visited by the girl, whose name was Joan d'Arc, a daughter of small cotters in the village of Domremy, and had sent her forward at her own request to have an audience of the king. Strange things were told them of this audience : how that Charles, partly for amusement and partly to test the reality of her mission, had disguised himself in plain apparel, and dressed one of his courtiers in the royal robes ; and how Joan had gone straight up to where he stood, and had said, "Gentle Dauphin, I come to save the heir of France, and restore you to the crown. Orleans shall be saved by this hand, and you shall be crowned at Rheims by the help of God and my Lady St. Catherine." Next it was told to the wondering people, and reached, at last, the soldiers of both the hosts, that Joan, with the banner of France in her hand, mounted on a white charger, and clothed in complete armour, was advancing to the Loire, and on the 29th of April, 1429, in the sixth month of the siege, bells were ringing, and cannon fired, and processions gathered to the cathedral; for Joan, at the head of a great company of gentlemen and men-at-arms, had entered the fainting city, and promised deliverance within a certain time. Here was a thing which the spearmen of Warwickshire, and the archers of Nottingham, and the fighting chaplains of Bury St. Edmunds and Netley Abbey, could by no means understand. They heard of a young maiden leading battalions of warriors, and prophesying defeat to the leopards, and rousing a million hearts by a few simple and noble words, and immediately set her down for a witch. All over France by this time she was known as Joan the Maid, and when the excited courage of her followers, and her own example in marching against the enemy, had scattered dismay among the besiegers; when their intrenchments were thrown down and their batteries stormed; and finally, when they were terror-struck by the supernatural success which followed the maid wherever she appeared, and hurriedly left their tents on the 8th of May, and retreated beyond the river, it appeared that her mission was at an end. But "No," said Joan, "I have promised to lead the gentle Dauphin to Rheims to be anointed with the holy oil, and wear the crown of his noble fathers;" and she rode off and presented herself once more to Charles. The generals and wise men all said the way to Rheims was impassable on account of the garrisons of the enemy, but Joan said she heard voices telling her that all would be well; and at last it was thought good policy to give in to the popular belief, and the wonderful march began. The English were paralysed,—no opposition was made to the heaven-guarded procession,—and when the ceremony was over, and the rightful heir was placed on the throne with the blessings of Church and people, Joan knelt at his feet and said, "Gentle King,"—he had only been Gentle Dauphin till the coronation was over,—"my duty is fulfilled. I wish to go back to feed the sheep with my brothers at Domremy, for they love me better than all the thousands I have seen since I left home." But more work was expected from the high-souled maid, and she was reserved for a different fate.

From this moment the whole face of affairs was changed. The honour of the land had been avenged, not by mailed knights and nobles of high descent, but by one of the daughters of the soil. The true chord was struck at last, and the people felt that liberty and regeneration must come from themselves. And well and nobly they rose in the great cause. Talbot, the gallant and good, had been taken prisoner, and the Earl of Suffolk and many other noble Englishmen. Nothing resisted the oncoming wave of popular enthusiasm. Onwards towards Paris itself the growing torrent flowed. Saon, Soissons, Chateau Thierry, Beauvais, Compiègne, hauled down the English flag. From Paris, however, the invaders were repulsed, and Charles, the careless king, retired again to the Loire to listen to some overtures for a compromise which the Duke of Burgundy commenced. When the first steps were taken, Bedford grew as distrustful of his ally as of the French king himself, and hit upon a notable device to attach the Burgundian more firmly than ever to the English cause. This was to resign the regency in his favour ; and the moment the astonished Philip found that the English interests were his own, and that every sacrifice he proposed for the attainment of peace would be at the expense of his own influence, he would not yield a point, and broke off the negotiation as injurious to the dignity of his lord, Henry the Sixth, by the grace of God King of England and France. The Regent Burgundy was a fiercer opponent of French independence than the English Bedford. He besieged the town of Compiègne which Joan had taken and now defended ; but her feats were no longer inspired by the same high confidence she had hitherto possessed in herself and her vocation. She was as honest in mind as she was bold in action ; and felt and publicly proclaimed that her holy call was completed at the coronation of Rheims. Still the heroic heart remained. She fought among the foremost, and in a sortie was taken by Philip on the 24th of June, 1430. And what was to be done with the conqueror of so many fields, the deliverer of Orleans, and Champion of the peasantry of France ? Bedford claimed her as a rebel to the English Henry ; the Bishop of Beauvais, in whose diocese she was taken, as a lapsed child of the Church. At last the illustrious John of Luxembourg, to whom Philip of Burgundy had presented her to make what ransom he could, sold her to the English duke and French prelate for the sum of ten thousand francs. For four hundred pounds, England and Rome had the gratification of burning to death a rebel and a sorceress. It was so easy to prove her guilt in both these characters. She had carried havoc with her sword among the English ranks, and had heard voices in the solitude of woods and the gloom of cathedral aisles, calling on her to buckle on her armour for the rightful king. And there, before her judges' eyes, was the actual sword which had done the mischief, and the armour she had buckled on. Nothing could be clearer to the zealous Bishop of Beauvais and the other intelligent ecclesiastics who presided at her trial ; and after an imprisonment, embittered by many insults on the part both of priests and soldiers, the noblest woman of all history was put to a painful death, and expired by a slow fire in the middle of the old marketplace of Rouen.

Write down this date, the 13th of May, 1431, as the death-doom of the chivalry of France. For many months the Maid lay in chains and darkness, and Dunois threw down no glove in her defence, no La Hire offered to do battle for her deliverance, and Charles—the Gentle Dauphin, but most forgetful king—made no effort in her behalf. He feasted and toyed with knights and mistresses, but left the village maiden to her fate. Only one princely heart in all the country was touched by her miserable end, and that was the heart of Philip Duke of Burgundy, the main support of the English claimant. He began to remember that he was a born noble and a French subject. In both these capacities he felt the shame of his present position ; persecutor of Joan the brave and simple, and enemy of Charles his natural king. The treaty of Troyes, which threw France under the proud feet of her conqueror, rankled in his mind as first collateral of the blood—and in the same year which saw the sacrificial fire at Rouen, the Burgundian gave in his adhesion to the national cause. Bedford, indeed, brought over the English pretender, and had him crowned by an English bishop, and surrounded by English guards in the cathedral of Paris. But men began to compare the two coronations ; one, where all France put up its vows at Rheims, and the heaven-appointed champion stood with the banner of the fleur-de-lis in her hand—and this, where there was no promise vouchsafed from heaven or gratulation permitted upon earth. Paris received the ceremony in stubborn silence, and Bedford saw his hopes of ultimate success destroyed. He restricted himself to Normandy, the ancient apanage of the English kings, and from Rouen and Caen issued his edicts, which, however, had no currency unless within reach of his retainers' swords. Charles, on the other hand, rose up from his sybarite dreams, and bestirred himself as one who at last was fighting for a throne. Wherever he showed himself the love of the inhabitants awoke. In Picardy the peasantry rose up in arms ; in Paris the excitable multitude were arraying themselves against their English oppressors. Dunois was master of Chartres and other towns, and Richemont, the brother of the Duke of Brittany, was again on the patriot side. Conferences for peace were opened at Arras in 1435 ; but the English self-reliance as usual kept the plenipotentiaries of Henry from seeing the change in their circumstances. They stood on as lofty ground as at Troyes, when Agincourt was recent and Harry the Fifth had all the strength of England at his back. All the princes of Europe were represented on this occasion. Cardinals from the Pope and nuncios from the Emperor endeavoured to lower the English pride. But all in vain. Bedford would not descend a hair-breadth from his demands, and died when he had given in his final answer. But the whole of Christendom was not to be kept in uneasiness because a king of England determined also to be king of France. Burgundy stept into the place of leader of the negotiations, and made his peace with Charles. He claimed a small tract of country to round his dominions on the Somme, and a formal disavowal of the crime of the Bridge of Montereau. Charles resigned the territory and disavowed the murder, and the first vassal of the Crown was again the defender of the kingdom. Great hopes sprang up from this reconciliation, and were not disappointed. The English garrison of Paris was besieged in the Bastile, and having capitulated on terms, retired to their countrymen at Rouen. Charles made his triumphal entry into the capital in the November of 1437, and from henceforth was looked on by all as King of France. Rescripts dated from Paris seemed corroborative of an undisputed government, and once more the English were mere invaders, holding some small portions of the land, but retaining them by no title but that of the strong arm. The strong arm, however, was weakened, since Bedford's death brought dissension into the councils of Henry the Sixth. Parliament, which was thoroughly English in its habits and desires, would vote no supplies for what they considered a foreign and unnecessary war. Symptoms were already not undiscoverable of the furious passions which gave such prominence to the wars of the Roses in the history of England ; and the French king could apply himself without fear of interruption to the internal reforms which the long struggle for existence had made necessary. Two things struck him as indispensable in order to preserve the independence of his crown : one was a compromise with the pretensions of the Pope, which might place some bound of separation between the spiritual and temporal powers ; and the other the creation of some regular and reliable force, which should place him beyond the caprices of his military tenants and the great feudatories of the Crown.

He therefore established what is called the Pragmatic Sanction, which guaranteed the liberties of the Gallican Church, and established a standing army. By these two regulations he took the power of the keys from the hands of Rome, and the power of the sword from the hands of his nobility.

Martin the Fifth, who had been chosen pope in place of the three pretenders to the holy chair, had summoned a council at Basle, in 1431, which had sat for some time with the concurrence of all the States. But Eugenius the Fourth, who succeeded Martin, wished for a council of his own; and on the plea of facilitating the reconciliation of the Greek Church, convoked a meeting at Bologna. The council of Basle declined to move—declined to dissolve—declined to give up its measures of reform. A religious war was on the point of breaking out, when Charles summoned a National Council to meet at Bourges. All the peers and officers of the Crown, and judges of the tribunals, were there; a very august assembly, presided over by the king, who was attended by the Dukes of Burgundy and Bourbon, and supported on his right hand by the frail person and cunning face of his son the Dauphin, a youth of fifteen, who will soon be better known to us as Louis the Eleventh. His national reformation was very moderate in its extent. It re-affirmed the subordination of popes to general councils; it bound the Pope to summon one of those plenary assemblages at least once in ten years; it secured freedom of election to the higher ecclesiastical dignities—the settlement at eighty of the number of cardinals—the reduction of appeals to the Court of Rome—the suppression of annates and other payments to the Pope. It insisted, also, on the curtailment of the power of excommunication, so that henceforth that sentence was never to be universal in its application, but limited to the individuals who had deserved the ban of the Church. Eugenius the Fourth anathematised the Council of Bourges, and all concerned in these inroads on the apostolical authority. But the Council of Basle published letters of approval, and encouraged the council of Bourges to persevere. The Pope was more recalcitrant than ever, and was only silenced when the Council of Basle deposed him as rebellious to his jurisdiction, and nominated to the chair of St. Peter, Victor Amadeus, a duke of Savoy, who had retired from the cares of his petty principality to devote himself to privacy and a life of riotous luxury on the banks of the Lake of Geneva. This rubicund recluse took the name of Felix the Fifth, and prepared to do battle with Eugenius. But France was contented with the triumph she had achieved; and as she had gained all she wished in the diminution of the papal power and the stoppage of the papal supplies, she declined to acknowledge her Savoyard neighbour as controller of the spiritual interests of France, and continued her empty-handed adhesion to the potentate who remained at Rome. A plebeian prelate she probably thought was more easily dealt with on the distant banks of the Tiber, than a prince-pontiff, who might perhaps transfer the seat of his hostile and independent government to the banks of the Rhone.

The other great stroke of policy was the creation of a standing army. Ecclesiasticism and feudalism had had their trial and had failed. Each in its proper day had done the duty for which it was ordained, and had lingered on after its active utility was over. The Church no longer fulfilled its office of comforter and consoler of the nation; and feudalism no longer fulfilled its duty as defender of the land. The seeds of Christianity had been widely and healthily spread in the early time of the struggle between faith and barbarism. Great truths had taken root, which had never been eradicated from the general mind; and even in the dark days of superstition, and the wilder period of unbelief, the divine prospects of the gospel have had their teachers and disciples. But the attempt on the part of priests and bishops to Christianise the State by investing the dignitaries of the Church with secular authority, ended by making the Church itself a secular institution. Prelates took rank with counts and marquises, and were generally more worldly and ambitious than their competitors. It was useless now for the oppressed serf to fly for protection to a holy abbot or spiritual overseer. He found the abbot with a sword by his side, and the spiritual peer at the head of his armed array. Time was when the voice of the gentle priest would have been heard in soft appeals against the tyranny of the oppressor ; but the oppressor now was a priest himself, and the interests of his order prevailed over his feelings as a Christian. There are still preserved some doggrel verses which, during the English occupation, travelled from cottage to cottage, and are inexpressibly pathetic in spite of the want of poetic power. It is a cry of distress and agony wrung from the heart of the people. They have no longer anybody to apply to in their misery. Poor Jacques Bonhomme is without a friend in all the world, high or low, and looks round on all the orders of the State with the same miserable conclusion that he has none to succour him.

> " Ah, princes, prelates, valiant lords,
> Lawyers and tradesfolk small and great,
> Burghers and warriors girt with swords,
> Who fatten on our daily sweat;
> To labouring hinds some comfort give,
> Whate'er betide we needs must live.
>
> . . . .
>
> Pity our faces poor and wan,
> Our trembling limbs, our haggard eyes,
> Relieve the fainting husbandman,
> And heaven will count you truly wise ;
> For God declareth great and small
> Who lacketh kindness, lacketh all ! "

More than forty verses are employed in running through the catalogue of hopelessness and neglect. All have failed in their duty to the poor. Barons oppress—bishops will not interfere—knights will not defend—lawyers will not cease from cheating. But in the utter misery of the "labouring hinds'" condition, there now rose a hope. The king has received a crown, consecrated by unnumbered prayers. He is the anointed shepherd of the people, and wears a sword for justice, and a shield for protection. More visibly God-appointed than the swaggering bishop who seizes their corn, and at length guarded and led through difficulties and dangers by a Maid whose words and actions reveal unmistakably that her mission is from above—a Maid sprung from their own rank of life, and devoting her courage, and finally her life, to the strengthening of the throne—the monarch became the central light of all the suffering population. It little mattered to them whether he was personally a self-indulgent epicure, or a vigorous ruler of men ; to them he was the personified safeguard of the weak. If they had no arms, and no wealth, and no authority, he had them all. No wonder, therefore, when Charles, after consulting the States-General assembled at Orleans, issued an ordonnance converting the military service of the feudal tenures into a tax for the payment of troops, raised for the national defence and commanded entirely by the Crown, that the great mass of the people hailed the alteration with delight. They were no longer to be exposed to the predatory bands of ambitious chiefs ; for any one found in arms, unless the Franc-archers and cavalry of the king, was to be considered a robber and a rebel.

The ranks of this national force were soon filled, and were in no long time called upon to show what metal they were of ; for the discontented nobles, headed by the Dauphin, the wickedest son, as he was afterwards the worst father in French annals, would not surrender their monopoly of arms without a struggle. The service they had been of in resisting the English, had awakened their hope of the complete independence of their fiefs, and they perceived that, by this politic act, the whole nation was enlisted on the suzerain's side. Glittering files of helmeted cavaliers again took the field, and dukes and princes gave the splendour of their standards to the rebel cause. But Charles, who threw off the carelessness of his character when great conjunctures arose, hurried into Poitou and the Bourbonnais, where the enemy were strongest, and at the head of his faithful soldiers, and with the aid of the peasantry and townsfolk, trampled the Praguery—as the insurrection called itself, in imitation of the Protestant Hussites in Prague—before it had time to spread. He mingled honour and generosity with justice, and extended his pardon to his ungrateful son, and to his misguided kinsman the Duke of Bourbon. Accessions from the highest orders of the State now came to strengthen the throne, which rested on the love and gratitude of the people. Charles of Orleans, who had pined since Agincourt in the chambers of the Tower, was restored to France by the pecuniary aid of the Duke of Burgundy, and continued the poetic studies, still worthy of the highest admiration, which had alleviated his captivity of five-and-twenty years. The nobility began to recognise the new place assigned to it in the polity of the kingdom. Subordination to a general law, and rank and influence for the benefit of the State, these were what many of the greater vassals accepted as the alternatives of their position. But many could not give up their hereditary notions of the private right to work public wrong, and ravaged peaceful districts on their own account. But Charles was no longer the unobservant titular of Bourges. He took with him his more sagacious nobles, and appointed them to commands in his plebeian army. The robbing and reiving magnates were astonished to see their brothers of the peerage employed as officers of the peace to arrest them for high crimes and misdemeanours, and fear fell upon the evil-doers when they heard that Charles had ordered Alexander de Bourbon, one of the most far descended of the culprits, to be sewn up in a sack and drowned at Bar-on-the-Aube. Another novelty was introduced with still greater effect in his treatment of a captured town. He took into the "royal peace" all the labourers, and all the women and children, and all who should fly for protection to the churches. The Praguery died out for want of recruits to so unpopular a cause, and trade took a start as if a great weight had been lifted off, when the roads were made safe, and the exactions of the nobles forbidden. Fairs were established under the king's safeguard in many of the towns. Charters were confirmed and renewed, and with a malicious ingenuity privileges were heaped on the districts contiguous to Normandy and the English possessions, and great commercial advantages in their intercourse with France guaranteed to the inhabitants of Burgundy. It was a more certain method of conquest than sword and gun ; and if the English invaders had not interfered with the peaceful acquisitions of the king, who was guided by the advice of the famous Jacques Cœur, the richest merchant and greatest shipowner then alive, the consolidation of France would have been complete. Commerce would have scaled walls and filled up ditches which no assailant could pass, and freedom of internal communication and protection to industry would have sunk all personal differences in the one great temptation of forming a constituent part of so secure and well-governed a realm. England occasionally made an effort to revive the terrors of its name ; but Henry the Sixth was easily daunted by difficulty and danger, and Parliament was soon disheartened by expense and unsuccess. Talbot seized Dieppe ; but the Dauphin and the now regular army retook it in a short time, and the luxurious English king and thrifty parliament thought it a good plan to agree to terms. Here the French historians break out into great rejoicings at the revenge their nation took for Agincourt, and the forced marriage of Catherine of France, by giving Margaret of Anjou to the son of Henry the Fifth—a hateful woman and fatal to her husband and her adopted country, as all French princesses married to English kings have been. By her arts and ambition the troubles of Henry's reign were embittered and increased. At this time, however, she was but fifteen years of age, and perhaps might have displayed a nobler character if she had fallen into more judicious hands.

A truce for two years was proclaimed on this joyous occasion ; but the short touch of war in the campaign of Dieppe had again awakened the evil passions of the land. Adventurers of nameless regions and every kind of arms were visible in the neglected fields. Charles remembered the policy of his grandfather the Wise, and proclaimed an expedition, in behalf of the Emperor, against the revolted Swiss. It was necessary, he said, to let out the peasant blood,—and he saw, with great satisfaction, a vast body of freebooters march off to measure swords for the first time against the men of Zurich. With prodigious bodily strength, and the wild courage of mountaineers, the savage Switzers appalled their assailants at the very time that, from the inferiority of numbers, they perished under the assault. But the cautious Louis, who commanded on this occasion, took a lesson from the terrible day of St. Jacques near Basle, and resolved on no account to quarrel with those indomitable barbarians, whom it was necessary to extirpate, old and young, as neither old nor young had learned the way to yield. At the same time that Switzerland was thinning the ungovernable swashbucklers of the Dauphin's army, his father carried all the remaining ne'er-do-wells of his kingdom to the siege of Metz in Lorraine. Metz bought off the assailants with a large ransom, and Charles applied the money to the enlargement of his regular force. He embodied bowmen in every parish, and so united the interests of every little community in the land with the feeling of national honour. A certain number of these archers were to be furnished by every district, and, besides their pay while in service, they received exemption from all taxes and other contributions except the rent of their little holdings. This arrangement was in full force when an effort was to be made to expel the English from the land. The opportunity was irresistible and easily seized. The Court of London had become the scene of crimes and artifices such as disgraced the reign of Charles the Sixth of France. Margaret had already begun to use her fatal influence. She had joined the party of the Cardinal of Winchester against his brother the Duke of Gloster. Gloster was accused of treason, and found dead one morning in his bed. Suffolk (the king's favourite) and the queen made bad use of their victory, and offended the good feeling of the nation. A tenure of the throne for fifty years, and all the glories of the Henrys had not so totally obliterated the usurpation of the family of Lancaster, that the claim of the elder branch, represented at this time by the Duke of York, was forgotten. A usurper, to be safe, should be generous and just. No prescription is sufficient to maintain a tyrant on a throne he disgraces. The passions of both parties were speedily irritated to the utmost, and the white and red rose were already talked of as emblems of the royal houses. Thirty years of dissension and civil war were now to open on England, at the very time when the wounds of her great rival were healed. The parts, indeed, played by the two kingdoms were completely changed, and though no Agincourt illustrated the French arms, their superiority was not less decided. One by one the conquests of the English were torn away. Wherever the king of France appeared, the gates, after a slight resistance by the garrison, were flung open by the townsmen; and on both sides the understanding was complete. Charles entered a city rightfully his own, and had no injuries to avenge; the inhabitants returned to their natural obedience, and had no danger to fear. He was not a foreign enemy subduing them by force, but a lawful king resuming possession of an unjustly withheld inheritance. Privileges and rewards were scattered with princely munificence among the newly recovered towns. A fervour of loyalty to the Crown of France spread from place to place, and at last, when the epidemic could no longer be restrained, the English leaders yielded to the universal movement. Rouen, though defended by Somerset and Talbot, capitulated in 1449, and Charles made his triumphal entry into the capital of Normandy. In the following years he stretched his power over Toulouse and Bayonne; and in the year 1453, when, after a revolt of the discontented nobility who adhered to the English cause, he finally, and for the second time, fixed his standard on the Castle of Bordeaux, nothing was left to England of all the possessions of the Edwards on the continent, the patrimony of the Conqueror, the dower of Eleanor, and the conquests of Henry, but the town of Calais. Glorious old John Talbot had died in armour at Castillon in Guienne, fighting with the courage of his youth, though more than eighty years of age. With him died out the long line of great captains, whom the wars of the Fifth Henry had formed. The swords of Agincourt were covered with rust, and the island visitor had given up the dreams of ambition, and sighed for nothing but repose. France was again a kingdom, the degrading treaty of Troyes avenged, and a career of internal improvement was opened which needed only a continuance of patriotic measures to conduct her to the noblest and happiest results. We shall see how this onward movement was turned aside to the profit of the most selfish of her kings, and how the spirit of loyalty which the sufferings of the people and the vigour of Charles had aroused, was converted into a blind submission to the throne, and a general prostration of heart and hope before the footstool of a despot.

As a fitting prelude to the reign in which he trampled on the new-found liberties of his country, the Dauphin embittered the last years of his father's life by his opposition and want of affection. Affection, indeed, was a feeling totally unknown to this man. Married in his youth to the beautiful Margaret of Scotland, daughter of the unhappy James the First, he had succeeded in so breaking her heart, that, when she was attacked with an illness which might easily have been cured, she rejected the medicines presented by the doctor, and said, "Fie upon life, speak of it no more." She had indeed no farther object to live for. A dull, brutal, selfish tyrant, poisoning all her enjoyment, and sneering with vulgar malice at the high thoughts which he could not comprehend, he had taught her to exchange the generous openness of her lively disposition for a sombre despair in all things. Poetry and hope were crushed out of her by the uncongenial harshness of her hateful mate. One day in her early time she saw Alain Chartier asleep upon a bench. Alain was acknowledged to be the best poet and ugliest man in France ; but Margaret slipped forward on tiptoe and kissed his lips without awakening him. "Don't think," she said to her ladies, "that it is the man I kiss ; I kiss the mouth from which so many beautiful words have flowed." The Dauphiness found her only escape from the machinations of the Court and the cruelty of her husband in death. Charles himself had a similar disgust of life, and produced by the same means. Already the fear of poison administered by his son made his festivals, and even his common meals, a torment to him. The courage and fidelity of the Scotch had induced him to engage the services of a number of those faithful mercenaries as a guard. Louis hated the Scotch—perhaps as representing courage and fidelity—and proposed to one of his confidants to attack them as they accompanied his father, in complete security, on some party of pleasure on which he had resolved. "I shall be there," he said, "for the sight of my father's face seems to terrify people unless I am by." What else he meditated besides attacking the escort was never found out; for the confidant, struck with horror, informed the king of the design, and Louis retired to his principality of Dauphiny. About the same time the services of the wise counsellor we have already mentioned—the great merchant and shipowner, Jacques Cœur—were lost to the State. This man was accused of malversation in his office of treasurer of the Crown. He was said to have heaped up incredible riches; and on some occasions he made a display of his wealth, which in a great measure compensated for the evil proceedings, if such they were, by which he gained it. He furnished funds for fleets and armies out of his private stores, when they could not otherwise be had; and continued his sage advice to the king, inculcating economy and repose. Charles was still indolent and self-indulgent when no great national effort was to be made. He allowed the prosecution of his faithful servitor, accepted the sentence of death which was passed upon him, and only started up to the kindness and generosity of his character when he remembered his services; and granted him his life. The rest of the treasurer's story is very strange. Jacques Cœur found refuge at Rome—was appointed admiral of the Italian fleets against the Saracens—trafficked in goods and money while sweeping the infidels from the sea—and died richer and more honoured than he had ever been in Paris. The king must have seen, when it was too late, that he had banished a financier whose advice on public affairs was cheaply paid for by the acquisition of private riches. Losses accumulated as his age increased. Though affectionately attached to his queen, he had for many years loved the beautiful Agnes Sorel. He had consulted her on the weightiest matters of state, and found her a counsellor worthy of him. The French for a long time believed that the noble change which took place in the monarch's character, and converted him from a cold-hearted lover of pleasure into a brave and patriot king, was owing to the indignant remonstrances of the favourite. Francis the First clothed this sentiment in these quaint and pleasant lines—

"More honour, gentle Agnes, hast thou won,
For that thy voice our France recoverèd,
Than could be achieved by cloister-prisoned nun,
Or holiest beadsman to the desert fled." *

But the delicacy of modern times has induced some authors to reject the assistance of so doubtful a character, and attribute the alteration in Charles's actions to a higher source. Whether she was the inspirer of his great deeds or not, she was at all events the person he loved best; and at this time, when his son was threatening his life, and his counsellor was removed, the "gentle Agnes" also was taken from his side. Darkness indeed closed thicker and thicker round the old man. Louis retired to the Court of Burgundy, from which he meditated mischief against his father and his native land; and though Charles kept up the appearance of activity, and even of ambition, by entering into a contest for the supremacy of Italy, and accepting the sovereignty of Genoa, his heart was no longer in the glory of arms or the strengthening of his kingdom. For whose benefit would all his labours be? At length in 1461, when his realm was placid, and all the storms which had agitated his first appearance were apparently quelled, the broken-hearted father and very desolate king died by what was almost a voluntary death. He abstained from food for six days, in the fear that Louis had

* "Gentille Agnès, plus d'honneur tu mérites,
La cause étant de France recouvrer,
Que ce que peut ledans un cloître œuvrer,
Clause nonain ou bien dévot hermité."

bribed his cook, and might thereby heap the guilt of parricide on his soul; and the Dauphin—in the midst of his life of deceit and hypocrisy, as a guest more honoured than desired at Ghent—was suddenly informed that his object was attained without an additional crime, and that he was King of France.

CHAPTER VII.

FROM LOUIS THE ELEVENTH, A. D. 1461, TO HIS DEATH, A. D. 1483.

Louis the Eleventh was nine-and-thirty years of age when he began to reign. His conduct had been long enough before the world to allow all men to form an estimate of his character; and it was therefore with no feelings of gratification that the nobles, whom his father had led in war, and associated with in the dignified solemnities of peace, beheld a person placed at the head of affairs on whom neither war nor pleasure seemed to have any effect;—a cold-blooded, watchful, unscrupulous tyrant, whose steps, like the tiger's, were noiseless, and whose object was only known by the rapid spring when he had got within distance, and the shriek of the victim. This man's character, strangely compounded of sagacity and superstition, of relentless cruelty and humorous peculiarities, has been the theme of novelists and poets; and though, for the purpose of dramatic action, his extraordinary qualities are brought into more startling contrast than ever occurs in real life, the judgment of history confirms that of fiction, that a more unlovable, untrustworthy, bad-hearted man, and selfish, unprincipled ruler, never was known in any country, nor any one who had so injurious an influence on the future progress and rational liberty of mankind. Charles the Wise would have founded the greatness of his kingdom on the elevation of the great body of the people. Henry the Fourth would have attained the same object by attaching a chivalrous nobility by mutual interests to the support of a popular throne; but this man commenced his reign with a determination to humble all classes alike—to make his nobles servants and his people slaves. It will be interesting to watch the steps he took; for it is as well to understand the methods by which liberty is either destroyed if it exists, or repressed if it threatens to appear. It is not impossible that in the history of our own time the struggle between power and independence may reappear under only slightly modified forms; and we shall be able to guess at the principle of both parties when we see what their earliest movements are.

Louis cast his ill-omened eyes around the land he was now about to "bring into order," and was alarmed at the condition of the national church. A national church it really deserved to be called; for, while confessing the superiority of Rome in antiquity and rank, it rested firmly on the decision of the Council of Basle, and acknowledged a power superior to the Holy See. It defended, also, freedom of election to vacant benefices, and refused the annates, or first year's income of bishoprics and incumbencies, to the exchequer of the Pope. Louis saw that the first advance against the citadel of civil liberty was a return to the obedience of Rome. He gave up at once all the franchises and exemptions wrung with such difficulty by the Church of France. He placed it again, bound hand and foot, under the heel of the successors of St. Peter, and even gave advantages to the ecclesiastical ruler which he had never held before. In return for this, the faithful son of the Church was sure of the Pontiff's support. He was a king who could do no wrong; for though he oppressed his subjects, and deceived his friends, and murdered his enemies by treachery, he had shown a most religious regard for the interests of the Papacy, and was honoured with the title, which his successors have retained, of "The most Christian King." The least Christian monarch of his time being elevated by popish gratitude to this lofty position, it was only left for the adulation of the courtiers to bestow upon the most ungraceful and undignified of rulers the title of "Majesty." This great word had not yet been applied to the persons of the sovereigns of Europe; but Louis the Eleventh set the example of claiming the highest-sounding and least-deserved epithets, and cheated and grovelled through a long reign of trickery and meanness as His Majesty the most Christian King. When the Church was again governed by a foreign master, whom it was easy for the king to win over to his side, the next important step in the progress of his design was to render the people powerless. For this purpose he did away with the Franc-archers of the previous reign. No village was allowed its butts and shooting-grounds. The parish was relieved of the expense of finding an "archer good" for the interior defence of the country, and the spirit of emulation in warlike sports was discouraged. But the land was not to be left unprotected. So in addition to his Scottish allies, he took into his pay large bodies of Swiss mercenaries, whose valour had struck him with such admiration at the battle of St. Jacques near Basle. He now more than doubled the taxes ; and as, although saving and grasping from personal disposition, he was liberal and even generous from policy, he derived great support from the absence of a home force of his own subjects, and the devoted adhesion of penniless mountaineers from the two poorest and most courageous populations in Christendom. We will only insert a word of surprise here with regard to the Swiss, that a people who are honoured throughout the world for the defence of their liberties at home, should be the scorn and shame of all generous minds by furnishing their strength and valour for the maintenance of the worst tyrannies abroad.

The nobility saw the object of the king, and took arms to prevent the extinction of their order and the diminution of their individual power. A cry is never wanting when people are determined to quarrel, and as the feudal chiefs could not, with any decency, state openly the reasons of their opposition, they placed it upon the two grounds of the sacrifice of French ecclesiastical liberty by the abrogation of the Pragmatic Sanction, and the intolerable weight of taxation which the new king had imposed. This, therefore, was called the War of the Public Good. Princes and feudatories, and all who had a lingering regard for the grand old days of license and free quarters, took up the patriotic cause. Charles of France, the king's brother, was the nominal chief, but the real head of this league was Charles the Rash, at this time called Count of Charolais, eldest son of the good Philip, Duke of Burgundy. In the list besides him were read the names of St. Pol, Brittany, Lorraine, Alençon, Bourbon, Armagnac, and Dunois. In short, the two parties were perfectly aware of each other's intentions, and met face to face. If the league succeeded, Louis's life would have been short, and a regency was openly promised. If Louis was successful, farewell to the great nobility, its independent power and hereditary magnificence; it must sink into an ornament of the court, or be exterminated altogether. It was the life of one or the other which lay upon the scales; and though the swords were sharpest, and the cause apparently the freest, on the side of the great vassals, the cunning, the policy, the perseverance, were all on the side of the king. Suddenly the oppressors of the towns and the harsh masters of country populations, affected a deep interest in the common weal. With haughty condescension they assumed the championship of the overburdened Commons, and kept them at the same time from coming "between the wind and their nobility," as if contact with them would have stained their coats of arms. But Louis, dressed in very undignified apparel, looked like a small shopkeeper, and affecting no airs of grandeur or superiority, entered into familiar talk with any well-to-do citizen he encountered, joked with him about his family, poked him under the ribs to give emphasis to his innuendoes, and strolled off to have a merry conversation with somebody else. Nobody could believe that so free-spoken a gentleman cared less for the common people than the Prince of Charolais, who would have put a townsman to death if he had stood in his way; and in a short time the people liked better to pay taxes to a man who put them at their ease, than to owe their deliverance to a set of champions who despised them in their hearts, and insulted them in their manners. Louis saw his advantage, and after trying to gain his object by a battle with the confederates at Montlhéry, where neither party was decidedly victorious, he suddenly discovered that the imposts he had laid on his dearly-beloved subjects had been advised by evil counsellors, and took off every payment which had been exacted since the time of Charles the Seventh. Poor man ! he had never heard that his good Parisians and affectionate gossips of Tours were discontented with the amount. Why hadn't they spoken before ? Tender-hearted, excellent Louis the Eleventh ! When he had thus soothed the pecuniary sufferings of his subjects, he put on his very simplest manner, got into a little boat, and paid a visit almost unattended to his dear friend and near kinsman, the Count of Charoläis. Who could resist such a mark of confidence and friendship ? Louis bestowed on the chiefs of the conspiracy everything they asked ; never hesitating for a moment, as indeed there was no occasion to do, for he had made up his mind to take everything back again on the first opportunity. He gave away towns and governments and offices, and as a parting gift presented the Count St. Pol, of the Imperial House of Luxembourg, who was the favourite of the passionate and jealous Charolais, with the sword of Constable of France. The Constable and Charolais hated each other ever after, which was the only object the king had in view. For consistency's sake, they insisted on his pretending to re-establish the Pragmatic Sanction ; but beyond this the cry of the Public Good was never heard. And Louis commenced anew.

He must have had as much enjoyment in the game he now played as if it had been a game of chess. How to move a castle to resist a knight, or a number of pawns to surround a bishop, how to keep Normandy in order by stirring up the enmity of Brittany, how to paralyse the motions of the young Duke of Burgundy—for in 1467 Charolais succeeded his father—by exciting insurrections among the men of Liege : these were the problems worked out in the solitude of his own thoughts ; for he boasted that he formed all his plans without the aid of others. The Marshal de Brezé said accordingly, that "the horse the king rode was a much stronger animal than it looked, for it carried the whole Council on its back." The results of the deliberations of this unanimous assemblage were soon visible in the vengeance which fell on the heads of the late confederacy. Charles of France, when all the others were getting lofty offices and rewards, had been presented with the Dukedom of Normandy. The people of Rouen, who had at first taken part against the Crown, received the first prince of the blood with acclamations, as a champion of their cause: and the king determined to show them they had chosen the wrong side. He raised an army, and hurried down to Caen; bought and bullied the Duke of Brittany, whom he found in that town, out of his friendship with Charles; and then fell upon the capital of the duchy, as if it had been in open rebellion. His right-hand man on this, as on similar occasions, was the famous Tristan l'Hermite, the executioner. Tristan's hands were soon full, for the king, with a vigorous impartiality which showed he was not a bigot to either side, cut off the heads of the aristocracy who had helped the princes, and threw hundreds of the commonalty, who had grumbled at his taxes, into the Seine. The Church, which he had bought over by the sacrifice of the Pragmatic Sanction, and still kept in awe by threatening to restore it—as he had engaged to do by the treaty with the Leaguers—was next to be taught that, however much he prized its friendship as a politician, its loftiest officers were the mere creatures of his breath. The system he pursued of excluding the higher orders from civil employments, had been introduced into ecclesiastical affairs. Wherever the sharp eye of Louis detected a fitting instrument for his purpose in the person of a penniless adventurer, or townsman of the lowest rank, he was very soon invested with the necessary authority, and perverted justice in the character of President of a court, or vilified religion in the office of a Bishop. The son of a small tradesman of the name of La Balue, had early shown such amazing want of principle combined with quickness of talent and audacious self-reliance, that he gained the notice of the king, then his confidence, then his friendship. The Pope made great efforts to win over this ornament of the faith, who was now Bishop of Evreux, and promised him the cardinal's hat if he persuaded his master to enregister the suppression of the Pragmatic Sanction in the rolls of parliament; and in foolish reliance on the promises of La Balue, sent him the blushing sign of his dignity before the service was performed. La Balue relaxed in his endeavours, as his wages were already received, and gained additional favour with the king for ceasing to trouble him on the subject. The favour continued for a long time, but at last, when Louis, in reliance on his powers of persuasion, and the counsels of his friends, trusted himself again within the power of Charles of Burgundy, and hoped to win him over as he had done in the former interview which destroyed the League of the Public Good, the advice given by the cardinal was found to lead to very dangerous results. The king had no sooner entered the town of Peronne, where the Rash Duke resided, than he found the trap he had fallen into. The vassal treated him as an enemy in his power, and gave evident indications of the violence he might have recourse to. Louis smiled, and flattered and promised in vain. One day it was reported to the duke that the men of Liege were in rebellion, that they were murdering his officers, and throwing off their allegiance, and that French agents in the pay of the king were prominent as ringleaders in the revolt. Louis's life hung by a single thread. He humbled himself in the dust, and accepted his host's invitation to accompany the army which was appointed to punish the citizens. He had, unfortunately, forgotten to tell his emissaries to remain quiet while he was in the duke's castle, and now the danger was growing with every hour. Before further discoveries were made, Louis put on the uniform of his subject, and cried, "Burgundy for ever!" as loud as the commonest soldier. Liege was taken, and the slaughter was dreadful. Louis encouraged the murders, to hide his complicity in the resistance; and after further humiliations and many faithful promises, he found himself once more safe in his own kingdom. Here strange discoveries awaited him. He intercepted letters from his favourite the cardinal. He found that his friend and gossip was the friend and gossip also of the Duke of Burgundy, the adviser of all that had happened at Peronne, especially of his forced presence at the siege, the degrading clauses of the final treaty, and the general harshness of his treatment. He found at the same time that the cardinal was in correspondence with his brother Charles, late leader of the League, who was still in resistance to his authority ; and, in short, that he was betrayed in every point. The king was offended at the perjury of his subject, but the man was a thousand times more angry at the error in his judgment. The son of the tailor, in the red stockings, had outwitted the son of St. Louis with the crown on his head. La Balue, though prince of the Church and bishop of a diocese, was imprisoned in an iron cage, about eight feet square, and kept like a wild beast in his den for eleven years in the castle of Loches. All that can be said in extenuation of this pitiless proceeding was, that the man was the disgrace of his order and his country, and that the instrument of his torture (as the natural justice of mankind is so prone to make out in other instances) was of his own invention.

Nothing seemed either above or below the vengeance of the humiliated king. In those days there were no newspapers to find fault with public men, or witty publications to make them ridiculous ; but the citizens of Paris had supplied the place of their *Times* and *Punch* by teaching an infinite number of jays and magpies, which they hung in cages along the line of the king's first entrance into the city after his escape from Burgundy, to utter the word "Peronne," with uncomplimentary epithets applied to Louis himself. Tristan l'Hermite was immediately busied in vindicating the royal honour. The necks of the unfortunate birds were unmercifully wrung, and the liberty of the press was at an end. Princes, cardinals, townsmen, and mocking-birds, all felt the strength of the relentless hand, which sometimes wielded a sword, and sometimes only flourished a whip. But there were some institutions, as well as individuals, which it was now his purpose to get within his power. Edward the Third of England, reposing upon the laurels of Crecy, had founded the Order of the Garter in 1349. John of France, in rapid imitation, as we have already seen, founded the Order of the Star. Philip of Burgundy had founded the Order of the Golden Fleece in 1430, and the principles of all these lordly confederations were derived from the ideas of chivalry which the romances had spread among the people. They were to be brotherhoods of noble knights, bound together by the bonds of mutual honour; they were to succour the weak, bridle the strong, and pay honour, as they fantastically expressed it, by purity of life and courage of conduct, to God and their ladies. But the Garter was a foreign badge; the Golden Fleece was a symbol of his subject and liegeman; the Star had fallen into disrepute from his promiscuous distribution among the favourites of the Crown; and Louis the Eleventh determined on instituting an order of chivalry himself. It was to be select in its membership, limited in its number, generous in its professions, and he fondly hoped the Garter and Fleece would soon sink into insignificance compared to the Order of St. Michael. The first brethren were named from the highest families in France; the remaining great feudatories, who had preserved some relics of their hereditary independence, were fixed upon to wear this mark of the suzerain's friendship. But when they came to read the oaths of admission, they found that the Order of St. Michael was in reality a bond of stronger obligation than the feudal laws had ever enjoined. It was a solemn association for the prevention of disobedience to the sovereign. The members were to swear submission in all things to the chief of the Order; they were to enter into no agreements with each other, or any one else, without the king's consent; they were to submit to such punishment, in case of breach of the rules, as the Order might appoint; and, in short, the brotherhood of noble knights sank, in the degrading treatment of its founder, into a confederation of spies. Armed with this new weapon, the king tried its effect on the Duke of Brittany, who was discontented with many things that had occurred. If he accepted, he would be bound by the statutes; if he refused, it would be an insult to the dignity of the king. The duke temporised, and consulted the Duke of Burgundy. The fiery Charles saw through the design, and swore to defend his neighbour in case of a quarrel with the Crown. Louis, nothing daunted, sent the collar of the Order to Burgundy himself. Burgundy refused it, and Louis's object was gained. He discovered who was bold or strong enough to stand out against him, and the war began. Not openly—it was not yet time to make it a matter of national honour—but the angry subject and hostile king were perfectly aware of each other's designs. Their animosity first broke out in the sides they chose in the great struggle then going on in England, called the Wars of the Roses. Edward of York, representing the direct line of Edward the Third, had taken arms against the feeble and dissolute Henry the Sixth of the Lancastrian house. Margaret of Anjou had mingled in the fray, and embittered it. We know how fortune alternately swayed to the red and the white of the emblematic flowers. Warwick, who is known in our history as the King-maker, had just established Edward the Fourth on the throne, and then failed, when he had quarrelled with the monarch he had set up, in restoring Henry. While preparing an expedition for this purpose in France, he had fitted out privateers, who enriched themselves equally on the English and Flemish traders, and then found refuge in the French harbours. Charles of Burgundy complained; Louis retorted with accusations of his having aided the new King of England in his attacks on the coasts of Normandy, and of having accepted the English Order of the Garter, though he had refused his own St. Michael. He summoned the vassal to appear before his parliament in Paris, and the vassal threw the summoners into prison. Louis saw the game now in his hands. He had put his enemy legally in the wrong, and, moreover, he had all the counsellors, and favourites, and warriors, by whom Charles was surrounded, in his pay. We need not, however, waste much pity on the duke. He was nearly in the same situation with regard to the courtiers and officers of the king. When the armies lay face to face, and famine had almost placed the Burgundians in Louis's hands, Charles sent a flag of truce with a statement and proofs of the infidelity of half the princes and feudatories who commanded the royal troops. Charles of France, now Duke of Guienne, was at the head of the deceivers, and was anxious to gain Charles's good will, in hopes of obtaining the hand of his daughter and heiress, Mary of Burgundy. Battle, with traitors commanding both the armies, would have been madness, and Louis agreed to a truce. Bitterer thoughts than ever, about the pride and falsehood of the nobility, rankled in that ignoble heart. Another incident soon occurred that brought affairs to a crisis. One of his spies, being in the castle of the Count de Foix, saw a mass of torn papers in a corner of his room, which had previously been occupied by a messenger of the Duke of Burgundy. The man gathered up the fragments, saw a name or two that excited his attention, pasted them all together, and was enabled to present to the king a bond of firm alliance, and the signatures of enemies whom he might well have trembled to see united against him,—Edward of England, triumphant at the battle of Barnet, where his enemy Warwick was slain, and now firmly established on the English throne; the Duke of Burgundy, Nicolas of Lorraine, the Duke of Brittany, and, above all, Charles of France, Duke of Guienne. These were all to be on him at once, and, as one of the papers said, were to set so many greyhounds at his heels that he could not know where to fly for safety. Louis, however, was more of the fox than the hare. He doubled on his pursuers, and tempted the Duke of Burgundy with the promise of restoring him some towns on the Somme, and letting him have his full revenge on his former favourite, the Constable St. Pol, who had betrayed him to the king. Charles, on the other hand, was to let Louis do as he chose with the Duke of Brittany and Guienne. The Rev. Abbé of St. Jean de l'Angely, soon after this honourable agreement, gave a supper to the last named of those princes, and his mistress, the Lady of Monsoreau. The Abbé had some famous fruit, and the pair of lovers divided a peach between them. In a few minutes the miserable lady died in torments, and Guienne was writhing in pain. His strength, however, enabled him to resist the effects for some months; but his confessor, as Louis boasted, was in the king's pay, and gave daily bulletins of his penitent's health. "He cannot last a fortnight," Louis wrote to Dammartin, who was commanding his troops in Guienne, "and you will take your measures accordingly." The prince died, as the monk predicted, and Louis's most dangerous enemy was withdrawn. The ostensible murderer, however, was to be punished. He was forcibly carried off by the friends of the deceased, and given into the justice, as it was called, of the Duke of Brittany. But the duke was afraid of bringing matters to an extremity with Louis, who was openly accused as the real instigator of the crime. He kept the culprit in confinement for some time, but before the public trial could be arranged, Louis had managed to be perfectly reconciled with the man who had so valuable a pledge in his hands. The new friends were soon after this astonished with a well-authenticated report of what had happened in the prison where the Abbé who was such a judge of peaches was detained. There was heard every night for some time a great clanking of chains, fearful outcries succeeded, then prodigious storms of wind and claps of thunder. At last, one night when the lightning was very vivid, the noises were redoubled, doors clanked and shrieks resounded, and on the following morning the body of the Abbé was found reduced to cinders, the enemy of mankind himself having first broken his neck. As the deposition of the jailor to this effect was carefully recorded, nobody could have the effrontery to suspect that the king had anything to do with the crime.

Now, then, there was to be war to the knife carried on by the Crown against the nobility. Burgundy was bought off by promises and gifts; England was soothed by concessions.

But within the boundaries of France itself, no limit was put to the vengeance and cruelty of the king. He arrested the Duke of Alençon in full peace, and immured him in a dungeon in Paris. He sent an army into the territories of the Count of Armagnac, and a detachment of it burst into his house, and murdered him in his bed. They also forced his wife, who was pregnant, to drink a mixture which produced immediate death. His brother was thrown into the Bastile, and kept in a cave below the level of the Seine, so that the water penetrated the floor. The wretched prisoner lived for eleven years in this manner, without shoes or proper clothing; and when released at the end of that time, on the accession of Charles the Eighth, was found to have fallen into a state of fatuity. A short cessation in this career of murder and revenge was produced by a new combination against Louis's life and crown. French honour and patriotism had now fallen so low that the princes and great vassals, in order to get revenge upon their oppressor, agreed to assign the crown of France to Edward the Fourth of England. He was to be crowned at Rheims, and already he bestowed rewards upon his adherents as if he were in possession of the kingdom. The treaty united many contending factions with but one object in common, the destruction of him whom all now knew to be their destroyer.

Burgundy and Brittany and St. Pol forgot their animosities and signed the bond. But Louis detected the plot. The old plans were tried and succeeded. Promises scattered the confederates, and they became distrustful of each other. Edward had disembarked in France at the head of an English army. Louis sent for great bags of coined money from Paris, and signed several papers, with the names in blank, bestowing salaries and pensions for distribution among the English Council. He disguised a common lackey as a herald, and sent him to an interview with the invader. The lackey was as clever and subservient as if he had been bred an ambassador, and won over the luxurious king. Louis flattered his ambition and bribed his avarice. He called him "King of

England and France, and Lord of Ireland," contenting himself with the title of "King of the French." He gave him sixty thousand crowns on condition of withdrawing his forces at once, and promised him fifty thousand crowns a year so long as they both lived. Edward was so captivated by the arts and liberality of Louis that he agreed to visit him at Paris. But Louis repented of the invitation he had given, and put him off, for fear he should grow too fond of the most fascinating of towns. "It is better," he said, "the sea should be between us;" and to obtain this object no expense was spared. Gifts were heaped upon the officers, and all the public houses were made free to the retiring army. The English pocketed the money, and marched from pothouse to pothouse with the greatest satisfaction.

At last it was reported to Louis that his invaders were safe home, and he resolved to make use of his victory. The fate of the Constable St. Pol was sealed. Conscious of his approaching doom, he threw himself on the protection of his former friend, the Duke of Burgundy. Charles hated him for his falsehood, but could not reject a suppliant. He told him to take shelter in St. Quentin. Louis, however, was at his heels with twenty thousand men. He fled, and Charles, rash in promise but infirm of purpose, forgot his chivalry, and surrendered him on the threat of hostilities against himself. He was tried for treason at Paris, and condemned to lose his head on the Place de Grève. Thousands of the brave and noble have spilt their blood since that time in the great square that faces the Hôtel de Ville, and allows a last view of the towers of Notre Dame; but this is the first occasion in which a prince, a near ally of the throne—for he had married a sister of the Queen—was exposed to the sword of the headsman for a crime against the Crown. The supremacy of the king's will was now so well established that there was no further use for secret assassination. A public execution struck more awe into the populace, and kept the nobility in more subjection, than a stab in the dark or a poisoned peach. Tristan l'Hermite, almost equally with Louis, was from henceforward the acknowledged Governor of France. But as long as Charles the Téméraire, or Rash, preserved his independent attitude in Burgundy, the discontented had always a refuge from the justice of the king. Fortunately at this time the overweening Burgundian became engaged in controversy with the strong-armed highlanders of Switzerland. They had offended him, by refusing compensation for some injury they had done to one of his adherents. To be resisted by a set of republican shepherds was too much for the knightly pride of the most touchy prince in Christendom. A great army was raised, and poured down upon the town of Granson. The inhabitants were put to the sword or drowned in the Lake of Neuchâtel. All the cantons were irritated at the shameless deed, and rushed to rescue or revenge. Charles met them in a narrow defile at the head of his horsemen, who could not act on such unequal ground. The first rank fell back upon the second, the second carried confusion into the rear. The quick-footed Swiss still pressed on, and at last a complete panic seized the Burgundian host. Charles himself spurred out of the confusion, and galloped as far as his horse could go. Never had the eyes of the mountaineers rested on such wealth and splendour as met them in the tents of the discomfited army—silken curtains, golden vessels, barrels of money, and armour of the finest polish. A jewel was taken by a soldier from the private chest of the duke, sold to a priest for a florin, sold by him for five shillings, and is now considered the greatest ornament of the French crown, and one of the richest stones in Europe. Louis did not know how to proceed in these astonishing circumstances. He had signed a treaty to maintain the peace towards the duke, and yet could not resist showing his approbation of the Swiss. With the Swiss also he had signed a treaty, by which he was bound to give them aid in men and money whenever they were attacked. He compromised the two obligations by abstaining from assaulting the Burgundian, and from sending assistance to the Swiss. He could not fulfil both stipulations, and it was more economical to execute neither. He gave the mountaineers, however, unmistakable evidence of his sympathy in their cause ; and when Charles, in the same year, came forth at the head of another powerful army, Louis encouraged the cantons to resist. The same thing as before occurred, with only the variation of place. Morat was a repetition of Granson. The slaughter of the defeated Burgundians was so great that, till the latter end of last century, a vast monument was still to be seen upon the field of battle, built up of the bones of the slain, and called the Bone-Hill of Morat. The battle of Nancy followed in 1477, and raised the Swiss to the summit of military fame, besides weakening Burgundy so as to render it for ever powerless against France. In the midst of winter, ill-provided, and doubtful of the issue themselves, the hosts of Burgundy moved on, and laid siege to the town of Nancy. Charles was no longer the impetuous warrior he had been. He was broken in spirit, and at times almost mad with disappointment and regret. He had even summoned to command his army an adventurer from Italy, of the name of Campo Basso. Campo Basso was, as might be expected, a correspondent of Louis, and had offered to place Charles in his hands. But Louis played, of course, a double game with the deceiver and his dupe. To show how generous he was, he warned the duke of the insincerity of his general, feeling well assured that his advice would be attributed to dishonourable motives ; and accordingly it was thought a weak invention of the enemy, and Campo Basso was more trusted than before. Again the Swiss battalions, aided by the forces of René of Lorraine, began to appear. In the midst of a great storm, and in a hard frost, Charles resolved to attack them. Campo Basso sent over an offer of his treachery to the gallant mountaineers ; but they despised a traitor, and scorned the disgrace of having such an auxiliary. He therefore retired to the rear of the Burgundian line, to intercept the fugitives, and enrich himself with their ransom. There were few fugitives, however, to ransom ; for as the horses slipped upon the icy plain, the victory was easier than at either Granson or Morat. The earth was heaped with corpses, and among them, after a long search, was found the body of the fiery duke, fixed in the snow, and so disfigured that he was only recognised by a scar on his face and the length of his nails, which he had allowed to grow, as a sign of mourning, ever since his calamities began. Not deserving of a very favourable epithet, this harsh and arrogant potentate closed a life of violeuce with a death of defeat.

But now all men's eyes were turned with earnest expectation to the first move in the great drama of intrigue and policy which his demise was certain to produce. His daughter had been the great card which he had held in his hands for many years. Lady of Hainault and Flanders, and all the Low Countries, she was a bait which none of the princes could resist. Charles had silenced enemies and gathered friends, by a mere hint of the bestowal of Mary's hand. He had played it against the name of king, and promised it to the son of Frederick the Emperor, if that successor of the Roman Cæsars would consent to convert his ducal coronet into a royal crown. The treaties and arrangements, and all the preparations for the betrothal and the creation, would be amusing, if they did not show how low morality and honour had fallen in those days. The Emperor said, "Let the young people marry, and I will name you king." But the duke, who gave no credit, said, "Make me king, and I will give your son my daughter." Neither would trust the other. The Emperor hurried off by stealth from the place of meeting, when he found the duke had summoned an increase to his escort; and Charles, vowing vengeance, and fearful of ridicule, packed up the royal crown he had brought with him beside the sceptre and mantle, and took his way to his states with no higher rank than he came. Other expectations had been equally disappointed, and now, in the year 1477, Mary was an orphan twenty years of age, handsome and well-informed, with a portion in her own right which would make any man she chose a sovereign prince, or double the grandeur of the greatest potentate. When Louis heard of the father's death, his first thought was, of course, to secure the daughter's succession. He knelt to all his saints in gratitude for the defeat of his rival, walked on a pilgrimage of grace to a church in Anjou, and vowed silver bannisters to the tomb of St. Martin of Tours. Having purified his mind by these religious exercises, he sent a peremptory demand for the restoration of the two Burgundies to the Crown, as they lapsed for want of male heirs. Of this there could be no doubt with respect to the duchy, which had been conveyed by John to Philip the Hardy; but the county of the same name was capable of feminine holding; and if Mary had been in a condition to assert her claims, might have refused obedience to the king. Mary, however, was lonely in the midst of all that wealth. She had no disinterested guardian to apply to, and made only a feeble protest when the Parliament of Burgundy, purchased or intimidated, recognised its feudal obligation, and transferred its allegiance to the French crown. Holland, however, and Flanders, and Artois, and large territories in Germany, and the disputed cities on the Somme, belonged to her still. If she had given her hand to some gallant soldier who would have defended her states, she might have aroused the chivalrous feelings of all the gentlemen in Europe on her behalf. But this she did not try, knowing too well, perhaps, that chivalrous feelings were limited to books of fiction. The encumbered heiress wrote in her despair to Louis himself. Louis was her godfather, and she had no other friend. She sent four trusty counsellors to lay her case before him. She begged his protection, and made a confidential request that he would conduct all his correspondence with her through no one but these trusted friends. "You want, of course, to know what I intend to do," said Louis, when he had read the letter on the day of audience; and the four envoys bowed. "I will marry my godchild Mary to my son, the Dauphin. I will rule her states in their joint names, till she is old enough to do homage. I will take possession of the male fief at once, and if any one opposes my decisions, I have forces enough to make my will obeyed." There was no circumlocution here, and the ambassadors were silent with surprise. The Dauphin was a sickly boy of eight years old, and their young mistress, as we have seen, was in the flower of her age. The king, in return for the visit of the Burgundian envoys, sent an envoy of his own. His barber was a quickwitted unprincipled adventurer, of the name of Oliver le Daim. He had come originally from Ghent, and was, of course, master of the Flemish tongue. This was the dignified emissary whom France despatched to the highest princess in Europe. He covered his original baseness with a pinchbeck title, and the barber took his northward way under the name of the Count of Meulan. But the Count of Meulan smelt dreadfully of the shop. He never could get the shaving-basin out of his countrymen's sight; and at his first reception he behaved so unlike a royal ambassador, that he was hissed by the audience, not without allusions to the propriety of throwing him out of the window. He was hustled down stairs, and was glad to slip out of his house and out of the town in the darkness of the night, and make his way back to his employer without having presented his letters of recall. Louis was delighted, for, while these things were going on at Ghent, he had succeeded with the messengers of poor Mary, and did not care if they had hanged the barber-ambassador on a lamp-post in the street. The trusty counsellors, won over by his address and protestations, surrendered Artois to his honourable keeping; and on their return were executed by the States of Flanders, in spite of the prayers and intercession of the princess. The accusation was not for having betrayed their mistress, but for having constituted themselves members of the Council of Four, in whom Mary had told Louis she put all her confidence. She had told nobody else, and declared the innocence of her hapless friends. But Louis, with his usual generosity, had forwarded the letter in which his god-daughter made the fatal avowal, and the discovery was almost fatal to herself. The States were republican in tendency, and resolved to submit as little as possible to the governance of a woman. They tormented her with their advice and wearied her with their reclamations, till she fortunately escaped their further importunities by persuading them to consent to her marriage with Maximilian, the son of the Emperor, the man to whom her father had resolved to give her in return for the title of King. Louis was quieted for a time by the fear of offending the Emperor, but carried on more fiercely than ever his war against feudalism, as represented by the great nobility at home. Burgundy was gone—Artois was his own—Normandy had long been attached to the Crown. Brittany remained, and looked uneasily at the rapid extirpation of his brethren. He intrigued with England ; but Louis intercepted the letters, convicted him by his own handwriting, and forced him to a treaty which rendered him utterly dependent. The duke had seen that a cloud was gathering from the increased religious fervour visible in the king. When a murder or a treachery was on hand, his activity in visiting shrines and vowing church ornaments became remarkable. People trembled when they saw the meanly-drest, slouch-gaited, sallow-faced old man travelling from altar to altar, and sticking his bonnet full of little images of saints, and pouring out flatteries and adulations to the statues of the Virgin. A tale of blood was sure to follow ; and in 1478 the wildest expectations of Paris were surpassed by the horror of one of his executions. There had been no such cold-blooded monster since the days of Tiberius. The Duke of Nemours was representative of the great house of Armagnac, and was married to a princess of Anjou, first cousin of the king. A headstrong, discontented, and ambitious man, he had joined in the League of the Public Good, and in many of the intrigues against the monarch since that time. Louis had taken no notice till he could secure his revenge. But two years before this, he had got him in his power, and kept the unfortunate man in chains. He was now tried for treason, and condemned. This was by no means unexpected. But men's hearts were revolted by the proceedings that ensued. The duke was taken to a wooden scaffold, the planks of which were loosely joined, and below the platform were placed the children of the culprit, three boys and two girls, the eldest twelve. When the axe had done its work, slowly, drop by drop, their father's blood fell upon their heads; and by this dreadful lesson the discontented were everywhere informed that nothing—not even relationship to himself—stood between the king and his revenge. Louis had been praised for the one solitary good act of his reign—his declaration of the unremovability of the judges; but on this occasion he displaced four of the counsellors of parliament, by his own authority, for wishing to moderate the punishment.

His pilgrimages and prayers must have increased in frequency shortly after this, for a tremendous thought had come into his head, and it would require a vast amount of saintly aid to make it tolerable to his subjects. This was no less than the trial for felony and treason of the deceased Duke of Burgundy. A court was called, the culprit was summoned, barristers were appointed to support the accusation; his whole life was inquired into, his faults pointed out, and malicious antiquarians ascended to the actions of his ancestors; and the murder of the Duke of Orleans, in the reign of Charles the Sixth, was urged as an aggravation of his crimes. After so much eloquence and such convincing proofs, the verdict could not be doubtful. The Duke of Burgundy was sure to be found guilty of the crimes laid to his charge, and his estates forfeited to the Crown. Maximilian, the husband of Mary, took the alarm. He begged his father the Emperor to interfere. He was afraid that action would follow the judgment, and tried at least to delay the sentence. The Diet of the States of Germany was about to meet, and might take up the cause of their chiefs. Louis therefore allowed the trial to expire, and had merely the satisfaction of showing that a grand vassal was not safe from his insults and vengeance even after death. Yet the daughter and son-in-law of the insulted potentate could not be expected to remain satisfied under so insolent a proceeding. Maximilian collected his forces, and declared war against the King of France. A battle at Guinegate satisfied neither party, for each in turn was victorious. The Germans remained on the field, but the French had lost fewest men and taken most prisoners. Louis, however, was in the end the greatest gainer by the engagement, for he had acquired the knowledge that cavalry was no match for well-trained footmen. His Swiss auxiliaries were the best portion of his army, and he increased his infantry, and brought it more under his personal control by taking the appointment of the officers into his own hands. Hitherto that patronage had belonged to the dukes or princes who commanded the forces, and bore too great a resemblance to the feudal system of benefit and obligation to find acceptance with the king. In fact, the object of his reign was by this time nearly accomplished. The Crown and the populace had united in compressing the upper class, and despotism received its accomplishment in the establishment of a standing army. Not much to be lamented individually, the great feudatories of France had established still fewer claims to their countrymen's regret at their fall, by the debilitating effects which their divisions and ambition had had on the strength of the kingdom. At first, perhaps, they were useful in forming little settlements of wealth and influence in regions too remote for the central authority to reach. The luxurious courts of Aquitaine or Burgundy civilised the manners and encouraged the arts, and by their tournaments and festivals opened a theatre for the display of feminine influence, which could not be without a humanising effect on the surrounding populations. But when power had disappeared, there was absolute mischief in pretending to keep up the appearance of independence. Instead of rival potentates, they sank into discontented subjects. From a confederation of almost equal authorities, they became an archipelago of insubordinate and disunited princes, exercising the petty tyrannies of local oppressors without the dignity of national requirements, and by their attempt to strengthen themselves against the monarch's domestic supremacy, weakened the power of the country in its relations with foreign states. The misfortune was, that this state of society, necessary and salutary, as a preparation for the future, tried to continue its existence when the time of its disappearance had arrived. Unfortunate also for its memory, is the reflection that its death-wound was not inflicted by the honourable hand of some great-hearted conqueror who respected it at the very moment of striking the inevitable blow, but that it was done to death by weapons which degraded as well as slew. There was no dignity in its closing scene. A wretched pettifogger, without a touch of sentiment or romance, put an end for ever to the fairy realms in which Arthur and his knights were supposed to hold high court. The sword was turned into a white rod or a silver stick, and the descendants of Oliver and Roland walked backward in grand processions, drest in the livery of their master, and quarrelled for precedence in the offices of the court. Nothing but the sound of a historical name remained to distinguish the De Coucis and Montmorencies from the herd of titled and landless adventurers who vied with them in the depth of their obeisances in the antechamber of the king. If any other distinction survived, it was the frequency with which their heads were submitted to the axe of the executioner. A nobility derived from Charlemagne was a sure passport to the scaffold. Louis was even witty on the subject, and when he was going to employ his friend Tristan in his melancholy office, he would write to the intended victim, "Cousin, come and give us your advice; we have need of so wise a head as yours." The need he had of his cousin's wise head was to put it into a basket filled with sawdust. It was seldom, however, that he condescended to be jocular with a noble. To the citizen and servants of his house he was full of quips and quiddities, and there is no doubt that the familiarity of his manners made him popular with the towns. But the towns had other reasons for liking this first of absolute kings, for in his desire to humble the great aristocracy, he conveyed privileges to the cities which placed their office-bearers on a level with the loftiest of the lords. In some instances he bestowed nobility on the members of town-councils, exempting them at the same time from joining the army in the field, being complimentarily held as always engaged in the defence of their own walls. But Louis, in aggrandising the burgesses, only carried out more boldly the policy of his predecessors, who, from an early period, had found a remedy in the franchises of the communities against the aggressions of the nobles. None of his ancestors, however, had bestowed such unremitting attention on the internal administration of the rising towns. Innumerable royal letters still remain regulating their affairs. The dress and decorations of the municipality were arranged with the utmost minuteness, the salaries of the different ranks, and even the wages of the ringers of the great and little bells. These, however, were not merely the noisy summoners of a meeting, but were the outward sign of freedom and independence. When a suzerain attacked a refractory town, the greatest proof of his anger, and the severest punishment he could inflict, was the interdiction of its bells; they were like the colours of an army, and represented the honour of all who served under them. Trade had greatly increased in several places in the midst of national distress, and was encouraged by the sagacious Louis as a surer guarantee against the power of the great vassals, than the written privileges he could bestow on the governing body. He even recommended the lords and ecclesiastics not to keep aloof from the profits of commerce, and gave increased rank and franchises to those who trafficked by sea. But in 1483 his health gave way. Two years before, he had suffered from a stroke of apoplexy, from which he recovered with undiminished intellect, but shaken frame. Every effort was made to retain the fleeting strength. Medicine, and prayers, and offerings were tried; and a holy hermit, when all science seemed to fail, was summoned to his aid; but St. Francis de Paul (that was the hermit's name) could not stop the downward course. He did not even attempt it, though the king fell on his knees to him, and blasphemously said, "If thou wilt, thou canst make me whole." He was more useful in earnest and pious conversation, and perhaps had a momentary effect on the conscience, which seemed seared beyond sensation. The penitent, if such he was, went by painful journeys, and visited his son for the last time; broke forth in a passion of regret into confessions of his crimes and frailties, and went back to Plessis le Tours to die. Yet to the last he cherished hope. A chaplain was praying for the health of his body and soul. "Pray for the health of the body," said Louis; "you should not ask too many things at a time." At last the fatal hour arrived. He had told the attendants not to mention the word *death*, but, when his final agony came on, merely to tell him not to speak. The word was said, and he remembered what it meant. He muttered a few syllables to his "sweet lady and great friend" the Virgin, and expired. If any one had looked out of the window of that sombre room, he would have seen a long narrow avenue, barred across at intervals as if to resist a charge of cavalry; sentinels stationed at each wicket; and along both sides of the approach a ghastly row of gibbets, with the decaying bodies of his enemies depending from the cords. Inside the house he would have seen double-barred doors, and guards again in every passage—a prison more than a palace; and in this gloomy den, for three years, had resided the invisible, inscrutable power, whose word was heard in the farthest parts of the earth, and whose hand pulled the strings by which the policies of many nations were ruled.

This reign has been dwelt on at greater length than is required by any of the others, as it is the turning-point of French and even of European history. The face of affairs between his accession in 1461 and his death in 1483 was entirely changed. A great gulf was dug between the centuries which comprehended the rise of chivalry and the Crusades, and that other and brighter period, which was to comprehend the diffusion of learning and the reformation of the Church. The middle ages, in the course of this one man's lifetime, had passed away, and modern life had begun.

CHAPTER VIII.

CHARLES THE EIGHTH, A. D. 1483, TO THE DEATH OF LOUIS THE TWELFTH, A. D. 1515.

CHARLES the Eighth was now thirteen years of age, feeble in health, and systematically kept ignorant by his father. His life had been spent, not in the joyfulness of childhood or the studies of youth, but in the solitude and restraint of the castle of Amboise. From that old fortress he was never allowed to travel. A prisoner more than a prince, he now found himself on the throne, which Louis appeared to have planted in safety on the humiliation of the nobles, and the submission of the people. But liberty leaves recollections, if no more valuable memorials, of where it once has been; and in the first glow of their delivery from a tyrant whom both parties hated, the aristocracy and the commons met in a parliament at Tours, and proceeded to abrogate some of the oppressions laid on them by the late king. Again the connection between the claims of Rome and national freedom was shown by the first demand made by the citizens and the inferior clergy for the restoration of the Pragmatic, by which the Pope's influence was curtailed. But the bishops opposed the demand, and paid their court to the foreign pontiff by the sacrifice of the franchises of the Church. The nobility also made a claim for the restoration of the right their ancestors had exercised, of defending the frontier against an enemy; and the burgesses agreed in the request, though for a different reason. The nobles saw in the renewal of their military services the only chance of recovering their old preponderance; and the burgesses saw in the dismissal of the foreign mercenaries not only a diminution of the power of the Crown, but an alleviation of their taxes. The taxes, indeed, were nearly intolerable. A review was taken of the state of the country, and the distress was fearful to contemplate. With the exception of some trading towns, and some of the seaports, which had been forced into unnatural prosperity by royal favour, poverty was spread over all the land. The royal assessments were immensely increased since the good old time of Charles the Wise, and the private exactions of the proprietors were increased in the same degree. The numerous days of forced labour for the landlord's benefit,—the supplies in lieu of rent,—the contributions exigible at his will, were bitterly complained of before this, the first national assembly which had been summoned for many years ; for it came out, on closer inquiry, that Louis's policy in degrading the nobles extended no further than to weaken their opposition to himself. He had left them still as untrammelled as ever in their authority over their dependants. He had taken away their dignities, but left them their privileges. They were exempted from public burdens, and only interdicted from public duties.

In the midst, however, of their hopes and complaints they voted a subsidy, but only for two years, and passed a resolution that after that period the assembly should again meet. The king, now fourteen, and therefore nominally of full age, could understand nothing of what was going on. He was rejoicing in his new-gained liberty and unaccustomed power, and devoted himself, when he read at all, to the perusal of the lives of Cæsar and Alexander, and took them for models of his own performances. He determined to be a conqueror, and was only uncertain in what quarter to commence his triumphs. Anne of Beaujeu, his sister, who was married to a brother of the Duke of Bourbon, was a more worthy child of the sagacious Louis than the frivolous boy. She ruled by her influence over her brother, but never showed she ruled. Wise regulations were issued in his name, bold steps taken without apparent hesitation, a firm system established ; and

France very soon felt that a strong hand was at the helm, and anticipated great things from so auspiciously commenced a reign. Some of the discontented lords were brought over by promises of advancement, and some of the towns and communes by promises of relief from their burdens; and though this policy was evidently borrowed from the late king's, it differed from his in so far that the promises were kept. But Anne could not hope to satisfy ambitions which could not be allayed without the sacrifice of herself. Louis of Orleans, nearest to the throne, and three-and-twenty years of age, was displeased at the supremacy of a woman. He had made up his mind to be virtual ruler of France, in expectation of his natural succession to the throne on the death of its sickly tenant. But Anne was on her guard; and Louis, forgetting his duty and patriotism, sought allies, both within and without the realm, to aid him in overturning her power. "Better to reign in a subject province of Germany or England than to be second man in the free and noble kingdom of France," was his motto at that time—how admirably to be exchanged for principles and conduct which gained him the name of Father of his Country, when he came to the throne as Louis the Twelfth, we shall soon see. But in the mean time, more ambitious and unprincipled than his grandfather, the murdered Duke of Orleans, he offered any terms, however humiliating to himself and France, for assistance in his personal schemes. Brittany and Lorraine were discontented vassals; England and Austria were rival powers; and he applied himself to all the four. We saw René of Lorraine triumphant over Charles the Rash at the battle of Nancy. The fame, however, was all he obtained; for Louis the Eleventh availed himself of the extinction of the house of Burgundy to lay firmer hold than ever on the territories of Provence, which René claimed as an appanage of his family. Francis of Brittany was drawing near his death, and was disquieted with thoughts of the future fate of his two daughters, who were his only heirs. Hating the power of France, his great anxiety was to prevent its aggrandisement by the absorption of any portion of his states when his orphans were left undefended. He listened accordingly, well pleased, to any proposition which promised to disturb the repose of his ambitious neighbour. From England little aid was to be expected, for our Richard the Third was on the throne, and the guilt of murder and usurpation weakened his power. Austria could not with any decency take part with Orleans, as Maximilian had engaged his daughter Margaret to Charles the Eighth, and sent her, though only two years old, to go through the ceremony of betrothal, and be educated at the court of her future husband. Maximilian had perhaps another reason for remaining quiet. He was now a widower by the death of Mary of Burgundy, and hoped to make nearly as fortunate a second marriage as his first had been by obtaining the hand of Anne of Brittany, who was at this time fourteen years of age. Anne of Beaujeu proved herself a true daughter of Louis the Eleventh. To keep Richard, who promised assistance to the discontented Orleans, quiet, she gave men and money to Henry of Richmond, who claimed the throne as descendant of the Lancastrian line. In August 1485 the battle of Bosworth placed the crown on Richmond's head, under the name of Henry the Seventh; and Orleans had an enemy instead of a friend on the English throne in his opposition to his native king. Maximilian, unlucky in all things except his marriage, was taken prisoner by the revolted Flemings, and kept in durance vile till he conceded their demands. France was therefore in the ascendant. An army was sent into Brittany under De la Tremouille, and Charles and Anne conducted another into Guienne. Orleans was forced to rise in insurrection at the very time that he must have seen that the movement was useless. Too far advanced in his plans to hope for pardon, and not far enough to succeed, he fought one or two small engagements, and was taken prisoner at St. Aubin de Cormier in 1488, and kept from doing further harm by imprisonment in the tower of Bourges. Francis of Brittany, the rebellious vassal, died, and the calamities he had foreseen fell upon his children. The dukedom was overrun by various nations—Englishmen, Spaniards, and Flemings; and at last, in despair of escaping by any other means from her persecutors and foes, and anxious to secure herself the favour of some person able to protect her, the heiress, Anne, the eldest daughter of the deceased duke, agreed to carry the dowry of Brittany to Maximilian, as Mary of Burgundy had enriched him with Holland and Hainault. In the year 1490 the marriage was celebrated by proxy, and the lucky wooer added one of the great provinces of France to his hereditary States of Austria, and boasted now of territories sufficient to maintain the dignity of King of the Romans, to which he had been elected some time before. He had never seen his bride, and was engaged at the time in a campaign in Hungary. The move paralysed all the players in the game. Henry the Seventh of England was alarmed at the increased strength of Maximilian. Ferdinand of Aragon, who had tried to weaken France by supporting the rebellion in Brittany, in order to recover the ancient possessions of Spain in the south, was equally dissatisfied with the turn affairs had taken. The head of the house of Albret had drawn the sword against France, in hopes of winning the heiress of Brittany for himself, and the alliance, in fact, dissolved in the very moment when Maximilian's triumph was apparently secured. But Maximilian forgot that Anne of Beaujeu was the real governor of France. No state of a game could be too desperate for so skilful and unscrupulous a player. An army was instantly poured into the revolted duchy; a parliament of Bretons summoned by the king to meet at Vannes; Rennes, where the weeping duchess, or Roman queen, resided, was seized; and Charles the Eighth, suzerain of the land, and Most Christian King, presented himself before his vassal on the 15th of November, 1491, and forgot in a moment, by command of his sister of Beaujeu, the little daughter of Maximilian to whom he was betrothed, and the betrothal of Maximilian to the fair young heiress to whom he now paid his obeisance. On the 6th of December he married her with royal solemnity, and on the 10th crowned her at St. Denis Queen of France. Never had a marriage even of a crowned head created such a sensation before. Maximilian lost his wife and the duchy of Brittany, and received back his daughter with nothing but the betrothal ring. Bitter upbraidings followed, of course ; for though neither engagement had gone beyond the ceremony of espousal, the result was considered equal to that of a double divorce. It was also a surprise ; for nobody but Anne of Beaujeu (who was now, by the death of her brother-in-law, Duchess of Bourbon) had imagined such a method of stifling the rebellion of a province and weakening the hands of a rival. The action, however, was successful, though manifestly unjust. France reposed for some time, freed from domestic troubles and foreign attacks.

But France, the moment she grows rich, grows ambitious too. Trade was flourishing, the public burdens were mitigated, the classes were more united ; and when the treasury had begun to fill, Charles, remembering the old connection between his country and Italy, between the house of Anjou and the kingdom of Naples, between the house of Orleans and the duchy of Milan, resolved, in imitation of the heroes of his choice, the Roman and Macedonian conquerors, to acquire a deathless fame by feats of arms. He made preparations for a march across the Alps, and a conquest of the whole of the peninsula. After that, he saw no difficulty in a voyage across the sea at the head of his admiring chivalry, to expel the Turks from Europe, and plant the fleur-de-lis on the walls of Constantinople. Expectations so extravagant had their natural result. We need not pause over the individual events. French impetuosity carried the army and the king, at the first dash, through Tuscany, and on to Rome, and further on to Naples. The separate principalities of that distracted land, where genius seems indigenous and union impossible, were in a high state of prosperity. Combined, they might have resisted this new invasion of the Gauls ; but the curse of envious factions vexed their councils, and one by one they fell. The Pope was besieged in the castle of St. Angelo ; Ferdinand of Naples was dethroned, and Charles made his triumphant entry into the city in February, 1495. On this occasion, as on many others, the famous lines might have been repeated, which say—

> "A king of France, with forty thousand men,
> March'd up a hill, and then march'd down again."

For, now that the gallant invaders were at the summit of their march, their eyes were anxiously directed to the possibility of a return. To march down again, was very soon the great ambition of the forty thousand warriors who had climbed the hill. Ludovic of Milan, who had been the partisan of Charles in his advance, was organising a league to intercept him on his homeward route : England, Aragon, and Austria, were getting ready for the invasion of France ; and Venice had an army of thirty-five thousand men waiting for him in strong positions at the foot of the Apennines. Charles compensated himself with an increase of rank and dignity, for the mournful condition of his affairs. He proclaimed himself Emperor of Constantinople, by donation from Andrew Paleologus, King of Jerusalem and the two Sicilies ; and made another solemn entry, clothed in the emblems of his new dignity. He made a silent exit in eight days after that, and fought his way through many obstacles, conquering in fair fight, although outmarched and outmanœuvred by the native levies ; and finally, after a really decisive victory over the Venetians at Fornova on the Taro, and a disadvantageous treaty with Ludovic of Milan, he led the remains of his forces back to France, and learned in a short time that every one of his Italian acquisitions had fallen from his hand. D'Aubigny, a relation of the Stuarts of Scotland, the general he had left behind, capitulated in Calabria, and with difficulty got home. All that was left to the youthful king from his transalpine journey, was a knowledge of actual war, and an enthusiastic love of the fine arts. He caught a new idea from the rising glories of architecture, sculpture, and painting ; and resolved to make his castle of Amboise a rival to the marvels of Florence and Rome. While engaged in ornamenting this residence, where he had spent his youth, he took the Queen one day to see a racket-court he was building, and hurt his head against a beam in one of the dark passages. Disregarding the accident, he continued his walk ; but, on returning through the same gallery, suddenly fell back in a faint. He was left where he lay, for fear of the effects of moving him in that condition, and died in the course of the same day. A thoughtless, weak, but generous-minded prince, showing the fault of his early education in the eagerness with which he grasped at the pleasures of wealth and ostentation so long denied him, and offering a hope of amelioration, both for himself and his country, at the very moment he was taken away. This was on the 7th of April, 1498, and a very different man came to the throne,

LOUIS THE TWELFTH,

different, fortunately, from Charles the Eighth, but still more fortunately, different from himself. You remember the rebellious, intriguing, discontented Duke of Orleans—the man who was only quelled by the sagacity of Anne of Beaujeu, and who had stooped to the infamy of begging foreign assistance to aid him in his personal designs. He was now in his thirty-seventh year, tall and well made ; his courage had been shown in many fields, for he had been distinguished in the Italian expedition, and displayed the valour of a Paladin, as well as the unselfishness of a hero, in the defence of Novarra. His talents were well known, though hitherto the use he had applied them to was not uniformly good ; and nobody doubted that, if he devoted himself to the duties of his high office, he would raise his country to a station it had never reached before. The misfortune, however, of his previous career was that it had placed him in opposition to many of the very individuals with whom his new position brought him into contact. The faithful advisers and generals, friends of the late king—had all exerted themselves against him, either in council or the battle-field. Though formally recon-

14

ciled to them during the lifetime of his predecessor, they were well aware what secret enmity might coexist with the outward manifestation of a different feeling; and many were conscious of the harshness and injustice of their treatment of the prince. The first movements, therefore, of the dreaded monarch were watched for with anxiety. His speech on taking his royal seat was the key-note of all his future life: "The King of France takes no revenge on the enemies of the Duke of Orleans." From that moment all the past was forgotten. Royalist, Orleanist, noble and burgess, all rallied to the Crown. The efforts of Louis the Eleventh, hateful in their nature and cruel in their execution, in lowering the power of the nobility, now showed their proper fruits. The king was surrounded by nobles who strengthened his throne, and were prevented, by his watchful superintendence, from oppressing the people. The provincial parliaments, in which the local legislation was carried on, and which had a voice even in the national affairs, were further protections to the lower class; and at this period the stage we alluded to in the usual course of nations was reached—the aristocracy had yielded to the Crown, but the Crown was still kept in check by certain institutions which had derived their authority from antiquity, and secured the liberty of all by the privileges of many. The feudal peers, limited in number and selfish in their objects, were guarded, in their high and palmy days, by their union among themselves, and the exclusion of the other orders in the State. Their struggle was against the predominance of the Crown, and in this they had not the sense or generosity to enlist on their side the sympathies of the masses. The kings, even the worst of them, without foreseeing the elevating effects of their proceedings, had attached the multitude to their cause by establishing franchises in the towns; and long after the nobility had sunk into courtiers, and the Church into slavery, the municipalities nourished a love of self-government, and hatred of tyranny, which the woes and struggles of so many intervening years have not altogether extinguished at the present time

But Louis ran a great risk of alienating the affections he had gained, by the next step he took. It was to secure his domestic happiness, and prevent the loss of his authority ; and again, in one of the most extraordinary marriages on record, Anne of Brittany, who had been betrothed to Maximilian, and was now the widow of Charles the Eighth, was a performer. Charles was of small size, and very ungainly figured ; but in both these respects his unhappy sister, Jane, was still more remarkable. Very plain in features, and greatly deformed in shape, she had been forced, two-and-twenty years before this, upon the unwilling Duke of Orleans by the tyranny of her father, Louis the Eleventh. To marry his daughter, and destroy at the same time the happiness of his kinsman, was a gratification of the old man's malice, which he could not forego ; and Jane, timidly acknowledging her deficiencies, but earnestly loving the fair young man who had been given to her as husband, tried to compensate for the want of personal beauty, by the meekness and tenderness of her disposition. A more gentle or uncomplaining sufferer never was the heroine of a romance. The generous heart of Orleans was sometimes touched by these virtues, but though he respected he could not love ; coldness succeeded, and, at length, the forced appearances of affection, exacted of him by his position and the watchful malignity of his father-in-law, degenerated into hatred, and Jane learned the terrible truth that she was an object of disgust and repulsion to the person on whom she had lavished all her heart. Anne of Brittany, the Dowager of France, was under thirty years of age, the widow of a man she could not greatly lament, and was visited in the first hours of her affliction by the new occupant of the throne. The visit was ceremonious, and exacted by the ordinary usage—but it was frequently repeated ; and while the deserted wife was lamenting in solitude the increased grandeur of her husband, which would place a greater barrier between them than before, an understanding was come to between Louis and Anne, that if a dispensation from his marriage with Jane could be obtained, she would again mount the throne she had so lately left, and carry once more the

Duchy of Brittany as an appanage to the Crown of France. There could be no possible difficulty in obtaining a divorce from the Pope who at that time represented Christianity in Rome, for he was the infamous Alexander the Sixth, more famous under the name of Borgia—a man who ostentatiously gloried in crimes and sins, and polluted the recesses of his palace with iniquities of which Tiberius and Nero might have been ashamed. To this monster Louis applied. A favour requested by the Most Christian King was a delightful opportunity in the eyes of the most Christian pope. He sent his son Cæsar Borgia, who had been a cardinal, but was now secularised, after having murdered his brother, the Duke of Gandia, and assumed his name, to convey to the monarch the dispensation he required. Cæsar, however, kept the object of his visit concealed—affected doubts of his father's acquiescence, and exacted as his own reward in the negotiation, a grant of the territories and title of Valentinois. With his title of duke instead of cardinal, however, he did not change his nature, for on hearing that the nuncio at the French court had detected his manœuvres, he caused that functionary to be poisoned, and maintained his influence by the bowl or dagger, as if he had been at Rome. Anne, to conceal her ambition or her love, made stringent covenants in favour of the liberties of her duchy. It was to be ruled in her name, to retain its privileges, to revert to her second son if she had more than one—and Louis promised all. There was always a Pope to deliver him from any embarrassing obligation, which must have been a great satisfaction to all the parties to engagements of which they were likely to grow tired. Jane of France retired to the convent of the Annunciadas, at Bourges, and died in 1505.

Happy man, in love and policy, the husband of Anne and Duke of Brittany began the regulation of his kingdom. He established a fund for the pay of his troops, and made pillage, to which they had been accustomed as one of the privileges of their profession, punishable with death. He gave regular salaries also to the judges of his various courts, and established a competitive examination before they were invested with their rank, to secure a competent knowledge of their profession. Bribery and gifts, from which their incomes were avowedly derived, henceforth ceased to be openly practised. The Pragmatic Sanction was re-established with greater authority than ever, and measures taken to prevent simony, purchase, or intimidation, in the obtaining of church livings. Attempts were also made to remedy the trickery and dishonesty of the lower practitioners of the law ; but at that time—and ever since—in vain. To provide for the increased expense of some of these alterations, he diminished his personal expenditure to the lowest sum. "I would rather," he said, when some of his friends accused him of parsimony,—"I would rather hear the complaints of my courtiers at my meanness, than the sighs of my subjects at my exactions." But when economy was found insufficient, he had recourse to the temporary expedient of selling the offices of his court and parliaments to the highest bidder—a fatal step, which only put off the evil day, for the money paid for the office required interest to make it a good investment, and who was to pay the interest but the body of the people by whom, in the last resort, all the burdens of the State are borne? The immediate supply, however, enabled him to bribe our Henry the Seventh with the payment of his yearly pension of fifty thousand crowns, and to win over his councillors with handsome gifts. He also made an advance, even before it was due, of the stipulated salary to the Swiss Cantons ; and no surer way could be discovered of securing the gratitude and attachment of those brave and mercenary allies. The politicians of that time must have been blinder even than their successors in the present day, if they had not seen the reason of all this bribery and preparation. Italy rose before him, as it has always risen before the eyes of the French, as the promised land. The retreat of Charles the Eighth, and all the calamities of the campaign of 1495 were forgotten ; nothing was remembered but the triumphant march upon Florence, and Rome, and Naples. All the plains of France were soon covered with marching thousands, anxious to renew the glories and avenge the misfortunes of their gallant predecessors. And as a prelude to the final blow, Louis published a declaration of his rights to the two Sicilies, derived from the grant of Joanna long ago, and his individual claim to Milan, as descendant of the unhappy Valentine, whom we remember demanding vengeance for the slaughter of her husband, the handsome Duke of Orleans, in the reign of Charles the Sixth; Valentine was his grandmother, and her transmitted claims had been ratified by the Pope. But what one Pope could ratify another could disallow. Ferdinand of Aragon, the least scrupulous of princes where his interests were concerned, joined in the invasion of Italy, and determined to make good his pretensions to Naples, when his more confiding ally should be elsewhere engaged. French courage and Spanish solidity found no opposition among the Italian States. Frederick of Naples surrendered on terms, trusting to the good faith of D'Aubigny, who commanded the French force, and Ravestein, who commanded the French fleet. He was sent into France, and exchanged his rights to his late kingdom for a pension and honourable treatment. He lived more as a subject than a prisoner, and died at Tours in 1504. Ferdinand, his son, trusted in the same way to the honour and generosity of Gonsalvo of Cordova—the Spanish general who has gained his name in history of the Great Captain—and was sent into Spain, where he was kept in close and rigorous confinement.

The object of the expedition was gained, and the difficult operation of the partition had now to be performed. Ferdinand took the portion assigned him with apparent satisfaction, and Louis was contented with his. But Machiavel, whose book was at this time being composed, might have borrowed a chapter from the policy of the Most Catholic King. Aggressions were made on the French possessions; troops were surreptitiously added to the army of Gonsalvo, and when an infectious disease weakened the French, while their allies, being more accustomed to the climate, escaped comparatively free, the insolence of the Castilian could no longer be borne, and war broke out. D'Aubigny, who had unfortunately been superseded by the incompetent Duke of Nemours, gave all the assistance in his power in a subordinate situation; and Bayard, the last of the knights, distinguished himself on this occasion by the personal courage and heroic attachment to his king, which have given him the name of "the Chevalier without fear and without reproach." Different, however, was the estimate which Ferdinand the Catholic entertained of the duties of a king and gentleman. A success lost half its charm unless it was accompanied with the triumph of being a trick at the same time. With this noble principle in view, he sent his son-in-law, Philip the Handsome—better known as the father of Charles the Fifth—to the unsuspicious Louis at Lyons. A treaty was entered into. Charles, the infant son of the negotiator, was to marry Claude, the infant daughter of the deceived. The two children were to be put in possession of Naples; and what occasion was there for farther quarrel about a property which was to belong to the heirs of the contending parties? Louis was blinded, and despatched immediate orders to abstain from attack, and to send back a portion of his army. Ferdinand, with a chuckle of gratification, commanded Gonsalvo to fall on the unprepared enemy; and in a short time D'Aubigny was defeated at Seminara, and the Duke of Nemours killed at Cerignolles. Gonsalvo entered Naples as its master, and the French interest was destroyed. Philip the Handsome was still in Louis's power. To secure his zeal in the cause, Ferdinand had concealed his intention to deceive; and the ambassador was alarmed when the news of the Italian battles came to Blois. "Don't be afraid," said Louis, reassuring him; "it is better to lose a kingdom which can be taken again, than one's honour which can never be regained." But noble sentiments have their reward only in the admiration of the hearers. The fate of war turned against the French. Their armies perished from want of care—their generals were unskilful—a storm dispersed their fleet; their resources became exhausted; and in 1503 they were reduced so low that they lamented the death of Alexander the Sixth, whose favour they retained to the last by prodigal generosity to his hateful and favourite son. The succeeding Pope died in a few weeks, and there then sat on the papal throne a man of indomitable energy and almost insane ambition, whose whole heart was set on the one design of expelling the barbarians from Italy, and who, to gain this object, would stop at no action however cruel, or deception however base. This was Julius the Second, the most warlike of the Roman pontiffs, who loved battle for its own sake, but in a double degree when it led to the withdrawal of the foreigner. His plottings and intrigues began at once. Spain was in his interest, and Gonsalvo sent the execrable Cæsar Borgia to expiate his crimes by perpetual imprisonment in Castile. An opportunity soon offered, as Julius hoped, to embroil the two powers against whom his wrath was principally directed.

The great idea of the Balance of Power—that is, such a just distribution of force, either by alliance or internal resources, between the different States, that no one shall preponderate over the others—began to be adopted as the policy of Europe. Louis was therefore uneasy when he reflected, that if he executed the covenants of the Treaty of Blois, and gave his daughter Claude to the heir of Ferdinand and Isabella, the power of the Spanish house would be paramount. The young Charles, the grandson of the Spanish monarchs, was already destined to unite under his crown Germany, and Naples, and the Netherlands, and Spain, and the illimitable domains newly discovered in America.. If, in addition to these, he obtained all the female fiefs of France, the counties of Burgundy and Artois, and the duchy of Brittany, besides the Italian rights of his proposed bride to Milan and Genoa, nothing would be left to his successor on the throne of France which could withstand so mighty a confederation. Yet he was bound by the contract; and unluckily the new Pope was more afraid of the Castilian Ferdinand than of him, though he equally hated both, and could be of no use in releasing him from his oaths. He threw himself on his people in this great emergency, and summoned a general parliament at Tours. He explained the state of his affairs, and asked the counsel of the States. They thanked him for his regard for the future interests of the land, and passed a unanimous resolution that the Treaty of Blois should not be executed. They farther humbly requested that, to prevent the possibility of so great a wrong, he would at once marry his daughter to the young Duke of Angoulême, who stood next in succession failing his heirs-male; and sheltering himself under the plea of this national demand, he bestowed the hand of Claude on her youthful cousin, who will take a more prominent part in these pages as Francis the First. It was for this he received, by public acclamation of the States assembled at Plessis les Tours, the glorious title of Father of his People. Meanwhile the mad Pope went furiously through the land, vowing vengeance equally on Frenchman and Spaniard, and anxious to set them at war. The wrongs and disappointment heaped on the young Charles of Austria would stir up his guardians and relatives, he fondly hoped, to revenge. But Ferdinand the widowed King of Spain, and Maximilian the penniless Emperor of Germany, the two grandfathers of the future Emperor, were more jealous of each other than anxious for the abasement of France. Louis also had managed to bribe the old Aragonese to quiescence by giving him his niece, Germane de Foix, a girl of eighteen, to replace the aged Isabella of Castile; and, with excellent judgment, took the opportunity of presenting the beautiful bride with all his rights to the kingdom of Naples by way of a marriage gift. Maximilian could do nothing, as he was in his usual frightful state of impecuniosity; but as he kept a "Book of Insults" in which he entered a list of his enemies, he inserted Louis's name at full length in the reddest possible ink, and locked it up in his drawer till an opportunity of revenge should occur. Julius, disappointed in his expectations of an attack on Louis from foreign powers, was busied in weakening him by other means. Genoa, stirred up by his emissaries, rebelled ; and it required the presence of the king in person to restore it to his authority. But great as was the holy pontiff's wrath against France and Spain for polluting the Italian soil with their degrading presence, he hated the republican freedom and commercial activity of the Venetians more. He entered, therefore, with all his accustomed zeal, into the League of Cambrai, for the destruction of those lordly and ambitious traders. George of Amboise, a cardinal and politician of a different sort from the generality of his brethren, had been the only counsellor of Louis since his accession to the throne. A favourite without being a flatterer, and a churchman without losing his patriotism, king and people trusted equally in his honesty and wisdom. Why he took so prominent a part in this onslaught on the Venetians it is difficult to divine. It was perhaps a sop to the Pope, who expected to recover the portions of St. Peter's patrimony which, he said, the nation of shopkeepers had seized ; perhaps it was a method of uniting on a distant expedition powers whose enmity would be more dangerous at home. The Emperor, the King of Spain, the Governess of the Netherlands, the Pope, and several of the smaller potentates, combined against the carriers of the Adriatic, and swore to drive them back into their lagoons. Louis passed the Alps, and, as a matter of course, spread over the plains of Lombardy. The Venetians, no whit daunted, met him at Agnadello, and kept the victory doubtful for a long time. The issue of the contest at last was the same as it has always been between the Gauls and Italians since the Roman discipline disappeared. The troops of Venice dispersed, and the fortunes of the republic seemed desperate. But the Venetians were Italians ; they spoke the same language as Julius, and acknowledged him the true successor of St. Peter. They also had money in their coffers, and territories which once had appertained to the Church. They sent his holiness some coin, and resigned the lands into his hands. Julius blessed them with apostolic and personal benedictions, and turned his arms against his Transalpine allies. His vengeance, however, was principally directed against the French. He won the Spaniards to his side by giving Ferdinand the investiture of Naples : he won the Swiss infantry from Louis by offering them higher pay. He formally constituted the inhabitants of the mountains the Defenders of the Holy See, and immediately let them loose on their former friends. He sent them against Milan ; and himself, armed cap-à-pied, and vowing vengeance in his heart, led his late enemies the Venetians against the Genoese, who still yielded homage to the stranger. He thundered with his cannon against the citadels of the French as a General commanding-in-chief ; and with excommunications against their leaders and supporters as Father of the Faithful—a bold, bitter-hearted, obstinate old man. Louis replied with the usual weapons, and, in conjunction with Maximilian, called a general council at Pisa, who declared against the Pope, and talked of his deposition and a wide reformation of the Church. Julius was not to be beaten in the matter of councils any more than in war. He summoned a meeting of his adherents at Rome, supported by Henry the Eighth of England and the Spanish King, and fulminated ferocious edicts against the schismatical assemblage at Pisa. War, therefore, went on as before. Gaston de Foix made but a brief appearance in history, but left his mark in it by the brightness of his course. Nephew of Louis, he shared the cool head and determined bravery of that great ruler, but he added a dash and impetuosity which had no equal, except in the first campaign of the great Condé. Of Gaston de Foix, the first campaign was the last. He conquered Italy in as short a time as the marvellous Napoleon, and died in the great victory of Ravenna in 1512. With their triumph clouded by such a loss, the glories of the French arms in Italy came to an end. Driven in on all points, as seems always to be the result of a French invasion of that easily subdued but hardly retained country, Louis saw no safety for France itself but in the discord of his enemies. The English were now added to his foes, and though, fortunately, they were so disgusted with the dishonesty of Ferdinand of Spain that they ceased to-coperate in his plans, their name was still given to the coalition which was rising against him between Maximilian and the new Pope, Leo the Tenth. The Battle of the Spurs, as it is called from the rapid retreat of French cavalry at Guinegate, near Calais, gave Henry the Eighth the additional excitement of military fame, but no results followed this first essay, and in the following year Louis, surrendering the point of honour, and only reserving his care for the happiness of his people, signed a treaty at Orleans, on what were thought disadvantageous terms ; and the realm breathed awhile from its exertions. What were those exertions worth ? What fruit had they produced? The useless and ambitious marches beyond the Alps are the only blemishes on the kingly wisdom and patriotic sentiments of this father of his people. In his domestic proceedings he was mild, economic, and benevolent, almost to a fault ; but the blare of trumpets and fluttering of flags he was unable to resist. The years he wasted in attempts to conquer Italy would have sufficed to establish France in wealth and liberty. And now at the end of his days, humiliated in his dreams of glory, but active as ever in his designs of improvement, a private grief was added to his official sufferings, for Anne of Brittany died. In his characters of husband and father, he shone equally as in those of king and warrior. It may even be doubted whether the purity of his court and simplicity of his manners were not of more effect in raising him in public estimation than his policy and battles. With Anne disappeared the modest dignity of his establishment, and he retired too much from public life. With the marriage of his daughter Claude to the Duke of Angoulême, his cousin and nearest heir, his circle was still farther narrowed. It was therefore with surprise, not unmixed, perhaps, with ridicule, that the nation heard in October of the same year that its worn-out and mourning sovereign had given his hand to a girl of sixteen, the gay and frivolous sister of our Henry the Eighth, and that he was affecting all the life and joyousness befitting a happy bridegroom's place. Tournaments in the morning, balls at night, councils, banquets, masquerades,—all these came upon the prematurely old man of fifty-three, after a long experience of a very different mode of life. In his old queen's time he had risen at an early hour, met his council, ridden out for exercise, dined in quiet, and gone to bed at nine o'clock. Nine o'clock was now the commencement of the day. Mary of England was unhappy unless she could drown the remembrance of her own regret, for being sacrificed to a political union, in gorgeous festivities and dances till early dawn. Louis sat up, feasted and danced till the hypocrisy of enjoyment fell from him at once, and on the 1st of January, 1515, three months after his wedding, he died. France paid noble tribute to the merits of its excellent king. There was not a hall or a cottage, or even a monastery, where his name was not reverenced as the lover of his country and defender of its rights. The enthusiastic cry of the assembly of Tours was ratified by the calm judgment of his contemporaries, and in spite of the faults of his youth and the unwise enterprises of his maturer years, his real intentions were always perceived to be so honourable and so good, that he was pronounced once more, without a dissentient voice, the Father of his People.

Who were that people, and what had they become, since we took our last survey, and found them rising by slow degrees from their state of ignorance, oppression, and almost hopelessness, under the weight of an unsympathising church and trampling aristocracy? Two hundred and forty-five years had passed since the death of St. Louis, at which we last paused, and things had greatly changed. Many abuses still remained, and many wrongs to be complained of; but the improvement consisted in this, that the abuses were recognised as such, and there were modes of appeal against the wrong. The rights of all classes were more clearly ascertained than in the times of the strong hand and obstinate will. The people, indeed, properly so called, had no separate or recognised existence in the State. The States-General, in which they were supposed to be represented, were rarely summoned, and the delegates of the Tiers Etat were chosen principally by the townsmen, and were outvoted by the other orders. But the gain to the commonalty was very great in the mere diminution of the aristocratic power. Legalism had done its work, and tied up the sword of the nobility. It had filled the country districts with representatives of the Crown who laid no claim to antiquity of birth, but who, in course of time, became elevated by their merits, or eloquence in the local parliaments, into a species of nobility of the robe, which held equal rank in the discussion of provincial affairs with the proudest of the neighbouring lords. Sickened with their inferiority in legislative or judicial ability, the relics of Creçy and Poictiers and Agincourt sank into a body without duties, who derived all their eminence in the realm from the favour of the sovereign. Yet, with a fond clinging to the forms of the past after its realities had passed away, they retained some of the shows of their former supremacy, which might be irritating, indeed, to their neighbours, but could add nothing to their dignity or importance. They still held their courts; but they were more like our courts-baron for the settlement of dues and quit-rents than for the decision of causes. The castles were themselves made to give outward demonstration of their fallen grandeur; the towers and battlements which the symbolising spirit of chivalry had limited to the magnates with the right of holding courts of justice, with power over life and limb, were taken down by royal order. An unbartisaned wall meant a dependent owner, as a town deprived of its bells was considered disfranchised. It was only by special favour that a few of the representatives of the Great Vassals were allowed in their residences to retain those emblems of independent authority. But the ordinary nobility clung to whatever fragments of ancient superiority the law or custom left them. A list of those fantastic privileges would be ridiculous, if we did not see how they increased in after times the dislike between the classes. Some proprietors, for instance, in remembrance of the old days of their predecessors' powers, ornamented their lawns, with more vanity than taste, with two gibbets—one in emblem of their civil, and the other of their criminal jurisdiction. They clung also pertinaciously in theory to the right they had possessed of putting their wives to death, when they had offended them past forgiveness, with the edge of the sword ; whereas, the vulgar townsman, under the same provocation, was limited to his fist as his instrument of castigation, and took the chance of having his face scratched or his hair pulled in return. Empty boasts and foolish pretensions of this kind may seem no very considerable element in the consideration of a national position ; but at that time, and for many years afterwards, the consciousness of present weakness and personal uselessness on the part of the gentry of the land led them to the most offensive reminiscences of their former supremacy, and to an open contempt for the Roturier or unennobled families, for which a mere exemption from the legalised oppressions of the nobility was an inadequate compensation. An aristocracy which is deserving of national gratitude for its activity and patriotism, is uniformly respectful of the feelings no less than the rights of the other classes.

But, surer guard against either insults or oppressions, by the diminution of the nobles' power, and the jurisdiction of local parliaments, and the freedom of powerful cities, was the great invention which put new armour into the hands of the middle class, and enabled a knowledge of rights and duties to be universally diffused. In 1455 the first printed book appeared in France. Guttenberg and Faust had perfected the wondrous art ; and from thenceforward men's thoughts were stamped in imperishable material, and found their way into all corners of the land. Before this time the tedious process of transcribing with the pen was the only means of multiplying copies of a work. Froissart, himself the prose poet of expiring knighthood, and the most interesting of all the authors of his time—and Alain Chartier, the first of French versifiers—and others who charmed wherever they were heard, were only known in the halls of the nobility by being read aloud, and then the volume was locked up as something too precious to be exposed. Books were of enormous price, for a lifetime was bestowed upon their transcription. But with the first turn of the Press, the poor man, or at least the comfortable shopkeeper, was placed on a level with the highest. He read the volumes upon volumes which the first impulse of publicity poured out ; and now the chronicler, the dramatist, the poet, the preacher, all found that their audience was immeasurably increased. The town halls began to possess libraries, which were hitherto limited to the richest monasteries and the palaces of kings. Charles the Fifth, who was devoted to the improvement of his people, possessed only nine hundred volumes in 1380 after the accumulating labours of his life. Now, in the first forty years of Guttenberg's invention, there were thousands of separate works poured forth upon the world. The Bible, first in place as in honour, led the way. The authors of ancient Rome and modern Italy, the theologians of Spain, and the "Tale of Troy" in England, with Chancer the foremost of our poets—these felt the new impulse, and not only spread a reverence for the past, but awakened the ambition of living men. There was now a wider theatre for glory—a stronger court of appeal than had ever been known before. Where power was insufficient to repel an injustice, there was the frightful punishment, to be dreaded by the wrongdoer, of a satirical attack which would fly from town to town on sheets of printed paper ; and where the love of right was not powerful enough to make a great man just, the Press was at hand to stir him to good actions by the hope of praise. The age of patrons began when the scholar's pen was found an instrument of weight. In former ages he would have been flogged and imprisoned for his importunity; he was now caressed as the arbiter of taste and giver or withholder of fame.

A new language and literature had risen from the grave at the very time that men's minds were thus prepared to give it a noble welcome. Constantinople, in 1458, was taken by the Turks, a set of irreclaimable barbarians who are allowed to defile the finest situation for a capital in the world, by the fear of the advantage which might be taken of it by a power which could grow with the growth of wisdom and strengthen with the strength of experience; and great colonies of scholars and philosophers, entertaining the thoughts, and understanding, if not speaking, the language of Plato and Aristotle, settled in all parts of the West. Greek became a study among all the curious and intelligent. The narrow circle of Roman learning and European infant literature, was widened so as to give a full view of the vanished past and embrace the prospect of a hopeful future. But the effects of this importation were not permanent on the mind of the recipients of the newly reacquired ideas. The word had been given, "Forward!" and not the magic of Homer or sweetness of Plato could hinder the great march. It was like the recovery of some vast treasure hid for a long time at the bottom of the sea ; it added to the essential wealth, but was not admitted into the currency. The metal was solid, but the impress put it out of date, and fitted it to be heaped up in college halls, to be played with as valuable counters, or shown as specimens of a vanished coinage. There were riches enough of its own discovery to satisfy the ambition of the time. In Italy, rising as if by enchantment, the Fine Arts awakened after a sleep of a thousand years. Architecture reached its proudest moment at the end of this period, when St. Peter's began to rise from the ground, and the great works of Perugino, Leonardo, and Raphael, showed painting in the palmiest state it has ever attained ; elevated above the mere reproduction of colour and outline by ennobling its subjects with sentiment and imagination, and exchanging the trivial accuracy of detail for the noble concentration of the whole on the grand ideal conveyed by the story delineated. Everywhere rivals and disciples of those illustrious men enriched chapels and galleries with their fresh creations. Michael Angelo and his pupils designed temples worthy of such transcendant ornaments ; and the heart was in danger of forgetting the object for which Christian churches were erected, in what might have seemed a restoration of the old classic paganism, where

Art was itself a religion, and admiration of the beautiful a duty and worship.

But the impulse thus given was not limited to Florence and Rome. The public mind was everywhere alive, so many things had occurred in a short time. France had actually become one undivided realm; there was one people and one king. Printing had stirred the most sluggish imagination with anticipation of what was to come; the rise of Greek studies elevated the dullest with remembrances of what had been. Uniting these two—opening out a page in a mysterious history of the ages which had been passed in darkness, and of the coming times in which their course would be performed in the light of day—the vast countries of America had burst upon the knowledge of Europe in 1492, and filled the hearts of thoughtful men with a wonder not unmixed with awe. France, always the liveliest of European nations, grudged to the sombre Spaniard the mastery of these strange realms, to which its own brilliancy would have been more adapted, and blamed its king for rejecting the offer of Columbus, which would have opened such a field for its enterprise and genius. But it was on this account more watchful of the proceedings of its successful neighbour, and when Francis the First came to the throne, the patriotism which bound it to its native king was heightened by fear of the preponderating forces of a rival monarchy, on which already, it was boasted, the sun never set. The French had tasted so much liberty, under the benevolent Louis the Twelfth, that they were prepared to guard the blessings they had obtained against the assaults of so ambitious a potentate as now threatened them on every side; and the great feature of the coming time is submission to the Crown and jealousy of Spain.

CHAPTER IX.

FRANCIS THE FIRST,—A.D. 1515 TO A.D. 1547.

WHEN Louis the Twelfth was dying, his thoughts travelled from the past to the future. He said, "I have done all for the best, but that big boy—*gros garçon*—d'Angoulême, will spoil all." A self-willed, brave-hearted, luxurious, and unprincipled youth of twenty-one at the time of his accession, Francis the First seemed only too likely to justify his predecessor's prophecy. Instead of the policy of emulation and improvement by the encouragement of self-reliance and mutual confidence which had earned Louis the noblest title known in history, he inaugurated a system of concentration of all the powers of the State in his own person, from which in the succeeding reigns many calamities proceeded. Despotism could not exist in the time of feudalism, on account of the resistance of the nobility. It could not finally establish itself on the overthrow of the great vassals, on account of the franchises of the towns, and the number of independent courts and councils. It was the aim of Francis, the lover of the arts and encourager of literature, the friend of learned men and pupil of Bayard, to combine the hero and the statesman—to rule in all the departments of the nation, not for the avowed or even unacknowledged purpose of curtailing its liberties, but simply from the conviction he entertained that he was the wisest man in France, the most honest of her statesmen, and the most patriotic of her soldiers. By dint of some years' perseverance in this persuasion, he succeeded in impressing it upon the belief of all his subjects. It was, therefore, in this reign that the germs of the faith which afterwards grew into the avowed identity of the King and the State, began to flourish. Patriotism limited itself to loyalty to the king. The will of the monarch became law without the sanction of a parliament. Counsellors who used to direct the public acts of Louis the Twelfth, were mere clerks to register the decrees of his successor ; and at the very time when the mind of Europe had finally thrown off the turbulent supremacy of armed barons, and was about to shake off the more incumbering chains of the Church of Rome, the peerage, and the bar, and the people of France, put themselves willingly into the tutelage of a single power, gallant and generous in this individual instance, but leading to deep sufferings and tremendous catastrophes in future years. The trustful suicides of the days of Francis the First were the primary origin of the regicides of the Great Revolution. Liberties surrendered so lightly had to be reclaimed with terrible throes.

The first step by which he showed his wisdom, was to repeat the only great failure in the reign of Louis the Twelfth. He marched across the Alps, showed great personal valour at the showy battle of Marignano, and made himself master of the Milanese. Establishing a viceroy in his new acquisitions, he returned to enjoy the adulation of Paris, and give proofs of his superiority in other directions. It is a curious evidence of the high position held by the Doge and Senate of Venice, that the Most Christian King, the conqueror of upper Italy, considered it one of the highest compliments he could receive, when the Seigneury of the commercial city in the Adriatic constituted him and his descendants "Noble Venetians." In the course of this campaign he had an interview with the Pope, and his next move in the aggrandisement of his authority was the old one we have seen so often made by his predecessors—a sacrifice of the liberties of the Gallican Church. The Pragmatic Sanction had never virtually been repealed ; the aggressions of Rome were always fully met both by king and clergy. But Francis saw that a national establishment would add immense weight to the national cause, unless controlled by a power in his own interest ; and a concordat, the sure pillar of tyranny, placed the Church helplessly at the feet of Leo the Tenth. Great opposition was made to this capitulation, by parliaments and people ; but the feeling of loyalty and implicit obedience was already strong, and the submission was at last made. The rescripts henceforth ran in the avowed style of despotic power, "For such is our good pleasure." Two years after the victory of Marignano the Emperor Maximilian died. The chief kings at this time in Europe, you are to remember, were all young and vigorous men. Henry the Eighth of England, manly and open in manner, excellent handler of the quarter-staff, and champion of the tournay ring, was twenty-eight ; Francis of France, handsome as an Apollo, and strong as a Hercules, was twenty-five ; and Charles of Spain, small in stature, plain in feature, and very reserved in disposition, was nineteen. The place of Emperor was the highest dignity in Europe. It entailed great trouble, and as it was endowed with only a formal sort of authority, such as is vested in the president of a council of equals, it needed the support of some external influence to contain within any moderate bounds the unruly feudal nobility which still flourished undisturbed in the different states of Germany. But the name of the Empire set the three young potentates on fire. Our blustering Henry was soon disposed of as more unmistakably a foreigner than either a Frenchman or Spaniard. The other two entered into active opposition. Both bribed, —Francis with lavish generosity, but the cautious Charles with more judgment. He gave his doubloons to the right men, and won the prize. The Electors assembled at Frankfort pronounced their award, and Francis prepared to punish his rival for his success. Whenever these three rulers appear, we see their characters come out as if the creations of a skilful dramatist : Henry, arrogant and ostentatious, good-natured, and easily led by flattery and admiration ; Francis of a higher class of mind, but covering his worst qualities under an affectation of generosity and chivalrous sense of honour ; and Charles, self-contained, firm-willed, false, and cold-blooded. Constantly the victor over his competitors, we turn with a kindlier personal feeling to the bluff murderer of his wives, and the knightly trampler on his people, than to the sagacious, scheming, half-Fleming, half-Spaniard, with the grasping acquisitiveness of the one, and the proud fanatical unforgiveness of the other. An old head upon young shoulders—often used as a phrase of commendation—is the most disgusting sight in the world. And this man's head was as old and his heart as callous at twenty as at fifty-seven. The difference between Francis and Charles was shown in their respective treatment of Henry the Eighth. Francis vied with him in the gorgeousness of his appearance at the famous Field of the Cloth-of-Gold, where the monarchs met, and displayed the wealth and folly of their retainers, and hampered their future proceedings by the extravagance of equipage and dress. The two kings feasted, and laughed, and even wrestled together; but nothing resulted from their meeting but the bankruptcy of half their courtiers, and the waste of a vast quantity of silk and feathers. Charles sailed quietly over from Gravelines to Dover; talked long and solemnly with the English sovereign, and gave Cardinal Wolsey—in strict confidence—a promise of his interest at the next election for Pope. This was better than wasting a realm's income in wine and fine clothes; and accordingly Wolsey, who was all-powerful with his master, turned his influence in favour of the sedate young man who looked so modest but soared so high, and had the good taste to think him a fitting occupant of St. Peter's chair.

That chair, unluckily for Charles, became vacant too soon. Leo the Tenth, having achieved his victory over the Gallican Church by the concordat of 1517, showed no great gratitude to his benefactor. He sided against the French; and when Francis sent Lautrec into Italy to defend the Milanese, and that unfortunate general, thwarted by enemies at home, and hated by the Italians for his pride and insolence, was driven back over the Alps, Leo was so enraptured by the news of the French humiliation that he died of the unexpected joy, and Wolsey looked across towards the judicious Emperor in momentary expectation of a summons to Rome. Adrian the

Sixth, an old Dutchman, who had been Charles's tutor in the Netherlands, was installed in the Vatican, and Wolsey transferred his affections to Francis. Yet, for a while, his favourite derived no benefit from the change. Henry the Eighth was tempted by offers which Francis himself could not equal, for treachery had got into the court and family of the French King, and Henry was ready to profit by the crime. The identity which Francis had even now established between his royal person and the land he governed, made a quarrel with himself equivalent to hostility to France. To be disloyal was to be unpatriotic. The Constable de Bourbon was a near kinsman of the Crown, and had the misfortune to offend the King's mother, by refusing her advances when he was left a widower in 1521. Repulsed in her love, she made him feel the bitterness of her hatred, and brought claims before the tribunals which crippled him of the possessions conveyed to him by his wife. The chancellor sided with the offended widow, and the parliament decided in her favour. Bourbon, discontented with the king's judges, hated the king. He entered into correspondence with the enemies of France, because he could not see the distinction between the land and its ruler. A treaty of spoliation and partition was signed. England was to have the northern counties, and Spain the provinces in the south. Between them, Bourbon himself, a popular king, was to supplant the unjust Francis, and show what a potent enemy could be made out of a discontented friend. He left the court in disgust, after a hypocritical interview with the king, traversed the whole of the country from Moulins to the Alps, and at last found a safe asylum at St. Claude, on the Jura, in the territories of Charles the Fifth. There he openly renounced his allegiance, and turned his dishonoured sword against his countrymen. The Admiral Bounivet, hot upon the heels of Bourbon, hurriedly laid siege to Milan, and hoped to reduce it to obedience to the king. But everything went unfavourable for the French. Milan was relieved, and Bounivet crossed the Ticino in retreat. After him came Bourbon, burning with personal animosity, at the head of the Italians and Spaniards. We have already named the Chevalier Bayard, and seen how, in spite of his want of interest and his slow advancement, his glory had become a boast of the whole of France. Francis had honoured himself by receiving knighthood from the sword of a man who held no higher rank than that of Captain in his military array ; but on this occasion, when danger had opened the way for merit, the dukes and marquesses were passed over; Bounivet, wounded at the bridge, gave his general's baton to the plain chevalier, and for a moment the command was in fittest keeping. But an arquebus ball crushed his side, and he was carried from the field. Past him poured the pursuing enemy, and among them Bourbon the traitor. All the good qualities of that misled but generous nature, were called forth by the piteous sight. He pulled up his horse and said, how much he grieved to see the condition of his friend. "Grieve not for me, sir," said Bayard, "I die like an honest man. But blush for yourself. You are a Frenchman and a prince, and yet you carry on your shoulder the livery of Spain, and your armour is dashed with the blood of your countrymen." Bourbon was silent, and passed on. Bayard confessed himself to one of his attendants, as there was no priest to be found, and said his last prayer with his eye fixed on the cross formed by the hilt of his sword. The descendant of Amadis de Gaul died of a musket bullet, to show that chivalry was out of date.

Chivalry, happiness, and self-respect, were all out of date in the heart of the wretched Bourbon. He pushed his forces into France, and found that he was deserted and despised by the adherents whom he had expected to follow his example. Forced to lay siege to Marseilles by the express command of his new master, it must have been some consolation to him to see the Spanish squadron defeated by Andrew Doria, who commanded the fleet of France. He retreated across the Alps, and led the fragments of his gallant army, in pitiable condition, to Genoa. Francis determined to follow his enemy to his lair ; and again there streamed towards the Alps, an array of armed men, which seemed to have sprung from the ground at the mere announcement of an Italian campaign. It was more like a continuation of the Field of the Cloth of Gold than an ordinary army : all the princes superbly armed, and surrounded by their personal attendants ; the marshals of France, the great nobles, down to the simple barons, all vying with each other in brilliancy of appointments and beauty of their horses. These alone formed a powerful cavalry. There were thirty-thousand foot-soldiers, the best in Europe, and a field artillery worthy of the other arrangements of the march. The magnificence of the army was its ruin. Francis burned to distinguish his courage, which nobody doubted, and despised the delays of generalship, which would have secured him an easy triumph. From Milan, which opened its gates without resistance, he despatched a strong force towards the kingdom of Naples, on which he already meditated an attack ; and as an occupation in the mean time, laid siege to the strong city of Pavia. Bourbon had not been idle. He had raised new levies in Germany, and obtained a loan of money in Savoy. Lannoy, the Neapolitan Viceroy, and Pescara, the Spanish commander, had also increased their troops. "Wait but a short time," said Chabannes and Montmorency, and the other experienced leaders of the French : "rest quietly upon your arms, and these discordant elements will dissolve." "What ! interrupt the siege," replied Francis, "and withdraw at the threat of a traitor like Bourbon ? No ! I will fight." He drew up his army in a plain, and the Imperialists saw a chance for escaping from their position, which had, in fact, become untenable. What valour could do was done. The French rushed on with their national impetuosity, and were mown down by the well directed artillery of the enemy, and the distant fire of the musketeers. Confusion at last fell upon them. Chabannes was taken prisoner, and d'Alençon, the next in rank, withdrew. Francis fought as if the sword of Bayard were in his hand. But crowds kept pouring on. He was gradually hemmed closer and closer, and some of the devoted band who combated at his side, advised him to surrender to the Constable. "Better die," cried Francis, "than yield to a traitor. Call Lannoy." The viceroy of Naples dismounted and received his royal prisoner's sword upon his knee.

Such a disastrous day had not gloomed upon France since Agincourt. Knights and nobles encumbered the plain. The captives were of great value, and every house in the country had to lament a member slain or in durance. Francis wrote to his mother, whom he had left as regent: "Madam, all is lost except our honour." But honour, as Falstaff says, could neither set a leg nor compensate for so ruinous a blow. The honour he prized was the paltry reputation of not being afraid. No Frenchman is when there is any witness to admire his bravery. But the calm young man at Madrid had a different estimate of honour. He had his rival brought into Spain, and kept him in severe confinement. He had the soul of a pawnbroker, and resolved to make the most of his pledge. A new advantage promised itself when the sister of Francis, the fair and fascinating Margaret of Alençon, hurried to Madrid to console her imprisoned brother. Her safe-conduct was only for three months, and Charles consulted his almanac to see the exact day of its expiry. In the mean time Margaret exerted all her powers. The Spanish nobles were won over by so graceful and fascinating a pleader; Charles himself appeared to yield, and Margaret might have been deceived. But as time went on, preparations were made for her arrest, and emissaries were reported to be gathering between her and the borders. Warned of these proceedings, the duchess hurried from Madrid, and put the Bidassoa between her and the magnanimous Emperor, on the very day her safe-conduct came to an end. Charles was now at the summit of his ambition. He had Italy at his feet, and his enemy in his hands. But a premature assurance of success was the rock on which he split. He neglected his instruments now that the work was done: he offended Henry the Eighth by his silence, and Wolsey by the coldness of his letters; the Pope was afraid of so powerful a neighbour; Pescara was disgusted with so ungrateful a master; Bourbon was disappointed at the breach of his engagements. Nobody continued heartily in the cause of a man who was so evidently "concentred all in self." Francis looked out of his dismal window, and thought how brightly the sun was shining at Fontainebleau, and how beautiful the woods upon the Loire. Charles worked upon his regrets and hopes. A paper was brought in for him to sign, and the captive would have signed anything for a breath of native air and the familiar sound of his native tongue. He agreed to resign his claims on Italy—to surrender Burgundy to the Emperor—to give him up towns and counties, and relieve him from homage, and marry his sister, and pay his debts, and do anything he required. Among other things, he bound himself to obtain the sanction for these surrenders from the courts and parliaments, and the chief municipalities of the realm. A strange pit, this last article, into which the despotic Charles fell, and the last help bestowed upon the Crown of France by the liberties of the towns and burghs; for who could expect that such shameless extortions would be ratified by the basest of burgesses, or enregistered in the records of any assemblage where Frenchmen were convened? The signature was made; the hostages, the two sons of Francis, were given up; a horse was waiting, saddled and bridled, on the opposite shore of the boundary river, and Francis, raising his hat, and sinking the rowels into the flanks, galloped and galloped, without rest or pause, till he reached St. Jean de Luz. Dreading still an ambush of the Spaniards, and hating more and more the sombre dungeon he had inhabited, he pushed on, till at last he breathed in safety and happiness within the stout walls of Bayonne. There he felt he was a gentleman and king once more. He showed he was a scholar too, and talked a good deal about Regulus, the Roman general, who had returned to his chains among the Carthagenians when he found the conditions of his deliverance could not be fulfilled. He showed himself a good Catholic also, and made terms with the Pope—very advantageous terms for that astute old man. Henry of England came over to his side ; for Wolsey was more incensed against the Emperor than ever by a new disappointment in his hopes of the tiara. All the little princelets of Italy joined his cause, in dread of the Spanish power ; and in a few months the emancipated captive was able to show the envoy who was sent from Madrid to remind him of the treaty, not only a flat refusal from every one of the courts and municipalities of France to dismember the kingdom of a yard of ground, but an alliance sworn and sealed between the different powers named above, which would enable him, if he chose to join it, to deliver his hostage children by force, and drive the Imperialists out of Italy. This league was under high auspices. Henry the Eighth was its protector, and the Pope was its head. It was therefore called the Holy League ; but, like all holy things in those days, it was not treated with the reverence its name seemed to demand. Bourbon, the renegade Frenchman, still in the service of the Emperor, showed himself a recreant son of the Church. Having a corps of Germans and other people who had imbibed the religious faith of Luther, and entertained a prodigious idea of the wealth of the luxurious clergy, he appealed to their new-found Protestantism and long established-poverty, by promising them the overthrow of the Pontiff's authority, and the sack of Rome. The Old Testament furnished those Bible students with their models for the treatment of the Idolaters, as the New had given them arguments against the riches of the priests. In a mingled fury of fanaticism and avarice, they forced the walls of the Eternal City, though Bourbon himself was killed at the first discharge, and all the horrors of religious hatred, and desire of gold, and the unbridled license of a dissolute soldiery, were let loose upon the town. Clement, the pope, fled to the castle of St. Angelo, and for several months heard the cries of his tortured subjects. At the end of that time he surrendered himself prisoner to the Spanish commander. Charles heard of his success in Madrid, and immediately set on foot processions of weeping monks, to bewail the calamities of the holy city, and to recite prayers for the deliverance of the father of the faithful. He also afflicted himself, and fasted on the same melancholy occasion, but wrote to his general to keep the Pope in sure custody, and to extort from his holiness the towns of Piacenza and Placencia, and to place a Spanish garrison in the castle of St. Angelo itself. His prayers were less successful than his secular instructions, and for a while the hypocritical deceiver rejoiced in his duplicity. But deliverance came from another hand. Lautrec, the French general, appeared before Rome, and the Pope was given over to him by the satiated occupants of his capital. They retired from the States of the Church, and left the field open for the enemy. Lautrec wreaked a useless vengeance on Pavia as the scene of the discomfiture of his master, and laid siege to Naples itself. There the usual result occurred—success in actual war, followed by defeat and calamity, caused by the hatred of the people. The besiegers' supplies were cut off, the heat became oppressive, Lautrec died, and the army was decimated by pestilence and want. One campaign in Italy is so like another, that it would serve to describe them all if we said the French burst triumphantly on the land, and after a short time were expelled with half their number. The episode of Bourbon's desertion and the sack of Rome are the distinguishing features of this particular war, and after those events the interest, even at that time, gradually diminished.

Francis, after many alternations of fortune, agreed to a peace at Cambrai, called the "Ladies' Peace," because it was negotiated by the sisters of the contending potentates, Margaret of Austria and Margaret of Angoulême—one, governess of the Netherlands—the other, regent of France in the absence of the king. The hostage-princes were to be restored on payment of two million crowns; but in other respects so many compromises were made on each side, that things were brought as nearly as possible to the condition they were in before the war began. Italy was surrendered by the French king, and Eleanor of Portugal, the sister of the Emperor, bestowed on him in return. These terms were proposed years before; and all the blood and suffering of the fairest portions of Europe might have been saved, if two guilty and ambitious monarchs had accepted them in peace. A discontented and troublesome conquest like Milan, which Francis was compelled to surrender, was not a more desirable acquisition than the middle-aged widow with whom he was forced to content himself. But family interests played a greater part in the policy of the world at that time than they are allowed to do now. This peace of 1529, which re-established the Pope, and gave the Milanese to the Sforzas, and confirmed Florence to the Medicis, was owing in a great measure to a marriage and a divorce. Charles the Fifth, having obtained a husband for his sister, was now called on to preserve a husband for his aunt ; for Henry the Eighth at this time found his remorse insupportable, for the sin of having wedded his brother's widow. He felt it, also, his imperative duty to strengthen the succession to his throne by leaving a legitimate son. For this purpose the aged Catherine was to be got rid of, and the young and blooming Anna Boleyn installed in her place. But Catherine had strong allies. The Emperor was her nephew, the Pope was her friend, and she had given birth to a daughter, who was now growing up to womanhood, and whose conduct was irreproachable. The Emperor, however, was not popular in England. The grave and thoughtful part of the community had doubts about the claims and authority of the Pope ; the frivolous probably wished an enlivenment of the court, over which the dull and ascetic Castilian threw a constant gloom. Anna Boleyn was gay and beautiful, gifted with all the graces of form and manner, and rich in all the accomplishments of the time. The minute steps by which the divorce was gained belong more to the history of England than of France ; how by degrees the passions of the king became enlisted on the side of the Reformers ; and how, probably with perfect sincerity, he persuaded himself that the dictates of his desire for marriage with Anna were the result of inward conviction of the truth of Protestantism. We have only in this place to see the effects of this strange incident on the affairs of Francis, who was deterred by no delicacy or scruple from the gratification of all his fancies, and therefore had no occasion to consult either pope or presbyter on their theological views of matrimony or divorce. Another weapon, however, he now felt was placed in his hands by the sensitiveness of his English neighbour. A promise to use his influence with the pope to sanction the separation from Catherine insured him the assistance of England in opposing Spain. A kind of triangular duel, as it has been facetiously called, was fought between those three. If Charles fired at Francis, Henry fired at Charles. But the game they played was too full of *finesse* to be understood by the observers. Clement desired to hold all within the power of the Church, and coquetted with Charles at one time and Henry at another. At last Henry lost patience altogether, and married the object of his affection, less disgusted with popery than with the Pope. Anathemas and excommunications were the music of his wedding-feast, and England threw off her allegiance to the chair of St. Peter.

Henceforth Francis saw his policy made more difficult. How could the Most Christian King give aid and countenance to a schismatic and rebel like Henry in his controversies with the Most Catholic of Emperors? And yet, without his support to the struggling interests of the Protestants and the recreant King of England, that Most Catholic of Emperors would attain the undisputed mastery of Europe. For a long time the preaching of Luther had made no impression in France. It was only when the German adherents of the great Reformer grew numerous enough to become worthy of political notice that the nature of his doctrines was closely examined. Already the vices of the clergy and the assumptions of Rome had created thousands of opponents, who spoke out against the corruptions of the papacy without an idea that they were Protestants by so doing. Margaret, the beautiful sister of Francis, who made her escape so opportunely from Spain, was now Queen of Navarre by her marriage with Henry d'Albret, the monarch of that toy-like kingdom, and gathered round her a court of the most determined reformers, whose weapons were not text and history, but song, and epigram, and satire. First among the poets was the fair Queen herself; and dogmas, which might have survived, though proved false, expired when they were discovered to be ridiculous. Francis, also endued like Margaret with a love of literature and taste for the arts, pursued the same course of encouraging the wit and talent and scholarship of the time by appointments to professorial chairs, and pensions on his private purse, without perceiving that he was nourishing Protestantism by every gift he bestowed upon genius, for all the intellect of the time was engaged on the side of the Reformation. Even the scholars and statesmen who professedly adhered to the ancient faith, were unrestrained by any considerations of reverence or obedience in the torrent of epigram, satire, and denunciation they poured forth on the abuses of the Church and the vices of the clergy. Monks of all colours, black and grey, with all their trumpery—luxurious abbots and dissolute bishops, found less favour at the hands of Sir Thomas More and Erasmus than in the writings of Luther and Hutten Yet no art or entreaty was left untried to induce Erasmus to domicile himself in France. The Princes of the League of Smalkald, which was formed in 1529 for the protection of liberty of worship, were kindly treated. Solyman himself, the greatest enemy of the faith and most celebrated Sultan of the Turks, found favour with the Most Christian King when he applied for help against the Emperor in Hungary.

But suddenly he saw the fault he had committed. Catholic Christendom suspected his religious truth, and a suspicion of this sort would weaken his sovereign power. It is almost impossible for a king to be a despot unless he is supported by a despotic church. And despotism was the work of Francis's life. He entered, therefore, into competition with his great rival in showing his attachment to the Holy See. He burned heretics in the great cities, and made adhesion to the new opinions a crime against the Crown. Charles on the other hand, led an expedition into Africa, and slaughtered the infidels in a new crusade. Victorious over Barbarossa, the usurper of Tunis, and followed by the blessings of the thousands of Christian captives whom he had delivered from slavery, he made his way to Rome. There, in presence of the Pope, he stood forth and made his complaint against Francis. He declared his readiness to invest one of his sons with Milan, on such conditions of suzerainty and subjection as he should afterwards choose to name; failing that, to meet his enemy foot to foot, on horseback or in a boat, armed cap-à-pied or naked to their shirts; or, finally, to declare internecine war upon him, binding himself by an oath never to sheathe the sword till he had made him the poorest gentleman that ever lived. After this decent and courageous bravado, at which the pontiff must have been no little amazed, the assembly broke up in most admired disorder, and the dogs of war were let loose. An invasion of France was resolved on, and Charles already counted his victory so secure that he distributed the estates of the French nobility among his favourites. An army of Spaniards and Italians was to overrun Provence, and another of Flemings to break in on Picardy. Between the two, Francis was to be crushed. Misfortunes crowded, not in single file but in battalions, upon the thoughtless but affectionate king. His eldest son Francis, the Dauphin, died at this time, of poison; but whether administered with the cognisance of the Emperor, or whether the fairer hand of Catherine de Medicis, the wife of his younger brother, did not begin its triumphs of cruelty and murder by opening the way to the crown for her husband Henry, is left in doubt. Defection deprived him of some of the strongest fortresses in Savoy; and the forces of his enemy were reported to be on the soil of France. Instantly the courageous Francis was roused from his grief and dejection. The territory in front of the Spaniards was made a desert; the cattle driven away, the villages burnt, and parties of resolute horsemen sent forth to harass them on the march. Charles expected that all would be risked on the arbitrament of one great engagement, and was foiled by the unexpected tactics. He marched without glory, for he saw no enemy; and without food, for every field was

16

bare. Sickness came to aid ; and, in frightful disorganisation, the starving hordes hurried across the Alps, slain and pillaged on their way by the angry peasantry, and perishing in the clefts of the rocks of hunger and fatigue. Thus fell the pride of the invader almost without a blow.

Francis took now the lofty part which hitherto had been played by his rival ; and at a Bed of Justice in the palace of the Louvre, summoned his rebellious vassal before his feudal court, stripped him by solemn sentence of his tenures of Artois, Flanders, and Charolais, which always had been held of the French crown, and of which his renunciation at the treaty of Madrid was null and of no effect, as having been obtained by violence and fraud. Beside him, on this great occasion, sat the King of Navarre and James the Fifth of Scotland, who had just married the short-lived Madeleine of France ;—a more dignified, though not a more useful demonstration than the quarrel-scene of his rival at Rome. The forms of feudalism were occasionally revived to gratify a hatred, as the forms of chivalry were retained to justify a duel ; but the hatred of the two greatest soverėigns in Europe carried them beyond the bounds both of feudalism and chivalry. Their language, by their respective heralds, would have done honour to two English prize-fighters. They interchanged the names of perjurer and liar, and reminded each other of the discomfitures they had sustained ; Charles being particularly caustic on the subject of Pavia and the prison of Madrid, and Francis retorting with reminiscences of the Emperor's overthrow in Provence, and starvation among the hills. Yet, in a year after this time, the enemies met, and spent four of the happiest days of their lives in unrestrained intimacy at Aigues Mortes, a small seaport on the Mediterranean. Charles arrived in a galley. Francis went on board, and grasping his hand said, "My brother, you see I am your prisoner again." Charles returned the visit on shore ; listened well pleased to the open unsuspecting talk of his companion, and put down all his sayings and plans, and recollections in his memory, to be used against him at the proper time. He promised him great things in return for all his confidence ; the investiture of Milan for his son, and aid in all his schemes. A French king at that time would have sacrificed anything for the vainglory of establishing himself in Italy. Charles saw his triumph, confirmed it by a friendly visit to Paris, and made use of it by obtaining permission to pass through France to punish the men of Ghent who had rebelled. And, when thus the whole advantages of his superior policy were secured, he denounced his friend to the indignation of every Christian, as an ally of Solyman the chief of the Unbelievers, and bestowed the Duchy of Milan on his own son, Philip, the prince of Spain. Five armies sprang up at the king's lifting his hand, to revenge this wrong and insult. But indignation may raise troops, but cannot raise money. Fresh burdens were imposed ; church ornaments were coined into crowns, but still the chest was empty. La Rochelle set the dangerous example of rebellion on account of its over-taxation, and was only quelled by alleviation of its payments and pardon of its behaviour. Assistance was greedily looked to by both parties. Solyman, the champion of Mohammedanism, on the side of Francis, was balanced by Henry, the defender of the Protestant faith, on the side of Charles. The Turks, under the same Barbarossa whom Charles had displaced from Tunis, besieged Nice, and ravaged the shores of Catalonia. Henry did little but keep Scotland from aiding France by the intrigues and menaces with which he sued for the hand of the unfortunate Mary Stuart, now Queen, for his son Edward. A great victory at Cericolles, in 1544, added another useless wreath to the chaplet of French achievements, and for a moment Milan opened its gates. But Charles and Henry were by this time on the soil of France. The Spaniards were at St. Dizier, the English at Boulogne. Troops were summoned from Italy, and collected from all quarters. Charles steadily advanced, seized Epernay, and rested in Chateau-Thierry. Paris almost heard the thunder of his guns ; and, flushed with the possession of Boulogne, Henry was reported to be upon the march to join the army.

But other sounds reached the ears of the belligerents The Protestants in Germany were sharpening their swords, and Charles feared the men of the Confession of Augsburg more than the Catholic French. A peace was patched up at Crespy in the Valois, which left things as they were, and enabled the two monarchs to turn their religious minds to the extirpation of heresy. The royal heretic who had been the faithful ally of one of them, and the considerate foe of the other, contented himself with demanding a bribe of two million crowns for the restitution of his conquests. Our character at that time was more economical than heroic ; and we seldom set our foot in France, unless on the careful calculation of how much the enemy would give us for going away again. From this time Francis and Charles had more interests in common than opposed. They both glowed with a hatred of the Reformation which only tyrants can feel. They persuaded the Pope to summon a general council to extirpate Lutheranism and Calvinism at once, and while the famous Council of Trent was gathering from all the orthodox nationalities, they occupied themselves in cruel persecutions of their suspected subjects. The valleys of Provence, the ancient seats of the Albigenses, were depopulated by the fury of this modern and sensual De Montfort. But the extirpation was incomplete ; a terrible foundation, the hatred of the survivors, was laid for the religious animosities which in after years scattered such misery over the land. Old and worn out with labours and debaucheries of every kind, the king, at fifty-two, felt all his energy decayed. Henry the Eighth had closed his troubled reign in the January of 1547. Francis brooded over the event as if it had some mysterious connection with his own fate. Fevered and ill at ease, he hurried from place to place to shake off the dark presentiment ; but journeys, and hunting-parties, and more elegant relaxations, were all in vain. The machinery would no longer move, and on the 31st of March in the same year, he followed his rival to the tomb.

The effects of this man's reign on French history, and

even on European manners, was greater than might be expected from the frivolous nature of most of his qualities. That his influence was injurious no one can doubt who reads the memoirs of the time ; for it is apparent that vice under him became systematised, and a dissolution of morals which, in previous periods, would have been at all events concealed from public observation, was blazoned forth as the accompaniment and proof of gentle blood. The coarseness and degradation of the courtiers and gentry were not so much meant to be hidden, as ornamented by the dressing of polish and sentiment in which they were involved. Female innocence and manly independence were laughed at as the virtues of a more savage state or of a lower order of society. Gallant as one of the ancient Paladins, and elegant in dress and attitude as an ideal of Titian, the king set an example of unbridled profligacy, which is only protected from the horror with which we read of the revels of Nero, by the chivalrous grace with which his wildest excesses were accompanied. A colouring of romance was added to the grossest and most ignoble of his attachments, and some of these were elevated into something which he considered higher than legitimate affections by the affectation of purity and respect. The modern politeness which bestows lenient names on very wicked actions, took its rise in the luxurious court of Francis. People who could not imitate him in his valour or his wit, or his love of genius, or his patronage of the arts, paid him the easy compliment of resembling him in his faults. They could not fight as he did at Marignano, nor extemporise a sonnet, nor receive the last sigh of a Leonardo ; but they could sneer at holiness and goodness ; they could support the abuses of a corrupted and tyrannic priesthood ; they could consider the sweet domestic charities as vulgar and out of place ; and they could spread the contamination of their heartlessness and sensuality wherever their power extended. It was better for the morals of a nation that a Henry should send half-a-dozen Anna Boleyns to the block, than that a Francis should place a succession of his favourites on the topmost step of the throne.

CHAPTER X.

HENRY THE SECOND, A. D. 1547 TO A. D. 1559.

THE new king, Henry the Second, was eight-and-twenty years of age, and had been for a long time admitted by his father to the conduct of public business. The nation, therefore, felt little change when the guiding hand was withdrawn. Francis for the last five years of his reign had gone back to the principles of his predecessor Louis the Twelfth, and had pursued the surest path to popularity by sparing the property of his people. He became economical of the public income, and left a considerable sum in the coffers of the State. The part played by the discontented feudatories of a former time, when a great vassal of Languedoc led an army into the field against a great vassal of Guienne—or when both directed their forces against the royal power—was now exchanged for the secret cabals and wretched combinations of beauties and sycophants. The struggle was now to get the name of the king on one side or the other, and under the cloak of that legal authority to grasp all the patronage and influence of the realm. It was like the state of affairs where the ancient mayors of the palace reigned in their puppet's name ; only in this case the mayor of the palace was a lady founding her empire on the sweetness of her face ; or a courtier gaining his master's ear by flattery and submission ; or a queen claiming her share in right of her position, and regarding no law, human or divine, to attain her object ; or, finally, a firm-willed, strong-handed warrior recommending himself by the unfaltering execution of the cruellest or most illegal decrees. The friend and courtier of Henry was the Constable Montmorency; his favourite was Diana of Poictiers; his wife was Catherine de Medicis; and his grim and ambitious general was Francis Duke of Guise. All these personages performed distinguished parts in the history of the time, and Henry himself emerges from obscurity only by the light their quarrels and reconciliations cast upon the central figure. "Beware of Montmorency," said Francis the First to him when he was dying; "he is false and pitiless. Beware of the House of Guise; it is unprincipled and ambitious." He did not warn him against Diana or Catherine, for he probably thought the influence of the mistress would cease with the failure of her beauty, and the character of the Queen had not yet come into display. But Diana was one of the women who either never grow old, or whose loveliness depends on some higher element than freshness of feature, for at all periods of her life she was the fairest ornament of the Court, and retained her influence over the king long after youth or even middle age was past. Brantôme says she was beautiful at sixty-five. Catherine as yet eluded discovery, for she had the family arts of simulation and concealment, derived from the Medicis, in addition to the Italian steadiness of purpose and recklessness of means. She bided her time in all changes of circumstances, as a shark follows a vessel through storm and calm in expectation of its prey.

The first days of his accession were employed by Henry in royal progresses through his dominions, shows, and spectacles. In the last of these he was himself a chief performer, and no one held the lists with a firmer lance, or overthrew his opponent with a more scientific thrust. It must always be remembered that kings are uniformly successful in bodily exercises and in playing chess. To unhorse or checkmate the sovereign would be high treason as well as bad taste. His amusements were diversified by sights of another kind. There was a duel which made a great sensation, and is now quoted as illustrative of the manners of the time. Two young nobles, De Jarnac and La Chateigneraie, had been intimate friends in the reign of Francis. Their friendship was cemented by a community of vice, and therefore did not stand the shock of their first disagreement. One of them, in boasting confidentially of his evil courses, whispered scandal on a lady of the court. The confidant confided it under the seal of secresy, to somebody else. Somebody else spread it under the same precautions, and when it was known to all the world, Jarnac, the original propagator, denied the whole statement, and threw the accusation of falsehood on Chateigneraie. Chateigneraie took up the gauntlet; and when Henry was returned from his provincial visits, the barriers were fixed in Paris, and the judicial combat was allowed. The king and all his court were there, and bets were high in favour of Chateigneraie, who was tall and strong, and one of the best swordsmen in France. But Jarnac, who was little and active, dashed in below the guard of his scientific rival, and brought him to the ground by two strokes behind the knee, and contemptuously gave him his life. A noose depended over the lists for the use of the defeated combatant, and Chateigneraie escaped the death of a felon by his adversary's moderation; but his vanity was more fatally wounded than his body, and he died of grief. This was not a softening or ennobling kind of entertainment to present to lords and ladies. It was therefore, perhaps, with a view to compensate for such profane enjoyments that Henry next proceeded to the slaughter of such of his people as began to think for themselves on religious subjects. Gibbets were erected on the side of the road by which he made his entrance into the good city of Paris, and unhappy Protestants were suspended from them by cords round their bodies, and dropped into a slow fire, which was kindled under them, till they expired. These operations endeared him to the Church; and the Pope, as Father of the Faithful, made advances to so obedient a son. It was high time, for the Most Catholic Emperor was more surely shaking the temporal throne of the ruler of Rome than Luther had ever done the foundations of his spiritual authority. The Protestant Princes of the League of Smalkald had been completely beaten at the great battle of Muhlberg within a month of Francis's death. The Elector of Saxony and the Landgrave of Hesse were taken prisoners, their military followers dispersed, and to all human appearance the cause of the Reformation on the Continent was at an end.

But fortunately the popes were sovereigns as well as pontiffs, and Paul the Third was alarmed at the irresistible power of Charles. He was offended, also, at the Emperor's acts; for the greatest prince in Christendom had not scrupled to profit by the murder of his son, Peter Farnese, whom he had invested with the duchies of Parma and Placentia. There were always after this date a number of delightful principalities, in which the popes installed their nephews or cousins, or less reputable connections. Nepotism, no longer limited to red hats and rich abbeys, extended its views to dukedoms and alliances with royal lines. Charles, with the intuitive dislike of his race and country, looked with contempt on the mushroom potentates, and besides, had a very considerable affection for the snug little Duchy of Placentia for himself. Spanish troops were therefore in waiting outside the walls of the beautiful little town; and when the wicked and wretched Peter was stabbed by the conspirators and torn to pieces by the mob, the soldiers rushed into the city, and the Imperial standard was raised upon the castle. Paul the Third was an affectionate father, we have seen, as well as Catholic chief. In one character he hated the Emperor, whom he suspected of being accessory to his son's death; and in another he had great reason to be satisfied with the proselytising and obedient king. He therefore sent to Henry, and told him that if he would come to the assistance of his family, he would aid him with blessings and coin, and if their joint efforts failed he would seek an asylum in France. His offer was not to be resisted, for even a defeat would give him a visitor of inestimable value, and preparations were made. Before the fruits of the battle of Muhlberg could be gathered by the victors, news reached the confederated Protestants that a quarrel had broken out between the French King and the Emperor, and between the Emperor and the Pope. They actually became the arbiters of these great dissensions, and were courted by all parties. Charles, in order to intimidate his Holiness, insisted on the return of the General Council to Trent, where it had been originally summoned in 1544, and its removal from Bologna, to which it had been transferred by Paul. This was to place it where the influence of Protestant belief was greatest, and already there were hopes of a compromise, by which Germany might become an undivided power. England was under an eclipse at this time, and was nearly forgotten outside of her guardian seas. Edward the Sixth was on the throne, Somerset was Protector, and both were too weak to do anything more than defend their authority against the cabals of the political and religious parties into which the nation was split. The career was therefore open to the rival crowns. Charles, in entering on the new contest, showed his usual sagacity, and made concessions after having obtained all the advantages of force. He granted liberty of worship to the Protestants by an Imperial rescript, marriage of their priests, and communion in both kinds, till the Council of Trent should come to a final decision. But this was assuming too much of the pontifical authority to be pleasing to Paul. He protested against the Interim, as this act was called, and prosecuted his schemes in favour of France more zealously than ever. Persecution and toleration therefore became the conflicting arms of the champions in this great struggle ; and it shows us how completely the political view at this time excluded the religious, that the heretics were slain and tortured by a man who was utterly regardless of the great question in dispute, while their liberties were defended by a gloomy and unrelenting bigot, who looked on them as the enemies of God and man. Henry, too thoughtless to take warning by the sudden change in his adversary's treatment of the innovators, sought to strengthen his cause, and increase the papal influence, by double severity against the new faith. The massacres and atrocities perpetrated under Francis at Merindol and Cabrières, rested for a long time in the memory of the people, till they were expelled by still wilder excesses of fanaticism and hatred. Rebellions, prompted by despair and over-taxation, broke out in several places, and an expedition into Italy was thwarted by the necessity of hurrying back to punish refractory Bordeaux. Disregarding the protest of the local parliament, the edict of the king had imposed a duty on salt, which maddened the consumers; for the article lay at their doors, and the commissaries were inquisitorial as well as unjust. Montmorency, the favourite, was in his element now. He was sent down to execute justice on the revolters, and spared neither sex nor age. A hundred of the chief artisans of Bordeaux were ignominiously hanged; crowns of red-hot iron were placed on the sufferers' heads while they were broken alive on the wheel. The bells were taken down, in sign of the withdrawal of the city's municipal powers; and a breach made in the walls, in sign of its subjection to military law. Wherever the Constable went, he was preceded by the executioners of his vengeance; and having spread desolation and misery through the whole south of the kingdom, he returned to Paris in time to take part in the rejoicings which had been going on while these terrible events occurred, for the marriage of Anthony of Bourbon with Jane d'Albret. The mother of this Jane was a Protestant and poetess, Margaret of Navarre, the sister of Francis the First, and the eldest son of this marriage was Henry the Fourth. These blood-stained espousals were the connecting link between the follower of Bayard and the friend of Sully. It is a great step when we come, with only one life between, from the armed bravo of Marignano to the author of the Edict of Nantes.

At this time also another marriage was resolved on, and another royal bride made her appearance at the court of France. A beautiful and graceful child she was, whose life has been studied with more zeal, and fate lamented with more tears, than those of any other queen; for it was the fair and unfortunate Mary of Scotland, transplanted now, in her sixth year, from the bleak land which scarcely owned its allegiance, and always refused its affections—to appear for a brief moment on the brightest and gayest throne in Europe, and go back to the toils and struggles, and errors and sorrows, of her native realm. She was betrothed in this year to Francis the Dauphin, who ascended the throne as Francis the Second. The rejoicings on these two auspicious events were soon interrupted; for all the nations were in a roused and unsettled state, and every day brought forth some new complication of parties, or totally unexpected turn in the progress of affairs.

A distinction seems always to have been drawn between the doctrines of the Lutherans and Calvinists. The Lutherans were considered merely dissidents from the Papal Church, but the Calvinists were thought rebels against royal authority. Excesses on both sides justified to superficial observers the opinion, which inflamed the Catholics and Reformers with unappeasable rage, that their joint existence was impossible. Catholicism, when it was triumphant, trampled on the faintest spirit of dissent; and dissent, when it had the opportunity, retorted with almost insane retribution. The release from the darkness in which all men's minds had been avowedly kept, was too sudden to be wisely borne. The light blinded their eyes, and the persecutors could point to their victims' acts in justification of their own. This will account for the tragedies and nameless horrors of the next half-century in France, in which the national character entirely changed. Jacques Bonhomme became a ravening savage instead of a complaining drudge, and knight and cavalier became brutalised below the standard of a Chinese mandarin or maddened Hindoo. National efforts, however they might ostensibly be only on temporal or political subjects, borrowed their spirit from these theological dissensions. Wars, sieges, marriages, all had reference to the great argument of the time; for it was felt on both sides that the preponderance of either of the parties in the religious struggle would decide the predominance of the political opinions which were supposed to be involved. Protestantism and free government, if not the cry, was already the sentiment of all the peoples, and Catholicism and loyalty to the Crown were the counterblasts on the other side. If Charles the Fifth therefore, at any time, perceived that the Pope himself relaxed in his opposition to the Calvinist reformers, he opposed the person of his Holiness without the least compunction, but with an unabated reverence for his office ; and if Henry the Second saw, in the midst of his executions of the Protestants of his own kingdom, that encouragement of the Lutherans of Germany would weaken his rival's force, he sent assistance to the confederated princes. But both were equally bent on maintaining their individual authority. It will therefore not surprise us when we perceive that, in the year 1552, the part played by these unprincipled potentates became reversed. Charles, the publisher of the Interim which secured the Protestant demands, is at open war with them in Germany, and Henry, the torturer of the reformers of his own kingdom, is armed in their defence. Maurice of Saxony, however, saved the French king the trouble of crossing the Rhine, for he secretly placed himself at the head of a band of determined Protestants, forced the passes of the Tyrol, and scattered the Council of Trent, which was still carrying on its labours. Without check or pause they marched without beat of drum, and got so close to the house in Innspruck where Charles was in bed with a slight illness, that his Imperial majesty had to fly with no more dignified apparel than his shirt and stockings. While the confederated princes were lamenting the escape of their expected prisoner, they were cheered with a message from the Emperor himself offering terms of accommodation. The rapidity of his flight had been increased by the knowledge which reached him in his retreat, that Henry, with a great French army, was on the borders of Germany, and ready to cross over to the assistance of his enemies. Better, he thought, to yield at once than allow his French rival to gain the glory of a reconciliation. The princes accepted the offer, and wrote to beg Henry to discontinue his advance. A French king at the head of a French army would think himself disgraced if he disbanded it without a triumph, even if all the objects of its assemblage were obtained. Henry, therefore, yielded to their request by discontinuing his advance; but indemnified himself by turning to one side, and seized by main force the cities of Metz, Toul, and Verdun, spread his legions over Lorraine, and made an attempt on Strasburg and the county of Alsace. In this he was only repulsed by the Protestantism of the people. They feared the Most Christian King and had more confidence in the Catholic Emperor, who, to the great satisfaction and at the powerful request of sixty thousand armed Lutherans, had just signed his name to the Treaty of Passau. This Treaty of Passau was the termination for a long time of the German strife. Equal rights were secured by it to Protestant and Papist; equal eligibility to seats in the Great Council of Spires, and mutual freedom of worship in the states of both communions.

The war henceforth became a petty personal quarrel between the sovereigns. Charles, having pacified the reformers, swore he would die before the walls of Metz, which the king had taken, before he would raise the siege; and Henry swore he would lose his last man before a Spaniard crossed the ditch. It was a duel, with the world gathered round the lists. Metz was a wretchedly placed town, with no regular fortifications, no bastions or towers, and was commanded by hills in the immediate neighbourhood. But Francis, Duke of Guise, threw himself into the place, and made preparations for defence. He knocked down the houses which weakened his position, dug ditches, raised earth embankments, mounted his cannon, and hung out a flag for all the gallantry of France to rally round. All the brave youth flowed northward as to a tournay. Counts, marquesses, and chevaliers, poured into the devoted town, and were instantly formed into companies for work and fighting. Fine feathers and jingling spurs disappeared. There were pickaxes, and spades, and sharp swords, and matchlocks, and tight discipline, and hearts burning for distinction. Charles came on with a hundred thousand men, with officers and nobles collected from every portion of his vast domain. Flemish infantry, Spanish cavaliers, German lansquenets, seven thousand pioneers, and a hundred and twenty guns. It was a presentment, before the time, of the more celebrated siege of Sebastopol. Guise was the Todtleben, as well as the general in command. Fresh defences were raised in the night, to be demolished again in the morning. Advances, sallies, assaults, and all the changes and chances of a continued battle, in which the besieged had only the advantage of a little more shelter than their assailants, marked the progress of this obstinate struggle. Time, however, was always on the side of the garrison. The winter rains came on. The exposed battalions suffered from cold and wind, and finally from hunger, on the heights above the town. If they descended near the ditch, they sank in the tenacious clay; if they forced their way to a redoubt, they were repelled with shot and spear. Reports also spread through the camp that Henry was coming with all the remaining power of France, and Charles, sick, wearied, but still breathing vengeance, was forced to forget his oath, and raise the siege in the first days of January, 1553, leaving forty thousand dead as witnesses of the obstinacy of the attack. The scattered fragments of the army were followed, and at first destroyed ; but compassion blunted the pursuers' swords. Such squalid forms, it was unworthy of a soldier to kill, such starving multitudes had no thought of resistance. They cried only for bread. The gallant Frenchmen fed them, clothed them, placed them in houses of shelter, and sent them to their own countries cured and gratified. It would be pleasant if we saw that this generous conduct had been met in a corresponding spirit. But Charles was more imbittered by disappointment than soothed by these Christian attentions. Perhaps he did not understand them, for his whole career shows no touch of anything higher than selfish policy, unredeemed by sympathy or romance. And let us not despise this latter quality, which, however laughable when combined with a weak judgment, is in great characters the foundation of all the virtues, for it is a lofty rising out of the everyday suggestions of interest or ambition; and makes a man who, without it, may be an object of awe or admiration, into a hero reverenced and loved. England might have boasted of Nelson as much, if he had been of sterner mould, but it was his tenderness, gentleness, in short, his romance, which makes him still talked of with the warmth of personal attachment. Cold-blooded, self-sufficient—rejecting sympathy because incapable of feeling it—Charles pursued his plans. All his Estates were taxed for men and money, and before the wounds of Metz were healed in the hospitals of the French, an immense array hung on the frontier of France. In some places where the Emperor was not present in person, it is delightful to see that the generosity of Guise was not thrown away. In Italy a gentler spirit was introduced into the war. De Buissac, the French commander, spared the peaceful populations, and was followed, in this unprecedented course, by the Spanish generals. The usages of civilised warfare existed for a while, till fanaticism again mingled with the contest, and warriors who fought like gentlemen in their character of soldiers, fought like wild beasts in their character of Christians. Let us therefore pray that in all the calamities that may be reserved for our country, she may escape the lowest and bitterest a distracted nation can feel—a religious war.

But Charles, as if fatigued with war, now turned his vengeance into softer channels. The successful move which Henry had made in securing the Scottish queen for the heir of France, was replied to this year, by the gain of the hand of Mary of England for the heir of Spain. A more ungainly couple never disgraced the bands of Hymen, by pretending to marry for love. Philip of the Asturias was now in his thirty-second year, and already the sullen, unforgiving bigot history still shudders to contemplate in the annals of the Netherlands. Narrow in heart and intellect, he was not more favoured by nature in his person than in his mind. An expression of stolid ferocity may yet be traced upon the coins which bear his image, as on the parchments which contain his words. In both we read, legibly written, the harsh will which trampled on every feeling, and the lust of blood which dominated every thought. All Catholic Christendom rejoiced at the nuptials. England was again to be restored to the patrimony of St. Peter, and heresy to lose its greatest shield. But the English themselves were very far from seeing the advantages of the Spanish match. The Parliament was altogether uncomplimentary and suspicious. It would give no power to the nominal king, nor admit foreign councillors, nor hold itself bound by continental alliances. Mary, the enraptured bride, regretted the rudeness of her people, and though she said nothing, took care to nurse her wrath in secret, to keep it warm. She was nearly forty years of age, gaunt and grim in her expression, the true daughter of Henry the Eighth, without his bluff openness, but as resolute in will and relentless in nature, as the repudiator of her mother, and the murderer of Anna Boleyn.

France was not long in perceiving that the English marriage was no gain to the cause of Charles. It had, indeed, a contrary effect; for the cruelties which the sanguinary pair perpetrated on the Protestants, filling the prisons with chained victims, and the fires of Smithfield with triumphant martyrs, awoke sentiments of pity in the dullest English hearts, and excited other feelings in so quick-witted and proud-spirited a people as the French. The despotic and demoralising teaching of the Jesuits was denounced by the University of Paris, and the Order was condemned to silence, and deprived of the mastership of schools. Henry, to gratify the Pope, had agreed to admit the Inquisition into his states; but at a great meeting of the Parliament, the famous Segnier, the advocate-general, protested against the measure. He knew what an inquisition meant, and warned his colleagues against submission. "You think you are all safe now, because you have the favour of the king, and are orthodox in the faith of the Church. Wait till an inquisition is installed, with the powers the Pope demands. When the king is in want of money, the inquisition will promise him the confiscation of your estates; and once before the officers of Rome, it needs but an accusation and two false witnesses, and if you were saints you would be burnt as heretics. Therefore, beware." The Parliament took the orator's advice, and the king withdrew his consent. But never was man so regardless of the happiness of his subjects when his own luxuries were to be supplied. To keep up the most dissolute court which had hitherto been seen in France, he stretched the ordinary taxation to its utmost limits. He then sold the offices round his person down to the assistant cook's. He created such an infinite number of fresh places, setting them all up for sale, that the whole land was filled with officials, whose business consisted in remunerating themselves for the money their appointments had cost. And all this time, while the Calvinists and Puritans were being cast into chains and hanged on the highways, the veil was occasionally lifted up from the orgies of the palace, and men shuddered at the profligacy revealed. Quarrels arose among the high-born ornaments of the court, which came before the tribunals of the judges, and witnesses on either side related incidents in the course of their examination which would have brought a blush on the forehead of Tiberius; for immorality had assumed that awful type, prophetic of the fall of nations, when it glories in its shame. Even the gallant De Buissac had a bodyguard in his Italian campaign, composed of the refuse of jails and galleys, but all of noble families. Not one was unstained by murder or robbery, or still wilder crimes. "I send them on desperate enterprises," he said, "for if they fall their lives are already forfeit to the law; if they survive, they in part efface their wickedness by usefulness to the State." But the troop was proud of its notoriety. It was an honour reserved for the most ambitious of gentle footpads to be admitted a member of the "Brave and Bad." We need not enter into the particulars of a state of manners so little satisfactory to contemplate. We must only bear in mind that this is the turning-point in human affairs, for the Reformation was yet unsettled, and the old religion had nothing to show in opposition to the sentence passed against it, but the vices of all the courts, the sufferings of all the peoples, the anarchy of Rome itself, and the rise of that portentous star of blood and infamy which filled Europe with fresh calamities under the name of Philip the Second. For Charles was worn out. He saw no steadiness in man, nor honour in kings. His wisest schemes broke down under the weight of prejudices and deceits. At the very time, in 1556, when he was concluding a truce with France at Cambrai, he found that Henry was entering into an alliance of the bitterest hostility against him with the Pope at Rome. To punish Charles for not having annihilated the Protestants in the field, and for continuing to observe the Treaty of Passau, the furious old Caraffa, who took the name of Paul the Fourth, offered Henry the old bribe of the kingdom of Naples. War was, therefore, about to break out more bitterly than ever at the very time when the Turks were riding triumphant in the Mediterranean, and the Lutherans establishing their power in Germany, and riots arising from utter want and despair in various nations. Charles withdrew from the scene disappointed in his personal schemes, but unsoftened by the influence of years, breathing vengeance as sternly as ever against heretic and rebel, and giving the truest proof of his enmity and ambition by resigning his kingdoms and all his dominions to the younger and more unrelenting hands of Philip. He retired into a convent in Estremadura, where the records of his monkish days are still preserved. They portray a small mind and self-indulgent nature. He existed for two years a martyr to gout and gluttony; mixing anxiously in public affairs when the helm was in other hands; a marvel to the friars, a torment to himself; and then died at the age of fifty-six. A vulgar Napoleon with his St. Helena at St. Just.

Philip the Second was now king of Spain and the Indies, of England, and Naples—the greatest potentate in Europe. He detected the false play of Paul the Fourth and his nephews, and in no long time saw the treachery of the Pope and his Camarilla to the Spanish cause rewarded by the descent upon Italy of a French army sent to their assistance, commanded by the Duke of Guise. A sign was easily made to the ambitious Caraffas by the crafty Philip, and those honourable gentlemen deserted their uncle as they had formerly deserted the king, and put every obstacle they could devise in the way of the French expedition. Henry was too deep in his pleasures at Paris to attend to the request for succour made to him by his general at Rome ; and while he was wondering at the insolence of the man who requested him to spare the expense of a banquet or tournament, and send the money to the starving army, he heard that Mary of England had at last prevailed on her Parliament to take part in the war, that ten thousand English had joined the Spanish array, and that an army sixty thousand strong, under Imanuel Philibert, Duke of Savoy, had poured into Picardy, and was investing the town of St. Quentin. Coligny, the nephew of the Constable Montmorency, was in the place with only three hundred men. But he refused to surrender. Montmorency hastily advanced to the rescue, and so weakened his force by bad generalship and an apparent ignorance of the locality, that the Anglo-Spaniards found it an easy matter to put him to the rout. St. Quentin became a word of evil memory in Frenchmen's ears. The half of their troops were killed or taken, the rest scattered in irremediable confusion. Not a soldier was left between the scene of the battle and the capital, and Paris was at the mercy of the enemy. But Philip was afraid of so distant an advance. He kept the army, which he joined shortly after the victory, occupied in petty details, and gave up the neighbouring towns to pillage and conflagration. The army as usual became demoralised by these assaults and spoilings. Careful Flemings slipt off with the silver of plundered churches and the jewels of murdered women. Greedy Germans also stole away with all they could carry. The English, who were never hearty in the Spanish cause, grumbled at being sent home from a land where pillage was so easy, to resist the Scotch, who were gathering, at French instigation, on the border ; and of the conquerors of St. Quentin, none remained but the Spaniards and Italians, who were too distant from their homes to hope to reach them with their booty. Guise also had hurried back from Rome ; troops of Swiss and other mercenaries came in ; and Philip derived no real advantage from the greatest victory the Spaniards ever won over the French, except the glory of the day and the plan of the great palace of the Escurial, which is built in the parallel rows of the bars of a gridiron, in honour of St. Lawrence, on whose day the battle was fought, and whose martyrdom consisted in being broiled over a slow fire. The triumphant Philip, therefore, slunk off in a very undignified manner ; and the defeated French made a dash in the midst of winter where they were least expected, followed the enterprising Guise over the frozen marshes in the neighbourhood of Calais, and on the 9th of January, 1558, pulled down the English flag from the walls of the town, which had braved the breeze ever since the memorable conquest of Edward the Third in 1349. The acquisition of Calais, which was rapidly followed by the reduction of Dunkirk and some other maritime towns, was an ample compensation for the disaster of St. Quentin. France had now the key of her own house, and saw a new barrier to her domain in the sea, in which she had formerly seen only a highway for her enemy's approach. Mary was weak and ill when this news reached her. "Calais will be found written on my heart," she said, when she lay dying ; and many other terrible things must have been written there, unless the sharp point of conscience was blunted against fanaticism and zeal. With a great shout of joy the Spanish alliance was given up when Elizabeth took possession of the throne, and Henry the Second saw his two highest hopes fulfilled—England detached from his great rival's cause, and Scotland assured to his side by the marriage which took place at this time between his son Francis and Mary Stuart. A marriage of a more sombre augury was celebrated six months after the capture of Calais and death of the English queen, for Philip sent as his representative to wed the fair Elizabeth of France, the sister of Henry, no other than the most fierce and bloodthirsty of all the generals of the time, the grim and malignant Duke of Alva,—a man without pity or remorse, whose presence must have been an omen to the unhappy bride of the fate reserved for her at the Spanish court—a life of uninterrupted grief and disappointment, terminated by a violent and mysterious death. She did not know the unimaginable villain to whom she gave her hand. She only regretted, with the natural feelings of youth, that Philip had demanded her for himself after she had been promised to his son. This is a portion of royal experience belonging less to French than Spanish history. We will therefore only say, the wife was made miserable by the jealousy of the husband, and the son imprisoned and put to death by the hatred of the father.

The marriage of the heir of France and Queen of Scotland took place the 20th of June, 1559. For many days the bells rang out rejoicings, and cannon fired off their salutes. Tournaments were held from morn till eve, and on the 29th Henry held the lists against all comers, and challenged the knights of France and Spain. He resisted the attack of his first assailant, the Duke of Savoy, who courteously turned his spear and retired. The Duke of Guise was likewise gracefully repelled; the two best generals in the service of France felt the skill of the monarch's arm, and ladies and nobles vied in their show of admiration. But a big rough Scotchman, of the name of Montgomery, advanced as the third assailant, and by some mismanagement did not succeed in giving the king the best of the shock, but shook his feet out of the stirrups. Henry insisted on another course. Montgomery obeyed, and held the lance so straight—so firmly pointed—that it broke in his opponent's visor, and a splinter went into his eye. A shrill cry was all the spectators heard; but the king lay forward on his horse. He was taken off and visited by the best surgeons; the wood had penetrated to the brain, and on the 10th of July he died. The strange thing connected with this man's reign is, that in spite of the progress of the press, by which knowledge was communicated a thousand times quicker, and in many more directions than before, a greater contempt for public opinion was displayed than in the comparatively unenlightened times of Louis the Eleventh ; and at the moment when Protestantism was eagerly watching the lives of the great and powerful, as evidences of a perversion of the Christian faith, the wildest excesses of debauchery were shamelessly exhibited in the persons of kings and nobles —as if the monarchy was already above both public and religious considerations, and tasted the first draught of absolute and irrepressible power. A worthless voluptuary is little regretted, even by the companions of his debaucheries, and all the courtiers turned their eyes to the new occupants of the throne—Francis the Second and the Scottish Mary.

FRANCIS THE SECOND.

Monarchy, in this instance, was represented by a sickly boy of sixteen, and a thoughtless beauty of about the same age ; and yet never was a time when a strong hand and powerful will were more required to protect the royal authority. While Francis was carefully nursed and pampered in all his desires, and Mary was singing ballads and dancing at masquerades, strange thoughts had taken possession of the general mind. The profligacy and extravagance of the last reign had borne their natural fruits. There was anger and discontent all over the land ; the towns complained of their privileges being destroyed, the country people of the exactions of the Crown commissioners ; prices were raised everywhere by the monopolies bestowed on court favourites, or purchased by greedy speculators ; and when the more inquiring spirits looked round, and saw that all these calamities were inflicted on them with the support and at the instigation of the champions of the Romish Church and the persecutors of the new opinions, they came to the conclusion that their chances of future liberty were connected indissolubly with the cause of the Reformation. All the liberalism of France became Huguenot or anti-Papist. In the same way, when the leaders of Catholicism, who were also the holders of office, perceived that opposition to their measures, complaints against their rapacity, and demands for freer government, proceeded from the followers of Calvin and other teachers, they confounded seriousness in religion with discontent in the State, and looked on every Protestant as a rebel in disguise. The last public act of the late king was ordering the arrest of an advocate who had undertaken the defence of some person accused of heresy. For this great crime he was tried and condemned. Francis and Mary inaugurated their reign by attending his execution.

The managers of the Court were the two brothers Guise—Francis the general, and the Cardinal of Lorraine. Uncles of the fair young queen, and guardians of the feeble sovereign, they had no enemy to fear except the public discontent, which they determined to put down by force; and nobody could see a cloud upon their prosperity when they peremptorily banished their rival Montmorency, and dismissed Diana of Poictiers, who was now Duchess of Valentinois, and immensely rich. They banished also Anthony of Bourbon and his brother the Prince of Condé, by sending them to escort the unhappy Elizabeth to her husband, Philip of Spain; and when thus freed from dangerous competitors, they gave a loose to the ferocity of their nature. A system of inquisition and extermination of the Protestants was established all over France, from which neither religious dissident nor political adversary could escape. The market halls were blackened with faggot-smoke, and yet the Bible grew more dear, the preachers more courageous. The great masses of the peasantry were, of course, immersed in ignorance, and were so scattered, and had such slender means of intercommunication, that the priests were still powerful in the remoter parts of the land; but towards the south the old Albigensian spirit survived. In the counties near Switzerland, the facility of intercourse and community of language spread the tenets of Geneva far and wide among the people. Half the nobility was in favour of the new opinions. The King of Navarre, Jane d'Albret his wife, and Condé his brother—the first princes of the blood after the sons of Henry—had publicly made profession of the new faith, and attended the Huguenot promenades in the "Priests' Meadow," on the banks of the Seine. Marot's hymns were sung in every hall; for Calvinism, wiser in France than in our own land, enlisted the gayest of poets and sweetest of musicians in its service; and now, when discontent with the management of the Guises was embittered by anger and fear, the Protestants could submit in silence no longer. A great though secret gathering took place at Nantes, where nobles met in large numbers. It was arranged to march on Blois with all the forces they could raise, and seize the king and the princes of Lorraine. But traitors were in the camp. The Guises were told of the plot, and carried the king to the castle of Amboise, which they had prepared to withstand a siege. Coligny and his brothers (nephews of the Constable Montmorency) were ordered to appear at court, and obeyed the summons. Condé presented himself without invitation, and offered to maintain his innocence by personal combat. The chiefs of the Conspiracy of Amboise, as this attempt is called, were now in the power of their enemies; and when the remaining confederates, even after the discovery, persisted in their plan, and broke out into open rebellion, they were crushed one by one. Promises, threats, and force—any means were equally welcome to the remorseless rulers at Amboise—were employed as occasion required, and the Huguenot nobles were everywhere seized. The only amusements now offered to the frail Francis and his bride were the executions of the vanquished. They were burnt as heretics rather than beheaded as rebels. The spectacle by this means was more appalling, and lasted a longer time. We are told, though the information was scarcely needed, that those shows were graced by the presence also of Catherine de Medicis, the mother of the king. In other places tortures were applied, so frightful that the priests themselves were revolted by the sight. The great bitterness of a war of faiths had not yet hardened them beyond compunction. To legalise and justify these measures, the Guises insisted on introducing the whole machinery of the

Inquisition. The benefit would fall to them—the odium on Rome. The great chancellor, Michel de l'Hospital, a man whose character shows that, even in the worst periods of history, the individual may obtain influence and glory by displaying the virtues befitting a happier time, opposed the fatal measure, and, as a compromise, conveyed the power of inquiring into false opinions to the bishops of France. To counterbalance this increase in the episcopal power, he proposed at the same time the summoning a national council (with liberty of worship to all sects till its decision should be known) and the convocation of the States-General. We shall find that this last was always a proposition of despair, when no other way was left to introduce good order in the realm. But the time for a States-General had long gone by. The monarchy had swallowed up the nation. It had lost the corporate capacity in which it gathered round Clovis and the early kings, and took part in the organisation of the State; and had not yet reached that other form of national influence which speaks through representation. The nation was now embodied in the Crown, and a restoration of old forms might lead to the revival of old attributes. The States-General might inquire too curiously into the origin of the monarchical power as it existed now, and the Guises opposed the proposal of De l'Hospital with all their force. A parliament of notables, however, was called as a middle course. But the first vote of the notables was for the assemblage of the States. They were therefore dismissed in disgrace, and the mask was taken off on both sides. The opponents of the Court declared themselves Huguenots; the Court declared them traitors. Anthony of Navarre and the Prince of Condé were invited to Orleans, where the king resided. They were arrested on their arrival, and Condé put on his trial. Coligny and his brother d'Andelot were also pressed to spend a few days at the palace; but while lawyers were preparing to plead, and soldiers were gathering to seize the other expected guests, Francis suddenly died. Everything was at a stand. The Guises, paralysed, let slip the golden opportunity of continuing their power by force. Emerging from the obscurity in which she had restrained her ambition till this time, Catherine de Medicis claimed the custody of her next son Charles the Ninth, who was still only nine years old, and before the court circle recovered from its consternation, the dark and blood-stained Italian was guardian of the king, and in fact, if not in name, regent of the kingdom.

Francis had reigned, if such a word can be applied to so nominal a sovereignty, for seventeen months. But in that short space the floodgates of evil were opened on the land. The country was divided into two apparently irreconcilable camps; and both stained with the lowest vices which ever mingled with high endeavours. The defenders of the ancient Church saw no dignity in the office they so pompously assumed, for they were conscious of no higher principle, in the maintenance of the old faith, than the aid it afforded them in keeping a blinded population in subjection. The reforming leaders degraded no less the loftiness of their design, by turning the great truths in whose cause they took arms into mere instruments of political and personal ambition. There were few on either side who cared for the things in whose name they fought. The Huguenots in general cared as little for the Bible as the Catholics for the Pope. And yet the bitterness of cruelty in this struggle transcends all example. It united the bigotry of fanaticism to the lawlessness of unbelief. Friends murdered friends; neighbours rushed armed into their neighbours' houses and slew them in cold blood. Torture of prisoners was almost universal, and mutilations, which are doubted of in India, were common in every province of France.

CHAPTER XI.

CHARLES THE NINTH, A. D. 1560, TO THE ACCESSION OF HENRY THE FOURTH, A. D. 1594.

THE dangerous experiment of the States was now unavoidable, and all parties paused for a while to see what the result would be. The result was not so considerable as either side expected. The universal voice was for reform in the management of the State and diminution of taxation. Reform also in the Church was strongly advocated; but the priests voted that it could only be procured by strengthening the laws against the Protestants; the Third Estate voted that the object was to be gained by freedom of conscience, and the nobles were almost equally divided in their votes. All, however, agreed in re-establishing the "Pragmatic," and diminishing the contributions to the Pope. After a session of six weeks the States-General were prorogued, and factions breathed again. Guise reconciled himself to his enemies the Constable and the Marshal St André, and the three put themselves under the protection of Philip of Spain in defence of the Catholic Church. This gave them the name of the Triumvirate. Condé and Coligny, on the other hand, strengthened their relations with the Huguenots. They looked in all quarters for assistance, and the Protestant prospects were not so desperate abroad as to discourage their hopes at home. In Germany the Huguenots, indeed, were at that moment triumphant. Not more than one-tenth of the people had retained their allegiance to the Pope. The great Elizabeth of England was a tower of strength, by the spectacle she afforded of a firm and beneficent rule, deriving its strength and consistency from a departure from the authority and traditions of the Church. Her counsels and good offices were never wanting to the Reformers in whatever part of Europe they might be, and by her active interference in the affairs of Scotland, in which the Guises were playing the same game of oppression as in France, she gave very perceptible evidence of what might be expected if she threw herself openly into the Huguenot cause. The court party temporised when they saw the disposition of their opponents. Catherine, the queen-mother, pretending an impartiality she did not feel, condescended to listen to a controversy carried on in her presence between the doctors of the contending faiths. She was struck with the ability of the Huguenot champions, whom she had considered hitherto as mere fanatical enthusiasts, and the admiration of such an enemy is more dangerous than her contempt. From this time she brooded over plans for the extermination of a sect who could argue so well and fight so bravely, and in the mean time gave them some delusive privileges, which irritated their opponents and dissatisfied them. They were permitted to worship outside the walls of a town, but they must go to the meeting unarmed, and disperse when ordered to do so.

It chanced that Francis of Guise was travelling with a stout escort near the little town of Vassy, in Champagne, on a Sunday in the March of 1562. The Protestants were worshipping in and around a barn beside the road, and the gallant escort drew sword upon the unhappy congregation, slew sixty of them on the spot, and wounded almost all the rest. Guise, who had been struck by a stone upon the cheek, rode on and took no notice of the outrage committed by his guard, but it spread from town to town. The trick was discovered. Permission to attend prayers unarmed was a plot to give them into the hands of their enemies. There was war in every province, and almost in every parish. Massacre was the rule on both sides. Catholic leaders hung their prisoners without trial, or shut them up in buildings which they set on fire ; Protestant leaders retorted, and drowned their enemies in sacks ; and one, the Baron des Adrets, made them leap down from a high tower while he and his friends pricked them on with sword and spear. The waste of peasant life was dreadful; many also of the chiefs died, and Anthony of Navarre, prince of the blood, was wounded to death in 1562. This weak and despicable Bourbon had been easily won over to the Triumvirate by the arts of the queen-mother, and jealousy of his brother Condé. Catherine was directed in the choice of the ladies of her court by their possession of beauty and the power of captivation. As other potentates sent forth a grey-haired ambassador to unravel a knotty point, the Italian ruler despatched a maid of honour beaming with youth and loveliness; her secretaries also were the fairest maidens in France; and it was generally found that they were successful in the object of their mission. Anthony of Navarre had no chance against the smiles and diplomacy of the young envoy who exposed to him the superior attractions of the Catholic cause. He was bribed on all sides. The Guises offered him the hand of Mary their niece, with the present Thistle of Scotland, to be compensated with the future Rose of England. The Nuncio of the Pope quelled any little hesitation in Anthony's mind on the slight impediment which existed to this plan in the fact that he had already a wife, by offering to dissolve the marriage on the plea that Jane d'Albret—who had brought him the crown of Navarre—was an avowed and open heretic. Anthony, however, was not tempted by the prospect of listening to John Knox, and being trampled on by Lord Ruthven, and declined the hand of the hapless Mary. He declined also the hand of Margaret of Valois, the daughter of Catherine, and contented himself with the promise of the kingdom of the Isle of Sardinia, which, as geography was not a common science in those days, was described to him as an earthly paradise, with no drawback to its perfect bliss. When he was wounded at the siege of Rouen, in October, 1562, he was attended by the ladies of the court, who soothed his weakness with all their arts. Their conversation was about the delicious life he would lead in the rich valleys of Sardinia, in the midst of pomegranates, and jasmines, and orange trees : and while indulging in these bright anticipations the deluded man expired.

Guise was assassinated in the following year by a Calvinist named Poltrot de Mené. Coligny was accused of complicity in the murder, and it was impossible to say whether the Catholics were more offended by the slaughter of their leader, or the Protestants by the libel upon theirs. Hatred grew warmer than ever ; and even the intervals which a treaty of peace now and then offered seemed only to increase the strife. Twice there were pacifications which brought no peace. Foreign affairs exercised their influence on these domestic struggles. The preparations of Philip against the revolted Netherlands gave hope to the Catholics ; the assistance of Elizabeth, and the supremacy of the reformers in Scotland, gave confidence to the Huguenots. In 1567 the war was at its height. Old Constable Montmorency mounted his horse once more, and commanded at a great battle near St. Denis. His enemies, Coligny and Condé, were forced to retreat ; but he himself was surrounded by a party of horsemen, and shot with a pistol by a Scottish cavalier called Robert Stewart.

A treaty, called the Peace of Longjumeau, gave rallying-time to both sides ; and in the next year the third war broke out. The same alternation of slaughter and violence characterised it as the last. The Battle of Jarnac revenged the murder of the Constable at St. Denis ; for Condé, being wounded and taken prisoner, was shot in cold blood by Montesquieu, the Captain of the Swiss Guard of the Duke of Anjou. This young gentleman, who was only nineteen years old, saw the bloody deed, and showed so much joy on the occasion that he has been accused of having ordered it. The rest of his life, for we shall soon recognise him as Henry the Third, does not go far in discountenancing the suspicion. A prince does not always require to give a positive order to have a crime perpetrated which is sure to give him pleasure. It is impossible to give a sufficient view of the utter dissolution of all the bonds of society in those dreadful years. In our Wars of the Roses, a century before this time, the battles had been as frequent and the sides as openly taken ; but there was a scrupulousness of honour which led the chiefs of the contending factions to spare the great towns and peaceable inhabitants. A Yorkist army encamped before a city which was supposed to lean to the Lancastrian side, and endeavoured to win it over by the gentleness of its treatment. A Huguenot troop would have rushed into the streets and filled the whole place with blood and rapine, even if the authorities had favoured the Huguenot cause. A royalist army in the same manner pillaged and destroyed the towns and territories equally of friend and foe. The result was, that the towns took arms, and the burghers kept watch and ward. The farmers and peasants, with axe and club, massacred the soldiers who fell into their power whatever party they belonged to. All France was a battle-field. Perhaps the universal soldiership of the nation may be traced to this ferocious period, when no man's life was safe unless by the strength of his own arm. Fighting, robbery, waylaying, were the occupations of high and low. A man's house was his castle, not in the figurative sense that we use the word, but by dint of bridge and iron gate. A gentleman with a loaded musket sat on the flat roof of his mansion, and observed the visitor who might be coming up the avenue. As he came near, he either gave orders to open the door, or shot him without further notice. Even if he saw his most intimate acquaintance, he called out to him from a slit in the wall, to leave his arms outside before he got admission. Old Montaigne, a French nobleman of no great wealth, but the most extraordinary genius of his time or country, tells a story of this period, which shows the state of manners. He was visited by a neighbouring gentleman, a kinsman of his own, who by some oversight was admitted with the friends who had accompanied him in his ride, without the preliminary laying aside of their pistols and swords. Montaigne did not know what to do. They were both on the same side in the politics of the time ; no quarrel had occurred, they were old friends, and yet the host saw very well the in tention of the callers, which was to turn him out of the house, and seize the possession of lands and goods. He was the wittiest, pleasantest, cleverest man in France, and he so received his visitors—was so agreeable, so polite, so friendly in giving them lunch, and so delightful in conversation, that the intended pillager had no opening for his design. How could he turn fiercely round on a gentleman who was offering him such civilities? Could he pocket a spoon by force, when its owner was bidding him dip it into the richest soup? Hospitality and jovial conversation had their reward. The crest-fallen visitor went away, and Montaigne put fresh bolts to his door, and determined to be more careful of how he admitted his dearest relations within the walls of his house. Yet in the midst of all this hurry of violence, and apparent love of confusion, there must have been longings, earnest and deep, for a restoration of repose. Catherine de Medicis was the evil spirit of all these miserable campaigns. Fascinating, we are told, in manner, and still beautiful in face and figure, nobody could have suspected that such a depth of perfidy, of self-will and cruelty, could lie beneath that fair and smiling outside. Brilliant in conversation, her delight was to form a circle round her of the gay and witty. Dances, fêtes and shows, succeeded each other from day to day. Protestations cost her nothing, for she broke them without remorse. To be niece of a pope was sufficient guarantee, she thought, of the orthodoxy of her religious creed; and yet to blind the Huguenots, she wrote to the Holy Father suggesting that they might be good enough Christians without believing in the mass, and excellent subjects though they did not attach any importance to the apostolic succession. A letter like this, on which such important interests depended, was written between a ball and a masquerade. But her plans in the main were as serious as if she had never smiled. She pursued a system—carrying it to its most rigid conclusion—which no other mother has heard of without horror. For the sole purpose of retaining the management of affairs, she deliberately and resolutely sank her son in the lowest and most degrading vices. She surrounded him with the worst specimens of both sexes, whom she could pick out of the demoralised and impoverished families in the kingdom. Drunkenness, gambling, debauchery of every sort, were the atmosphere in which the poor young man breathed. Uneducated, uncontrolled, with all his passions excited to the utmost, he knew no restraint upon the wildest excesses of his temper and desires, except the awe inspired in him by his mother. His spirit, feebly aiming at the beginnings of wrong, quailed before that incarnation of the bad and remorseless, whose gloomy heart had been meditating for years the awful deed which has made her name immortal. In solemn conference with the Duke of Alva, who was filling the Netherlands with the blood of half the inhabitants, and the groans of all the rest, she had come to one fixed and terrible resolve, and never, in all the gaieties of the court, or strifes of the battle-field, or apparent reconciliations with her enemies, had she forgotten it for a moment. The Protestants were to be extirpated from the land, and murder was to be the instrument employed.

The third peace was therefore negotiated and achieved at St. Germain, in August 1570. The terms were extremely favourable to the Protestants. They had liberty of worship, equality before the law, and admission to the universities ; and as a guarantee of safety, the four towns of Rochelle, Montauban, Cognac, and La Charité, were put into their hands. Chief of all the Huguenots, brave, generous, and accomplished, was Henry of Navarre, now barely seventeen years of age, but already displaying the same talents and qualifications which made him in after years Henry the Great, as well as Henry the Beloved. To get him into the power of the court, no labour was spared. He was invited, with the other nobles and princes of the Reformers, to attend at the nuptials of the King with Elizabeth of Austria, in 1571, but the rejoicings for the auspicious marriage had no temptations for the cautious chiefs. They remained in safety at Rochelle. At this time a great triumph accrued to Christendom, by the victory obtained at Lepanto by John of Austria, a natural son of Charles the Fifth, over the Turks. The argument was irresistible in the minds of popes and cardinals: "If heaven has given such a proof of its favour by the destruction of the unbelievers, how much more will it not strengthen our hands in the annihilation of heretics and schismatics?" Catherine was logician enough to accept any premises which came to their conclusion in blood. She made up a match between Henry of Navarre and her daughter Margaret, and felt sure the whole party of the Reformers would attend the marriage of their chief. Notre-Dame, the grand old cathedral which still looks grim and horror-struck with the thousand tragedies which have passed within its view, never presented so gay an appearance, as on the 18th of August 1572. As a compromise between the rival faiths, the ceremony was performed in the clear space outside, leaving the bride and bridegroom, after the blessing was said, to go to their respective places of worship,—Margaret into the church, and Henry to the chapel, as if, by an undesigned symbol, to show that sectarianism is the work of man's hands, with its separations and animosities, while religion is all-embracing, like the great light of day. On the raised platform, in the square before the church, all the parties in the State made their appearance. Great historic names were sounded on both sides; Teligny, Rochefoucauld, and Rohan, replied to by Guises, Tavannes, De Retzes; all the beauties of the court, all the leaders of the armies, the queen, in sullen gratification, hidden in maternal solicitudes—and the king.

Henry took Margaret's hand, and all Paris grew watchful when the triumphant artillery proclaimed the great event. The Protestants thanked God for the reconciliation which was now so securely guaranteed; the Catholics had other thoughts, but kept them to themselves. On the following day Catherine held a secret council in her room. The Duke of Anjou, the Keeper of the Seals (an Italian bishop), and some other favourites, were divided in opinion. Some wished to include the Guises themselves in the approaching massacre; some wished to spare the young Henry of Navarre; all insisted on the blood of Coligny ; and when the time drew near, the king, maddened by the malicious representations of his mother, who alarmed him for his life and crown unless the blow was struck, cried out, "Kill all—kill all ! Let not one escape to reproach me with the deed !" He was taken at his word. On the 20th of August, two days after the wedding, the bells of the Church of St. Germain l'Auxerrois rang out for matins. This call to early prayer was the signal for the slaughter. Instantly the streets were filled with armed Catholics, who, to distinguish themselves, wore a white cross on their hats, and a sash on the left arm. Coligny's was the first life aimed at. He was murdered in his lodging, and his body thrown into the courtyard, where it fell at the feet of Henry of Guise, who had sent the assassins in. Firing was now heard in every lane and street. Women, men, children, were remorselessly shot or struck down ; the obscurest haunts were searched, and nobody was spared. Some wonderful escapes, however, are recorded. Henry himself saved his life from the personal fury of the king, by submitting to go to mass. Charles ordered him to forsake his heresy, and revere him as the image of God, and cease to be an enemy to the image of God's mother. He then took his fowling-piece, and fired out of the window of the Louvre upon his subjects, who were trying to escape by flight. After three days of dreadful noise and confusion—the discharges of pistols, the shrieks of the wounded women, and the shouts of the assailants—there fell a dead silence upon the streets of Paris. There was nobody left to slaughter, and perhaps repentance began. Not, however, in high places did this holy feeling make its way. Catherine wrote triumphal accounts of her achievements to Alva, and Philip, and the Pope. Innocent the Third went in solemn procession to render thanks for the victory vouchsafed over his enemies, and struck medals in honour of the deed. Has that medal been yet thrown out of the collection of the Vatican, and broken to pieces by the hangman's axe ? Philip and Alva rejoiced at the happy news, and expected favourable results to their operations in Holland, from the effects of this unpitying energy in France. A great groan burst from the heart of England, which was instantly turned into a shout of execration. Germany was horror-struck at the atrocity, and Charles himself—debauchee, bigot, murderer as he was—was touched with sorrow. "Ambrose," he said to his confidential physician, Ambrose Parè, "I know not what has happened to me these two or three days past, but I feel my mind and body as much at enmity with each other as if I was seized with a fever. Sleeping or waking, the murdered Huguenots seem ever present to my eyes, with ghastly faces, and weltering in blood. I wish the innocent and helpless had been spared." Orders, however, were sent round in his name to all the governors of provinces, and all the commanders of towns, to follow the example of the capital. Most of them obeyed, and shrieks and lamentations filled the villages and cities; but yet not altogether extinguished were French generosity and honour. Many rejected the hateful orders with contempt. Dauphiny was protected from the horrors of assassination by Claude of Savoy; Chabot saved Burgundy from the stain. One whose name should never be forgotten, the Viscount of Ortez, wrote from the frontiers of Normandy: "Sire, I have communicated your majesty's orders to your faithful inhabitants, and to the troops in the garrison. I found there good citizens and brave soldiers, but not one executioner."

Men who had learned their Ava Marias at their mothers' knees, and loved their sisters, and played with little Protestant cousins in their boyhood, could not shut their hearts from the natural feelings of compassion. A great reaction took place. Henry of Navarre was a man to love and be proud of, though he was a disobedient son of the Church. There were seventy thousand French corpses spread over the face of the country in this, which has the black name of the Massacre of St. Bartholomew, and people began now to reflect it was their own countrymen they had slain. In the first glow of the success the fourth war broke out, and the Catholics besieged Rochelle, but, after great suffering and heroism, they were repulsed, and the Duke of Anjou was forced to retire. But the bitterness of former struggles was absent. The Catholics lost the ferocity which had characterised the frightful 20th of August, for a strange revulsion had taken place. Charles, haggard with remorse, and tormented with some inward suffering, turned with suspicious eyes upon his mother. She was versed, he well knew, in all the arts of poisoning. Could this wasted frame be the result of something she had poured into his drink? Were those dreadful recollections not enough, without the further aggravation of feeling that his mother was the cause of his decay? He turned his broken heart to the Protestants; he tried, by kindness to the living, to bury the accusations of the dead. His brother Alençon and the Montmorencies had formed a middle party, to which the King of Navarre and the Prince of Condé gave in their adhesion. They resolved to bring in peace and concord, by silencing the extremes on both sides. But the evil spirit of France was on the watch: Catherine stirred up the bad passions on both sides. Alençon betrayed their plans to his mother, and the leaders were arrested. Montgomery, the big rough Scotchman whose uncourtliness had put a splinter in the eye of her husband, Henry the Second, paid with his head, at the interval of fifteen years, the penalty for his maladroitness as well as his Calvinism. Executions were plentiful as before, and Catherine gazed on them with unabated satisfaction. But the king, wearied and desponding, had no taste for these things any more. He was tortured with new and mysterious pains of body, and old and very easily explained agonies of mind, and died on the 30th of May, in the year 1574, with the Massacre of St. Bartholomew weighing upon him to the last.

HENRY THE THIRD,

his successor, was in his twenty-fourth year, and had succeeded during that short period of life in deceiving every friend, deserting every duty, and nullifying every hope. We have seen this Duke of Anjou mix freely in the perils of war, conquer at Jarnac and Moncontour, and displaying among all his deficiencies the solitary virtue of personal courage. Even that deserted him from this time forth. As in our own James the Second, whose earlier days had shown some symptoms of manly enterprise, but whose timidity became as manifest as his cruelty, the possession of supreme power made Henry the Third a voluptuary and a coward. Tyranny, after crushing others, exercised its degrading influence on himself. After being employed by his mother as a bait to secure the assistance, or at least the neutrality, of Elizabeth, by the offer of his hand, he had been elected to fill the throne of Poland by a venal and discontented nobility, who showed, even at that early date, the germs of the perfidy and party-spirit which finally expunged their country from the nationalities of Europe; and accompanied by numbers of his favourites, he had presented himself to his amazed people in the character of the most unmanly sybarite that ever disgraced a crown More bigoted than the most fanatical of enthusiasts, flogging himself in the public street, and joining in the processions from shrine to shrine, the man, with mocking lips, jeered at the very saints he pretended to reverence; and while elevating the Polish hopes and filling his private exchequer, he devoted the chief part of his time to the company of his sycophants and comrades, talking over their adventures in the Court of France, and praying for a speedy return to that infamous society. Charles died suddenly; and the news was thought to travel with great rapidity when it reached Cracovia in thirteen days. Nothing could restrain the impatience of the French nobility to get back to Fontainebleau and the Louvre. Poland was in confusion; there were enemies on the border and malcontents within. The loyal servants who had obtained his election derived their only safety from his presence; the army would resist his departure; so the noble monarch disguised himself as if he were escaping from a prison, slipt out of the palace at midnight, rode without stopping till he had reached the borders of his kingdom, and sent a messenger to the Austrian ruler that his Majesty the King of Poland and France was at his gates. Great receptions gratified his puerile vanity at Vienna, and Venice, and Turin. He was fêted with more zeal as he drew nearer the seat of his power, and on the fifth of September, 1574, he crossed the boundary line into his own dominions, and was received at the Bridge of Beauvoisin by his brother Alençon and Henry of Navarre.

Disgust in a short time took possession of all men's hearts. They saw the descendant of St. Louis and Francis sink religion into ridicule, and knighthood into disgrace. They saw a king of France, surrounded by his minions or favourites, dress himself in woman's clothes, and sing infamous ballads in a public meeting, and on the same day sing psalms through the streets dressed in the robe of a penitent—a Christian Nero, with the solemn voice of Coligny scarcely hushed, and the grim eyes of the Bible-reading Huguenots fixed on all his proceedings. No wonder there was strife and misery in the land. Alençon, wicked as the king, and not so clever, joined the levies which were gathering round the old leaders. Henry of Navarre escaped from his honourable and close-watched detention by the swiftness of his horse at a hunting-party, and bade his adherents, who came to him in great numbers, once more "to follow the White Plume which was always in the front of battle." He celebrated his recovered independence by resuming the exercise of the Protestant faith. But the great families of the Montmorencies and others, who were merely discontented with the government, were disinclined to mix their standards with the avowed Huguenots. It was, therefore, easy for the queen-mother to break up the ill-assorted union. She sent embassies of her bedchamber-women to wait on the Duke of Alençon, and in a very short time that feeble prince was detached from the cause. He, however, mediated a peace which was very favourable to the Reformers. Their worship was permitted in all parts of France except in Paris; all edicts against them were withdrawn; the massacre itself was disavowed; and several additional towns were surrendered to them as pledges. This was the fifth peace since the religious wars began, and was called the Peace of Monsieur, in honour of Alençon. The contemptible being who called himself king, and appeared at ball and theatre with rich necklaces round his bare neck, and affected the appearance of a female beauty, had no wish, in signing this pacification, but to be left undisturbed by the anger of faction or the ambition of his brother. To separate Alençon from the Huguenots, he would have made greater sacrifices still. But the sacrifice he made was quite enough. The Catholics saw the overthrow of their faith in the terms of the treaty; the Huguenots the finger of God in the spread of their opinions.

The Holy League began in 1576—a league which bound itself by the most awful sanctions to extirpate heresy—to spare neither friend nor foe till the pestilence was banished, and even, if need be, to alter the succession to the throne. The next heir after the childless Alençon was a Huguenot; but ascending far above the successors of Hugh Capet, Bourbon, or Valois, there was a prince whose whole heart was devoted to Rome, and who traced up in lineal descent to Charlemagne—and this was Henry of Guise, son of that old Francis who was assassinated by Poltrot, and who himself bore marks of his Catholic soldiership in a wound upon his face, which made him known as the Balafré. "No Protestant King of Navarre! We will have Catholic Henry of Guise!" But Alençon was by no means pleased with this part of the League's intentions. He threw himself into its ranks by way of stemming its course, and was lost or forgotten in the tumult which raged in every heart. The king summoned the States to meet at Blois, but the States showed the somewhat contradictory symptoms, not only of hatred of dissent, but of something very like republicanism. They wished to control the royal power by commissioners appointed by themselves, whose decision on any disputed question was to be final; and being bribed and bullied by the party of the Guises, they passed an edict interdicting the Huguenot faith, and withdrawing all the guarantee towns from their hands. This was, in fact, a declaration of war; the white plume was waving in the breeze in a moment, and all the party were in arms. More sincerity arose on both sides in viewing the matters in dispute, and amalgamation became almost impossible. The king brought discredit on the League and on himself by joining it as a member. This move degraded him from being monarch of France to being one of a faction, and not even chief of it; for in spite of Henry's calling himself the leader of the confederacy, the real authority remained with Henry of Guise. The king, for instance, wished to raise money, but the Balafré frowned, and the Catholic purses remained closed. He could neither command nor persuade. His thoughts, therefore, were soon bent on peace. He managed to obtain a treaty at Bergerac in 1577, by which the former state of affairs was restored. A compliment at the same time was paid to the Huguenots, and a triumph gained to himself, by the abolition of the League. But one of the articles of the League was the indissoluble "association and brotherhood of its members till its objects were obtained." Now, its objects could not be obtained while a Huguenot was favoured, or even tolerated in France, or while there was a chance of the accession of so dangerous a heretic as Henry of Navarre. War after war broke out, to the number of seven in all, and with still increasing hatred; but it is useless to particularise them. It will serve to show the curious mixture of motive and action that one of these is called the War of the Lovers, because it arose from the jealousies and rivalries of the leaders who were invited to meet at the palace of the queen-mother. That astute Italian introduced a sort of chivalry of vice in the prosecution of a campaign. She invited the young prince of Navarre—for he did not take the name of king while his mother, Jane d'Albret, lived—to come to her court with all the cavaliers he chose. There were balls and dances every night, and the appearance of the greatest cordiality; for a radius of a mile and a-half was established round the house, within which quarrels and fighting were unknown. It was an oasis consecrated to the coarser Venus. But outside those narrow limits the war raged with undiminished ardour. A Huguenot lord, after joining in the same dance with a Catholic, would ask him to accompany him for a ride across the line, and the survivor came in with bloody sword to boast of the result. One night Henry gave a return entertainment to the queen and all the court. When the supper was over, and the dances were resumed, Henry slipped out of the garden, joined Sully and some other young nobles who were waiting his arrival, and rode all night. On the following day the queen-mother heard that one of her towns about thirty miles off had been surprised and pillaged ; and when Henry rode back within the peaceful circle, complimented him on the success of his stratagem.

But gloomy forebodings began to mingle with these festivities. Alençon, to weaken the power of Spain, was allowed to place himself at the head of the revolted provinces. The revolt was religious as much as political, and the furious Leaguers saw the brother of the king and heir of the throne enlisted against the Church. His visit to London, to prosecute his claim to Elizabeth's hand, also, though terminating in ridicule and disappointment, showed his want of attachment to the true faith. He came back to Paris humiliated and unsuccessful, both in love and war. His want of zeal was discovered, and not much reliance could be placed on a man who supported the rebels of Holland and wooed the great heretic of England. His death, in 1584, was not lamented on any other account than that it advanced by one step the cause of a far more hated, because far more terrible opponent. The king, however, was more alarmed by the League than by his cousin of Navarre, and threw himself upon his counsels for support. Henry of France and Henry of Navarre were presented as allies to the public mind in opposition to Henry of Guise ; and the war which broke out in 1585 was called the war of the Three Henries. But the weakest of the three threw the game away. He joined again the Catholics who despised him, and neglected the party who, requiring his countenance, would have repaid him with devoted allegiance. The conduct henceforth of Navarre and Guise proved a remarkable contrast. It was the interest of the Bourbon to elevate and dignify the throne to which he saw himself likely to succeed; he therefore treated with profound reverence the office of the king, and his person with outward respect. It was the business of the Guise to degrade the crown, which would otherwise have been too sacred for a sacrilegious hand to touch; he therefore treated the king with marked indignity, and stirred up the lowest passions of the mob in opposition to the highest authority in the land. By his success in this policy he made a narrow escape of exciting feelings of hatred to royalty itself, which would have punished his ambition by taking away the object of it. On the 18th of February, 1587, the execution of Mary Queen of Scots fell like a firebrand on the Catholic plans. She had once been Queen of France, and was the nearest relation to the Guises. She had been true to but one object throughout her life, but that object justified and ennobled all her deeds, for it was the supremacy of the Church. The violences of the League, the curses of the Pope, and the threats of Philip of Spain and of all the Catholics of Europe, had led to the sad catastrophe, by showing the wise counsellors of Elizabeth, that while Mary lived and plotted there was no safety for Protestantism or freedom; and now the blow recoiled with tenfold force on the persons who had made it unavoidable. Philip began his preparations for the Armada. Guise concealed no longer his enmity to the king, and roused the populace and parliament of Paris, both of which were entirely at his command, against him. The infatuated monarch showed his usual want of judgment. He replied to the reclamations of the magistrates by confiscating their salaries, and threatening to throw them in sacks into the Seine. But no course of proceeding would probably have altered the result. Victories and defeats had all the same effect. Henry of Navarre beat an army of Papists commanded by Joyeuse, one of the minions of the court; and Guise repulsed the enemy from the soil of France in Alsace. The defeat was attributed to the king, and the victory to the duke,—a fatal contrast between him and Guise, of which he could not weaken the effect by comparison with Navarre. The two uncrowned Henries were held up as models for the third, for even the Catholics saw with a sort of pride the achievements of Henry, who, though a Huguenot, was a prince and a Frenchman still. This state of affairs could not last long. Guise made a solemn entry into Paris, and was recived with all the ceremony usually reserved for a king. Henry was at the Louvre, and trembled at his subject's approach. When the interview was over, Guise returned to his house and surrounded it with armed men, as if to hint that his life was in danger from the king; a very old trick, and very often successful. Everything continued quiet on both sides till some Swiss royal guards marched into the town. In a moment the mob were up in arms. Barricades were erected in the streets; pistols were fired at the passengers. The Swiss were attacked, and indiscriminate massacre began. Catherine strove in vain to induce her unworthy son to go and show himself to the malcontents. He heard the firing on his troops, and had not the courage to order them to defend themselves; and while his mother rode boldly into the streets to quell the insurrection, he slipt noiselessly to his stables, where the Tuileries gardens now are, and galloped without pause to Rambouillet. On the following day he got safe within the walls of Chartres. This was called the Day of the Barricades, and for a while it certainly advanced the cause of the Duke of Guise. With affected moderation he rejected the acclamations of his party, allowed the Swiss guards to escape, and in other ways endeavoured to pacify the adherents of the king. But dark thoughts were already fermenting in that most unkingly and uncourageous mind. He redoubled his religious observances, a sure sign in him, as in Louis the Eleventh, that some wickedness was in the wind, and signed a ferocious edict against Protestantism in all its branches, banishing its professors from the land, and excluding all heretic princes from succession to the throne. Having done so much for the cause of Catholicism and Guise, could the Balafré refuse his invitation to visit him in his poor house at Blois? The States would be summoned at the same place, and all the difficulties of the country satisfactorily arranged. The Balafré went—the States assembled. A meeting was to be held early in the morning of the 23d of December, 1588; and the king, it was observed, was at his prayers from four or five o'clock. Guise came in at eight, and as he crossed the hall that led to the great staircase the attendants locked and barred the gates. The Balafré entered the council-chamber, and was warming himself at the fire, and eating from a box of bonbons. A message came that the king wished to see him in his room. As the duke lifted up the curtain at the door he was stabbed by a dozen armed men, and only dragged himself into the king's chamber, where he expired. Henry looked at him with a cowardly delight, and kicked the dead face as it lay grim and bloody on the floor. Next day the Cardinal of Lorraine was slaughtered in his room up-stairs by the king's guards, and all the adherents of the two brothers were arrested. Catherine de Medicis, who was confined to her bed, had only time to perceive the success of her lessons of cruelty and dissimulation, for she died in a fortnight after. She was at first appalled at the deed, but ratified it by asking the safety of only two of the Guise family. "Give me the Duke of Nemours," she said, "and the Duke of Joinville: they are young, and may live to serve you." "Willingly, madam," said the king, with a bitter smile, "I will give you their bodies, but I must have their heads."

Heaven and earth rose against the massacre of Blois. It seemed a wilful playing into the hands of the Huguenots to remove the Catholic chief, and the Pope looked on the deed not only as murder, but as heresy. The unruly capital burst into a cry of disobedience, and the Sorbonne formally withdrew the allegiance of the people from an unworthy king. The name of Royalist was as fatal as that of Huguenot had been. The president Harlay, and sixty of the councillors, who bore the royal commission, were only saved from death by being taken to the Bastile. When the meeting at Blois was dissolved, the members spread the flame of disaffection through town and country. The Duke of Mayenne, brother of the murdered Guise, was declared by the Council of Sixteen, consisting of deputies from the sixteen quarters of Paris, lieutenant-general of the kingdom, till the States-General could be assembled. In short, the king was deserted by his people, and nothing was wanting but the formal sentence of his deposition. Henry of Navarre saw his inheritance endangered, and came to the rescue. An interview took place between the cousins ; the Most Christian King, and the most chivalrous Bourbon. It was not altogther regard for his own interests which moved the new ally. In so unsettled a nation as France then was, a forcible change of dynasty would have led to unending conflict, for there was no power like our Houses of Parliament, in the cases of English ejections from the throne, to give it any higher sanction than that of force. To save his country from perpetual civil war or total anarchy was the object of Henry's efforts. His plans were bold and masterly. The few devoted adherents who still clung to their sovereign, from hereditary attachment, or from the poetic compassion which binds noble natures to a fallen race, accepted the guidance of the Huguenot chief. Mayenne was repulsed from Tours, and when men saw such measures of tenderness, as now distinguished the royal army, announced in the royal name, and such admirable military tactics displayed under the royal banner, the personal vices of the nominal monarch began to be forgotten. Opposition was paralysed by the consciousness that the royal authority was now supported by conduct worthy of a king ; and at the end of July, an army of forty thousand men, confident in their leader, and restored to the full feeling of loyalty to the throne, commenced the siege of Paris. Henry of Valois gazed on the hated battlements with delight. "Farewell, Paris," he said ; "from this time your towers and pinnacles shall offend my eyes no more. I will make it difficult to discover where your position was." But Henry of Navarre was more wisely employed. He was superintending the placing of the troops, bringing up the guns, arranging the tents; and it was understood that the day of assault was fixed for the 2d of August. Mayenne saw no chance of safety. His garrison was weak and dispirited; the populace, with its usual fickleness, was cowardly where it was not mad. But among the rabble there was a youth of twenty-two, who had been a Jacobin friar for some time, and had degraded the cowl by the wildest excesses, both of debauchery and blood. Every crime was sweet-smelling odour to Jacques Clement the monk. He wore a dagger which was displayed with ferocious energy in every quarrel, and yet was fanatical in his religious beliefs, and carried the practices of superstition and idolatry to an almost insane extent. This was a sort of man who might be extremely useful in the distress to which the Catholic party were reduced. He was sent for by the Duchess of Montpensier, sister of the Duke of Guise, a woman so wicked that her conduct drives us into a charitable unbelief of its reality, and used such arguments and arts with the blinded, arrogant, sensual young fanatic, that he went forth on the 1st of August, determined to repay his benefactress for her goodness and condescension in the way she herself had prescribed. Letters were furnished to him, which were obtained by false pretences from the president Harlay in the Bastile, and on presenting them he was admitted to the camp of the besiegers, and taken into the presence of the king. While Henry was reading the missive which Clement put into his hand, the Jacobin drew a knife from his sleeve, and stabbed him in his chair. It was not at once fatal. The king started up, and drawing the weapon from his side, wounded his assailant in the face, thus mixing on the same blade the blood of the assassin and his victim. The attendants rushed forward and killed the murderer at once. A happy chance for his employer, for her name escaped the formal revelation which a trial would have produced. Henry was placed in his bed, and for a while hopes were entertained of his recovery

Nothing in his life became him like the leaving it. An undiscovered spring of goodness welled forth as his last hour drew nigh. He forgave his enemies, recommended himself to his friends, embraced the hero of Navarre, and thanked him for all his aid. He turned to the crowd in the apartment, and declared Henry his rightful and true successor, and added, "Dear cousin and brother-in-law, be sure of this, you will never be King of France unless you profess yourself a Catholic." If the dignity and tenderness of a deathbed could have wiped out the vices and deficiencies of all his former years, Henry the Third might have been reckoned among the kings who have done honour to the crown. But the inflexible verdict of history must be delivered upon the course of a man's life, and not on the expressions or aspirations of his last hours; and the last of the Valois must be pronounced a king without honesty or patriotism, and a man without courage or virtue.

Meanwhile he is lying dead upon his blood-stained bed, and Henry of Navarre has proposed an immediate assault upon the devoted town. Some of the assembled nobles have kneeled in sign of fealty to the rightful heir; but many deeds are yet to be done before he can be written of as the acknowledged King of France. At present he is a politician and a warrior, and in both capacities a great field is open for his skill. When the Catholics within the walls heard of the success of their emissary, their joy knew no bounds. The Duchess of Montpensier fell into the arms of the messenger who brought her the news, and kissed the lips which conveyed such tidings of great joy. She got into a carriage, and shouted the intelligence through the streets. The churches —so dreadful was the perversion of men's minds—were filled with triumphant worshippers returning thanks. Jacques Clement was declared a martyr to the faith, and his mother was compared by the blasphemous assemblage to the Holy Virgin who had carried the Saviour of mankind upon her breast. When the intelligence reached Rome, the rejoicings were still more revolting. Sixtus the Fifth pronounced the assassin's praises in full consistory, and compared his achievement in usefulness and self-sacrifice to the incarnation and crucifixion. In Germany and England the deed was differently viewed. Elizabeth got ready troops to be landed in Normandy in aid of the new king. Lutherans and Swiss came pouring into France. Yet Henry's position was dangerous and undefined. The nobles who commanded his armies were Catholics as zealous as the enemy. Before the corpse of the late king was cold, they proposed to his successor a retractation of his Huguenot errors, and conformity to the Church. "You don't know what you ask," replied Henry. "You require a change which would argue no sincerity either in one faith or the other. If you think to terrify me to so sudden an alteration, you know neither my courage nor my conscience." "Sire," cried the gallant Givry, and kneeled at his feet, "you are the true king of the brave, and none but a coward would desert you." The others, however, hung back. The spirit and principles of the League remained unbroken. The Cardinal of Bourbon was even proclaimed by Mayenne under the name of Charles the Tenth. All the victories which made Henry's name distinguished had been gained over Catholic foes. If full powers were conveyed to him, would his policy of depressing the Leaguers not be continued? Henry came to an agreement. He consented to accept a conditional allegiance, binding himself to study the doctrines of the Catholic faith; to summon a States-General at Tours; to restore to the churches the goods of which they had been despoiled; and to limit the privileges of the Reformers to the places in which they at present existed. These things were all to be done within six months. In reliance on these terms, he was recognised sole sovereign of France, and entitled to the obedience of all. But Paris still resisted, and riots and massacres were continually renewed under pretence of religious fears, till Mayenne himself was glad to leave that city of contention and misrule, and take the field against the Man of Béarn, as he was insultingly called. The quality and composition of the contending forces had greatly changed. Mayenne, at the head of preponderating numbers, besieged Henry in Arques, and was only repelled by the union, which his great rival displayed, of the courage of despair and the calmness of military skill. With a mixed army of English, French, Germans, and Swiss, he found it difficult to keep them together, as his purse was low, and the diversity of tongues and nations prevented the unity of the force. To fight was the only way to combine those discordant elements; and at Ivry, on the 13th of March, 1590, he obtained a brilliant success. Mayenne fled. "Save the French!" cried Henry, when the pursuit was hottest; "down with the foreigners! Strike and spare not!"—an unacceptable observation, if understood by his mercenaries from England and other lands. Let us hope it was spoken in purest French, and unintelligible to strangers' ears. It referred to the Spaniards who had been sent by Philip to aid the Catholic cause, and prepare a way for his own ambition. He desired a repeal of the Salic law, and the acknowledgment of his daughter Isabella as heiress to her grandfather Henry the Second.

After this a new power displayed itself, which had never played a part in the quarrels of a nation before. It was the brilliancy of the sayings of the new king, which spread all through France, the land of all others in Europe where a brilliant saying has most weight. After the combat of Arques, where he had been foremost in the attack, he wrote to his friend the Duke of Crillon, "Hang yourself, brave Crillon; we have fought at Arques, and you weren't there." "Gentlemen," he said before the battle of Ivry, "if you miss the standards at any time, look for my white plume; it will lead you to honour and victory." At supper, on the night before, he had spoken harshly to an old German of the name of Schomberg; and while he was marshalling the troops before the charge, he stopped his horse. "Colonel," he said, "we have work before us, and it may chance I don't survive; but I must not carry with me the honour of a gentleman like you. I beg your pardon for what I said last night, and declare you a brave and honourable man." He embraced the colonel. "Ah! sire," said the German in his broken language, "you kill me with your words, for now there is nothing for it but to die in your defence." Schomberg did so. He rode up to the rescue of the king in the hottest of the fight, and fell before Henry's eyes. When he besieged Paris, Mayenne sent out the useless people, who had been starving for some days. Henry fed them, and soothed their fears. Some peasants were brought before him for having introduced provisions into the beleaguered town, and expected to be hanged for aiding the rebels. He gave them all the money he had in his purse. "The Man of Béarn is poor," he said; "if he were richer, he would give you more." One of his captains, the Sieur de Barri, was governor of Leucate, a small place near Narbonne. He was taken prisoner by the Catholics, who carried him before the wall, and threatened to hang him if his wife would not surrender the town. She refused, and the Leaguers killed her husband. She had a Catholic prisoner of equal rank in her hands, but she disdained reprisals, and let him go. Henry heard of her conduct, and this was her reward:—He appointed her governor (not governess) of Leucate till the majority of her son; thus giving a man's honour to her who had shown a man's heart. Compared to these actions and words of Henry, the conduct of his opponents was not only unchivalrous but unpopular. Divisions raged high among the leaders of the League. Mayenne wished to be king; the Duke of Lorraine wished his son to be king; and when Henry of Guise, the son of Balafré, escaped from his prison of Tours, and joined the garrison of Paris, he also wished to be king. The Infanta, or daughter of Spain, wished to be queen; and it did not need half the quickness which is always found in the French to perceive that, compared with any or all of his competitors, the man of the white plume and the generous spirit was the fittest occupant of the throne.

But a rigorous pontiff filled the Roman chair. Sixtus the Fifth would hear of no accommodation with a heretic, and Henry would hear of no recantation when his motives might be suspected. "Master first, disciple afterwards," was his motto, and the war went on. The Sixteen, as the sections of Paris called themselves, were in the pay of Spain. Availing themselves of the absence of Mayenne, they encouraged the brutal populace to break out into a riot; they tore the more moderate of the judges from their seats, and hung them with their president, above the doorway of the court. Mayenne came back. Great was his fear of Henry, but greater his wrath against the Sixteen. He hanged four of them from lamp-posts in the street, and restored the ordinary municipal officers to their authority. But regular authority dislikes rebellion, and the now pacified city looked kindly on the legitimate heir. Other opponents were driven over to his side by the injudicious aid his enemies received. Alexander Farnese, Duke of Parma, was the most famous general of the time, and had been chosen to bring the legions of Spain and the chains of the Inquisition over here in the year of the Armada, 1588. He was now selected to head the same legions to support the fantastic claim of his master's daughter. Henry was driven to extremities, for Alexander was unluckily the most cautious of commanders, and always refused a battle. The daring gallantry of the royalists, with Henry at their head, fell back like sparkles of foam before the imperturbable solidity of the Spanish lines. They would not fight—they would not retreat—they solemnly performed the work assigned to them, the protection of a border or the relief of a town, but they would do nothing more. Alexander of Parma was not at all like Alexander of Macedon, for he had nothing of the hero in him except his courage, and trusted nothing to chance. Against policy like this the Man of Bêarn had no defence. His allies were not united in their desires. The English wished to drive the Spaniards from the shores of Brittany and Normandy, where they would have been dangerous neighbours to Elizabeth ; Henry wished to drive them from the middle of France and send them to the shore, where they could do least harm to himself. He could raise no taxes by the legal machinery of Parliament and Council, and would not lay hard contributions on the districts he held. He was the poorest of gentlemen, this most lovable of kings; and hints are given that his Majesty's apparel was not altogether free from darns, or his boots from holes in the leather. Nothing kept its gloss but the plume of white feathers which swayed above his head, and his bright sword and imperturbable good-humour. While in this condition his great adversary, Alexander of Parma died (December, 1502), and his fortunes revived. He gathered all his forces for a last attempt upon Paris, and his enemies as usual played into his hands. The same cowardly bigot, Philip of Spain, who had united all classes and creeds of Englishmen in favour of Elizabeth by his insolent Armada, now was the creator of French union by his domineering conduct in France. Mayenne summoned a States-General at his request, and Philip there in no courteous terms stated his royal will; it was very short and very decisive—they were to accept his daughter as queen, that was all. A compromise was attempted; they would declare the Duke of Guise king, and he should marry the Infanta. Philip refused; his daughter should be queen in her own right, and then would marry Guise. Mayenne, who saw, whether it was king or queen, his pretensions were at an end, procured a resolution of the Parliament of Paris, that "any sentence, decree, or declaration, contrary to the Salic law, should be void and of non-effect." Whatever strengthened the Salic law and the direct succession was a vote on the side of Henry of Navarre. The royalist army, the lawyers of the League, and now the Parliament of Paris, had virtually pronounced in favour of his claim. Nothing was wanting to secure the unity and peace of the kingdom but the acceptance by the king of the religion of the majority. If he could only believe that the Pope was the first Bishop of Christendom—that mysterious power rested on the consecrated priest—that the holy men who carried humanity to its highest point by the virtues of their lives, were now, with increased authority, permitted to watch over human affairs—if he could only believe that images and pictures were aids to pure devotion, and that only within the boundaries of a divinely-founded, divinely-supported Church, salvation was to be found, what blessings could he not shower down on twelve or fourteen millions of people—what laws might he not enact—what charities might he not bestow—what glory might he not obtain! It does not become us to pass judgment on the sincerity of his conversion. The inclination to believe was strong, and to some minds we find even now the romantic and poetic element contained in the old faith, with all its recorded martyrdoms and miracles, is irresistible, at the sacrifice, instead of the gain, of worldly standing; and we must accept the declaration of faith which Henry gave in the Church of St. Denis, on the 25th of July 1593, as the sincere expression of his heart and mind. Best proof of the sincerity of his Christian feeling and of the reality of the sentiments he professed was this, that he did not turn a persecutor—he did not sneer at the party he had left, or hold them up as hypocrites or knaves. He acknowledged, with the self-respect he knew to be his due, that it does not require a man to be a traitor as well as a convert, or to gain favour with his new communion by mean insinuations or bitter invectives against his old. Henry did not run the risk of being considered a dissembler in both his religions—a false Protestant feigning an opposition to the Papists which he did not feel—a false Papist scattering libels upon the Protestants which he could not believe—for he was manly and above board, not less in his conformity than in his resistance. And now the Catholic Henry was crowned king of France, 27th February 1594.

CHAPTER XII.

HENRY THE FOURTH, A. D. 1594, TO THE DEATH OF LOUIS THE THIRTEENTH, A. D. 1643.

CROWNED king, with a hand equally fitted to hold the sceptre and wield the sword, Henry the Fourth made the nation feel the beneficial effects of a strong government at once. Twice he had besieged Paris—twice he might have taken it: once by famine, and he fed the wretched inhabitants; once by storm, but he would not expose it to the horrors of an assault; and we may guess with what feelings he was now received within the reconciled and grateful city. In this great contest the delightful thing was that both parties thought they had won: the Leaguers, because they had put a Catholic on the throne; the Huguenots, because their leader and champion had gained all he desired. God save the king! was shouted all day long when he entered into the capital, which, however, at that moment was garrisoned by Spanish troops. The united Leaguers and Huguenots stood round their sovereign. He politely invited the foreigners to leave his good town, and stood at the Porte St. Denis to see them go. They defiled past him, and in answer to their salute, he said, "Good-by, gentlemen. My compliments to your master, but don't come here any more." The only two powers who delayed the recognition of the king were the Pope and Philip. The former intended to make a bargain for his complaisance, and the latter never forgave any one who ran counter to his plans. The Catholic Henry availed himself of the Pragmatic which had conveyed the patronage of abbeys and bishoprics to the Crown, and turned the tables on the Holy Father by employing the honours of the Church in pacifying the State. If a zealous Leaguer still held back, hesitating to believe the sincerity of the conversion, he was convinced of the Catholicism of the most Christian King by the bestowal of the revenues of a vacant stall or rich deanery. Villars Brancas, a zealous papist and gallant soldier, who was governor of Rouen against the king, never gave credit to Henry's attachment to the Church till he was presented with two or three abbacies for his own enjoyment. Rouen then opened its gates, and the military abbot did suit and service to his orthodox and discriminating patron. All the leaders were softened by the same arts, and at last Guise and Montmorency were admitted into favour. Guise, a disappointed opponent, was made governor of Provence; and Montmorency, a discontented supporter, received the constable's staff. Hatred, doubt, and bitterness, of course lay for a long time in the hearts of the fanatical and ambitious. Clement the Eighth, the fifth Pope who within four years had sat on the Roman throne, had not pronounced the absolution of Henry's previous unbelief, and a youth, a pupil of the Jesuits, imbued with their principles, if not incited in this instance by their advice, attempted the murder of the king. His knife slipped, and only inflicted a trifling wound; but the whole nation was awake to the indignity of the action. The University and Parliament pronounced against the Jesuits, and they were ordered from the soil of France. Henry confessed the step was necessary, but it was not legal, and in a few years he revoked the sentence of banishment, and allowed the society to return.

Meanwhile he required some outlet for the national spirit, some point of union for the national animosities. All Frenchmen hated Philip, and he declared war on Spain, January 1595. Henry kept himself in the centre, ready to fly to the rescue of any of his peers. Biron was hard pressed in Burgundy, and retreated on the Marne;—Henry hurried down and won a brilliant victory at Dijon. An adherent at Marseilles slew the traitorous consul of that city, and admitted Guise, who was now a true servant of the Crown, within the walls. Henry was received with acclamations, and the Spaniards who held the citadel were expelled. At last, when all the gallant soldiers of the realm were anxious for an opportunity of display, and none had any theatre for their talents unless under Henry's command, the gratifying intelligence was given to the king that Mayenne himself, the general of the League and competitor for the Crown, was coming in to make his submission. He was immensely fat, and very short of breath. Henry received him in a broad walk of his garden, and after listening to his complaints, kept him in earnest conversation, walking all the time at a far quicker pace than usual. Panting, puffing, red in the face, and very weary on his legs, the Duke de Mayenne did not dare to interrupt the king's talk, and on they went, the king pacing as if for a wager, and the prodigious bulk of Mayenne visibly melting away with heat and agitation. At last he could hold out no longer, and begged to be allowed to rest. "Cousin," cried the king, bursting into a laugh, "I'm glad you've spoken at last, for this is all the punishment I intend to inflict on you for your opposition." And severe enough punishment it was, for another half hour would probably have been the death of him.

Measures were now taken to improve the internal administration of the country. An assembly of notables was convoked at Rouen, and Henry granted them full powers, telling them he had summoned them, not to register his commands, but to give him their advice. The design was admirable, but the principles of civil government had fallen into disuse. There were blind monarchists in the meeting, and blind republicans too. Some thought it treason to interfere with the royal prerogative, and others thought that no interference with it could be too much. While these discussions went on, the Spaniards surprised Amiens by a sudden march, and the war interfered with reform. Henry showed all his ancient valour, and some of his ancient foolhardiness. "I have played the king of France too long," he said, "I must give them a specimen of the king of Navarre." He attacked the Archduke Albert of Austria at the head of a small body of horse, and the Spaniards, persuaded that such audacity could only proceed from an enemy with immense support in the rear, retreated before a twentieth of their force. All France was soon cleared of foreign enemies, and domestic factions were now to be reconciled. Peace! peace! was as earnest a cry of Henry as of our own Lord Falkland; and in that sacred word, as he called it, he included the closing up of religious differences. On the 13th of April 1598, he issued the celebrated Edict of Nantes, conveying toleration in its widest sense to the dissidents from the established faith. Peace with Spain was signed at Vervins on the 2d of May of the same year, and a greater security was given for the repose of France, and the pacification of Europe, than the signature of so false and truculent a tyrant as Philip, by his death, which occurred in September. He had offended every State by his ambition, and sickened every heart by his cruelty. His country retaining its size and the appearance of power and grandeur, lay in reality like a water-logged first-rate on the sea, with its crew in mutiny, and its guns dismounted. It needed only a storm or an enemy to make it founder or strike.

With peace a great king only changes the field of his labours. There was the devastation of thirty years to be repaired, irregularities in government to be corrected, and contentment to be restored to the great body of the people. But the talent of a great king is not less shown by the choice of his counsellors in peace than of his generals in war. Henry had remarked from an early period the wisdom and self-command of a young Protestant of the name of de Rosni, who had been presented to him in 1571, when he was only eleven years old. Cautious and calculating, as befitted his Scottish blood (for he was of the family of the Bethunes), but bold and enterprising, when occasion offered, as his master himself, de Rosni found himself consulted on affairs of the deepest importance before he had risen above a captain's rank in the military array. Ever rising with the fortunes of the king, de

Rosni, at the time we have now reached, was intendant of the finances, and grand master of the artillery of France. But, more than all these, he was the king's friend, without a touch of courtiership, and his adviser, without a thought of self-interest. With the help of a man so wise and so patriotic, affairs rapidly began to mend. The income of the State was raised without exaction, and spent with economy. The first reform was in the mode of raising the taxes, of which it was discovered that not more than a sixth part reached the royal exchequer. This was put an end to by the dismissal of almost all the intermediate receivers, and a direct payment being made to the treasury, by which the expenses of collection were afterwards paid. The next and more difficult reform was the abrogation of certain exemptions which diminished the number of contributories to the public finances, and of course increased the liabilities of the tax-paying class. By a fatal retention of feudal privilege, the French nobility had asserted their freedom from the ordinary taxation of the State, even after their feudal obligation of personal service in war was commuted for an equivalent in money. Payment of a national burden would have been degradation to their rank as nobles. Now it had also become an established rule, during the wars and struggles of the last half-century, that the profession of arms ennobled, that is, that active service in the field withdrew a man, whatever his birth might be, from the list of roturiers or taxable plebeians, and made him so far on a level with the highest in the land. Another class had availed itself of the exemption conveyed by the possession of certain estates which were suffered to carry a title of nobility with them; and rich tradesmen and successful lawyers had purchased "ennobling lands," for the double purpose of assuming a territorial title, and delivering themselves from the burden of taxation. If we consider the number of fighting captains and purse-proud receivers, and others who had either carried a sabre or filled their pockets since the reign of Francis the First, we shall see what a host of enemies was raised by the undaunted de Rosni, when he withdrew the rank and privilege both from soldier and landowner. There was to be no title to true nobility except descent from noble fathers, or direct creation by the king. The nobles of the sword, and acquirers of seignorial fiefs, were therefore plain misters again, and contributed to the public income in proportion to their means.

But the counsellor and the king were equally fitted to each other in other respects. If Henry had the misfortune to retain the fire and passions of his youth till long after his hair was grey, and threatened never to grow old, he had the counterbalancing advantage, in the sagacious de Rosni, of a guide and adviser who had never been young at any period of his life. Always steady, and unbiassed by the tastes or frivolities of the time, the youth of nineteen had had the calmness of a sage of forty, and now at forty he had the affectionateness and zeal of a youth of nineteen. All his affectionateness and zeal were brought into play by the divorce the king insisted on in 1599. Margaret of Valois was the bride, you remember, whose marriage was celebrated with the bloody rejoicings of the Bartholomew massacre seven-and-twenty years before. Her life had answered to that fearful beginning; for she was one of the most debased and infamous of women, in a time when the standard of female virtue was not so high as it is at present. Reception into the Romish Church opened a way for the dissolution of the marriage, and the newly-converted Henry applied for it as a favour as well as a right. Nothing could resist the evidence, but the Court of Rome is famous for its delay. In the interval Henry was captivated by the beauty of a young lady of noble family, and was prepared to offer her a promise of marriage. De Rosni was consulted on the point, and tore the proposed engagement to pieces, when the king showed him the paper he had written, exposing himself by the action to the rage of his master and the hatred of the powerful family of the disappointed damsel. To prevent similar imprudences, a marriage was hurried on in a few months after the sentence of separation was pronounced by the Pope, and another de Medicis mounted the throne of France. Mary de Medicis had no brilliant virtues to extinguish the memory of her relative and predecessor Catherine, but she had none of the darker vices to recall that personage's reign. It would be pleasant if we could say that the charms of domestic happiness weaned the king from the course of life he had so long pursued ; but the truth must not be concealed that his career of sensuality continued to the close. His reign is marked by the succession of his favourites as well as of his victories and laws ; and these love-passages, as they were called, entered so deeply into the popular view of the monarch, and became so mixed up in the ballads and memoirs of the time, that many who know nothing about the battle of Ivry or the Edict of Nantes, derive their idea of his character from the story of the Fair Gabrielle or Marie de Beauvilliers. Nothing could be more misleading than any belief of the kind. His true lineaments were drawn in the cabinet of de Rosni, who is better known as Duke of Sully, and not in the boudoir of contending beauties. It was there that, in 1602, he had to make head against a revolt—not of his people, whose heart he had won by the care he took of their interests, and the homely but noble wish he expressed that the time might soon come when every Frenchman might have a hen in his pot—but by a contention of nobles whom his great qualities alarmed, and who were forced to raise upon their side, against a patriotic king of the seventeenth century, the prejudices and ignorance of the thirteenth.

The great chiefs of the old nobility, whom he had appointed governors of counties, or who retained in their genealogical books records of the time when they were equals of royalty and independent within their own domains, entered into absurd plots to bring back the days of Richard of England and Philip Augustus. Foremost and most foolish among these was the Marshal de Biron, Henry's chosen friend and fellow-soldier, and the last man he would have suspected of treachery or disaffection. But Biron was the vainest of men, and was deluded into the hope of a duchy, or even a kingdom, by the aid of Spain and Savoy, and of his discontented brethren, the Guises and de Bouillons and Montmorencies. Biron's movements, however, were known; and Henry sent for him, and told him his plots were discovered. In a fit of repentance or of returning friendship, Biron renewed his fealty, and half-confessed his crime; but the tempters were at work as before. He transgressed again—was arrested, imprisoned, tried and beheaded—the last example of a conspiracy for the recovery of feudal rights—the first example of a great dignitary judicially convicted of high treason, and executed in course of law. The terror was greater that the leniency of the king was known, and his anxiety to pardon the culprit if he would only condescend to confess his fault. The companions of his crime were, therefore, either silent and submissive, or fled to foreign lands. It was thus that, before the crown had been twelve years upon his head, Henry had no enemy and no gainsayer in all the realm of France. Protestant and Catholic vied with each other in affection to his person, and for the first time in all the weary years we have surveyed, from the disturbed times of Charlemagne and his sons, to the victories of England and the Wars of the League, the kingdom was at unity in itself. An heir to the throne, born in 1601, had given another support to the house of Bourbon, and another security to France. There was no chance now of a change of dynasty, or a dispute about the succession. After consolidating his power at home, and endearing himself to his people more and more by his care of their pecuniary interests—with his arsenals filled with stores, his harbours with ships, and his army ready for summons at a moment's notice—Henry looked across the borders of his beloved and happy France, and made up his mind to carry into effect a plan which he had entertained for many years. It is called in history the Political Design of Henry the Fourth, and has generally been treated with opposition as injudicious, or with contempt as impossible.

We, who only know Spain in its decay and Austria as an ill-compacted power, can form a very slight estimate of the fears caused at this time by the preponderance of the House of Hapsburg. The two branches into which it was divided held more than the half of Europe. But greater than the influence they had exercised through their territorial pre-eminence, was the might they possessed in countries under other crowns, by their being recognised the chiefs and supporters of Catholicism wherever it was to be found. At this time the bent of men's minds, and the force of circumstances, had led to the combination of various hitherto discordant states. The counties and dukedoms of France, we have seen, had all become welded into a firm and solid domain. England and Scotland, forgetting their political animosities, accepted the decree of geography, and were one Great Britain under the same king. Switzerland had increased the closeness of the ties between its cantons. The provinces of the Netherlands, subdued and powerless under their foreign yoke, had formed themselves into a compact confederacy in successful resistance to Philip and his son. To make up for this loss, Spain had amalgamated Portugal; and the Peninsula presented an appearance of union from the Pyrenees to Gibraltar, and from the Mediterranean to the Atlantic. Gathered in rich dependence on this enormous realm lay Naples and Sicily, Sardinia and the States of Milan; and far away, magnified by distance, and awful from their unknown dimensions and population, the vast regions that owned its sway in America. The other branch held the Empire, which gave it a supremacy over the whole of Germany, while the Emperor, in his separate capacity, was king of Austria, Bohemia, Hungary, and Transylvania. The union between the houses was strict and indissoluble; and when Protestantism examined the strength and number of its opponents—in which formally it was forced to include the Most Christian King, who had only attained his throne by forsaking its communion—the prospect seemed dark and almost hopeless either for religious or civil freedom; for the more attentively we examine history, clearer and clearer rises before us the great and sacred truth that these two are inseparable. Besides the dominions held in direct sovereignty by Spain and Austria, there were all the little potentates of Italy to weigh down the already overloaded scale. The Pope, the Duke of Mantua, and the Commonwealth of Genoa, were so surrounded by the possessions of the Hapsburgs, that they had no liberty of action even if their religious tenets did not lead them willingly to adhere to the Catholic cause. Great Britain, on the other hand, was a Protestant power ; so were Holland and the northern states of Germany, and Denmark and Sweden. What was there laughable or impossible in the creation, out of these elements, of a counterpoise to the dangerous overweight of the two great and allied monarchies ? We of the present generation, who see the fulfilment of Henry's object in the established balance of power by the erection of a tribunal of war and peace, constituted of the five great monarchies of Europe, can do little more than admire the wisdom of a statesman who, two hundred and fifty years ago, had the foresight to desire a central court of arbitration and government, in which every European community should have a voice. We need not follow the plans by which it was proposed to achieve this end ; but the things aimed at have almost all been accomplished. Spain was to be reduced to her peninsular domains ; America and the West Indies thrown open to trade ; the House of Savoy strengthened by a great increase of territory in Piedmont, and eventually by the possession of Lombardy. More independent authority was to be given to the princes of Germany ; and the crowns of Spain and the Empire were to be rendered incapable of being held by members of the same family. From the early part of 1601, the great arrangement had occupied the thoughts of Henry and Sully. In that and succeeding years a correspondence on the subject was carried on with Elizabeth, who suggested several articles in the plan; and though James occasionally agreed to it, and even professed himself willing to immortalise his name by taking all the honour of the original idea to himself, he was of too feeble a mind, and frivolous a character, even to understand a scheme which might have realised the dreams which political enthusiasts already began to entertain, of a perpetual peace, where civilisation and Christianity should rule over different kingdoms as if they were merely provinces of the same realm, and the barbarian Turks, expelled beyond the Bosphorus, should terminate their debased and brutal national existence in the wildernesses from which they sprang. Christendom for Christians, and Europe a Brotherhood of States, might have been the motto inscribed on the banners of the confederates in this holy cause. In 1609 the incident occurred which had been waited for as the signal for action on the part of France. The dukedom of Cleves became vacant by the death of John William, without children for his succession. The candidates were the Catholic Duke of Saxe, and the Lutheran Elector of Brandenburg, and the Calvinist Count Palatine of Neuburg. The Emperor pronounced for the Catholic, and Henry took part with the Protestant princes. War burst out like a fire that has smouldered in secret. The German rivals were anxious to decide their quarrel before the arrival of the King of France. The territory in dispute was therefore, as is usual in struggles of this sort, made the theatre of incalculable sufferings ; it was made a desert by both parties, because it could not peaceably be enjoyed by either.

But however the contest might appear to vary in details, the result was evidently foreseen. Henry, the foremost warrior of his time, was again in the saddle with thousands of the men of Arques and Ivry, ready to follow him as of old, in company with their sons. The Popish prospects, on the other hand, were gloomy in the extreme. The Swiss and Savoyards were interposed as barriers between the forces of Spain and Italy and the plains of Germany. Venice protected the shores of the Adriatic, and the Emperor was engaged in quelling revolts in Hungary and Bohemia. All the Catholics of Europe who preferred the supremacy of the faith to the liberties of their country, cried shame on the eldest son of the Church, who deserted his mother in her distress. Lutheranism, Calvinism, Anglicanism, all raised their heads and prayed for the success of the Most Christian King. On the 14th of May 1610 the king got into his coach to go to the arsenal and take leave of Sully, who was Grand Master of the Artillery. He was on the eve of parting for the Rhine, and great schemes were revolving in that now grizzled head whose active fancies age had failed to subdue. Beside him in the great vehicle, which was almost as large as a modern omnibus, sat seven noblemen of his court. They had turned from the Louvre into one of the narrow streets, and were interrupted by some encumbrance on the road. While the carriage stopped till the obstacle was removed, a man of great height, muffled in a cloak, and with a broad-brimmed hat over his brows, stood up on the spokes of the wheel, dashed his arm into the window, and struck Henry with a knife. A second stab pierced the most gallant and loving heart in Christendom, and the king fell back dead. There was awe and consternation all round. The murderer was not struck down at once, or torn to pieces, or trampled by the crowd. His name was Francis Ravaillac, a fanatic, though in the calmest possession of his senses—a man of incredible firmness of mind, who bore all the tortures of his trial and execution without departing from the silence he had enjoined himself. No art or cruelty could extract a confession of his confederates, if any he had. All he revealed was merely his hatred to the Protestant faith, and zeal to force the professors of it to recant on pain of death. He had taken the habit of a lay brother in the monastery of St. Bernard. He there was troubled with a strong inclination to kill the king—visions pushed him on to it. It was evidently the will of Heaven, for the king intended, he was told, to make war on the Pope, the highest of earthly sins, inasmuch as "the Pope was God, and God the Pope." Whatever secret lies under the silence of this misguided enthusiast, the suspicions of the Protestants throughout the world were raised and justified by the rejoicings caused by the execrable deed. Catholicism was saved in Germany by the death of the great protector of the Protestants, and howls of execration were uttered over the dead soldier in all the pulpits of Rome. Francis Ravaillac was spoken of after his execution as an instrument raised by divine justice; and, scarcely stopping at the word martyr, many went so far as to consider him a saint.

Meanwhile the victim, after life's fitful fever, slept in an honoured grave among the great monarchs of his race, and in every heart in France was written his epitaph—Henry the Great the Father of his Country.

LOUIS THE THIRTEENTH.

Henry the Fourth was fifty-seven years of age when he died, and left a son of nine, the heir of his throne and reputation. A few more years of life might have enabled the affectionate father to mould the son's mind to higher purposes, and instruct him how to carry on with firmness and wisdom the scheme of government he had commenced. But Louis the Thirteenth was the spoilt child of a weak and selfish woman. Deceitful, timid, unprincipled, and capricious, Mary de Medicis was as injurious to France by the lessons of dependence and favouritism she gave her son, as the darker de Medicis of a former time by the bad instruction in violence and tyranny she had given to Charles the Ninth and Henry the Third. A king perpetually in search of support, clinging to every flattering or bullying courtier who can gain the upper hand, entering into the cabals of his court with the keenness and dishonesty of a candidate for place, imprints a character of meanness and pusillanimity on his reign which may be as hurtful to the interests of his people as the bolder vices of more wicked and unscrupulous natures. It is perhaps safer for a monarch to be hated than despised. Fortunately for Louis, or his mother, who was appointed Regent, the crop of great princes in Europe had died out; and as we have often in the course of this history seen a similarity of character in the kings of the time—the Richards of England replied to by the Philip Augustuses of France; the Henry the Eighths matched with the Francis the Firsts—so, at this period, the frivolous and unworthy favourites of the court of France corresponded in a remarkable degree to the wretched parasites and intriguers of the court of James the First. Spain, as we have seen, had sunk into premature decrepitude under Philip the Third. A feeble potentate hardly retained the Empire from slipping from his hand. The minor states were ruled by persons who made no mark in the annals of the time. Undisturbed, therefore, by foreign interference, uncontrolled by internal government, rioting in debauchery in Paris, caballing with their confederates in the provinces—the nobles, who had yielded a willing obedience to Henry, broke out into the wildest excesses of personal independence, or vied with each other in selling their support to the trembling and capricious Regent. It might have been taken for a sudden leap backward into the feudal times. The princes of the blood, the chiefs of the Guises, the Duke of Nemours (of the house of Savoy), the families of Rohan and Soubise, of Longueville and Saint Paul, the Dukes of Bouillon, Joyeuse, and Epernon, were by no means disinclined to assert their dignities, and gathered round them a crowd of retainers who vowed suit and service to them with more unreserved allegiance than the ancient homage. But when their pride was farther increased, and their power augmented, by appointments to the great governments of the realm—when Mayenne kinged it in the Isle of France, with Paris as its capital, and Vendôme in Brittany, and Epernon in the Anjoumois, Montmorency in Languedoc, and the others in like manner from Picardy to Béarn—no limits could be put to their insolence and encroachments. Sully was early disgusted with the intrigues of the court-circle, and retired to his government of Poitou ; and then the weak Italian was left to her own devices. Her own devices extended no farther than the selection of some stronger and firmer nature on which her feebleness could rely.

In her suite, when she came to France in 1601, was a certain very inferior officer called Concino Concini, and with him his wife, Eleanora Galigai. This Eleanora was the ruling spirit in the councils of the Crown. Her influence was so striking, that we can scarcely wonder if, in that superstitious age, it was attributed to magic. Whatever she said was law, and Mary de Medicis was the mere secretary to record her wishes. Her husband was made Marquis d'Ancre, first Minister of State, and finally Marshal of France. The nobility could submit to a good deal; and it was observed that as long as Concini distributed among them the treasure which the late king had collected for the expenses of the war with Spain, their objections were mildly stated and easily withdrawn; but when the exchequer was exhausted and a foreign menial was made Marshal of France, their patriotism rose. They retired to their respective provinces, and prepared for an insurrection. The threat, however, was sufficient; Mary promised to summon a States-General, and hurried her son, who had just reached his thirteenth year, before the Parliament of Paris, and had him declared of full age, and qualified to commence his reign. The States-General assembled in the midst of high-raised expectations, and separated, as usual, with universal disappointment. The discussions showed the want of a centralising patriotism, or even of administrative adroitness. There was no order in the debates; the nobility complained of the privileges showered upon the people; the people, or Third Estate, complained of the pensions settled upon the nobility; the clergy complained of the non-publication of the decrees of Trent and the toleration extended to Protestants. The assembly was dissolved in a few months, and the name of the States was never heard again, till the fearful days of the great Revolution, when men looked anxiously back to get a foundation in the past for their proposed edifice of liberty and justice, and found nothing more to the purpose than the archives of this long-forgotten and abortive convocation.

The leaders of the nobles had hoped to gain all their ends by the votes of the States-General; but they did not know the arts of Concini, or the talents of his wife. Spain, they thought, was to be conciliated, and the enmity of the great Henry atoned for, by the submission of his son. The hand of a Spanish princess was therefore applied for in 1615, and Louis was espoused to Anne of Austria, the daughter of Philip the Third, while Elizabeth of France, his sister, was sent to Madrid as bride to the Prince of Spain. The double marriage was expected to strengthen the faction of the Italians, but the feeling of independence the ceremony had impressed on the young king was a circumstance for which neither Concini nor Galigai was prepared. Mary, however, was still kept in complete subjection, and Louis appeared also, for a time, to have no will of his own. He was confined to the grounds of the palace, and was never allowed to show himself to the Parisians. The Tuileries garden, where so many happy children are daily to be seen, when the trees are in full leaf, and the parterres filled with flowers, was the sole scene of amusement or recreation permitted to the youthful king. A few friends were allowed to join him in his sports; among others, a gentleman of the name of Albert de Luynes, whose genius does not seem to have been of a very lofty order, since it was limited to a marvellous skill in the handling of hawks and other birds of prey. However, the sportsman-like Albert was the dearest friend of the desolate son of Henry. Meanwhile, the great nobility had gone into open insurrection. They formed a confederation for the Public Good—hoping by that name to enlist the favour of the poorer classes on their side; but Concini offered places to some, increased rank to others, and money to all, and the public good was forgotten in the private benefit. Condé, the chief of the association, went to court—insulted the queen—threatened the favourite, and so broke through the terms of the Treaty of Loudun, by which the differences were arranged, that in a fit of rage and insulted dignity, the three Italian adventurers, the queen and the Concinis, signed a warrant, and committed Condé to the Bastile. Condé was first prince of the blood, and nearest relation of the king. All the promoters of the Public Good were in arms at once. Troops were marshalling over all the land; but Concini kept his nerve. He called into the councils of the queen a quiet-looking young ecclesiastic, who had spoken with great eloquence at the meeting of the States-General, two years before, and had been appointed Bishop of Luçon. His name was Armand Duplessis de Richelieu, and he attached himself to the interests of his patron and the queen. Something already told him perhaps that he was doomed to be the most fatal foe the nobility had ever seen. Of this, however, he gave no sign, but kept his eyes and ears open to the incidents which were evidently on the eve of appearing The first event seemed fatal to all his hopes.

Louis and de Luynes were in the Tuileries gardens one day, in 1617, and the conversation fell upon the Regent and her favourites ;—the mother was harsh and fickle—the Concinis arrogant and neglectful ; Louis hated them all three; and listened to his friend well pleased. The friend told him "he did not know what was the extent of his power, or how much the people wished him to reign in reality and not in name. Who were those low Italians who drove the queen-mother in whatever path they chose? Would the Parisians rise in their defence—the Parisians who had tamely seen Condé, a Bourbon and a Prince, conveyed through the streets to prison? It needed only a little signature—all else would follow. He should soon feel what it was to be a king." The little signature was given, and as Concini entered the Louvre, a band of gentlemen surrounded him ; one demanded his sword, and while he was drawing it out in sign of his surrender, the others shot him with pistols, and stabbed him in fifty places, till he lay stark dead upon the courtyard pavement. Immediately the young king threw open a window, from which he had seen the exploit, and went out on the balcony and thanked his loving subjects for the great action they had performed. He then agreed to the banishment of his mother to Blois, and the arrest and trial of Eleanora Concini. It would have been kinder to have put her to death along with her husband. She was arraigned of high crimes and misdemeanours, but principally of having obtained her power over the queen by sorcery. "The only sorcery I employed," she proudly said, as she went to execution, "was the sorcery which a strong mind exercises over a weak one." The fierce love of blood which has always characterised the Paris mob burst forth on this occasion ; they carried the head of the unhappy woman through the streets upon a pole, and tore her body to pieces.

De Luynes, the skilful fitter of hawks' hoods, was no less

skilful in profiting by the royal favour. He was made Duke, Marshal, Constable, in a very short time, and appointed inheritor of all the wealth of his predecessors. From this time the politics of Europe were regulated not by kings, but by their favourites. Lerma or Olivarez, in Spain, Buckingham in England, and de Luynes in France, degraded the royal dignity to such a degree that the three most despised men in their own dominions were Philip, and James, and Louis. Each was so absorbed in the petty cabals of his own court, that he could take no part in the great affairs which were shaking the world beyond his own realm. The Thirty Years' War broke out in 1618, by which it was to be determined whether religious liberty was to survive in any portion of Europe; immense interests, territorial as well as theological, were at stake. But James was busied in composing the quarrels of his courtiers, or writing counter-blasts against the smoking of tobacco. Philip was sunk in gloomy and enervating superstition. Louis was led by the will of de Luynes; and that manager of falcons, now converted into a statesman, saw no higher duty before him than that of increasing his influence and riches. Religious jealousies also mingled with other causes of disturbance, and kept men's attention at home. The Protestants were alarmed at the absorption of the state of Béarn into the realm, and the restoration of all Church property in that state to the Catholics. Rochelle became the headquarters of the malcontents, and Paris replied to its declarations of armed independence, with cries against the toleration of any form of dissent.

After a period of doubt and indecision, with no strength in the government and little union among the discontented, the accumulation of petty grievances, and the insolence of a court which knew how to insult but not to govern, became intolerable in all parts of the country, and civil war in its wildest form burst forth. In any other kind of contest the personal courage of the king would have redeemed him from the contempt of his people. In 1620 he put himself at the head of the lords and cavaliers who were true to his person, and carried havoc and desolation among his foes. But his foes were his own mother and the nobility of his realm. He showed some sparks of the paternal fire, and fought well and bravely, but against his own subjects. Two years of siege and skirmish showed him how impossible it was to restore union to the nation by the mere exercise of force ; and neither he nor his councillors had wideness of view enough to re-establish tranquillity by introducing fixed principles of action into the government instead of trusting to the sword. The sword could not restrain the ambition of the nobles, for the sword was wielded by themselves. When a rebel was struck down, the victorious royalist grew discontented with the smallness of his reward, and became a rebel in his turn. All parties soon tired of a war which led to nothing, and longed for quieter times. Many obstacles to the renewal of repose were now moved out of the way. De Luynes, the favourite, had died in 1621. The queen-mother, desisting from opposition, and forgetting the fate of the Concinis, returned to the court, and almost resumed her old authority. Not now was her influence supported by foreign adventurers whose pre-eminence offended the self-respect of the peerage, but by the same quiet-mannered man whom we saw admitted to the council in 1616, and who had been lost to public view ever since, either in his little bishopric of Luçon, or in an honourable banishment at Avignon. "The man's ambition is immeasurable," said the king, and refused some applications his mother made in his favour. But in 1622 the interest of Mary prevailed. The Pope sent her favoured adviser the Cardinal's hat, and Louis agreed to admit him to the cabinet. He was only to give his opinion ; but he was to affect no state, to hold no levees, and to behave in all respects as a simple, quiet, humble-minded ecclesiastic, who had written dreadfully dull books against the Protestants, and in favour of Christian Perfection. Swelling, however, with grandeur, robed in the mantle of his rank, and with the banner borne before him, his eminence the Cardinal de Richelieu took his seat at the board. In a moment there was no doubt whatever that the true man was found. He never even consulted his colleagues, but did everything with a high hand. The king looked on him with wonder, the queen-mother with a kind of fear, and the nobles of all ranks and persuasions perceived that their master had appeared in the land. His conduct was inexplicable to people who did not know that the two objects of his life were, to extirpate the Protestants at home and weaken the throne of Austria abroad. To attain either he neglected the other for a time, but returned to it with fresh vigour when the opportunity occurred. If he seemed for a moment to favour the Calvinists in France, it was to enable him to present a united front to the pretensions of the Austrian despot. If he crushed the Huguenots at Rochelle and elsewhere, it was to enable him to turn with undivided power to assist their co-religionists in Germany.

And it was high time that the attention of France should be directed beyond the Rhine. After six years of war, in the year 1624 Catholicism was triumphant ; the Lutheran princes were everywhere subdued ; Spain sent money to the Emperor ; England sent nothing but vain good wishes to the reformed. In their desperation, the oppressed confederates had turned their eyes to the far north, and summoned to their aid Christian the Fourth, the Danish king. They little suspected that the orthodox and tyrannical Prince of the Church, who now governed the politics of France, and oppressed their brethren wherever they could be found, was only waiting for an opportunity to attack their enemy in his own country, and renew the plans of Henry the Fourth in opposition to the Hapsburgs. But first the citadel of French revolt and Protestantism was to be levelled with the ground ; Rochelle was to be restored to the Catholic faith. A great army was collected, and the capital of the Huguenots besieged. Richelieu was general, engineer, prime minister, and bishop ; he directed all the operations, raised a dyke which was the admiration of all the soldiers of the time, and shut out the fleet which England pretended to send to the support of the beleagured town. Having forced an entrance, he rode in beside the king at the head of the troops in velvet and cuirass ; and performed mass in the great church in rochet and stole, in honour of the victory. Louis the Thirteenth, assured of peace and submission in his own kingdom, led an expedition into Italy, and, after a brilliant campaign, brought his army back by way of Languedoc. There they seized Nismes and the other towns which had been rallying-places for the Reformers, and Richelieu hurried to the scene of action. The walls of the captured cities were thrown down, their cannon removed, and the inhabitants expected some measure of intolerable severity, from the bigotry of the priest and the arrogance of the conqueror. He issued an edict containing the greatest indulgences ! He secured them in all their rights and privileges—freedom of worship and equality before the law—only they were not to hold political assemblages on pretence of religious meetings. They might pray and preach, but they must not conspire. This was in 1629. In the very next year Richelieu gave all his assistance to the great Gustavus of Sweden, the Lion of the North, who crossed the Baltic with thirty thousand men to the aid of the Protestant cause, and the fortunes of the House of Austria were rapidly reduced to the lowest ebb. The active but unscrupulous Wallenstein had been displaced by the Emperor, at the instigation of secret and unsuspected emissaries of the Cardinal ; and there was no one able to resist the triumphant battalions of the warrior king, who carried the Bible in his breast, and commenced all his battles with prayer. He marched through the length and breadth of the land, shouting the war-cries of the Old Testament, and considering himself a chosen instrument to overthrow the images of Dagon and the plans of Antichrist. Richelieu rejoiced in the success of his schemes, and for a moment did not perceive the change which was arising in the king's mind. Louis grew jealous of his minister's glory, and listened to the slanders which the queen-mother and Marillac the Treasurer, and all the opponents of a domineering favourite, were ready to pour into his ear.

He even went so far, on the 11th of November, 1631, as

to yield to the prayers of his mother, and order the Cardinal into exile. The sentence of banishment was signed, but the king dared not look on the countenance of the man he wronged. He retired to hide his fears and regrets in the solitude of a little chateau he had built at Versailles. While there, waiting till the minister had departed from Paris, the door opened, and the well-known face of the Cardinal met his eyes. There was a sudden revulsion of feeling. He remembered only the triumphs he had attained by the labours and genius of the great ruler and politician, who now came to throw himself at his feet, and say farewell for the last time. Meanwhile the palace of the Luxembourg, the residence of the queen-mother, was alive with lights and laughter. The nobles gathered round Mary, and celebrated their victory with uproarious rejoicing. Places were distributed among the successful faction, governments promised, and vengeance concerted against the adherents of the priest. Suddenly a chill fell upon their gaiety—the great minister was known to be closeted with the king, and more in favour than ever. This was called the Day of Dupes, and the unfortunate conspirators paid dearly for their momentary triumph. Marillac was imprisoned, his brother the Marshal executed, the queen-mother sent into exile. The French courts of justice were busily employed in trying the accused, and the axe was never idle in carrying the judgments into effect. It was a reign of terror directed by one man, and pressing heavily only on the great and powerful. Gaston, the king's brother, whom the Cardinal had married to Mademoiselle de Montpensier by main force, was chased from Paris; and the queen herself, the young and handsome Anne of Austria, the favourite of the court, and not disliked by her husband, was treated with suspicion, her desk searched for letters, and her waiting-women interrogated as to her correspondence. Louis the Thirteenth was brave in battle, but the most timid of poltroons in presence of a loftier nature than his own. Richelieu used his soldiership by employing him at the head of the French armies, and hid his deficiences as a king by the aquisitions of lands and influence he added to the Crown in his name. The few remaining privileges of the Parliament, even the right of protest, were taken away. The royal power saw no rival either in town's franchise or noble's privilege. In attainment of his object of elevating the throne, the pitiless churchman gave over the loftiest heads to the block, and scarcely spared his own brethren when they ran counter to his plans. He travestied, indeed, the highest officers of the Church into the strangest shapes—making an archbishop admiral of the fleet, and portly abbots colonels of artillery. It was difficult to distinguish the bishop in the field from the major of dragoons; for they all handled the sword with equal skill as the crosier—the only distinction being that, when a high church dignitary offended the Cardinal by backwardness in an attack, or bad discipline in his regiment, he sent him back to his diocese, and condemned him to ecclesiastical punishments. He shot the refractory brigadier, and only sentenced the military prelate to bread and water, and self-flagellation in his cell. But military prelate and refractory brigadier knew that there was neither pity nor remorse in the imperturbable heart of the Cardinal or the insensible bosom of the King. That unworthy son of the generous and affectionate Henry saw his wife insulted by an overbearing churchman, and his brother, Gaston of Orleans, treated with indignities at which a slave might have revolted, with no participation in the indignation either of brother or wife. Everything was to be placed helplessly at the feet of royalty, and queen and princes must share the common lot. This was the great effort of the Cardinal's life—to establish a central power, uncontrolled by lords or parliament; and the very incompetency of the personage who profited by the success of his endeavours, shows the depth of his sagacity and the strength of his will. Louis gave no active aid to this creation of an absolute monarchy. He saw opposition cease, and adulation surround him, and everything attributed to the royal office; and was only grateful to the devoted servitor who raised him to the unexampled height. In the cold regions of that sterile elevation he lost all the feelings of our ordinary nature ; he lost even his pride of family and his national affections. Mary de Medicis had been the wife of Henry the Great, and was mother of the king ; but Richelieu, with the full cognisance of his master, left her to the extremity of poverty and neglect at Brussels or London, and finally at Cologne, where she died in 1641, without a reconciliation with her son.

It is useless to enter minutely into the external policy of France under Richelieu's administration, for the great actions of the time were performed by other nations, and all that he did was to maintain what he conceived the balance of European power, by allowing no State, or even religion, to preponderate over all the rest. His internal policy may be briefly stated to consist in depressing all orders of the State in unreasoning subjection to the King. There were revolts in various quarters to resist this yoke, but they were quelled with uniform success. Once, and once only, the fate of the Cardinal seemed finally sealed. The Count de Soissons, a prince of the blood, headed the discontented gentry in open war in 1641, and established the headquarters of revolt in the town of Sedan. The Empire and Spain came to his support with promises and money. Twelve thousand men were under his orders, all influenced with rage against Richelieu, and determined to deliver the king from his degrading tutelage. Richelieu was taken unprepared, but delay would have been ruin. He sent the Marshal Chatillon to the borders of Sedan to watch the proceedings of the confederates, and requested the king to summon fresh troops and go down to the scene of war. While his obedient Majesty was busied in the commission, Chatillon advanced too far. Soissons assaulted him near the banks of the Meuse, at a place called Marfée, and gave him a total and irremediable overthrow. The cavalry on the royalist side retreated at an early part of the fight, and forced their way through the infantry, not without strong suspicions of collusion with their opponents. Paris itself was in dismay. The King and Cardinal expected to hear every hour of the advance of the rebels; but no step was taken. It was found, when the hurry of battle was over, that Soissons was among the slain. The force of the expedition was in that one man; and the defeat was as useful to the Cardinal as a victory would have been. The malcontents had no leaders of sufficient rank and authority to keep the inferiors in check; for the scaffold had thinned the ranks of the great hereditary chiefs, and no man could take his first open move against the Court without imminent risk to his head. Great men, indeed, were rising into fame, but of a totally different character from their predecessors. Their minds were cast in a monarchical mould from their earliest years, and they considered submission to the Crown the highest of earthly duties, irrespective of the justice or wrongfulness of the orders it conveyed. From this time subserviency to the king became a sign of noble birth. Feelings of patriotism, liberty, and self-respect, were considered old-fashioned and absurd; and Richelieu has the boast, if boast it can be called, of having crushed out the last spark of popular independence and patrician pride. A strange spectacle it must have presented to foreign lands to see the most gallant nation in Europe—the people who had dethroned, before they murdered, the last of the Valois, and resisted Henry of Navarre—lay itself, powerless and contented, beneath the feet of a man like Louis the Thirteenth. And at the very same time the scene was presented in England of a nation, which had submitted to Henry the Eighth, and borne the degrading authority of James, rise in open rebellion in defence of its rights and liberties when they were threatened by Charles the First.

One more effort was made to shake off the trammels of the hated Cardinal. A conspiracy was entered into to deliver the land by the old Roman method of putting the tyrant to death; and the curious part of the design is, that it was formed almost in presence of the king. His favourite friend young Cinq Mars, son of the Marshal d'Effiat, his brother Gaston of Orleans, and his kinsman the Duke de Bouillon, who were round his person at all hours of the day, were the chief agents of the perilous undertaking. Others, and with them de Thou, the son of the great French historian, entered into the plan, but wished the assassination to be left out. They would arrest and imprison him ; but this was evidently not enough. While Richelieu lived, no man could be safe, though the Cardinal were in the deepest dungeon of the Bastile. Death, however, was busy with their victim, without their aid. He was sinking under some deep but partially-concealed illness when the threads of the plot came into his skilful hands. He made the last use of his strength and intelligence in unravelling and punishing the rebels, as he called them, against the king's authority. The paltry and perfidious Gaston was as usual penitent and pardoned, but on Cinq Mars and de Thou the vengeance of the law and the Cardinal had its full force. The triumphant but failing minister reclined in a state barge upon the Rhone, towing his prisoners behind him to certain death. On their arrival at Lyons the process was short and fatal. The young men were executed together, and the account of their behaviour at the block is one of the most affecting narratives in the annals of France. Carried by slow degrees from Lyons to Paris, the inexorable Richelieu reached his noble mansion called the Palais Cardinal, and prepared to die with as much dignity as he had lived. With declarations of the virtuous aim of all his actions, and vauntings of his exemption from personal considerations, which it is painful to read after the perusal of his career, he bequeathed his princely residence to the king (which has therefore been known since that time as the Palais Royal), and ended a strange and eventful life on the 4th of December, 1642.

What amount of vanities and weaknesses is sufficient to diminish the effect of a really great and self-sustaining nature, it is impossible to say. France seems more tolerant than we are, if not of spots and blemishes in her great men's characters, at least of absurdities and contradictions. This fearful Cardinal, for instance, was the vainest and most pretentious of tenth-rate poets, and hated the first glory of the French stage, Corneille, for having written the fine tragedy of the "Cid." He bribed and bullied people to write against it, and collected, paid, or frightened audiences in the private theatre of his palace, to listen enraptured to his own amazing bombast in the tragi-comedy of "Mirame." In war we have seen with what pomp he entered a hostile town. At all times when he commanded the troops in person, he wore a military dress, which reminded the spectators of the Knights of the Round Table. He had steel breastplate, and cap with long feathers; a sword at his side; and was preceded by two pages, one carrying his helmet and the other his gloves. But his triumphs in war were not so dearly valued as his irresistible attractions in the eyes of the beauties of the court. A thin, haggard, sallow-faced man—with the manners of a sycophant or a bully—speaking a fantastic jargon, such as was introduced in the romances from which he derived his idea of fascinating conversation—stained at the same time with the blood of so many victims, and terrifying wherever he went, with the fear of the vengeance of an easily-offended but unforgiving temper—he considered himself the most perfect example of a gay young cavalier who ever made war on ladies' hearts. No rank nor beauty hindered him from considering himself an acceptable wooer. He threw himself at the feet of Mary de Medicis, the mother of his sovereign, and of Anne of Austria, his wife. The laughter or disgust of those ladies is said to have been the origin of his hatred to both. A pretender in poetry, a charlatan in war, and an old beau in love, it would have needed stronger and more satisfying qualities than this man possessed, to have saved him in England from unmitigated contempt. But ridicule would not have preserved him from the bitterer feelings which would have been roused by his perseverance in his policy of depressing the people and exterminating the nobles. If we can imagine his failure in those attempts, and the survival of a patriotic aristocracy and free people, we can imagine also what would have been the place which Richelieu would have held in French history. We can realise it more clearly to ourselves, if we fancy what would be at present the position, in our annals, of his contemporary Stafford, if his plans for elevating the Crown at the expense of all the other Estates had been successful. Greater than Richelieu, far bolder in design, and more manly in execution, more dignified in manner, with fewer personal infirmities to neutralise the colossal magnitude of his plans and principles, the historians of an absolute monarchy created by his genius, if under such it were now our fortune to live, would have had no occasion to blush for the littleness of their champion and hero. But the bold bad man of the English Rebellion is execrated for his attempt, while pitied for his fall. The French Cardinal is slightly blamed for the enormities of his guilt and the paltriness of some of his aspirations, but is held up as the great statesman who destroyed the liberties of a nation, and established a despotic throne upon the ruins. The French, more than any other nation, seem worshippers of Power, without inquiring how it was attained, or on what foundation it rests. Provided a sceptre be firmly held, and is feared and respected enough by others, they do not seem to care how blood-stained its handle may be, or how terribly it oppresses themselves.

Louis the Thirteenth survived his minister but five months. Conscious of his weakness, he felt miserable when the controlling hand of the strong cardinal was withdrawn. Cabals and parties were getting together in the very room where he retired to die ; and, wearied of life and disgusted with power, on the 14th of May, 1643, in his forty-second year, he closed his eyes upon a world which to him had been a scene of bitterness since his first entrance upon the stage, leaving the reputation of personal courage combined with a weak understanding and callous heart.

CHAPTER XIII.

LOUIS THE FOURTEENTH.—THE MAZARIN MINISTRY, 1643 TO 1661.

THE natural advantages of France in compactness of territory and richness of soil, enable her to recover more rapidly from the effects of civil commotions than any other land. All through the earlier years of Louis the Thirteenth's reign, there had been a succession of riotous disturbances, which must have interfered with the comforts and prosperity of the people. Villages were burnt and chateaux overthrown; towns were amerced in heavy fines, and estates confiscated to the successful side. But when the steady hand of the remorseless Cardinal held all the orders of the State in unresisting quiet, the farms regained their fertility, the towns resumed their trade, new castles were built over all the country, and, best effect of all, the confiscated estates gave rise to a new order of proprietors. A vast mass of the soil of the country was set free from the hereditary hold of an impoverished aristocracy, and rich merchants and the smaller tradesmen of the local centres of industry, became deeply interested in the efficacy of the public law and the improvement of their newly-acquired domains. France has had three aristocracies in the course of her annals from the Crusades to Louis the Fourteenth. After the time of Louis the Eleventh, the representatives of the first or old feudal aristocracy, the descendants of the men who were in reality the king's peers, and not his actual subjects, were few and far between. They were left like pillars in an almost universal inundation, and were finally sapped and overthrown by the force of the prevailing tide. These were the holders of vast principalities, who maintained a kind of royal state in their own possessions, and kept high courts of judicature over life and limb in the whole extent of their hereditary fiefs. In the long English wars, from Creçy to Agincourt, the great body of them disappeared, and only here and there a Great Vassal was to be seen, distinguished in nothing from the other nobles except in the loftiness of his titles and the reverence that still clung to the sound of his historic name. The second aristocracy arose among the descendants of the survivors of the English and Italian wars. They claimed their rank, not as coming down to them from the tenure of almost independent counties and dukedoms, but as proprietors of ancestral lands, to which originally subordinate rights and duties had been attached. Mixed with these, we saw the Noblesse of the Robe, as the great law-officers were called, who constituted a parallel but not identical nobility with their lay competitors; and later still, enriched tax-gatherers and others who had fattened on the royal favour, ascended above their original position, by the purchase of what were recognised as ennobling estates, and formed indeed so numerous a portion of the acknowledged nobility, that an edict was passed to deprive them of a pre-eminence derived solely from the acquisition of those lands. The third aristocracy was now about to make its appearance, the creation of court favour and badge of personal or official service—possessors of a nominal rank without any corresponding duty—a body selected for ornament, and not for use—and incorporating with itself, not only the marquis and viscount, fresh from the mint of a minister or favourite, but the highest names in France.

The aristocracy of the sword and of ancient birth had itself to blame for this degradation. Before any of the great alterations in manners or government which give a new character to human affairs, there seems always some strange relaxation of morals, or atrocity of conduct, which makes society anxious for the change. The unfortunate custom in France, which made all the members of a family as noble as its chief, so that a simple viscount with ten stalwart and penniless sons gave ten stalwart and penniless viscounts to the aristocracy of his country, had filled the whole land with a race of men proud of their origin, filled with reckless courage, careless of life, and despising all the honest means of employment by which their fortunes might have been improved. Mounted on a sorry horse, and begirt with a sword of good steel, the young cavalier made his way from the miserable castle on a rock, where his noble father tried in vain to keep up the appearance of daily dinners, and wondered how in the world all his remaining sons and daughters were to be clothed and fed, and made his way to Paris. There he pushed his fortune, fighting, bullying, gambling, and was probably stabbed by some drunken companion and flung into the Seine. If he was lucky or adroit enough, he stabbed his drunken friend and pushed him into the stream, and after a few months of suing and importunity, obtained a saddle in the king's guards, or a pair of boots in the musqueteers. At this time it came out that in twenty years of the reign of Louis the Thirteenth there had been eight thousand fatal duels in different parts of the realm. Out of the duels which were daily carried on, four hundred in each year had ended in the death of one of the combatants. When the fiercest of English wars is shaking every heart in the kingdom, there would be wailing and misery in every house if it were reported that four hundred officers had been killed in a year. Yet these young desperadoes were all of officer's rank, and the quarrel in which they fell was probably either dishonourable or contemptible. Men fought and killed each other for a word or a look, or a fashion of dress, or the mere sake of killing. Where morality is loosened to the extent of a disregard of life, we may be sure the general behaviour in other respects is equally to be deplored. The rule holds good in the present instance in France. There was great, and almost universal, depravity in the conduct of high and low. Vice and sensuality found refuge and protection even in the presence of princesses and queens. People residing in remote places heard only of the gorgeous license in which the great and powerful lived. They knew them only during their visits to their ancestral homes as worn-out debauchees from the great city, who brought the profligacy of the purlieus of the Louvre in the peaceful cottages of the peasantry on their estates. It was, indeed, so much the fashion to be wicked, that a gentleman was hindered from the practice of his Christian or social duties by the fear of ridicule. The life of man, therefore, and the honour of woman, were held equally cheap ; and the blinded, rash, and self-indulgent nobility laid the foundation, in contempt of the feelings of its inferiors and neglect of their interests, for the terrible retribution which even now at intervals might be seen ready to take its course. Worst feature of all, the clergy, the appointed guardians of religion and morality, were neither religious nor moral. They might be proud of their brother Richelieu's power and intellect, and of the achievements of his naval archbishops and fighting prelates, but they could not be edified by the Christian example either of cardinal or bishop. Abbés and confessors began already the career of drawing-room trifling, and avowed disregard of the decencies of their position, which characterised the reign we are now entering upon, and embittered the people against the Church and Christianity itself more than any writings of philosophers or essays of unbelievers.

The country, however, in spite of these depressing circumstances, had grown, as we have already said, in wealth and comfort. There was a good deal of trade in the Atlantic and Mediterranean ports. Henry the Fourth and Richelieu had improved the internal communications, and already planned the Canal of Languedoc, which was to unite the two seas. The highways were well paved and guarded, to the admiration of all other nations. The Gallic genius had burst forth in all the arts and embellishments of life. Architecture was pouring fourth its triumphs both in town and country. The drama had sprung full-grown into existence with the first masterpieces of Corneille. The conversations of "lords and ladies bright," though tinged with the ribaldry and immorality of the time, were models of elegance and ease ; the manners were courtly and refined ; and Louis the Fourteenth was about to assume the nominal kingship—for he was not yet five years old—of a kingdom which the virtues had deserted, and which only the graces and accomplishments were left to guard and beautify.

The principles of Cardinal Richelieu were so securely planted that nothing could eradicate them from the soil. Like some shrubs that flourish best in tempestuous situations, the storms which burst over France seemed only to fix their roots deeper. The efforts to shake off the yoke he had laid upon the land appeared vigorous and sincere ; but the whole policy of his life had been to frivolise and debase the minds of the new generation ; and we shall see the spectacle of a great and powerful party, fighting for the highest and holiest of causes, behaving like the mimic heroes of the stage ; changing their dresses and characters with every change of scene ; and at last, convinced, apparently, of the unreality of their endeavours, and hastening to sheathe their imitation swords, and take off their tinfoil helmets, to assume the livery and decorations of a master as vain and theatrical as themselves.

Louis the Fourteenth was left in the guardianship of his mother, who was also appointed "regent, to be assisted by a council wherein questions were to be decided by a plurality of votes ;" and already the grandeur of the king's name gave an overwhelming authority to whatever party had the custody of his person. Anne of Austria summoned to her aid, not a council of the nobles or magistrates of France, as had been provided by her husband's will, but a certain Italian of the name of Mazarin, whom Richelieu had distinguished with his favour, and nominated for the scarlet hat in 1641. Cardinal Mazarin was the guide and master, and finally the unacknowledged husband, of the weak and self-willed queen. He applied to the Parliament of Paris to cancel the testament of Louis the Thirteenth, and to nominate Anne "regent with unlimited powers." In reading the history of France, we are very apt to be led astray by a confusion of names. When we speak, for instance, of a parliament, we are disposed to think of a body of representatives selected by the nation, and endowed with authority to make and modify the laws. But in France a parliament meant nothing of the kind. It was merely the court of justice under its president and other officers, whose utmost right extended only to make respectful remonstrance when any new tax was about to be imposed. Its dignities were not even attained by proficiency in the law ; they were to be had by purchase, and, once bought, they became hereditary. It was only a blind playing with a great name, or a profound ignorance of the jurisdiction of such a society, which tempted the alien minister to apply to a parliament like this for the alteration of a form of government. But there was danger even in this application for a useless sanction. The lawyers who presided in that court perhaps cast their eyes across the Channel, where the great struggle between Charles and his parliament was at its height. They might fancy some resemblance between their own position and that of the stormy assemblage at Westminster, which claimed an equal authority with the king. Happy, at all events, to be admitted to a public participation in national concerns of so much importance, they gave a willing consent to all the Cardinal demanded. The council was abolished, the queen established in absolute governance, and the Parliament of Paris had its first taste of power.

The regency of Anne began with internal trouble and foreign glory ; for almost at the same time that the parliament transgressed its limits in Paris, the young Duke d'Enghien, better known as the Great Condé, won a brilliant victory over the Spanish forces at Rocroy. Prodigies were told of the vigour and skill of this youthful commander. He was but twenty-one years of age, and was opposed to the oldest and wisest generals of Spain ; but he made all his dispositions as if by the inspiration of a natural genius, and dashed on with such intrepidity, that in one tremendous charge he broke and scattered for ever the famous Spanish infantry, which had so long been the terror of other armies. The Viscount of Turenne, whose name is still included in the list of generals of the first class, was hard pushed by the superior forces of the Bavarians in the defiles of Switzerland. Condé hurried across the Rhine, and, accomplishing a junction with Turenne, poured their united power upon the enemy. Three days the combat lasted, and on one occasion the impetuous Condé cast his baton of command among the enemy and retrieved it sword in hand. At last his perseverance had its reward, and another great victory was written on the standards of France with the name of Friburg. The Duke of Orleans in the mean time had driven the Spaniards backward on the Scheldt; the ground was therefore prepared for the campaign of the following year, and Turenne was again at the head of the French army. But again Turenne met with a resistance he could not overcome, and the conqueror of Rocroy and Friburg flew to his assistance. The rival friends combined their forces at Nordlingen, a town in Bavaria, and inflicted a memorable defeat on the Imperialists on the same spot which had seen the overthrow of the Protestant princes eleven years before. These three successes were enough to establish the fame of a lifetime; and henceforth Condé's battle-cry consisted only of the words, "Remember Rocroy, and Friburg, and Nordlingen!" The cry, however, was not always successful, for in 1647 he was repulsed from the siege of Lerida, and left the province of Catalonia in possession of the Spanish kings. In this same year the famous insurrection of Naples took place, of which the hero was a poor fisherman of the name of Thomas Agnelo—which we have corrupted into Masaniello—and caused a great diversion in favour of the French in their contest with Philip. For though the reign of the usurping fisherman was not long, it led to an invitation, addressed by the people, to the Duke of Guise, the grandson of Balafré, who, with all the pride and ambition of his family, hurried off to avail himself of their offer of the presidency of the Neapolitan republic.

But Guise was not the sort of man either to found or retain authority. His haughtiness offended his friends ; he had little money and few troops ; and a new demagogue rose up among the people. This was a butcher of the name of Annessa, who soon disgusted the population by his cruelties, and then surrendered the city to the Spaniards. Those ungrateful conquerors rewarded him by hanging him on the spot, and carried off the Duke of Guise as their prisoner into Spain. This, however, was but a slight drawback to the military fame of France. Condé gained another great battle at Lens, in the neighbourhood of Calais, to which the Archduke Leopold had advanced ; the Marshal de la Meilleraie had sailed with a powerful fleet, and seized some harbours on the coast of Tuscany ; and, in consequence of these exertions, the terms of the Peace of Munster, in 1648, which put an end to the Thirty Years' War, and established the liberties of Protestantism in the larger part of Germany, were very favourable to the French. They obtained possession of the higher and lower Alsace (with the exception of the town of Strasburg, which was not added till a later date), and some places both in Germany and Italy, which they did not long retain. They forced the Emperor also to agree to a free navigation of the Rhine, and to bind himself to build no fortress on the right or German bank. The contest, however, with Spain still lingered on ; but affairs of more importance were occurring at home, and we must go back, from international transactions and incidents on a great scale, to the tricks and troubles of the Court and people which ended in civil war.

The first disagreement, of course, took place about a tax. Patriotism and loyalty can stand very severe trials, but generally fail when they press too heavily on the pocket. The Parliament of Paris, which had stretched its authority so far as to establish the queen and Mazarin in their supremacy, now came forward as the guardian of the people's interest, and protested against five edicts which had gone forth for the increase of the national payments. But it was a different thing to protest against a dead king's will and a living cardinal's proclamations. The Cardinal led the young Louis, now ten years old, to what is called a Bed of Justice—a solemn assemblage of all the courts of law and finance, and the nobles of the realm—wherein it was illegal to offer any opposition to the royal mandate openly expressed. Louis sat in state, and uttered the words "I wish it," and the lips of the parliament were closed.

Revenge followed rapidly on triumph. The offices of the courts of law, of the accounts, and of the aids as they were called—the magistratures of the country towns, and the dignities of the provincial assemblies—were all become freeholds, transmissible like other property, subject to the formal renewal of their duration, which was pronounced every ninth year. This right of hereditary tenure was called the Paulette, because it was first established by a man of the name of Paulet, and was so far beneficial to the exchequer that the holders of office paid a sixtieth of their income to the State every year. The time had now arrived for the renewal of the Paulette, for nine years had elapsed, and the king's grace was looked on as a matter of right. Mazarin determined to try the question, and would only continue the tenure of office in all the courts of the kingdom on payment of four years' income of each. From this he excepted the Parliament of Paris, perhaps with the object of making it hateful to the other parliaments, perhaps with the mean idea of buying off its opposition by sparing its money. But the parliament saw the snare, or scorned the bride; and a Resolution of Union, which was published as its reply, took away the hope which the minister had entertained of producing discord between the different courts. Anne was alarmed, and yielded to the remonstrances of the union delegates, and allowed them to propose some measures of reform. The reforms they proposed were of the most universal kind. From justice, finance, police, commerce, pay of the troops, and royal domains, down to the management of the private household, nothing escaped those lynx-eyed purifiers in a session of only ten days. The citizens were amazed and gratified beyond measure. Witty lampoons, sparkling sayings, epigram and ballad, circled though the town. Young barristers, who were only in want of clients and fees, crowded the streets and squares with their inflammatory harangues, and gave their legal opinions for nothing. They were called Protectors of the People by the mob, and Disturbers of the Peace by the authorities. As little boys used to be hustled off by the police when they were engaged in mimic fights with their slings, and returned in greater force than ever when the sergeant had withdrawn, the combat between court and city swayed to alternate sides ; and some ingenious person therefore called the reformers the Slingers, or Frondeurs. The name was taken up at once—everything was the Fronde. Ladies' dresses were ornamented with slings in embroidery ; their lockets were in the form of a sling ; and perhaps the bonnets which we see in the prints of the period, with the lappets brought over the ears, and tied with long coloured ribbons under the chin, owe their fashion to the same design.

The Fronde was fairly established before the queen and Mazarin were aware of its existence. Its objects ostensibly were to diminish taxation and to correct abuses ; its more important aims were to supplant the foreign minister and divide his spoils among its leaders. The queen looked for a long time in vain to discover who its leaders could be. She suspected everybody—the Duke of Vendôme, and the Duke of Beaufort, his son, among the first ; but their papers, which she seized, showed nothing, and she was forced to withdraw her accusations. There was a young ecclesiastic at that time, of the name of John Francis Paul de Gondi, of the family of de Retz, who rose into great favour with the serious and religious portions of the public. He was nephew of the Archbishop of Paris, and was himself Archbishop of Corinth ; but as his flock in that metropolitan city were schismatic (except those who had turned Turks), he had leisure to assist his uncle in his high office, and was appointed his coadjutor and successor. He preached at all the churches, and held visitations at the monasteries, and catechised the young, and consulted the aged clergy on the management of the diocese

When he rode though the streets, he was saluted with cheers and blessings, and the orators of the Fronde held him up as the pattern of all the Christian virtues. At night he put off his episcopal robes, disguised himself as a trooper or tradesman, and attended the meetings of the discontented. In a short time he had distributed seven or eight thousand pounds in stirring up the passions of the people, and was in daily expectation of being summoned by his patroness the queen to give his influence in quelling them. The queen at last suspected the worthy archbishop of being not quite the simple and self-denying individual he appeared. She had him watched and followed, and Mazarin determined to strike the blow.

A vast assemblage crowded the spaces of Notre Dame, to celebrate a Te Deum for the great victory of Lens, of which the young Condé had just sent home the news. When the multitude were dispersing, a dash was made upon three of the obnoxious councillors who had animated the discussions of the Fronde. Two of the intended persons escaped, but a surly, burly demagogue, of the name of Broussel, was tracked to his house in the mechanics' quarter of Paris, and arrested by an armed force. His daughter flung open an upper window, and called "Rescue, rescue!" Thousands gathered at the cry, pressed in upon the carriage into which he had been hurried, and upset it. They then threw furniture in the way of another vehicle into which the prisoner was removed, and stopped its farther progress. All the streets were filled with excited spectators. "Broussel and Liberty!" sounded from every throat; and though the man was safely lodged in prison, the uproar did not cease. The archbishop hurried to the palace. Consternation had already given way to insolence. The courtiers gibed and jested on the impatience of the people, and there was a great amount of wit expended on the looks and appearance and manner of poor old Broussel, who was eighty years of age, and whose daughter was past her prime. But de la Meilleraie, a marshal of approved courage, came in and said how serious the matter looked. Gondi, who entered at the same time, whispered to the queen, "Madame, it is a revolt!" "It is a revolt!" she replied in an angry tone; "to imagine a revolt possible!" Gondi bowed and was silent. Meanwhile Paris was rising fast. The jokes ceased; there was a talk of pardoning Broussel, and Gondi was empowered to promise his release if the multitude would disperse. He went to the chief seat of the commotion, and was in great danger before he was recognised. A man was mortally wounded by his escort, and the shouts and threatenings were appalling. Gondi jumped down to where the sufferer lay, administered the last rites of the church, and was instantly known as the Coadjutor, the friend of the poor, the guardian of the city. He led back forty thousand quieted and submissive men to the windows of the Louvre. Anne was less pleased at the pacification of the riot than pained at the influence of the archbishop. She frowned upon him, sneered at him, menaced him; and the soul of the churchman was vexed, but not subdued. This was called the Day of the Barricades, and reminded the historic student of the troubles of the Orleanists and Armagnacs, of the Huguenots and the League.

The Court was beaten in spite of its haughty language. Broussel was set free, and, boiling with wrath and disappointment, the queen left Paris, and carried her son to St. Germains. The Cardinal had no peaceable means left to resist the victorious Fronde, and the warrior Condé was summoned to bring his glory and his sword in support of the Mazarins. But the French are the last people in the world to yield to personal intimidation. They may obey a tyrannical government, whether of one or of many; but though politically submissive, they are personally brave, and the sight of a hot-blooded, haughty-voiced soldier, vowing vengeance on the disaffected, called forth a corresponding haughtiness on the other side. The Prince of Conti was Condé's brother, and could not submit to his arrogant pretensions. He joined the Fronde. The Duke of Vendôme, the Duke of Nemours, the Duke of Bouillon, and in a short time the heroic general the Viscount Turenne, followed the example. Gondi was indefatigable in keeping up the agitation in the capital; and the dazzled Parisians devoted themselves to the cause of so many princes, and gathered all day long round the windows and balconies of the town-hall, where the two most beautiful women in France—the real chiefs and supports of the insurrection—the Duchesses of Longueville and de Bouillon, addressed them in exciting little speeches, or, at all events, rained on them their sweetest nods and smiles. The queen banished the courts of justice—the courts of justice banished Mazarin ; Condé collected troops in defence of the minister, and Conti was declared " lieutenant-general of the kingdom, under the orders of parliament." The queen's faction had secured the adhesion of de Grammot, de Chatillon, and all the personal hangers-on of the profligate court. Other beauties contested the palm in policy and conquest with the celebrities of the Fronde, and courtship and admiration had a great deal more to do with the proceedings on both sides than patriotism or conviction. The contest was a shame from the beginning. Conti did not care more for the Parliament than Condé did for the Cardinal. A few skirmishes were fought more for show, than use. Both parties celebrated the result in little songs or vaudevilles, and nobody was either better or worse. But the more serious spirits of the Fronde desired something more decisive, and made overtures to Spain. The sense of honour, however, awoke in the reasonable members of the faction at the prospect of a foreign enemy being appealed to in their cause ; and Matthew Molé, a most honoured name for several generations in the legal annals of France, brought about an accommodation to prevent so great a scandal. Concessions were made on both sides. The parliament was reinstated in Paris, and Mazarin restored to power. The saloons of the beautiful duchesses were crowded with the heroes of both the camps, and the cry of " Broussel and Liberty ! " was the laughing-stock of all the drawing-rooms in Paris. Louis the Fourteenth was about eleven years old, and never forgot the discomforts and alarm of his seven month's retreat at St. Germains. Fronde and Mazarin, princes and people, parliament and cabinet, were equally disgusting in the boy's eyes ; and he only longed for the moment when he could trample on them all. If he had never at any time been so utterly powerless, he perhaps would never have been so ambitious of power.

Gondi was at his old arts again—preaching in public, and conspiring in the dark. Condé became intolerable for pride and arrogance ; he despised the Cardinal and insulted the Queen : his retainers fell off from his side, and the Graces of the Fronde spread disaffection among all the young cavaliers of his party. The mob continued true to its idols—the wily, double-faced, unprincipled Archbishop, and the Duke of Beaufort. This was the handsomest man of his time—gay, dissipated, easy-mannered, liberal of his money, and still more of his smiles and speeches ; and above all, endeared to the populace as grandson of Henry the Fourth, to whom he bore a striking resemblance in manner and dress.

The rapid evolution of stratagem and plot which distinguished this period, is perhaps best shown by an incident, frivolous in itself, but from which serious consequences flowed. Some of the lower partisans of the Fronde determined to raise the popular indignation against the friends of the Queen and Cardinal ; and a certain syndic of one of the trades, of the name of Joly, was fixed upon to fire the train. His clothes were put upon a wooden figure of his height and size, and a marksman put a bullet though the sleeve at the upper part of the arm. Joly marked himself with some scratches and blue paint at the exact spot where the hole would fit, and took his seat next day in his carriage, in his wounded coat. The marksman aimed at the carriage with an unloaded musket, and disappeared in the crowd. There was, of course, great uproar ; and shouts of execration, begun by the Frondeurs, were uttered against the Court. On the same evening the opposite party had determined on a similar trick. The Prince of Condé was, or appeared to be, fired at in his carriage, and equally violent accusations were made against the Fronde. Condé was irritated to the last degree, and accused of premeditated murder the holy and charitable Coadjutor, and the merry, jovial, gallant-hearted Duke of Beaufort.

They appealed to the parliament, which acquitted them at once. He then carried his plaint to the queen, but the queen was in no humour to listen to his demands: he had offended her by his overbearing obstinacy. And the Italian cardinal glowed with a hatred which would have stopped at nothing for its gratification: he laughed and jested, or flattered and soothed, the object of his wrath. He turned the Archbishop of Corinth into ridicule when Condé blamed him for his duplicity. "If I catch him," said the Cardinal, "in the disguise you speak of—in his feathered hat, red cloak, and military boots—I will get a sight of him for your highness;" and they roared at the idea of discovering the intriguer in sc unfitting an apparel. But one night, in the winter of 1650, disguised beyond the reach of detection, and guarded by a passport from the Cardinal himself, the Archbishop of Corinth was admitted by a secret door into the Regent's room at the Palais Royal, and deep conference was held between the two. In a few days afterwards it was announced in Paris that the Prince of Condé was arrested, and sent close prisoner to Vincennes, along with his brother the Prince of Conti, and his brother-in-law the Duke of Longueville. All day long the populace shouted before the gates of the archiepiscopal palace, and Gondi was at the summit of his ambition. Pleasanter to him was the triumph that it had been obtained, in a great measure, by a deception which a dramatic author would scarcely introduce in a comedy. Anne had obtained from Condé an order for the seizure and detention of three or four persons whose names were left in blank; and, on the authority of his own signature, the hero of Rocroy was led quietly down a back stair and given over in custody to the police. The ground, however, was now clear for farther effort, for the brother leaders of the Fronde and of the Mazarins were both in confinement; and the husband also of the fascinating politician who had lately begun to scatter her blandishments equally upon all, was kept as a pledge of her sincerity to the old cause. Others now rapidly rose to the surface who had not been heard of before. Condé's wife was a niece of Richelieu, and inherited her uncle's love of power. She presented herself in Bordeaux, and roused the population to arms against the tyranny of the Crown. But Mazarin led the queen and the young king against the city, and it yielded to its sovereign. He also obtained the victory in a combat against Turenne, who had entered the service of Spain and fired upon the fleur-de-lis. But with the momentary success of the Cardinal's cause rose his pretensions and demands; and the Fronde, alarmed at his recovered authority, changed its tactics, as a clown in a pantomime changes his clothes. It demanded the trial or liberation of the prisoners it had helped to send to Vincennes, without delay, and Mazarin removed them for safe custody to Havre. It then pronounced sentence of banishment, by the voice of the Parliament, on the obnoxious minister, and ordered him to quit the kingdom within fifteen days. The town militia kept watch and ward over the queen, by command of the Coadjutor, and hindered her flight to join the favourite. She could offer no further resistance to those who called themselves the friends of Condé, but who were the very same persons who had fought him in the field a few months before. Orders were given to set the captives at liberty. Mazarin himself communicated the news of their freedom in person, and, with great acclamations, and bonfires, and firing of guns, Condé made his triumphal entry into the city. He was now master of the situation, and was equally courted by the two other parties into which the State was divided—the Queen's, which was supported by the Duke de Bouillon and the now repentant and pardoned Turenne—and the Fronde, which had fallen into the guidance of the Duke of Orleans, uncle of the king, the Coadjutor, and the Duchess of Chevreuse. His own was called "the Prince's," and comprised the Duke of Rochefoucauld and other personal friends and military admirers. The old influence began to work. The Cardinal, from his place of retirement (for he had thought it safest to betake himself to Cologne), governed the queen with as absolute a sway as ever, and recommended her, as a stroke of policy which would silence all the parties, to take the king to a Bed of Justice, and make him declare his majority. But the majority of a boy of twelve is scarcely more legal than real; and Condé, perceiving the object of the move, prepared for war. In a moment we hear of towns besieged and dances attended, fights in the field and masquerade balls in the city, as if the two sorts of operations were of equal importance. In the midst of all, we see the plotting, lying, fawning, bullying Archbishop of Corinth rejoicing, like a bird of ill omen, in the storm he had created, and believing that civil commotion was the ground on which his talents had the greatest room for display. Rank, beauty, youth, and accomplishments, were all ranged on one side or the other, and with shameless immodesty sacrificed themselves to win over the wavering chiefs. The Duchess of Chatillon, the Princess-Palatine, the Duchess of Longueville, Madame de Monbazon, trafficked with their fascinations, and made what now is called political capital out of their charms and characters. Anne of Austria herself displayed all the attractions her age had left her, and occasionally won over an enemy by pretending to admire his person or his wit. Gaston of Orleans was the weak puppet with which all parties played alike, but he relied on the Coadjutor, who had at this time (1651) been created a cardinal by Pope Innocent the Tenth, for the purpose of opposing him to Mazarin, whom his Holiness hated with very unholy hate; and all the arts of that unscrupulous politician were required to keep up even an apparent agreement between the two chief enemies of the Court. Gaston feared Condé, and Condé despised Gaston; yet both were indispensable to the Fronde. When hostilities broke out on a large scale, Turenne, the same who had deserted to Spain and fought against the queen, took command of the royal army; and Condé was proud of an opportunity of measuring himself with his rival. The gallantry of the French was now regulated by the two best generals in Europe. When Turenne was looking one day at the movements of some troops he had thrown into disorder, he perceived a change in their position that pleased his professional eye, though contrary to his interests. "The Prince has arrived," he said, and withdrew to make farther preparations. The tendency of both parties was to hold themselves in the neighbourhood of Paris. The chiefs of the Fronde hurried into the city, to receive the congratulations due to their exploits from the fair politicians who had won them to their cause. The queen also established her headquarters near the capital, to be ready for any turn of popular sentiment in her favour, and to hear the reports of her spies on the proceedings of her enemies. She knew what dances were to be given, and who were to attend the assemblies of the duchesses of the Fronde. On one occasion, when Turenne knew that half the officers of Condé's army were engaged to a brilliant fête at the Duchess of Monbazon's, he made an attack on the enemy's camp, and was only repulsed by the steadiness of some old soldiers, who gave time for reinforcements to arrive. But the crisis was at hand ; for each party began to be suspicious of the other's gaining over its supporters—Mazarin lavishing promises of place and money, and the Duchess of Chatillon, invested with full powers by Condé, appearing in the opposite camp as the most irresistible ambassador that ever was seen.

Turenne held his force well together on the plain of Grenelle. His rival was on the other side of the Seine, at St. Cloud. It was necessary for Condé to relinquish that position when he heard of a great increase of the royalist troops, and he determined to take post at Charenton, on the east of Paris ; but how to reach that safe position was the point of difficulty. He resolved at last to cross the bridge at St. Cloud, skirt the Bois de Boulogne, and, keeping outside of the barriers, but under protection of their guns, get round by the north, and elude the army of Turenne. In this he nearly succeeded, but Turenne was not altogether deceived. By the time the retreating army had reached the gate of St. Antoine, the cavalry of the royalists were launched upon its rear-guard by Turenne in person, and Condé saw there was no alternative left but to fight to the last extremity. Gaston had retired and locked himself in the safe obscurity of the Luxembourg. The Cardinal de Retz was engaged in theological studies at the archbishopric, but occasionally sent messengers to Orleans to tell him on no account to open the gates to the outnumbered Condé. If Condé were got rid of, argued the prince of the Church, there would be nobody to stand between me and either the absolute command of the Duke of Orleans or the favour of the queen. The citizens ranged themselves on the walls ; the king was placed by Turenne on an elevation at Charonne, where he could see the impending engagement in security, and, after a pause for the formation of ranks, the great struggle began. French gentlemen dashed, in opposing battalions, against their countrymen and ancient comrades. Turenne was calm and resolute ; Condé felt the old flame of Rocroy and Nordlingen firing his blood, and fought like the boldest of his dragoons. Splendidly dressed ladies waved signals to their champions and lovers below, and the streets became alive with shouting and armed citizens, who desired to be let out to the aid of their defenders, and could not see in cold blood the slaughter of their friends. Thousands went to the Luxembourg to beseech Gaston to open the gates of the city for the reception of the wounded and protection of the overmatched. For a long time he resisted, and only when the grace of the action was lost by his delay, granted the request. Long trains of wounded and dying young men began to be carried in ; the groans and blood were horrible to hear and see ; and the women of all ranks and ages were frantic with sympathy and grief. Condé himself came for a moment within the gate ; his sword was in his hand ; his face was flushed with exertion ; his garments dripping with gore. He threw himself on a chair, and burst into tears. "I have lost all my friends," he said, "the gallant young hearts that loved me." "No, they are only wounded," said his cousin, the Princess of Orleans ; "they will recover and love you still." Condé sprang up at the good news, and rushed back into the fight. At the head of all his capable horse, he made one desperate long-continued charge, and drove the enemy backward for a mile. In the mean time the gates were opened wide, and, file after file, the weary soldiers marched into the city ; and, dashing homeward after his successful charge, Condé and his squadrons galloped in the last : but when the ponderous bars were once more put across the portals, it was felt that the combatants indeed were saved, but that the Fronde was destroyed. The Princess of Orleans, as if to render reconciliation impossible, ordered the cannon of the Bastile to be fired upon the royal army ; and Louis the Fourteenth had been present at his first battle.

Quarrels soon arose between the townsmen and their military guests. Taxes were oppressively raised, and shops were pillaged ; royal offers of clemency and peace, on the other hand, began to be stuck up on walls and public places, and the fear of anarchy was an irresistible argument in favour of despotism and order. Condé saw how affairs were going, and retired to the Netherlands. It was not long before it was known, with national humiliation, that the best soldier of France, a prince of the blood and protector of the people, had followed the recent example of his conqueror, and sold his services to Spain. The king made his triumphal entry into Paris, accompanied by his mother and Turenne. He convoked the courts, and received them into favour, "provided they returned within the limits of their duties, and abstained from interfering with the government." Gaston was sent into honourable exile, to his castle in the beautiful town of Blois, and the Cardinal-archbishop, the evil spirit of the Fronde, was received with apparent cordiality, and began to entertain hopes of supplanting his rival ; but when he had fallen into disrepute with the citizens, he was quietly carried off to Vincennes, and left to meditate on his plots and schemings within the bars of his apartment. The Parisians were now so changed from what they had been, that they received their old enemy, the Cardinal Mazarin, with demonstrations of delight, when he made his solemn entry into the repentant city with Louis as an attendant at his side.

A struggle began between Condé and Turenne, which raised the military reputation of both to the highest point.

Turenne, perhaps because his conscience told him he was now on the right side, fought with more than his ordinary vigour against the degenerate Bourbon who commanded the enemies of his country. He retook the cities and fortresses which Condé had seized at the commencement of the campaign. The Spanish forces were gradually driven back, and the warrior prince must have had strange misgivings when he retaliated on the successes of Turenne, by capturing the town of Rocroy: the first victory which made him famous was won on the same spot; and perhaps to some recollections connected with that happier time is owing the strange impulse which moved him to send back to Louis, who was in the camp of Turenne, some French standards which had fallen into his hands. "The Spaniards are so little in the habit," said Louis, "of taking French colours, that I scorn to deprive them of their present trophy," and returned them to the traitorous chief. The military apprenticeship of the king under Turenne was of the greatest benefit to his character and position. Away from Mazarin, he gradually became confident in himself; and, as the effeminate cavaliers of all the factions saw a long perspective of wealth and glory in the court and camp of a ruler of twenty-two, adhesions poured in from every side. The Duchesses of the Fronde and Princesses of the Cardinal concentrated all their arts on the youthful Louis, and in a moment, as if by the turn of a conjuror's wand, the monarchic spirit fostered by Richelieu revived in greater intensity than ever. Slavery became a passion, and Condé himself, when peace had been declared with Spain, was drawn within the vortex of flattery and obedience, and knelt before his placable but contemptuous sovereign. "My cousin," he said, in answer to his excuses, "after the great service you have rendered to the Crown, I have no wish to remember any action of yours which has only done harm to yourself." The Treaty of the Pyrenees, concluded in 1659, contributed to the young king's glory and the power of France: it secured to his crown large portions of Flanders, Hainault, and Luxemburg; Roussillon and Perpignan were confirmed to it in the south; and the friendship of the rival nations was farther consolidated by his marriage with Maria Theresa, the daughter of the Spanish king. To prevent at any time the union of the two crowns, the Infanta, in the articles of marriage, made a solemn renunciation of all her rights to the Spanish succession. Louis contented himself with her dowry of five hundred thousand golden crowns, and led her into Paris in August 1660.

Worn with years and labour, regretted by the queen, and respected, from the force of youthful habit, by Louis, the Cardinal Mazarin died in a few months (March 1661). Cabals, plots, opposition, were all at an end, and the reign of Louis the Fourteenth may be said to begin at this date. He has fifty-four years of life and authority before him, and in the course of that time the whole state of European society will be changed. After the troubles of the Fronde in France, and the great rebellion in England, which may be named more as contrasts than resemblances, one of those ebbs which occasionally occur in the advancing tide of liberty and progress made itself perceptible in both nations. The supporters of the Grand Remonstrance, the men of Dunbar and Marston Moor, fell at the footstool of the falsest, basest, meanest of monarchs and buffoons ; while the intriguers of the boudoir, and traitors of every party, the followers of De Retz and sycophants of Anne, rose to a higher sort of servitude, which was almost dignity, when they bent their foreheads to the ground at the audiences of the pompously-worded and gorgeously-arrayed potentate, who already professed to represent in his own person the glory and majesty of France.

CHAPTER XIV.

THE KING REIGNS AND GOVERNS, A. D. 1662, TO THE PEACE OF NIMEGUEN, A. D. 1678.

LOUIS THE FOURTEENTH was now every inch a king, and France, tired of the exactions of delegated power, and humiliated by the government of two foreign ecclesiastics, was delighted to be trodden under foot by a monarch of her own blood, who oppressed her in his own name. Mazarin had died, with his conscience and pocket equally burdened under a fortune of eight millions sterling—a sum representing an infinite amount of suffering in the then impoverished land, and contrasting strangely with the actual poverty in which the royal treasury was found. Louis spared the iniquitously-acquired hoards of the avaricious Cardinal, but turned his eyes on the ill-judged magnificence of the Superintendent of the Finances. His name was Fouquet, of whom it is only necessary to say that he laid out nearly a million on the erection of his house at Vaux, and had spent forty thousand pounds in a fête he injudiciously gave in honour of the king. The king at that time had difficulty in maintaining any sort of establishment at all, and never forgot the absurd ostentation of the entertainment, or the gorgeous grandeur of the mansion. He took one for his model in the assemblies he held at court, and the other for the enormous proportions of his palace at Versailles. Fouquet must have regretted the splendours of the supper and the size of the banqueting-hall, for they were evidently the cause of his disgrace. His transactions were inquired into, his extortions found out, his defalcations to the exchequer calculated, and his goods and chattels forfeited to the Crown. We do not read of any of the surplus being refunded to the taxpayers ; but a greatei favour was bestowed upon them than if they had been admitted to a share of the Intendant's spoils, for a new man was appointed to his place—a man of perfect honesty, though the temptations were so great ; of purest patriotism, though his country was now represented by one man ; economical with dignity, and just even in the partition of public burdens ; and this was a favourite clerk of Mazarin, who is known in contemporary history as the great Colbert. No monarch ever had a more sagacious or honourable servant. The finances were put into a clear and intelligible form, the expenditure was regulated by the receipts, useless pensions cut off, generous allowances made, and still the country was less oppressed than it had ever been before.

The services of a man like Colbert had perhaps an injurious effect on the young king. He saw his treasury regularly supplied, his people contented, his courtiers obedient, and he determined to make the other nations of Europe know that he was a sort of personage they had not met with for a very long time. Europe, indeed, was regulated by externals at that period more than it ever has been before or since, and Louis was the exact king required to take cognisance of outward show. The Spanish ambassador took precedence of the French at the court of our Charles the Second. A quarrel in the street, between the respective footmen, made the occurrence public. Louis withdrew his minister from Spain, sent the Spanish minister out of the country, and told his astonished father-in-law that, if he did not send an envoy to make open renunciation of all claims to pre-eminence over the ambassadors of France, he would declare war without a moment's delay. The Spaniards were very proud, but they were also lamentably poor ; and a Don of the greatest magnitude was sent over the Pyrenees, and made solemn declaration that the representatives of the sovereign of Spain and the Indies held only a secondary place in presence of the representatives of the Most Christian King. At the same time, his ambassador at Rome was insulted by the Corsican guard of the Holy Father. The poor islanders were the lowest of all the military servants of St. Peter, and limited their duties to forming a guard of honour round a scaffold when anybody was going to be hanged or beheaded ; but Louis chose to make it a question of state. He seized on Avignon, which was still the property of the Church, and was looking with horrible eyes upon the wealth of some of the French cathedrals, when the Pope, for the first time in the history of the Papacy, sent a cavalcade of nuncios and bishops to make a humble apology. Nuncios had visited all parts of the world with threats and denunciations, but Europe stood aghast when it saw the sacred embassy on its knees before the violator of the papal territory, and heard it agree to erect a pyramid where the insult had occurred, recording the event, and the reparation exacted for it. When a man has bullied the King of Spain and the Pope, he may, of course, trample on his own people to the top of his bent. The poor remains of a parliament, therefore, which reminded him of the troubles of the Fronde, underwent the humiliating process almost in its literal sense, for the monarch, accompanied by his courtiers, entered the Hall of their sittings, whip in hand, and ordered the members to disperse. Cromwell had given the same invitation to the parliament of England, but it was with the Ironsides at his back, who would have needed but a nod of his head to put the senators to death. An insult is more fatal to the independence of an assembly than a violence; and perhaps the riding-switch in the hand of Louis did more harm to the parliamentary idea in France than the bayonets of the grenadiers, whom we shall soon see clearing the Legislative Council at the order of Napoleon.

There is seldom a period of struggle and transition in a State, without creating some great and preponderating personage, who becomes the representative of the time. Our English Rebellion ended in Cromwell, the American troubles produced Washington, and the French Revolution Napoleon. But clustered round them all were the secondary heroes of the day—Pyms, Hampdens, Elliots, Falklands, Straffords, and Clarendons ; the chief became but the central figure of a constellation which made itself visible in the troubled sky. Washington had his Franklin, and the other fathers of the great republic ; and Napoleon had the companions of his glory, who were brought forward by the same causes as himself. But Louis the Fourteenth stepped into the rewards of activity and courage, without having shared in the labour and heat of the day. The foreign policy of Richelieu and the intestine contentions of the Fronde had called forth a vast amount of energy and experience in every department of the State. Sword and pen, political wisdom and administrative skill, were all at the command of the young sovereign, who had hitherto lived in degrading subjection to a foreign priest and domineering mother, and who suddenly, and without any effort of his own, found himself at the head of a more subservient nobility than Francis the First, and a more devoted army than Henry the Fourth. He had Condé, Turenne, Grammont, Crequy, and Luxemburg, ready to execute his orders against foreign powers. He had Colbert, the best of administrators, and Louvois, the best of secretaries-at-war, to superintend the internal interests of the nation and the discipline of the forces. He had the gallant Francis, duke of Beaufort, the handsome Frondeur, the favourite of the Parisian mobs, the grandson of Henry the Fourth, as admiral of his fleets, and spread the fear of France over all the islands of the Mediterranean. Painters and poets were waiting in silent expectation for the proceedings of a reign which had so hopeful a commencement, and Louis was not wanting to himself in this respect. He put the muses into his livery, as he had already done the nobility ; and literature and art became not so much the bestowers of fame as the receivers of wages. Bossuet, the greatest of French orators, and Molière, the greatest of French dramatists, were equally at the orders of this portentous autocrat, to praise, to delight, to flatter and amuse him. Fame, genius, intellect, or science, had no chance against the preponderating majesty of this very ill-educated, very narrow-hearted young man. If he smiled, the most dignified of bishops condescended to the lowest and most degrading employments; if he frowned, the loftiest of poets retired in despair from his presence, and died of a broken heart. Adulation had not reached such a pitch since the time of the old Roman Empire, when the patricians said prayers before the altars of Claudius or Nero. And as the circle of his admirers increased, it extended beyond his own dominions, and he had paid panegyrists and salaried applauders in all nations. He made a yearly allowance to our dignified Charles the Second, and gave gifts and annual pensions to our Right Honourable and Honourable Houses of Parliament. It will perhaps help us to understand some of the causes of his prosperity, when we remember that he was the only sovereign in Christendom at that time who was absolutely and entirely master of his own kingdom. In other realms there were conflicting powers. Spain was reduced, by the jealousies of its constituent kingdoms, almost into a confederation of small and ill-assorted states; Germany was divided by religious enmities; England was demoralised by the return of its impoverished and embittered exiles, and betrayed by its own king; Holland was not yet consolidated after its tremendous struggle with Spain, and was torn by internal factions, and intent on conquest in the Brazils; Prussia was not yet a kingdom; and czars of Muscovy were looked on as we now look on the kings of Cabul or Nepaul—savage chiefs ruling a savage people, and so far removed as to have no weight in the policies of civilised states. This was the condition of France and the surrounding nations before Louis had been five years on his independent throne (1666).

It was in the year 1658 that, for the first time in history, a firm and hearty alliance was in full force between England and France. Cromwell had sent six thousand of the soldiers of the civil wars to serve under Turenne, who led them against the Spaniards commanded by Condé, and after a great victory over them at the battle of the Dunes, took the strong town of Dunkirk, and delivered it to the English flag. The English flag at that time was the standard of the Commonwealth; and the first care of Louis, after the Restoration, was to purchase from the royal Charles the trophy of so many gallant Englishmen's blood. Charles sold Dunkirk to the French king for a sum of money for his private purse, and in a short time the nation heard with dismay that the harbour was deepened, and the fortifications made impregnable, and a fleet collected safely behind its bulwarks, which at any moment might be launched against the eastern coast. But Louis was not yet ready to risk the existence of his marine. He waited till the maddened English swept the seas of the infuriated Dutch, and crippled their own resources in the effort. In the mean time he built his vessels, enlarged the port of Brest, dug a harbour at Cette, and covered the coast round Rochefort with docks and arsenals.

When all these preparations were completed, he looked round for a cause of quarrel, and found it in the right of his wife to the succession of her father, Philip the Fourth, who died in 1665. We remember with what solemnity Maria Theresa, at her marriage with the king in 1660, made renunciation of all her rights of succession to the states of her father. The dowry of half a million of crowns was supposed to be in full payment of all her claims; but the lawyers of the young monarch now found out that the sum had never been paid, and that the renunciation extended only to the Spanish kingdoms, but had no reference to the other dominions of the late king; and the judges and bishops vied with each other in declaring that Flanders and Brabant belonged to the Queen of France by all laws, human and divine. The Emperor Leopold, who was head of the house of Austria, and traditionally jealous of the Bourbons, received hush-money from the surplus treasures of Colbert, and a promise of the succession to Spain itself when the feeble and unhealthy Charles the Second—the brother of Maria Theresa by a second marriage of her father—should leave it open by his death. While the ambassadors and statesmen were toiling at the best means of concealing the dishonest intentions of the two greatest potentates in Europe, magazines of artillery and provisions were scattered thickly on the road between Paris and the Netherlands. The ways were levelled, cattle collected, peasants engaged to aid in the transport ; and when the time was come, and the justice of his cause proved to the satisfaction of thirty thousand men, equipped, armed, and victualled by the efforts of Louvois, the secretary-at-war, war was openly declared, and the whole force of France—its nobles, generals, soldiers, and engineers—followed Louis to the field in the assurance of victory, and were not disappointed. Town after town opened its gates to the brilliant Court, who transferred the luxuries of the Louvre to the trenches of a besieged city. The army from this time became a profession in which merit was sure to rise, and supplied the want of noble birth or hereditary fortune. A few words of praise uttered by Louis to a young man who distinguished himself at the head of his company, was equal to a peerage. Military rank, in short, became a recognised standing in the State ; and when a tax-collector's money had purchased a lieutenancy in some aristocratic regiment for his son, his position was assured, and he might have horsewhipped his former equals with impunity, as if he had been born a lord.

In one campaign the whole of Flanders was overrun. Names of places very prominent in succeeding wars, occur as yielding without a blow—Charleroi, Ath, Tournay, Lille, and Douay. Brussels would have fallen with the same facility, if it had not been thought better to secure the posts already captured. The great Vauban, who introduced a new species of fortification—of which the main characteristic is, that it places its citadel almost on a level with the ground, and does away with the lofty buildings which used to carry the guns and stand exposed to the enemy's fire—tried his first experiment on a great scale in the defences of Lille. Offering no mark to an attacking force, but fenced in with ditch and sunken wall, the garrison lay secure within its ball-proof casemates, and poured destruction on any assailant who came within their fire, from loop-holed walls. Flanders, which had been conquered by the king, was now supposed to be guarded by Vauban; and Louis went back to Paris to receive the applauses of his enraptured subjects, and the incense of the painters and poets.

Turenne, who had in reality commanded all the movements, had no greater glory from the campaign than the triumph of exciting the jealousy of Condé. Franche Comté had obtained its name of Franche, or Free, by being held in only a nominal subjection by the kings of Spain. In all essentials the inhabitants ruled themselves, and, by the mere appearance of republican independence, must have been an eyesore to the surrounding monarchs. It lay like a wedge thrust in between Switzerland and Burgundy, and interrupted the communication between Dauphiny and Lorraine. Condé was governor of Burgundy, and made certain propositions to Louvois and the king. What the propositions were nobody knew; but in the February of 1668 the truth came out. Twenty thousand men, with the same admirable order as in the preceding year they had traversed the Spanish Flanders, crossed over into Franche Comté, with Louis at their head, but with the great Condé in command. In twelve days from the time of his leaving St. Germains, the king was received in Besançon, and hoisted his standard in every citadel of the land. The conquest of Flanders was no longer the wonder of the Court; the submission of Franche Comté had been enforced in less than half the time. But the glory of Turenne was more permanent, inasmuch as the new acquisition of Condé awoke the susceptibilities of all the powers. England, Sweden, and Holland, entered into an alliance to resist the further aggressions of the French; and in spite of Louis's contempt for Charles, whom he paid, and the Hollanders, whom he despised as republicans, and the Swedes who lay on the other side of the Baltic, he was obliged to yield. The obstinacy of the envoy of the United Provinces, a certain Van Beuring, prevailed. A combination of all the maritime states was threatened, and with a sulky submission Louis surrendered Franche Comté to its former sovereign, and vowed vengeance deep and lasting against the presumptuous Dutch. This sacrifice was forced from him by the peace of Aix-la-Chapelle, concluded in May of the same year, 1668. Conquest and treaties were more speedy in those days than they have often been since, for the Triple Alliance, suggested by our English Sir William Temple, was arranged with Holland and Sweden in five days; and the Treaty of Aix-la-Chapelle was signed in six weeks after the negotiations were begun.

To hide his discontent, or his desire of vengeance, the king threw himself into the whirl of gaieties and expenses which have made this reign as memorable as his greater actions. He began the palace of Versailles, and directed in person the laying out of the alleys and the planting of the groves. That vast mass of masonry still remains to attest the poverty of the architectural taste of the time, and the blindness of an absolute monarch in entombing himself in a place so vast, and so overwhelming in mere extent, that its inhabitant must have sunk into utter insignificance. There were beds and suites of rooms for many hundreds of people; and the palace, when it was fairly finished and filled, had as many cabals and as many lies and rumours in it as the most scandalous of country towns. Meanwhile Louis was in the heyday of his career, and was beyond all question the most popular man in France. He carried the graces of deportment to a point never dreamt of before. He walked with such a tramp of dignity, rolling his eyes and turning out his toes, that the courtiers could stand the sight no longer, and burst into loud applause. He wore red heels to his shoes, four inches high, which added greatly to his stature, and yet did not bring him up to the standard of ordinary men. His features were large and handsome; and when he danced in public, and stalked across the scene with the attitudes of conscious power, the French taste became perverted altogether. All gentlemen walked with a strut, and stuck out their elbows, and tied themselves in at the waist. They also wore immense wigs covered with flour, flowing over their shoulders, and silver-buckled shoes that came nearly up to the ankle. A hat it was impossible for a conjuror to balance on the top of the enormous periwig, so they carried the three-cornered cockaded superfluity under their arms or in their hands. Rich velvet coats, with amazingly wide skirts, brocaded waistcoats half-way to the knee, satin small-clothes and silk stockings, composed their apparel, which received its crowning adornment in gold-headed cane and diamond-hilted sword. It is perhaps unjust in us, who are still condemned to round hats, which shelter us neither from the sun nor rain, and tight-fitting neck-ties and swallow-tailed coats, to laugh at the fashions of two hundred years ago ; but there is always something characteristic of a period's sentiments in the clothes it wears. The thoughts of that time were as absurdly artificial as the dress. There was velvet and hair-powder in its poetry and theology ; and its admiration of power, as condensed in the puffed-out person of the king, outraged every feeling of manliness or self-respect.

Two things occurring in this year will show the change that had taken place since the days of the blind searching for independence, even of the Fronde, which were now looked back upon with shame. Condé, the conqueror of Rocroy, and latterly of Franche Comté, obtained the honour of a square hassock at the king's mass, as a reward for all his gallantry ; and the Duke of Vermandois, natural son of the king, was created Lord High Admiral. This distinguished naval commander was a child of the beautiful Duchess de la Vallière, and was at this time one year old. Du Guesclin would have seen no honour in kneeling on one sort of cushion more than another in presence of Charles the Fifth ; and Louis the Eleventh would not have ventured to give so high an office to an infant, though legitimate heir to the Crown. But the smiles of the king were valuable even at the altar ; and it was from this atmosphere of sycophancy and devotion in which he lived, that he looked out upon the sturdy Hollanders, and thought the hour of his revenge was come. He sent the beautiful Henrietta of England, the daughter of

Charles the First, who had married his brother the Duke of Orleans, on a secret embassy to her brother Charles the Second. That craven king met her at Canterbury, and sold the alliance of the United Provinces for an enlargement of his allowance, and even went so far as to promise his aid in ships and men, provided he got some share of the spoil when the Protestant republic should be destroyed. Sweden, which had fallen into a minor's hands, was silenced by the same arts; and De Witt, the Pensionary or chief officer of the Netherlands, sent to inquire the causes of the great preparations going on in the arsenals of France. "I will do what consists with my dignity," replied the king, "and owe an account of my proceedings to no one." The Hollanders saw the approaching storm, and turned their eyes to a young man, the descendant of the great Nassaus to whom they owed their deliverance from the Spanish yoke, and invited him to take the military government into his hands. This was William, Prince of Orange, whom we shall afterwards see on the throne of Great Britain, under the name of William the Third. He was nephew of Charles by his mother, and the honest burgomasters of the towns thought it a master-stroke of policy to appoint him to the command—it would be such an unnatural thing for an uncle to help in the ruin of his own flesh and blood. Charles counted his pension, and mourned the untimely death of the fair ambassadress Henrietta of Orleans, who died, within a few weeks of her return, of some unknown and mysterious malady, which, however, at that time, was not uncommon among ladies who had the misfortune to offend their husbands. And things took their course. A hundred and thirty thousand men, under the command of Turenne, Condé, and Luxemburg, poured to the north-eastern frontier. Louvois, as usual, had foreseen all the requirements of the war, and had even had the skill to diminish the military stores of the Hollanders by buying them at exorbitant prices for the use of France. Vauban was there with his skill, and General Martinet—whose name is still the word for a punctiliousness in discipline unknown before—attended to the order of march and the details of the drill. The men on this occasion were armed for the first time with the bayonet, the most tremendous instrument, when placed in proper hands, yet discovered by the ingenuity of man. The King's House —as a body of the young nobility all radiant in gold and lace was called—caracolled in gorgeous array round their master's tent at Maestricht; and if the poor Dutchmen had been as good scholars as they were fishermen and merchants, they would have been reminded of the myriads of Xerxes on their glittering march to Greece. In forty days Holland was overthrown, and the French were already within four leagues of Amsterdam. De Witt, the Grand Pensionary, was for unconditional submission, and sent an embassy to the camp. The embassy was insultingly dismissed, and the people of the Hague rushed desperately to the house of the great statesman, and tore him and his brother Cornelius to pieces. Everything seemed now settled, and rejoicings were already preparing to celebrate the final conquest of the country, when the calm and resolute William of Orange gave desperate proof of his firmness and sagacity. He opened the sluices throughout the land. The great German Ocean and the Rhine poured over all the plain, and the invading army was limited to the high grounds on which their citadels were placed. Better, he thought, give his country to the sea than lose its liberties. While pressed within the walls of Amsterdam, and with the enemy's army in full march against him, he had still sent forth the Dutch fleet to meet his enemies on the sea. Off Yarmouth a great battle was fought, with doubtful success, between the united French and English and the Hollanders. De Ruyter, indeed, was the Nelson of his native land, and had noble and worthy companions in the bold men who steered so unflinchingly against such desperate odds. In three other great combats the victory continued equally undecided; but in some cases not to be defeated is to win, and the squadrons of the Provinces sailed triumphantly into port. William was like a lion at bay. Shame took possession of the English parliament to see the Protestant prince left friendless in his struggle with the Great King ; and the exasperated nation forced the wretched Charles to sign a treaty of peace with his heroic nephew in February, 1674. It needed but an example, and every generous heart warmed to the defender of his country. Brunswick, Brandenburg (now Prussia), Münster, Osnaburg, Spain and the Empire, took arms against the oppressor. Louis had now all Europe opposed to him, and rejoiced in the opportunity of distinction by showing that he was equal to all other nations combined. France seemed, indeed, to grow with the magnitude of her efforts, and all the frontiers were covered with armed men. Louis himself marched once more against Franche Comté, and attached it for ever to the Crown. Condé fought a drawn battle at Senef with the indefatigable Prince of Orange. And Turenne, passing into Germany at the head of a numerous army, which had been reinforced by the conquerors of Franche Comté, defeated the combined forces of the Emperor and the Duke of Lorraine at Sintzheim. He then entered the Palatinate, the most rich and beautiful province upon the Rhine, fertile in wine and corn, and gay with many prosperous towns and happy villages, and brought shame and execration on himself and his unpitying master by the devastation he wrought. He burned the peaceful hamlets, and slew the unoffending people. He so destroyed the farms, and tore down the woods and vineyards, that three generations have not sufficed to restore its ancient fertility or wealth. The hatred of the peasantry still rests upon Louis and Turenne, and the curse of so many outraged homes lay heavy on them both. After several victories, by which the Imperialists were driven across the Rhine which they had crossed near Strasburg, the proposer of the devastation of the Palatinate and the executioner of his fury went to the high altar of St. Germains and returned thanks for their success. In the next campaign, Turenne was opposed by Montecuculli at the head of the German forces, and prepared to attack him in an unfavourable position into which his movements had drawn him at Saltsbach ; a bullet, which is still shown in the museum of the Invalides at Paris, struck him in the breast as he was inspecting the enemy's works, and the greatest of French leaders died a soldier's death, 27th July, 1675.

The loss was so great that it was equivalent to a defeat. Without striking a blow, the army recrossed the Rhine, and Louis looked uneasily at the further progress of the European coalition. The Marshal de Crequy had been defeated and made prisoner at Treves, Alsace was threatened by the victorious Montecuculli, and the aspect of affairs was serious enough. Some traces of the old military organisation still lingered in the legal tenures of the landed properties, and Louis, in this extremity, called out the feudal tenants. Gentlemen from all parts of the country answered to the call. The realm was in danger, and old viscounts and vavasours left their patrimonial holdings, mounted on such horses as they possessed, and armed with such weapons as pleased their fancy. But when four thousand of those antediluvians, including their retainers, appeared with the regular army on the borders of Flanders, it was found they would be of no use, as they certainly were not at all ornamental; and this was the last appearance in history of the feudal chivalry which had existed in the armies of Clovis, and defended the kingdom in the days of Pepin, and suffered a glorious eclipse at Agincourt.

But Louvois, who hated Turenne, determined to show that France had many as worthy a son as he, and furnished an army to the Great Condé, who was nominated to the command in Germany, so excellently disciplined and plentifully supplied that the old days of victory were renewed. Condé, emulous of Turenne, adopted his tactics of caution and observation; and having checked the Italian general—who rivalled in the Imperial service the glories of his opponent in the French—he relinquished the command of armies at the end of this campaign, and lived to an honoured old age in his magnificent retirement of Chantilly. Montecuculli also retired into private life in this year, which saw the death of Turenne and the resignation of Condé. "A man who has had the honour," he said, "to oppose such generals, should not risk his laurels against tyros in the art of war."

In the two campaigns of 1676 and 1677, the king and his brother, Monsieur, attained almost equal distinction. Louis took Bouchain, Valenciennes, and Cambrai; and Monsieur won the battle of Mont Cassel against the Prince of Orange. The winner of a battle, however, is never without enemies at home; and Louis had the meanness to hate his brother for being so like a rival near his throne. Fame was also acquired on a new element in those eventful years. A privateer—not very far removed, in those days, from a pirate—of the name of Du Quesne, had distinguished himself, first in the management of a single vessel belonging to his native Dieppe, and then, as the war became more maritime, in the command of small squadrons. He had been rapidly raised in the ranks of his profession, and at this time was what the French call lieutenant-general of the naval forces, equal to our vice-admiral of the fleet. Du Quesne was placed in charge of a large fleet in 1676, and sailed into the Sicilian waters. De Ruyter, who had resisted with such valour the combined efforts of France and England, was now, by the strange revolution of politics, the admiral of the united fleets of Holland and Spain. He was blockading the harbour of Messina, and the French had been called to the aid of the revolted townsmen. On seeing the hostile flag, he sailed out into the open sea, and after an indecisive combat in January, he bore down upon Du Quesne, and commenced a general action. Those waters have often before and since been witnesses to the struggles of contending nations, and have heard the shouts of Carthagenians and Romans, Goths and Normans, English and French; but a more glorious career was never brought to a close than at the battle of Agosta, where De Ruyter received his death-wound. His name, indeed, survives the town which gave its designation to the combat, for it has long been swallowed up by earthquake. And even Louis, who had the faculty of making noble speeches, though without the power of entertaining noble thoughts, on being congratulated that a dangerous enemy was removed, replied, "It is impossible not to be affected at the death of a great man." Du Quesne, who expected a speech in his favour, of equal elevation, was disappointed. He received neither speech nor trophy, and the reason assigned by the king himself was, that he was a Protestant. "Sire," said Du Quesne, who had also the faculty of saying fine things, "when I fought your majesty's enemies, I did not inquire what religion they were of."

At this time, when people were blinded by the blaze of his glory, the sagacious councillors of Louis advised him to conceal that exhaustion, which is always the price of fame, had fallen upon the realm, and that his exchequer was nearly empty, and his levies insufficient. He therefore listened to overtures of peace, and was generous when it did not interfere with his own interests. He adroitly hinted at commercial privileges to the Dutch; and no consideration would persuade those mercantile patriots to continue the war which William of Orange recommended, as he saw the real motive of the conqueror's moderation. He took his last revenge on the oppressors of his country by thundering down upon the camp of Luxemburg, who, in reliance on the preliminaries being settled, was in no expectation of an attack; and thus gloriously concluded the campaign by driving the French from the field.

But nothing could resist the longings for peace which had seized on the heart of Europe. The Empire, and Spain, and Holland, and all the belligerents, great and small, determined to be at rest; and Louis signed the Peace of Nimeguen, first with Holland, and then with the other powers in succession, with the affected condescension of a benignant patron who bestowed repose on a suffering world, but with the skill of a politician who took possession of as much as he could comfortably retain. He kept the whole of Franche Comté and Alsace, and many of the strong fortresses and industrious towns of Flanders. He secured—perhaps with a prescient thought that Spain might some time or other have the same interest with himself—a strong boundary-line between the

Spanish possessions and the Netherlands ; and, as if merely to show his power, he forced the Elector of Brandenburg to restore the territories he had conquered from Sweden, and the King of Denmark to diminish the dues he had established on entering the Baltic. Having thus shown that his word was law from Calabria to Norway, he reposed upon his laurels, and applied the same care to the little quarrels of his court—the discussions about the precedence at a ball, or the order of being "incensed" at church—as he had bestowed so successfully on the machinations of the Empire and the enterprises of Spain.

CHAPTER XV.

GRANDEUR AND FALL OF LOUIS, A.D. 1678 TO A.D. 1715.

It was at this time that the municipal authorities of Paris conferred, in a formal manner, the epithet of Great on the king they delighted to honour. But the mayors and aldermen of towns are not the bestowers of fame. History has not ratified the title, and we may in a very short time be able to see the reason. To be great, a man must be generous and just; he must be unselfish, and have trust in other men. Alexander is called the Great, because the heroic and lovable portions of his character compensated for the darker parts. Frederick the Second of Prussia has been called the Great, to distinguish him from the exceedingly little Fredericks by whom he was preceded and followed; but nothing but the grossest flattery could affix a name indicative of the virtues of patriotism and noble thoughts on the tyrannical and inflated potentate who sat on the throne of France. The sentiments of his subjects, however, are not much more elevated than his own. At the commencement of his independent reign, at the death of Mazarin, the poet Racine dedicated to him his tragedy of "Alexander," and held forth the Macedonian destroyer of Persia as a proper model for a Christian king in the year 1663, "inasmuch as it needed only a little effort to make him redoubtable to all Europe. I foresee," he adds, "that your majesty will cover yourself with fresh glories, and at the head of an army complete the resemblance to your illustrious prototype, and add the title of Conqueror to that of the wisest monarch in the world."

The peace of Nimeguen put an end for a while to this career of wisdom and conquest. But no sooner were the swords of the belligerents sheathed, and the bills of their previous expenditures examined, than the various principalities and powers were astonished to perceive the proceedings of the French monarch. He doubled his fleet, he laid the foundations of the works at Cherbourg, which were only finished in 1858; he kept his army on its full establishment; he fabricated arms and accoutrements as if he were in the midst of a dreadful war; and having a hundred ships in his harbours, sixty thousand sailors in his pay, a line of strongly-armed fortresses on the frontier of his rule, and a vast array of soldiers cantoned throughout the land, he commenced the trade of spoiler on a very considerable scale, and seized several towns belonging to his friends and neighbours without giving them any notice of his design. The strong town of Strasburg, barrier and capital of Alsace, which covered the Rhine, and opened a passage into Germany by a commodious bridge, was pounced upon in profound peace, and then fortified by Vauban and victualled by Louvois, so as to place it beyond any probability of recapture. He demanded Alost in Flanders from the Emperor, on the sole ground that he wished to have it; and bought the town of Casal near Milan of its possessor the Duke of Mantua, who was very much in want of funds. The neighbouring nations looked on with awe. Singly, there was no chance for any of them, and the overwhelming master of such forces would give them no time to unite. Louis, indeed, owed as much to the insufficiency of his rivals as to his own self-will in the position he had assumed. England we need not speak of, for it was under the degrading influence of the Stuarts; Spain was sinking beyond hope in the apathy of exhaustion; Germany was tormented with internal struggles and the terror of a Turkish invasion. There was but one man of the time competent to the task of curbing the excesses of the great king, but he was only the hereditary prince and elective governor of one of the smallest of the states, and had nothing for some years but the glory of devising noble plans for the deliverance of Europe, without materials, in men or money to carry them into effect. This was William of Orange, who is reported to have said, that since he could not obtain Louis's friendship, he was determined to conquer his esteem. Fine speeches, however, had become so much the fashion at this time, that they were attributed to every body ; and it is not necessary for us to believe that William either valued the friendship of the devastator of his country, or paid him the compliment of supposing that a defence of popular freedom could acquire the despot's esteem. To give still further notice to his neighbours of the hopelessness of opposition, and keep up the military enthusiasm of his subjects, he sent a powerful fleet against Algiers, with mortars for the discharge of bomb-shells—a new invention, which was expected to alter the whole art of maritime war, as it gave an equality of force to an attacking fleet against stone batteries on land. The bombardment was successful, but at so prodigious an expense that the Dey is reported to have offered to set fire to the town himself if Louis would send him one-half of what the expedition had cost.

In three years after this, the corsairs were again visited by the gunboats and mortars of the champion of the Christian cause. The captives were given up to the French admiral, but as the English who happened to be among the slaves had the stubborn stupidity to say that the Dey had delivered them out of compliment to the King of England, the victorious Frenchman put them all ashore again, assuring them that the submission of the barbarians was made entirely to the flag of Louis the Great—a trait which, to the perverted taste of Voltaire himself, appears characteristic not more of English pride than of the respect paid to the French king. This dignified ruler took credit to himself for abstaining from the basest of crimes. There was a vast quantity of self-laudation when he refrained for a whole year, in a time of perfect peace, from warlike operations against the Emperor, who was at that time driven from Vienna by the Turks, two hundred thousand strong, and only saved his capital, and probably the remainder of his states, by the assistance of the heroic John Sobieski, king of Poland. A gentleman might as well take credit to himself for not running off with his friend's watch when he is attacked by highwaymen, and busied in the protection of his purse and life. It was not discovered for some time after, that the gentleman on this occasion from the first had been in alliance with the thieves. But the patience and long-suffering of the world were tried by still greater pretensions. The grand old republic of Genoa was so humbled that she sent her Doge to implore freedom in Paris. The other kings had yielded all his demands. It was only left to show his superiority to the superior of all crowned heads, and take an easy victory over the Pope. The ambassadors resident at Rome had agreed to surrender a certain privilege which they had acquired, nobody could say how, of exempting all the persons who lived in their palaces, or even in their quarter, from payment of the dues charged on importation at the gates of the city. Louis was requested to follow this example. He answered haughtily it was for him to set an example, not to follow it; and maintained the right of his representatives, though it interfered very materially with the police regulations and the revenue of the town. He sent an embassy which looked a great deal more like an attempt at conquest than a visit of peaceful friendship. The minister was attended at his official entrance by a thousand men fully armed, and took possession of his house as if it had been a citadel. He then placed sentinels round it, and seized a neighbouring church, which he turned into a military post. The high days of the Papacy had passed away, or an insult like this would have armed all Christendom in its defence. All that the Pope could do was to excommunicate the ambassador, but the Marquis de Lavardin only laughed at the harmless ceremony, which three hundred years before would have brought his master to the footstool of St. Peter.

Having thus attained the pinnacle of earthly glory by the personal abasement of the loftiest dignitary of his religion, he determined to show that it was from no leaning to the Protestant doctrines that he thus humiliated the Catholic chief. In the same year that he insulted the princely and pontifical dignity of the helpless Innocent the Eleventh, he signed the famous "Revocation of the Edict of Nantes." In 1598, the generous and sagacious Henry the Fourth had secured the peace and prosperity of the kingdom by the Settlement of religious disputes contained in the "Edict" he issued on changing his faith. Three generations of Frenchmen had grown up under this Christian comprehension, and had lost the asperity of polemic differences in the ennobling sentiments of their common duties. Sully and his Huguenot contemporaries had accepted their position as a tolerated and protected minority, and had performed their services to the State without reference to creed or communion. Louis himself was the first who introduced a distinction in the selection of his servants. Turenne, Schomberg, and Du Quesne, though of the proscribed persuasion, had been found indispensable, and were unwillingly given an opportunity of distinguishing their talents. Turenne, indeed, yielded to the arguments of Bossuet, and rose into unclouded favour with the king by his conversion to the Catholic faith; but the others were more stubborn or less enlightened, and suffered with the common herd under the great calamity that now fell upon the professors of the Reformed religion. Du Quesne was excepted by name, but died before he could avail himself of the indulgence. Schomberg joined the great stream of exiles who were driven into foreign lands by the savage and impolitic principles that had actuated the king. There was to be no toleration for dissent. The Huguenots were to disappear from the land they polluted with their presence, either by conformity to the Roman Church or banishment from their homes. What sufferings were included under that dreadful word, we can scarcely imagine now, for the hospitable shores of America are open to us, and the new regions of Australia invite us with outstretched arms. But the Frenchman was driven from his shop in the town and his country farm; from his cottage on the Seine, or his manufactory on the Rhone; his fortunes were ruined, his friendships and associations broken off; and hundreds of thousands poured across the ungrateful borders, harbouring an enmity to their country, which found indeed, on one or two occasions, outlet for itself in open war, but took a far surer revenge on their hypocritical and bigoted oppressors, by carrying their arts, their talents, and industry into other and hostile lands. The looms of depopulated Lyons hummed strains of vengeance in the now crowded workshops of Norwich; Germany, Switzerland, Sweden itself, received accessions of skilled and earnest workmen, who spread refinement and taste among the artisans of those simple countries, and enabled them to compete with the French in the markets of the world. Yet the agony must be great to leave the scenes of one's youth and manhood, for even an assured provision under other skies; and on this occasion grey-haired fathers and prattling children, strong-armed men and women in the bloom of beauty, were driven forth, with no home to receive them, and exposed to all the sufferings of friendlessness and want.

Louis rejoiced in the work of his hands when he saw the emptied villages, and felt that God was worshipped with no heterodox ceremonial from Calais to Marseilles. To this great act of religious fervour he was impelled by two considerations. One was, that he had conveyed his affections to a cold narrow-hearted woman, of the age of forty-seven, who had been companion and successor of his former favourite, Madame de Montespan, and was resolved to make up for the sins of her youth by rigid propriety in her old age. This was Madame de Maintenon, a successful adventuress, who had earned her first maintenance by giving her hand to a deformed buffoon of the name of Scarron, and achieved the highest of royal dignities by a private marriage with Louis the Fourteenth. The other consideration was, that an avowed and unflinching advocate of Popish doctrines was now seated on the English throne, and gave whatever influence could be derived from the co-operation of James the Second to any step which could be taken to injure the Protestant cause.

But Madame de Maintenon and James were equally disappointed in the result of the Revocation. The few recollections of liberty and self-respect still remaining in the hearts of the French, were turned to gall by the treatment of their fellow subjects. The spirit of opposition to the arbitrary proceedings of the English court was strengthened by the accession of so many thousand expatriated Frenchmen, who showed in their own persons the result of Romish supremacy. Never had the whole of Europe been nearer the loss of freedom than at this time. The North had forgotten its ancient glories, and erected despotic thrones in the Scandinavian kingdoms. Except in Great Britain and Holland, there was no approach to representative or liberal government. James fought with all his power to make his domains no exception to the universality of absolute rule, and pursued his schemes with so little judgment that a far more quiescent people than the descendants of the lords of Runnymede, and the gentlemen of the Petition of Right, would have been moved to rebellion. Rebellion, indeed, is scarcely a fitting word for the resolution which a great and outraged nation took to dismiss so disgraceful and contemptible an oppressor. A rebellion is a rising up against established power ; but this was a determination to abolish a newly-founded system of cruelty and weakness, which was in fact itself a rebellion against a nation's rights. The Prince of Orange had watched the gradual rise of English discontent. His wife was daughter of the infatuated king, and he himself was nephew. When the nation's patience at last gave way, the Prince appeared off the coast of Devon with a powerful fleet, which had been gathered without ostentation or notice in the ports of Holland, and landed with a few thousand soldiers at Torbay. Before Louis had time to recover from his surprise at the audacity of so small a potentate as the Stadtholder of the Provinces invading a great kingdom in alliance with himself, he received a visit from the fugitive Stuart, and perceived that the expedition of the Prince was not considered by the British people as an invasion, but a deliverance. He felt it, however, an increase of his dignity that he had a crowned head in his wages. He established the unlucky exile, therefore, in St. Germains, and treated him with the ceremony befitting a sovereign of England, and a dependant of his own.

But these stage antics at St. Germains were received with very little favour at St. James's, or in the Houses of Parliament. The British nation had declared that James the Second was no longer its king. Louis made equally solemn declaration that he was ; and issue was joined on this great question, where the pleadings were carried on with fleets and armies. James made his appearance in Ireland at the head of some French troops and made his disappearance at the Boyne, pursued by the French refugees. Schomberg was at their head, and when the uniforms of Louis's contingent were seen on the other side of the river, "Gentlemen," he said, "behold your persecutors," and the Huguenot cry was again heard as they charged upon their foes. The question was definitively settled, as regarded the possession of the English throne, by the flight of the dispossessed and dastardly claimant ; but the other matters in dispute, which had been cherished on both sides, between Louis and William, were now to be brought to the arbitrament of arms. "The bad that men do liveth after them," and England felt for some time the inefficiency or dishonesty of her former king. Charles, his jovial brother, had wasted in revelry the money devoted to the defences of the country. James had turned into polemic channels the sums voted for the maintenance of the fleet. Failing in his great effort of forcing the nation to embrace the Romish faith, he succeeded in stripping it of its natural bulwarks, and the harbours were either empty or thinly occupied by rotting ships and ill-paid crews. Tourville, the French admiral, was accordingly ruler of the sea. He defeated the English and Dutch squadron off Dieppe, and reigned supreme in the channel for nearly two years. Louis, availing himself of this circumstance made one more attempt to establish his puppet on the English throne. Fleets from the other harbours were collected at Brest, and an army was stationed in the neighbourhood of Cherbourg. When all preparations were made, the great expedition put to sea ; but William had wasted the supplies neither on suppers at Whitehall nor missionary labours among the clergy, and presented a rampart of a hundred vessels of war, that bore gallantly down on the fleet of Tourville, and put an end to the naval energy of France by the tremendous overthrow of La Hogue. James is reported by his apologists to have witnessed the engagement from a safe position on shore, and to have said, "See how my brave English fight!" But this is not in keeping with his character. It is much more certainly known that he volunteered to serve on board the French fleet, but probably with the hope of having his offer refused.

At the same time that he tried to impose a monarch on a neighbouring country, for the gratification of his pride, the French king was carrying on a war on the Emperor and the Duke of Savoy, in order to obtain as much as possible of a neighbouring country for himself. His first campaign had been as brilliant as usual : Luxemburg defeated the confederates (the Imperialists, English and Hollanders) at Fleurus. The Savoyard was defeated with still easier glory by Catinat at Stafarde, near Saluces ; and Piedmont was overrun in a very short time. In 1691 the town of Mons was captured by the king in person, and Liege mercilessly bombarded after its resistance had ceased. In the following year Namur was taken in the presence of Louis, who assumed the nominal command, and in the face of William and a powerful army. Leaving his conquest to be strengthened by Vauban, Luxemburg obtained another victory over the English king at Steinkirk. This battle is one of those of which the circumstances make it memorable in spite of its merely temporary results. William had detected a spy of Luxemburg in the camp. He made him write a false report to his employer, which would put him off his guard, and closed in upon the French army before it could recover from its surprise. But there was a great number of young nobles studying the art of war or of victory (for they seemed the same thing) under the Marshal Luxemburg. Princes of the blood, descendants of the Great Condé, great-grandsons of Henry the Fourth, and nephews of Turenne—these and others placed themselves at the head of their regiments, and bore up against the attack, till Luxemburg arranged his lines. The fight was the most critical of the war, and ended in a triumph of the French. But the danger had been great, and the enthusiasm of the whole nation gathered round the gay young cavaliers who had saved the reputation of its arms. They were met by crowds outside the towns as they returned to the capital. Flowers, crowns, and speeches were poured upon them all the way; and fashion completed their reward by inventing absurd pieces of dress in the shape of lace neckcloths and calling them Steinkirks. There were Steinkirk watch-chains, Steinkirk seals, Steinkirk bracelets, of which the names still remain, though the origin of them is forgotten. But this campaign of 1693 was famous for the bloodiest engagement of those times. At Nerwinde, William was nearly surprised, as Luxemburg had been at Steinkirk. He had only time to entrench himself during the night, and in the morning the combat began. It was fought with far more bitterness than is usual in civilised war; for the exiles of France, the sufferers by the Revocation, were again placed face to face with their oppressors, and religious fury was mingled with their military courage. Twenty thousand men were left dead upon the field; the wounded filled the villages of France and the Netherlands. There was great glory obtained by the French conquerors on this terrible day, but the glory of the vanquished Hollanders was no less. William was one of the men who rise with the necessities of their position. Almost always defeated, and never depressed—enabled, by some indomitable energy of his own mind, to resist a triumphant advance with the remnants of a scattered array—it is impossible to say whether his military fame would have been increased, in the opinion of qualified judges, by a series of successes.

The French began to tire of useless fame ; a victory never put them an inch nearer the object of their wishes. William would not yield them a foot of ground ; and England began to take an interest in the struggle, of which she had hitherto been rather an unconcerned spectator than a sharer. The national spirit of fair play was roused up to see the only champion of the cause of freedom overwhelmed by superior forces. A diversion was made in his favour on the real battle-field of English fame : vast fleets were fitted out, and traversed the sea in all directions. Calais, and Havre, and Dunkirk were bombarded, and Dieppe nearly reduced to ashes. William gained fresh vigour on land from the triumphs of the navy, and from other quarters clouds at the same moment came over the French cause. Luxemburg died, and left no successor worthy of his post. Louvois, a still heavier bereavement, had left his country without a competent administrator of its military force ; a famine fell upon the land ; the vigorous youth of the provinces was utterly exhausted; money it was impossible to raise ; and Louis, with the joy-bells for victories sounding in his ears, knew that the end was come. He appeared no more with his armies in the field, but became more strict in religious ceremonial and in devotion to Madame de Maintenon. William pushed forward, with unaccustomed hope ; he besieged and took Namur, in spite of the resistance of a numerous garrison, and the threatening position of a covering army of a hundred thousand men. By this wonderful achievement he raised the common estimation of his military skill and reputation ; for it was the first time that any of his continental deeds was gilded by the glory of success. News at the same time came frowning over the sea that the only French settlement in Hindostan, Pondicherry, which the great Colbert had planted as the stepping-stone to great commercial results, was seized on by the Dutch, and that the best of the French islands, St. Domingo, was wasted and ravaged by the English. Reprisals were attempted against these maritime powers, but no longer by the regular navy of France. It is an evident sign of national weakness when the sufferings and losses of a country are revenged by private hands. There were privateers from St. Malo, like Duguy Trouin, and corsairs like Jean Barte, who fitted out vessels and insulted the unarmed shores of Jamaica, and even made a dash on the treasures of Carthagena. But these desultory efforts had no effect upon the war. When we consider the condition of French affairs at this time—the impoverishment of Louis's finances, the wretchedness of his people, the disappearance of his fleets, the loss of his greatest generals and wisest counsellors—we shall not be surprised at his turning a longing eye to the possibilities of a peace. But we shall be greatly surprised—unless we take into consideration the blinding effects of his former pre-eminence—to see that he assumed all the airs of a conqueror using his power with the most generous moderation, in the terms he offered to Europe. Europe was as anxious for repose as he was, because she had never been anxious for war. The Peace of Ryswick, therefore, was universally hailed with joy. It gave back all the Flemish and other conquests of the French; it recognised William as the true king of Great Britain and Ireland; it demolished the fortifications of the frontier towns, on which so much science and money had been lavished; and, finally, Europe returned to the position it had been in nine years before—exhausted now of men, and wealth, and happiness, with many wide tracts of land made forever incapable of cultivation, and many flourishing cities reduced to a heap of ruins. The cause of all these woes conveniently forgot everything except that he was the first who proposed to put an end to them; and the salaried historians and slavish poets of the time sang in all tongues and nations the praises of the magnificent king who was deaf to the call of ambition, and listened only to the sweet voice of pity and compassion.

His people, however, were too much depressed to give way to rejoicings on the restoration of peace. The sacrifices had been so heavy that they destroyed the elasticity of the nation's resources as well as of its animal spirits. The Frenchman became less mercurial and more thoughtful than he had been before ; and the king, whether from advancing years or the necessity of retrenchment, curtailed the costly splendour of his domestic circle, which perhaps had hidden from him the sufferings of his subjects in the glare of his attendants' prosperity. He sank more and more under the domination of Madame de Maintenon ; and as he could no longer give the law to subject Europe, he indemnified himself with the most rigid government of his court and family. His habits were fixed with the regularity of the heavenly motions, and were looked up to with the same admiration by the smart astronomers of the bedchamber and audience hall. If there were injured cities in the Low Countries, or impoverished farms upon the Rhine, their hatred might have been appeased if they had known the degrading miseries of their destroyer's private life. Summoned at a certain hour from his morning sleep—dressed by duke and marquis—led by chamberlain and marshal, and surrounded at breakfast by lord and lady—preceded, attended, followed by some hundreds of greedy courtiers and other expectants of his favour, as he passed from his apartments to the palace chapel—waited on in his walks—watched in all his actions—never alone, never natural—never off the stage—the poor old man was as great a prisoner in his golden chains as any culprit in the galleys. He knew the atmosphere he breathed in—of false praise, secret enmity, grovelling meanness, and utter depravity of life—and yet could breathe no other.

The majestic fabric of Versailles, which was a triumph for the Peace of Nimeguen, was a libel on the Peace of Ryswick ; and complaints were heard, or suspected, against the magnificence of the royal establishment while poverty was eating into the comfort of every cottage in the land. Louis would not confess to himself that he had lived too long, and that he was the survivor of a state of things which had passed away. He still spoke with the voice of the master of Colbert and Louvois, and Turenne and Luxemburg ; and turned his eyes to Spain, as he had formerly done to the Netherlands, forgetting that the instruments of his former greatness had broken in his hands. His wife, Maria Theresa, had long been dead (1683) ; and now her brother, the feeble Charles the Second, was about to follow. Every politician in Christendom was on the alert for the expected event. Maria Theresa, we remember, had renounced her claim ; her sister had married the Emperor Leopold ; and though the ceremony of renunciation had been omitted at the time of the union, the Emperor had forced his only daughter by the Spanish princess to renounce all the rights derivable through her mother on her betrothal to the Elector of Bavaria. Of this Bavarian marriage there was a son. All parties, indeed, seemed to have insurmountable obstacles in the way of their accession ; and Louis, perhaps to blind the eyes of England and Holland to his possible proceedings, entered into a secret treaty with William and the United Provinces for the distribution of the Spanish monarchy, as if it had been the prize-money of a captured town. It is amusing to see our wary constitutional king, and the wary republican high mightinesses of Holland, giving countries here and countries there, without the least reference to the populations, or deigning to consult them as to their wishes on the point. France was to have the kingdoms of Naples and Sicily ; Austria was to have the Milanese ; and the young Prince of Bavaria to have the kingdom of Spain, the Low Countries, and the American colonies. But the young Prince of Bavaria died in 1700, and the web had all to be spun again. The Archduke Charles of Austria, second son of the Emperor, was now to have the share of the late Bavarian ; France was to have the Two Sicilies and Lorraine ; but Louis, who was fond of bestowing kingdoms which did not belong to him, generously offered to give the kingdom of the Two Sicilies to the Duke of Savoy, in exchange for his hereditary duchy and the territory of Nice. When this last arrangement was concluded, the contracting parties waited patiently for the demise of Charles of Spain ; but Charles of Spain was not so weak as he had been thought. He was offended at this sharing of his spoils before he was buried, and wrote a will. This will was the most important document of the time. Its object was to secure the integrity of the Spanish realm. Spain, whatever happened, was to be mistress of all her subject crowns; she was to have Milan and the Sicilies, the Low Countries, and the Indies. He would not have his country a dependency of France, by leaving it to the heir of that monarchy; nor of the Empire, by leaving it to the eldest son of Leopold; nor a prey to intestine division or foreign war, by leaving it in fragments, as proposed by William and the Provinces. He left it to the Duke of Anjou, second son of the Dauphin; failing him, to his brother the Duke of Berri; failing him, to the Archduke Charles; and failing him, to the Duke of Savoy. He let each of the competitors have a distant view of the inheritance; but the inheritance was to continue whole and undivided. The treaty of partition, however, was still in existence, duly signed and executed; and William and the Provinces waited to see how nobly Louis would fulfil the conditions, and preserve the balance of power in Europe, by not allowing the greatest monarchy of Christendom to fall into the hands of either a French or German prince.

Louis, on the 16th November, 1700, got up and dressed himself with care. He summoned the Marquis of Castel Rios, the Spanish ambassador, into his presence, and, at the same moment, his grandson, the Duke of Anjou, entered the apartment by another door. "Behold your monarch!" he exclaimed to the Spaniard, who fell upon his knees and kissed the young man's hand. The great doors were then flung wide, and the crowds in the outer gallery came forward to see what was going on. The old king said, "Gentlemen, I present to you the King of Spain; his birth entitles him to the crown; the late king has left it to him by will; the nation demands him,—I have yielded to its demand.—Sir," he added, turning to the King of Spain, "be a good Spaniard—that is now your first duty; your next is to remember that you are a born Frenchman; the Pyrenees have disappeared!" France heard the declaration with very different feelings from those which found expression in the cheers and applauses of the auditors of this speech. To lift away the Pyrenees, she felt, would exhaust her enfeebled strength; for it was certain that England, and Holland, and the Empire, would resist with all their power this effort to remove the landmarks set up by nature herself. And, in accordance with these sad forebodings, the War of the Succession began Thirteen years of the greatest sufferings which France had hitherto endured—of defeat in the field and discontent at home—were the terrible payment which she made for the glory her sovereign had arrogated to himself of creating a King of Spain.

People acquiesced in this unexpected proceeding for a time. Surprise paralysed the other parties to the secret treaty, and William and the Provinces went so far as to recognise the new king. The Emperor was indignant, but felt himself too weak to take active steps to assert his son's rights. And it was at this critical moment that Louis irritated the Crown and people of England by acknowledging the son of James the Second. He paid him a formal visit at St. Germains, on the death of his father, in 1701, and addressed him as James the Third. The maker of two monarchs thought he was renewing the great days of his youth, when he distributed ranks and territories as he chose; but different enemies were round him now. William, the calm placid Dutchman, who concealed beneath that impassive exterior the soul of a hero of romance, burned with the double indignation of a king and a soldier. Insulted by the recognition of his rival claimant to the throne, he felt there was now a fair field for the display of his military talents, and a chance of repaying the wrongs he had suffered at the hands of the haughty Frenchman. But, in the midst of his hopes and preparations, he died. Two men, however, rose in his place—one the greatest general, except one, in the annals of England—John Churchill, Duke of Marlborough; the other, Prince Eugene of Savoy. Equally unfortunate in the case of these two irresistible commanders, Louis remembered that the Englishman had obtained his scientific experience under

Condé and Turenne, and that he had rejected the services of Eugene when he applied for a colonelcy in his guards, and threw him, disappointed and irritated, into the hands of the Emperor.

England, Holland, the Empire, Prussia, Denmark, and Hanover, supported the claims of the Emperor's second son as King of Spain. He issued his orders and bestowed his decorations under the name of Charles the Third. Spain, France, and some of the Italian powers, drew sword for the king's grandson, who coined his doubloons and appointed to his armies as Philip the Fifth. Louis was defeated in all his plans. Marlborough sent his marshals in headlong flight from Blenheim, Ramillies, Oudenarde, and Malplaquet. Gibraltar was wrested for ever from Spain, and attached to England. His fleets were burnt at Vigo, and Toulon was besieged by sea and land. His grandson was driven from Madrid by the genius of Peterborough, and became a fugitive in his own nominal kingdom. Prince Eugene in the mean time crushed the French power in Italy, and approached the boundaries of France. And when the clouds were heaviest upon the outward prospects of his country, the old man's house was made more desolate than any of the cottages he had ruined in the Palatinate or ravaged in the Cevennes, by the entrance of death into the gilded halls of Versailles. The Dauphin, his son, died in 1711. The Duke of Burgundy, his grandson, and the duchess, followed their father within the year. The Duke of Brittany, now heir to the crown, and only five years old, died at the same time, and nobody remained in the direct line of succession to the old man of seventy-four but the Dauphin's third son, afterwards Louis the Fifteenth, a child in arms. While these reiterated blows were breaking the spirit of the king, and rousing a superstitious feeling in the nation that the end of their career was come, a gleam of light slowly broke forth from a death in another quarter; for the dread summons was delivered to the Emperor Joseph, who had succeeded his father Leopold in 1705, and followed him to the tomb in 1711. At first it made little change in the próceedings of Eugene. That greatest of soldiers passed across the boundary line and trod the sacred territory of the great nation. Louis was advised to retire to the Loire, but refused, and said he would mount his horse and die in battle rather than appear to yield. But the Tories of England took a politic view of the Emperor Joseph's death. They thought, why should we go on fighting on behalf of Charles the Third of Spain, who by the demise of his brother, is Emperor of Germany? Was it wise to resist Philip the Fifth for fear of the union of Spain and France, and now to persist in supporting the Austrian's claims with the certainty of seeing the Empire and Spain in the same hands? The Tories did not care much for the military glories of Marlborough, for they hated him as a renegade from their principles, and the meanest and most unscrupulous of mankind. At the end, therefore, of the thirteen years, Louis was surprised to find his nomination to the Spanish crown ratified by the English and Dutch. He attained the barren glory of having a grandson on the throne of the Castiles, but the Pyrenees remained as abrupt and mountainous as ever; for Philip made formal renunciation of his rights to France —a renunciation registered in the parliaments of Paris and Madrid—and the Peace of Utrecht was signed in 1714. By this England obtained many advantages. She retained Minorca in addition to Gibraltar, which gave her the command of the Mediterranean. She gained also the immeasurable territories of Hudson's Bay, Newfoundland, and Acadia, which made her paramount in North America. Austria kept possession of the Milanese and Naples; and Philip contented himself with the kingdom of Spain and the Transatlantic possessions of the Crown.

It was time the great War of the Succession should come to an end. A great change had taken place in the mind of France. The magnificence of the early years of Louis had turned men's thoughts only into the channels of glory and ostentation. The ascetic severity, with the religious intolerance, of his advancing age, divided his court into the two parties most fatal to a nation's happiness, the conscientious bigots and the men without a faith. Yet in outward observance there was no distinction between the two. No meeting of enthusiasts at an American revival showed deeper signs of devotion and contrition than the powdered and ribanded gentlemen and ladies who worshipped beside the king; no assemblage of avowed atheists and unbelievers could have equalled those same personages, when they met at supper in their luxurious apartments or paraded on the broad terraces of Versailles, in their sneers and epigrams against all that was pure and holy. But even the external observances imposed on them by the solemnity of the aged pair, who were strict to mark any levity of behaviour, however blind or indulgent they might be to the real vices of their attendants, became a weary servitude to the gay and young. They looked forward to happier times when hypocrisy would not be required, and when they would be encouraged in their greatest excesses by the example of the wielder of the royal power. On the outside of the courtly circle, deeply suspected of the most hideous crimes, and tolerated solely in consideration of his rank, was the Duke of Orleans, next in blood to the future king, and entitled on that account to the approaching regency—a man whose talent for society and freedom from all restraints would have made him merely the model of wit and wickedness if he had been born in a lower station, but whose character promised a complete realisation of the wildest dreams of luxury and abandonment when the reins of power were in his hands. Louis saw before his successor the dreadful prospect of a guide and governor in the person of the most fascinating and most debauched man of his time. He tried to guard against the danger by appointing a council of government; and farther to prevent the accession of the hated nephew, if his youthful charge should be removed—and Orleans was not only considered capable of any enormity of the kind, but was widely suspected of having already cleared a way for himself to the throne by the mysterious deaths of so many members of the royal line within the last few years—he nominated to the succession two of his natural sons, whom he had long ago legitimated by royal edict, and created Duke of Maine and Count of Toulouse. Town, court, and country were revolted at the notion of seeing those base-born and unpopular persons on the throne of St. Louis. Better the vices and joyous improprieties of the great-grandson of Henry the Fourth, than all the upstart insolence of the children of Frances Athenaïs de Montespan. People gathered round the coach of the old king as he travelled from Paris to Versailles, not to hail him with loud acclamation, or even respectful silence, but to count the growing care-lines on his face, and to calculate how long he would still survive. He did not survive long. Theatrical, even in the realities of life, to the last, he summoned a party round his bed on the 15th August, 1715, when the physicians had declared his state hopeless, and in their presence made a speech to his successor, a terrified little boy of five years old, who comprehended nothing of the exhortations addressed to him. He bade him take warning by his example, not to devote the public revenue to war or buildings. "It is the ruin of a nation. I have often commenced a war too lightly," he said, "and continued it for vanity. All your happiness will depend on your submission to God and the care you bestow on your people." These were almost his last words, and on the 1st of September he died—the last survivor of the period to which he had given his name, for with Louis the Fourteenth the "age of Louis the Fourteenth" expired.

The great characteristic of this age is its artificiality. In everything—in poetry, painting, ordinary conversation, gardening—in the highest and the lowest, the effort was to avoid the simplicities of nature, and make an ostentatious display of the resources of art. The government of one man, planted in unapproachable supremacy on the throne of twenty millions of people, distributing the blessings of law and safety by a line of servitors all deriving their authority from the Crown, and forming one unbroken chain from the chancellor or marshal of France to the usher of a local court, or the corporal of a company in a regiment; this was so artificial a system—

perplexed with so many difficulties, and therefore strengthened by so many regulations—that routine and custom banished every motion of spontaneity or independence. This slavish subjection to established forms extended, we have said, to literature and art. The Crown became strengthened by the definiteness of the duties of all inferior offices ; and the throne itself was forced to gain a condensation of power and interest, by a rigid adherence to the rules laid down for its direction. Not more despotic was Louis, or more unbending in the demarcation of the powers of his subordinates, than Boileau, the great critic and satirist of the time, was in the exaction of a certain style, of which the limits were arbitrarily fixed by himself, for dramatist and poet. There was to be no undress—no familiarity—no touch of nature making the whole world kin ; but the hero of Greece was to be my Lord Achilles of Phthia ; Hecuba was to be Madame, and Iphigenia, Mademoiselle. It is wonderful to behold at a pantomime what prodigious activity, and even what grace can be shown in a dance in fetters ; and no one can deny the possession of genius—even dramatic genius—of the highest order to Corneille and Racine ; but it will be sufficient to mark our present and wiser appreciation of the impediments which interfered with those great men's motions, to mention the judgments passed by the best critics in France on Shakespeare. To call him a savage was the mildest form of objection. He was too shocking in his tragedies to be sympathised with, and too vulgar in his comedies to be understood. The difficulty of bending the long formal Alexandrines, in which their plays are written, with the flexible grace of easy or natural conversation, was held forth as an additional advantage of the French style over the negligent facility of Shakespeare's versification, as it presented greater labour to be endured, and greater triumph to be gained. How long this adherence to the Louis the Fourteenth dignity might have lasted, it is impossible to say ; for the traditions of the great monarch survived the Revolution, and received a kind of pinchbeck renewal in the days of the first Empire ; but it was only when parliamentary government was established, and debates in the Chambers equalled in intensity of interest the finest passages on the stage, that a new race of dramatists arose in the land, who spoke in the language of ordinary life, and surpassed at one bound the stately declamations and rounded periods of their powdered and periwigged predecessors. Even while retaining their cumbrous versification, they out-shakespeared Shakespeare in their disdain of theatrical conventionalities, and strove to become natural, as the highest effort of their skill.

One good effect, however, proceeded from this fixedness of rule which petrified the higher productions of Louis the Fourteenth's time. People could not be always writing about kings and queens ; and if they wanted to mention minute circumstances—the dress of a heroic soldier, the beauty of a reigning toast, or the petty intrigues of the court, by which great events were produced—they were driven into the form of letters or memoirs ; a style of composition in which the French have never had any rivals, and from which we at this moment derive all the information worth having on the habits and thoughts of the time. Everybody was charmed with the elegant gossip and the familiar recollections of the fair leaders of the fashions and politics of the hour. The easiness of the style was so admirably adapted to the frivolity of the events, that it required neither criticism nor exertion to enter into its merits ; whereas the professed historian, who always wrote in ruffles and silk stockings, was read by an admiring and fastidious public, who always dressed itself in buckram and brocade. Each branch of letters had its glorious chief, who had given the model of that kind of composition ; and Boileau had threatened death and destruction to any one who departed from the mould. Racine was so painfully perfect that it was high treason to hint a fault, and positive rebellion to depart from his example. Tragedy, therefore, became as monotonous as a range of Assyrian kings, whose sculptors thought it impiety to give the slightest variety to their royal features. But it was theology which felt most the impress of that inexorable and exacting age. No pulpits have ever shaken to greater eloquence than those in which Bourdaloue, Bossuet, and Massillon, delivered their holy message. The message, however, was dressed in the livery of the court, and spoken in the ears of princes and courtiers, with bated breath and whispering humbleness. Highest of these—boldest in language—loftiest in idea—was Bossuet, the Bishop of Meaux; but his boldness of language was in praise of the king; his loftiness of idea, the elevation of the royal power. To attain that object he drew up the articles of the modern liberties of the Gallican Church, which took away the unquestioned supremacy and possible tyranny of the Pope, and transferred both—the unquestioned supremacy and the possible tyranny—into the hands of Louis. His natural impetuosity and haughtiness, along with the craven submission of his mind to established authority, threw him into perpetual contradictions with himself. Zealous adherent of his Church, and advocate of blind obedience to her commands, he aided in overthrowing her reign when she came into contact with the pride of his imperious master. Proud of his illustrious pupil, the saintly Fénélon, he wrote against him, appealed against him, and caballed against him, when he suspected him of faltering in the orthodoxy of his Catholic opinions, and succeeded in having him condemned by the Pope and humiliated by a public recantation. Yet there was no relenting in that impenetrable bosom; he rejected the advances of the man who was at that time the greatest ornament, not only of the Church of France but of Christianity itself. The Eagle of Meaux, as Bossuet was called, old and worn out, died unforgiving and unreconciled (1704). He died wasting his last strength in mounting stairs to waylay the king with his petitions, and to catch one other glimpse of the heavenly countenance which had been to him as the face of an angel. But his favour was past. Madame de Maintenon disliked and feared him. He had descended to the indignity of patching up the quarrels between Louis and his former favourite, Madame de Montespan; but secure in her character of wife, she did not require his assistance, and contented herself with the interested services and low intelligence of her confessor, Père la Chaise. In neglect, and even in penury, the great preacher, the universal author, the deep scholar, brought his troubled and many-coloured life to a close. He lived just long enough to perceive the nothingness of all his toils. He had advocated the revocation of the Edict of Nantes; had received accounts of the massacres which Louis perpetrated by his dragonnades against the recusant Huguenots, and his cruelties among the enthusiasts of the Cevennes, with almost idolatrous gratulations; had written a book proving the falsity of the Reformed religion, from the disagreements on points of doctrine among the Protestants themselves, in the midst of the quarrels of Jesuit and Jansenist, of Gallican and Roman, of the envenomed advocates of the different views of grace, and of the ferocious enmities of the maintainers of predestination or free-will; and he now expired with the infuriated exiles he had helped to expel on the borders of the kingdom sword in hand, and the people on whom he had bestowed so many lessons in the art of hating their heretical countrymen on the very eve of throwing off religion altogether. Bossuet has been dwelt on at some length as the representative of the ecclesiastic spirit of the time. In his dignity of demeanour and pomp of language, no less than in his crouching abasement before power, and pitiless support of authority, we trace the working of the great king's character on the highest intellects, as well as on the masses of his people. In every thing the same influence is to be seen. Walking amid the straight avenues and stately terraces of the palace of Versailles, on which he expended upwards of sixteen millions sterling—casting your eye over its immense proportions, its formal lines and rigid uniformity of design, you almost fancy you can see in stone and mortar, in alley and parterre, a reproduction of the age of Louis the Fourteenth. A grave solemnity and imposing grandeur still haunt the long-drawn corridors and dimly-lighted halls of that prodigious residence. The width of the walks, the gigantic scale of plantation and enclosure, the canal-like regularity of the lakes, and laborious artificiality of fountain and waterfall, all these remind you of the effect of lavished wealth and anti-natural effort. The vast place, with all its symmetry and grandeur, seems an embodiment of the fixed and ostentatious monarchy by which it was created. Versailles will be for ever a protest against the liberties of France and its occasional outcries for Equality and Fraternity ; for it bears in every line the impress of a grand and overbearing despotism, where the destinies of the whole nation are intrusted to a single man. It must have been on taking possession of the untasteful but immeasurable mansion, that the king felt in his inflated heart the sentiment to which he gave frequent utterance, "L'état c'est moi"—I am the State.

CHAPTER XVI.

LOUIS THE FIFTEENTH.—REGENCY OF THE DUKE OF ORLEANS, A.D. 1715 TO 1723.—1723 TO 1774.

At the moment when Louis, on his deathbed, was expressing his sorrow at having been the cause of unnecessary wars, his conscience must have reproached him with the proceedings he had encouraged in Scotland. Anne, the English queen, had died in August, 1714. Selfish enough to persist in excluding her brother from the throne during her own life, she had family affection or family pride sufficient to desire his re-establishment when her reign should end. There were cabals, treacheries, conspiracies on all sides, not without the knowledge of the weak-minded queen and her unprincipled ministers, in favour of James the Third, who had assumed the title on the death of his father in 1701; and Louis, yielding to the same mad ambition of king-making which had thrown him into the war of the Spanish Succession, furnished money, which he was fain to borrow, and promises—of which he had a more plentiful supply—to the infatuated young man in making an invasion on the coasts of Great Britain, a few months after George of Hanover had assumed his seat on the constitutional throne. The effect of the death of the great supporter of despotism was felt in the north of Scotland the moment it was known. James the Third slipped safely back to France, leaving his gallant adherents to perish on the English scaffolds, and disappeared from history in the dimness of his retreat in a little town in Lorraine. His name occasionally rises to the surface, according as the enemies of England find it useful as a threat against her repose ; but the first application of it to a political purpose, showed also how impossible it is for policy to contend with geography, for Spain and France were proved even then to be more divided by the barrier mountains than united by the relationship of their kings. The Spanish minister, Alberoni, had reduced the expenditure of his country, and had filled the treasury. Great things entered his mind as soon as he found himself freed from debt, and he proposed to enlist the military services of the famous Charles the Twelfth of Sweden, in restoring the exiled monarch of England to his throne. He proposed also to encourage the Turks to attack the Emperor ; and he tried to create a civil war in France. When the Christian prelate had completed the plan of these benevolent measures, he despatched a Spanish expedition to seize Sardinia, and an army at the same time to take possession of the island of Sicily. All nations were roused at the sight of so much insolence and injustice ; and the first spectacle which the promoters of the Spanish accession of Philip the Fifth and the restoration of the Stuarts saw, after the death of Louis, was a combination against Spain, of France under the Regent Orleans, and England under George the First. To complete the amazing contrast between the two periods, Marshal the Duke of Berwick, son of James the Second, was sent into Spain at the head of a French army to overthrow Philip the Fifth, the grandson of Louis the Fourteenth. Towns were taken, and provinces seized. England regained her old supremacy on the sea, and Admiral Byng exterminated the fleets of Spain in the Straits of Messina. Alberoni saw the badness of the move he had made, and patched up a dishonourable peace. England was glad to sheathe the sword to consolidate her domestic quiet ; and France was in such a dream of prosperity, such a fairyland of hope and brilliancy, that the grim realities of war had scarcely ruffled her repose.

Philip of Orleans, nephew of Louis the Fourteenth, and now ruler of the kingdom, saw nothing in glory but an interference with his pleasures, and nothing in supreme power beyond the means of gratifying his tastes for luxury and expense. The extravagances of wickedness perceived in the Roman Emperors were revived in the person of the grandson of Henry the Fourth, and pupil of Dubois. This was a man who seems to have been permitted upon the earth for the purpose of showing to what depths of infamy a human being could descend. Originally a menial servant in one of the colleges, he had been promoted to be sub-tutor to the Duke of Orleans when a boy. Worming himself into his pupil's favour by the basest compliance with all his wishes—aiding him in his profligacy, and encouraging him in his blasphemy and infidelity—he had risen to be abbé, bishop, cardinal, and prime-minister of France. Luxurious as his master, he had the essentials of vice without the refinement that makes it less dangerous to the mass, and without the decencies of concealment which betray a consciousness of wrong. Open in his iniquities, loud in his sneers at holy things, the Cardinal Dubois lavished the resources of the State at the same rate as the equally wicked but more popular prince. When those two sated voluptuaries and very needy politicians saw the approach of national bankruptcy with a dismay which arose from the certainty that the bankruptcy would end in revolution, they were enraptured with the appearance in Paris of a Scotch gentleman of the name of Law, who promised them unbounded wealth, and the country endless prosperity, if they would only adopt his scheme. It would be difficult to name any scheme, attended by such promises, which would have been rejected by Orleans and Dubois. The scheme was simply this: To institute a paper-currency resting for its security on some imaginary gold and silver mines on the banks of the Mississippi. But the delusion took: the Company of the West, as the joint-stock bank was called, could scarcely find clerks enough to deliver its scrip in return for solid coin. Shares went up twenty, thirty, a hundred, and at last three hundred per cent. Princesses, duchesses, ambassadors of foreign kings, crowded the antechambers of Law, the great financier; and the prince and cardinal filled their purses on the credulity of the people.

The ships, however, laden with gold, never sailed into port; the silver mines of Louisiana yielded no increase. A clamour began to be felt, and the Prince Regent took the most ludicrous means to appease it. He published an order that no one should keep in purse or drawer more than twenty pounds in cash, under a penalty of forfeiture of some share of it to any one who could prove the crime. Much money came into the bank under this threat; but ten times more was buried or went into foreign states. Then there was a law reducing the rate of interest; and finally, when the breakdown was unavoidable, and all the gold in Europe would scarcely have paid for the nominal value of the shares, preparations were made for a bankruptcy according to the sections of a royal edict. The shares were to fall gradually; they were to sink month by month till finally they stopped at half their original price. There they were to remain, and all would be well as far as a royal edict could make it so.

But panics are above royal edicts, or even acts of parliament, and the shares fell to nothing. Thousands of families were ruined: provisions rose in price; anger took possession of the offended multitudes, and Law escaped with the greatest difficulty with his life. It is only just to add that the projector was a believer in his own project, and carried nothing with him into his miserable exile at Venice but his poverty and broken hopes. Meanwhile Orleans and Dubois continued to the outraged citizens the spectacle of their vices and crimes. All orders in the State felt the effect of the recent speculation; high and low had equally sold their independence and honesty in pursuit of that sordid Mammon; and so thoroughly was the whole mass of society saturated with a spirit of gambling and intrigue—of base submission to those who could aid their fortunes, and insane contempt for those who would rebuke their excesses—that, on calmly looking back to that period, with its heartless glitter and utter prostration of the loftier faculties of the mind, we see no refuge for the past nor prospect for the future, but some great convulsion, which shall free us from the ungodliness of priests, the infamy of nobles, the profligacy of women, and the hopelessness of a brutalised and trampled people. This was still far off, and totally unnoticed till it actually appeared: but it was coming. Debasing tyranny like Louis the Fourteenth's, degrading viciousness like Orleans's and Dubois's, and the wider and more systematic demoralisation introduced by the king, who was now ready to assume the sceptre, could not fail, sooner or later, to produce fruits worthy of the altogether corrupted tree which had been planted in such soil and tended by such hands.

In 1723 the vain ceremony was gone through of taking Louis the Fifteenth, in his fourteenth year, to a Bed of Justice, and proclaiming his majority. He had been consecrated at Rheims the year before. The office of regent was now at an end, but the influence of Orleans remained in quality of prime-minister. It is pleasant to get to the close of so disgraceful a period as the regency of Philip and the career of Dubois. That unregretted adventurer came to his end, brought on by the debaucheries of his life, in August, 1723; and in four months he was followed by his congenial pupil, who died of apoplexy on the 2d of December.

The Duke of Bourbon, who was appointed premier, was a far stupider man than the Duke of Orleans, and quite as depraved in character. The Parisians were now treated to the sight of magnificence without taste, and luxury without refinement. The thinking portion of them were farther scandalised by the dreadful severities exercised against the Protestants by this man of no faith. An edict of intolerable harshness, in 1724, recalled the memory of the worst days of the Revocation; and at this very time the Church itself was divided into hostile camps, which threatened vengeance against each other and the abrogation of even the forms of religion throughout the territories of France. The Duke did not pretend to be a politician, and left the cares of state to his favourites, who, as usually happens in cases of this sort, were persons of the lowest rank. One of these, who called herself the Marchioness de Prie, persuaded him that the surest way to retain his power would be to bind the consort of the king to his cause by the chains of gratitude and interest. She advised him, therefore, to send back the little Spanish princess who had been received and lodged at the Louvre in 1722, in the character of future queen, and put some person in her place who would be mindful of the obligation. With this view the insolent adviser presented herself to the sister of the Duke, in order to make her the offer of the crown ; but was received with such haughty severity and contemptuous pride, that she left the princess to her solitary grandeur, and bestowed the hand of the king of France in a very different quarter.

The favoured candidate was the daughter of a simple and excellent gentleman who had been presented with the crown of Poland by Charles of Sweden, and stripped of it again by Catherine of Russia. He was now living in obscurity at Weissenburg, on the borders of Alsace, and was on the point of bestowing his daughter on a colonel of his acquaintance when the flattering offer of the Marchioness de Prie changed all his plans. Marie Leczinski, the daughter of the dis-crowned Stanislaus, was elevated to the highest rank in Europe, when her husband was but fifteen years old, and Bourbon expected interminable gratitude from the new queen. She was, however, of a dull and unimpressible disposition, and had no room in her heart for either gratitude or hatred. The insult bestowed on Spain was certain to lead to war, war to increased taxation, and increased taxation to—nobody could say what. So the Duke of Bourbon was banished to his estates, and an aged churchman of seventy-three, who had been preceptor to the king, was installed as prime-minister, and the peace-loving administration of Cardinal Fleury began. Peace-loving, but not peace maintaining ; for the powers in a few years became embroiled beyond the possibility of reconciliation. Hostilities with Spain were indeed avoided, in the meantime, by apologies for the sending back of the princess ; with England, by a rigorous non-interference with her superiority at sea ; with the Emperor, by withdrawing all designs upon Italy ; and with the rest of the world, by gentleness and forbearance. A kind, good old man, who hated war as a Christian, and feared it, in the present state of French feeling, as a politician ; he feared it also—and his enemies said still more—for the chance it would bring of his own dismissal from power, and the substitution of a younger and more vigorous rival ; for, in spite of his priestly profession, and his outward humility, and declarations of disinterestedness, it was believed that ambition never burned more fiercely in Wolsey or Richelieu than in the breast of that meek-looking, low-voiced, gentle-eyed old man.

Skilfully remaining ignorant of the infamous excesses in which his pupil indulged, he kept the noiseless tenor of his way, encouraging peaceful enterprise, and devoting himself to the material prosperity of his country. To maintain quiet he would sacrifice anything—the glory of his nation, a very common cry in French history, to the domineering haughtiness of England; the liberties of the Gallican Church to the ultra-montanism of the Jesuits. But good crops and cheap provisions, and lightened taxation, are powerful supports to a minister against the attacks of patriots and liberals. Voltaire had already established himself as the first wit in Europe, and the most dangerous enemy of all sorts of authority which did not repose on the bayonets of a powerful army. He had already tasted the sweets of living under a censorship of the press and a timid old cardinal, by having been twice imprisoned in the Bastile, and once banished to London. His sayings, his writings, his sneers and sarcasms, were recognised as one of the powers in the State ; and even at this early time we may divide the influential classes in Paris into the nobility, the churchmen, and the philosophers.

A spirit of ribaldry and disregard of the sanctions of religion pervaded the wonderful literature which now began to make its appearance—a literature with a fresher life in it than the formal correctness of the masterpieces of Louis the Fourteenth's time would have allowed. Running over with the ebullitions of a newly-discovered power—handling the highest speculations which can occupy the mind of man with a lightness of touch and brilliancy of expression which brought them within the observation of the most careless reader ;—over all —over the wit of Voltaire and the elegance of La Fontaine, the brilliant solidity of Montesquieu and the dreamy rhapsodies of Rousseau—was poured forth the jeering and contemptuous conviction of the unreality of all human endeavours, which Goethe has since that time embodied in his Mephistopheles. All the fiery youth of gentle birth and no occupation were devoted in a short time to the two absorbing desires of throwing off the vulgar obligations of a worn-out superstition, and flourishing their swords in a field of battle. Fleury, a priest and pacificator, had no mercy to expect from these quick-witted, out-spoken young gentlemen ; and perhaps even the war-detesting Cardinal was not sorry when a safety-valve was opened in 1733 to the irrepressible activity of a new generation, which had never known the sufferings of the last years of the grand monarch's reign. This was the death of Augustus the Second, whom Russia had placed on the throne of Poland when Stanislaus was expelled. Stanislaus, it was felt by every one, was now in a very different position from that he had held before. He was now father-in-law of the King of France, and that wearied voluptuary was not yet so entirely sated by his debaucheries as to be beyond the ambition of following his grandfather's trade in repairing the broken fortunes of kings. Charles the Sixth (the Emperor) supported the claim made to the vacant throne by his nephew, Frederick Augustus, Elector of Saxony ; and, in return, Frederick Augustus accepted a certain act which the Emperor had issued, called a Pragmatic, by which he abrogated the Salic law as regarded the succession to his hereditary States, and left them by will to his daughter, Maria Theresa. Russia also, which from this time threw its monster weight into the scales of all European settlements, defended his cause. Fleury, like all men of irresolute minds and petty views, did too much or too little : he allowed Stanislaus to hurry off to Warsaw, and aided him with a miserable flotilla, which found its way to Dantzic, conveying fifteen hundred men. Those who carried into the Baltic the glories of France and her fortunes, were taken prisoners by the Russians ; and Stanislaus was exceedingly happy when he succeeded in slipping across the borders of his by no means loyal kingdom of Poland, in the disguise of a peasant labourer, and re-established his quarters in the safer limits of France. But the pride of the nation was touched. Nobody cared much for Stanislaus or the Polish crown ; but the insult of defeat was to be avenged. We had at that time in England a minister of the name of Sir Robert Walpole, whose character as a statesman has been rising ever since. Without the slightest tincture of romance or heroism, this clear-headed, stout-hearted country gentleman was a type and representative of his country in one of the more level periods of our annals, when national prosperity is all in all, when honour is scarcely considered a national object, and where a desire to pick quarrels and take offence on trifling occasions is thought the sign of a weak and unmanly disposition. Sir Robert had the great task at home of composing internal dissension, and reconciling the population to the new dynasty under the first and second Georges, whose foreign accent and coarse manners contrasted in a very unfavourable light with the traditions of the stately Charles the First and his jovial, captivating and gentlemanly son. Nothing could be more agreeable, therefore, to the pacific and cautious Walpole than an invitation from Fleury to keep England out of the approaching troubles altogether. There was to be no increase of expenditure in fitting out ships of war or fortifying naval stations. Sir Robert put a few bribes of five hundred pounds into the hands of some of the more belligerent members of parliament, and let it be known that English commerce was unrivalled, and would continue unmolested on the sea, and that no other merchant-ships were safe. Vast prosperity accordingly poured into London, and Bristol, and Liverpool ; and we may blush while we make the humiliating confession, that we plumed ourselves more upon the monopoly established at this period in the catching and carrying of slaves than on any other part of our commercial career.

Slave-carriers of the world—smugglers in all lands—pirates and buccaneers in all the southern seas—we left France and Spain to fight for dispossessed monarchs, and Germany to maintain great armies and sustain great reverses. In the meantime we filled our treasuries, and perfected our maritime skill, in perpetual warfare beyond the line. We imported the cultivation of turnips into Norfolk, and began to look upon agriculture as a science. Manufactures also flourished under the peaceful protection of Sir Robert Walpole, and the excellent example of the French sufferers by the Revocation, whose sons had now all taken English names, or anglicised their French ones, and hated their former country with the bitterness of personal wrong.

France, in addition to the aid of Spain, had at this time the assistance of the King of Sardinia, who, in his quality of guardian of the Alps, held the keys of Italy on one side and France on the other. The heroes of the old wars of the Succession were still alive, but stripped of all their vigour by advancing years. Marshal Berwick, who had so successfully defended Spain, was in command of one of the French armies on the Rhine, and was killed by a cannon-ball while preparing for the assault of Philipsburg. When his death was reported to Marshal Villars, who commanded another army in Italy, the soldier's envy was roused by the news: "He was always lucky," he said, and in a short time felt that there was no chance of so glorious a conclusion to his own career. He retired weak and exhausted, to repose from his fatigues at Turin, and died in the same room where, eighty-five years before, he had been born, his father at that time having been Ambassador to the King of Sardinia. But the war went on with greater spirit when the opponents of Marlborough and Eugene were withdrawn. In every quarter the allied French, Spaniards and Sardinians, were successful. Paris became gay once more as in the first glorious years of Louis the Fourteenth, and Notre Dame again showed her walls hung with captured flags. But flags and gaiety do not constitute the strength of a nation ; and three years of victories and disappointments reduced all the contending parties to a thirst for peace, which it was impossible to satisfy too soon. Spain was the principal gainer here. She began the war to restore Stanislaus to the crown of Poland, and ended by placing her king's second son on the throne of the Two Sicilies. France accepted the Pragmatic of the Emperor, and guaranteed Maria Theresa's rights. Stanislaus himself was contented with the title of king, and the possession of the duchy of Lorraine, which he obtained in 1738, and which after his death was to lapse to the French crown. And here let us say, in passing, that no dethroned sovereign ever took such ample revenge upon fortune for her enmity, by showing what royal qualities of goodness, justice, and munificence he possessed. For eighteen years the one bright spot in Europe where gentleness and peace established their undisturbed reign, was the dukedom of Lorraine, where Stanislaus gave to all his people the example of a useful and virtuous life. His former oppressors, his rivals, his successors on the uneasy throne of Poland, all wrote of him and to him with the respect and affection his Christian qualities deserved ; and when he died, loaded with years and benedictions, in 1766, it was felt that royalty had lost its brightest representative, and humanity itself one of the fairest of its examples. It is a pity that the narrowness of the scene on which his actions were performed circumscribed his fame within such contracted limits ; but even the foolish vanity which has been called the dignity of history, has not disdained to commemorate that a grateful people knew this powerless but delightful potentate by no other name than that of Stanislaus the Beneficent.

During the whole of the war from 1733 to the preliminaries of peace in 1736, France had held the dignified place of righter of wrong and vindicator of her national honour. She had no hidden purpose of aggrandisement at the expense either of her friends or enemies, and Cardinal Fleury and Sir

Robert Walpole had such confidence in each other's honesty that each was left to pursue his own course of policy untouched by the other. Europe seemed at last to have achieved a solid foundation for peace. It had arranged for the present, and made preparation for the future, particularly by guarding against any complication which might arise at the death of the Emperor. The Pragmatic, securing the succession of the Austrian monarchies to his daughter, had been signed by France and Spain, by the King of the two Sicilies, and Russia, and peaceably accepted by England and Holland. France sighed for repose, and found none. The king and courtiers were regardless of the national poverty and the commonest rules of decency. Shocking equally the reflecting by their manners and the impoverished by their extravagance, they seemed to exult in their exemption from the restraints of law or reason. An endless succession of unprincipled and designing women, not taken, as in the haughtier days of preceding sovereigns, from the ranks of the aristocracy, but from the lowest born of the people, governed the brutalised and voluptuous king. The nobility, instead of joining in a feeling of disgust at the proceedings of the court, were only embittered with the commonalty for interfering with their monopoly of royal favour. There was as violent a rivalry between titled and illustrious fathers for the disgraceful elevation of their daughters to the position of king's favourites as for the highest offices of the State. Louis the Fifteenth is saved, indeed, from a close inquiry into the particulars of his private life, as some noxious and unsavoury animals are defended from capture by the odour they spread. But it needs to be remembered that the reign of this man was the turning point of aristocratic debauchery and degradation. Lower the upper ranks could not go ; and a rebound or an extrication was inevitable. Peace, long continued under such auspices, might have been more injurious to the real greatness of the country than the struggles and sacrifices of even a disastrous war. Personal courage and the love of glory were surer of a stage for their display in the field of battle than in the gilded drawing-rooms of slaves and paramours. There would be closer links established between the different classes—a community of danger or suffering would endear the general and the private to each other:—

> "And noble thought would be freer under the sun,
> And the heart of a people beat with one desire."

After four years' breathing-time, accordingly, an occasion was found for an appeal to arms, and ere many months were over, battle and siege were going on from one end of Europe to the other. Hostilities, we have already seen, were almost perpetual between England and Spain on the other side of the line; and in 1738 a "Declaration" had brought the enmity to our own hemisphere, and English and Spanish fleets were searching for each other on every sea, yet without disturbing the relations existing between other states.

Charles the Sixth, the Emperor of Germany, died in 1740 —a very natural thing for him to do, for he was not very young, and had for some time been in bad health. Now was the time to show the efficacy of signatures and solemn treaties. The Pragmatic was in full force, with the names and seals of almost all the potentates in Christendom, from Sicily to Denmark, appended. Nothing seemed more easy than for Maria Theresa to step into her father's possessions, guaranteed to her by so many kings; but the moment the game was on foot there was no keeping in the crowned pack from the chase, and all the parties to the Pragmatic made claims on their own behalf. Spain was representative of the old Austro-Spanish rights, though the family was changed. Bavaria was direct in the female line from Ferdinand the First. France itself was descendant from an elder branch through the wives both of Louis the Thirteenth and Louis the Fourteenth. Poland and Sardina put in their demands for separate portions, and the young and beautiful Maria Theresa had nothing to depend on but the letter of the agreement, and the charm of popularity with which she had already surrounded herself among the subjects of her father. Things might have been settled by compromise or bribery, or other diplomatic means ; but it chanced that on the borders of the Austrian States a new kingdom had sprung into existence nine-and-thirty-years before—in the year 1701—when the ducal house of Brandenburg was elevated to royal rank, and took the title of Kings of Prussia. The two first kings had been strange-mannered men—half-savage and half-inspired —coarse and cruel, yet pervaded with a consciousness of a great career laid open to their nation's talent and enterprise ; and with a curious long-sightedness the second of those scarcely civilised potentates had determined to prepare his country for great exertions, of which he himself was neither to be witness nor guide. He cultivated his estates ; imported artisans, farmers, and shepherds ; laid out millions of florins in reclaiming waste lands ; lived like a wretched miser ; thrashed his courtiers, male and female, with sticks, with his own royal hands ; starved and imprisoned his son ; and laid up forty thousand dollars every month in his treasury, whether he could spare the amount or not, and this, in a reign of eight-and-twenty years, accumulated to an enormous sum. His only expense was his army. He had seventy thousand soldiers, all picked men, tall and strong ; and he drilled them in a way never heard of before. He taught them to load and fire so quickly that he quadrupled their effective force ; he made them masters of the bayonet exercise, and was so unpitying in his discipline, and so marked and scarified the grenadiers themselves with canes and cats, that the greatest coward would have preferred being slain by an armed enemy in the front to the anguish the old tyrant would have inflicted on him if he had shown the slightest fear. This tremendous barbarian died in 1740, and his son, the starved and trampled-on Frederick, reigned in his stead. A very different man in outward form, for he was polite and intelligent, a poet and a friend of poets, but at heart as untamably self-willed and pitilessly exacting as his brutal predecessor. Ambassadors were driving hither and thither in the full glory of protocols and treaties on the death of the Emperor Charles, when Frederick the Second of Prussia, ferreting out some deeds in some old muniment-chest, by which his ancestors, many generations ago, had resigned all claim to the province of Silesia, protested against the deceased's uncertain right to deprive him of his legitimate succession, and led his army into the coveted ground.

He defeated the Austrians at the battle of Molwitz, and occupied the province without delay. Even peaceful Fleury saw that, as one portion of the young queen's states could be seized, France had a chance of getting possession of some other, and accordingly a treaty was entered into with Frederick, and an army of thirty-five thousand men was sent into Germany, to support the election of Charles of Bavaria, the candidate for the Imperial dignity, opposed to Maria Theresa's husband Francis Duke of Tuscany.

Chivalry and knighthood, however, were not extinct, though they did not appear in complete steel nor figure at tournaments. All England got up in arms. George the Second was an apathetic man, and thought the world was safe as long as the crown was undisturbed ; but the parliament, and the counties and the town-councils, besieged the throne with remonstrances against the assailants, and war was declared in defence of the woman-king. This was her noble title ; for when she presented herself to the Hungarian magnates, and addressed them in Latin—the language of public affairs in that country—they drew their swords, and waved them in the air, crying, "Let us die for our king Maria Theresa." Great subscriptions were made by the English ladies for their injured sister's cause, and sent over in hard cash when she was at her worst extremity. Fortunately, when the generosity of one portion of mankind had little effect, the rascality of another was of the greatest use. Maria Theresa offered to resign Silesia to its unprincipled invader, and immediately the Prussians looked coldly on their French associates. The Marshal de Broglie was blockaded in Prague, and lost more than half his army by cold and hunger in a disastrous flight through Bohemia. Charles of Bavaria, the nominal Emperor was driven from his hereditary dominions, and fled to Frankfort. The French armies from all directions retreated towards the Rhine, and George the Second made his appearance in Germany at the head of a considerable force of English, Hessians, and Hanoverians, and gained the battle of Dettingen, the last battle at which an English king has flourished his sword in person. No monument of this engagement survives at the present day, except the Te Deum in which the great Handel celebrated the victory. With so many kings in the field, it was necessary for the successor of Francis that he should buckle on his sword. Louis made a short and successful campaign in 1744, and in the spring of the following year was present at a victory over the English. The battle of Fontenoy has had the advantage of being narrated by Voltaire, a writer who, when he turned his mind away from the polemics and philosophy—falsely so called—by which his bad eminence was attained, is beyond all doubt the most fascinating, and even the most unobjectionable, author of his time ; and he contrives by the manly impetuosity of his statements, and the graphic brilliancy of his descriptions, to make the vanquished feel no degradation from the issue of their noble efforts. War resumed some of its old courtesies on this occasion, and the sad divisions produced by civil quarrels is painfully shown in the civilities exchanged before the engagement began between the French guards, in which were many of the Scottish Jacobite exiles, and their loyal countrymen who served in the British ranks. "Gentlemen of the French guards," said Lord Charles Hay, "it is for you to begin fire." But the Count of Hauteroche replied, "We never fire first ; 'tis for you to begin." The Duke of Cumberland, the brother of the king, was in command of the allies, of whom not quite eighteen thousand were English. Forming a column of fourteen thousand men, thirty or forty abreast, he marched straight forward, across even ground and uneven ground, turning neither to the right nor left, bayonets fixed, and steady as on parade—the most tremendous advance that ever was made in war. They were fired on in front and in the flank ; "cannon to right of them, cannon to left of them, volleyed and thundered ;" and still they pressed on, the same imperturbable mass of regulated strength as ever. Nothing could stop that terrible approach, and the Marshal de Saxe seized the king's bridle and begged him to leave the field along with his son the Dauphin. But they would not move, for even that heartless voluptuary was a true son of France as regarded personal courage. Things, however, grew rapidly worse ; orders were given to evacuate the village of Fontenoy, and a positive command was issued by Marshal Saxe to provide for the safety of the king. The English column meantime found itself at the end of its incredible march, and did not know what further to do. Everything had sunk before it ; but it had neither cavalry, nor guns, nor courageous allies to cover it on either side. The Dutch remained in the rear ; and the victorious English kept their ground, having fairly marched through the hostile force. While all was confusion round the person of the king, and the retreat was actually going on, a dashing young aide-de-camp, the Duke de Richelieu, came up at full speed, sword in hand. "The victory may still be ours," he said, "if you will only stop. Send five guns to the head of the column, and fire right down its extreme length, while we charge it on all sides at the same time." The king saw the only chance remaining ; the old Marshal was persuaded to make the attempt ; the guns were hurried into position : the King's House, with all the gallant adventurers of France, and the fiercer hostility of the Irish exiles, charged upon the flanks. The advance was a noble precursor of the heroic madness of Balaklava, and the retreat was as difficult, but more glorious. With the same unflinching gallantry as marked their advance, the troops faced about, and though officers were falling at every step, and hundreds were mown down by the murderous fire in their rear, their march was sullenly steady, and their ranks unwaveringly kept. They might have asked why they had gone on, and also why they were led back. There was no general among them to make use of their valour; and Cumberland lost as much glory as his army gained.

Cumberland, however, was to gather war's blood-stained laurels in Scotland in the following year; for Louis, continuing his career of success after the victory of Fontenoy—the first and last pitched battle of any magnitude which the French ever gained against the English—had made himself master of nearly the whole of Flanders, and by way of working a diversion in his favour, had approved of the romantic expedition of Charles Edward Stuart, the grandson of James the Second, who landed on the coast of Scotland in the month of June. The plan was successful; George returned to England, and Cumberland repaired to the seat of war in the north. It was not so much the unexpected good fortune of the Pretender, in defeating his English opponents in a few inconsiderable engagements, which exercised a favourable influence on French affairs, as the spectacle it afforded of the divisions existing in the kingdom of his most powerful and inveterate enemy. The divisions, however, were only temporary. England soon recovered from its surprise, and in a very few months enabled the cold-hearted Cumberland to trample out the last sparks of sedition in the blood of the gallant and generous Highlanders at the fight of Culloden in 1746.

In the mean time, while Louis and Frederic were pursuing their design against Maria Theresa in the Netherlands and Germany, the navy of England rode mistress of the seas. It seized Cape Breton and other colonies of France in America, and intercepted her ships from India. It almost paid the expenses of the war by the value of prizes taken from Spain, and prepared the way for greater triumphs by showing its triumphant flag off the coast of Hindostan. Great things indeed were taking place in that vast theatre of English enterprise. The story of France in those transactions is one of great efforts made in vain, and the gradual extinction of all her power. Louis the Fourteenth had established a French India Company, about the same time that the English Company was finally established by William the Third. At first the insinuating genius and showy qualifications of the French gave them the superiority in the contest for favour with the native princes. Dupleix, the Governor of Pondicherry, and de la Bourdonnais, were two of the self-taught warriors and politicians whom it seems the specialty of India to produce. Whether the natural vigour of the European intellect finds room for its display in a land where there is so varied a field for the development of different kinds of powers, or that the feeling of superiority over a whole race of mankind elevates the individual to higher actions than he would otherwise attempt, these two men—one originally a factor in a mercantile establishment at Chandernagore, and the other governor and superintendent of trade at the Island of Bourbon—stepped into a position which, in old and traditionary Europe, would have been reserved for kings and princes. They created a fleet and raised an army; and de la Bourdonnais dispersed an English squadron, and took possession of the settlement of Madras. Jealousy, however, sprang up between the two; and mutual complaints and accusations were sent home by every ship. The king and council could form no idea of such a proceeding as war and conquest by two personages whose duty it was to attend to the sale of indigo and silk; and when de la Bourdonnais arrived in Paris to support his cause in person, Dupleix had greatest influence at court, and the conqueror of Madras was thrown into the Bastile. Dupleix was now supreme, and succeeded in repulsing an English fleet which bombarded Pondicherry. When peace was restored between the rival nations in the West, by the treaty of Aix-la-Chapelle, in 1748, no sign of amity made its appearance between the rival merchants on the Coromandel coast. Dupleix sided with one of the princes of Arcot, replaced him on his throne, and was so carried away by security and ostentation, that he bought or forged the title of Viceroy of the Carnatic of the Great Mogul, and affected a greater magnificence than the native rulers. "High in a throne of royal state, which far outshone the wealth of Ormus or of Ind," the Frenchman "exalted sat" and received the prostration of nawabs and rajahs. But India had not been without its elevating effect on the genius of the rival nation. England saw the earlier services of Robert Clive, a merchant's clerk in a counting-house near Calcutta, at first with surprise and then with pride. He left his desk, and took the command in war with a self-reliant dignity which gave confidence to his companions. Step by step he followed the proceedings of Dupleix, and smote him hip and thigh at the siege of Madura, near Arcot. The native mind was subdued by the sight of a people who vanquished the French as easily as the French had scattered the Hindoos; and court influence at home completed the misfortunes which English superiority had begun. Dupleix was recalled, and, in spite of his title of Marquis, was again looked upon as a book-keeper in a stall, and died of a broken heart in the effort to induce his judges to leave him some small portion of the great fortune he had at one time acquired. The Count Lally, an Irishman by descent, was sent out to replace the plebeian Dupleix, and made matters a thousand times worse. Harsh, contemptuous, and overbearing, he was far more keenly dreaded by his friends than by the enemy. He so offended the inhabitants of Pondicherry, which was a second time besieged by the English, that they almost prayed for the capture of the town and the disgrace of the commander. The capture came; and the commander, storming, cavilling, and finding fault with everybody but himself, was sent home, and after some years' imprisonment in the Bastile, was executed as a traitor. De la Bourdonnais, Dupleix, and Lally, were the victims of French feeling in the matter of a colonial empire. Clive, on the other hand, was ennobled, Coote promoted, and honours and wealth showered on the bearers of the English flag. The issue of a contest in which the combatants were so differently treated by their employers, was easily seen. And with India laid open to her powers, with immense squadrons blockading Toulon and Marseilles, and her Austrian allies ravaging Provence, England looked on with patience at the momentary triumphs of France in Italy and Flanders.

The apparent object of the war existed no more, for Francis of Tuscany, the husband of Maria Theresa, had been raised to the Empire by an indisputable majority of the electors, including the vote of the versatile Frederick of Prussia, in 1746. The belligerents were farther induced to a renewal of peace by the ominous appearance of a body of fifty thousand Russians, despatched by the Empress Elizabeth to the aid of the Dutch. No one could tell what effect the swarms of an almost undiscovered desert would have on the future policies of the world; and it was thought wiser to prevent their first taste of the vintages of the Rhine, which might induce them to renew their visit, by an accommodation among all the states. The Peace of Aix-la-Chapelle, therefore, was hailed with great joy. It replaced everybody very nearly in the position held before the fight. England returned the greater part of her conquests; Frederic, however, retained his prey of Silesia; and now that Maria Theresa was firmly established on her father's throne, and had procured the Empire for her husband—Francis the First—the powers and potentates of Europe had the unblushing effrontery once more to sign the Pragmatic Sanction, which they had been labouring for eight years to destroy.

The history of France, for many years to come, is the history of decay and failure—not so much as regards the curtailment of her power or the unsuccess of her arms, as the internal corruptions by which nations more surely fall than by defeat. Lost provinces may be re-won, a false step in policy may be retraced, but the destruction of private virtue and public honour is irremediable. The indescribable luxuries of the royal establishment went on, not only unreformed, but increased, as the king advanced in years. To silence the professional accusations of the clergy, Louis, reeking from his debaucheries, threw himself unresisting into their hands. An archbishop, certain of the support of the Crown, published a sentence of excommunication against all who would not accept a famous bull called "Unigenitus," by which a certain pope had denounced a religious party in the Church called the Jansenists. An excommunication, an archbishop, a bull and a pope, in the days of Voltaire, and Buffon, and Rousseau, could have little to expect except the derision which an anachronism is certain to receive. The Parliament of Paris rose up in defence of the excommunicated. The king rebuked the parliament. The parliament renewed their order against the reception of the bull, and the king sent the parliament into exile. But the quarrel was made up on the occasion of the birth of the Dauphin's second son, the unhappy Louis the Sixteenth—who was thus the cause of the restoration of a popular assembly which had rebelled against the Crown, and the banishment of three of the bishops who persisted in preferring the pope's authority to the king's. This was in 1754. He lived to see the omnipotence of popular assemblies, and the death or exile of all the bishops in France.

In a few years after the Peace of Aix-la-Chapelle the reconciled opponents hated each other with a bitterer hatred than before. England had presumed too much on her superiority, and had issued her commands to France as to a subject state. She had insisted on the expulsion of the Pretender from the French soil, and took no notice of the circumstance that, while France obeyed her haughtily urged behest, she was building ships, and founding cannon, and establishing a nursery for sailors by great bounties on the cod-fishing on the banks of Newfoundland. In 1756 England awakened suddenly to the danger, and, availing herself of some boundary quarrel, unsettled at the last peace between her settlers in Acadia and the French inhabitants of Canada, she seized all the fishing-boats she could reach, and attacked a sloop or two of war. France retorted. Richelieu, the same whose advice had saved the day at Fontenoy, made a sudden descent on Minorca, which had been an English possession ever since the peace of Utrecht in 1697, and carried, by gallantry as much as by surprise, the strong citadel of Port Mahon. This expedition was protected by a French fleet under Galissonnière, which repulsed the attack of an inferior

English force under Byng. The pride of the country was so ridiculous that nothing would satisfy it for the absence of a victory at sea but the blood of the offending admiral; and Byng was shot at Portsmouth, "to encourage the others,' according to Voltaire. Whether this was the object or not, the face of affairs soon changed. From that moment there was no gleam of prosperity for the standard of France. There was a minister in England who threw such energy into the councils of the State, that defeat, or even disappointment, became unknown. His name was William Pitt, universally known as the Great Commoner, a designation he only lost when he sank almost into oblivion as Earl of Chatham. In all quarters France had to lament her losses. She heard day by day of the capture of some colony, such as Canada, torn from her by Wolfe at the great battle of Quebec—of all her West Indian Isles—and, finally, of all her fleets. In this war she had unfortunately exchanged the alliances which had always hitherto secured her support. She had united her fortunes with those of Austria, and neglected the interests of Spain. Maria Theresa, whom we admired in her adversity, does not take so heroic a position in the direction she gave her foreign policy. When she had achieved her place, she condescended to flatter Madame de Pompadour, the king's vulgar and ambitious favourite, by writing her letters filled with professions of friendship; but her object was gained, and France deserted her natural allies. Frederick, the moment he heard of the correspondence with Pompadour, marched his irresistible battalions, and took possession of the whole of Saxony. He conquered the Austrians at Losowitz; and instead of sending the Saxon army, which he took prisoners in a body, to waste their time in his citadels and jails, he mixed them up in small proportions in his own regiments, and subjected them to the same frightful drill as had converted his countrymen into a submissive and unreasoning machine. A victory in this way was the best of recruiting-sergeants. In 1757 he conquered the French at Rosbach, and compensated for the bad generalship of his ally, the Duke of Cumberland, who had been forced to consent to an armistice in the electorate of Hanover. Pitt, however, disallowed the convention, and drove the enemy out of Hanover by a successful battle at Crevelt.

But, while victorious in various fields, Frederick perceived that the number of his foes was continually on the increase. Austria, Russia, and France, were fearful odds against so new and unconsolidated a kingdom. The crown, however, lay on the bayonets of his soldiers, and wherever they went he was undisputed king. Austrians and Russians entered his capital, and put Berlin to ransom ; but he held his army together, and crushed his enemies separately. Fights and marches which set all the world wondering in those exciting years, but which had no permanent effect in the distribution of political power, have now fallen out of men's minds, except as curious studies of the art of war. But the changes of policy produced by deaths and disagreements were more effectual than battles in altering the state of affairs. Sensible at last of the mistake they had made in deserting their old connections for Austria and Russia, the ministers of France entered, in 1761, into a strict alliance with the Bourbons of Spain and the two Sicilies. This treaty was stigmatised in Europe as the Family Compact. But George the Third had succeeded his grandfather the year before. He hated Pitt, and was displeased with the aggrandisement of Frederick of Prussia. He listened to the detractors of the Great Commoner, and longed for peace. Not the less vigorously, however, did Pitt carry on his designs ; and the result was, that when Spain began arming in 1762, expeditions were fitted out in all the English ports, which tore from the Spanish crown its most cherished possessions—the great island of Cuba and the rich Philippine Isles. Farther resistance was found to be impossible ; and the disastrous Seven Years' War (1756–1763) was brought to a conclusion by the Peace of Paris.

A nation can submit to a good deal of suffering when it is the price of glory and success ; but France had no consolation, except in the acknowledged bravery she had displayed, for the weight of taxation that fell upon her when the contest ceased. It was necessary for the public discontent to find an issue somewhere. The king was still too sacred to be personally attacked ; for the attempt which had been made upon his life by Damiens in 1757 had for a moment blinded the people to his faults ; and an atonement for an extravagant court and an inglorious war was found in the society of the Jesuits. The Parliament hated them as enemies of civil freedom ; the supporters of the Gallican Church as the avowed champions of the Pope. Their own conduct had forfeited the respect of the public, and roused the jealousies of private life. They were now banished from the realm amid the lamentations of the bishops, the acclamations of the people, and the sneers of the philosophers. The principal personage who rose in this manner in defence of the national liberty, and the purity of society, was Madame de Pompadour! The Jesuits had the satisfaction of being sacrificed by a hand whose severity brought honour to the victim, and saw an avenging providence in the death which overtook their persecutor in the very hour of her triumph. Her place was supplied by Madame du Barri, a woman of the lowest rank and most depraved disposition ; and the king sank lower and lower in the gulf of self-indulgence and vice. The same clouds which had gathered round the closing years of Louis the Fourteenth, and darkened his old age, were unnoticed by the heartless Sybarite, who had been deaf all his life to the feelings of patriotism and affection. Maria Leczinski, the daughter of Stanislaus, died in 1768 ; the Dauphin, the Dauphiness, and their eldest son, were all dead. The heir to the throne was their second son, Louis, now ten years of age. His grandfather was lost in the obscure enjoyments of his private apartments, and took no thought either of the blanks which death had made in his family circle, or the cries of his oppressed and discontented people.

But we are now getting nearer what may be called our own times : names come constantly before us that have the sound of familiar friends. In 1769 the island of Corsica gave up its long struggle for independence under the heroic Pascal Paoli, and was incorporated with France. In two months afterwards, on the 15th of August, a child was born in Ajaccio, with all the privileges of French citizenship, though with all the fire and impetuosity of his Italian descent, who was afterwards known through all the habitable globe as Napoleon Buonaparte. It is strange that the most rugged of the small isles which dot the Mediterranean sea—more distinctive in its character, and less civilised in its habits, than any other spot in Europe—should have given birth to the most cosmopolite genius the world ever saw—the foreigner who sat on the throne of France with a deeper knowledge of French feeling than any native king—the Italian who subdued Italy at the head of an army of strangers—the conqueror of Germany and Egypt—who dated his decrees sometimes from the capital of Spain, and sometimes from the Kremlin of Moscow. If Paoli had continued the contest for one year more, Corsica would have been equally lost to its old masters, the Genoese, but its acquirer would not have been the exhausted Louis of France; England would have attached the island to her crown, and Napoleon would have been a subject of George the Third.

There is nothing better proved by a course of historic study than the strange fact, that the people on the very verge of change and revolution have no idea that anything is about to take place. A nation is always taken by surprise when its institutions are overthrown, like a child when its house of cards is toppled over by its own height. Contemporaries in other lands are generally quite as blind; but the spectator from a distance of time sees everything more clearly. There are no other foreign incidents to relate in the reign of Louis the Fifteenth; but his internal administration has a startling interest to us from the results which so soon followed. First of all, the finances, which are the real anchors by which nations ride in safety, were in a hopeless state. The expedients to fill the exchequer which proud and majestic personages like the French kings were reduced to, were worthy of sharpers at cards. The Grand Monarque himself discovered that the Crown had sold a great many titles of honour—such as countships and marquisates—during the last ninety years. He issued an order that all those ranks within that date of creation should be disallowed; and having thinned the peerage by such a wholesale clearance, he sold all the titles back again, with a guarantee against future deprivation. The offices of judge and pleader, of master of requests and clerks in chancery—in short, all the places in the high courts of equity and justice—were held by purchase. A man bought what we might perhaps call a chief-justiceship of the Queen's Bench, and sold it at an increased rate when he had enlarged the fees and perquisites by which he was paid. Louis the Fifteenth could not displace the holders of snug appointments for which they held the crown receipts; but when the war became very expensive, he created a great number of new berths connected with the different judicial bodies, and sold them for large sums. What may have been the feelings of the clients before such courts we are not told; but we know that the multiplicity of forms and tribunals through which the simplest cause had to pass, made justice impossible either to rich or poor. The collectorships of taxes in the same way, from the farmer-generalship to the merest messenger, were set up to sale. The municipal offices, to which incomes were attached, were also disposed of to the highest bidder; and the ingenuity of chancellors of the exchequer was not displayed in discovering new taxes, but in raising a revenue from year to year by the creation of titles and offices which the rich and ambitious would think it worth their while to buy. Sole residuary legatees of all the feelings of liberty which once were so widely scattered through the provincial governments in France, the parliaments professed a power of interfering with the outrages of the royal prerogative; a tradition still lived among them that, at one time, they possessed a potential voice in the allocation of the public burdens, and that, till within a short period, they had retained a veto on the proceedings of the Crown in the matter of taxation.

The Duke of Aiguillon was governor of Brittany in 1770, and was guilty of oppression in the levying of the public burdens and of some injustice in the application of them. The Parliament of Brittany accused him of these crimes. The Chancellor Maupeou, the sycophantish flatterer of the infamous Du Barri, tried to quash the trial, and succeeded in getting the case removed to the Parliament of Paris, where the Duke might be judged by his peers, who were ex-officio members of that court. All the parliaments from the different districts in France sent up their adhesion to the metropolitan tribunal. Parliamentary power was to be reorganised in this trial of one of the highest of the nobility, and each little provincial assembly saw its dignity and privileges vindicated by the restoration of ancient forms. The king interfered and forbade the proceedings, making it penal at the same time for the members to correspond with the other parliaments, or to give up their usual duties as magistrates of the land. But the wily lawyers saw their opportunity. Since they could not exercise their ancient authority as judges in the last resort, they would not entertain the ordinary pleas. All pleading ceased; and the king's next move was to appoint the accused man, the Duke of Aiguillon, prime-minister of France. Aiguillon went boldly to the point. Two soldiers appeared, late at night, at the door of each of the members. The simple question was asked, "Will you resume your duties or not?" Forty of the magistrates consented, but were ashamed on the following day when they saw their colleagues had stood firm. They retired; and next night the soldiers appeared again, and gave them notice that their offices were withdrawn, their properties confiscated, and themselves condemned to immediate exile. This triumph over the lawyers was received with universal applause. The nobility hated the upstart commoner, who had ventured to find fault with a duke; the philosophers sneered, as was their wont, at what they considered a quarrel for authority between the Crown and the courts. The people had no respect for magistrates who had bought their office for the express purpose of squeezing an immense return for their money out of the suitors before them ; and, finally, the wit and satirist had endless occupation in making songs and lampoons about the poor old dignitaries, who were marched off in spite of obesity and gout between two musketeers of the guard. The other parliaments were treated in the same way, and the new members were nominated by the king.

It was not perceived that even a purchased office, which was insured against removal by the supreme power, was some guarantee for personal independence. The courts of law were now the creatures of the crown ; and Madame Du Barri, insolent, ostentatious, and insatiable for power and money, was at the height of her evil power. There was no court, nor parliament, nor municipality in all the realm, that could find fault with what she did ; and Louis, as his advancing years made the spectacle of his excesses more offensive, had his tastes catered for by this woman with disgusting subserviency, and was drowned deeper than ever in his impurities and crimes. With liberty so entirely dead at home, no hand could possibly be raised in defence of it abroad. Russia, Austria, and Prussia fell upon Poland, while it was torn with domestic faction, and made the memorable partition of it in 1772, from which it may be questioned if any benefit has accrued to the parties engaged. It is painful to read that one of the personages implicated in this shameless wrong was Maria Theresa, who had so recently suffered from a similar dishonesty herself. It is said she perceived the atrocity of the deed when she signed the division of the spoil ; but her conduct received a kind of condonation in the apathy of France, the blindness of Sweden and Denmark, and the phlegmatic and unfeeling quiescence of England.

Meanwhile society went its foolish round. The salons of Paris were never more gay. Witty duchesses entertained men of genius, who had no other claim to such high distinction than the authorship of clever and sometimes very improper books. Young bishops of noble houses, and abbés of elegant manners, were the delight of those blue-stocking assemblages, and sneered at the Christian faith, and paid compliments to painted countesses, with great grace. Such a totally unreal state of manners and feelings never existed in a civilised land before. One good strong belief—even of something not worthy of approval in itself—would have been an improvement on that flippant, brilliant epicurianism of the hour, when there was no trust or faith either in God or man. Of this dismal period, it may be said, that the family had ceased to exist. The sacredness of the married bond was lost among all classes of the people. The labouring men of twenty years old, at this time, were the persons who, nineteen years afterwards, lapped with grinning lips the bleeding skulls they succeeded in seizing from the sawdust of the scaffold. The young girls of eighteen at this time were the matrons who, eighteen years afterwards, shrieked their unimaginable accusations against Marie Antoinette, the mother of the Dauphin. No government can endure,—no system can be built up,—except through a people's reverence for the domestic affections. All the fires that poets talk about on the altars of our country are lighted at the common hearth. The Romans were wrong in ordaining that if the vestal flame expired by the carelessness of the watcher, it could only be revived by beams gathered from the sun; they should have commanded it to be re-illumined from a parlour grate. It would not have had so noble a source, but it would have burned with a steadier heat. Let us shut up this miserable career with the statement, that Louis the Fifteenth—old, exhausted—hated and despised—descended to his dishonoured tomb on the 10th of May, 1774.

CHAPTER XVII.

LOUIS THE SIXTEENTH.—A. D. 1774 TO A. D. 1793.

ALL the performers in the great drama, of which we are not yet come to the final act, were now upon the scene. There were Louis the Sixteenth, aged twenty years, gentle and kind; Louis the Eighteenth, aged nineteen, clearer in intellect and more marked in character; and Charles the Tenth, aged seventeen, stubborn and proud. These were the three grandsons of Louis the Fifteenth, and all attained the throne. But there was another personage at that time alive who also the likeness of a kingly crown had on: it was a little child of seven months old, a grandson of the false and dissolute Regent, who, after a long period of struggle and obscurity, emerges at the end of his career as Louis Philippe. Four Bourbons and a Buonaparte were all preparing for their parts in the year 1774—three princes, a boy playing the hoop in the streets of Ajaccio, and a baby in arms.

A young king is always popular; he has made no personal or public enemies, and there is a length of reign before him which will enable him to reward his friends. But there perhaps never was so popular a king as Louis the Sixteenth. Married at sixteen to the beautiful daughter of the Emperor of Germany, one year his junior, he and Marie Antoinette, when their establishment was formed, presented to the admiring eyes of the Parisians the model of a perfectly happy life. They reminded the observers of some of those charming fairy tales where royal shepherds and shepherdesses exchange the cares of power for the enjoyments of Arcadia ; and if the enjoyments were a little expensive, and Arcadia a domain filled with princes and princesses, the interest of the story was only enhanced, and the voices of the real Corydons—the starving peasantry and angry men of the towns—were drowned in the shouts of jubilee. The finances were utterly ruined ; the expenses of the State greatly exceeded the utmost possible extent of its income ; and the goodness of the young monarch's heart came forth in the first speech which reached the public ear : "We will have no loans, no fresh burdens, and no credit ;" and, leaving his ministers to devise means of paying the army and navy, the interest of the funds, and the overwhelming salaries of the national servants, he conducted his gay and brilliant wife to Rheims, where he was crowned with greater splendour than Louis the Fourteenth, and with a prouder display of feudal ceremony and knightly magnificence than had been dreamt of by Philip Augustus. As if to make up for his own youth and inexperience, he called to his council the Count de Maurepas, at this time seventy-three years of age, who had been disgraced twenty-five years before by the favourite Pompadour, and had been busying himself ever since in studying the modern philosophies by which the world was going to be reformed. But there are some men whom years cannot make old, nor any study of philosophy wise and prudent. The new minister was as firm a believer in Arcadia as the Phillises and Strephons of Paris. He would bring back a golden age, where the dreams of philanthropists and the wisdom of statesmen should be united. He had read the glowing descriptions of a state of society where all men were equal before the law ; where the rich could not oppress the poor ; where the Crown was the fountain of perennial grace ; and where the obsolete prejudices of a useless and supererogatory church were reduced to the purest essence of the Christian precepts, and where there was neither heresy nor superstition. He put his theories into practice with the same thoughtless levity as he had maintained them in the sparkling conversaziones of the capital, and gave open manifestation of his principles and designs by appointing to the management of the finances, or chancellorship of the exchequer as we should call it, one of the least-known writers in the work called the "Encyclopædia," in which the most sweeping changes in government, society, and religion, were agitated with the greatest eloquence and amazing success: his name was Turgot. And with a prime-minister tapping his golden snuff-box and uttering declamations about the rights of man, and a chief of the finances, one of the most honest and intellectual men in France, and imbued with all the doctrines of the school of Voltaire and Diderot, the enthusiastic young marquises and abbés, who united politics and romance in almost equal quantities, saw an end of all the miseries of life. A new era had opened on mankind, and its inauguration was fortunately intrusted to a king of the most amiable disposition, and a queen who shrouded the grandeurs of the noblest place in Europe, and the pride of the highest birth, in a graceful simplicity of manners and the most childlike enjoyment of the pleasures of her age and rank.

The Parliament of Paris was in exile, embittered against kingly power by the tyrannical use made of it by Louis the Fifteenth; cherishing in its disgrace the privileges it had claimed, and to which it undoubtedly was not entitled by the terms of its constitution; and certain of the support of Parisian opinion, in the opposition it was prepared to continue to the despotism of the throne. The king's friends advised him to avail himself of this opportunity to make terms with the parliament—to define its powers, and to use it in advancing the measures of reform and retrenchment which he was resolved to introduce. But in the soul of the light-hearted and frivolous-minded Maurepas there was no room for enmity or suspicion. He restored the parliament without conditions; and the pardon thus generously extended by the young king was viewed in all quarters as a triumph of liberty over the Crown. The lawyers in all countries are the class which is least inclined to change, and the most tenacious of abuses. There was probably no member of that legal and magisterial court who did not feel that the propositions of Turgot for the reform of the law and of the system of taxation were founded in justice, and that sooner or later they would be found indispensable to the safety of the State. But they determined to show their authority on every occasion, and refused to enregister the royal edict for the suppression of the Corvée (or forced labour on the landlord's ground), and other seignorial rights. The king, at Turgot's instigation, persisted, and attended a Bed of Justice, where he gave orders for the registration in person ; but he saw the spirit in which he was met. Even Malesherbes, the President of the Court of Aids, a chosen colleague of Turgot himself, and strongly inclined to the liberal views of the Encyclopædists, resigned his post, and Louis lost confidence both in men and things. He was not sure of the benefits of so many alterations, especially if forced on an unwilling people, and dismissed Turgot from his place. If Turgot had had unlimited power, and a long life before him, he might have succeeded in carrying a portion of his plans. But "Raw Haste" was, as usual, "half-sister to Delay." He saw before him the whole scheme of a perfect and complete reformation, but he forgot the difficulty of fitting-in its separate parts. He proposed to abrogate the exemption from taxation which the nobility and clergy unblushingly enjoyed—to free internal commerce from the annoyances of local payments and trade monopolies—to introduce perfect liberty of conscience and uniformity of law throughout the provinces of the kingdom—to dissolve the monasteries, and apply the funds to a system of national education :—all very excellent and praiseworthy intentions, but not to be carried into effect by the stroke of a harlequin's wooden sword.

Neckar, a banker of Geneva, was called in to fill the place of Turgot, and endeavoured to apply the principles of his late trade to the affairs of a great nation. He considered credit the salvation of States as it was the prosperity of banks, and commenced a system of borrowing on the security of the country, as if a national debt was a sign of riches and power.

He introduced at the same time a system of carefulness and economy, which he hoped would speedily make the ordinary revenue sufficient for the expenses ; but the theoretic supporters of democratic simplicity deserted him when their pensions were diminished, and Neckar was also displaced.

The talent and honesty of three administrators like Turgot, Malesherbes, and Neckar, struggled in vain against the confusion of the state finances and the selfishness or ignorance of all classes of society. The numerous propositions of change had unsettled men's minds, and their withdrawal brought anger and disappointment. The peasantry were starving in a great many parts of France, and were instigated in others to outrages against law and property by parties who intended to give the philosophic ministers a hint of the danger of all innovation. Barns and stackyards were burned down in the midst of a loudly lamented scarcity of grain and the declared ruin of the agricultural interests. These crimes were meant to be a protest against the doctrine of political economy ostentatiously promulgated by the Government, "that the proprietor of corn was not *bound* to supply the markets with his grain, but might throw the whole of his crops into the sea if he chose." An injudicious declaration of a right which no farmer out of bedlam would have been likely to exercise, created a popular outbreak ; but the Economists, as the disciples of Turgot were called, persisted in the truth of their assertion, and could prove it, with the greatest syllogistic precision, to the satisfaction of the Tuileries and Versailles.

The antechambers of those princely dwellings laughed at both the contending parties—the argumentative Turgotists, and the starving people—and were far more deeply agitated with the results of the speculations on kings and governments in which they had indulged, the tidings of which were wafted over to them by every ship that came from the shores of America. Here were the very questions which had filled the works of the Encyclopædists ; carried out to the arbitrament of arms before their eyes : "no taxes without representation ;" "no supreme power except by the will of the people ;" "no dominant sect;" "no privileged birth;" "nc inequality of condition." Here were the exact statements in their theoretical essays translated into the reality of life—a vast struggle fairly entered upon between the British colonies, swelling with those new ideas of univeral freedom and fraternity, and the old British crown relying on prescription and experience. In 1774, the year of the king's accession, a Declaration of Rights had been sent over to Europe along with other documents, by which the sympathies of all the generous and enlightened were demanded on behalf of the patriotic cause. Already the American leaders had successfully resisted the Stamp Act of 1767. They had also opposed a newly imposed tax on tea and other commodities for the benefit of the mother country; and, as is generally the case between near relations, the quarrel became embittered by the identity of blood and character. Obstinate Jonathan would not hear reason, and obstinate John would not condescend to speak it. Washington was now appointed commander-in-chief of all the colonial forces by the different provincial assemblies; war broke out and blood was shed in April 1775, and on the 4th of July 1776 Congress issued a declaration of independence, and took the name of United States. Paris was in as high a state of excitement and exasperation as Boston or New York. The dreams of philanthropists had taken bodily shape, and it was indispensable for the glory of France and the dignity of human nature that the champions of liberty should be supported. Hundreds of young and ardent enthusiasts took out their coroneted swords from the chest crowned with armorial bearings, where their ancestors of the feudal times had laid them, to draw them in the cause of freedom, equality, and a republic. But a bolder step was soon forced on the unwilling king, and he dispatched an emissary in the name of France with credentials to the Congress of America, and soldiers in the uniform of France to support the insurrection. Twelve sail of the line, under the Count d'Estaing, were their convoy across the Atlantic, and it must have been only with an affected surprise that Louis reaped the fruits of this interference, in a war with England. In no other way, even by open hostilities, could he have equally benefited the men of Massachusetts and New York. The Marquis de Lafayette, one of the highest of the old nobility, was foremost in the combats on their side, and the promulgation of their principles. He was citizen Lafayette, and scorned the title of marquis as a mark of the inferiority of his brother the smith or ploughman. Smiths and ploughmen in all parts of France began to hear, from returning soldiers, reports of the proceedings across the sea. They heard of the gradual progress of the popular cause; of battles where the English, when conquerors, were not inclined to pursue their advantage against their countrymen of the colonies, who only fought on American soil for the same privileges which their ancestors had won with the sword at home; of the necessity the English government accordingly experienced of employing mercenary troops of Hanoverians, Hessians, and other continental populations, to coerce the free-spirited inhabitants of the long-settled provinces on the Hudson and Delaware, who had been as English in heart and feeling ten years before as the men of Warwickshire or Devon. They discussed all these things in their shops and barns, and began to think what an oppressed and cowardly race they were to submit to a frippery peerage and worldly church, while people of their own class were achieving liberty and good government by courage and combination. Louis the Sixteenth, as king and liberal, was in a most painful and contradictory position. Every success his confederates won over his enemies was a fresh blow at the monarchic principle; every success gained by his enemies over his allies strengthened the hands of his declared and inveterate foe. If England was weakened, monarchy felt the stroke; if England was strengthened, France would feel her vengeance. An unhappy fate where failure or triumph was equally to be feared. But of the two, it was better to deprive England of her power to harm; and the whole strength of France was therefore roused to avenge the humiliation of the Seven Years' War. France had come out of it stript of her ships and colonies. She had surrendered Canada and some of her western islands, and all her hopes in India. Her rival had planted her foot on the golden soil of Madras and Bengal, and was establishing an empire in the territories of the Great Mogul, whose very name was a mysterious sound of grandeur and wealth. From all that granary of riches and fame the French younger sons were kept out by the Treaty of Paris (1763), and they looked with disgust and hatred on the rapidly acquired fortunes of the civil servants of the English India Company, who went out poor and came back with the fabulous treasures of oriental kings. The bitterness of international hatred had never been so great. In all quarters of the world France had been forced to succumb, and now was the opportunity to be revenged for lost America, for lost Hindostan, for lost Senegal, for the lost Rhine, and the re-established Pyrenees. At first she appeared to have a certainty of success. The family compact had given her the assistance of the Bourbons of Spain and Naples. With the help of the Spanish fleets, a superiority was established for three months over the British Channel and the Mediterranean. Seventy sail of the line blockaded the approaches to Gibraltar, and appeared before Plymouth. An army was collected on the shores of Brittany and Normandy, intended for the invasion of England. Citizen Lafayette came over from America to take part in crushing the perfidious Albion, and there were preparations for his hospitable reception all along the English shore from Cornwall to Dover ; but the invasion never came. Admiral Hardy cruised in the Channel with thirty-eight men-of-war, and the combined French and Spanish fleet retired without a blow to their own harbours, with the loss of five thousand men from a pestilence which had raged in all the ships.

But other foes were gathering round England. She had irritated neutral nations by her exercise of the right of search, and had very probably turned it to the advantage of her own commerce by throwing obstacles in the way of the vessels of other nations. Russia, Sweden and Denmark entered into an armed neutrality for the defence of their mercantile flag, a proceeding which had exactly the same effect in hampering the movements of England as open enmity would have had. The Dutch were on the point of joining the northern powers, and thus retaining all the advantages of peace while inflicting the utmost injury on a rival; but England showed her appreciation of a disguised opposition by declaring war on the astonished Hollanders, and seizing all their possessions in the American seas. She also sank or destroyed all their vessels at home; and with all these enemies, open and concealed, upon her hands, prepared for the final relief of Gibraltar, which had been assaulted by sea and land ever since July 1779. France did not limit her support of this celebrated operation to the mere sending of her royal princes to perform their first feats of arms under the Spanish commander Don Alvarez. The Duke of Crillon brought also twelve thousand French soldiers to the standard of the Spaniards, making an army altogether of upwards of forty thousand men. The fleet was on a still larger scale, and the munitions of war had never been so prodigious in quantity and power since gunpowder was invented. The garrison consisted of seven thousand men; and it appeared as if the contending nations had chosen this as their field of trial, and rested the final result of their struggle on the fate of the rock. There were a thousand guns pouring night and day upon the fortress; fifty sail of the line, and numberless floating batteries with very heavy artillery, joined in the dreadful concert; and frigates, mortar-boats, and vessels of every size and armament, filled up the bay. The average number of shells discharged upon the town was six thousand a-day.

Elliot, the governor, however, and his garrison, were sustained by their own courage, and by the hope of a speedy and glorious deliverance by the fleet of Rodney, which had gained a great victory over the Count de Grasse on the 12th of April. On the 13th of September, the same year, the decisive trial was to be made by a number of fire-proof galleys of a new construction, and the English general waited with impatience the effect of the terrible attack. The flotilla was assisted by nearly two hundred cannon, which Crillon had directed against the fortifications, in addition to the usual broadsides of the united fleets. In the midst of the smoke and thunder of those innumerable guns, the English proceeded to the lower part of their walls, and discharged red-hot balls at the floating-batteries. In spite of their double-lining of wood, and their sheathing with sponge, and other appliances for the extinction of flames, one after another of the impregnable mortar-boats was enveloped in fire. Terror spread through the fleet. With a generosity little practised at that time, the English soldiers ran to the shore and saved several hundreds of their terrified enemies, who tried to swim to land; and all men perceived that the further prosecution of the siege was vain. Lord Howe threw provisions and reinforcements into the place, and the combined armies withdrew.

England, however, found it as much beyond her power to subdue the Americans as the allies had found it to take Gibraltar by force. It was found how impossible it is to break the spirit of a people who know the advantages of freedom, and are in sufficient numbers to give effect to their resolution to retain them. Defeat was of no consequence—the tide closed in after the successful column had passed on; and a triumphant march across half the country left no more mark of its passage than a ship in the sea. Great men arise in great emergencies, and America was happy in a band of patriots and gentlemen who gave a dignity to rebellion, by the solemn spirit of duty and moderation with which they carried it on. All the rules of honourable warfare were scrupulously observed, so that the "rebels" found themselves treated with a respect never shown to rebels before. Prisoners were taken and exchanged—even the amenities of life were reciprocated between the commanders; and perhaps this absence of insulting retribution, and of the accompaniments of prisons and scaffolds, which generally characterise a revolt, enabled both parties to retire from the contest with feelings unembittered and unhumiliated. French science guiding American courage, half-zeal in the cause of repression, on the other side the cares of a vast European war against France, Spain, Holland, and in reality, though not in appearance, against Russia, Denmark, and Sweden, were too much for the unassisted power of England. Peace was accordingly proclaimed on the 25th November 1783; mutual restorations were made by the principal belligerents; and "the United States of America" were recognised, in their treaty with the mother country, to be sovereign and independent powers.

To have added so great a people to the family of nations was a subject of pride to the French of all ranks and conditions. But the sight of their handiwork reminded them painfully of the position still occupied by themselves. They tried to commence a new career of equal laws and constitutional government, when the very traditions of equity or law had died out from every mind. For the succeeding six years efforts were continually made to arrest the onward course of events; but all efforts were too late. Sometimes there was an attempt made by the oligarchs around the throne to reverse the wheels, and retravel the same space that had been traversed since the death of the last king. A persistence in the backward journey might succeed, it was fondly hoped, in landing them in the happy days of Louis the Fourteenth and undisputed power; and their measures were as impolitic as their desires were impossible. At the very moment, for example, when the aid of France was given to the American revolutionists, an edict was issued limiting commissions in the French army to men who could prove a noble descent of one hundred years at least. At the same period, also, when the public thought was fixed on the amelioration of the condition of the lower orders, the military authorities tried to introduce the brutal severity of the Prussian system, which made the common soldier's position worse than the slave's, and substituted the sergeant's cudgel and drummer's lash for the milder discipline which had won the victories of Condé and Treunne. Debt went on accumulating all this time, and some few clear-eyed persons saw the inevitable end. The marvel now is how any one could be blind to it. There were only three classes in France—the nobility, the priests, and the "roturiers." The soil of the country was divided between them, but in very unequal proportions. The nobility and priests held fully two-thirds, and the remainder was parcelled out into infinitely small tenures, and belonged to the starving and unhappy millions. We are to remember that the Church and nobility were exempted from the greatest part of the taxes, and that therefore the whole burdens of the State fell upon the smallest portion of the land. We must remember, also, that the nobility were not resident on the estates from which their incomes were derived, and that the curés and inferior clergy, who represented the order in outlying villages and hamlets, were miserably paid, while the wealth of half the country went to the fashionable bishops and unbelieving abbés who glittered in the salons of the wickedest and gayest metropolis in the world. The lower priesthood was as discontented as the farmer and cottar.

The system of minute subdivision of the land had been long at work in France, and had weakened the power of resistance to injustice, which only territorial influence, on a great scale, can give. The landed pauper had no means of combination or enlightenment, and had sunk for many years into moody acquiescence in a state of affairs over which he had no control. The taxes absorbed nearly two-thirds of the gross value of his land ; and if he rented a field from a neighbouring noble, his share of the proceeds sank to almost a nominal sum. Yet he was one of a body who constituted in fact the whole of the country ; for the number of the upper classes was not more than a hundred and fifty thousand, and the population was already twenty-five millions of souls. Still, however, fresh taxes were imposed ; and still the expenditure exceeded the income by seven millions a-year. Calonne was appointed finance-minister by the influence of Marie Antoinette, and repaid his patroness by giving her unlimited sums from the exchequer to be employed in her feasts and balls. Within the charmed circle of Versailles and the Trianon, the dream of Arcadian happiness still went on. There were assemblages of the most amazing brilliancy, and court shows which had never been surpassed for beauty or extravagance, while France lay groaning and writhing beneath the weight that pressed it to the ground. At last Calonne could give no more; taxes would yield no return. The king heard of the distresses of his people, and pitied them; but what could he do? He was nearly as impoverished as the rest; and as a last chance of alleviating the burdens by increasing the number of contributaries, he had recourse to the dangerous expedient of summoning a meeting of the Notables—or chief nobility and magistrates—to consult on public affairs. The Notables assembled, and discovered that the source from which their pensions and bribes were derived was utterly exhausted, but declined to come to the rescue of the State by sacrificing a shilling of their wealth or one iota of their privileges. They made up, however, in malice what they wanted in patriotism, and scattered irritating reports of the national distress, and the expenditure of a dissolute court, in all parts of the country, when their session came to a close.

Affairs had now got beyond the possibility of being patched up by temporary expedients, and Brienne, Archbishop of Toulouse, who succeeded Calonne in the finances, talked flippantly and lightly of a new convocation of the States-General, without being in the least aware of what these terrible words implied. We have not heard of the meeting of such a body since the ominous days when Richelieu made his first appearance in the Assembly of 1614. Since that time the existence of a constitution had been almost forgotten, for the tyrannies of the three kings that intervened had been a virtual suspension of every power except their own. But the convocation of a States-General, where, as in an English parliament, every order in the nation had a voice, was hailed as an acknowledgment that power proceeded from the people. The statements of the philosophers were now to be verified, and king, lords and commons to be placed in their exact positions—no authority conflicting with another, but all working harmoniously to one end—the universal good. Never was such a unanimous acclamation of delight and anticipation uttered by a hopeful and enraptured people, as when the States-General assembled on the 1st of May, 1789. This was no creation of a royal edict like a new court of parliament, nor a nominated assembly like the municipality of a town. It was a great national convocation, founded on the principle of almost universal suffrage (for no vote was rejected at the polling-places throughout the land, which any tolerably dressed individual offered). Chosen in this manner by three millions of voices, it was evident the members of the Tiers Etat carried with them the influence of a representative body. They represented the whole of the untitled, unprivileged multitude by whom France was inhabited, while the Church and nobility rested on their own authority. It was a tremendous experiment, and never would have been tried if the upper ranks had known that the constituents of the assembly were starving, and embittered, to an unspeakable degree, against their oppressors, clerical and lay. These delegates of the poor were to meet under the same roof with the titled aristocrats who had trampled on their social rights and domestic affections so long, and with the mitred lords who had extracted their last sheaves of corn, and had grasped the lands which tradition told them had once belonged to their fathers. Under the same roof was near enough; but when it was arranged that they should meet in the same room, and have an equal number of votes in the decision of the question submitted to them, the friendly barriers of the tournament were thrown down, and the battle to the death began. The opponents sat face to face—the pale, thoughtful, emaciated face of the suffering and revengeful Tiers Etat; the bloated, handsome, contemptuous face of the high-born bishop and polished duke. They must have looked at each other with strangely ominous eyes when they met for the first time, and Jacques Bonhomme examined the Marquis of Carabas across the gulf of so many hundred years. But it was not only Jacques Bonhomme in his own person who came into such close proximity with his ancient lord. He might not have been so hostile, for his requirements might have been more easily satisfied. But the Tiers Etat, besides many men of its own order, had sent up, as its representatives, a more dangerous class than even the ruined shopkeeper or oppressed farmer. The struggling lawyers of the different county courts—the educated professional men, who looked down intellectually on the privileged vicomte, but were kept in perpetual remembrance of their plebeian birth by the social superiority bestowed upon the trifling and half-instructed noble ;—the aspiring youth, too wealthy for the ranks, too plebeian for the epaulets, who had read of the battles of his country, and had longed to follow to the field some warlike lord, with the hope of succeeding to the baton of Du Guesclin or Clisson. These were deputed to make a statement of their grievances in face of hereditary judges, ignorant of law and science, and of holiday soldiers who were covered with decorations, and had never fired a shot. The representatives of the Tiers Etat felt with bitterer enmity than their constituents the disadvantages of their position, for education and refinement had added a feeling of degradation to the other sentiments the aristocracy had excited ; and it is not too much to say that the desire to feed their great revenge against the tinselled and disdainful coxcomb, who plumed himself on his family name, was more ardent and sincere, even at the commencement, than the loftier ideas they professed to entertain. Down with rank became, therefore, the rallying cry of the lawyers, doctors, curés—for many of these were elected by the Tiers Etat—even more earnestly uttered than justice or reform. Dissensions began in a week after the meeting had been translated to Versailles. The priests and nobles still persisted in demanding to sit in a separate chamber from the commons. The commons, on the other hand, invited the other orders to join them in their hall, to proceed to the despatch of business ; and when their invitation was rejected, they solemnly constituted themselves into "The National Assembly," and by this measure excluded the recalcitrant aristocrats altogether from the management of public affairs. In vain did dukes and archbishops complain of this unexampled usurpation of supreme power. The king was undecided and alarmed : accordingly, his proceedings were fatal ; for indecision and alarm make all actions ill-timed, and injudiciously severe. He prorogued the Assembly for a month, and stationed soldiers at the door to prevent the members from going in. Their president, Bailly, when crossed bayonets refused them admission, led them to the Tennis Court of the palace, and there they took an oath never to dissolve till the object for which they met had been secured.

An attempted violence, like the unhappy king's, is either a victory or a suicide. A large secession, principally of clergy, took place from the other orders ; and transports of joy heralded the appearance in the hall of the Tiers Etat of three archbishops at the head of a hundred and forty-eight priests. The nobility gathered close upon the heels of the Church, led by the Duke of Orleans, who lent the disgraceful aid of his royal countenance to the popular cause, and recalled by his name and character the licentious excesses of his grandfather the regent, but without his redeeming virtues of courage and generosity. Beside him sat the hero of the late American struggle, the friend of Franklin and Washington —the Marquis de Lafayette—a figure whom we shall see at intervals holding a distinguished place on the historic stage, but yielding on all occasions to some higher and stronger nature than his own—an incarnation of mediocrity and good intentions. Incarnation of high powers and selfish motives, near them sat Mirabeau, the noble who had been a tribune of the people—the wickedest and most debauched aristocrat in France, who had given his unequalled eloquence and firmness of purpose to the regeneration of his country. All writers agree in describing the greatest genius whom the assembly contained, as the ideal of personal ugliness, but so redeemed by the expression of power which sat upon his harsh and striking features, that the most perfect of sculptured heads could not have possessed half their sublimity and fascination. He was like what poets have described " the archangel ruined," where the lightning-scars which have destroyed the symmetry of his face have ennobled it into a more awful kind of beauty. Different from him, and near him, was the small person and commonplace countenance of Robespierre,—grinning, smirking, and contemptible,—but ere many months were over, spreading a thrill of terror through the stoutest hearts, when his ill-omened calmness of look and manner appeared above the sides of the tribune. The king, who had at first refused the Assembly a place to meet in, now yielded all their demands. He abolished the privileges of birth and profession ; taxes were imposed upon all equally ; and the career of civil and military life was thrown open to every Frenchman. The public debt was secured, the press was declared free, personal and religious liberty was guaranteed, and municipal councils were constituted in all parts of the country. But the Tiers Etat were not satisfied with a mere declaration of the royal intentions, and declined to intermit their meetings till they saw these reforms in practice. The king again threatened, and again withdrew his threats. Confident in their power and numbers, the Tiers Etat disregarded equally the threats and the withdrawal. The authority of the king was openly overthrown, and the Assembly was paramount in the State. Meanwhile all Paris was in a state of insane commotion. Clubs, meetings, associations of all kinds, kept every quarter of the great city alive. Enthusiasm grew with every fresh event, and already the thirst for blood, which so strongly distinguishes the Parisian mob, began to fire the hearts of the rabble. The report ran round from the Hôtel de Ville to the Palais Royal that the soldiers were on their march to dissolve the National Assembly. A militia was instantly formed—guns procured—and tricoloured flags hoisted on public buildings. Huzzaing—maddened and drunk with wine and excitement—the populace rushed toward the Bastile. After a short resistance they burst into that old stronghold of despotism, and dragging the governor to the Place de Grève, they put him and his subordinate officers to death, and bore their heads fixed upon pikes through the streets. The tiger had now tasted his favourite feast, and there was no restraining him from his hideous repast. The nobility, however, continued still tc hope. They were misled by the respectful and graceful manners for which the French were famous, even in the lowest ranks. There was the same lifting of the hat, the same reverence of the body ; and they considered that all was well. But news, which travelled slow in those days, came up from their patrimonial castles. The peasantry had risen with torch and pitchfork. Their fine old buildings had been burned ; the charter-chests ransacked, and the title deeds of their estates committed to the flames. Their towns had been seized by the rabble, who had installed their favourites and flatterers in the chairs of magistracy. There was but one corner of all the country comparatively quiet, and that was La Vendée, a remote county on the shores of the Atlantic, where the patricians lived upon their lands, performed the duties of their station, and were kind to the poor and respectful to the Church. In every other province, and district, and parish, the same sanguinary scenes were enacted as in the capital. Nothing is more clearly ascertained than the fact of torture being applied to the unhappy victims who fell into the rabble's power. They burnt their former masters (sometimes their benefactors) before slow fires. They hacked them to pieces before the eyes of their wives and children ; and drove young and delicately nurtured girls into the woods, or left them to perish on the roads. Every locality had its civic or national guard. The regular army had joined the people ; and there were some half a million of armed men, wearing the three-coloured cockade, and preventing the possibility of a contrary opinion being heard. The king made his appearance before the Assembly at Versailles, and adopted the Tricolor. It must have been the severest of his sufferings at that time to exchange the time-honoured Lilies of France for the livery of the house of Orleans and the colours of Paris, which in union constituted the new flag. But he was rewarded by the enthusiastic shouts of a drunken and furious population, and thought he had saved the country by sacrificing his personal power. Other eyes saw clearer. His brother of Artois, afterwards Charles the Tenth, and many princes and nobles, deserted him in this great extremity, and carried their complaints and selfishness into other lands. If they had staid at home they might have arrested and regulated the torrent, or been nobly engulfed in its vortex ; but to beg and petition at the footstool of foreign despots, to desire the restoration of their rank and riches at the price of the conquest and degradation of France—this was the blot that never was cleared off from the shields of the old nobility. Their departure strengthened the enemies of their order, and gave them the excuse of a fear of foreign arms. Neckar, the banker of Geneva, had been recalled to manage the finances. There were no finances to manage, for how could taxes be collected when half the land was in flames, and all men either trembled for their lives or were struggling to distinguish themselves in the great contest going on between the past and the future ? The present was a narrow isthmus destined in the imagination of the patriotic dreamers, who called themselves politicians, to unite the solid qualities of the middle ages with the liberty, happiness, and equality of the coming time. It did not matter how rough its ways might be, since they conducted to so delightful a scene. And its ways became rough and terrible, and almost impassable, they were so slippery with blood.

A regiment had come up from the country, and relieved guard at Versailles. The regiment in garrison invited the officers to dinner. In the midst of their carousals the king and queen went into the room to congratulate them on their arrival. The officers were all noble and young ; they were heated with champagne—they saw their monarch and the still fair daughter of Maria Theresa smiling their welcome. They drank the dreadful toast of the king for ever ! and threw their tricolors under the table. Louis and Marie Antoinette retired pleased though alarmed, but the multitudes of Paris heard of the event. Thousands of women of the wild est appearance and lowest manners toiled down on the 5th of October to Versailles. They gathered round the Assembly Hall, and gained admittance to the king. They demanded two things—neither of which his majesty could bestow—a constitution and bread, for there had been a bad harvest; the fields had been neglected; there was no money to pay for imported corn. The population was roused—and hungry. Thousands of idle, dissolute, cruel, revengeful men followed the female procession. When they had had their smooth speeches from the king, and their vain assurances from the Assembly, they still lingered about Versailles. A great rain came on; they were tired and thirsty, and wet to the skin. Some of them, when it began to grow dark, discovered an entrance near the chapel, and were repelled by the guards. They persisted, and poured on. A foolish soldier fired upon the people, and the fight began. Shoal after shoal of the maddened furies of Paris—of the basest and most degraded wretches a great capital hides from the eyes of the better inhabitants, but nourishes in the darkness till some great convulsion exposes the hideous brood to the light of day—went up the princely steps of that palatial home. They forced their way even into the bed-chamber of the queen, who had only time to escape by a secret passage. Where were the two regiments which had uttered such shouts about the king for ever, and trampled the cockade under foot? If the officers had moved, their own men would have slain them without remorse. Versailles, therefore, was no longer safe. The king and all his family removed into Paris, amidst the acclamations of innumerable crowds on the following day, and never saw the stately alleys and majestic apartments of that royal residence again.

Things rolled onward with the force and impetuosity of some vast pinnacle which an earthquake has shaken from the summit of a mountain. The Assembly, in the absence of money, issued a number of "assignats," or paper obligations, which were to pass as coin. This currency, if good for little else, was good enough to buy the estates of the Church, which were secularised, and put up to open sale. A crown-piece in silver soon bought a hundred pounds' worth of these paper notes, for the flight across the frontiers continued. Dukes, marquises, bishops, abbés, disguised in many forms, effected their escape with all the goods they could carry. Gold in incredible sums was smuggled into foreign lands, or buried beneath well-known trees in secret parts of their parks and gardens. Ladies carried with them their jewels and ornaments. Even the friends of the Revolution hoarded all the silver they possessed, and a circulating medium actually disappeared. Faster and faster the stream of emigration flowed on. The Assembly imposed a treble tax on the property of the refugees, and decreed worse penalties on any who should henceforth leave the country. A line was drawn round the borders on all sides, and made escape more difficult. Mirabeau, however, the fiery master of the Assembly, had softened in his feelings towards the Crown. His youthful prejudices in favour of rank and antiquity began to revive. He thundered from the tribune against the excesses to which enthusiasm was pushing them blindly, and lost perhaps the glory of having moderated the Revolution into a reformation by an untimely death in 1791. The king despaired at last when the Titan in whose strength he trusted was laid low. He fled; but bad management, as usual, uncertainty, timidity, and want of counsel, ruined his plan. He was captured at Varennes, and from that time was a prisoner as if he had been taken in war. He was allowed, indeed, to go through the vain form of accepting the constitution the Assembly had prepared, with limits on the royal power and responsibility to the nation: but at that very time the great majority were in favor of a republic; and in all the clubs, furious demagogues excited the passions of the populace into hatred of the kingly name.

A new element came into the strife when Louis announced his constitutional royalty to the other crowned heads of Europe. They all felt their dignity outraged and their seats endangered. Armies were raised by Austria and Prussia, in readiness to defend the royal cause. The emigrants, who had been cowards enough to fly from their own land, were bold enough to vapour with sword in hand on the other bank of the Rhine. Nor was war a disagreeable movement to the opposite party. Dumouriez, a member of the Legislative Assembly, perceived that the only chance of domestic unity was in turning the national feeling into a new channel—a channel which, by carrying off the wilder spirits in a fresh and hitherto unexplored career, with the motto of "a fair field and no favour," would divert the republicans from their attacks upon the throne. War was, therefore, declared against the Empire on the 20th April, 1792. Never was prospect apparently so hopeless as met the generals in that eventful year. The treasury was empty, the nation divided, the government inexperienced and weak, and the king, in whose name the campaign was opened, the most hated man in his dominions. In Paris he continued, indeed, to be so grossly insulted, that Lafayette himself came to the rescue, and endeavoured to save him from insults and danger by his influence with the mob. The mob, however, allows no influence to any one who does not really or avowedly execute its will. Lafayette, therefore, went to the king, and told him the time was come for more resolute measures. He must leave Paris; but not disgraced and as a fugitive; but sword in hand, mounted on his horse, surrounded by his friends, and place himself at the head of the army. If Louis had been capable of understanding this counsel, it never would have been required. He would have risked or lost all long ago. He let "I dare not wait upon I would," and the opportunity was lost. Enemies assembled in growing numbers on the frontiers—Austrians, Prussians, and other Germans—and manifestoes were issued by the generalissimo of the invading armies, which irritated the people and ruined the king. The Tuileries was attacked by a furious multitude, though Louis had fled for safety to the hall of the Assembly; and all his servants and friends, and the gallant Swiss Guard, who defended their post to the last, were massacred on the stairs and in the corridors. Drunken revelry and heaps of dead defiled the palace of France. The Legislative Assembly was as furious as the wildest of the mob. It abrogated the kingly power, threw down the statues of all former monarchs, including Henry the Fourth's, and imprisoned the royal family in the Temple. To give force to these infractions of the constitution, to which all parties had so lately sworn, it summoned a National Convention. When the news of this proceeding was conveyed to Lafayette, he declared his intention of remaining true to his recent oaths. An order of arrest was issued, and the champion of liberty in both the hemispheres was forced to fly for his life. He came into the Austrian dominion, and as the republicans at home had denounced him as a royalist, the Emperor and the refugees denounced him as a republican. He saved his head from the French guillotine, and pined for five years in the dungeon of Olmütz ; a terrible state of affairs, when moderation comes to be considered a crime. It is only just to this true gentleman, whose talent was not equal to his heart, to record his noble words : "Let us have the love of liberty for our guide ; but let us never forget that liberty, severe in all its principles, fears license as much as tyranny, and that to conquer and retain it is less the reward of courage than the triumph of virtue."

Three men came prominently forward at this time, to show the triumph of virtue by which liberty is secured. Robespierre, Marat, and Danton, represented in their three characters the falsehood, selfishness, and fanaticism to which the excesses of the Revolution are due. Robespierre glosed and flattered till his opportunity came, and then he gave license to his hatred and suspicions. Marat proclaimed the equality of all men before the sword of the executioner and the word of a dictator giving utterance to the popular will. Danton was a sincere enthusiast, and perhaps was more dangerous on this account than the designing hypocrite or the raging madman, his compeers. A tribunal was erected on the 17th of August, 1792, by the Sections of the town, to take cognisance of political crimes more rapidly than the ordinary courts. Then began the system of indiscriminate slaughter which made Paris a byword among the nations, and affixed an ineffaceable stain on the French name. Thousands were arrested on suspicion, and murdered in the prisons. An armed mob waited at the doors of the different jails, where the suspected conspirators were undergoing a trial by members of the new tribunal ; and on the appearance of the culprits, whether acquitted or not, fell on them indiscriminately —for sex gained no distinction—and put them to death with clubs and stones. Priests were slain wherever they appeared. Rich and poor began to be so confounded in the common destruction, that beggars, shopkeepers, and starving artisans, were hurried to the guillotine as aristocrats. Higher and higher rose the tide, and at last reached the walls of the Temple, where Louis the Sixteenth was confined. He was tried on the 6th of November, for treason to the nation, and defended by Malesherbes, now old and feeble, whom we remember forming part of the government with Maurepas and Turgot in the first brilliant days of the unhappy prince's reign. He gained only the glory of having risked his life by saying a word in favor of the predestined victim ; and the most innocent and well-intentioned of all the monarchs of France was condemned like a common felon to the guillotine on the 21st of January, 1793. For a short time the strangeness of the spectacle imposed silence upon the brutalised crowd who had gathered around the scaffold. It was a king come to expiate the crimes of his ancestors and of his position, not his own. He had never made a personal enemy or lost a personal friend. He began an address to the spectators, but a sign from the harsh commander of the guard produced a roll of the drums which drowned his voice. The executioners seized him and laid him under the fatal axe. The priest in attendance said simply, " Son of St Louis, ascend to Heaven !" and all was over.

It was in the magnificent open space where the Tuileries gardens extend to the Place Royale that this miserable crime was perpetrated. All the fountains that now ornament the scene cannot wash away that innocent and uselessly shed blood. On looking up the long avenue of noble architecture on either hand, you see on one side the beautiful façade of the Church of the Madeleine, and on the other, the simple outline of the House of Representatives. A poet would be pardoned if he found Law and Religion looking with tearful eyes on the central spot where the great tragedy took place. The historian must be satisfied with the prosaic statement, that law and religion were equally outraged by the sufferings of this honest-hearted king and inoffensive man.

CHAPTER XVIII.

THE REPUBLIC.—THE CONVENTION.—A. D. 1793 TO 1795.

THE natural feelings of mankind would, under other circumstances, have rebelled against the atrocities which followed the execution of the king; but the atrocities were so vast and so overwhelming, that they prevented the natural feelings from finding vent. The wilder spirits of the movement expected their only security in the excesses of their behaviour, and a system was now commenced among the legislators of the land, of bidding for power and popularity by exceeding each other in the fierceness and infamy of their propositions. The Convention itself was divided into factions, who panted for each other's blood. Marat, the most brutal of men, for a long time contested the place of honour with the supple and insinuating Robespierre. Danton, the other embodiment of the evil passions of the time, had no thought of anything but perpetual excitements to the mob, and murder on the streets of Paris. The formation of a Committee of Public Safety, composed of the most ferocious members of the Convention, was a deathblow to any hope which might still have been entertained of clemency or reason. The party of the Girondists, who were respectable for their talent and eloquence, and the comparative moderation which distinguished their political views, were defeated in their efforts to resist the torrent of slaughter and demoralisation, and miserably perished either by the axe or by positive starvation on the public roads; for the enemy of the Convention, like the enemy of the Pope in the old days of excommunication, became an outcast whom no one would feed, or clothe, or entertain. A few struggled on, for a short time, in hopeless resistance to the demagogues who had set a price upon their heads; and some of them had found a temporary resting-place in the town of Caen.

From this old burial-place of our Norman kings a young woman made her way to Paris on the 11th July, 1793. The great agony of the period had extended to young and old—to girls and boys. This young woman, whose name was Charlotte Corday, was about four-and-twenty years of age, with a very noble figure and beautiful countenance. She had studied the career of the Girondists, and inflamed her mind with the picture they drew of the happiness of France if freed from the oppression of the tyrants who trampled on her in the name of freedom. A new Joan of Arc, she had fed her solitary imaginings with the idea of some great deed to be performed by herself; and, without counsellor or accomplice, she presented herself at the house of the redoubtable Marat. He was in his bath, and could not be seen. His mistress looked in the pleading face of the sweet-voiced, gentle-mannered young girl from Caen, and admitted her to the room. She stabbed the monster with a knife, and laid it on the floor. He shrieked for aid, and Charlotte was seized, standing quietly by the window; the work, she knew, was done, and she was ready to receive the wages. But assassination is always fatal to the party that descends to it. The illegal vengeance on such a person as Marat increased the evil it was intended to cure. Robespierre had now no rival in his mastery of the Committee, and carried intimidation to its utmost limits. He procured the condemnation, with equal ease and equal equanimity, of friend and foe. He guillotined the high-born Marie Antoinette, the queen of festivals in her youth, the queen of sorrows in her premature old age; he guillotined the Duke of Orleans—foul descendant of foul progenitors—who had voted for the death of Louis, and tried to curry favour with the mob by taking the absurd name of Philip Equality; he guillotined also the learned and philosophic Bailly, President of the Constituent Assembly, who had been Mayor of Paris in the first days of the Revolution, and only stopped short in his support of it when its excesses began.

Old friends come out upon us in this dreadful dance of death, whom we have not seen for many years—Malesherbes, the virtuous and courageous advocate of Louis—Danton himself, the mouthpiece of so many murders—and, strangest sight of all, an old woman dragged on a hurdle from the prison where she had lain a long time, and recognised, by the aged among the spectators, as the famous Countess du Barri, who had been the ruler and tyrant of the court of Louis the Fifteenth, and now, after an interval of upwards of twenty years, was paying the penalty of her dishonourable rise and ill-used power. It is a pleasant thing to observe that this destruction of all human feelings—this total reversal of all the dictates of justice, mercy, and truth—could not be carried on under even a nominal submission to the Christian faith. The same voices which proclaimed the slaughter of the inhabitants of a country town, abolished the worship and denied the existence of God. They raised in His place an idol to be adored—a woman of the lowest class, representative of a Grecian image before whom prostrations were made, and flambeaux kept burning to symbolise the Light of Reason; and before this frightful mockery bishops and priests fell down in reverence, and made open profession of their disbelief. Murders all this time were practised in the secondary towns and cities with as much vigour as in the capital. A man called Carrier is badly eminent among the commissioners of the Committee; he presided at Nantes. He seemed to have a morbid preference for the most revolting crimes: he ordered as many women as men to be shot in cold blood. Five hundred children of both sexes, the eldest being under fourteen years of age, were taken forth for execution. The shortness of their stature saved many from the range of the musket-balls. They broke their bonds, and ran for safety even among the battalions of the executioners. They crept between their legs, and embraced their knees, and looked imploringly and terrified into their faces. Nothing moved those exterminators' hearts ; they slew them as they lay at their feet. But shooting was tedious ; boats were filled with women, who in many instances had babies at the breast, and taken out into the middle of the Loire ; the plugs were withdrawn from the bottom, and the hapless cargo left to drown in sight of both shores.

These details will be sufficient ; but what the royalist historians dwell on most strongly is the extraordinary fact that, after the first delirium of revenge had soothed itself in the slaughter of nobles and priests, it was awakened to tenfold fury by the sight of its plebeian and powerless friends. Out of eighteen thousand six hundred and thirteen victims in the criminal lists made by the republican Prudhomme, there are only two thousand and twenty-eight aristocrats, male and female ; three hundred and fifty nuns ; eleven hundred and thirty-five priests ; but there are fourteen hundred and sixty-seven wives of *labourers* and *artisans*, and *thirteen thousand six hundred and thirty-three non-nobles* of different conditions. Some knowledge of this appalling fact must have begun to spread in the summer of 1794. The Convention itself became alarmed at the powers it had committed to the Revolutionary Tribunal over which Robespierre had established a complete mastery. His word was law ; and it was easy, from his obscure hints, and sometimes from his open threatenings, to perceive that no man's life was safe. Tallien, whose name ought to receive some redeeming light from the effort he now made, denounced the uncontrolled dictator and ruthless murderer in full assembly. If there had been a moment's hesitation, the assembly itself would have been massacred on the spot. But they assumed a dignity to which their previous actions had ill entitled them, and received the accusation. Robespierre fled to the Hotêl de Ville, to the protection of his dependant, Henriot the mayor. Attempts were made to excite an uproar in his favour ; but the populace hated where they feared, and refused the call. Troops were marched down with bayonet and cannon, and Robespierre, after an ineffectual attempt at suicide, was taken. Spiritless and subdued, he showed on the scaffold the cowardice which always accompanies cruelty, and was mocked for not knowing how to die after having sentenced so many to death. This most just retaliatory execution took place on the 28th July, 1794, and the Reign of Terror came to a close.

Now if we bear in mind the hideous scenes perpetually presented in the towns and villages of France, the frightful uprising of all the worst passions of our nature, and the apparent disruption of all the bonds of social existence, we shall feel our minds filled with involuntary admiration when we see the immense effort the country was making at the very same time against a coalition of almost all the powers of Europe. While she was marching her long array of sufferers to the guillotine, there were pouring out from the gates of all her cities interminable files of her defenders. The royal army had not been dissolved, it had only changed its colours. The ranks were filled with men who had seen the angry front of rough-visaged war, and their officers were now selected from among themselves ; no man was shut out from hope by the accident of his birth. And along all the roads that led to the frontier, thousands of stout young fellows, who had never handled deadlier weapon than hedging-bill or pruning-hook, were armed, drilled, and regimented in the course of the march ; and with the military instinct which has always characterised the French peasantry, they presented themselves to the delighted general on the Rhine, or in the Low Countries, not only conscripts who swelled his numbers, but trustworthy soldiers who stood as firm as the veterans of the host. All Paris, in the pauses between the butchery of the victims—while the guillotine for a short space stood still—accompanied the young volunteers a mile or two along the road, joining in the famous Marseillaise, a hymn of patriotism which is still cherished among the French as connected with the triumphs, however short-lived, of their efforts at liberty, and returned to the front of the Town-Hall, or the Place Royale, to attend the execution of the remaining aristocrats of the day. Meantime the soldiers increased their pace, and with great reason, for the Duke of Brunswick had passed the boundaries, and was besieging Thionville ; the Prussians were gathering for the attack, and the combined Imperialists were on their way to the Rhine. Before they had reached the scene of action the invaders had taken Verdun, and were in full march on Paris by way of Chalons and the forest of Argonne. Dumouriez had only time to summon Beurnonville from Lille, and Kellerman from Metz. The Prussians, by an able manœuvre, got between the French forces and the capital, and there seemed nothing to prevent their advance. But Dumouriez came up with them at Valmy, and after a connonade of fourteen hours and great exertions on both sides, the invaders were forced to retreat, and Paris was saved. This battle, the first of the revolutionary army against a foreign enemy, was fought on the 20th September 1792 ; and it was afterwards remarked, as a strange coincidence, that at the very time when Louis Philippe, the young Duke of Chartres, was distinguishing himself as an aide-de-damp of Dumouriez in defending the sacred soil, his father, the infamous Duke of Orleans, was taking his seat in the National Convention with the intention of procuring the murder of his cousin the king. The French army pursued its success, crossed over into Belgium, and, after a brilliant victory at Jemappes—where the same young aide-de-camp was of essential service in restoring confidence to a battalion which had begun to waver under the terrible Austrian fire—overran the whole country like a flood, and effected the conquest of the Austrian Netherlands. But the following spring brought a disaster to the army at Neerwinden, and the fickleness of the Convention was instantly seen. It suspected Dumouriez of betraying the country to the enemy, of hostility to the government, and even of a design to set the crown upon the head of the young Duke of Chartres, and establish him as a constitutional king. To be suspected or accused by that iniquitous assembly was to be pronounced guilty ; and Dumouriez, after trying in vain the personal attachment of his troops, despaired of stopping the horrors of the Revolution by force, and retired with his staff and a few friends into the enemy's camp. Among his aides-de-camp we have already mentioned Louis Philippe. He accompanied his chief into exile, and brought such discredit by this action on the name of Bourbon that his father was arrested as an aristocrat in disguise, and unable to conceal the anti-liberal feelings of a prince even under the nickname of Philip Equality. The defection of Dumouriez appeared fatal to the cause in a military point of view; and other calamities fell upon the Convention. La Vendée, in the extreme west, took up arms for Church and King; Brittany and Normandy protested against the powers of the Committee of Public Safety; the departments of the south were discontented with the predominance arrogated by the north; and in the midst of these domestic troubles Sardinia and Spain were arming behind their respective boundaries, and ready to pour down from their hills upon the plain. Nothing daunted, the millions were still ready to rise; a levy-in-mass was decreed, and the country declared in danger.

If ever country was in danger of falling into utter ruin from intestine quarrels and external assault, France was in that fearful state at this time, for Marseilles was in insurrection, La Vendée in arms, and successful over the few troops yet sent against it; and a new enemy was brought into the field in the shape of England. She had been driven into war by the proceedings of the Convention, and now accepted the custody of the great arsenal and fortress of Toulon, which the royalist insurgents delivered into her hands. England, Austria, Prussia, Spain, Sardinia, a third of her own population, and many of her strongest towns, opposed to her—a ferocious assembly howling mad imprecations against disobedient subjects and foreign foes—all the aristocratic prejudices of Europe roused against her by her treatment of the nobles, all the religious feelings of Europe united against her by her treatment of the Church, France yielded not a jot in heart or hope, but like the old Greek hero, stamped with her feet, and armed men arose. An army was sent to Marseilles;

fresh thousands poured into La Vendée ; another vast array was directed upon Lyons, and a fourth took station on the heights above Toulon. A wondrous view presented itself to their eyes, for the great basin was filled with ships, English, Spanish, and French. The English colours, joined to the fleur-de-lis, floated upon the walls ; and outside of the harbour an English fleet, commanded by Lord Hood, seemed to guard its acquisition with an impregnable line of power. The tremendous efforts made by France at this time might be the result of madness or despair, or heroic self-devotion, or patriotism, or whatever you like to name it; but they were successful. Kellerman in the Alps ; Houchard and Jourdan at Hondshoot, near Dunkirk ; and Hoche upon the Moselle, reaped the first harvest of the newly-unfurled tricolor. La Vendée was compressed if not conquered ; and men were at leisure to observe the progress of the great operations for the recovery of Toulon. It seemed, indeed, a vain attempt for the new levies of the Revolution to expel the English from a fortress so powerful in itself, and defended by so numerous a fleet. A bombardment was carried on from the elevations where the army stood ; but it produced little damage, and the great ships replied with almost as much effect, or at least with as much noise, from the harbour down below. Time was wearing out the besiegers ; and Dugommier, who conducted the operations, saw no chance of driving the leopards, as the English were contumeliously called, into the sea. But there was a young man of four-and-twenty, in command of a company of the artillery, who saw with clearer eyes; he asked the general to allow him to erect a new battery on a certain height which had not been occupied, and promised he would plant the tricolor upon the walls in a very short time. This was Napoleon Buonaparte, and he was as good as his word. Down with irresistible force, and inevitable precision, poured balls of heaviest metal against ship and town. No part of the basin was safe from his attack. The vessels were shifted into all quarters of the harbour, but still the bullets found them out. At last the place was declared untenable ; the fleets were withdrawn with as many of the inhabitants as could find room on board; the stores in the dockyard were destroyed, and Lieutenant Buonaparte was highly complimented for his zeal and talent. This was his first exploit in war, and was against the same enemies as his last. From Toulon in 1793 to Waterloo in 1815, he had never come into personal contact with the English arms. He must have had strange memories of the hills behind Toulon when, for the first time for two-and-twenty years, he again saw St. George's standard on the heights of Mont St. Jean.

With the death of Robespierre, in July 1794, the hopes of France began to revive. A more generous spirit pervaded the Convention: measures for the restoration of tranquillity were passed; banished members were recalled; offers of amnesty were made to the discontented in La Vendée and Brittany; and the infamous Carrier was condemned to death. It even went so far as to remove the body of Marat from the Pantheon, which had been dedicated to the great men of the country; and dissolve the club of the Jacobins, where the memory of that monster was cherished, as a saint of the new religion of blood and license. But the reins were relaxed too soon. The evil passions of the mob required the restraint of fear, and broke forth in riot and massacre again. The royalists encouraged the confusion in hopes of a recall; and, to complete the misery of the land, a very severe winter followed an insufficient harvest, and political discontent was aggravated by cold and hunger. It did little good to the starving thousands in Paris and Rouen that wonderful things were done by their countrymen in the south and north; that they advanced triumphant into Spain, and, after consolidating their authority in Belgium, marched into Holland, and dictated conditions at the Hague and Amsterdam. Pichegru, the conqueror of both the Netherlands, had performed the unexampled feat of taking a fleet by a charge of horse; for the Dutch ships were frozen up in the Zuyder Zee, and the French dragoons were ordered to assault them upon the ice. By skilful tacking, the mounted privateers managed to keep ut of the reach of the broadsides of the immovable ships, and made their advance where no guns could be brought to bear. We may suspect that the Hollanders were not very hearty in resistance to their brother republicans, for the whole nation peaceably acquiesced in the changes that took place in their name and constitution. The United Provinces disappeared from the map, and became the Batavian Republic.

These operations had a more decided effect on the foreign assailants of France than on her population at home. The King of Prussia, finding little chance of increasing his dominions by the spoil of his friends, easily reconciled himself to the murder of a neighbouring king, and the extermination of priests and nobles. He made peace with the Convention in April 1795—the first of established powers who recognised the competency of the revolutionary rule. But the crowds of Paris were more exacting. They did not ask for glory or an increase of dominion—they asked for bread, the only unappeasable cry which a government can hear. There was no bread to bestow, and the ferocious instincts of a famished population broke loose. The Tuileries was again invaded; the Convention itself insulted and threatened, as if it had been no better than a mere hereditary king; and the head of one of the deputies was carried into the hall of council upon pikes, as if he had been a marquess of the old regime. A demand was made for a new sort of government, to be nominated by the sovereign people, and the patience of the Convention could bear no more. When it was delivered by the military force from the hideous multitudes who surrounded the place of meeting, it retorted upon its assailants with numberless executions, and sent to the scaffold the few of its own body who had advocated their cause. Again the hopes of royalists and reactionists began to rise. The poor little Dauphin, who had been called Louis the Seventeenth, as if in mockery of his position, by the coalesced enemies of his country, died of poverty and cruel treatment, almost of want, at this time; and Europe, with insulting rapidity, recognised the Count of Provence, a refugee at Verona, as Louis the Eighteenth, King of France and Navarre. A man to lead them, a hero to fight at their head, was all the gallant exiles said they required. But the new king was neither manly nor heroic. His brother, the Count of Artois, was a libertine in his private life, and a devotee in religious faith; and if he had any share in the blood of Henry the Fourth, carried the white plume of Navarre, not in his helmet, but in his heart. Both the brothers talked of drawing the sword, and fighting for their rights; but they were greater performers with the knife and fork, and heard unmoved of the devotion and death of their followers. A few thousands of these were put on shore by a British squadron on the projecting point of Quiberon, and called the inhabitants to gather round the white flag of the king and their aristocratic names; but the peasantry showed no enthusiasm. Hoche, the republican general, the son of a cutler at Versailles, was upon them like a wolf on the fold, and the expedition of gentlemen fell a useless sacrifice—not one of them survived; for whoever escaped the slaughter of the battle was shot for treason after the engagement. The Convention was now drawing to a close, for it was to be superseded by a new form of government, consisting of two chambers, one called the Council of Five Hundred, the other the Council of Ancients; a committee nominated by them were to be called the Directory, and perform the duties of the governing power. In order to provide against the inexperience of men altogether unused to public affairs, the Convention inserted a clause that two-thirds of its present members should belong to the new legislative body. But Paris considered this an interference with its right of election, and rose in mutiny. Insurrection was openly proclaimed by the Sections of the spoiled and famishing city. Multitudes took arms, and appeared upon the streets. The Convention ordered General Barras, who had aided at the capture of Toulon, to provide for its defence, and he undertook the duty on condition that they gave him Lieutenant Buonaparte as second in command. The Convention agreed, and the young engineer took his measures at once. He planted cannon to sweep the long street called St. Honoré, and the two quays along the Seine. When the maddened multitudes appeared, he applied the match with pitiless firmness to the guns, and continued his discharges till not a vestige of the rioters remained. He had strong reserves in the courtyard of the Tuileries; the cross causeways were all secured, and the mob felt in a moment it had met its master, and was subdued and tractable from that hour. The Convention died with more dignity than it had lived, and illustrated its last days with wise and excellent laws. It held forth offers of amity to the disaffected, and, sickened of civil butchery and the sacrifice of compatriot lives, it decreed that, when peace was restored to the provinces of France, the penalty of death should be abolished for ever from the statute-book. On the 26th of October 1795 its session ended and its functions ceased—an assemblage which showed more mingled qualities, high and low, than any other of which the records remain—which, having commenced with the insensate fury of the proscriptions of ancient Rome, ended with the wide views and beneficent enactments of an English parliament.

And now that the sea of blood begins to subside, and the natural face of the land to be seen, let us compare its appearance before and after that devastating but reparative flood. First, the Church was in possession of half the territory of France. Enormous estates, including lakes and forests of the size of an English county, were the absolute property of the dignitaries of a cathedral or abbey. These tracts of country were not only free from ordinary taxation, but had privileges infinitely more galling than an exemption from money payments. Their cultivators were not farmers in our sense of the word, but serfs, and slavery was contagious in many of those domains; for they had the strange quality of making residents upon them forfeit their personal freedom. If a man occupied a house on one of those spiritual territories for a year and a day, he became "main mortable," or the thrall of the Church—he belonged to the monks of a convent or the canons of a cathedral; he could not leave his money by will, or bestow it during his lifetime; it lapsed to his lords. Up to the year 1780 it was no unusual thing to see an officer of the army, his breast covered with decorations, who was as much the property of some corporation of friars or clergy as the cattle in their stables. Attempts were made from time to time to check this glaring wrong, and the crime of holding bondsmen upon any estates whatever ; but the interests of the Seigneurs and the Priests always prevailed, and till the very beginning of the Revolution there was territorial slavery as one of the acknowledged institutions of the land. It will give us a better idea of the intolerable wealth of the French clergy, to remark that the extent of their possessions was nearly double the whole size of England. And the tendency of church lands was always to increase ; for the grasping prelates of the ages of ignorance and superstition had introduced a great number of regulations by which their holdings were made inalienable. Once in the clutch of the Church, they could return to civil or national uses no more. A great baron forfeited his lands by treason, or died without heirs : the monarch succeeded in both those circumstances, and regranted the property to other holders on condition of feudal service and defence of the kingdom. But the clergy, in their spiritual capacity, never could be guilty of treason, and the corporations of monks and friars never could die out. There was always a bishop or abbot, and the lands held under the crosier had no military or public duties, and merely fed the luxury or ambition of their venerable owners. Doles of bread at the monastery door degraded and fed the brutalised population; but even the doles of bread were grudgingly bestowed. The country was thinly peopled, and it was impossible for the peasantry in outlying districts to come from a distance even for their daily meals. They had therefore gradually submitted to their necessities, and bestowed themselves on the Church as its goods and chattels, in exchange for a permissive occupancy of a small portion of the soil. The soul of a Frenchman has always expanded at the sight of a very moderate portion of wretched land, if he could only call it his own ; and it was therefore with a thrill of rapture, and the first ennobling glow of self-respect he had ever felt, that the down-trodden church-tenant received the Revolution which secured him in property the little garden and field he had cultivated as a serf. In the next place, the Church was tyrannical and active in the exertion of its ecclesiastical power, almost in exact proportion as it was careless and neglectful in its territorial and spiritual duties. Twelve years before the accession of Louis the Sixteenth, while his degraded grandfather was offending the remaining good feeling of the country by the depth of sensuality into which he had sunk—while the chief clergy were contesting the palm for irreverence and debauchery with the wits and debauchees of the capital—while the decencies of life were spurned at as a hypocrisy below the regard of a gentleman or a lady—the Church was exercising an iron dominion over the minds and bodies of its victims which would have done honour to the founders of the Inquisition.

The story of the unfortunate Calas, a merchant in Toulouse, is well known. It has been dressed up in play and novel, but the simple facts are more appalling than any addition can make them. He and his family were Protestant, and were looked on with evil eye in the capital of what had once been the country of the Protestant Albigenses. Toulouse, as if to make up for that blot in her early history, was the most bigoted and priest-ridden city in France. One of Calas's sons being too idle for trade, and legally incapacitated by his religious tenets from going to the bar, was struck with despair about his future prospects, and hanged himself one night at the door of his father's shop. Instead of pitying his bereaved parents, the populace, stirred up by the shopkeepers and priests of the town, became persuaded that the young man had determined to conform to the Catholic Church, and that his father and mother, his brother, a visitor who happened to be in the house, and the servant-maid, had murdered him to prevent his recantation! We need not dwell on the proofs of the innocence of those unhappy people, for the mere statement of their accusation is sufficient; we will merely state that the father perished miserably by being broken alive upon the wheel, the sisters were immured in a convent, the brother was banished, and the mother, an Englishwoman, who was probably considered a more unpardonable heretic on that account, reduced to poverty.

Four years after this, in 1766—only three-and-twenty years before the Revolution—there was a young gentleman of Abbeville, of the name and title of Chevalier de la Barre, who had been brought up by his aunt the lady-superior of a convent in the town. He was now seventeen or eighteen years old, and was in expectation, through the interest of his relation, of getting a commission in the cavalry. His aunt had had the misfortune to attract the admiration of a man of the name of Belleval, an assessor of the taxes ; and the nephew had threatened the presumptuous wooer for his insolence. The abbess had pleasant little supper-parties at the convent, where young De la Barre and a friend of his own age, called Etallonde, were admitted, but from which Belleval was excluded. The terrors of the Church were invoked to revenge the contempt of the nephew and the haughtiness of the aunt, and the young men were accused of two great and unpardonable crimes. They had seen a procession of monks pass within thirty yards of them, and had not taken off their hats ; and the wood crucifix on the bridge had been slightly marked, as if with a cane. The clergy were aroused. The bishop took the lead, and instituted penitential processions to the injured crucifix, and threatened terrible things against the perpetrators. Belleval accused the young men. It was proved by several witnesses that the Chevalier had spoken disparagingly of a plaster image of St. Nicholas ; that he had sung certain songs as he passed along the street, which were not fit for ears polite ; and that he had been seen walking near the crucifix on the night when the injury must have been inflicted. None of all these accusations was clearly proved ; but the boy was put to the torture ; was declared contumacious and disregardful of church authority ; and, finally, was condemned to be burnt alive. The sentence was carried into effect with the merciful alleviation, that he was decapitated before he was thrown into the flames. Up to the last year of his life—which was 1778—Voltaire, who applied his genius and wit and eloquence to remedy these frightful ills as far as regarded the memory of the sufferers, was pursued by the unrelenting malignity of the Church, not so much for his opposition to its doctrines as for his exposure of its crimes. Let us remember that, when the day of trial came, the vast body of the clergy not only gave up the clerical profession, but trampled on the Christian faith, proving by these acts the hypocrisy which had guided them to such cruelties in all their previous lives, and we shall not wonder at the excesses of hatred displayed against the monks and abbés, however much we may regret the sufferings of the individual men. The Revolution made a tragedy like that of the Calas or De la Barre impossible. It threw open half the land of the country to the occupation and ownership of the people at large. It threw down the privileges of an effete and unmanly nobility ; and perhaps when the great balance is struck between the misery it produced and the misery it abrogated, it will be found that the momentary griefs of the struggle from 1789 to 1795 bear no relation to the immense mass of pain and degradation and hopelessness which had oppressed the multitudes of France for hundreds of years before, and threatened to crush them, with rapidly increasing weight, in the years which were to come.

If nations suffered like individuals from the stings of an uneasy conscience, England would take to herself a great portion of the sufferings of the French people, and of the excesses of the Revolution itself. The devastations of the English wars, which lasted for a hundred years from 1340, which sank the peasantry into hopeless want ; and the "wrongful masterdom" exercised by the Edwards and Henrys during all that time, have been blamed by French historians as the cause of the abnormal growth of French society and the absence of a true middle class. The defence of the country was thrown into the hands of the landed proprietors, who indemnified themselves with privileges of the most unpatriotic kind when the invaders were repelled. The shopkeeper in the town, exposed to the ravages of an English host, or the not less destructive defence of a French feudal army, had no security for his wealth if he had managed to attain it. He could not invest it in land, for the "roturier," or non-noble, was incapable of purchasing properties to which warlike duties were attached. There was, therefore, no answering class to that which, very soon after the Conquest, began to reappear in England, the free tenant who had land of his own, and was as secure of his tenure as the lord under whom he held. In France the population was, therefore, only twofold, the highest and the lowest. There was no "yeoman of Kent with his yearly rent" who looked with the same honest feeling of independence and self-respect on the lord and the labourer.

But things grew still worse when education came. The lawyers and financiers, and the other evil growths of a high state of civilisation, began to perceive that they had intelligence but no rights, and wealth and influence but no social rank. They hated the aristocracy they envied, and vowed its destruction when they could not share its advantages. We therefore find the intellect and energy of the country ranged against its titles and decorations. There was growing up a vast mass of cultivated refinement and hoarded wealth, and municipal ambition, and desire of literary and military distinction—all the elements, in short, of a strong and healthful middle class—and there was no room for it between the inane supremacy of the nobility and the half-savage apathy of the serf. It was necessary to sink one and elevate the other. If, at the furious outburst of the pent-up force, the first were annihilated and the second endowed with too great a power, it is not for us to find fault whom it took hundreds of years to consolidate our freedom; and who have had the good fortune to distribute the harshnesses and wrongdoings of the struggle over so long a period. The aggregate of our sufferings and crimes escapes our observation. If all the woes, violences, and iniquities of every kind, from the wars of the Barons to the expulsion of the Stuarts, which it has cost our country to assemble six hundred and fifty-eight gentlemen in council at Westminster, were compressed into four or five years, we should have little cause to look down scornfully or shudderingly on the atrocities of the French Revolution. There is, however, one peculiarity in which our battle for liberty has the advantage over our neighbours; it was unmixed, from the beginning to the end, with any element unworthy of the great inspiring cause. There is something august and elevating in the persistence of a nation in vindicating its inherent rights through centuries of varying fortunes, and sustaining the struggle with the solemn earnestness of men who have staked their lives upon the issue. The stern men of the Great Charter were but the forerunners, with the same type of character and face, of the men of the Grand Remonstrance and the Convention of 1688; Hampden might have worn De Montfort's armour, and appeared a lineal successor of the summoner of the burgesses to parliament. But in France, things of the greatest interest were so mixed up with unworthy accompaniments, that the vast aims of the leaders in the outbreak against corrupted authority are almost lost in the ludicrous dress they wear. It gives an appearance of mockery to the aspirations of those professed lovers of freedom, to hear that they left off their Christian names as badges of superstition and law, and took those of old Roman and Greek patriots who had never bowed the knee to kings. They called themselves Cato and Phocion, and Brutus, and Aristides; and these, with the very modern title of "citizen" before them, must have had rather an amusing effect. Citizen Agamemnon paying his respects to Citizeness Volumnia gives us no great idea of the truthfulness of his desire for sensible and useful changes. They altered also the names of the months, and dated, not from the birth of Christ, but from the origin of French freedom. They banished poor old January and his eleven successors, and installed a new family in their place. The assemblage of the Convention had happened on the autumnal equinox; they commenced with that date, and, calling the period up to the 21st October "Vendémiaire," went through the winter months as Brumaire and Frimaire: these may be translated, Vintagy, Chilly, Frosty. Then came "Snowy," "Showery," "Windy," for January, February, and March. Spring was represented by Buddy, Flowery, Meadowy; and Autumn by Harvesty, Hot, and Fruity. This fantastic nomenclature of the seasons lasted from the 21st September 1792 to the 11th Nivose of the year Thirteen, which had to be translated in ordinary books into the 1st of January 1806.

This mingled tale of great national convulsions and pitiless executions—of a total upheaving of new elements, and a total displacement of the old, with heroism, patriotism, and the loftiest aspirations combined with folly and charlatanism of the wildest kind—is now coming to an end. The separated fragments of a grand old building are now lying scattered and unconnected amid the dust and confusion its fall occasioned, but the master-architect is at hand who will apply them to their proper use, and build them up again into a new fabric, more symmetrical and according to rule than the old, but not more calculated to last. Napoleon Buonaparte is about to lay his hand on the Revolution, and guide it into the path he desires. The history of France condenses itself for the next twenty years into the life of one man, and the same thing may almost be said of the history of the whole of Europe.

THE DIRECTORY, A. D. 1795, TO THE FIRST CONSULSHIP, A. D. 1799.

The Directory consisted of five members, nominated by the Council of Five Hundred. Of these Barras and Carnot are the only names worthy of being recalled; Barras as the first patron and friend of Napoleon, and Carnot as the greatest military administrator the Revolution produced. The wonders of Louvois, in the early days of Louis the Fourteenth, were transcended by this fanatical regicide. He had a bankrupt exchequer and a disturbed country to deal with, and all the powers of Europe to resist. Yet the indomitable energy of his will, and the zeal of his followers, supplied the want of money and order, and enabled him to send armies to the field as perfect in equipment as if the taxes were collected in a time of prosperity and peace. Taxes, indeed, had nearly ceased, for the industry and agriculture of the land were at the lowest ebb ; but there remained to the financier, who had faith in the restoration of his country, the enormous mass of property of which the priests and nobles had been deprived, as security for any loan he could manage to contract. Two-thirds of France were a substantial pledge for the money required to defend the soil. Promissory notes on this vast deposit were issued at almost a nominal value, yet, from the immensity of the sums they represented, yielding a considerable amount in present coin or negotiable paper. The man who had lent on the assurance of those confiscated demesnes, was doubly bound to resist a restoration of their old proprietors and an invasion of foreign enemies. A loan, therefore, in the hands of Carnot, was both a present aid and a future support ; and though there was loud grumbling, and a great deal of suffering, and much political discontent, the great minister knew that a succession of victories would reconcile his countrymen to everything—would make the impoverished shopkeeper and the rebellious Vendean equally forgetful of their own grievances in the glory of their beautiful France. Victory was therefore as indispensable to the Directory as money ; and unlimited authority was given to Carnot. He used it with unsparing hand, and was seconded in all his labours by a series of generals who excelled the heroes and soldiers of the wars of the Grand Monarque, as if to prove that the enthusiasm of revolution had a greater effect than the excitement of loyalty. Princely Condés, and Turennes, and Luxemburgs were to be transcended by the plebeians whom the new order of things had thrown up to the surface. Carnot, however, was almost as fortunate in his enemies as in his agents. The Count of Artois (Charles the Tenth) at last summoned energy to leave his safe retreat in England, and professed to lead an expedition into La Vendée. A British fleet again bore a body of gallant emigrants to their native soil, and the loyal and priest-loving peasantry gathered to receive them. But the Count of Artois saw beyond the enthusiastic bands of armed peasants, and clergy brandishing the cross, the close-ranked battalions which Carnot was sending into the field. After an inglorious delay on the mainland, or rather on the Isle Dieu, as near to the mainland as his timorous disposition would carry him, he returned to his contemptible safety, and left his followers to their fate. More indignant at the desertion of their chief than quelled by his absence, the enthusiasts rushed upon their doom. The chiefs of the insurrection had no longer a rallying-point, or a supreme authority to keep them united, and by separation and disunion their strength was broken. Stofflet, one of their leaders, was taken and shot at Angers; and Charette, another, underwent the same sentence at Nantes. The Count of Artois was again happy with his priests and mistresses; the Count of Provence was inventing new dishes for dinner, and publishing the vengeance he would take on the disobedient when he returned to his country; and La Vendée submitted. The tricolor was hoisted with universal acquiescence on the walls of Rochelle; and France, as stated in the formal declaration of her rights, was a "Republic, one and indivisible."

Of the other generals of this one and indivisible republic, it is necessary to follow the separate steps, and observe the peculiarities of each battle and march. Few of them had succeeded, in previous campaigns, in forcing their enemies into more than one engagement, and both parties rested on the fame acquired by the solitary achievement; but with the young Buonaparte, who was now appointed General-in-chief of the Army of Italy, it is impossible to pursue this method. His blows were so rapid and so numerous, that it would require a large space to describe them in the order in which they occurred; marches—which in other commanders are generally movements from one secured ground to another, and directed entirely by the exigencies of their own troops—were positive acts of war under this new chief. A movement of his forces, which to ordinary spectators appeared a mere change of place, was felt by the enemy at a hundred miles distance to be a defeat. There never had appeared so theoretically accomplished a soldier since the days of Marlborough and Eugene. In those great leaders science regulated the proceedings of a campaign, and attained its object if no variation was required from the scheme originally laid down. And certainly it is an amazing display of mental power to provide for the thousand contingencies of a lengthened struggle, and foresee the combinations necessary to meet the possible arrangements of the enemy. Another general had risen since their time in the person of Frederick of Prussia, who left more room for divergence from an original plan, and relied on disconcerting his opponents by sudden changes of disposition, which the wonderful discipline of his armies enabled him to make. He overthrew the solemn traditions of the Austrians by a rapidity of movement, of which their slow and solid battalions had no conception; and made a great portion of his art of war to consist in surprise. As profoundly scientific as Marlborough or Eugene, and a hundred-fold more rapid in combination than Frederick, the new leader of the French army united the merits of all the three. He calculated time and distance with more than the accuracy of the Englishman or Savoyard, and flung his forces with more unexpected vigour on an unprotected position than the Prussian. His rule in a campaign on land was the same as our own Nelson's at sea—"the greatest force on the weakest point"—so that it did not matter whether those great chiefs of men had on the whole the largest fleet or army; it was sufficient for them if they could throw the numerical superiority on any one point. Nelson broke the line with his whole fleet, and enclosed half the opposite vessels in a double fire; Napoleon crushed the enemy's separated armies with an overwhelming force, and, before they could effect a reunion, destroyed the portion he had contrived to outnumber as well as take unprepared. We must trace this marvellous genius in his military achievements by campaigns, and not by separate engagements.

The campaign of 1796 began under very depressing circumstances. Pichegru, who was in command upon the Rhine, was either a traitor or incompetent; he was bought over by the Prince of Condé, who headed some of the emigrants in that quarter, or was out-generalled, and Austrians and Piedmontese again threatened an incursion on the soil of France. Moreau, a man of unbounded reputation at that time, and who afterwards was considered by the enemies of Napoleon the only leader capable of holding the field against him, was ordered to advance into the States of Germany; and Buonaparte at the same time joined the army he was appointed to command in the south of France. Carnot had not yet had time to attend to the commissariat; the clothing was deficient, the troops in arrear of pay, and nothing in perfect order but the artillery and ammunition, and the hearts and spirits of the men. Over the mountains marched thirty thousand soldiers in the apparently disorganised, starved, and shoeless condition which characterises a defeated force. But they were all young and hopeful; their general was six-and-twenty years of age.

Italy was the traditionary land of French glory. Its fields were fertile, and its palaces and churches filled with uncountable wealth. In four days they won four victories, and forced the Piedmontese king to furnish food and clothing to his victors, on condition of being left on his throne. The Directory gave positive orders to leave no monarch in power; and perhaps Buonaparte considered he was obeying their command when he stripped the rulers he came into contact with, of all their authority, and only left them their royal, serene, or imperial titles to facilitate the requisitions he made. On the 12th of April he had begun his march; in twenty-five days he had silenced Sardinia, laid enormous contributions on the Dukes of Modena and Parma—of money to please Carnot, and of pictures and statues to delight the Parisians—and passed the Po. On the 9th of May he forced the bridge of Lodi across the Adda, seized Milan on the 15th, and gave his men a treat in the village of Pavia on the 23d. While he was fighting, raising money, laying in stores, sending eloquent bulletins to the Directory, and receiving humble messages from princes and potentates, the scarecrows of our former acquaintance had become the most glorious army in the world. Living like the most ferocious of brigands, spreading disaffection to settled governments wherever they went —offending the prejudices of birth by their boisterous contempt of rank—offending the feelings of the middle class by their lawlessness and license—they redeemed all by an obedience to orders in the field, a courage in actual battle, and an endurance of fatigue such as has not been seen since the Tenth Legion of Cæsar had conquered their predecessors in Gaul. Like the Tenth Legion of Cæsar, too, they derived all their high characteristics from a glowing admiration of their leader, which rose in those enthusiastic youths into idolatry. To live for him, to fight for him, to die for him, was the highest hope of veteran and conscript; and if service had been counted by victories and not by years, the deeds of this first campaign would have given the name of veteran to the youngest soldier of the force. Twelve battles, besides numerous small engagements, laid all upper Italy at their feet, and at the beginning of September it was supposed, according to the usual routine of warfare, that active hostilities were at an end. Austria, however, showed astonishing vigour: she poured fresh thousands into her Lombard provinces, and succeeded in hemming in the French within the walls of Verona. But Buonaparte interrupted for a moment the peaceable labours in which he had been engaged, of pillaging the trembling sovereigns of the duchies and marquisates which dotted the face of the land and converting the principalities of the recusants into republics after the model of the French; and, leaving the Cispadane constitution unfinished, achieved a secret march from the besieged town. The first news of his evasion was conveyed to the capitals of Europe—which had begun to rejoice in the approaching annihilation of the invaders—by the reports which immediately reached them of the tremendous battles of Arcola and Rivoli. The first was so obstinately contested that it lasted four days ; the second consisted of three separate victories won over the three divisions into which scientific strategy and a very old man had divided the Austrian army, so that each was thoroughly dissolved before the other came to its support ; and finding that obstinacy, and science, and fortified positions, and superior numbers made no difference, and that winter was just as congenial to those sons of the south as summer, the Austrian party began to despair ; the Pope long ago had sent in his submission ; the populace rejoiced in seeing their oppressors humbled by their fellow-peasants,—and Mantua, the chief stronghold of the Imperialists, surrendered. Italy was a conquered land, and the glories of Francis the First were renewed without a Pavia, and of the earlier Anjous without an insurrection of Naples. On the 17th October 1797, Napoleon Buonaparte granted the Emperor of Austria the peace which both countries required, though only one demanded it. He secured to his country the long-coveted limits of the Ocean, the Alps, the Pyrenees, and the Rhine. Belgium was amalgamated with it, and all the imitative constitutions, wherever they were established, were guaranteed by the triumphant Republic.

When the conqueror in so many battles, the author of so many magnificent descriptions, the bestower of so honourable a peace, made his appearance in Paris, the enthusiasm of the public knew no bounds : wherever he appeared, the noble-featured, quiet-mannered little Corsican was hailed as a hero and benefactor ; but he laid aside his military dress, attended no meetings which he could possibly avoid, and when his appearance was indispensable, wore only the simple uniform of a member of the Institute. He knew that the guillotine-axe was still sharp, and was conscious that the members of the Directory were hostile. Carnot and another of his personal supporters had been displaced ; factions had arisen also in the Council of Five Hundred and of the Ancients. The old state of affairs had still its adherents. The emigrants, availing themselves of a lull in the popular feeling, had returned in great numbers to France. The excessive depreciation of the paper money in which government obligations were paid, enabled the old proprietors, in many instances, to recover a portion of their patrimonial estates at a very small sum. They were aided in this, in some instances, by the good feeling of the local authorities, who winked at their proceedings; and if the fortunate recoverers of their position had had the sense to remain quiet, they might have excited a change of sentiment in their favour, which was impossible while they had continued in open hostility to their country. The priests also came back in whole battalions, and awoke the fanaticism which only fear had laid for a short time to sleep. They were received in country houses, and re-established in their offices of confessors and directors; a hierarchy was secretly instituted on the model of the old, and, in fact, there was an organised body, bound together by religious and political beliefs, busily at work for the overthrow of all that had been done for the last ten years. Nor was there the same unanimity as before in the army itself. The coarse and furious adventurers of Italy were jealous, in the midst of all their laurels, of the praises lavished upon the Army of the Rhine. The refinement of these comparatively civilised troops made them hateful to the scum and offscouring of the cities of the south which had humbled Mantua and Rome. When detachments from the forces of Bernadotte and Moreau joined them in Lombardy, they had perceived with disgust that the new-comers had the audacity to call their officers "monsieur," or "sir," instead of "citizen;" and this was treason to the Republic and the equality to which all men are entitled. The soldiers sacrificed more lives in duels on this momentous subject than would have filled the list of casualties in a pitched battle; and as the discussions went on, no obscure intimations were given that the Army of Italy was ready to cross the Alps, and massacre all persons, whether rich or poor, whom they were pleased to call the aristocrats of Paris.

A fresh ebullition of violence among the lower orders in

the city itself, was feared by the timid and the comparatively wealthy. Even at this time voices were heard in favour of a military despotism to preserve society from dissolution a second time. Buonaparte listened to these voices with greedy ears, but gave no answer. He lived in complete retirement with his wife Josephine, whose first husband, General Beauharnais, had perished in the Revolution. Still young and captivating, she employed herself in the education of her two children, Eugene and Hortense. Josephine had been very useful to her husband in securing him friends and supporters; for her manners were irresistible, and her love to the young conqueror unbounded. But Buonaparte and Josephine, and all their friends, waited in silence and patience till the proper time for his reappearance on the stage. Conscious that, amid the struggles of party, in which he took no share, his name might grow dim—conscious also that the enmity of the Directory would be softened by his absence from the scene of these disreputable quarrels—he determined to apply for employment in a distant quarter. The Directory, with presumptuous pride, desired him to make a descent upon England, and convert it into the British Republic. It was the spring of 1798; Nelson was on the waters with a fleet, and every square mile of the British Channel was watched by sloops and frigates. Portsmouth was filled with ships, and Buonaparte knew that, unless he had two months' undisputed command of the sea, his expedition to England would end in surrender and imprisonment.

But he saw a far-off land, where a glory was to be won which would gain a new charm in the eyes of his countrymen, by the romance and mystery which hung upon the scene. Egypt, the land of the Pharaohs and Ptolemies, would be a noble field for new triumphs. Its acquisition would also weaken England, by enabling him to intercept her Eastern trade, and, in the dreams of the Corsican, the desert became but a starting-point for the overthrow of Persia and the conquest of Hindostan. The Nile and the Ganges drew him towards them with the force of fascination, and on the 19th of May he sailed from Toulon, escaped by his usual good fortune from the English cruisers, took Malta from the Knights of St. John after five days' delay, and effected his landing with forty thousand men near Alexandria. The battle of the Pyramids and capture of Cairo showed the same irresistible skill and courage as the great fights of Italy ; but they were rendered useless by a catastrophe which came upon the fleet. The admiral who had guarded the expedition to Egypt had taken up his position in the bay of Aboukir, and had made every preparation against an assault by Nelson, who was known to be in search of him in all parts of the Mediterranean. His vessels were drawn up so near the coast that no enemy could get between them and the land, and they would therefore have the advantage of presenting an unvarying and raking broadside to the advancing foe ; they were, in fact, converted into stationary batteries, and, by concentrating their fire, could defeat any separate attack. But Nelson, seeing they were riding at anchor, said to his second in command, "Wherever the French can swing, there is room for us to pass," and ordered his whole line, one by one, to take up a place on the landward side of the anchored fleet. Seventeen hours of unceasing cannonade alarmed the inhabitants for miles inland ; Arabs and Egyptians crowded the commanding stations, and, when the cloud cleared up, they saw the power of France utterly annihilated—fragments of ships floating about the bay, and, far off, the sails of two or three which had contrived in the heat of the engagement to slip their cables and escape. The Mediterranean was an English lake from henceforth ; the tricolor was banished from its whole extent, from Alexandria to Gibraltar, and the forty thousand French soldiers, led by the first generals of the time, were prisoners in a foreign land.

Cut off from European help, perhaps the conqueror of Italy saw the commencement of his Oriental career. The plains of the Indus—the capital of Delhi—the crown of the great Empire of Hindostan—and the spoils of Calcutta—were all in the excited anticipations of the young man of twenty-nine, intoxicated with conscious power and the fumes of success. He accommodated himself to Eastern habits at once, and rode a dromedary across the desert with the simplicity of an Arab sheik. Forming his army of thirty thousand men into a caravan, and holding high discourse with learned muftis and other interpreters of the Koran—professing great respect for Mahomet, and giving hopes of a sincere conversion to Islam—he arrived in Syria. There he took the town of Gaza, and besieged St. Jean d'Acre, anciently called Ptolemais. At the foot of Mount Tabor he defeated the Turks with enormous slaughter, and spoke with more confidence than before of a march on Constantinople and the throne of the Great Mogul. But a check was received in the siege of Acre which awoke him to the realities of his position. Sir Sidney Smith, an English commodore, landed with a few blue-jackets and marines, and defended the beleaguered town. The French retired, discomfited and wearied out, on the 20th of May, and, after a toilsome and disastrous march to their old quarters in Egypt, gained the last glory of their arms in the battle of Aboukir. This victory was doubly valuable, as it restored to the French annals a name which Nelson had banished from the lips of Frenchmen—they could now speak of Aboukir with as much triumph as the English. This was on the 25th of July, and the Turks were utterly destroyed as a disciplined force.

Before leaving the Egyptian campaign, it will be necessary to mention the two actions which have thrown the darkest shade on the reputation of Buonaparte—the massacre of the Turks at Jaffa, and the murder of his own men. The fate of a town taken by assault is too well known to attract any particular consideration, if it is unaccompanied by circumstances of unusual barbarity. The defeated defenders and the innocent townspeople suffer the utmost violence which the rage of an irritated soldiery can inflict. While the conflict lasts, or before discipline can be re-established, no life is safe ; but after the first burst of wrong the perpetration of murder or robbery becomes a crime. At Jaffa it was the policy of Buonaparte to strike with terror ; and he gave up to indiscriminate destruction every inhabitant of the devoted town. Five hundred Turkish prisoners were killed in cold blood, and the peaceful citizens were ruthlessly slain. The slaughter lasted for two whole days, and the general-in-chief ordered it to continue. This sanguinary act brought its legitimate punishment. The corpses of men, women and children, encumbered the streets, and their reeking blood ascended to heaven, and came down upon their murderers in the shape of pestilence. The French army was stricken down ; and though the general endeared himself more than ever to his men by visiting the hospital wards, and touching the hideous swellings which characterise the disease, with his hands, nothing would reanimate their courage. The remembrance of their suffering comrades in the lazar-house at Jaffa paralysed the assailants of Acre ; and when the siege was raised and the French were forced to evacuate Syria and find refuge in Egypt, those plague-struck soldiers embarrassed the commander more than all the rest. Some he sent by sea to Damietta, others to Gaza by land. But with the remainder, seventy or eighty, lying helplessly on their beds, expecting to die, incapable of being moved, with no sufficient force to leave for their protection, what was to be done ? He ordered the doctors to prepare a soporific draught which would easily end their pains, and though one of the physicians refused the office, some others obeyed. The patients drank the medicine, and never woke again. Now, these were two dreadful crimes against humanity and Christian feeling ; but the defenders of Napoleon say that war is not a Christian or humane operation at all, and that there are cases in which a massacre like that of the Turks at Jaffa may be really a work of necessity, and a murder like that of his own countrymen an act of mercy. The prisoners, they say, were too numerous to be guarded, as the detachments necessary for this purpose would have exposed the whole army to great risk. If, on the other hand, they were dismissed, they were certain to join the enemy and increase his already great numerical superiority. They were, therefore, slain, not cruelly or unnecessarily, but that they might not weaken Napoleon nor strengthen Djezzar Pasha.

The poisoning of his countrymen is placed on different ground. The infuriated enemy, savage and relentless, were in full advance. It was out of his power to retain the town. The sick would be slain, not with sword or gun, but with tortures of the most intolerable kind. Their lives were already despaired of; was their death to be agonised and dreadful? A slight overdose of opium, and they were beyond the reach of Turkish cruelty. If he was himself in their place, could there be a doubt of the choice he would make between a peaceful slumber and a tortured end? These were the defences urged by his friends, and by himself in his conversations at St. Helena. We cannot judge of military necessities; but ere we let the curtain fall upon these frightful departures from the code of ordinary morals, let us give the unhappy director of them the benefit of the fact, that they are the principal instances of personal cruelty adduced against him; and that with regard to the massacre, it raised him in the estimation of the Egyptians, and with regard to the poisoning, it did not lower him in the affection of his men.

In the mean time strange events occurred at Paris, of which the watchful Josephine sent reports as often as possible to her husband. The guiding hand was absent from the army, and the glories of the Italian campaign were followed by disasters, when the war broke out again in 1798. The first glow of patriotic ardour was past, and many thousands of the youth of France were buried in the lands they had subdued. Piedmont, Italy, Flanders, French soil itself, were covered with their graves, and the ranks of the regiments were scantily supplied. The system of forcible conscription was introduced, and discontented all classes of the community. The Council of Five Hundred, the Council of Ancients, and the Directory, were trembling for their re-election, and occupied a large part of the military force in maintaining order at home. On the frontier, affairs were worse and worse. The

Archduke Charles—the only man of talent the royal family of Austria has produced—defeated Jourdan in Germany: the savage and inspired Suwarrow at the head of an army of Russians, as wild and desperate as himself, overthrew Scherer, the republican general, in Italy, and continued his advance in spite of the science of Moreau. Macdonald flew to the rescue from Naples; but the united skill of the French leaders failed before the brutal immobility of Muscovite serfs. A great defeat upon the Trebbia made France tremble for her southern boundaries; Suwarrow continned his march; Sardinia threw off her hated subjection to the tricolor; the Russians entered Milan and Turin; and crowds in coffee-rooms and in barrack-yards, and in the streets of all the cities of the Republic, talked of nothing but the little olive-complexioned man who had conquered Italy in two months. Popular discontent vented itself on the Directory: the members were terrified, and resigned or changed their places, and no one was left of its original body except Barras, the patron and friend of Buonaparte. There was a man of the name of Abbé Sièyes, who is chiefly remarkable for the ease with which he manufactured a constitution, and imposed it on his country. In about a week he could produce a code of laws more complete than the regulations of Lycurgus and Solon, and more minute than the British constitution, which, without being written down, has taken a thousand years to grow into its present state. He began, for the twentieth time, preparing a change. But people were tired of changes; they longed for something to keep them steady and unmoved; some strong hand to hold the sceptre, even if its weight was sometimes oppressive to themselves; and again all the politicians and country farmers, and men of peace, joined with the soldiers and citizens in talking of the little dark man who maintained such perfect discipline, and did such marvellous works. Enemies were gathering thick and fast. A mixed expedition of Russians and English landed in Holland. Suwarrow gained another victory at Novi; and one momentary glimmer of success, gained by Massena at Zurich, did not restore the public confidence. There were Austrians, Russians, English, Piedmontese, menacing the soil; and now the murmurs grew louder and louder against the Directory for having banished, out of hatred and jealousy, the only soldier of France who was equal to the occasion. What was he doing on the banks of the Nile, or under the shadow of the Pyramids, when the Alps were alive with enemies, and Belgium was bristling with bayonets from the Neva and the Thames? The soldier of France came. He had left the army to the care of Kleber, a great and just commander; and had ventured in a small frigate down the whole length of the Mediterranean. It is a strange incident of the voyage that stress of weather kept him in the harbour of Ajaccio, his native place, for nearly a week; when he again took the sea a fog concealed him from the English cruisers. He landed at Frejus, posted to Paris without a moment's delay, and surprised Josephine with his appearance in the small house where he had left her.

All things were prepared for a decisive movement. Everybody knew it was coming, but nobody knew what it was to be. Sièyes got ready a constitution. Barras yielded to Buonaparte's advice in everything; the army was in his favour, and the peaceably inclined invoked him as their deliverer. The Council of Five Hundred and the Council of Ancients were summoned to assemble at St. Cloud on the 10th of November. On that day General Buonaparte, who had been appointed to the command of all the troops, entered the Chamber of the Ancients, and protested against the constitution under which they were formed. Leaving the senators overwhelmed with surprise, he proceeded to the Council of Five Hundred. There he was more noisily received. The benches were occupied by many who had been active in the Convention and the Committee of Public Safety. Buonaparte looked round at the furious visages of the majority, whom his brother Lucien, the president, found it impossible to restrain. He hesitated, he grew pale, and would have lost the opportunity he desired, if his grenadiers had not rushed into the hall, and protected him from the personal violence of the members. For a moment the resolution of the new Cromwell had given way, but it was only for a moment. Next minute a file of soldiers entered the assembly. Bayonets fixed, and drums beating, they marched up the whole length of the apartment. The members saved themselves by the windows at the upper end, and the Hall of Legislature was filled with armed men. The constitution of the year Three was at an end, but Sièyes was ready with half-a-dozen, and a new one was promulgated on the 24th of the same month. By this, three Consuls were appointed for ten years. The First Consul was to have the patronage of all the offices of administration, of the army and navy, and of the magistracy ; the promulgation of laws, and the declaration of peace and war. This First Consul, it is useless to say, was Napoleon Buonaparte ; and it is equally useless to say, that his two colleagues, Cambacérès and Lebrun, were merely additional clerks to register his decisions. The French rejoiced still in the name of republicans, though they had a ruler who possessed all the authority of the crown. They likewise thought they were constitutionally governed by the fiction of a Senate and a Legislative Body, and a Tribunate, though the same grenadiers were still in arms who had dissolved the Councils of Five Hundred and of the Ancients. The First Consul took rank with kings, and wrote letters announcing his accession to all the crowned heads of Europe. But he was as yet too plebeian a person to be admitted to such distinguished correspondence, and he was obliged to wait patiently for a time when the descendants of the Hapsburg Cæsars, and the Hohenzollerns, and the Romanoffs, watched for a note from his hand as if it were a condescension from a superior being.

CHAPTER XIX.

THE FIRST CONSULSHIP, A.D. 1799, TO THE EMPIRE, A.D. 1804.

THE four months of winter, from January to May, 1800, were sufficient to prove that France had changed her constitution more completely in reality than in name. We may have observed in the earlier period of this history, that when an ambitious king wanted to extend his authority, his first care was to buy over the assistance of the clergy by sacrificing the pragmatic, by which the liberties of the Gallican Church were secured. The Pope was not worth the buying at the end of the eighteenth century; and Buonaparte perceived that the liberties of the country were no longer suppressible through the priesthood, but were confided to the championship of the press. Henceforth the first assault on the freedom of the nation is always made through a censorship on the newspapers. It was with this step that the First Consul inaugurated his reign. He placed all publications under the severest restrictions, and shut up the debating clubs and political assemblies throughout the Republic. The wealth of the country was lying unemployed for want of a medium for its diffusion; he established the Bank of France, guaranteed by the State. He increased the revenues by fresh burdens upon realised property, and aided local trade by relaxing some of its restrictions. He strengthened the power of his government by concentrating it in fewer hands; and replaced the municipal and county commissioners by the appointment of prefects responsible only to himself. The central bureau in Paris contained all the information poured in from the provinces and from all the powers of the State. Of this central bureau he was the sole guide. A system of police, governed by certain rules and elevated into a department, was substituted for the uncertain methods of former rulers who depended on the reports of the local authorities. There was nothing going on in any town or district, from Strasburg to Brest, from Calais to Bayonne, that was not accurately known.

He founded also the Military College of St. Cyr, which should furnish scientific soldiers to the nation ; and schools of primary instruction in all directions, to give her, if possible, a peaceable and educated population. He devoted himself, as the chief of all his labours, to the consolidation of the statutes and the simplication of the law, a work which, under the name of the Code Napoleon, has more endeared him to the French people than all the victories which fed their military pride. Paris became a place of settled ideas ; and the show and ostentation which are signs of assured property began to be perceived. People were still simple "citizens ;" but carriages began to roll about the streets ; the official robes of senators and legislators were of the gaudiest kind ; the genius of Parisian milliners invented the most becoming and fanciful costumes. A lady in a richer dress than had adorned the person of a duchess could not retain the pristine simplicity of mind and manners in which the Republic professed to delight. The wives of the ministers of state remembered the noble festivities at which they had enviously wondered, in the gay days of Marie Antoinette and the beautiful Madame de Lamballe. There were ladies as fascinating as Marie Antoinette, and as beautiful as Madame de Lamballe, who did the honours of the reception-room of the First Consul, and only required a change of name to convert it into a court. Josephine was the most expensive dresser, and tasteful leader of the fashions, among all the belles and ornaments of the new regime. Buonaparte's sisters also were celebrated for talent and beauty. The young fellow-soldiers of the master glittered in brilliant uniforms, and made the assemblages as bright with plume and epaulet as, and more interesting with heroic names than, the Tuileries balls of the royal time. Murat, the handsomest man and finest swordsman in France ; Lannes, the favourite of his general ; Desaix, who had followed his leader's example, and left the worn-out Eygpt for the conquest of Europe,—and fifty others, gave animation to the social life of Paris. The populace did not grudge those enjoyments to the soldiers who had earned a right to them by courage and intelligence, especially as they knew that the campaign might possibly elevate the sentinel at the door into a guest within the chamber ; and nothing was wanted to confirm this happy state of circumstances but an honourable peace. Peace accordingly was the object of the First Consul's public endeavours ; yet it may be doubted whether the failure of his negotiation with the German Emperor, and our stubborn and firm-hearted George the Third, was not rather a pleasure than a disappointment. Austria rejected all his advances, and the royalty of England would not deign him a reply. We still acknowledged Louis the Eighteenth as the only legitimate authority in France, and General Buonaparte was manifestly a usurper. The usurper, however, felt every inch a king when he put on his cocked hat and plain grey riding-coat, and mounted his Arab horse : ball-rooms were emptied ; and Lannes, and Murat, and Desaix, rode by his side.

The old rapidity of march and conquest was renewed, as if the enchanter had found his wand again. Leaving Paris on the 5th of May, 1800, Buonaparte scaled the Alps in a quarter where the feat was thought impossible, on the 16th ; on the 20th the plains of Italy lay like a picture beneath the eyes of the soldiers, who were astonished no less than the Austrians at what they had done ; and on the 1st of June they made a triumphant entry into Milan, where the streets were spanned by arches, ladies waved fans and handkerchiefs, and the populace hailed them as their deliverers. But the enemy were gathering round the invaders. Outnumbering them—two or three to one—the Austrian generals chose the great level of Marengo, near the fortress of Alessandria, as the field of battle, and assaulted the French columns as they approached the river Bormida. The French columns were not in the habit of being attacked with impunity, and the Austrians were courageously received. Thousands after thousands, however, poured on; their superiority of numbers began to tell. Not all the eloquence and skill of the First Consul could keep his men together under the charges of innumerable horse and foot; and four times the line was broken, and a retreat begun. On the last occasion, when Buonaparte in vain had set the example of the most desperate courage, Desaix, at the head of the last reserve, crossed the plain at a rapid rate, rushed into the disordered masses of the enemy, and forced them into irremediable rout. He scarcely lived long enough to know the success of his movement, for a bullet hit him in the moment of victory; and Buonaparte, without a rival to his fame, was left to the full enjoyment of all the results of this greatest of his early battles—the battle of Marengo. This was on the 14th of June, five weeks after he left Paris, and he made his public re-entrance into that enraptured city on the 1st of July. Austria was humbled as in the former Italian struggles. Genoa and Lombardy threw off her yoke, and the Ligurian and Cisalpine republics were the result of a two months' campaign. Europe looked aghast at the change produced by the presence of one man—that one man was felt both by countryman and foreigner to be the sole obstacle to the overthrow of French power, and the restoration of the old line.

Nothing could persuade either friend or foe that the action with which this momentous year came to a close was not the result of these beliefs. As the First Consul was going to the opera, on the 23d of December, a machine was exploded on his way, which destroyed houses and other buildings on both sides of the street, but missed the object of its attack by a very few paces. The carriage went on uninjured; but the enthusiasm of the nation knew no bounds. If the emigrants planned the attempt for the purpose of procuring their return, they shut the doors on themselves more rigorously than before; if the foreign potentates encouraged the design, to weaken and divide the people, they united the whole nation, royalist and republican, in the most unlimited admiration of the first of soldiers, whose existence was now seen to be its surest defence against invasion from without and anarchy within. The victory of Hohenlinden, which was won by Moreau on the 3d of the same month, lost half its brilliancy in the agitation caused by the First Consul's escape: but its effects were felt at Vienna almost as much as those of Montebello and Marengo. Austria signed a treaty of peace at Luneville in February, 1801. In this she ceded Belgium and the left bank of the Rhine to France; and acknowledged the four republics which had been carved out of her dominions or created against her will—the Batavian, Helvetic, Cisalpine, and Ligurian. Bavaria and Portugal lost no time in following the example of Austria; and by the autumn of the same year, the Corsican engineer was acknowledged one of the governing powers of Europe, and received the consummation of his wishes, and the ratification of his rank, by the recognition of the Pope and the blessing of the Church.

The Christian worship was re-established; and with a cry of joy, as when sailors are delivered from a shipwreck and touch the land again, the people hailed the restoration of the services to which they had been accustomed in their youth. They felt on surer ground when they entered the sacred aisles that connected them so solemnly with the past; and Buonaparte, whose name might have taken many years to reach the isolated and illiterate peasantry in many parts of the country, was now brought home to them every day, for he was prayed for at morning and evening service. The few among the more educated classes who had not abjured their faith, not only saw in him the hero of the military glories of the nation, but the protector of the national religion. Far-seeing politicians perceived in this act of the free-thinking First Consul, who had taken such a deep interest in the doctrines of Mahomet when he was in Egypt, a step in the direction of highei power. A consul for ten years did not require the aid of a Pope, whose tenure would probably not be so long ; and these forebodings or hopes received a further proof when the man who had commenced his authority by silencing the press, now entered into a concordat or agreement with the Papacy, by which many of its ecclesiastical privileges were restored. Buonaparte gave some advantages to the Church that he might gain its support against other orders in the State. The Church was contented with the little it received, as furnishing a stepping-stone to more. It was a great move for one of the contracting parties to have regained its legal existence and authority in France ; it was a still greater gain to the other to have obtained the support of a strongly organised body of men, who acted as a moral police in the rural districts, and gave only such views of public affairs as suited the ruling power.

There was now peace round all the borders of France except the sea. On that perpetually hostile element the English rode supreme. A race of captains had been trained in the eight years of war such as no nation had ever possessed. Dashing and sagacious at once, the commanders of British ships were a parallel to the leaders on land who lent their aid to the First Consul. What Buonaparte was to the French army, Nelson was to the English fleet. He was its chief and model at the same time. While the First Consul was working in his little study in the Tuileries, holding the threads of all the Continental policies in his hands, intimation reached the English government of a hostile armament going on among the Northern Powers. Denmark, Sweden, and Russia, were won over to throw off what he had persuaded them to consider the galling yoke of British supremacy. But while their ships were getting ready, and the French partisans were rejoicing in the anticipated blow, his hopes were overthrown in the most unexpected manner. A fleet was sent to the Baltic under the flag of Sir Hyde Parker, but under the guidance and command of Nelson, the passage of Elsinore was forced, and the Danish fleet exterminated at Copenhagen on the 2d of April. While the French occupiers of Savoy and the Prussian seizers of Silesia were lost in virtuous indignation at this nefarious attack on a neighbour in a time of peace, the English admiral spread all sail up the Baltic in search of the Swedish fleet,—which, fortunately, had time to ensconce itself under the defences of Carlscrona,—and continued his career till he presented all his broadsides in front of the town of Revel (14th May). Napoleon had suffered a greater loss than the destruction of the Danes in the death of the Russian Paul. The mad admiration of that savage ruler had placed the resources of all the Russias in his hands; but it scarcely needed the sight of so many guns to persuade his successor, Alexander, to resume his friendly relations with England. Sweden was glad to escape with only a passing view of Nelson; and Denmark, without a mast to hoist a flag on, surrendered her attempt to aid the Emperor with her maritime strength.

But though undisputed mistress of the seas, Britain saw no use in maintaining the struggle, in which she was left alone. What were the objects she contended for? The nation at large had no interest in the restoration of the fanatical or sensual Bourbons. Many persons maintained already that one people had no right to interfere with the internal arrangements of another. Others thought that Buonaparte, being satisfied with his success, would have no farther ambition; and the great body of the nation were tired of paying taxes, and wished to be left alone. On the 25th of March, 1802, the Peace of Amiens, between France and England, gave some breathing-time to both. But neither trusted the other. The sword was half-drawn at the moment the pen was signing the ratification. Buonaparte pursued his schemes of aggrandisement while the preliminaries were being arranged. He obtained a change in the government of some of the republics he had established very favourable to himself. He fitted out an expedition against St. Domingo, which spread alarm among our West-Indian possessions. The small province of the Valais in Switzerland was detached from the Helvetic Republic, and furnished an unencumbered access to Italy. The great causeway of the Simplon, on which armies and artillery could be moved as on a level, was begun; the whole kingdom of Piedmont was incorporated with France, and every camp and barrack throughout all that vast extent, from the Channel to Lombardy, was filled with fresh-raised troops. Drilling went on as in the heat of a war, and six hundred thousand men slept, as it were, upon their arms. This was not the sort of peace that England had agreed to. The First Consul had added millions to his subjects and thousands to his army, almost before the ink of the treaty was dry; and surrounded by his new populations and his recently enrolled battalions, he insisted haughtily and insultingly on England fulfilling her part of the agreement to the letter. She was to surrender Alexandria, which she had won with the sword after defeating the relics of the French expedition which Buonaparte deserted. She had to resign the Cape of Good Hope to the Batavian Republic, of which he was now virtually the chief; Malta to the Knights of St. John, who could not resist him for an hour. The circumstances were entirely changed, and England declined to denude herself of her conquests till he replaced himself in the position he held at the date of the peace. Heroic in some of his aspirations, unequalled as a leader in the field, unmatched as a politician, Buonaparte was at the same time as impetuous and uncivil in manner, and coarse in language, as the lowest frequenter of the canteen. Ignorant altogether of the polish and self-respect which we distinguish with the name of gentlemanly conduct, he knew neither how to behave with dignity to his equals nor kindness to his inferiors. He attacked the English ambassador with the most vulgar insolence in presence of the court—scolded, stormed, and threatened like a drunken grenadier, and finally bounced out of the apartment like a sulky child. He had said, if England drew the sword he would throw away the scabbard. England was not in the least afraid, and declared war on the 18th of May, 1803.

She commenced by the harsh, though not unexampled, proceeding of laying an embargo on all French vessels in her harbours. Buonaparte retorted by the unheard-of cruelty of consigning to his military prisons all the English travellers whom the peace had attracted to every part of France. They were condemned to linger far from home for many years—men and their wives and children, who could have had no possible effect on the course of hostilities, but whose detention embittered the feelings of the British nation to a degree which only the death or overthrow of the oppressor could diminish. False accusations of complicity in designs to murder him—because the misguided fanatics who meditated the crime proceeded to the scene of their attempts from England—still farther heightened the indignation of the British public. But when, in addition to these insults to our honour, our safety became endangered by the parade of a vast army at Boulogne, called the Army of England, and flat-bottomed boats for its conveyance to our shores were collected from all the harbours of France, a mad enthusiasm of hatred and patriotism took possession of the whole people ; and while a hundred and sixty thousand sailors defended the meteor-flag at sea, there were more than half a million armed men lining all the heights from Dover to the Land's End. Austria was also on the watch : she had been alarmed by Buonaparte's seizure of the Electorate of Hanover, which, though a hereditary possession of the English king, formed a portion of the German Empire ; and all the other kingdoms were uneasy, and carried on their preparations without noise.

Events meanwhile were taking place at Paris, which furnished new allies to his English foes. A conspiracy to put him to death was discovered by the police ; and Pichegru, the old general of the Republic, and Moreau, the conqueror of Hohenlinden, were implicated in the accusations. These, whether true or false, led to the imprisonment and suicide of Pichegru and the exile of Moreau. But to strike terror into the Bourbons, whom he suspected to be the real originators of the attempt upon his life, he determined to show that no consideration of pity or justice would stand between him and his revenge. He ordered the young Duke d'Enghien, a son of the Prince of Condé, to be seized on the neutral territory of Baden; and his secret and positive orders, joined to the officious zeal of his friends, put the unhappy prisoner to death beneath the walls of Vincennes after the mockery of a trial. The circumstances spread abroad: the solitary lantern on the breast of the sufferer, the dark ditch of the rampart where he was placed, the file of soldiers, and the hour of midnight—these, with the noble bearing of the young man, gave the incident the appearance of an assassination rather than the result of a judicial sentence. Injustice to an individual comes more home to the general bosom than the oppression of a nation. All hearts were shocked by this unprovoked and apparently useless murder: but the supporters of the policy of terror determined to cover the blot of the execution of the young Condé with a proof of the national approval of the principal delinquent. A few days after the tragedy of Vincennes, a proposition was made in the Tribunate to create the First Consul hereditary Emperor of the French. The proposition was received with acclamations. The Senate made him a formal presentment of the crown, and on the 18th of May the great drama of 1789 came to an end.

Here was a ruler with more despotic authority than Cardinal Richelieu, and a more implacable hatred of popular freedom than Louis the Fourteenth. Yet the implements of tyranny had become so defective by the disuse of a few years, the traditions of unreasoning submission and divine right had been so washed out by the blood of the Revolution, that the position of the French was infinitely happier, both in its present circumstances and its future prospects, than at any former time. The dominance of the priest, the insolence of the noble, the exactions of the farmers-general, the exemption of favoured orders, the uncertainty of law, the galling inequalities of social ranks, had all passed away. If taxation pressed, it was at all events equal in its pressure. It did not spare the chateau to fall with tenfold weight upon the cottage;

even the conscription made no invidious distinctions, but fell on all alike. The French were contented with the equality about which they had raved so loudly, even when they discovered it was an equality of submission. But there were reasons which justified a strong and repressive government, arising from the very novelty of their emancipation from former wrongs. If they had been allowed to riot in their ill-consolidated liberties, the Austrians and Russians would very soon have encamped upon the Seine. The curtailment of their theoretical rights was compensated for by the protection of society from the outbursts of discontent. It was a temporary sacrifice to secure their eventual claims ; and over all that might be disagreeable in their political condition, there was thrown the halo of military renown. The Frenchman consoled himself with the reflection that he might be trampled on a little at Versailles and Fontainebleau, but that he was immensely feared at Vienna and Berlin. Napoleon the First, like a new Charlemagne, made a tour to receive the gratulations of his subject states. All the European kingdoms recognised his new dignity except Russia, Turkey, and England ; and Catholic Christendom put the seal upon his elevation, when the Pope crossed the Alps to anoint him with the holy oil on the 2d December 1804. On the 26th of May of the following year he placed with his own hands the iron crown of the Lombard kings upon his head, and assumed the name and title of Emperor of the French and King of Italy.

THE EMPIRE, A. D. 1804, TO THE MARRIAGE, A.D. 1810.

Honours and decorations were heaped upon State and army, to accommodate them to the glories of an imperial reign. The two Consuls were rewarded for their obsequiousness in offering their resignations, by being created Lord-Chancellor and Arch-Treasurer of the Empire. These were intended to be the chiefs of a new social nobility, and did honour to the

Emperor's selection by the magnificence of their balls and the unmatched excellence of their cooks. Eighteen men of a very different kind were elevated to a higher military grade, and added new triumphs to the title of Marshal of France. The most observable of these are Massena, Soult, Lannes, Ney, Davoust, and Kellerman. Two of them, Murat and Bernadotte, were afterwards kings—the first for a brief space at Naples, and leaving no marks of policy or wisdom behind; but Bernadotte was more wise and fortunate, and founded a royal dynasty in Sweden, which has endeared itself to its subjects by justice and moderation, and is acknowledged among the established royalties of Europe. The institution of the Legion of Honour gave Napoleon the means of appealing to the nobler feelings of his soldiers; and the equality expressed by the medal on the breast of general and private had an elevating effect on the great body of his men. It was fondly remembered in the conversations of the camp that Soult had been in the ranks like themselves—that Bernadotte, a few years before, was a sergeant—that Murat had been a simple dragoon; and they felt prouder in themselves, and more trusting in their chief, when they reflected that there was no soldier's knapsack which did not possibly contain a marshal's baton.

Such intensity of hatred as burned between the new Emperor and England never disturbed the councils of Carthage and Rome. The system represented by each was utterly inconsistent with the very existence of the other. Military aggression, and the maintenance of internal tranquillity by an overwhelming force wielded by one man; a settled order of things, even if not the best in itself, and a government in accordance with the general will of the country, constitutionally expressed—these were such antagonistic principles that either the despotic propagator of new ideas must fall, or the defender of existing institutions be rendered powerless. The fight, therefore, became more like a duel between two irreconcilable adversaries, in which the seconds occasionally took part, than a war urged for European or national purposes. It was for the complete destruction either of England or of Napoleon, and the enemies felt from the beginning that the battle was to the death.

The first act of the Emperor was to place himself on an elevated throne above the town of Boulogne, and distribute the ribbons of the Legion of Honour to the soldiers who had distinguished themselves in previous campaigns. His face was turned to the White Cliffs all the time of the ceremony, and he pointed across the Channel with a promise of guiding their next manœuvres in the fields of Kent. In all England, Scotland, and Wales, there were not above ten millions of souls. France, in addition to the twenty-five millions of her own population, was backed by the millions of Germany and Italy and the Netherlands. But no man in all the Island ever lost a night's sleep from alarm at an invasion of the French; that seems to be a plant of a later and less honourable growth. While a hundred and thirty thousand men were within easy summons to Boulogne, and boats for their conveyance were assembled in all directions, intimation reached the boastful threatener of the "nation of shopkeepers" that a hundred and eighty thousand Russians were on their march to the south, supported by English subsidies; that Austria was fully armed by largesses from the same inexhaustible exchequer; that Prussia was trembling in the scale, as in all her history she has never been guided by any higher principle than her own immediate advantage; and the plans of Kentish manœuvres, if ever entertained, were surrendered at once. Marches were silently made, ammunition and all the instruments of war moved without ostentation beyond the Rhine, and the dreadful intelligence reached the German courts in September and October, that Napoleon had penetrated the Black Forest, and placed his troops between the Austrian army and the capital; that the great fortress of Ulm was besieged; that it had surrendered with its garrison of thirty thousand men; and that the victor was in full march to Vienna. On the 15th of November, Napoleon made his triumphal entrance into the residence of the Cæsars, and the unhappy Francis the Second fled to Olmutz, where he awaited the arrival of Alexander and the Russians. The Archduke Charles was approaching from another quarter, and Napoleon determined to destroy the Austrians and Russians before his arrival. He advanced into Moravia, deceived the allies by a pretended uncertainty of movement, and tempted them to their doom in the plains near Brünn, upon the Schwartza. The Emperors of Germany and Russia placed themselves on the heights of Austerlitz as spectators of the approaching battle, and saw the bright sun of the 2d of December rise to illuminate a certain victory. But the sun shone brighter for Napoleon than for them. Murat, at the head of a powerful cavalry, swept the extremities of the field; Lannes pushed at the centre, after overthrowing their left wing; Davoust repulsed them when they advanced; Soult was upon their rear when they retired. One great effort was made by the Russian mounted guard; but Rapp, the favourite aide-de-camp of Napoleon, carried a reinforcement to the French, and the combined Russians and Austrians were annihilated as a resisting force. Some fled for safety to a frozen lake at the end of the field, but the artillery poured upon their crowded masses, and tore up the fragile floor on which they stood. Whole battalions went down under the fearful fire, amid the broken fragments of the ice. The fugitives in other directions were pursued by the unpitying horse, and, two days afterwards, Francis of Germany appeared as a suppliant in the conqueror's tent. "We can oppose you no longer; what terms will you give?" "Will you give up your alliance with the English, and help me to ruin them with all your power?" was the first thought of Napoleon's heart. He trampled on the majesty of the loftiest throne in Europe, and aggrandised himself at its expense. He rewarded his supporters with its spoils, and created the Electors of Bavaria and Würtemberg kings, enriching their crowns with provinces of their ancient master. He created his marshals dukes and princes, and carved out whole countries to maintain their new dignity from the states of friend and foe. Prussia, with which he was at peace, furnished the grand-duchy of Berg for Murat, and the principality of Neufchatel to Berthier.

His family might have been jealous if rewards of such magnitude had been given to merit alone ; so he silenced the people who found fault with his want of natural affection, by giving the viceroyalty of Italy to his stepson Eugene de Beauharnais, and two kingdoms to two very incompetent men—the kingdom of the Two Sicilies to his brother Joseph—the kingdom of Holland to his brother Louis. Surrounded by tributary kings and ennobled marshals, he returned to Paris to enjoy the delirious congratulations of his friends, and prepare for fresh conquests in the following year. But his remembrance of the year's events was not uncheckered with darker shades. On the 21st of October the combined fleets of France and Spain were defeated off Cape Trafalgar by Nelson, who died with the shouts of victory in his ears. It was not an ordinary defeat, which a little extraordinary exertion might repair ; it was a total annihilation of the very elements of maritime power. The allied nations had henceforward neither ships nor men. The very desire of naval rivalry disappeared from the hearts of the French and Spaniards : and while the tricolor was advancing in irresistible strength from capital to capital, there was not a shore or harbour in the whole extent of Europe which did not see the English flag undisputed and alone. The great question was now to be decided—and all men watched it as a philosophic no less than a political problem—whether eventual supremacy belongs to the land or the sea ? A great French author had already said, "The trident of Neptune is the sceptre of the world ;" and now came the realization or disproval of the saying.

The year 1806 opened with negotiations that led to nothing, and the great struggle went on between the hereditary foes. England lavished promises and money, formed alliances, strengthened her fleet, pushed her commerce into quarters unvisited before, and kept up the resolution of her people by speeches, pamphlets, and state-papers. All the theatres rang every night with "Hearts of Oak" and "Britannia Rules the Waves." Napoleon retorted on his side by squeezing French subsidies from subject nations, by tightening the reins of his own authority, by splendid reviews in the Champ de Mars, and real ameliorations in the machinery of government and simplification of the law. But the pride that cometh before a fall already showed itself in his contempt for other powers. Some highwaymen in English annals have relieved their victims of watches and money with such a gentlemanly air, and even accompanied their crime with such complimentary speeches, that the ladies were more charmed than angry at the loss of their rings and jewels; but Napoleon was not a sentimental footpad. He tore away a province as a more commonplace robber might tear away an ear-ring —inflicting almost as much suffering by the insolence as by the pain, and continued incredulous of the effect of his behaviour on the nations he outraged, merely because they made no open demonstration of self-defence. Prussia—always selfish in her aims, always dilatory in her exertions—had waited with anxious inaction while her rival Austria was crushed. She availed herself of the dangerous friendship of Napoleon to lay hands on the electorate of Hanover, the territory of her ally George the Third; and having steeped herself not only in the shame of spiritless acquiescence, but in the crime of an actual dishonesty, Napoleon considered her too contemptible and too guilty to be defended by the other states if he trampled on her neck. After waiting, however, till she had irritated Austria by her desertion, and England by her injustice, Prussia began to writhe under the heel of France. Napoleon had established a great society of secondary princes, which he called the "Confederation of the Rhine," and declared himself its "Protector." Prussia endeavoured to found a counterbalance to this in the combination of the other German states, of which she hoped to be the head. But the clear-eyed man in the Tuileries was across the Rhine in a few hours after her purposes were discovered. On the 9th of Ocber 1806 the campaign began. It is called the campaign of Jena, for at that place the crowning victory was obtained. It was the Trafalgar of the Prussians, and from that time they ceased for some years to be a military power ; order, discipline, numbers, all were gone.

The conqueror bore his success with none of the meekness or moderation of a great mind ; he merely saw another kingdom at his feet, and pressed on it with all his weight—nobody could resist, nobody dared to complain. It began to be felt that a personage had arisen whom it was useless either to oppose or blame. His marches were like the exaggerations of romance—his battles like the strokes of an avenging fate. The dates of that memorable month of October are the mere resting-places of the Eagles in their flight from field to field. Saalfeldt, Jena, and Auerstadt (the two latter fought on the same day), Greussen, Halle, Erfurt, Leipsic, Magdeburg, Göttingen, Spandau—these are the names of the places where victories were gained by the Emperor or his lieutenants, on a march of conquest beginning on the 9th of October and ending on the 27th with the entrance of Napoleon into Berlin. It verified what he had written in his address to the soldiers on their departure from Paris : "There is not one of you who would wish to return to France by any other path than that of honour ; we must not re-enter our country except under arches of triumph." The Eagles continued their career without a moment's delay. Murat captured the whole army opposed to him at Prentzlow on the 28th, and secured the town of Stettin and the line of the Oder. By the end of the following month, Silesia and Prussian Poland were overrun, Glogau yielded to Jerome Buonaparte, and Posen to Davoust. All the country from the Rhine to the Baltic was traversed by the French, and their standards flew at the same time at Cologne and Dantzic.

Victorious over the bodies of men, Napoleon now determined to interfere with their individual interests, and to exterminate England altogether by overthrowing her trade. His armies could perform wonders, but to stop the desire for

English manufactures, or the love of English gold, was a miracle beyond his power. Russia, Austria, Prussia, failed against his forces; but Lancashire vanquished his Berlin decrees. There was something almost ludicrous in the blindness of his rage. He put England into a state of blockade, though he had not a ship upon the sea, and ordered all his subject-peoples to do without English supplies, though he had not a broadcloth or cotton-mill in all his dominions. Artillery, horse, and infantry were always defeated when opposed to his battalions; but printed ginghams were irresistible. There were conspiracies, beyond the reach of his spies, in every parlour where the daughters were dressed in coloured muslins, and cloths, cutlery, and earthenware were smuggled wherever an English vessel could float. The Emperor was at last compelled to witness the failure of his plan in the apparel of his wife and her ladies of honour; for they got their Indian shawls from London, and their light dresses from Manchester.

The critics of Napoleon's career have traced his first great mistake in his publication of this ban against the commerce of the world; and his next in the non-restoration of its liberties to Poland. A nation, however, of fourteen millions of people, which values its liberties so little as to allow them to be taken away, and so riotous and unpatriotic in the use of them while they retained the semblance of independence, would not have added to his strength against Russia and Austria so much as it would have weakened his designs against the very appearance of freedom at home. He recruited his regiments, therefore, among the countrymen of Sobieski; but left them as denationalised as before. The bitterness of the struggle made the combatants forgetful of the inclemency of the season, and hostilities went on throughout the year. Russia had come into the field, and brought her climate along with her in the winter of 1806. She, however, brought her Cossacks also for the first time into European conflict; and for a moment the trained troops of France were embarrassed by the irregular assaults of those sons of the frozen steppes. Wheeling round their march like carrion-crows expectant of a meal, those frightful little Tartars, on their equally frightful little steeds, left no repose to the flanks of an advancing column. In the midst of a storm of hail, the pulks—divisions of forty men into which these cohorts were formed—dashed furiously down upon the blinded French; their long lances pierced far into the line, and ere the musket could be raised, or the thickened air cleared sufficiently for a mark, the thousand dwarfs, laying themselves almost full length along the backs of their ponies, and grasping the neck in their arms, hid themselves from the enemy among the hairs of the mane, and disappeared in the falling sleet. On the 8th of February, 1807, the great battle of Eylau was fought between the French and Russians. The cold was intense; the ground was covered with snow; there were three hundred cannon pouring their destructive fire during the whole day. A great tempest dashed the snow-flakes into the combatants' faces, and interfered with the sight of the commanders. There was little room for manœuvring, and the steadiness of the Muscovites presented an impenetrable barrier to the French attack. The sons of the Seine and the Po, and all the sunny plains from which their armies were now supplied, had never experienced a climate so fierce, nor enemies so immovable. At length, however, the Russians, in excellent order, and with all their guns and colours, removed from the field of battle; they chanted the Te Deum for their success, next day, and were ready for another trial. But Napoleon, who knew how effective names were upon the susceptibilities of his countrymen, dated his bulletin from the scene of the combat, and occupied it for eight days to show how complete his victory had been. This was the most murderous battle he had hitherto fought; and as he was farthest from his supplies, his losses were less easily repaired. The Senate voted eighty thousand men of the conscription of the following year, thus commencing the system of drawing bills upon human life, which were discounted with the blood and suffering of the whole of France. Eylau was practically a check if nominally a victory; and it required the great achievements of the assistant generals to raise the spirits of the army.

A succession of triumphs by Bernadotte, Suchet, and Oudinot, closing with the undoubted victory of Friedland, won by the Emperor in person, brought Russia to terms. Sixty thousand of his subjects destroyed or captured on this dreadful day, wrung the heart of Alexander, both as a benevolent man and an ambitious ruler ; his Prussian ally could give him no farther aid ; and in a few days after the combat the vanquished potentates had interviews with the conqueror at Tilsit on the Niemen. He received them in his tent and listened to their entreaties, but finally granted peace on his own conditions. The two sovereigns were to accept the Continental blockade of England ; to recognise his three brothers as kings of Holland, Sicily, and Westphalia ; and Prussia was to pay enormous contributions towards the expenses of the war, and furnish large tracts of her territory to enlarge the neighbouring powers which had been true to France. Having humbled two of the haughtiest magnates in Europe, and had the opportunity of showing his supremacy by his insulting and contemptuous treatment of the beautiful and patriotic Queen of Prussia, who came to implore his clemency and generosity, he returned on the 27th of July to Paris, the most powerful individual in the world, and the most idolised ruler the nations had ever beheld. In spite, however, of his rigorous measures against the liberties of the land, and his silencing of all newspapers and pamphlets except such as the censorship approved, his efforts at an entire suppression of public opinion on some portions of his conduct were ineffectual, for the convulsive energies of the Revolution had given a totally different character to the population of France. Jacques Bonhomme was no longer either the wretched unidea'd serf we saw him in the cruel time of the dominant church and feudal chiefs, nor the unreasoning madman and blood-stained savage we knew him in the Reign of Terror, but he retained just enough of the memory of his former ill-treatment, and his former supremacy, to be watchful for any assaults upon the liberties guaranteed him by the laws.

Napoleon perhaps forgot that, by the admirable theory of equal rights and duties which he published as the jurisprudence of France, he gave a firm foundation for opposition to the acts of tyranny in which he frequently indulged. The force of an inundation is not known unless where there are banks by which to measure its height. There was now a standard by which a government's actions could be judged; and oppression, besides being impolitic, now became illegal. The conscription, even at this period, began to be hated, and the love of conquest to be blamed in the midst of bonfires and processions. For though Napoleon had got the command of the press, and the tribune, and the pulpit, and nobody could either write an attack on him or make a public speech in opposition, there were thousands of living gazettes in all the villages of France, who discussed his measures with the utmost freedom, and uttered curses not loud but deep. These were the soldiers who had served their time, or were home on furlough, or had lost their healths in the service. While the glow of military ardour was upon them, they marched merrily against a foreign foe: but when they came back, and found the small field of their inheritance a wilderness for want of culture, their relations starving, their brothers and friends already called away to fill up the ranks of the army, they took a different view of public proceedings. Every year, from the first wars of the Revolution in 1793, had probably sent back among the ordinary population twenty thousand discharged or invalided soldiers. In the thirteen years which had now elapsed, the number of these experienced men was very large; and at the same time that their apprenticeship in arms enabled them to understand and glory in the bulletins which told of Prussia vanquished and Russia humbled in a single campaign, their intelligence also pointed out to them how useless these barren laurels were for the real improvement of their lot. They longed for a cessation from wars and victories, and blamed the ambition of the Emperor though it brought all the kings of Europe to their feet. From this time, therefore, Napoleon's cry against England was that she was the sole obstacle to a peace. Formerly his appeals to his countrymen were about palms and glory—captured standards and statues brought to Paris. Now he talked of corn and oil, sighed for the time when he might apply his mind to agriculture and trade, and bitterly inveighed against the selfish islanders for preventing him from turning his sword into a pruning-hook and his barracks into mills.

Portugal, however, attracted his notice during these plaintive regrets and anticipation of the golden age, by admitting the manufactures of England in contravention of the Berlin blockade. He prepared an army at Bayonne, and obtained permission to march it through Spain from the infatuated rulers of that decrepit power. Shortly after the appearance in the *Moniteur* of the words, "The House of Braganza has ceased to reign," Marshal Junot entered Lisbon at the head of a large force, while the Portuguese royal family sailed out of the harbour in an English squadron to seek a refuge in Brazil—a severe price to pay for wishing to exchange the wines of Oporto for the woollens of Leeds! But with an army in Portugal, and another at the foot of the Pyrenees, the Emperor determined to make another royal family "cease to reign." The Bourbons met him more than half way. The old King of Spain, Charles the Fourth, complained to Napoleon against his son; and the prince—afterwards Ferdinand the Seventh—complained against his father. He was constituted arbiter and master of both. He beguiled them to a pretended conference at Bayonne; took them into custody; obtained a renunciation of their rights in favour of himself; and, abolishing the Bourbons from the list of European royalties, appointed Joachim Murat King of the Two Sicilies—*vice* Joseph Buonaparte promoted to the throne of Spain. Joseph, the elder brother of Napoleon, was a good and easy man, not without talents, but with none of the energy that had lifted five of the family of Ajaccio into royal rank. He felt some reluctance in leaving the land of music and maccaroni, for the land of the bull-fight and stiletto. While he was on his way an insurrection, with frightful massacre—quelled also with frightful cruelty by Murat—broke out at Madrid ; the Junta, or national government, assembled at Seville, and proclaimed their legitimate king in spite of his forced renunciation. The old Spanish pride was up, without any of the old Spanish courage ; and Napoleon was obliged to fight for the crown he had so ingeniously conveyed.

The fight would not have been long or the issue doubtful, if it had been left to Spain and France ; but a new combatant came upon the ground, who altered the position of the belligerents. On the 31st of July, Sir Arthur Wellesley landed in Portugal with eight or ten thousand men, and on the 22d of August won a great victory at Vimeira, which so disheartened the French army that they applied for a convention by which they evacuated the whole of Portugal, and left the English in possession of the field. Dupont, the French general in Andalusia, was also forced to surrender to an overwhelming force of Spaniards, and the tide of victory seemed fairly turned. Murders and treachery were rife, over all the land of Castilian honour. More French soldiers perished by the knife than by the musket. Catechisms were published by the monks, where, in answer to the question, "Is it sinful to kill a Frenchman ?" the Christian student replies, "No, the kingdom of heaven is gained by the slaughter of one of those heretical dogs." In every city the populace, led by the friars, broke out into hideous excesses. They tortured and slew the upper classes who wished to maintain order in the place, brandished their bloody daggers before the faces of the saints in their churches, and fled to hide themselves in the hills the moment a French company was reported within ten miles. A coward inspired with religious fanaticism is the cruellest of men ; he thinks the sufferings of his opponents a new tribute to the faith. Napoleon, to place a bridle on this demoralising warfare, dashed across the mountains in November, 1808 ; gained three great battles against the regular army of Spain in the course of a fortnight; and on the 4th of December made his entry into Madrid. If there seems a sameness in the expression of "making his entry into a town," it is owing entirely to the repetition of the event. There were but two capitals of first-rate magnitude into which he had not marched in triumph. These were Moscow and London. As to Vienna, Berlin, Dresden, Milan, and the rest, he walked into them as he might into one of his own villages; and it is not unlikely, at this very time, when Russia seemed his most trustworthy ally and obsequious servant, that visions of the Kremlin rose before him, and of a peace dictated from the grand old city, which represented equally the East and West—the east by the oriental style of its buildings; and the west by the luxury and refinement which characterised its society.

Alexander was closely watched while he was flattered, and perhaps despised: but it was so evidently the interest of all legitimate authorities to weaken the power of this new colossus which overtrode them all, that the sagacious Corsican could not rely on the sincerity of the Czar in the support he ostensibly gave him. Prussia also began to move; England poured her subsidies into the greedy hands of all the German princes, and bribed the Austrians to fight for their own existence. While Napoleon, therefore, was busy in Madrid reducing the chaos into some sort of order, the hated and perfidious Albion made a diversion on the banks of the Rhine and the Danube, which carried him back to Paris to be nearer the centre of affairs. Spain and Portugal were indeed only second-rate questions in the terrible events which were about to occur. We may leave them for a rapid review, when we come to the time when all the different cords which were held by outraged Europe drew closer and closer to the lion they were meant to enclose—when we shall see the meeting of all the converging armies, and compare the share they bore in the grand catastrophe; but at present we have to follow Napoleon into Germany, where a tremendous spirit had been aroused. It was not limited this time to the rich and great, or to regular armies or constituted governments. In Prussia a simple major (Schill) had organised a body of volunteers, who spread the flame of patriotism through the country. In the Tyrol an inn-keeper, Hofer, made himself a name as honourable as that of Wallace or Tell. Everywhere the young were on the side of fatherland and freedom ; enthusiastic students left the university to shoulder a gun ; and unless speedily quenched, it was evident the conflagration would spread from the Baltic to the Bosphorus. It was quenched in blood by the pitiless hand of the alarmed master. He made one of his furious clutches at the heart of his victim before it was prepared to guard its breast. He crossed the Rhine on the 3d of April ; on the 10th of May he was residing in the Austrian Emperor's palace at Schoenbrunn, and on the 12th he took up his quarters for the second time in Vienna. The interval had been filled up with the battles of Abensberg, Landshut and Eckmühl (where twenty thousand prisoners were made), and the bombardment of the capital itself. Battered and ruined by his shot, and ominously discontented with his exactions, Vienna was no safe place for a foreign army. The Archduke Charles also was in the neighbourhood with a large force. Boats were thrown over the Danube a little way below Vienna, and the French army went across. They seized the villages of Essling and Aspern, and fought against the Austrians with such doubtful success that the combat was renewed by the enemy on the following day. Never was the glory of the Eagles in such danger as here ; for a sudden rise in the river enabled the Austrians to float down immense balks of timber, which broke the bridge by which Napoleon had crossed, and he was himself cut off from his supports under Davoust, and his military supplies. Powder even began to fail ; and after repelling the enemy by the bayonet, the wearied conquerors were led backwards in retreat. They effected with great difficulty a crossing to the island of Lobau, and soon converted it into an impregnable position. But an impregnable position is of no use if it cannot be made a base for offensive operations. For a whole month the victorious invaders were cooped up on that isle, carefully watched by the Archduke Charles; and watching, in their turn, the proceedings of the enemy. If the Archduke made a false step, he knew his fate was sealed; to be quite safe, he made no step at all. Napoleon had, therefore, time to arrange his plans, and combine the movements in the farthest parts of his positions in Italy and northern Germany with his strategy on the contemptible piece of land he occupied in the middle of the Danube. Everything turned out as he wished. The Duke of Brunswick was driven out of Bohemia; the Austrian princes, Ferdinand and John, were defeated and pursued into Hungary by Eugene Beauharnais; the heroic Major Schill was taken and slain at Stralsund; and finally the armies of Italy, led by the Viceroy, and of Marmont from Dalmatia, joined the great army, and Napoleon was at the head of two hundred thousand men.

On the 1st of July, in the midst of a storm of thunder and rain, he led his troops across wooden bridges to the opposite plain. The Archduke's artillery was scarcely distinguishable from the noisy skies, as it poured its volleys from a hundred pieces of cannon on the long lines which marched towards the shore. Two hundred thousand Germans were drawn up in battle array to receive them as they defiled into the plain of Vienna, where they had already immortalised the names of the villages of Essling and Aspern. A little way up the stream lay the village and height of Wagram; and here the great contest was to be decided. The inhabitants of Vienna climbed to their house roofs and the tops of towers, and, stretched out before them, perfectly visible in all their movements, were four hundred thousand men trained and disciplined, and now placed foot to foot for the purpose of putting each other to death. The Emperor of Germany had placed himself on one of the hills on the other side; and we may easily fancy the feelings of the Viennese and of their ruler when the first cannonade declared that the deciding battle was begun. The cavalry was launched forth in reiterated advances against the Austrian centre; the artillery poured upon it at the same time; the attention of the wings was occupied by furious assaults, and by mid-day the centre was pierced, the wings enveloped, and Wagram was added to the crowded list of Napoleon's victories. The Viennese saw their defenders slain from end to end of the extensive plain, and twenty villages, which had formed the great charm of the prospect from the walls, devoured by the flames. Francis had seen the destruction of his hopes, and ridden rapidly away.

A humiliating peace was the immediate result of this overwhelming blow; but its consequences were more fatal to the victor than the vanquished, for in the intoxication of that final triumph over the oldest of European powers, he resolved to unite himself to the glories of antiquity by marrying one of the daughters of the house of Hapsburg. The French people had thrown off their reverence for the glories of antiquity, in which their order had no share; and were revolted as politicians and as men by the ill-starred ambition that carried their chief among the royalties for his bride. They saw Josephine day by day before them, gentle and captivating in all her ways, and recognised in her a child of the middle class like their own wives and daughters; a type and guarantee of the new order of things. A crowned citizen was the symbol of the great revolutionary principle which displaced legitimacy to make way for merit. The French were proud of the plebeian origin of their Emperor and Empress, as other people are proud of the mythic pedigrees of their kings and queens. A man of the people was a far higher individual, in their eyes, than a prince born in the purple; and for the sake of his father, an humble advocate, and his mother, a shopkeeper's daughter, and his uncle, a simple priest, they forgave him many things which they would not have pardoned in a descendant of their ancient monarchs. What *he* did appeared their own work. *They* conquered at Marengo, and Austerlitz, and Jena, and Wagram, because their equal had done so. And all the tender feelings of husbands, and all the sympathies of wives, were excited to the utmost when the generous and loving Josephine sacrificed her happiness to the

Emperor, as she had sacrificed her riches and influence to the young Lieutenant of Artillery, and accepted a divorce, to make room for a daughter of the Cæsars. Austria gave her princess with a shudder of humiliation and regret, and France received her with a sigh of pity for her predecessor, when, on the 30th March, 1810, the uncle of the Emperor—now created Cardinal—pronounced the nuptial benediction on the married pair, and Maria Louisa became the wife of Napoleon Buonaparte.

CHAPTER XX.

THE EMPIRE—FROM THE AUSTRIAN MARRIAGE, A. D. 1810, TO THE RESTORATION, A. D. 1814.

If Napoleon, as was said at that time, in divorcing Josephine, divorced France also, he did not succeed in quieting the fears of Europe by his Imperial marriage. England persisted in her obstinacy, "insular and brutal," as the *Moniteur* called it, and only added to the bitterness of her satires and caricatures, and sang "Rule, Britannia" louder than ever. Disagreeable news came by every post to the Tuileries from Spain, and secret reports brought information of the discontent of the German States. The letters and embassies of congratulation the Emperor received on the birth of his son—whom he created King of Rome—on the 20th of March, 1811, did not blind him to the real state of feeling. It seemed, indeed, a confirmation of his power, and an establishment of his dynasty. But that was precisely what his allies did not want, and his enemies would not acknowledge. Russia began to be uneasy at the continued prospect of being shut out from commerce and aggrandisement. The self-willed despot in France would neither let her trade with England nor enrich herself with the spoils of Turkey. She could not lie idle, with neither the sword nor the yard measure in her hand—at all events, without the taxes upon imports in her exchequer; and in 1812 she opened her harbours to British manufactures, and persuaded Sweden to join in breaking the imperial decrees. To trade with England was to fight with Napoleon; and Russia prepared for the combat by raising soldiers against the one and getting subsidies from the other. The conduct of Sweden was more unaccountable; for one of the generals of the Empire had been adopted into the royal family, and was acknowledged heir-apparent and regent of the kingdom. This was Bernadotte—a true Frenchman in his genius and courage; but the vulgar insolence of the Emperor's manners had offended his pride—his contemptuous commands offended his patriotic feeling towards the new country which had placed its crown on his head—and he threw his weight into the scale, not against France, which he still loved with filial affection, but against Napoleon, whom he considered its tyrant and oppressor.

Muttering denunciations against the ingratitude of his subordinate officer, the great soldier set out on his campaign against the north. Six hundred thousand men were rapidly converging towards the Niemen; two hundred thousand were left to support the intrusive king in Spain; three hundred thousand were scattered over the different fortresses at home and abroad; three hundred thousand mercenaries were held at his orders by various powers; and, with a military establishment of fourteen hundred thousand men, he left Paris on the 9th of May 1812, and made his first halt at Dresden. The only kings Louis the Fourteenth ever saw as his dependants were the mean-spirited James of England, whom he fed with scraps from his table, and his young grandson, the King of Spain, whom he treated like a child. More mean-spirited than James, and more childish in their submission than Philip of Bourbon, was the mob of emperors and kings who now paid court to Napoleon in the capital of Saxony. Princes, dukes, arch-chancellors, and other high-sounding potentates, were delighted if they succeeded in crouching and bribing their way to the antechamber. Crowned heads jostled each other in the hall of audience, and laughed at the jokes or trembled at the bursts of passion of the rude and unchanged student of Brienne and barrack-room lieutenant. There were the Emperor of Austria, the Kings of Prussia, Saxony, Bavaria, Würtemburg, Westphalia, Naples, and Spain—and Eugene, the son of Josephine, Viceroy of Italy. Madame Tussaud's waxworks in London, where all the notorieties of the world were crowded in one room, are the only parallel to this assemblage; and those waxen images are as capable of independent thought or action as their prototypes were in the presence of the man who had marched through the civilised world at the double-quick step, and was now about to trample out the pride of Russia as he had trampled out the liberties of Europe. This was the last time he held a levee of kings, and was the solitary glimpse of the great scheme he once entertained of establishing an Empire of the West, where the kingdoms should be ruled by nominated kings, and all be responsible to the central authority. Their majesties, on this occasion, were humiliated while they staid, and embittered when they went away. There was not one of them whose self-respect and dignity had not been wounded by insult, or whose people had not been ruined by exactions. There might be festive toasts drunk at their stately dinners of "Success to the imperial arms," but in their secret hearts they loved and reverenced the Emperor Alexander, who resisted the plebeian tyranny by which they were all oppressed.

The advance was as wonderful as the preparations for it had been. Napoleon crossed the Niemen in the end of June, and felt the magnitude of the risk when he trod on Russian ground. The Russians, we may almost say, were fortunately in that state of the progress of nations when the peasantry were mere machines, and the upper class undisputed lords. There was brute force in those countless multitudes, and intellectual power to guide it. The land was everywhere laid waste, and the armies retired behind the desert they had made. Barclay de Tolly, the commander-in-chief, had the magnanimity, like Fabius of old, to allow himself to be considered too cautious, and would not risk a battle. But the impatience of his countrymen at last prevailed: a new commander was appointed, and Napoleon was filled with delight. To tempt them more surely to a combat, he besieged the town of Smolensk, garrisoned by thirty thousand men, and protected by a hundred thousand outside the walls. The slaughter of his forces was prodigious, and the gain very slight; for, on entering the town, it was found to be evacuated both by garrison and inhabitants. In the deserted streets of the burning town, the conqueror considered his position. Before him were the sterile levels which led to Moscow—the natives hostile—the enemy hovering round his march, and the winter not far off. But to return would have been nearly as difficult, considered as a march, and more unfortunate as a political move. He gave orders for the advance, and the fate of his great army was sealed.

After struggles at every river, the Russians ventured on a great battle at last at Borodino, on the Moskowa. They displayed their usual stolid gallantry, and received their usual reward: they were defeated, but with such loss to the victors that the practical advantage was on their side. The field of Borodino was covered with more corpses, and retained with greater difficulty, than the snow-covered ground at Eylau. But the invaders moved on, and on the 14th of September the gilded roofs of Moscow, and the imposing masses of the Kremlin, were seen from the heights of Mount Salutation above the town. The army hurried gaily down; but the streets they entered were deserted, the public buildings were stripped carefully of ornaments and archives—there was no official left to ask for terms; it was a city of the dead. There was no cheering among the troops when they perceived the solitude through which they marched, and gloomy forebodings fell upon the whole force. These were justified to their worst extent ere many hours elapsed. Lurking in the lanes and alleys, the convicts and criminals, who had been let out of prison when the town was deserted, set fire to some of the houses. The French saw the conflagration spread, and trusted it would die out when it came to the open spaces where the buildings ceased. But there were other performers in this extraordinary work besides the sweepings of the jails. Whenever the flames expired in one quarter, they broke out in another. Raging, smoking, and surging on their way, they constantly turned their fiery tongues towards the Kremlin, where Napoleon had fixed his headquarters. If the wind changed, the fire sprang up in the same direction, and always pointed to the citadel. Napoleon left the town for a while, but still the conflagration went on. Alexander disdained to answer the letters in which the invader proposed an honourable peace. Cold winds began to sweep over the ruined and unsheltered plains; and France was fifteen hundred miles off, and a desert swarming with enemies lay between. He left the ashes of Moscow on the 19th of October, and the greatest tragedy of modern times, perhaps of all history, began.

In one unbroken chain of disasters and disappointments the army continued its retreat. Followed, met, surrounded by hordes of Kossacks of the Don, and nameless children of the farthest deserts of Asia—intercepted by the regular army, and cut off from supplies by the devastation of all the fields and the desertion of the villages—the French left many dead at every mile of their march; for, in addition to all these calamities inflicted on them by war, the elements let loose their fury on the straggling host. They were frozen to death as they walked; if they rested, they never rose again. They were footsore, hungry, and diseased; but neither the sky nor Kutusoff, the Russian pursuer, softened at their griefs. Still poured down the unpitying hail, and still rained on them the unpitying cannon. They were at last a mere herd of fugitives; order was at an end; and Napoleon, perceiving that his functions as general of the expedition were over, resolved to use his energies as Emperor to retrieve the glory of France. He left the wretched remains of his army at Smorgoni on the 5th of December, stopped at Warsaw on the 10th, and on the 18th, in a dull, dark night, when nobody expected his appearance, drove through the silent streets of Paris, and reached the Tuileries at one o'clock.

Half a million of men, in the flower of their youth, had died in these mad six months. There were, therefore, many thousand cottages in France, and Italy, and the confederated states, which were darkened by the shadow of Moscow. The survivors, one by one, arrived to give a livelier image of the sorrows they had endured, by the sight of their emaciated bodies and frostbitten limbs. Discontent spread among the people when the extent of the calamity became known ; the Emperor's name was hated in many quarters, and couriers upon couriers hurried into that busy room in the palace where he sat at the plain wooden table which served him for a desk, and told him Austria had deserted the alliance, "the Prussians have joined the enemy—we are driven back from the Vistula—from the Oder ;" and at last, "we have been pursued as far as Berlin," and "the foe is in full march towards France."

It was fortunate, perhaps, for Napoleon that there was danger as well as sorrow to excite the people. The thought of France being invaded had never entered any one's mind since the alarm of 1793. The military enthusiasm of the nation prevailed over the grief of individuals, and by the end of April 1813, three hundred thousand soldiers were on their way to the Rhine. The Emperor was fully awake to the perils of his situation. He resolved to put his house in order before he joined the army, and entered into negotiations with a prisoner whom he had seized some years before, and tried to coerce into obedience to his will. This was the venerable Pius the Seventh, the Pope of Rome. After keeping him at Savona for some time he brought him to Fontainebleau, and now forced or deluded the old man into a Concordat which allowed him, indeed, to execute the spiritual offices of the chief pontiff, but restored him the domains of the Church shorn of their independent rights. He was to be Pope of Christendom, but no longer sovereign of an earthly state.

Having thus got quit of a rival potentate in his kingdom of Italy, he hurried to the frontier. Two brilliant but ineffective battles at Lutzen and Bautzen (May 20) served only to encourage the united Russians and Prussians, by showing that they could resist him in fair fight. They were not unwilling, however, to listen to his overtures for peace. But their demands were still too high ; they required a restoration of his conquests beyond the Rhine, and the withdrawal of all his forces into his own country. The report which arrived at this time of Wellington's great victory at Vittoria, which overthrew the throne of Joseph, strengthened their position ; but Napoleon was moved by the same event to a different line of conduct. If there had been a victory in Spain, in addition to those he claimed in Saxony, it might have been possible to concede their claims. But the French nation, he thought, would not ratify a peace concluded on the news of a defeat. He rejected all accommodation ; and Austria, which had acted as mediator, declared war.

Russia, Austria, and Prussia, seemed great odds against the fugitive from Moscow ; and the time had passed away when the soldiers of the republic hurried to his standards, and conquered Italy in a fortnight and Austria in a month. All the young blood of France was poured out on foreign fields. There were no husbandmen at home to hold the plough—no merchants to push their trade. The land was half desolate, and the population perceptibly decreased. Yet against all, the proud heart of the "child of victory" bore up ; the defection of the Bavarians who had served for many years in his armies, and now turned their arms against their companions, did not change his purpose. He retreated to Leipsic, resolved to set all upon the hazard of one cast, for he felt certain that in that position he could draw all his opponents into a decisive battle. It was the greatest battle of which any record is kept. The huddled millions of Xerxes, or any Indian invader, present nothing to the mind but confusion and disorder. But at Leipsic the numbers of those ancient and barbaric hosts were nearly equalled, and all the skill of modern warfare, and the destructiveness of modern weapons were brought into play. There were seven hundred thousand combatants on this great occasion, and a thousand cannon. Indecisive on the 16th October, it was renewed, after a feeble attempt at an armistice, on the 18th ; and the

French sustained, for the first time with Napoleon in command, a palpable and undeniable defeat. The Saxons, a body of thirty thousand men, went over to the enemy in the middle of the engagement, and disordered his plans: his ammunition also began to fail; fifty thousand Frenchmen were killed in the two days' battle, and twenty-five thousand prisoners were taken in the retreat. The charm of invincibility was broken, and the allied kings now pressed forward with more emulation to destroy the man they feared, than they had formerly displayed to court and flatter him. Distresses of all kinds gathered around him thick and fast. Every day brought him the news of some prince turning against him; and at last it was reported that the king of Naples, his brother-in-law and most devoted of his adherents, had left the camp, and the cup of bitterness was full. The time had come when the hunters were round their prey. Wellington was within a few marches of Bayonne, flushed with a score of victories over the Marshals of France; Holland was in rebellion; Italy powerless; Hanover restored to her elector; Naples on the eve of treachery; Westphalia expunged from the map; and Poland blotted out as a nation. A million soldiers formed a wall of steel round his narrowed dominions, and England over the sea continued pouring forth her inexhaustible treasure, and guarding every outlet with her fleets. A bold spirit might have been pardoned for quailing before such a combination. The love of glory in preference to repose had at last been expelled by suffering from the hearts of the French people: "Give us peace," they cried to the Emperor as he galloped past upon the street; "Give us peace—peace on any terms," exclaimed the Legislative Body, "and guarantee to us for the future the liberties you have destroyed." Napoleon did not reply to the people, and dismissed the Legislative Body in a rage. He was the sole representative of the nation, he said, and he would defend its honour to the last. He sent off Ferdinand the Seventh to Spain, in hopes of exciting a civil war; he also released the Pope, in hopes of conciliating the Catholic party; and then mounting his horse, and wearing the little cocked hat and grey greatcoat, he began the most wonderful, the most scientific, and the most varied of all his campaigns. His old genius and youthful activity came back again. The other commanders seemed paralysed by the fact of hostile armies being on the French territory. They could not bear up against the degradation of their country, where even a victory would lose half its glory by being gained on an invaded soil. But Napoleon made head against all. Galloping great distances by night, through miserable roads and in the midst of storms of rain and snow, he seemed to be present everywhere. With a fifth part of the forces of his enemies he threw them into confusion, and nearly into despair. At one time they meditated a retreat, so rapid were his blows and so unexpected his cross marches from one line of their advance to the other. Negotiations were opened for peace, but with sincerity on neither part. The Bourbon party began to raise its head, feeble and disunited, but supported by the feeling of the Allies, who allowed the Count of Artois, and his sons the dukes of Angoûleme and Berri, to enter France.

There was no further hesitation on Napoleon's side. "All or nothing" was his motto, when he found the legitimate claimant supported by the very powers which pretended to be treating for peace. A series of manœuvres recommenced, which military historians dwell upon with delight; but science and manœuvring were of no avail against an innumerable array in front and disaffection behind. Paris was in agitation. The threat of pillage had terrified the hearts of the shopkeepers, and the Allies steadily pushed onward to the metropolis. The feelings of the nation had become estranged. And although the Emperor had still a hundred thousand soldiers holding fortified places in the heart of Europe, he would not relax his grasp even upon the distant Dantzic or commercial Hamburg, to increase his present force. On the 30th of March the whole confederated army, the dwellers in all the nations of Europe, caught sight of the capital of the world. They filled the vast plain from the Marne and

Charenton to the Seine and St. Ouen, and sent their flying parties to the outskirts of the town. The young men of the Polytechnic School, and the soldiers of the garrison, were eager to fight, and defended the suburbs with the utmost courage ; but Paris could not trust to the results of a battle under its walls. Joseph, the commandant of the city, retired ; Maria Louisa and the King of Rome had been sent away to Blois ; and the great city lay at the mercy of the enemy. Marmont surrendered on guarantees of protection to life and property, and the sovereigns at the head of their troops defiled along the Boulevards on the following day. At that very hour Napoleon arrived in hot haste from Troyes, at Juvisy, a small hamlet between Paris and Fontainebleau. If he had been twelve hours earlier, who can say what effect his presence might have produced ? Now, indeed, all was over. He got certain intelligence of what had occurred, and in deep thought rode back to Fontainebleau.

Did he hear at that time that the entry of the Allies was a triumph and ovation from end to end of the fickle and thoughtless capital of France ? The Emperors and Kings were received as conquerors and deliverers. The rough thousands from unheard-of lands, the Cossacks and Bashkirs, were run after as curiosities ; the bronzed men of Austria and Prussia were welcomed as victors whom it was an honour to receive. Never were operas so crowded, or meetings so enthusiastic, as those where the Calmuck countenances of hideous dwellers of the Ukraine looked up towards the beauties and celebrities of Paris from the pit, and the kings and generals glittered with gold and jewellery in the boxes. Louder and more brilliant demonstrations even than these celebrated the entrance of the Count of Artois in state, to take possession of the vacant throne in the name of his brother Louis the Eighteenth. Long lines of enraptured spectators received the white cockade of the Bourbons with tumultuous applause. The tricolor—dyed in so many victories, waved from so many captured capitals—disappeared. Napoleon in the mean time had resigned the crown; and in the courtyard of Fontainebleau had bidden adieu to his Old Guard, and kissed the glorious colours he was never to see again; and was now taking his way in silence and neglect towards the island of Elba, which the wisdom of his enemies had appropriated for his residence. In clear weather he could almost see the shores of Italy, of which he had been king; and in a few hours could hear from France, of which he had been absolute lord; and there, in solitary rides over his lilliputian domain, or engaged in reviewing the four or five hundred soldiers of Jena and Austerlitz who had been allowed to follow him as a guard of honour, he meditated great things for the future, and left his good citizens of Paris to admire the panorama which kept revolving its variegated canvass before their eyes.

When the main figure of the spectacle made its appearance, the Parisians were somewhat disappointed when they saw in the person of their legitimate king an old man of prodigious obesity, with heavy brooding features and perpetual gout. Sitting by his side, however, was another resuscitation of the past, which awoke more painful feelings still. It was the Duchess of Angoûleme, the unfortunate daughter of Louis the Sixteenth, and so long a prisoner in the Temple. She now advanced with pale and withered countenance along the same road, covered with arches of triumph, leading to the Tuileries, over which her mother had been so pitilessly dragged to the scaffold. The representatives of the ancient line had disappeared for more than twenty years, and so many wonderful incidents had occurred, so many changes in position and opinion, that their very existence had vanished from men's memories. But now old names began to be heard again which had had a great sound before the Revolution, the possessors of which had learned nothing—and forgotten nothing—during their exile. They were only bent on making up, by insolence and superiority, for their humble position and scanty fare in Leicester Square and other haunts of expatriated men. More respectable while submitting to their fate, and teaching languages or dancing to the citizens of London or Vienna, than when they tried to exert their ancient privileges over a people who had ceased to remember the old order of affairs, they quickly converted the compassion their protectors had felt for their sufferings into dislike. They reclaimed estates which had passed through great numbers of hands since they were confiscated in 1793. Houses had been built upon their lands; canals dug between their villages; rents had been paid to the intrusive proprietors, and Monsieur le Marquis would not be satisfied without a full and free restoration of all he had been defrauded of so long. And Louis the Eighteenth was scarcely in a position to resist his claims, for he himself was playing, on a still greater scale, the same game. He reclaimed all the rights, powers, and supremacies of the royal crown; assured the people, while he was guarded to church by Russian and Austrian bayonets, that he reigned by divine right; and even in the bestowal of the Charter, affected the airs of a man conferring a benefit out of his free grace and favour, and took no notice of the toils and struggles by which the people had won the right to be more freely governed than before.

THE CHARTER AND THE HUNDRED DAYS, A. D. 1814–1815.

The Charter, however displeasingly granted, was a document of inestimable value: it consecrated by legal sanctions all the true victories of the Revolution, and gave a point of departure for the gaining of more. It is only surprising how a man of the sagacity of Louis the Eighteenth could believe for a moment in the coexistence of the feudal feelings of his personal supporters and the clauses of so liberal a constitution. The liberality of the constitution was in fact its weakness. The standard of good government was raised too high, and the oldest established monarchy could not hope to reach it. A nation still heaving with so great a storm, with people embittered by the animosity of five-and-twenty years, with so many injuries to avenge on both sides, and such a total prostration of dignity and honour as the rapid alternation of success and defeat had produced, found it impossible to fulfil the conditions of the compact it had made between the past and present. It could not satisfy the disinherited seigneur, nor dispossess the roturier of his lately purchased estate. "Seigneur," indeed, and "Roturier," had lost their signification, but not their recollections. The seigneur remembered his rights and immunities—his donjon keep and gilded chair at court ; the roturier, within a month of the publication of the Charter, began to remember the little man in the grey riding-coat who had kept those harpies so gallantly from the land, and scowled with ill-concealed hatred as he saw the tents of the Tartars and Croats pitched all down the beautiful avenues of the Champs Elysées, and met long trains of priests and bishops going to return thanks to God for the humiliation of their country. Priests and bishops were busy in all directions. Over every deathbed hung a priest denouncing endless woes unless the sufferer restored his secularised lands to the Church, or his government-guaranteed lands to their legitimate owners the refugees. The Charter, indeed, became a dead letter, from the incapacity of the whole people to understand what liberty was. It guaranteed, 1st, Equality before the law ; 2d, Admission to all employments ; 3d, Unity of administration ; 4th, Representative government ; 5th, Taxation only by the votes of the representatives ; 6th, Individual liberty ; 7th, Liberty of worship ; and 8th, Liberty of the press. To this Charter all the officials of the court and dignitaries of the kingdom were duly sworn ; but it was observed that the Most Christian King did not swear to it himself. It was his gift to a grateful and obedient nation, and he would observe it only so long as its conduct deserved the boon. Its conduct became displeasing very soon. It read the clause about employments being open to all ; and it saw every position in the law, the church, and the army, customs, excise, and post-office, filled by retainers of the old school. It read of individual liberty, yet there was no protection against false arrest, and imprisonment of undefined duration before trial. Liberty of worship became a mockery under the privileges arrogated to themselves by the refugee priests; and liberty of the press was represented by a censor who prohibited all publications which had not received his permission to appear.

All this time there was an immense army of the Allies to be maintained at France's cost, and an enormous war-contribution to indemnify the invaders against the expenses of their campaign. It was such a new thing for the French to pay the expenses of a war, that they were doubly disgusted to be forced to remunerate the destroyers of their fields and devastators of their towns. The taxes from ordinary sources were dried up; there was little commerce, and agriculture had come to a stand-still from the uncertainty of political events. The returned exiles had no money, and the whole burden fell on the comparatively opulent middle class, who had saved some hard coin, and were now forced to bring it out from their depositories under the thatch or in the dry well of the orchard, and pour it into commissioners' hands for the enrichment of Prussians and Muscovites. Unhappy Frenchmen! who used to hear the hundred cannon of the Invalides announcing the seizure of another kingdom or the gain of another victory—they had never formed an idea before of the meaning conveyed by the words capitulation or conquest. And now in their distress they had nobody to turn to in whom they could trust. The generals of Napoleon had gone over to the Bourbons; his secretaries and councillors exerted all their ingenuity in blackening his name. Talleyrand, the incarnation of selfishness and falsehood, who had begun in the rage of the Revolution by throwing off his dignity of bishop and his belief in anything,—who had wormed his way to power under every form of government—bloodthirsty with Robespierre, constitutional with the Directory, patriotic with Napoleon, and witty, pleasant, heartless, and deceitful with them all,—this man of much cunning and no virtue was raised not less by his supple talents than his family rank to be chief adviser of the king. It was only natural that a Bourbon should take counsel from a Talleyrand-Perigord—the loftiest of kings and the first of nobles. And the first of nobles wrote proclamations against Napoleon, who had used him as an instrument and despised him as a man, in which he attributed all the ills of the country to his baneful influence, and sneered at his countrymen for having submitted to an adventurer "who was not even a Frenchman." Deserted thus by their natural leaders, the military chiefs following the example of Berthier and Soult in slavish adulation of the returned king,—Seguier and the other eminent civilians aiding the reactionists in every infraction of the spirit of the Charter, the press muffled and the law courts prejudiced,—the people of Paris were reduced to the gay and bitter verses of Beranger, and laughed at the caricatures he gave them of the reinstated marquises as loudly as they dared. Very slight were their hopes of amelioration from the Congress which commenced its sittings at Vienna. There, scissors in hand, sat the delegates of the allied sovereigns, ready to clip off bits of territory, and round the national maps to their own satisfaction. Talleyrand was there using his bad eloquence in defence of every wrong. England and Russia, who recommended milder councils, were outvoted ; and Louis heard, well pleased, from day to day, that the monarchical spirit was greatly encouraged at this court of kings and renegades, and put more trust in the divine right by which he governed than ever.

Meanwhile a hundred and thirty thousand soldiers had returned to France ; two hundred thousand more were scattered through the villages and farms. They found their fields neglected and their cottages in disrepair, but the object of their indignation was changed. They no longer blamed the conscription for the want they saw around them, but the foreigner who had trod their soil, and the wretched poltroons who, in their absence beyond the Rhine, had allowed the tricolor to be trampled in the dust. "If we had been there," they said—"if the Little Corporal had had the men of Marengo and Eylau at his side, this would not have happened." And everywhere, shortly after this, there were whispers about great things that would occur when the violet appeared in spring. Ladies wore violets in their bonnets, and little sketches were circulated, in which the figure of a violet was so disposed that the interval between the leaves formed the well-known countenance of the Emperor, with his plain grey riding-coat and little cocked hat. He was talked of as Corporal Violet ; and the tedious winter wore away.

The insolence of the returned emigrants increased : the Duke of Berri gave a decoration from his own breast to a gallant major of his regiment, who had earned it by many years' service of his country. A refugee marquis saw the act, hurried up, and expostulated with the duke, demanding the decoration for himself as more deserving than a plebeian officer who had fought under the usurper. The argument of nobility was irresistible to a Bourbon prince : he took the ribbon away from the major, and gave it to the seigneur. All spirit, however, was not defunct in the regiment : the colonel rode up and accused the prince of injustice ; high words ensued, and at last the colonel said, "If you had offered such an insult to me, I would have put you to death." The end of the story is, that the major lost the ribbon, and the colonel was broke. But the electric chain was touched ; the anecdote spread through the army,—and the spring was coming near, and the violet just ready to bud. All this time the Charter lay nearly dormant ; the Congress sat at Vienna, and consulted wisely all day and danced indefatigably all night. Paris was in uneasy expectation of something, it knew not what ; and the son of St. Louis and descendant of Henry the Fourth could not ride upon a horse, and astonished the spectators of his dinners with the voracity of his appetite and the size of his royal limbs. Citizen, villager, soldier, civilian, everybody in France felt, by a kind of instinct, that something was in the wind—everybody except the returned emigrants, the fashionable milliners, and the ministers and statesmen of the king. Renegade marshal and reinstated refugee were equally satisfied that their tenure of power was secure ; and though at times a glimpe of the unreality of his position broke upon the sagacious and gastronomic Louis the Eighteenth, his apprehensions were treated as visionary; and yet the violet was just about to appear.

It did not seem that the bursting forth of that pretty but common flower excited much attention in Elba. The island was guarded by English cruisers, and commissioners from various nations were resident to watch that the newly-appointed monarch of the Elbese territories did not leave his domains. There appeared no wish on the part of that somewhat petty potentate to withdraw his paternal care from the empire, across which he could ride in a couple of hours; and he was busy making roads, building bridges, and calculating the expense of a better pier to his imperial city of Porto Ferrajo. His only relaxations were scientific discussions with his friends, and quiet evening-parties at the house of his sister Pauline.

It chanced, on the 26th February 1815, that the ball at Pauline's was deprived of much of its usual brilliancy. The captain of the English cruiser had taken his ship for a few days to Leghorn; the commissioners of the allied powers were absent on leave or otherwise engaged; and at ten o'clock at night a small cannon discharged on the rampart did not interfere with the enjoyment of the supper that followed the dance. The report, however, had great effect in other quarters. Six hundred men of the Old Guard marched silently down to the harbour; there they were joined by four hundred Poles and Corsicans; and the whole force embarked in a brig called "The Inconstant." Just before the sails were hoisted, the men caught sight of the grey riding-coat and cocked hat as the wearer stepped upon the deck. Not a word was said; the anchor was raised, no obstruction was offered; the little vessel left the lights of the town behind it—and the Violet was in full flower. Three tedious days were passed upon the voyage; English frigates were swarming everywhere, and some one or two passed in sight of the Inconstant. At length French soil was seen, and the invading army landed in the Gulf of Juan, near the town of Cannes. The few inhabitants of that district were too remote from public affairs, and too ignorant, to be much moved by the strange apparition of a thousand men disembarking from a brig from some unknown region beyond the sea. It was only on the 8th of March that the Parisians read in the *Moniteur* that Napoleon was in France. By this time he was in Lyons at the head of a considerable army. All the forces hitherto sent to oppose him had gone over at sight of the tricolor. At Grenoble he had been met by a regiment of seven hundred men, who prepared to resist his advance. He walked slowly forward to the front line, and said, "My friends, if there is one among you who wishes to kill his emperor—his general—he has it in his power!" He unbuttoned the little grey coat to receive the ball, and shouts arose of "Vive l'Empereur!" while he continued his march with an addition of seven hundred men. The same enthusiasm arose among the soldiers wherever he appeared—the ranks rushed into each other's arms, and the officers shook hands. Ney, "the bravest of the brave," was sent to arrest the audacious madman, and promised largely before he took leave of the king; but when he came within sight of his ancient chief—when he saw the colours he had fought under, and heard the shouts of the men he had so often led to battle—above all, when he saw the sorrowful but benignant countenance of his friend and master—all his old love and reverence returned: he put his sword into its sheath, and was again the Ney of former days—the sword of France and follower of Napoleon. There was no longer either the power or the will to resist. The exiled nobility rushed off in headlong panic to resume the scissors and dancing-kit in their ancient haunts; the shopkeepers looked dubiously on at the flight of their new opponents, and the approach of their old oppressors; the king himself, on the 20th of March, left the Tuileries at one o'clock in the morning for the Flemish frontier, and three hours afterwards, in the early glimmer of a spring dawn, Napoleon entered the palace of Fontainebleau, from which he had taken his departure exactly eleven months before.

The Congress was still pursuing its labours at Vienna;

discussions were going on about the boundaries and populations of newly constituted states, when, on the 25th of March, the Duke of Wellington entered the council-chamber, and informed the plenipotentiaries that their work was all to do over again, for the Emperor was in Paris, and the grand army as numerous and enthusiastic as ever. The anger caused by this unexpected intelligence was perhaps embittered by the excessively ludicrous position in which it placed the Allies. They had been friendly enough with each other while employed in the parcelling out of Europe, but now that the struggle was to be renewed, mutual distrust took the place of previous confidence. Prussia and Russia were doubtful of the continued aid of Austria in the humiliation of the Emperor's son-in-law; Austria was suspicious of the effect a great victory won by Napoleon might have upon the wavering faith and selfish ambition of his German rival; England alone, of all the powers, felt no doubt or hesitation. She knew she would have to fight and to pay—to fight her own battle under her own Wellington, and pay her hard-earned treasures for the enrolment, equipment, and maintenance of all the whiskered pandours and the fierce hussars whom the other empires and kingdoms would pour across the Rhine. War resumed its sway over men's hearts and hopes. Napoleon was declared a pariah, and beyond the protection of the law. Thousands of soldiers were gathered into camps, and there was the sound of marching battalions all over the plains and mountains from the Niemen to the Seine. Louis the Eighteenth resided in the mean time in Ghent, where he was surrounded by a small court of hopeful politicians, who told him all would be well; and tried to forget Versailles and the Louvre, by weekly parcels of oysters and other edibles from England.

On the evening of the 20th of March the streets of Paris were still in commotion. The king had eloped the night before, and the details of Napoleon's advance were confused and contradictory. Suddenly lights were seen in rapid progress along the bridge of Louis the Sixteenth, now called the Pont de la Concorde; horses' feet were heard in great numbers;

and at a furious pace a carriage dashed on with the blinds shut, and enclosed by lines of cavalry, with swords drawn, at full gallop by its side. It stopped at the first wicket into the Tuileries gardens, and Napoleon was lifted out and triumphantly carried into the palace. Paris was quiet from that hour. It knew that the arbitrament was taken out of its hands, and all men stood in silent expectation of what was about to come. In the little study, still shown to the visitors, Napoleon worked as never man worked before. He re-established the finances ; reinstated the office-holders dispossessed by the late authority ; dismisssed the Swiss Guard and the "House of the King ;" ratified the sales of national domains which the emigrants disputed ; dissolved the Chamber of Peers and Deputies ; and summoned a great meeting of the electoral colleges, for the 1st of May, to aid in the revision of the constitution and its adaptation to the wants and wishes of the people. The conqueror was now a legislator : the despot was now a reformer. The acceptance of the charter of Louis the Eighteenth had shown him that the time for irresponsible authority had passed away, unless it could be disguised in legal forms ; and he professed his adhesion to the Charter, with a firm resolution at the same time to adapt it to his purposes when the time of his revived power should come.

Meantime he laboured night and day. Everything passed through his hands ; accounts, diplomacy, law, and the organisation of his forces. These came rapidly in. His old companions-in-arms took the command. Once more the tricolor waved from spire and tower ; and lying on the floor with great maps spread before him, the Emperor designed the approaching campaign by means of differently coloured pins —one colour for Austrians, one for English, and so on for all the nations. Red-headed pins were very thick in Belgium, for Wellington had gone over to Brussels, and was at the head of an army of seventy thousand men, of whom thirty-four thousand were British. Green-headed pins were also plentiful in that quarter, for Blucher with a hundred and forty thousand Prussians was established on the Sambre. All the farther portions of the map were dotted over with the contingents of Russia, Bavaria, Hungary, Italy—of all the peoples who could be roused by patriotic feeling or British gold. Thirty-six millions were lent by this country to the various powers ; our annual expenditure was raised to a hundred and twenty-six millions ; our ships were sent forth again to guard the sea, and the ring grew narrower and narrower every hour which encircled the French soil. Nine hundred and fifty thousand men were summoned under arms by the Congress of Vienna, and they obeyed the summons. Four hundred and ninety-six thousand two hundred men, on the other side, garrisoned their country, and kept watch round Napoleon ; and the great contest began. If he could succeed in preventing a junction between the Prussians and English ; if he could beat them in detail, and secure himself in possession of the Netherlands, he might be ready with an army, flushed with victory, to meet his other enemies before they approached the Rhine. But he did not prevent the junction, and did not beat the armies of the English and Prussians separately. We may therefore take it as an ascertained fact that he failed in the execution of both parts of his design—that he did not conquer the British soldiers, nor take Wellington by surprise.

On the 15th of June he advanced to Charleroi, and sent Ney on to occupy the English army while he attacked the Prussians. On the 16th the battle of Ligny was fought, where the French had the apparent triumph of remaining on the field of battle. Blucher had something better to do, and retired to keep open his communications with Wellington. On the same day the combat of Quatre Bras introduced the old antagonists of the Peninsula to each other once more ; and the same cheers were heard which had resounded at Vittoria and Salamanca. The French had a slight superiority in numbers, and an absolute monopoly of artillery and cavalry. We had not a horse or gun, and yet the British line resisted attacks of cuirassiers and volleys of cannon all day long. At last the Duke himself came up with a reinforcement ; and when, later in the evening, the guns and dragoons also came up, the enemy withdrew from the field, and must have looked forward with sad forebodings to the future chances of the campaign. On the 17th the chiefs collected their forces for the decisive struggle. Grouchy was despatched by Napoleon to hold the Prussians in check; and on the 18th the two greatest generals the world ever saw alive at the same time, met face to face, with the contending glories of a lifetime to come into collision, and with all the breath of Europe hushed to catch the first sound of the momentous result. This was at Waterloo. Wellington had seventy-two thousand seven hundred and twenty men under his orders. Napoleon had seventy-four thousand. Blucher with seventy thousand was expected to aid the English, and Grouchy with forty thousand to aid the French. The object of each of these subordinate generals was to prevent the advance of the other; and so to leave the battle to be fought between the champions in the field.

Napoleon was no longer the clear-eyed, firm-nerved commander of other days. A fate seemed upon him. He could neither avail himself of success, nor provide against misfortune, as in the times of Austerlitz and Friedland. With apathetic indifference, or blind obstinacy, he had refused assistance to Ney at Quatre Bras; with equal blindness he allowed a day to intervene between Ligny and his onslaught on the English: and Wellington had taken all his measures, had secured the best fighting-ground in Belgium, and was ready for any thing that might occur. It was a Sunday; and while all the church bells in England were calling the people to prayer, the cannonade commenced. Everybody was in expectation of a battle. It was known in England that Napoleon had crossed into the Netherlands, and that Wellington was ready to meet him. News was slow of coming, and people's hearts were sick with the expectation of the next mail. It chanced that, between the services on that eventful Sunday, a clergyman in Kent was walking in his garden. His gardener was an old soldier who had fought in Spain. He said, "There's a fight going on, sir, somewhere; for I remember when we were in the Peninsula we always knew when a cannonade was taking place, wherever it might be, by a crumbling of fresh mould." He took a spade and dug down a single foot, and along the smooth surface left by the steel an imperceptible trembling shook down little pellets of the soil. "That's it, sir," said the gardener; "they're at it sure enough."* Before the next Sunday came round, the news had spread "from end to end of all the sea-girt isle;" joy-cannon had sounded from all the castles in the land; and it was known that the greatest victory of modern times had crowned the British arms. A great price was paid for it in the deaths of many gallant men; but lamentation was lost in the general rejoicing. For many successive hours the imperturbable line of red-coats had stood the charges of the furious battalions which fought under the eye of the Emperor, and felt that the glory of France was intrusted to their keeping. The squadrons of horse, the discharges of artillery, and finally the advance of the Old Guard, had made no impression on the soldiers of England. And when the decisive moment came, and the distant guns of the Prussians proclaimed that Blucher was at hand, the great word was given, the inert masses which had remained immovable so long, rose up with a shout that reached the ears of Napoleon, and the irresistible bayonets poured on. Down in dreadful power swept the regulated torrent of horse and man; and the French, surprised and terrified, were huddled into broken heaps. The day was won. Napoleon turned his horse in the bitterness of despair, and silent, moody, and bewildered at the frightful scene, made his way to Paris before the intelligence of his disaster had arrived, and gave up the struggle as hopeless.

This, be it remembered, was a war of armies. The French population had never heartily rallied round the Emperor, or the event would have been very different. All the

* This curious anecdote was communicated to the author by the son of the clergyman, as a fact well proved at the time, and before intelligence of the battle had arrived.

nations of Europe could not have forced their way into a realm guarded by the courage and patriotism of thirty-five millions of Frenchmen. But there was now no object round which the courage and patriotism of France could gather. Doubting—fearing—divided—disinclined to the Bourbons, as representing the tyranny of the past—dreading and disliking Napoleon as representing the sufferings of the present, the people were everywhere quiescent and expectant. Again the hordes of strångers polluted the pure air of Paris with their presence as conquerors and avengers. Louis the Eighteenth came back with his hungry satellites and royal and imperial supporters. Napoleon surrendered himself prisoner to the English, and was carried to the dreary imprisonment of Saint Helena ; and it was not till Time, the beautifier, had hidden the harshnesses of his reign, and the bitterness and darker vices of his character, that romance and patriotism gathered round his story. At that fearful time the population only saw in him the cause of their degradation and distress. It was not till the memory of their losses and sacrifices was softened by his death in that distant isle, that the glories of his early victories and unequalled genius came back to their hearts. But in a gradually increasing volume the stream of his popularity flowed back to its ancient channels ; and when the generation which saw his defeat and suffered for his ambition had passed away, his fame became as dear to the French at large as it had been to his immediate followers ; and Waterloo was forgotten in the earlier blaze of his Marengo and Jena. Poetry and imagination had never produced a career equal to that of the student of Brienne, the son-in-law of the Cæsar and arbiter of the world. Dull Bourbons with their ancient descent, and wily Orleanses with their vulgar cunning, were unfavourably contrasted with the winner of so many battles, the conqueror of so many kingdoms ; and it was foreseen by sagacious observers that the power of his mere name would be irresistible if properly applied, so deep was its sway in the hearts and passions of the most imaginative and military nation in Europe.

A.D. 1815 TO A.D. 1824.—LOUIS THE EIGHTEENTH RESTORED CHARLES THE TENTH.

While Napoleon was sailing to his destination in the "Northumberland," and winning all hearts by his gracious manners and delightful conversation, the king came back to Paris. The feelings of the parties were more embittered than before. Royalist and Imperialist were scarcely restrained from personal violence, and Louis himself was forced to appeal to the Charter he had granted the year before as a defence against the outrageous loyalty of his friends. He was forced also to appeal to the declaration of his allies, many times repeated, that their war was with Napoleon, not with France; for hostile views were entertained by Prussians and other Germans, who wished to dismember the country and render it powerless, since they could not hope to keep it quiet. A more difficult position was never occupied by any king before. His adherents were resolved on undoing the whole work of the Revolution, and the nation, though repudiating the word, were equally resolved to retain the improvements it had produced. Exasperated monarchists in the south showed the spirit of their creed, and thought to curry favour with the government by the massacre of Marshal Brune and other supporters of the Empire. They were gratified with the faint disapprobation expressed by the government, and its exhortations to patience. Louis gratified them still farther by declining to interpose the royal pardon between Marshal Ney and the sentence of the Chamber of Peers, which condemned him to death. Wellington, the great and good, has been blamed for allowing the execution of so brave a soldier—having been a party to the capitulation of Paris, which contained a stipulation against any inquiry into previous acts; but he had no power over the proceedings of the highest criminal court in the realm, and still less to enforce mercy on the irritated mind of the unforgiving king.

The Chambers were more monarchical than the monarch

they tried to serve; and the ameliorations in law and justice which the last twenty-five years had produced, were looked on with evil eye as badges of slavery to a set of republican theorists and an imperial chief. The family of Buonaparte was banished for ever from the soil of France. The peers included in the same sentence all who had consented to the death of Louis the Sixteenth. Up to this time the perplexed king had endeavoured to conciliate the supporters of the Revolution by calling to his service the two basest characters it had produced. He had made Talleyrand his minister for foreign affairs, and Fouché, the spy and traitor of every cause he had espoused, his minister of police. But the Revolution and the Empire were equally scandalised by such representatives, and Louis gratified his own feelings and the prejudices of his partisans by giving the supreme direction of government to the Duke of Richelieu, a returned emigrant who had been in the Russian service twenty years, and had not acquired any violent love for liberty during his governorship of Odessa. He managed, however, to obtain from the allied powers a reduction of the war-contribution and of the period of the occupation of the country. France had now to pay only seven hundred millions of francs (£28,000,000), and maintain an army of a hundred and fifty thousand foreigners for five years instead of seven. While in this exceptional state, torn with party, labouring under exorbitant taxation, and guarded by garrisons of English, Russians, and Germans, in every town, the Chambers held their first session, and gave an opportunity for the display of hitherto unheard-of talent and eloquent political debate, but did nothing more. They were dissolved in 1816, and were summoned to meet under a new qualification of the electors, by which a contribution of twelve pounds a-year entitled to a vote. There was no material in the country at that time for the production, not merely of a parliament, but of a constituency. There were no constituted bodies in the State to set an example of local government. There were no corporations to gain strength by union, nor any independent clergy, nor magistracy, nor landed proprietors of hereditary wealth and influence, to act as defences between the two extremes into which society was divided. The interference of the State with the subject had been carried to such an extent that the subject could do nothing for himself. So many bonds existed between the simplest individual and the central power—there was such a system of passports and inspections, of permits and regulations, that the citizen forgot the traditions of individual independence. The law interfered with everything, and left no part of a man's life to his own direction. Under the specious name of a repeal of the law of primogeniture, a system of superintendence of a person's fortune had been introduced which was a complete denial of the rights of property. A father was prevented, not only from leaving his estate to his eldest son, but from distributing it according to the merits or the wants of his children. The former custom, which merely (as is still the case in England) provided that, in case of no will being made, the landed estate should go to the eldest son, giving at the same time ample power to the possessor to leave it as he thought proper by testamentary disposition, had been abrogated by the Revolution, and lands and houses and money were divided between a family, not according to the wishes of the parent, but in certain proportions fixed by law. This regulation, which was intended to introduce equality, produced, by the pounding down of large properties, a sort of macadamised road along which the car of despotism can most easily move.

A constitution cannot be created in an hour, and the curious spectacle was now presented of a king and a people anxious to settle the government on the sure foundation of mutual rights and reciprocal obligations, and unable to do so. France was a collection of individuals, and properly speaking was not a nation. Its nationality, however, revived when the foreign armies were withdrawn in 1818, and the sword was again in French hands. With this sword they were to do terrible things. With a court and nobility little altered from the times of Louis the Sixteenth, and a population madly zealous for the personal equality which the Revolution and even the Empire, had secured, every incident in Europe stirred up the prejudices of the opposing sides. The monarchs of the Alliance had generally promised free governments to their peoples while the struggle lasted, and now used all their arts to escape from the obligation, or to withdraw the concessions they had already made. Insurrections broke out in various lands : the royalty of France was anxious for their suppression, the population of France for their success. The Duke of Berri, second in succession to the crown, was assassinated in 1820, and the monarchic enthusiasts viewed the deed as a declaration against kings. Stringent laws were introduced, individual liberty was curtailed, and the liberty of the press withdrawn. A revolution at the same time broke out in Spain. Ferdinand, the basest of poltroons and cruelest of tyrants, had refused the reforms he had sworn to introduce. The constitution of 1812 (an imitation of the French constitution of 1791) was proclaimed. The example was followed by Naples, which had a similar king to complain of. The States of the Church threw off the hated yoke of the cross-keys and the three-crowned hat, and Benevento and Pontecorvo declared themselves republics. Piedmont was not left behind in its fight for freedom. A cry was even heard at the extreme east of Europe for a new life and a resuscitation of ancient glories. It came from Greece, which for centuries had been trampled down by the brutal and utterly irreclaimable Turks ; and, in fact an outcry for change and improvement arose from all the nations which had aided or even wished the fall of Napoleon. The countrymen of Miltiades were favourably regarded, or at least not forcibly repressed, by the classical potentates—who, besides, were not displeased at the commencement of the dismemberment of Turkey ; but the Neapolitans, Romans, and Piedmontese, had no dead and innocuous Demosthenes to plead their cause, and the armies of Austria were employed in extinguishing the hopes of freedom from Turin to Naples.

While the fever for constitutional government was raging

like an epidemic in all the Continental states, the island of St. Helena was visited by a great storm on the 5th of May, 1821. In the midst of the noisy blast and flashes of tropical lightning, Napoleon was lying almost insensible on his bed. Something in the tempest, or something in the lightning, recalled his wandering mind to the scenes of his former life. His eyes opened for the last time, as if to survey a battle-field, and muttering the words "Tête d'armée," he sank back on his pillow, and his wondrous career was closed. For six years he had complained of his fate with undignified lamentations, and tried to excite the sympathy of the world by exaggerating the miseries of his position. Quarrelling over trifles, stickling for punctilios, and avenging his misfortunes by insults and calumnies on the mere officials whose disagreeable duty it was to see to the safe custody of the prisoner who had so strangely escaped from Elba, he compensated for all his littleness, and all his faults of temper and disposition, by the revelations he made of his former acts. Such a repository of intuitive wisdom, and almost prophetic enunciation, as the reports of his conversations and his dictated recollections at St. Helena, is nowhere to be found. Those marvellous writings, like the Despatches of the Duke of Wellington, have given their author an undying name as a far-seeing, combining, and deep-thinking master in the art of war. By their published works, those two greatest of military chieftains are lifted out of the class in which their detractors had placed them: Napoleon from among the rash and fortunate gamblers in the lottery of glory who risked all, and generally won; and Wellington from the catalogue of commonplace commanders, who, with a good deal of common sense and some knowledge of details, were indebted for their success to the unequalled resources of their country and the dogged stubbornness of their men. But Cæsar never equalled either of them in military tactics, or political organisation, or literary skill.

The field was now free for a new order of affairs. The French broke forth at once into a wild passion for parliamentary government, which was inflamed by the belief they had in the efficacy of eloquence alone to cure all the evils of the State. No such orators as now ornamented the tribune of the House of Representatives had ever been heard before. Public speaking had never been a power in France, for the censorship over lip and pen had existed for hundreds of years. A good speaker was now thought a greater personage than a scientific and successful general. Soult and Massena, and all the marshals of the Empire, sank into contempt compared with the thunderers of the Chamber—Foy, Benjamin Constant, Manuel, Sebastiani, and Royer-Collard. These were all orators of the highest class, and all on the Opposition benches. The ministerialists had no batteries of noble language with which to reply to the fire of their assailants ; but they had power on their side, and the fear of change, and the support of foreign sovereigns, and the zealous aid of the heir to the crown, the bigoted, narrow-minded, and furiously reactionary Count of Artois. Attached to neither of these parties—scarcely supporting the constitutional parliamentarians, but steadily embarrassing the government by his ostentatious adhesion to the principles of 1789—was Louis Philippe, Duke of Orleans, chief of the collateral royal line, and restored to the enormous wealth of his ancestors.

To try the firmness of Louis the Eighteenth in support of the monarchic cause, the sovereigns assembled at Verona committed to France the task of putting down the Spanish liberals who still maintained their constitution of 1812, and reinstating Ferdinand on his absolute throne. A hundred thousand men crossed the Pyrenees, under the command of the Duke d'Angoulême, and were joined by the remains of a Catholic army called the Army of the Faith, which the priests and other absolutists had raised in defence of the irresponsible Crown. These apostolical and cowardly allies brought more dishonour and dislike on the invading forces, by their cruelty and insubordination, than were compensated for by their numbers or moral weight in the country. The Cortes (or parliament of Spain) carried Ferdinand in honourable durance with them to Seville. D'Angoulême entered Madrid, and, after a heroic resistance on the part of Mina, Quiroga, and Ballasteros, succeeded in the object of his mission. The constitutional regency was dissolved, and a loose given to the feuds and passions of the triumphant Army of the Faith. But d'Angoulême was a French gentleman, and not a Spanish butcher. He bridled the lawlessness of both mob and army, and placed the late rebels, and all who were suspected of disaffection, under the protection of French tribunals and impartial law. Impartiality in the eyes of the Spanish enthusiasts was worse than hostility; and a royalist insurrection was with difficulty prevented against the protectors of royalty, since they would not condescend to be also the oppressors of the people. At length the struggle came to an end. A hundred thousand trained soldiers will always walk from end to end of the distracted and demoralised land of the Cid and Gonsalvo. The king was liberated, freedom withdrawn, and a frantic mob received their monarch when he returned to his capital with cries of—"Long live the absolute king! Death to the liberals! Perish the nation!" By an unfortunate coincidence—though perhaps designed by his admirers—the Duke d'Angoulême made his entry into Paris on the anniversary of the battle of Austerlitz. The arch of triumph, which forms so splendid a termination to the view from the Tuileries, had been left uncompleted on the downfall of Napoleon; but wooden scaffoldings were raised on the unfinished walls, painted carpets were suspended from the top, and the arch itself garlanded with laurels. The ridicule, however, was not of the duke's seeking, and even Beranger spared him for the sake of his moderation and love of justice.

The monarchy appeared strengthened for a while by the Spanish crusade; and the minister, de Villèle, thought he might venture on the introduction of various measures which had the appearance of a more liberal tendency, but was thwarted by the secret influences round the throne. His propositions were well intended but impracticable; they only set men's minds into a state of vague activity, canvassing theories of government and examining the foundations of political power. One law, however, proposed at this time, had a greater effect than the bills on Worship, Civil Rights, Politics, and Finance. It was a law to make sacrilege in a church punishable with death! Profanation—of which the priests were to be the expositors—was subject to the same penalty as murder. The peers passed it without difficulty; but the press was in an uproar: people began to remember the tyranny of the Church in the days of Calas and de la Barre; and Villèle withdrew it before it was discussed in the lower house—withdrew, but did not annul it. To secure more power by means of the subservient though eloquent Chambers then existing, he prolonged its duration unchanged to seven years instead of five, and symptoms were soon visible of the uneasiness and indistinct expectation which are precursors of changes in a nation's state. Villèle increased the public anxiety by declaring that he should now be able to close up the last wounds of the Revolution by making the national resources indemnify the returned emigrants for the loss of their estates. The Church in supremacy, and the ancient nobility in power, were the prospects which encompassed the deathbed of Louis the Eighteenth. "My brother," he said to the Count of Artois, "go you to your duties; leave me to my prayers." He died on the 16th September, 1824, and the intelligent portion of the country regretted the loss of a well-intentioned though selfish man, whose philosophic indifference to everything but his own comfort had led him to keep a comparatively impartial course between the claims of the future and the past; feeling little gratitude, probably, to a past which had treated him so unkindly, and no affection for a future which his sagacity enabled him to see would treat him or his successors in the same way.

CHAPTER XXI.

CHARLES THE TENTH.—A. D. 1824 TO A. D. 1830.

THE tide of affairs set faster than ever in the direction of feudalism and oppression. A secret influence had begun the reaction at the end of the last reign, and now there was little moderation observed. The Jesuits had poured back into the cities, and were reinstated in the governance of schools and colleges. Propositions were made in the Chambers to restore their revenues to the clergy; and twenty-one new bishoprics were created to increase the influence of the Church. All the years between the Revolution and the accession of Louis the Eighteenth were studiously forgotten. One enthusiastic abbé went so far in his prostration before existing power, as to describe the Emperor winning battles and dictating treaties as the "Marquis Buonaparte, lieutenant-general of the armies of the king." Chateaubriand, the most celebrated author of his time, liberalised in his feelings though strongly monarchical and Catholic in his principles, had been dismissed from the ministry with less ceremony than is generally shown in the discharge of a servant. And even relics and indulgences from Rome were received by the princes and nobles upon their knees. A procession was formed on the 15th of August —the day now dedicated to the fête of the Emperor,—"in memory of the vow of Louis the Thirteenth against the Protestants;" and in this procession the King, the Dauphin, and the Dauphiness appeared on foot. The veil was openly withdrawn, and the nation saw what it had to expect. The great orator Manuel had been expelled from the Chamber, and dragged out of it by force for an opposition speech. Beranger's ballads had been suppressed, and the popular songster imprisoned. A bill was introduced in 1826 for the restoration of the law of primogeniture ; and in the following year, notice was given of an alteration in the form of trial by jury, and of a new law for the regulation of the press.

At the same time the weight of authority was used with harshness and injustice to crush any person who opposed these propositions by word or deed. The Academy of Sciences ventured to prepare a petition in favour of literary freedom ; the king refused to receive it ; and the two persons who had taken the chief part in the preliminary discussion were dismissed from their employments—Villemain from his office of Master of Requests, and Lacretelle from his Readership of Plays. The Duke of Rochefoucauld-Liancourt, a member of the Chamber of Peers, died at this time ; and some of the old pupils of the Academy of Chalons, to whom he had been very kind, endeavoured to show their gratitude to their neighbour and benefactor by bearing his body to the Barrier, where the hearse was waiting to convey it to his estate. In the Church of the Madeleine the police seized the coffin—unwilling that such a mark of respect should be shown to a member of the Opposition ; the pupils resisted : in the struggle the coffin fell to the ground, and the authorities in triumph carried it off in a fly.

Wherever the king went, shouts of "No censorship of the press!" saluted him. He reviewed the Civic Guard in the Champ de Mars : the usual cry was raised. "Sir," he said to one of the citizen soldiers, "I come here to receive your homage, not your counsel." And in the evening of that day the whole force was dissolved. Paris, in fact, was disarmed, and the army constituted the sole support of order. What that order was to be was now very plain to all. A law was proposed in the upper house, establishing a police of the press, and was rejected. Seventy-six new peers were named ; the Chamber of Deputies, from which still less subserviency was expected, was dismissed ; and the gauntlet was fairly thrown down. In this year the battle of Navarino—which practically delivered Greece from its oppressors, and was hailed as the first national resurrection to freedom since the reaction had begun—was viewed with very different sentiments by the peoples engaged in it. The English and French navies, which were united in the entire destruction of the Turkish fleet, took also different views of the result of their valour and preponderating force. France was so enraptured with a naval victory, however obtained, that even the supporters of the ministry rejoiced in an action which greatly excited the Liberal hopes throughout Europe. The English, on the other hand, perceived too late the fault they had committed in exposing Turkey unprotected to the maritime attacks of Russia, and called the victory of Navarino "an untoward event." Yet, as naval victories were of more importance to France than England, an opportunity was found for another triumph in an expedition against the Dey of Algiers. Successful to a certain degree, but not so brilliantly decisive as its promoters had expected, the squadron came back with its work only half performed, but furnishing information which led to a greater effort and more satisfactory result in a future year.

In spite of government influence, which was unscrupulously used, the elections of 1828 returned a Liberal majority to the Chamber. There were riots with loss of life in Paris and other towns. The Villèle ministry retired for fear of the coming storm ; and the helm was taken by Martignac, who, however, steered only as the higher authorities directed. The same struggle was repeated,—ordinances of repression on one side and bills introduced in favour of freedom on the other,—arrest of members and denunciation of ministers. Martignac, afraid or unable to go any farther, resigned in favour of Polignac, a personal friend of the king, and blind and foolish enough neither to see nor understand the tendency of the actions he was induced to perform. In this exasperated state of parties, and while a new election was going on, the expedition long meditated against the Algerine pirates took place.

Algiers capitulated on the 5th of July, 1830, and the result of the elections was known on the 22d. The Liberal majority was overwhelming; and the king and courtiers had nothing to show on the other side, except the military glory of the conquest of a new colony to France. Relying too much on this support, and confident in the assurances of the Archbishop of Paris, who had been his evil genius so long, the king determined, by a bold stroke, to prevent the meeting of a hostile assembly, and issued, on the 25th, the fatal ordinances which rendered his farther occupancy of a constitutional throne impossible.

These ordinances were three: 1st, The liberty of the press was suspended; 2d, The Chamber of Deputies was dissolved before it had met—by this proceeding annulling the election; and, 3d, The law of election was changed, and the returns placed entirely in the hands of the prefects who were in the pay of Government.

The fatuity of king and minister was shown in the little effect they expected from the publication of this monarchic revolution. Polignac did not increase the garrison of Paris by a single soldier, and Charles was hunting rabbits at St. Cloud. But, on the morning of the 28th, Paris came forth upon the streets. From every shop and manufactory emerged the members of the Old Civic Guard, which had been so contumeliously disbanded three years before. Loud exclamations in favour of the Charter were heard in every quarter of the city. Meetings were held by the deputies who had been dismissed before their powers were verified, and the military authorities were uncertain how to proceed. Muskets at last were fired, barricades erected, and the excited multitudes bore steadily on from point to point. Marshal Marmont, who was in command of the troops, was unequal to the situation, and could neither fight with vigour nor temporise with wisdom. The king, still deaf to reason, persisted in ordering the revolt, as he called it, to be put down; and for this purpose there were not more than twelve thousand soldiers of all arms, and some were disaffected, and all taken by surprise.

On the 29th the revolt became a revolution; a form of government was established at the Hôtel de Ville, and Lafayette, whom we remember as the young marquis who aided the Americans in their resistance to the English, took the command of the municipal forces. The young pupils of the Military School applied their science to the selection of the most available points of attack, and Marmont retired to St. Cloud. Charles awoke to the danger at last; he sent messengers to say he revoked the ordinances, ratified the Charter, and withdrew his alterations. A voice rose from the provisional committee, "It is too late!" and the great struggle was over. A lieutenant-general of the kingdom was appointed in the person of Louis Philippe, Duke of Orleans, and he assumed the place at once. He issued a proclamation on entering Paris, which indissolubly connected his fortunes with the result of the Three Days. "I have not hesitated," it said, "to place myself in the midst of your heroic population, and to make every effort to preserve you from the calamities of civil war and anarchy. In coming among you, I have carried with pride the glorious colours (the tricolor cockade) which you have resumed, and which I myself have long since adopted. The Chambers will be assembled, and will take measures for the maintenance of the laws and the rights of the nation; the Charter henceforth shall be a reality."

The establishment of the Charter prevented the chance of the restoration either of the Republic or the Empire. Charles the Tenth made the last use of his power in confirming his cousin in the lieutenancy of the kingdom, and abdicated in favour of the young Duke of Bordeaux. Louis Philippe, however, declined to receive his office from the authority of the king; and on the 4th of August the last of the legitimate Bourbons took his departure from France, and hid his weakness and disappointment in foreign lands. Once more he took up his quarters in Holyrood, the old residence of the Scottish kings, and, on entering its gloomy portal, must have mused deeply on the instability of earthly grandeur; for that grey old pile had been the home of Mary,

Queen of Scots, of Henry Darnley, and of James the Second, and had been the scene of more suffering and sorrow than any royal dwelling in the world.

LOUIS PHILIPPE, A.D. 1830 TO A.D. 1848.

A few days of earnest application, aided by the universal anxiety to restore a settled government to the country before the revolutionary passions excited by the struggle should break out into uncontrollable excess, enabled the peers and deputies to make certain alterations in the Charter, and nominate Louis Philippe King of the French. The alterations in the Charter and the change in the royal title were all in a popular sense. "King of France" was an embodiment of the feudal idea of the universal proprietorship of the sovereign; "King of the French" made him the leader of the people, but not the owner of their soil. The modification of the Charter in the same way tended to an assertion of equality and freedom. The Roman Catholic religion was declared, in the first article, to be merely the religion of the majority, but was not the religion of the State, or the dominant faith. The press was declared to be delivered from a censorship for ever, and the Charter itself was placed under the protection of the National Guard. The Lieutenant-General of the Kingdom accepted the throne on the terms offered to him by the Chambers, and began his reign, on the 9th of August, as Louis Philippe the First. No monarch ever had a more difficult part to play, or fewer adventitious circumstances in his favour. He was a usurper in the eyes of the Legitimists, a tyrant in the eyes of the Republicans, and an illegally nominated ruler in the eyes of the Imperialists. His birth, his title of king, and the absence of the national suffrage (on which the Buonapartists relied), weakened his position both abroad and at home; and both abroad and at home "high the winds whistled and the billows roared."

A priest-led revolt in La Vendée, in favour of the ancient

line, was put down by force; the suspicions of other nations were soothed by a declaration of non-intervention; England fortunately acknowledged the Revolution, and, by her politic moderation, secured a fair field for the new dynasty; Belgium, excited by the example of its neighbour, dismissed its king, and was clamouring for an incorporation with France, to prevent its reannexation to Holland. But Louis Philippe had the wisdom to perceive that the absorption of Belgium would be war with Europe, and came to terms with England on the settlement of the question.

Leopold of Saxe-Coburg, who had been husband of the Princess Charlotte of England, was elected King of the Belgians, and speedily married the eldest daughter of Louis Philippe. Peace was restored in the course of a few years to the interior of France, and dignity maintained abroad. Fifty thousand men were marched to the defence of Belgium, which was invaded by the Dutch, and the citadel of Antwerp was taken after a lengthened siege. Portugal was overawed by a French fleet, and reparation exacted from the usurping king, Don Miguel, for an injury to French merchants. Austria overran the States of the Pope, and a French expedition was despatched to keep the invaders in check, by the seizure and occupation of Ancona. His Holiness must have been divided in his feelings of gratitude between his assailant and his defender; for one took possession of his inland towns, and the other made himself at home in his principal port. Meanwhile the tide of success swelled higher and higher round the throne of the Citizen King. Riots, indeed, broke out in Paris, but were put down before they grew into revolutions. Napoleon's son, the Duke of Reichstadt, who had been brought up at the Austrian court, and who at all times might have excited the feelings of the nation by his birth, and as the representative of the universal vote by which his father had been declared Emperor, died. The Duchess of Berri, mother of the Duke of Bordeaux, endeavoured to excite an insurrection in favour of her son in the western provinces, but brought an air of ridicule upon her endeavours by the absurdity of her appearance, and more serious feelings of reprobation and disdain by the degrading immorality of her conduct. At the same time a sympathy was established between regenerated France and Portugal and Spain, which both adopted constitutional governments; and England, proud also of her parliamentary rule, lifted Louis Philippe into the great family of recognised and rightful kings, by entering with him and the sovereigns beyond the Pyrenees into a Quadruple Alliance.

The more, however, Louis Philippe became invested with power, the deadlier grew the enmities of the factions who saw, in the consolidation of his authority, the death of all their hopes. Attempts were made upon his life—first by an unknown hand, and then, in 1835, by a Corsican of the name of Fieschi, who discharged what is called an Infernal Machine as he passed along the Boulevards, and killed fourteen spectators, but missed his principal aim. The fiery spirits and inflammable intellects of the French seem incapable of the moderation which accepts a governing power, and gives it no excuse for going beyond its limits by the commission of crimes against which every honourable mind revolts. The freedom of the press rose into license, freedom of discussion into incentives to rebellion, and freedom of accusation into provocatives to murder. Wise and good men gathered round the throne when it became the object of these detestable attacks. Guizot, Thiers, Molé, and Dupin endeavoured, by moderation in the tone of their addresses in the Chambers, to set an example of peaceable argumentation to the parties outside the walls. But political animosity rose into madness; and though there were probably few of the opposition writers who openly advocated assassination, there were many who were perfectly ready to profit by its fruits.

The "Laws of September" were passed, putting some limit to the liberty of political pamphleteering, and Louis Philippe became a traitor in the eyes of the silenced libellers, as well as a tyrant: he was false to the Charter, and truculent to the people. To turn the attention of the nation to more distant objects, Monsieur Thiers commenced a vast scheme for the propagation of French glory in the newly acquired territory of Algiers. A conquest of the whole land was meditated, over which the Kabyles and other inland tribes exercised a nomadic proprietorship; and treasures of great amount and the blood of innumerable men were poured out, to produce a crop of barren laurels in the great Sahara, and give a safe field of operation for the exuberant energies of France.

Assassination still went its hateful way. Alibaud and Meunier, by failure in their attempts, seemed to render the king callous to the conspiracies of the disaffected; and in the same year he extended his clemency to an opponent of another kind. Louis Napoleon, a nephew of the Emperor, had cherished for many years the most chimerical hopes of a restoration to the soil of his country and the rights of his birth. A formal instrument of Napoleon had nominated him his heir in failure of the Duke of Reichstadt; and in all the struggles of his adversity—in the total desertion of friends, and even the want of a sufficiency to live on—the Tuileries and Versailles never left his thoughts. "I shall be Emperor," he said, "before I die; I will govern France in the ideas of my uncle, and then perish with a bullet in my brain."

Considered a half-witted enthusiast by those who did not know the hidden recesses of that dark and mysterious intelligence, the news of his appearance at Strasburg, and attempt to overthrow the throne of Louis Philippe with the help of a few disaffected soldiers in that distant garrison, was received with laughter by the public in England. Something of the same feeling must have existed in France; for Louis Philippe declined to bring him to trial on the capital accusation of invasion or rebellion, and sent him to America unscathed.

From this time the parliamentary system was in full force for some years; and henceforth we find a new characteristic in French history, and the names of ministers become more prominent than those of warriors, or even of kings. The Chamber of Deputies was divided into three parties. Odillon Barrot was leader of the dynastic opposition which accepted the royalty of July, but wished to surround it with democratic institutions. Thiers was the chief of another party which accepted also the Citizen King, but qualified its adhesion with the maxim, "The king reigns, but does not govern"—an epigrammatic condensation of the English maxim of the responsibility of ministers; and Guizot, an orator, philosopher, and historian, of whom his country is justly proud, was leader of the third or conservative party, which admitted the policy of the last revolution, and the changes it had introduced, but resolutely opposed any farther progress in the same direction. The first would have made Louis Philippe the chief of a hereditary republic; the second would have made him a powerless ornament of a court; and the third would have made him king on the same principle as the legitimate predecessors he had displaced.

If the monarch of July had adopted the view of any one of those divergent parties, he might have established his throne on the security of the Charter to which he had sworn. But he was false to all in turn. Selfishness, displayed in the meanest form which selfishness can take—the acquisition of money for himself and family—was the leading feature of his mind. A master of the arts of cajolery and deceit, it added a new charm to victory if he could achieve it by a trick or falsehood. He demanded dotations for his sons on the most unfounded pretences, and was the most importunate of beggars at the treasury door of an impoverished country, while he was the richest individual, in his private possessions, in Europe. French honour and French economy—two prodigiously strong passions when they are combined, were roused against the insatiable pillager of the public wealth. The dotations were refused or modified, and still the old man persevered. He dragged his ministers one after the other through the odium of asking and the shame of being repulsed; and carried his duplicity into foreign policies as well as domestic aggrandisement, to the endangerment of the national peace. England, which had been on the kindest and most confidential terms with him from the first, began to find that his friendship was not to be relied on if the chance of a present benefit came in the way. In 1840 the relations of the two countries waxed cold; and Thiers, who was at that time in power, was encouraged to talk boldly of war and conquest, and to boast of the superiority of the French fleet in the Mediterranean, and the duty of France to support her ally, the rebellious Pasha of Egypt, against the oppressions of the Porte and the threats of England. Louis Philippe, whose motto was "peace at any price," encouraged his bellicose little premier till withdrawal would make him ridiculous, and then accepted the acts of England as wiser than his own, and turned out his minister, in the midst of much laughter at his expense on both sides of the Channel. During the alarm caused by the vainglorious crowings of M. Thiers, the king had persuaded the Chambers to surround the great city of Paris with a fortified wall and majestic detached forts, which might put it beyond the attack of the enemies of France. The sight of the rising battlements reminded the middle-aged of the strange visitors they had seen in 1814 and 1815; and visions of red-coated English and kilted Scotch, and all the national armies of the Continent, began to rise before their eyes. Can this be the Citizen King, they asked, who gave us such solemn undertakings against war and taxes? They did not perceive that the walls were protections against mutiny within as well as assaults outside; and strengthened in the belief that the fortifications were the bulwarks of his throne, the king called M. Guizot to his councils as premier, and hoisted the standard of resistance to all innovation.

By this time the glories of Napoleon had shone through the dreadful setting with which they closed. Tired and perhaps ashamed of the peaceful policy of their present ruler, the youth of France looked fondly back to the days when the eagles flew from steeple to steeple, and the little grey riding-coat appeared in the front of battle. But again an air of ridicule was thrown upon the Emperor's triumphs and recollections by what appeared the insensate conduct of his nephew and representative, Louis Napoleon. He had returned from his deportation to America, and in the August of this year made an attempt on the kingdom of France by landing on the coast of Boulogne, and invoking his great uncle's name. That name appeared to be an abstraction unconnected altogether with his earthly relationships, for no murmur was perceptible when the invader was sentenced to imprisonment in the castle of Ham, and a tame eagle, which he had carried over to be his standard, was confiscated to the zoological garden of Paris. From this tedious detention we may anticipate the story so far as to mention that the ambitious prince effected his escape in 1846, and cherished undiminished hopes of his eventual recall in the midst of the sneers and obloquy of London.

But not the less deep was the newly awakened admiration for Napoleon. Far off amid the melancholy main the ashes of the great man reposed under a willow he had planted with his own hands, and pilgrimages had been made by admirers from every land to visit the solitary grave. All at once, while his nephew was contemptuously detained in prison, the name of Napoleon became a rallying-cry of all the parties in the State. An application was made to England for permission to bring the remains of the unequalled soldier to the banks of the Seine, to rest among the people he had so dearly loved ; the Belle Poule, under command of the Prince de Joinville, a son of the king, brought back the sacred relics, and they were deposited with reverence and triumph under the dome of the Hospital of Invalides, and guarded night and day by veterans of the Grand Army. Paris was filled with the Presence of the Emperor. In 1833 his statue, dressed in his habit as he lived, had been inaugurated by the Citizen King, and looked down from its pillar in the Place Vendôme over the prostrate city. Sentinels, ancient soldiers of the Imperial Guard, were employed to show the column to admiring visitors, and never omitted to state that the metal composing it had once been twelve hundred Austrian and Prussian guns. The honours paid to the Conqueror of Italy were intended to reconcile the present generation to its inaction ; and no cloud appeared upon the horizon to give a warning of the effect of these warlike recollections.

But in 1842 a stop was put to the career of personal prosperity which the king had run since his accession. A family of five sons, respectful and affectionate, had spread the charms of domestic life over the hours of his retirement from the cares of State. Enriched with the fortunes he had procured them from their relations, or wheedled for them from the country, the princes had a course before them on which the farthest seeing could not discern a cloud. They had acquired military fame in the campaigns of Africa, and de Joinville, the sailor-prince, was expected to elevate the navy of France to an equality with England's. On the 13th of July, the heir of the crown, the Duke of Orleans, was thrown from his carriage and killed. The mourning was universal and sincere ; he was the most popular of the new family, and gave a prospect of stability to the throne, by his possession of courage and vigour. But Louis Philippe saw deeper than others the fatal results of this sad bereavement. The deceased left a son, the Count of Paris, an infant of four years of age ; and all the uncertainties of a long minority, in the present unsettled state of the government, rose before him. Yet, if money or influence could be procured, at any sacrifice, for the survivors, the chance was not to be thrown away ; and in 1846 every intrigue was set in motion to secure the hand of the Queen of Spain for one of the fortunate youths. But the vigilance of England had for some time been excited by the aggressive and insulting attitude assumed by France. Islands had been seized in the Southern Seas for no purpose but to show the independence of M. Guizot, and to blind the public to the reaction at home by an apparent activity abroad. A quarrel, nearly ending in war, had arisen about the French occupation and protectorate of the island of Tahiti, and the expulsion of some English settlers ; and while a secret enmity was fermenting in the mind of both the ministries, a rapid political blow was struck, which gained its object for a while, at the expense of the respect of all the nations concerned.

Louis Philippe affected to yield so far to the reclamation of England, as to declare that he would be satisfied with the hand of the sister of the Queen of Spain for his fifth son, the Duke of Montpensier, and made an engagement by his word of honour, which was ratified by an equal obligation on the part of M. Guizot, that the marriage should not take place at the same time with that of her sister, but be postponed, as was understood by all parties, till the marriage of the queen should have given promise of an heir to the Spanish throne.

The sagacious Louis Philippe discovered a certain half idiotic cousin of Isabella of Spain, deficient in every power both of body and mind ; and in a secret and underhand manner, he celebrated the wedding of this miserable being with the queen ; and immediately afterwards that of his son with the handsome, blooming, and wealthy Maria Louisa, who, in addition to her present possessions, which were very large, carried to her husband the succession to the Spanish crown, in the absolute impossibility of any issue from her sister's unhappy marriage. Good feeling and political opposition were roused by this degrading trickery—and England learned, with a sentiment of regret and compassion, that M. Guizot, whose talents and character had hitherto commanded her respect, had been deluded by the crowned tempter at his ear to defend his conduct on the quibble that the marriages were not celebrated at the same time—some little interval having occurred between them—and that this was all he had promised. Suspicion and jealousy took the place of the former cordial relations. Losing the fervent friendship of the only constitutional neighbour on whom it could rely, France, like a beggar with its bonnet in its hand, waited at the gates of Austria and Russia, and begged the moral support of the most despotic of the powers. The moral support of Austria and Russia there was but one way to gain, and that was by an abnegation of all the principles represented by the accession of Louis Philippe, and an active co-operation in their policy of repression.

At this time the Swiss broke out into violent efforts to obtain a reform ; and the strange spectacle was presented of a Pope talking glibly about the rights of men, and proclaiming himself, as some of his boldest predecessors had been, a protector of the peoples against the tyranny of kings. Austria quelled the Swiss aspirations with the strong hand, and took up a menacing attitude towards the weak and benevolent pontiff, Pius the Ninth. France was quiescent ; and the Opposition rose into invectives, which were repeated in harsher language out of doors. The stout shopkeeper, who now occupied the throne of Henry the Fourth, thought that all the requirements of a government were fulfilled if it maintained peace with the neighbouring states. Trade he thought might flourish though honour and glory were trampled under foot. He accordingly neglected, or failed to understand, the disaffection of the middle class, whose pecuniary interest he was supposed to represent, but whose higher aspirations he had insulted by his truckling attempts to win the sympathy of the old aristocracy and the foreign despots. Statesmen like Thiers and Odillon Barrot, when the scales of office fell from their eyes, and the blandishments of the sovereign were withdrawn, perceived that the parliamentary government of the Charter had become a mockery, and that power had got more firmly consolidated in royal hands under these deceptive forms than in the time of the legitimate kings. A cry therefore suddenly rose from all quarters, except the benches of the ministry, for electoral and parliamentary reform ; and there was also heard the uniformly recurring exclamation, premonitory of all serious disturbance, for a diminution of the taxes. The cries were founded in justice, and urged in a constitutional manner. Corruption had entered into all the elections—parliamentary purity had become a byword under the skilful manipulation of the purse-bearing king—and the expenses of the country far exceeded its income, owing to the extravagant building of forts and palaces, with which, in the years of his prosperity, he had endeavoured to amuse the people.

People of all classes had become wearied of so undignified a reign. The National Guard, under whose protection the Charter had been placed, was systematically neglected. Its ranks had become open to the holders of various and hostile opinions. The nobility, such as it was, which had survived the Revolution, and had glittered its uneasy day in the antechambers of the restored Bourbons, had never deigned anything but looks of disdain on the Throne of the Barricades. The populace had kept their irritated minds fixed on the Reign of Terror and the triumphant days of the guillotine. It was in this state of feeling that a banquet of opposition deputies was announced to be held in the twelfth arrondissement, the lowest and most excitable portion of the town. The ministry took the alarm, and prohibited the dinner. Attempts to enter the tavern were repulsed by force—a crowd collected—seditious cries were uttered. Some squadrons of cavalry trotted up the street—a musket or two was discharged; but fresh troops came on, and the riot was at an end. Louis Philippe thought all danger was over, and congratulated himself on his firmness in preventing the opposition orators from exhaling a portion of their zeal in eloquence which would have died in the hour it was uttered, for the press was already chained. Next day, however, there came out upon the streets the mysterious and unaccountable multitudes which great occasions bring to the daylight from the cellars and garrets of Paris. Strange-looking, hideous-featured, wildly-dressed beings, who are never seen in quieter periods, but who appear, when blood is wanted, like phantoms summoned by magical incantations on the stage. They swarmed all over the town—gloomy, dark, unpitying, and there was no one to oppose them. They erected barricades, and gave utterance to a word which had not been heard for forty-four years. In a moment the word was taken up, and "A Republic!" was shouted at every discharge of musketry, and in answer to every appeal. A republic was an apparition which struck Louis Philippe with horror. He ordered the troops to put down the insurrection, but the troops, as in that other revolt which placed him on the throne, were ill commanded. Doubt and uncertainty paralysed every force—and still the dreadful cry and infuriated mob came on. He heard them on the outside of the

Tuileries, and his heart sank within him. After the vain ceremony of an abdication, he slipt out through the palace garden, passing the site of Louis the Sixteenth's execution, and shook the ungrateful city's dust from off his feet. His sons, equally regardful of their safety, changed clothes with some workmen near the grounds, and slunk into safe obscurity; while the widowed Duchess of Orleans, taking her son in her hand, presented herself, undaunted and calm, before the Chambers which had assembled to decide on their future course. She plead the cause of the orphan prince with an eloquence which was unaffected by the danger of her position; with hundreds of muskets in the hands of a furious rabble pointed at her head. She reminded them of the suppliant's father whom all men had loved and trusted; and promised them, under the royalty of her son, the true fulfilment of all the promises which his grandfather had broken. But a voice was heard from the tribune, uttering the same words which had broken the hopes of Charles the Tenth, "It is too late;" and the Republic took its course. The generous heart of France was moved equally with pity and admiration of the impassioned mother, who defended her child's cause so nobly, and with contempt of the spiritless princes who carried their wealth and pusillanimity into other lands.

It is not intended in this short sketch to enter on the events which have occurred since the fall of the Orleans dynasty. The circumstances are too recent, and the action still in such rapid progress, that it is not possible to pass a judgment on the characters or prospects of the momentous drama. It will be sufficient to say that the shifting canvass of the last ten years has presented scenes and combinations never dreamt of before. The despised adventurer, who raised the pity of his countrymen by his attempt on Strasburg in 1837, and their laughter by his expedition to Boulogne in 1842, has for six years been Emperor of the French by the elective votes of an overwhelming majority of the nation. France, under him, has attained a stronger position in Europe than it has held since the calamities of his uncle began. He has persuaded the proudest and most boastful of peoples to accept protection from the dangers of domestic factions, as the price of the last vestige of its public or individual freedom. The elect of the whole nation, and the offspring of a popular revolution, he has accumulated on his own head more power than was acquired by the sword of Philip Augustus, or the policy of Louis the Fourteenth ; and yet his subjects are more liberty-loving than their mediæval ancestry, and more intelligent than their predecessors of the Fronde. It is not for us to foretell what the end of these strange circumstances will be. We can only watch and be prepared, having no wish but for the honour and happiness of France.

INDEX.

A.

D

E

F

I

J

K

L

Q

R

S

T

U

V

THE END.

LIST OF WORKS

PUBLISHED BY D. APPLETON & COMPANY,

Nos. 443 & 445 Broadway, New York.

A Descriptive Catalogue, with full titles and prices, may be had gratuitously on application.

Baxley's West Coast of America and Hawaiian Islands.
Beach's Pelayo. An Epic.
Beall (John Y.), Trial of.
Beauties of Sacred Literature.
Beauties of Sacred Poetry.
Beaumont and Fletcher's Works. 2 vols.
Belem's Spanish Phrase Book.
Bello's Spanish Grammar (in Spanish).
Benedict's Run Through Europe.
Benton on the Dred Scott Case.
—— Thirty Years' View. 2 vols.
—— Debates of Congress. 16 vols.
Bertha Percy. By Margaret Field. 12mo.
Bertram's Harvest of the Sea. Economic and Natural History of Fishes.
Bessie and Jessie's Second Book.
Beza's Novum Testamentum.
Bibles in all styles of bindings and various prices.
Bible Stories, in Bible Language.
Black's General Atlas of the World.
Bloomfield's Farmer's Boy.
Blot's What to Eat, and How to Cook it.
Blue and Gold Poets. 6 vols. in case.
Boise's Greek Exercises.
—— First Three Books of Xenophon's Anabasis.
Bojesen's Greek and Roman Antiquities.
Book of Common Prayer. Various prices.
Boone's Life and Adventures.
Bourne's Catechism of the Steam Engine.
—— Hand-Book of the Steam Engine.
—— Treatise on the Steam Engine.
Boy's Book of Modern Travel.
—— Own Toy Maker
Bradford's Peter the Great.
Bradley's (Mary E.) Douglass Farm.
Bradley's (Chas.) Sermons.
Brady's Christmas Dream.
Breakfast, Dinner, and Tea.
British Poets. From Chaucer to the Present Time. 3 large vols.
British Poets. Cabinet Edition. 15 vols.
Brooks' Ballads and Translations.
Brown, Jones, and Robinson's Tour.
Bryan's English Grammar for Germans.
Bryant and Stratton's Commercial Law.
Bryant's Poems, Illustrated.
—— Poems. 2 vols.
—— Thirty Poems.
—— Poems. Blue and Gold.
—— Letters from Spain.
Buchanan's Administration.
Buckle's Civilization in England. 2 vols.
—— Essays.
Bunyan's Divine Emblems.
Burdett's Chances and Changes.
—— Never Too Late.
Burgess' Photograph Manual. 12mo.
Burnett (James R.) on the Thirty-nine Articles.
Burnett (Peter H.), The Path which led a Protestant Lawyer to the Catholic Church.
Burnouf's Gramatica Latina.
Burns' (Jabez) Cyclopædia of Sermons.
Burns' (Robert) Poems.
Burton's Cyclopædia of Wit and Humor. 2 vols.
Butler's Martin Van Buren.
Butler's (F.) Spanish Teacher.
Butler's (S.) Hudibras.
Butler's (T. B.) Guide to the Weather.
Butler's (Wm. Allen) Two Millions.
Byron Gallery. The Gallery of Byron Beauties.
—— Poetical Works.
—— Life and Letters.
—— Works. Illustrated.

Cœleb's Laws and Practice of Whist.
Cæsar's Commentaries.
Caird's Prairie Farming.
Calhoun's Works and Speeches. 6 vols.
Campbell's (Thos.) Gertrude of Wyoming.
—— Poems.
Campbell (Judge) on Shakespeare.
Canot, Life of Captain.
Carlyle's (Thomas) Essays.
Carreno's Manual of Politeness.
—— Compendio del Manual de Urbanidad.
Casseday's Poetic Lacon.
Cavendish's Laws of Whist.
Cervantes' Don Quixote, in Spanish.
—— Don Quixote, in English.
César L'Histoire de Jules. par S. M. I. Napoleon III. Vol. I., with Maps and Portrait. (French.)
Cheap Edition, without Maps and Portrait.
Maps and Portrait, for cheap edition, in envelopes.
Champlin's English Grammar.
—— Greek Grammar.
Chase on the Constitution and Canons.
Chaucer's Poems.
Chevalier on Gold.
Children's Holidays.
Child's First History.
Chittenden's Report of the Peace Convention.
Choquet's French Composition.
—— French Conversation.
Cicero de Officiis.
—— Select Orations.
Clarke's (D. S.) Scripture Promises.
Clarke's (Mrs. Cowden) Iron Cousin.
Clark's (H. J.) Mind in Nature.
Cleaveland and Backus' Villas and Cottages.
Cleveland's (H. W. S.) Hints to Riflemen.
Cloud Crystals. A Snow Flake Album.
Cobb's (J. B.) Miscellanies.
Coe's Spanish Drawing Cards. 10 parts.
Coe's Drawing Cards. 10 parts.
Colenso on the Pentateuch. 2 vols.
—— On the Romans.
Coleridge's Poems.
Collins' Amoor.
Collins' (T. W.) Humanics.
Collet's Dramatic French Reader.
Comings' Physiology.
—— Companion to Physiology.
Comment on Parle a Paris.
Congreve's Comedy.
Continental Library. 6 vols. in case.
Cooke's Life of Stonewall Jackson.
Cookery, by an American Lady.
Cooley's Cyclopædia of Receipts.
Cooper's Mount Vernon.
Copley's Early Friendship.
—— Poplar Grove.
Cornell's First Steps in Geography.
—— Primary Geography.
—— Intermediate Geography.
—— Grammar School Geography.
—— High School Geography and Atlas.

Cornell's High School Geography.
—— " " Atlas.
—— Map Drawing. 12 maps in case.
—— Outline Maps, with Key. 13 maps in portfolio.
—— Or, the Key, separately.
Cornwall on Music.
Correlation and Conservation of Forces.
Cortez' Life and Adventures.
Cotter on the Mass and Rubrics.
Cottin's Elizabeth; or, the Exiles of Siberia.
Cousin Alice's Juveniles.
Cousin Carrie's Sun Rays.
—— Keep a Good Heart.
Cousin's Modern Philosophy. 2 vols.
—— On the True and Beautiful.
—— Only Romance.
Coutan's French Poetry.
Covell's English Grammar.
Cowles' Exchange Tables.
Cowper's Homer's Iliad.
—— Poems.
Cox's Eight Years in Congress, from '57 to '65.
Coxe's Christian Ballads.
Creasy on the English Constitution.
Crisis (The).
Crosby's (A.) Geometry.
Crosby's (H.) Œdipus Tyrannus.
Crosby's (W. H.) Quintus Curtius Rufus.
Crowe's Linny Lockwood.
Curry's Volunteer Book.
Cust's Invalid's Book.
Cyclopædia of Commercial and Business Anecdotes. 2 vols.

D'Abrantes' Memoires of Napoleon. 2 vols.
Dairyman's (The) Daughter.
Dana's Household Poetry.
Darwin's Origin of Species.
Dante's Poems.
Dasent's Popular Tales from the Norse.
Davenport's Christ. Unity and its Recovery.
Dawson's Archaia.
De Belem's Spanish Phrase-Book.
De Fivas' Elementary French Reader.
—— Classic French Reader.
De Foe's Robinson Crusoe.
De Girardin's Marguerite.
—— Stories of an Old Maid.
De Hart on Courts Martial.
De L'Ardeche's History of Napoleon.
De Peyrac's Comment on Parle.
De Staël's Corinne, ou L'Italie.
De Veitelle's Mercantile Dictionary.
De Vere's Spanish Grammar.
Dew's Historical Digest.
Dickens's (Charles) Works. Original Illustrations. 24 vols.
Dies Irae and Stabat Mater, bound together.
Dies Irae, alone, and Stabat Mater, alone.
Dix's (John A.) Winter in Madeira.
—— Speeches and Addresses. 2 vols.
Dix's (Rev. M.) Lost Unity of the Christian World.
Dr. Oldham at Greystones, and his Talk there.
Doane's Works. 4 vols.
Downing's Rural Architecture.
Dryden's Poems.
Dunlap's Spirit History of Man.
Dusseldorf Gallery, Gems from the.
Dwight on the Study of Art.
Ebony Idol (The).
Ede's Management of Steel.
Edith Vaughan's Victory.

Egloffstein's Geology and Physical Geography of Mexico.
Eichhorn's German Grammar.
Elliot's Fine Work on Birds. 7 parts, or in 1 v.
Ellsworth's Text-Book of Penmanship.
Ely's Journal.
Enfield's Indian Corn; its Value, Culture, and Uses.
Estvan's War Pictures.
Evans' History of the Shakers.
Evelyn's Life of Mrs. Godolphin.
Everett's Mount Vernon Papers.
Fables, Original and Selected.
Farrar's History of Free Thought.
Faustus.
Fay's Poems.
Fenelon's Telemaque. The same, in 2 vols.
—— Telemachus.
Field's Bertha Percy.
Field's (M.) City Architecture.
Figuier's World before the Deluge.
Fireside Library. 8 vols. in case.
First Thoughts.
Fiji and the Fijians.
Flint's Physiology of Man.
Florian's William Tell.
Flower Pictures.
Fontana's Italian Grammar.
Foote's Africa and the American Flag.
Foresti's Italian Extracts.
Four Gospels (The).
Franklin's Man's Cry and God's Gracious Answer.
Frieze's Tenth and Twelfth Books of Quintilian.
Fullerton's (Lady G.) Too Strange Not to be True.
Funny Story Book.

Garland's Life of Randolph.
Gaskell's Life of Bronté. 2 vols.
The same, cheaper edition, in 1 vol.
George Ready.
Gerard's French Readings.
Gertrude's Philip Randolph.
Gesenius' Hebrew Grammar.
Ghostly Colloquies.
Gibbes' Documentary History. 3 vols.
Gibbons' Banks of New York.
Gilfillan's Literary Portraits.
Gillespie on Land Surveying.
Girardin on Dramatic Literature.
Goadby's Text-Book of Physiology.
Goethe's Iphigenia in Tauris.
Goldsmith's Essays.
—— Vicar of Wakefield.
Gosse's Evenings with the Microscope.
Goulburn's Office of the Holy Communion.
—— Idle Word.
—— Manual of Confirmation.
—— Sermons.
—— Study of the Holy Scriptures.
—— Thoughts on Personal Religion.
Gould's (E. S.) Comedy.
Gould's (W. M.) Zephyrs.
Graham's English Synonymes.
Grandmamma Easy's Toy Books.
Grandmother's Library. 6 vols. in case.
Grand's Spanish Arithmetic.
Grant's Report on the Armies of the United States 1864-'65.
Grauet's Portuguese Grammar.
Grayson's Theory of Christianity.
Greek Testament.
Greene's (F. H.) Primary Botany.
—— Class-Book of Botany.
Greene's (G. W.) Companion to Ollendorff.

Greene's (G. W.) First Lessons in French.
—— First Lessons in Italian.
—— Middle Ages.
Gregory's Mathematics.
Griffin on the Gospel.
Griffith's Poems.
Griswold's Republican Court.
——— Sacred Poets.
Guizot's (Madame) Tales.
Guizot's (M.) Civilization in Europe. 4 vols.
—— School edition. 1 vol.
—— New Edition, on tinted paper. 4 vols.
Gurowski's America and Europe.
——— Russia as it is.

Hadley's Greek Grammar.
Hahn's Greek Testament.
Hall's (B. H.) Eastern Vermont.
Hall's (C. H.) Notes on the Gospels. 2 vols.
Hall's (E. H.) Guide to the Great West.
Halleck's Poems.
—— Poems. Pocket size, blue and gold.
—— Young America.
Halleck's (H. W.) Military Science.
Hamilton's (Sir Wm.) Philosophy.
Hamilton's (A.) Writings. 6 vols.
Hand-Books on Education.
Hand-Book of Anglo-Saxon Root-Words.
Hand-Book of Anglo-Saxon Derivatives.
Hand-Book of the Engrafted Words.
Handy-Book of Property Law.
Happy Child's Library. 18 vols. in case.
Harkness' First Greek Book.
——— Latin Grammar.
——— First Latin Book.
——— Second "
——— Latin Reader.
Hase's History of the Church.
Haskell's Housekeeper's Encyclopædia.
Hassard's Life of Archbishop Hughes.
——— Wreath of Beauty.
Haupt on Bridge Construction.
Haven's Where There's a Will There's a Way.
—— Patient Waiting no Loss.
—— Nothing Venture Nothing Have.
—— Out of Debt Out of Danger.
—— Contentment Better than Wealth.
—— No Such Word as Fail.
—— All's Not Gold that Glitters.
—— A Place for Everything, and Everything in its Place.
—— Loss and Gain.
—— Pet Bird. [in case.
—— Home Series of Juvenile Books. 8 vols.
Haven (Memoir of Alice B.).
Hazard on the Will.
Hecker's Questions of the Soul.
Hemans' Poems. 2 vols.
—— Songs of the Affections.
Henck's Field-Book for Engineers.
Henry on Human Progress.
Herbert's Poems.
Here and There.
Herodotus, by Johnson (in Greek).
Herodotus, by Rawlinson (in English). 4 vls.
Heydenreich's German Reader.
Hickok's Rational Cosmology.
—— Rational Psychology.
History of the Rebellion, Military and Naval, Illustrated.
Hoffman's Poems.
Holcombe's Leading Cases.
——— Law of Dr. and Cr.
——— Letters in Literature.

Holly's Country Seats.
Holmes' (M. A.) Tempest and Sunshine.
——— English Orphans.
Holmes' (A.) Parties and Principles.
Homes of American Authors.
Homer's Iliad.
Hooker's Complete Works. 2 vols.
Hoppin's Notes.
Horace, edited by Lincoln.
Howitt's Child's Verse-Book.
—— Juvenile Tales. 14 vols. in case.
How's Historical Shakspearian Reader.
—— Shakspearian Reader.
Huc's Tartary and China.
Hudson's Life and Adventures.
Humboldt's Letters.
Hunt's (C. H.) Life of Livingston.
Hunt's (F. W.) Historical Atlas.
Huntington's Lady Alice.
Hutton's Mathematics.
Huxley's Man's Place in Nature.
—— Origin of Species.

Iconographic Encyclopædia. 6 vols.—4 Text and 2 Plates.
Or, separately:
The Countries and Cities of the World. 2 vols.
The Navigation of all Ages. 2 vols.
The Art of Building in Ancient and Modern Times. 2 vols.
The Religions of Ancient and Modern Times. 2 vols.
The Fine Arts Illustrated. 2 vols.
Technology Illustrated. 2 vols.
Internal Revenue Law.
Iredell's Life. 2 vols.
Italian Comedies.

Jacobs' Learning to Spell.
—— The same, in two parts.
Jaeger's Class-Book of Zoology.
James' (J. A.) Young Man.
James' (H.) Logic of Creation.
James' (G. P. R.) Adrien.
Jameson's (Mrs.) Art Works.
——— Legends of Saints and Martyrs. 2 vls.
——— Legends of the Monastic Orders.
——— Legends of the Madonna.
——— History of Our Lord. 2 vols.
Jarvis' Reply to Milner.
Jay on American Agriculture.
Jeffers on Gunnery.
Jeffrey's (F.) Essays.
Johnson's Meaning of Words.
Johnson's (Samuel) Rasselas.
Johnston's Chemistry of Common Life. 2 v.

Kavanagh's Adele.
——— Beatrice.
——— Daisy Burns.
——— Grace Lee.
——— Madeleine.
——— Nathalie.
——— Rachel Gray.
——— Seven Years.
——— Queen Mab.
——— Women of Christianity.
Keats' Poems.
Keep a Good Heart.
Keightley's Mythology.
Keil's Fairy Stories.
Keith (Memoir of Caroline P.)
Kendrick's Greek Ollendorff.